FIFTH EDITION

Real Writing

with Readings

Paragraphs and Essays
for College, Work, and
Everyday Life

Susan Anker

Bedford / St. Martin's
Boston ◆ New York

For Bedford/St. Martin's

Executive Editor: Carrie Brandon
Senior Developmental Editor: Martha Bustin
Senior Production Editor: Deborah Baker
Production Supervisor: Jennifer Peterson
Marketing Manager: Casey Carroll
Senior Art Director: Anna Palchik
Editorial Assistant: Sophia Snyder
Copyeditor: Linda McLatchie
Cover Design: Billy Boardman
Cover Photos: Front: Jonathan Stark; *Back (Student Edition):* Pelle Cass
Composition: Graphic World, Inc.
Printing and Binding: RR Donnelley and Sons

President: Joan E. Feinberg
Editorial Director: Denise B. Wydra
Editor in Chief: Karen S. Henry
Director of Marketing: Karen R. Soeltz
Director of Editing, Design, and Production: Marcia Cohen
Assistant Director of Editing, Design, and Production: Elise S. Kaiser
Managing Editor: Elizabeth M. Schaaf

Library of Congress Control Number: 2009924676

For information, write: Bedford/St. Martin's, 75 Arlington Street, Boston, MA 02116
(617-399-4000)

ISBN-10: 0-312-59632-4 *(Real Writing)*   ISBN-13: 978-0-312-59632-3
          0-312-53904-5 *(Real Writing with Readings)*   978-0-312-53904-7
          0-312-56711-1 *(Instructor's Annotated Edition)*   978-0-312-56711-8

Acknowledgments

Janice E. Castro with Dan Cook and Cristina Garcia. "Spanglish." From *Time* magazine, July 11, 1988. Copyright © 1988, Time, Inc. Reprinted by permission. TIME is a registered trademark of Time, Inc. All rights reserved.

Judith Ortiz Cofer. "Don't Misread My Signals." Published in *The Latin Deli: Prose and Poetry* under the title, "The Myth of the Latin Woman: I Just Met a Girl Named Maria." Published in *Glamour* magazine under the title, "Don't Misread My Signals." Copyright © 1993 by Judith Ortiz Cofer. Reprinted by permission of the University of Georgia Press.

Patrick Conroy. "Chili Cheese Dogs, My Father, and Me." Initially published in the November 4, 2004 issue of *Parade*, pages 4–5. © 2004 Pat Conroy. Reprinted by permission of Parade and Marly Rusoff & Associates, Inc. All rights reserved.

David Dosa. "A Day in the Life of Oscar the Cat." From *The New England Journal of Medicine*, July 26, 2007. Volume 357: 328–329, Number 4. Copyright © 2007 Massachusetts Medical Society. Reprinted by permission. All rights reserved.

Stephanie Ericsson. "The Ways We Lie." Originally published in *The Utne Reader*, November/December 1992 issue. Copyright © 1992 by Stephanie Ericsson. Reprinted by the permission of Dunham Literary as agents for the author. This essay also appears in *Companion Into Dawn: Inner Dialogues on Loving* by Stephanie Ericsson, published in 1997 by HarperCollins.

Dianne Hales. "Why Are We So Angry?" Initially published in the September 2, 2001 issue of *Parade*. © 2001 Dianne Hales. Reprinted by permission of Parade Magazine and the author. All rights reserved.

Eric Liu. "Po-Po in Chinatown." From *The Accidental Asian: Notes of a Native Speaker* by Eric Liu. Copyright © 1998 by Eric Liu. Used by permission of Random House, Inc.

Noreen Malone. "What Happens If You Fall into a Black Hole?" Appeared on www.slate.com/id/2199664 on September 9, 2008. Copyright © 2009, Washington Post. Newsweek Interactive Company, LLC and Slate Magazine. All rights reserved.

Brief Contents

Contents

*For other useful materials, such as vocabulary-building tools and a step-by-step guide to conducting a job search, visit the *Real Writing Student Center* at **bedfordstmartins.com/realwriting**.

Thematic Table of Contents

Preface

Since the first edition of *Real Writing*, the basic goal of this book has been twofold: to show students how writing is essential to success in the real world, and then to help them develop the writing skills they need to succeed in their college, work, and everyday lives. *Real Writing* shares this goal with the other *Real* books: *Real Skills* and *Real Essays*.

As always, our first job as educators is to meet students where they are—to understand who they are and what they bring to the college writing class. Only then can we make a connection with them and guide them along the path to success. Because this book is grounded in the real world, the content of each edition must reflect changes in that world and its requirements for success. Honestly, that is what I love about having the chance to revise every few years. What happens in classrooms, boardrooms, and living rooms is not static, and as an author I have the opportunity to incorporate what is needed to help students become successful college students and citizens. So, in this fifth edition, *Real Writing* has the same basic goals and some of the same core content that has worked for so many instructors and students. It also reflects important new research into what helps students connect to college life and their communities, and thereby succeed academically and identify and achieve their own goals.

Core Features

The core features of *Real Writing* that have made it successful are here again, with changes based on the thoughtful suggestions of reviewers, both users and non-users of the book, and longtime writing teacher friends.

Motivates Students as No Other Text Does

College can be intimidating, so *Real Writing* is designed to get students off to a good start and remind them that they can survive and thrive in college.

- **"Profiles of Success" show that writing skills are important to workplace success.** Inspiring case studies of former students who have overcome

---

PROFILE OF SUCCESS

Argument in the Real World

The following profile shows how Reggie uses writing and includes an example of how he uses argument in his work.

Background I grew up in a family of six brothers and sisters, raised by a single mother. I was an athlete and in high school was voted Most Valuable Player in both football and baseball. When I arrived at Hinds Community College, I realized that my reading skills were weak, so I took developmental reading with a teacher, Vashti Muse, who became my mentor. In the supportive environment of Hinds, I thrived. I was a member of the Fellowship of Christian Athletes on campus, a group that meets to share ideals and find ways to help the campus and other communities. I became a big brother to a local high-school student and have been rewarded by helping others.

After getting a B.A. from Delta State, I returned to be a college recruiter for Hinds, where I now oversee recruitment, supervising three other recruiters and enrollment specialists. I visit local high schools to give presentations and talk about the many advantages Hinds offers students. I encourage students who are not confident in their academic skills to try Hinds, and I tell them that if I could do it, they can too.

Degrees/College(s) B.A., Delta State University; M.Ed., Jackson State

Reggie Harris
District Recruiting
Coordinator

challenges to succeed in college and in life, "Profiles of Success" include photos, short autobiographies, and authentic workplace writing samples. The people profiled work in a wide range of careers, including nursing, law enforcement, teaching, business, non-profit community development, entertainment, and academia. As part of each chapter in Part 2, "Writing Different Kinds of Paragraphs and Essays," these popular profiles now function integrally as readings, accompanied by questions that encourage careful reading and analysis. Students can now relate these real-life examples of each mode of development more easily to the two other brief illustrative readings that follow: a paragraph model and an essay model, both by student writers.

- **Chapter 1, "Course and College Basics," begins with practical, candid advice about how to be a successful student, offered *by students*** (with photos and quotations) who, perhaps like your students, did not know at first how to navigate within their college environment. This chapter's can-do, practical attitude sets the tone for the rest of the book.

Shows Students That Good Writing Is an Achievable Goal

Real Writing's message to students is clear: Good writing is not magic, nor is it something that only "born writers" can do. Good writing has certain basic features, and by focusing on and mastering these, any student can become a better writer.

Description translates your experience of a person, place, or thing into words, often by appealing to the physical senses: sight, hearing, smell, taste, and touch.

Four Basics of Good Description

1   It creates a main impression—an overall effect, feeling, or image—about the topic.
2   It uses specific examples to support the main impression.
3   It supports those examples with details that appeal to the five senses: sight, hearing, smell, taste, and touch.
4   It brings a person, place, or physical object to life for the reader.

In the following paragraph, each number and color corresponds to one of the Four Basics of Good Description. A student sent this paragraph to helium.com, a Web site for writing, sharing information, contributing to organizations, writing contests, and much more.

Scars are stories written on a person's skin and sometimes on his heart. **1** My scar is not very big or very visible. **2** It is only about three inches long and an inch wide. It is on my knee, so it is usually covered, unseen. **3** It puckers the skin around it, and the texture of the scar itself

- ◄ **Helps students focus on the most important elements first.** Each chapter in Part 2 opens with a list of four basic features of the type of writing, followed by meaty annotated models that are color-coded to show the four basics at work.

- **Step-by-step checklists give specific guidance.** Students can use these detailed checklists to write and revise their papers, following the steps listed and doing the concrete activities that will lead to effective writing.

Makes Grammar Less Overwhelming

Real Writing helps students gain confidence and see grammar in a new light, as useful in achieving their own goals. It does not need to be an inscrutable set of rules known only to instructors. Instead, like other skills or bodies of knowledge, it can be learned and bring satisfaction.

- **Focuses first on the four most serious errors.** The Part 4 chapters on fragments, run-ons, subject-verb agreement problems, and verb problems help students find and fix many of the mistakes that mar their writing. They have heard the grammar rules and terms before, but often these student writers get lost in the details. Grammar success becomes possible when students focus on the most important errors first and absorb explanations and strategies that make sense to them. When they master these four topics, they know they will not make the serious mistakes that count against them most, in college and in the real world, and this fact gives them a firm foundation from which to proceed to other grammar topics.

- **Review charts at the end of the grammar chapters visually summarize key information.** The "Finding and Fixing" charts are excellent review and reference tools. ▶

- **"Language Notes" help students with tricky English language rules.** For nonnative and native speakers alike, these "Language Notes" help students write correct academic English.

Shows Students How to Be Active, Critical Readers

Like writing, reading is essential for success in college, work, and everyday life. *Real Writing* gives students more help with the essential skills of previewing and active reading, skills they can use immediately in all their courses.

- **"Reading Basics" is now a complete chapter (Chapter 2).** This new chapter includes boxes that highlight basic active and critical reading strategies for absorbing information from various college documents, such as essays, syllabi, and tests, along with other real-world documents such as advertisements and product labels.

- **Marginal prompts help students engage with readings moment by moment and note key elements.** In all Part 2 models and in all the selections in "Reader" section (in the version of this book with readings), prompts get students to identify, summarize, and reflect on what they are reading. ▶

mundane: ordinary
proximity: closeness
What do you think "change a sow's ear into a silk purse" (para. 1) means?

Dale Hill

How Community College Has Changed My Life

After graduating from Kaskaskia College, Dale Hill went on to receive an M.A. in English from Southern Illinois University in 2008 and currently teaches English at Kaskaskia, his community college alma mater. Hill most enjoys reading "short stories and essays, since the work must be done with precision and power," and he aims to achieve a similar level of conciseness in his own writing. He encourages other aspiring writers "to read widely in order to absorb the beauty of the language, to write constantly even if your writing seems inadequate at first, and to set realistic goals that you never give up on."

PREDICT Read the title and the first paragraph. How do you think the writer's attitude might have changed?

_____

_____

Grandpa was a sharecropper. With only a second-grade education, he planted his seeds and raised his family of seven sons and three daughters. My father, third eldest of the sons, broke new ground when he became the first person ever in the family to graduate from high school. Although Dad was very bright, it never occurred to him to go on to college. He and Grandpa shared the attitude that college was only for rich people and that you cannot change a sow's ear into a silk purse. Dad was expected to work to help sup-

New to This Edition

When I wrote the first edition of *Real Writing*, I was proud that it was the first writing text to link writing and real-world success. It was a breakthrough, and the reason, I believe, that the book was successful from the start was that it reflected what teachers were doing in their classes and was a good extension of that teaching.

This edition of *Real Writing* is similar in breaking new ground. Through research, countless campus visits, and conversations with instructors and students, I became convinced that not only did we need to connect to students, but we also needed to help students connect to the college and their own community. For many students, college is a part-time occupation, wedged in between multiple other demanding commitments. They come to school unaware that colleges offer much more than classes, that colleges are teeming with resources and learning opportunities of all sorts, waiting to enrich those who seek them out. When students are involved in their college communities, they are more likely to stay. When students have a chance to write about these real, voluntary activities, they draw from a rich pool of experience. Many find their voice for the first time, and many find that their writing is both easier and better than ever.

So, for the first time, this edition of *Real Writing* includes a strand on the theme of **making connections to college and community**. Crafting this feature was the hardest thing about the revision, but it was also the most rewarding. And it is unique to this book. It will be, I believe, another way *Real Writing* can be a solid extension of your classroom practices.

More Strategies for Success in College

In Chapter 1, the "College Basics" section introduces a new emphasis on making connections to help students become engaged in college, in their communities, and in their writing.

- **"Know Your Resources"** activities and writing practices help students become aware of and use campus resources, including the writing center.

- **"Connect to the College"** features the profile of a young woman who attributes her academic success and transfer to a four-year college to her involvement in first one, then several college clubs.

- **"Know Your Learning Style"** coverage utilizes the VARK Questionnaire to help students determine their learning style—whether visual, auditory, read/write, or kinesthetic—and gives specific strategies for using it to read, study, write, and take tests.

More Models and Tools for Successful Writing

- **In Part 1, Chapters 4–9 now begin and end with the instant-messaged exchanges of two students.** Chelsea Wilson has been assigned to write a paper, and her friend, Nick Brown, who has taken the taken the course already, serves as an unofficial peer tutor and sounding board. This illustrated case study shows students how it is possible to work through their writing questions and frustrations and proceed step-by-step through all stages of an assignment, in this case Chelsea's paper on the topic of "My Career Goal." Part 1 chapters on the writing process also now include new writing assignments.

- **Part 2 continues the strand of making connections with a new "Writing about Connections" assignment, at the end of each chapter.** These assignments ask students to respond to an exciting new kind of student profile called "Community Matters." Each one tells the story—complete with a photograph and quotations—of a student who was busy and overloaded, as most of yours are, but who attributes his or her success to taking time to get involved. The writing of the students profiled in the "Community Matters" boxes is included as a model. ▶

- **More examples of real student writing provide realistic models.** In addition to Chelsea Wilson's writing in Part 1, Chapters 10 through 18 each have three models of student writing, and each chapter of the "Readings" section (Part 8 in the version of the book with readings) now includes a student essay along with the two professional essays.

- **An explanation of rubrics helps students write with the criteria in mind.** Chapter 3, "Writing Basics," now includes a description of grading criteria, along with annotated examples of unsatisfactory, satisfactory, and good writing on the same topic.

More Grammar and Editing Practice

- **New comprehensive Editing Review Tests** cover increasingly comprehensive clusters of grammar issues, culminating in tests that require students to apply what they have learned in all of the grammar chapters. ▶

- **New grammar practices in each chapter reflect common student problems.** New practices are realistic and touch on wide-ranging topics of interest to students.

ASSIGNMENT 2   Writing about Connections

Read the following account of Jorge Roque before doing the assignment below.

COMMUNITY MATTERS

Jorge Roque

Jorge Roque is a veteran of the Iraq War, where he served in the Marine Corps and was partially disabled. When he returned after his tour ended, he had trouble finding work and ended up living in his car. He was referred to Veteran Love, an organization that helps soldiers returning from the war.

He started at Miami-Dade Community College in 2007, taking developmental reading, writing, and math. On his own, he organized students to write letters to soldiers in Iraq because he knew how much letters helped morale. Then, he made fliers on how people could help and posted them around the campus. He also gives presentations to classes about Veteran Love. Billie Jones, the faculty adviser for Omicron Delta Alpha, a service fraternity, heard of Jorge's work and asked him to join. He did, and his first project was to organize a food drive for the homeless. He is vice president of Omicron Delta Alpha and has since created and served in many community events while still taking classes and working at the financial aid office. He is also active in the Student Government Association.

Here is part of an argument Jorge presents for getting involved in service work while you are a student.

Even for the busiest student, getting involved in service organizations is worth the time and effort it takes. At one point, after I had returned from Iraq, was homeless, and was experiencing post-traumatic stress disorder, I was referred to Veteran Love, a nonprofit organization that helps disabled ex-soldiers, and they helped when I needed it most. When I was back on track, I

NAME _____   SECTION _____

1

Editing Review Test 1
The Four Most Serious Errors (Chapters 21–25)

DIRECTIONS: Each of the underlined word groups contains one or more errors. As you locate and identify each error, write its item number on the appropriate line below. Then, edit the underlined word groups to correct the errors. If you need help, turn back to the chapters indicated.

Two fragments _____   Two verb problems _____
Two run-ons _____   Four subject-verb
                              agreement errors _____

1 Every time you step outside, you are under attack. 2 Which you may not know is hitting you, but the attack is truly happening. 3 Invisible storms of sky dust rain down on you all the time. 4 It does not matter if the sun is shining, and the sky are bright blue. 5 The dust is still there.

6 Sky dust consist of bug parts, specks of hair, pollen, and even tiny chunks of comets. 7 According to experts, 6 million pounds of space dust settle on the earth's surface every year. 8 You will never notice it, scientists, however, are collecting it in order to learn more about weather patterns and pollution. 9 Using sophisticated equipment like high-tech planes and sterile filters to collect dust samples.

10 Dan Murray, a geologist at the University of Rhode Island, has began a new project that invites students and teachers to help collect samples of cosmic dust. 11 Murray says that collecting the dust particles are quite simple. 12 It starts with a researcher setting up a small, inflatable swimming pool. 13 Next, this investigator leaves the pool out in the open for forty-eight hours. 14 Finally, the researcher uses a special type of tape to pick up whatever have settled over time. 15 The tape is put into a beaker of water to dissolve a microscope is used to analyze what comes off the tape. 16 The information finded there will help scientists predict insect seasons, measure meteor showers, or even catch signs of global warming.

More Tools for Successful Reading

- **New marginal prompts promote active, critical reading.** In addition to the prompts in the "Readings" section, now all models in the Part 2 chapters have marginal prompts to get students in the habit of active reading.

◄ **Additional selections in the "Readings"** section include a new student-written essay in each chapter. Of the twenty-seven essays in Part 8, eighteen are new and chosen for both their excellence as models of the methods of development and their high-interest value.

- **More vocabulary glosses develop language skills.** All readings in Part 2 and in the "Readings" section now have more vocabulary words, shown in boldface. Students are instructed to highlight these vocabulary words, read the definitions, and later use the words in sentences of their own.

Monique Rizer
When Students Are Parents

 Monique Rizer graduated from Gonzaga University with a journalism degree in 2001 and received an M.S. in information management from Syracuse University. As the mother of a young son while in college, Rizer was presented with an unusual challenge, one that she says inspired her to "share a unique experience about college life and offer suggestions on how to support other non-traditional students." She also kept an anonymous blog while her husband was deployed to Iraq, sharing her stories and experiences with other military spouses. She offers this encouragement for other student writers: "Read. Read. Read. Along with just writing frequently to build that muscle, reading is probably just as important."

GUIDING QUESTION
Do you know about resources that could help you on your campus?

Crammed behind my desk, I **fidgeted**[1] and shifted my eyes to observe   1
the other students in the room. I tried not to look the way I felt—like I
didn't belong there with them. I couldn't help noticing that all the other

---

More Student Presence Throughout, and More Visuals

More concrete student presence creates a clear, engaging, student-centered textbook.

- Most student writing models now include photos and biographical notes.

- The subjects of the "Profiles of Success" features appear at the beginning of their respective chapters with a quotation giving student-to-student advice, and previewing the full "Profile of Success," now integrated more fully with follow-up questions and activities that help students actively engage with the profiles.

- The new "Writing about Connections/ Community Matters" assignments include photos of the students being featured, along with biographical notes and quotations.

- The photos of Chelsea Wilson and Nick Brown, along with their typed exchanges, help bring the writing process alive for students in Part 1, Chapters 4–9.

◄ Part 2 chapters now contain a new series of photographs or drawings by students from around the country, bringing in the student perspective. Accompanying writing prompts give students a chance for journal writing and visual analysis.

STUDENT PHOTO

`write` What is the story here?

Ancillaries

Real Writing does not stop with a book. Online and in print, you will find both free and affordable premium resources to help students get even more out of the book and your course. You will also find convenient instructor resources, such as downloadable sample syllabi, classroom activities, transparency masters, and more. For ideas and assistance on using these ancillaries in your course, please see the Resource Integration Guide on pages xxviii–xxix. To order any of the products below, or to learn more about them, contact your Bedford/St. Martin's sales representative by e-mailing Sales Support at sales_support@bfwpub.com, or visit the Web site at **bedfordstmartins.com/realwriting/catalog**.

Real Writing Student Center **at bedfordstmartins.com/realwriting** Send students to free and open resources, or upgrade to an expanding collection of innovative digital content—all in one place. The *Real Writing Student Center* Web site provides access to *Exercise Central*, the largest free online database of editing exercises (see p. xx). Additional free resources include help with taking tests, building vocabulary, making oral presentations, and conducting a job search; annotated student paragraphs and essays; the VARK Learning Style Questionnaire; *Grammar Girl* podcasts; useful forms mentioned in the book; and a guide to writing a research paper. Premium resources available through the *Real Writing Student Center* site include *WritingClass* and *Re:Writing Plus*.

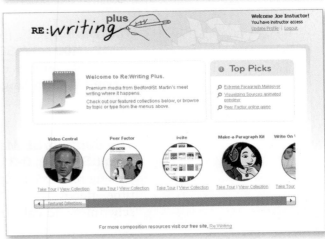

WritingClass **at yourwritingclass.com** Students are online all the time. *WritingClass* keeps them on target. At one easy-to-use site, students can see if there is a new assignment, click through and complete the activity, and check back to find out how they did. *WritingClass* makes it easy for you to set assignments—and see when students have done them. There are options for building online discussions, adding multimedia tutorials, and more—but you choose how much or how little you want to do online.

***Re:Writing Plus*, now with *VideoCentral*, at bedfordstmartins.com/rewritingplus** This impressive resource gathers all of our premium digital content for the writing class into one online collection. It includes innovative and interactive help with writing a paragraph; tutorials and practices that show how writing works in students' real-world experience; *VideoCentral*, with over 50 brief videos for the writing classroom; the first-ever peer review game, *Peer*

Factor; *i-cite: visualizing sources*; plus hundreds of models of writing and hundreds of readings. *Re:Writing Plus* can be purchased separately or packaged with *Real Writing* at a significant discount.

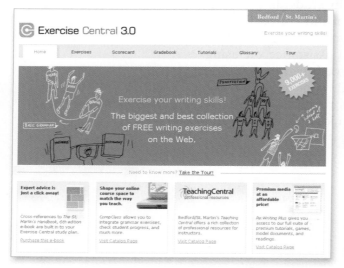

***Exercise Central 3.0* at bedfordstmartins.com/ exercisecentral** Completely free, and offering the largest database of editing exercises on the Internet, *Exercise Central 3.0* is a comprehensive resource for skill development as well as skill assessment. In addition to over 9,000 exercises offering immediate feedback and reporting to an instructor grade book, *Exercise Central 3.0* can help identify students' strengths and weaknesses, recommend personalized study plans, and provide tutorials for common problems.

***Supplemental Exercises for Real Writing*, Fifth Edition (ISBN-10: 0-312-56708-1 / ISBN-13: 978-0-312-56708-8)** This book supplements the exercises in the editing and research chapters of *Real Writing* with more than one hundred additional practices.

Quick Reference Card (ISBN-10: 0-312-61816-6 / ISBN-13: 978-0-312-61816-2) Students can prop up this handy three-panel card next to their computers for easy reference while they are writing and researching, or they can bring it to class. It contains the basics on writing, editing, and research and documentation. Available packaged with *Real Writing*.

***Make-a-Paragraph Kit with Exercise Central to Go* (ISBN-10: 0-312-45332-9 / ISBN-13: 978-0-312-45332-9)** This fun, interactive CD-ROM includes "Extreme Paragraph Makeover," a brief animation teaching students about paragraph development. It also contains exercises to help students build their own paragraphs, audiovisual tutorials on four of the most common errors for basic writers, and the content from *Exercise Central to Go: Writing and Grammar Practices for Basic Writers*.

***The Bedford/St. Martin's ESL Workbook*, Second Edition (ISBN-10: 0-312-54034-5 / ISBN-13: 978-0-312-54034-0)** This comprehensive collection of exercises covers grammatical issues for multilingual students with varying English-language skills and cultural backgrounds. Instructional introductions precede exercises in a broad range of topic areas.

***The Bedford/St. Martin's Planner with Grammar Girl's Quick and Dirty Tips* (ISBN-10: 0-312-48023-7 / ISBN-13: 978-0-312-48023-3)** This appealing resource includes everything that students need to plan and use their time effectively, with advice on preparing schedules and to-do lists and blank schedules and calendars (monthly and weekly) for planning. Integrated into the planner are pointers on fixing common grammar errors, with tips from Mignon Fogarty, host of the popular *Grammar Girl's Quick and Dirty Tips for Better Writing* podcast, and from other podcast hosts. Also included are advice on note taking and succeeding on tests, an address book, and an annotated list of useful Web sites.

Journal Writing: A Beginning (ISBN-10: 0-312-59027-X / ISBN-13: 978-0-312-59027-7)   Designed to give students an opportunity to use writing as a way to explore their thoughts and feelings, this writing journal includes a generous supply of inspirational quotations placed throughout the pages, tips for journaling, and suggested journal topics.

Notebook Dividers for Real Writing, Second Edition (ISBN-10: 0-312-62063-2 / ISBN-13: 978-0-312-62063-9)   Prepared by Lois Hassan, this set of eight sturdy dividers is pre-printed to help students organize their papers and succeed in their writing course. Each divider contains a relevant quotation and a list of writing or college success tips.

From Practice to Mastery (for the Florida College Basic Skills Exit Tests) (ISBN-10: 0-312-41908-2 / ISBN-13: 978-0-312-41908-0)   Full of practical instruction and plenty of examples, this handy book gives students all the resources they need to practice for—and pass—the Florida College Basic Skills Exit Tests on reading and writing.

For Instructors

Instructor's Annotated Edition of Real Writing, Fifth Edition (ISBN-10: 0-312-56711-1 / ISBN-13: 978-0-312-56711-8)   This annotated edition gives practical page-by-page advice on teaching with *Real Writing* and contains answers to all exercises and suggestions for using other ancillaries.

Practical Suggestions for Teaching Real Writing, Fifth Edition (ISBN-10: 0-312-56712-X / ISBN-13: 978-0-312-56712-5)   An ideal resource for teachers new to teaching or to *Real Writing*, *Practical Suggestions* contains information and advice on bringing the real world into the classroom, using computers, teaching multilingual students, and more. It also includes advice for responding to the most difficult student papers.

Additional Resources for Real Writing, Fifth Edition (ISBN-10: 0-312-56709-X / ISBN-13: 978-0-312-56709-5)   This book supplements the instructional materials in *Real Writing* with a variety of transparency masters, planning forms, handouts, and other reproducibles for classroom use.

Testing Tool Kit: A Writing and Grammar Test Bank (ISBN-10: 0-312-43032-9 / ISBN-13: 978-0-312-43032-0)   This test bank CD-ROM allows instructors to create secure, customized tests and quizzes from a pool of nearly 2,000 questions covering 47 topics. It also includes 10 pre-built diagnostic tests.

***Teaching Developmental Writing: Background Readings*, Third Edition (ISBN-10: 0-312-43283-6 / ISBN-13: 978-0-312-43283-6)** Edited by Susan Naomi Bernstein, this professional resource offers a collection of essays on topics of interest to basic writing instructors, along with editorial apparatus pointing out practical classroom applications. The new edition includes revised chapters on technology and the writing process and focuses on topics relevant to instructors who work with multilingual students in the developmental writing course.

***The Bedford Bibliography for Teachers of Basic Writing*, Third Edition (ISBN-10: 0-312-58154-8 / ISBN-13: 978-0-312-58154-1)** (also available online at **bedfordstmartins.com/basicbib**) Compiled by members of the Conference on Basic Writing under the general editorship of Gregory R. Glau and Chitralekha Duttagupta, this annotated list of books, articles, and periodicals was created specifically to help teachers of basic writing find valuable resources.

TeachingCentral at bedfordstmartins.com/teachingcentral Offers the entire list of Bedford/St. Martin's print and online professional resources in one place. You will find landmark reference works, sourcebooks on pedagogical issues, award-winning collections, and practical advice for the classroom — all free for instructors.

Content cartridges These are available for the most common course management systems—Blackboard, WebCT, Angel, and Desire2Learn—allow you to easily download Bedford/St. Martin's digital materials for your course. For more information about our course management offerings, visit **bedfordstmartins.com/cms**.

***CourseSmart e-Book for Real Writing* (ISBN-10: 0-312-60136-0 / ISBN-13: 978-0-312-60136-2)** Bedford/St. Martin's has partnered with Course-Smart to offer a downloadable version of *Real Writing* at about half the price of the print book. To learn more about this low-cost alternative visit **www.coursesmart.com**.

Ordering Information

Use these ISBNs to order the following supplements packaged with your students' books:

***Real Writing with Readings* with:**

- *The Bedford/St. Martin's ESL Workbook*, Second Edition
  ISBN-10: 0-312-62727-0 / ISBN-13: 978-0-312-62727-0

- *The Bedford/St. Martin's Planner*
  ISBN-10: 0-312-69166-1 / ISBN-13: 978-0-312-69166-0

- *Exercise Central to Go* CD-ROM
  ISBN-10: 0-312-62611-8 / ISBN-13: 978-0-312-62611-2

- *From Practice to Mastery* (for Florida)
  ISBN-10: 0-312-62721-1 / ISBN-13: 978-0-312-62721-8

- *Journal Writing: A Beginning*
  ISBN-10: 0-312-64363-2 / ISBN-13: 978-0-312-64363-8

- *Make-a-Paragraph Kit* CD-ROM
  ISBN-10: 0-312-62723-8 / ISBN-13: 978-0-312-62723-2

- *Merriam-Webster Dictionary*, Tenth Edition
  ISBN-10: 0-312-64364-0 / ISBN-13: 978-0-312-64364-5

- Quick Reference Card
  ISBN-10: 0-312-64733-6 / ISBN-13: 978-0-312-64733-9

- *Re:Writing Plus* Access Card
  ISBN-10: 0-312-62725-4 / ISBN-13: 978-0-312-62725-6

- *Supplemental Exercises*
  ISBN-10: 0-312-64366-7 / ISBN-13: 978-0-312-64366-9

- *WritingClass*
  ISBN-10: 0-312-62726-2 / ISBN-13: 978-0-312-62726-3

Real Writing with:

- *The Bedford/St. Martin's ESL Workbook*, Second Edition
  ISBN-10: 0-312-62975-3 / ISBN-13: 978-0-312-62975-5

- *The Bedford/St. Martin's Planner*
  ISBN-10: 0-312-62970-2 / ISBN-13: 978-0-312-62970-0

- *Exercise Central to Go* CD-ROM
  ISBN-10: 0-312-62968-0 / ISBN-13: 978-0-312-62968-7

- *From Practice to Mastery* (for Florida)
  ISBN-10: 0-312-62971-0 / ISBN-13: 978-0-312-62971-7

- *Journal Writing: A Beginning*
  ISBN-10: 0-312-64134-6 / ISBN-13: 978-0-312-64134-4

- *Make-a-Paragraph Kit* CD-ROM
  ISBN-10: 0-312-62972-9 / ISBN-13: 978-0-312-62972-4

- *Merriam-Webster Dictionary*, Tenth Edition
  ISBN-10: 0-312-64135-4 / ISBN-13: 978-0-312-64135-1

- Quick Reference Card
  ISBN-10: 0-312-64734-4 / ISBN-13: 978-0-312-64734-6

- *Re:Writing Plus* Access Card
  ISBN-10: 0-312-62973-7 / ISBN-13: 978-0-312-62973-1

- *Supplemental Exercises*
  ISBN-10: 0-312-64133-8 / ISBN-13: 978-0-312-64133-7

- *WritingClass* Access Card
  ISBN-10: 0-312-62974-5 / ISBN-13: 978-0-312-62974-8

Acknowledgments

As always, this edition of *Real Writing* stems from the efforts of many people, not just myself. Together, we created so many new and exciting features, that I have to keep this part of the preface brief to accommodate the space that the description of the new features and ancillaries required. So, my thanks will be short on length but long on gratitude.

Editorial Advisory Board

We always have each edition of the book reviewed widely, but we also ask a few colleagues to scrutinize the contents more intensively and provide in-depth suggestions. I fully rely on the advice of these people and give them profound thanks for their help. New to our advisory board with this edition are Jan Bishop, Greenville Tech; Laura Jeffries, Florida State College at Jacksonville; and Theresa Johnson, Troy University. I am so grateful to these new recruits. And although she was not an official adviser, Robin Ozz, Phoenix College, bff, has certainly played a big role in the development of the book.

Three other people have become integrally blended into the book because of their many years of critical review and friendship; I could not have done this edition or any of the previous ones without them, so special thanks to longtime advisers Karen Eisenhauer, Brevard Community College; Tamara Shue, Georgia Perimeter College; and Bill Shute, San Antonio College.

Student Advisory Board

I continue to thank the students who helped me develop Chapter 1, "Course and College Basics." They had at that time recently passed the course using *Real Writing*, and their candid and insightful advice to incoming students forms the basis of the chapter. Their comments also helped me revise the book. Those students are Mark Balderas, San Antonio College; Michelle Bassett, Quinsigamond Community College; Nicole Day, Brevard Community College; and Katilya Labidou, Brevard Community College. Nicole has now graduated and is featured in a "Profile of Success" in this edition (Chapter 14).

Other Student Contributors

This time around, many more students have shaped the revision. The students who are profiled in Part 2 chapters ("Writing about Connections") were inspiring to talk with as they make a difference in the world. Those students are: Dana Cardona, Montgomery County Community College and Bucknell University; Alessandra Cepeda, Bunker Hill Community College and Worcester State College; Corin Costas, Bunker Hill Community College and University of Massachusetts, Boston; Shawn Elswick, Mott Community College; Jenny Haun, Brevard Community College; Caroline Powers, St. Anselm's College; Evelka Rankins, Urban College of Boston; Jorge Roque, Miami-Dade Community College; Lynze Schiller, Middlesex County College and Marymount Manhattan; and Robin Wyant, Ivy Tech.

The students whose writing is included (in addition to the student volunteers listed above) are: Kathleen Aharonian, John Around Him, Jasen Beverly, Carlton Brown, Jackie (Davison) Linstead, Lou Enrico, Jim Green, Samson Green, Brian Healy, Dale Hill, Abigail Klatt, Rollina Lowe, Jelani Lynch, Rose Martinez, Lorenza Mattazi, Casandra Palmer, Robert Phansalkar, Caitlin (Prokop) Flynn, Vanessa Radzimski, Monique Rizer, Ruth Russell Van Anden, Kimberly (Sharpe) Hyatt, Cathy Vittoria, Kelli Whitehead, and Michele Wood. I also want to thank Nick Brown and Chelsea Wilson, whose exchanges on writing open and close all of the Part 2 chapters. The student photographers were Jenn Ackerman, Andrew Dillon Bustin, Harrison Diamond, Josh Ferrin, Caleb Miller, and Kate Napier. Several other students have helped as advisors and have provided inspiration: David Ayers, Chelsea Kerrington, Nick Van Buskirk, and Chelsea Tolle. Thank you to all these people.

In addition, many thanks for Jessica Felizardo, Bay State College, for coordinating a photo shoot of students and classes and for allowing me to observe a number of her writing classes.

Reviewers

In addition to the Editorial Advisory Board, a large group of reviewers helped to develop the fifth edition. Thank you to Désiré Baloubi: Shaw University; Elizabeth Barnes, Daytona State College; Renee Bell, DeVry University; Jan Bishop, Greenville Technical College; Randy L. Boone, Northampton Community College; Cynthia Bowden, Las Positas College; Michael Boyd, Illinois Central College; Cathy Brostrand, Mt. San Jacinto Community College; Dawn Copeland, Motlow State Community College; Claudia Edwards, Piedmont Technical College; Deb Fuller, Bunker Hill Community College; Frank Gunshanan, Daytona State College; Tatiana Gorbunova, Owens Community College; Vivian Hoskins, Phillips Community College of the University of Arkansas; Blaine Hunt, Tacoma Community College; Brenda J. Hunt, Western Piedmont Community College; Laura Jeffries, Florida Community College at Jacksonville; Theresa Johnson, Troy University; Peggy Karsten, Ridgewater College; Merle K. Koury, College of Southern Maryland; Cathy Lally, Brevard Community College; Tricia Lord, Sierra College; Monique N. Matthews, Santa Monica College; Aubrey Moncrieffe, Housatonic Community College; Matthew Petti, PsyD, MFA, Instructor of English, University of the District of Columbia; Sandra Provence, Arkansas State University; Rick P. Rivera, Columbia College; Neal Roche, Adjunct Professor, Essex County College; Ann Smith, Modesto Junior College; Catherine Whitley, Edinboro University of Pennsylvania; Lisa Yanover, Napa Valley College; Rose Yesu, Massasoit Community College; and Guixia Yin, Bunker Hill Community College.

Contributors

In addition to all the advisers, students, and reviewers, others made significant contributions to this edition. Sandra Roy and Tamra Orr helped with grammar practices, and Jeff Ousborne and Candace Rardon created apparatus for the reader. Jonathan Stark took the student photos that appear on the title page and part openers. Eve Lehmann cleared permissions under the guidance of Sandy Schechter, and Linda Finigan secured permission for photographs and other art.

Bedford/St. Martin's

Bedford/St. Martin's richly deserves its reputation as the premier publisher of English texts. It devotes extraordinary time, brainpower, and plain old blood, sweat, and tears to each of its books, even one in the fifth edition. Each project is a messy, collaborative, and ultimately rewarding effort for the many people who are involved. Everyone at Bedford/St. Martin's demands much and gives much more.

Sophia Snyder, editorial assistant, was new to the job when we started the revision, but she had perhaps the steepest learning curve I have seen. She was an invaluable help on a wide variety of matters, not the least of which was keeping track of the myriad details of two similar projects when I faltered. Thank you, Sophia. I know you have a bright future. I was pleased to work again with Deborah Baker, senior production editor, who ably managed the very, very complicated and demanding production process.

Casey Carroll, marketing manager, is always a joy to talk with and conveys all sorts of information and creative ideas with intelligence, diplomacy, and an incredible dry wit. He does a great job of interacting with a large and diverse group of people. He has also been an early and strong supporter of the "Writing about Connections" feature in this edition. I also thank Dennis Adams, humanities specialist manager, an unflagging advocate for my books who, like Casey, always brightens my day. Jim Camp, national specialist, brings a lifetime of successful experience to his job and adds much to our team.

We created a new look for *Real Writing* with this edition, and I am very grateful to Claire Seng-Niemoeller, who has worked on the book from the start, for her creativity, flexibility, and patience as we all weighed in. Anna Palchik, senior art director, also brought her considerable talent and experience to the new design. And Billy Boardman, senior designer, with characteristic creativity and grace, came up with wonderful ideas for the cover and part openers. Thanks also to Pelle Cass, who brought his artistic vision to the brochure.

The remarkable New Media group continues to develop some of the most useful teaching tools available. Special thanks to Katie Schooling, assistant director of new media, for her work on *WritingClass*, and to Kim Hampton, new media editor, and Katie Congdon.

I am forever grateful to founder and former president Chuck Christensen, president Joan Feinberg, editorial director Denise Wydra, and editor in chief Karen Henry, busy executives who remain devoted to each book and author. Their ideas are very much a part of this revision, and their friendship and support through the years means much to me. I am also delighted to have executive editor Carrie Brandon's practical and sound advice as she builds and shapes the list of Bedford/St. Martin's offerings.

Finally, I was reunited with Martha Bustin, senior editor, whom I have known and worked with before, but not as an author. She, like Sophia Snyder, was new to the company, and joined me in a particularly challenging year, when we worked on two books simultaneously, trying to keep them straight and develop sound new features for each. In addition to bringing wonderful new ideas and a fresh vision, Martha is seemingly unflappable, a serene and steady antidote to my frequent flapping. Thank you, Martha.

And then there's my husband, Jim Anker, who helped me through a rough year. His surname is supremely fitting.

—Susan Anker

Real Support for Instructors and Students

GOALS AND LEARNING OUTCOMES	SUPPORT IN *REAL WRITING*	SUPPORT IN STUDENT ANCILLARIES	SUPPORT IN INSTRUCTOR ANCILLARIES
Students will connect the writing class with their goals in the larger world.	■ "Course Basics" in Chapter 1 ■ "Profiles of Success" and "Community Matters" in Part 2 ■ Student writing with biographical notes and photos	■ *Notebook Dividers:* Aids to organizing course materials ■ **Quick Reference Card:** Portable tips for writing, editing, and more ■ *The Bedford/St. Martin's Planner* ■ *WritingClass:* Online course space with helpful materials and activities	■ **Instructor's Annotated Edition:** Tips suggest activities to engage students ■ *Practical Suggestions:* Chapters on useful instructional approaches, ways to bring the real world into the course, and more
Students will write well-developed, organized paragraphs, essays, and papers.	■ Thorough writing process coverage in Part 1 ■ Coverage of various rhetorical strategies in Part 2, with detailed writing checklists; a focus on the "Four Basics" of each type of writing; and a special emphasis on main point, support, and organization ■ Models of writing throughout Part 2 and in Part 8 of *Real Writing with Readings*	■ **Quick Reference Card:** Portable writing advice and more ■ *Real Writing Student Center* site: Additional model readings and writing advice (**bedfordstmartins.com/realwriting**) ■ *Make-a-Paragraph Kit* CD-ROM: Paragraph development advice and exercises ■ *Exercise Central to Go* CD-ROM: Writing exercises (even more exercises available at **bedfordstmartins.com/exercisecentral**) ■ *Re:Writing Basics:* Additional writing support at **bedfordstmartins.com/rewritingbasics** ■ *WritingClass:* Online course space with writing materials and activities	■ **Instructor's Annotated Edition:** Tips for writing instruction ■ *Additional Resources:* Reproducible planning forms for writing ■ *Practical Suggestions:* Help with assessment and ideas on various approaches to helping students with their writing ■ *Testing Tool Kit* CD-ROM: Tests on topic sentences, thesis statements, support, organization, and more
Students will build grammar and editing skills.	■ Thorough grammar coverage and many opportunities for practice in Parts 4 through 7, with a focus on the "Four Most Serious Errors" (Part 4) ■ "Find and Fix" charts ■ Grammar review charts	■ **Quick Reference Card:** Portable advice on editing the "Four Most Serious Errors" and more ■ *Real Writing Student Center* site: More grammar exercises, with instant scoring and feedback (**bedfordstmartins.com/realwriting**) ■ *Supplemental Exercises:* Editing exercises ■ *Make-a-Paragraph Kit* CD-ROM: Tutorials on finding and fixing the "Four Most Serious Errors" ■ *Exercise Central to Go* CD-ROM: Editing exercises (even more exercises available at **bedfordstmartins.com/exercisecentral**) ■ *WritingClass:* Online course space with grammar and editing activities	■ **Instructor's Annotated Edition:** Tips for grammar instruction ■ *Additional Resources:* Reproducible exercises and transparencies for modeling correction of the "Four Most Serious Errors" ■ *Testing Tool Kit* CD-ROM: Test items on every grammar topic
Students will build research skills.	■ Step-by-step advice on writing research essays in Chapter 20	■ **Quick Reference Card:** Portable research and documentation advice ■ *Supplemental Exercises:* Research exercises ■ *Re:Writing Basics:* Research and documentation advice at **bedfordstmartins.com/rewritingbasics** ■ *WritingClass:* Online course space with research activities	■ *Additional Resources:* Reproducible research exercises and other handouts

GOALS AND LEARNING OUTCOMES	SUPPORT IN *REAL WRITING*	SUPPORT IN STUDENT ANCILLARIES	SUPPORT IN INSTRUCTOR ANCILLARIES
Students will read closely and critically.	■ Advice in Chapter 2, "Reading Basics," on reading in college and beyond ■ Critical reading questions with Part 2 models and in Part 8 of *Real Writing with Readings*	■ *Real Writing Student Center* site: Additional model readings, annotated for important features (**bedfordstmartins.com/realwriting**) ■ *WritingClass:* Online course space with critical reading activities	■ *Instructor's Annotated Edition:* Tips for teaching with the selections in *Real Writing with Readings*
Students will think critically.	■ Critical reading questions with Part 2 models and in Part 8 of *Real Writing with Readings* ■ Checklists encouraging students to think critically about their own writing and writing process	■ *Journal Writing: A Beginning:* Includes inspirational quotations and journaling tips ■ *WritingClass:* Online course space with critical thinking activities	■ *Instructor's Annotated Edition:* Tips for encouraging critical thinking and class discussion ■ *Additional Resources:* Reproducible writing checklists for students ■ *Practical Suggestions:* Advice on integrating critical thinking into the course
Students will prepare for and pass tests.	■ Advice on reviewing for tests in Chapter 2 ■ Practice tests at the ends of chapters ■ Appendix A, "Succeeding on Tests"	■ *Real Writing Student Center* site: Grammar exercises, with instant scoring and feedback advice (**bedfordstmartins.com/realwriting**) ■ *Supplemental Exercises:* Editing exercises ■ *Exercise Central to Go* CD-ROM: Editing exercises (even more exercises available at **bedfordstmartins.com/exercisecentral**) ■ *From Practice to Mastery:* Study guide for the Florida Basic Skills Exit Test ■ *WritingClass:* Online course space with test-taking activities	■ *Additional Resources:* General diagnostic tests as well as tests on specific grammar topics ■ *Practical Suggestions:* Advice on assessing student writing, with model rubrics, advice on marking difficult papers, and more ■ *Testing Tool Kit* CD-ROM: Tests on all writing and grammar issues covered in *Real Writing*
ESL and multilingual students will improve their proficiency in English grammar and usage.	■ "Language Notes" throughout the grammar instruction ■ Thorough ESL chapter (Chapter 33) with special attention to verb usage	■ *Real Writing Student Center* site: ESL exercises, with instant scoring and feedback (**bedfordstmartins.com/realwriting**) ■ *The Bedford/St. Martin's ESL Workbook:* Special instruction and abundant exercises ■ *Exercise Central to Go* CD-ROM: Includes ESL exercises (even more exercises available at **bedfordstmartins.com/exercisecentral**) ■ *WritingClass:* Online course space with ESL materials and activities	■ *Instructor's Annotated Edition:* Tips for teaching ESL students ■ *Practical Suggestions:* Advice on teaching ESL students and speakers of nonstandard English ■ *Testing Tool Kit* CD-ROM: Test items on ESL issues

To order any of the ancillaries for *Real Writing,* please contact your Bedford/St. Martin's sales representative, e-mail sales support at **sales_support@bfwpub.com**, or visit our Web site at **bedfordstmartins.com**.

A Note to Students from Susan Anker

For the last twenty years or so, I have traveled the country talking to students about their goals and, more important, about the challenges they face on the way to achieving those goals. Students always tell me that they want good jobs and that they need a college degree to get those jobs. I designed *Real Writing* with those goals in mind—strengthening the writing, reading, and editing skills needed for success in college, at work, and in everyday life. Here is something else: Good jobs require not only a college degree but also a college education; knowing not only how to read and write but how to think critically and learn effectively. So that is what I stress here, too. It is worth facing the challenges. All my best wishes to you, in this course and in all your future endeavors.

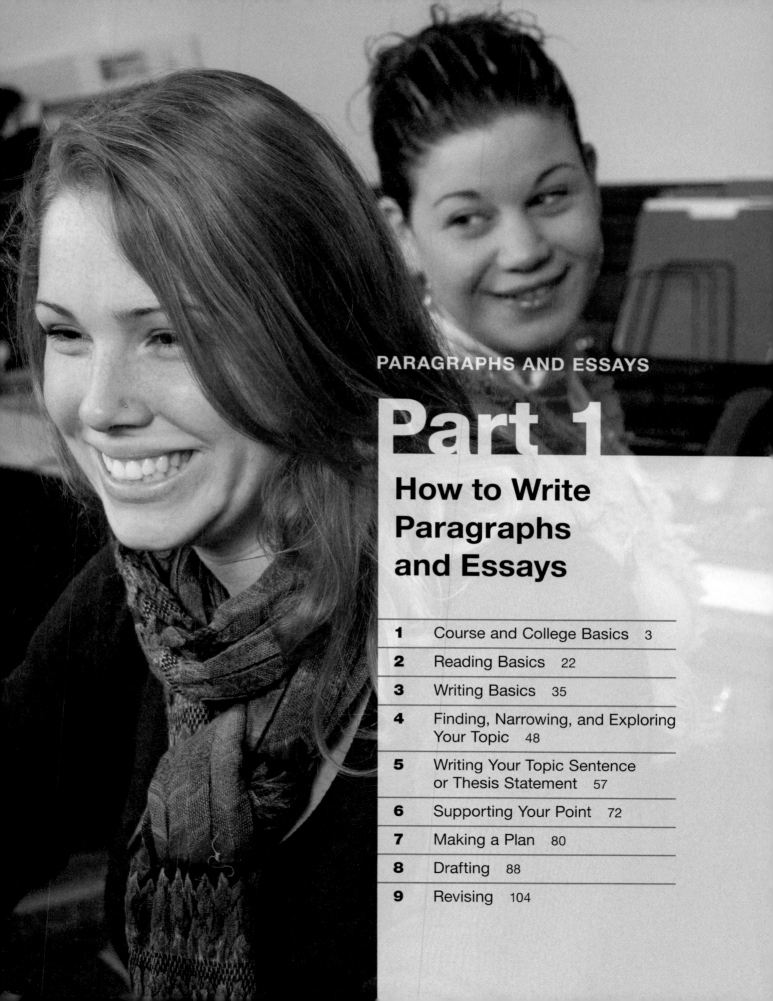

PARAGRAPHS AND ESSAYS

Part 1

How to Write Paragraphs and Essays

YOU KNOW THIS

You already have experience using the skills necessary for college success:

- You juggle work and life responsibilities.
- You schedule your daily activities.

think What do you know about being a successful student? What do you know about college?

1

Course and College Basics

What You Need to Know

This chapter reviews basic information you will need to get off to a good start in your writing course. It then gives you other strategies for success in college.

Course Basics

The students pictured in this chapter recently completed the course you are now taking. For this section, we asked them to tell you "things they wish they had known." In the margins, you will find their best tips for succeeding in the course.

Take the Course Seriously

A few of you may think that you do not belong in this class because you always got good grades in writing when you were in high school. If you were given a test that determined you should be here, accept this fact and think of this course as an opportunity. Get everything you can from the class: You will need to write in every other course you will take and in any job you will want.

Also remember that you get from this course only what you give. Your instructor does not decide what grade to give you: He or she evaluates and grades the work that *you* do—or do not do.

(See Nicole Day's **PROFILE OF SUCCESS** on page 196.)

3

NICOLE DAY: "Doing the assignments is crucial to your grade in the class and to your future. By doing the assignments, you might learn something that you never knew before."

TIP For help planning your assignments, visit **www.ucc .vt.edu/stdysk/control.html**.

MICHELLE BASSETT: "You'd be surprised at how much you miss when you're absent for just one class. As for getting there on time, two things: Many instructors give out important information right at the start of class. Also, many consider coming in late an absence."

Do the Assignments

Take the course and the course work seriously. Do not make the mistake of thinking that you can do nothing and still manage to pass. If you choose not to do the work, you risk failing the course. More important, you will not learn to be a better writer, and that will affect your future plans.

If you cannot do the assignment, either because you do not understand something or for a personal reason, do not make up excuses. Talk with your teacher, explain what you did not understand when you tried to do the work, and get help. If you will be turning in an assignment late, ask for a new due date. Then, make sure you get it done by that date. Remember: Late papers are often graded down.

Also, make a schedule for doing a big assignment: Do not leave the assignment until the last minute because then you will rush and cut corners. Allow yourself plenty of time to do a good job.

Make Sure You Understand, and Get Help If You Don't

If you do not understand a concept during class, the quickest way to clear up your confusion is to ask the instructor to go over it again or to give another example. If you don't understand, probably others don't either, so don't feel foolish asking for clarification. Or, ask your question after class or by e-mail.

Don't be embarrassed to ask for help. See your instructor during office hours, or make an appointment for another time if you have a conflict. Also, if your college has a writing center, writing lab, or writing tutors, get help from these people: That is what they are there for. Whatever you do, don't stay confused or give up.

Manage Your Time

Passing this course requires that you attend class and that you complete the homework and writing assignments. To do so, you need to manage your time effectively.

Get to Class (on Time) and Stay until the End

Make a commitment to go to every class. Things come up that may conflict with your class, but if you are going to miss a session, be late, or leave early, let your instructor know in advance, if possible, and ask what you should do on your own. Get assignments or handouts you missed.

Make a Calendar

With so much going on, it can be hard to remember what is due when. Using the syllabus that your instructor gives you, make a calendar that covers the whole course, listing due dates for papers, tests, and other assignments. Papers take more than one night to write, so make sure to schedule in the various steps, as shown in the partial course calendar that follows.

You can find many free online calendars (type "free online calendars" into a search engine) that cover months, a week at a time, or a day at a time. Keep the electronic calendar on your hard drive in a folder with the course title, and do the same for other courses. Or, use one calendar for everything: college courses and personal responsibilities. You can put papers and other course documents in this folder too. Or, you can print out or draw a calendar and staple it to the front of a paper folder for the course. This way, you can look at the calendar without going through the whole folder.

TRADITIONAL COURSE CALENDAR

English 098, Tuesday/Thursday, 8:30–10
Professor Murphy
Office hours: T/Th, 11–12:30 and by appointment

		1 Prewriting for narration paper due	2	3	4	5
6	7	8 Draft of narration paper due	9	10 Test, fragments	11	12
13	14	15 Final narration paper due	16	17	18	19
20	21	22 Review, test on subject-verb agreement	23	24 Test, subject-verb agreement 11—Appt. with Prof. Murphy	25	26
27	28	29 Prewriting for description paper due	30	31		

You should review your calendar at the start of every month or week. Make it a habit.

Connect with the Class

As we all know, it is possible to go to every class and still not be part of it. Decide that you will be an active part of the class. If you connect with the class, you are more likely to do well.

TIP For lots of good tips on time management, reading and study skills, and more, visit **www.howtostudy.org** or **www.studygs.net**.

TEACHING TIP Devote a few minutes of class time to allowing students to get to know their neighbors and to exchange contact information if they wish.

KATILYA LABIDOU: "I'm not one who grasps things easily. I had to go to my instructor's office every chance I had, both before class and also on days when I didn't have to be at school. I finally understand my writing better as well as my speech."

Make a Friend

Students sit usually in about the same place for each class. Exchange names, phone numbers, and e-mail addresses with students who sit near you. Get to know at least one other person in the class. That way, if you cannot make it to a class, you will know someone who can tell you what you missed. Also, if you find you do not understand an assignment, you can double-check with another student. You might also want to study with other students.

Get to Know Your Instructor

Your instructor wants you to succeed in the class. It helps him or her to know you a little bit: who you are, what you do, what you need help with. Make an appointment to visit your instructor during his or her office hours. When you go, ask questions about material you are not sure you understood in class or problems you have with writing. You and your instructor will get the most out of these sessions if you bring examples of your writing or specific assignments you are having trouble with.

MICHELLE BOSTICK: "Going to see your instructor in her office allows you to identify areas where your writing is weak, and you can get help that might embarrass you if you had to ask in class. It helps you become a more confident student. It also shows the instructor that you are concerned about your writing and will take initiative."

If you e-mail or text your instructor, avoid using the casual language that you might use with your friends. Though an e-mail or text message can be less formal than a writing assignment, it does not make a good impression to write informally, as one student did to her instructor:

> Hey! i just recieved yr message. yes, i have the questiones downloaded and i will write and email u the assignment uve noted.

Use more formal English to e-mail or text an instructor, and read it carefully before sending it.

Sit Near the Front

Do not hide in the back of the class, texting or sleeping, hoping that no one will notice you. Instead, when you go to the first class, sit in one of the first few rows. It really is easier to learn when you are closer to the instructor.

Speak Up

For many students, speaking in class is difficult: You are not sure you have the right answer, or you think your question might be stupid. But speaking up in class is important, and participation is often part of your grade. School is exactly the right place for getting over the fear of talking in a group, and the ability to speak to people in a group will help you at work and in your everyday life. Speaking up also allows you to get answers to questions and to take part in class discussions. If you wait until later, you may forget your questions or the points you wanted to make.

Once you get used to speaking in class, you will find that it is not hard. Challenge yourself, early on, to participate orally: Volunteer to answer a question or to ask a question. Here are some tips that might help you:

- Don't be afraid to make a mistake. No one in the class, including your instructor, will make fun of you. As teachers are fond of saying, "There's no such thing as a dumb question."
- When you speak, look at your instructor (or whomever you are speaking to).
- Speak loudly enough for people to hear; otherwise, you will have to repeat yourself.

Identify Your Course Goals and Needs

What do you, personally, want from this course? Once you have a good idea of what you want, you will be more able to focus on what you need and to get specific help from your instructor.

First, what are some of your real-world goals, both small and large, right now and in the future? Some short-term goals might be persuading your boss to give you a raise, getting a bank loan, or getting a promotion. Longer-term goals might include deciding what kind of job or career you hope to have or what degree you want to finish. Do some thinking and list at least five short-term and longer-term goals, making them as concrete and specific as you can. (For example, "be happy" is too general and abstract.)

Once you have some real-world goals in mind, link those goals to the writing skills you want to learn or improve in this course. For example, if one of your real-world goals is to convince your boss that you deserve a raise, you might want help with making a good argument for that.

Hang in There

Don't give up on yourself if things get hard. You can get help, and you can become a better writer and pass this course. If you drop out, you will either have to take the same course next term or have the same writing problems that you had coming in. This course is the time and place to improve your writing, and better writing skills will give you more control over your life and how you communicate with others.

Believe in your ability to pass this course and stay focused; do not panic and run away. For inspiration, check out the former students highlighted in the Profiles of Success in Chapters 10–18. All of these people are successful,

NICOLE DAY: "Sitting in front is very beneficial to your learning. You can see everything, and it lets your teacher know that you want to learn and not just hide in the back."

RESOURCES *Practical Suggestions* includes more advice on fostering class participation.

MARK BALDERAS: "Be sure to set your *own* goals. They will help you succeed."

KATILYA LABIDOU: "Acknowledging your faults is the first step. I was really surprised when I first got a failing grade. Wanting to be better than average is what got me through. Sometimes, I wasn't sure I could do it, but I stuck with it and spent time learning about writing and grammar."

yet all of them had to overcome some major obstacles, often their own fear of writing.

College Basics

Many of you may not know much about your college: You come to the campus for classes but spend most of your time working, taking care of family, and handling other responsibilities. Beyond the classes and instructors, colleges offer a whole world of help and hope. This section shows you some of what is available to you—free—as a student at your college.

Know Your Resources

You might have visited the college's Web site to get basic information before you enrolled. Now that you are here, it is time to go back and find out what resources the college has. Following is an example of a college home page showing the wide range of services and support available. If you do not have your own computer, use a library or lab computer to view your college's home page.

When you scroll down the menu bar on the left to "Students," you can then click on any of the items listed under "Students." Clicking on "Support Services" brings up the following page.

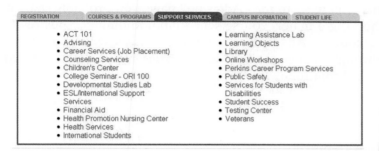

On this page, many free support services are listed, such as ACT 101, which is a special support program for first-year students, as well as the Health Promotion Nursing Center, the Library, and Student Success. Clicking on any of the entries will take you to a page that gives you detailed information about each service. Take the time to go through these resources: They provide help of all sorts.

ACTIVITY 1 Scavenger Hunt

Go to your own college's Web site. First, click on "Students" or "Current Students" and then on "Support Services" (it may have a slightly different name). After locating each of the services or resources listed below (column 1), fill in the chart with the information you learn.

SERVICE/RESOURCE	HOW CAN THIS SERVICE OR RESOURCE HELP ME? (LIST AT LEAST THREE SPECIFIC WAYS.)	LOCATION	
Advising			
Career Services			
College/Student Success			
Financial Aid			
Health Services			
Writing Center			

Make a Plan

As Ed Powell, who has mentored and advised many students, always tells students, "Those who fail to plan, plan to fail." Think about that.

When you went to the "Advising" page, you probably saw information about choosing a major, course scheduling, finding campus resources, and changing courses. All of these advising services will help you chart your course through college to your degree. Start making a plan by completing steps 1 and 2 that follow.

1.   What Do I Want to Be?

I want to be _____

TIP For tools to use in getting a job, visit the *Real Writing Student Center* at **bedfordstmartins.com/ realwriting**.

If you have only a general idea, for example, "I want to be a businessperson" or "I would like to work in the health-care field," try taking some time now to narrow that field. If you know you are interested in health care, break this large area into smaller, more specific or specialized subfields, as the photos and this diagram show.

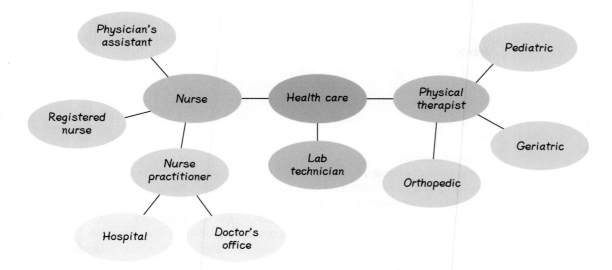

Try making a similar diagram to narrow and explore a general field you are interested in. After breaking a large area into more specific subfields, you will be able to fill in the statement "I want to be . . ." in a more specific way.

2. Talk with Your Academic Adviser and Plan Later Semesters/Terms

Make an appointment with your adviser to talk about what classes you will need to take. Try to plan out the next couple of semesters, even though class times might change. It is good to have a plan for beyond the next semester.

Then, working with your adviser, make a rough plan of the sequence of courses you need to take to graduate. For example, if you can take two courses a semester, plan what these courses will be, and figure out when you will be able to complete your requirements. Your plan may change later. Still, the important thing is to have a working plan for getting your degree or certificate.

Connect to the College

Many students do not know about their college's "student life," a rich array of activities, events, organizations, clubs, and projects that bring students together. Even if you commute to class, you can still become involved with student life and be a greater part of your college community. Why is this important?

The most successful students feel connected to the college, whether through a relationship with a teacher, coach, adviser, or someone they have met through participation in a college activity. Students involved in college activities are much less likely to drop out. They know more people who can help them when they have trouble, and they make good connections, for the present and for the future. Involved students also develop their interests and take advantage of different kinds of learning experiences. Many successful students believe that if they hadn't connected to the college in some way beyond classes, they would not have stayed.

TIP For more on connecting to community, visit **bedfordstmartins.com/ realwriting.**

COMMUNITY MATTERS

Dana Cardona

How I got connected to the college: I got dragged to a student government meeting by a friend, and then I got hooked. I became vice president and started a program that distributes "Love Bags," canvas bags filled with age- and gender-appropriate items for children recently put into foster care. Many of the children are taken from their homes suddenly and don't have a chance to gather their possessions. These bags help them a little. I got a local business that makes canvas bags to donate some. Doing this project made me very involved with my life at the college and also the larger community.

How the connection changed my life: When I started college, I didn't know about how much I could get involved. I wasn't a rich kid: I live in low-income housing with my mother. I went to a community college, and I took four years to get an Associate of Arts degree.

What I learned: I learned so much from my connection to student government and also a community service club I became president of. I learned that each person can make a difference: It only takes one. That realization changed my life. And because I was so involved in the college community, I did better in school. I started out taking a developmental course, but now not only have I graduated, but I've transferred, with a scholarship, to Bucknell University, a great four-year college.

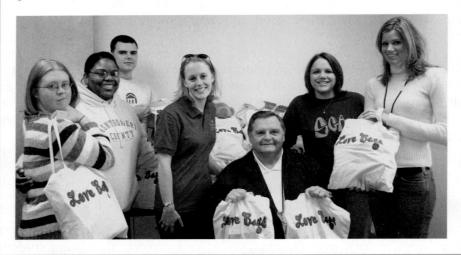

Look back at your college's Web site, and find "Student Life" or "Student Activities." Click there to find a page that lists general categories of student life, such as Cultural Diversity, College Radio, Intramural and Extramural Activities, and Student Activities and Clubs.

Here is a partial list of the student clubs and activities found at one college.

Adventure Club	Dance Group
Asian Club	Dental Hygiene Club
Community Service Club	Environmental Club
Criminal Justice Club	Guitar Club
Culinary Club	International Club

· ·

ACTIVITY 2   Interesting Clubs

Find out about three clubs at your college that you might be interested in, and fill in the following chart.

CLUB NAME	DESCRIPTION	LOCATION, MEETING TIMES

You will benefit in many ways by getting involved at your college: Data show that students connected to the college community do much better academically and graduate at higher rates. Find out what clubs and activities your college has, and go to one or two meetings.

· ·

Know Your Learning Style

People have different ways of learning, and knowing how you learn best is another strategy for success in college, at work, and in your everyday life. Take the following questionnaire to find out what your learning style is. Then, read about how to use your own learning style in college.

· ·

The VARK Questionnaire

Choose the answer that best explains your preference and circle the letter(s) next to it. **Please circle more than one** if a single answer does not match your perception. Leave blank any question that does not apply.

TIP To take the Learning Styles questionnaire online, go to **www.vark-learn.com**.

1. You are helping someone who wants to go to your airport, town center, or railway station. You would:

   a. go with her.

   c. write down the directions.

   b. tell her the directions.

   d. draw, or give her a map.

2. You are not sure whether a word should be spelled "dependent" or "dependant." You would:

   a. see the words in your mind and choose by the way they look.

   b. think about how each word sounds and choose one.

   c. find it in a dictionary.

   d. write both words on paper and choose one.

3. You are planning a holiday for a group. You want some feedback from them about the plan. You would:

   a. describe some of the highlights.

   b. use a map or Web site to show them the places.

   c. give them a copy of the printed itinerary.

   d. phone, text, or e-mail them.

4. You are going to cook something as a special treat for your family. You would:

   a. cook something you know without the need for instructions.

   b. ask friends for suggestions.

   c. look through the cookbook for ideas from the pictures.

   d. use a cookbook where you know there is a good recipe.

5. A group of tourists want to learn about the parks or wildlife reserves in your area. You would:

   a. talk about, or arrange a talk for them about, parks or wildlife reserves.

   b. show them Internet pictures, photographs, or picture books.

   c. take them to a park or wildlife reserve and walk with them.

   d. give them a book or pamphlets about the parks or wildlife reserves.

6. You are about to purchase a digital camera or cell phone. Other than price, what would most influence your decision?

   a. Trying or testing it.

   b. Reading the details about its features.

   c. It is a modern design and looks good.

   d. The salesperson telling me about its features.

7. Remember a time when you learned how to do something new. Try to avoid choosing a physical skill, for example, riding a bike. You learned best by:

   a. watching a demonstration.

   b. listening to somebody explaining it and asking questions.

    c. diagrams and charts—visual clues.

    d. written instructions—for example, a manual or textbook.

8. You have a problem with your knee. You would prefer that the doctor:

    a. gave you a Web address or something to read about it.

    b. used a plastic model of a knee to show what was wrong.

    c. described what was wrong.

    d. showed you a diagram of what was wrong.

9. You want to learn a new program, skill, or game on a computer. You would:

    a. read the written instructions that came with the program.

    b. talk with people who know about the program.

    c. use the controls or keyboard.

    d. follow the diagrams in the book that came with it.

10. I like Web sites that have:

    a. things I can click on, shift, or try.

    b. interesting design and visual feaures.

    c. interesting written descriptions, lists, and explanations.

    d. audio channels where I can hear music, radio programs, or interviews.

11. Other than price, what would most influence your decision to buy a new nonfiction book?

    a. The way it looks is appealing.

    b. Quickly reading parts of it.

    c. A friend talks about it and recommends it.

    d. It has real-life stories, experiences, and examples.

12. You are using a book, CD, or Web site to learn how to take photos with your new digital camera. You would like to have:

    a. a chance to ask questions and talk about the camera and its features.

    b. clear written instructions with lists and bullet points about what to do.

    c. diagrams showing the camera and what each part does.

    d. many examples of good and poor photos and how to improve them.

13. Do you prefer a teacher or a presenter who uses:

    a. demonstrations, models, or practical sessions?

    b. question and answer, talk, group discussion, or guest speakers?

    c. handouts, books, or readings?

    d. diagrams, charts, or graphs?

14. You have finished a competition or test and would like some feedback:

    a. using examples from what you have done.

    b. using a written description of your results.

    c. from somebody who talks it through with you.

    d. using graphs showing what you had achieved.

15. You are going to choose food at a restaurant or café. You would:

    a. choose something that you have had there before.

    b. listen to the waiter or ask friends to recommend choices.

    c. choose from the descriptions in the menu.

    d. look at what others are eating or look at pictures of each dish.

16. You have to make an important speech at a conference or special occasion. You would:

    a. make diagrams or get graphs to help explain things.

    b. write a few key words and practice saying your speech over and over.

    c. write out your speech and learn from reading it over several times.

    d. gather many examples and stories to make the talk real and practical.

(© Copyright Version 7.0 (2006) held by Neil D. Fleming, Christchurch, New Zealand, and Charles C. Bonwell, Green Mountain Falls, Colorado 80819 USA)

The VARK Questionnaire Scoring Chart

Use the following scoring chart to find the VARK category that each of your answers corresponds to. Circle the letters that correspond to your answers; for example, if you answered "b" and "c" for question 3, circle "V" and "R" in the question 3 row.

QUESTION	A CATEGORY	B CATEGORY	C CATEGORY	D CATEGORY
3	K	(V)	(R)	A

SCORING CHART

QUESTION	A CATEGORY	B CATEGORY	C CATEGORY	D CATEGORY
1	K	A	R	V
2	V	A	R	K
3	K	V	R	A
4	K	A	V	R
5	A	V	K	R
6	K	R	V	A
7	K	A	V	R

QUESTION	A CATEGORY	B CATEGORY	C CATEGORY	D CATEGORY
8	R	K	A	V
9	R	A	K	V
10	K	V	R	A
11	V	R	A	K
12	A	R	V	K
13	K	A	R	V
14	K	R	A	V
15	K	A	R	V
16	V	A	R	K

CALCULATING YOUR SCORES

Count the number of each of the VARK letters you have circled to get your score for each VARK category.

Total number of **V**s circled = ___

Total number of **A**s circled = ___

Total number of **R**s circled = ___

Total number of **K**s circled = ___

Use Your Learning Style in College

To figure out how to apply your learning style in college, look at the following sections and read the one that matches your style. If you have a preference for more than one learning style, read all the sections that apply.

Visual

Visual learners learn best by drawing, looking at images, or "seeing" things as they read, write, and listen.

Using Your Learning Style

To read/study →
- Draw pictures or diagrams of concepts.
- Use colored highlighters to mark what you want to remember.
- Note headings in texts, and look at diagrams, charts, graphs, maps, pictures, and other visuals.

- Write symbols that mean something to you in the margins. (For example, write exclamation points by the most important information in a chapter.)
- Make your own flowcharts or timelines.
- Make outlines in different-colored inks.

To write →	• Use mapping or clustering to get ideas. (See p. 53.) • Use charts or outlines to plan, write, and revise. • Use correction symbols to edit. (See the symbols at the back of this book.)
To take a test →	• Highlight important information, or put checks or other symbols by it. • Make a flowchart or outline of your answers.

Auditory

Auditory learners learn best by hearing things.

Using Your Learning Style	
To read/study →	• Read aloud notes, texts, handouts, and so on. • Tape lectures and class discussions (but don't forget to take notes, too). Later, you can listen to the recordings. • Listen to course-related audio CDs or tapes. • Talk to other students about course material. • Work with other students to prepare for class, complete activities, and so on.
To write →	• Get ideas by talking to yourself or others. • Read your writing aloud as you draft. • Read your writing aloud as you revise and edit.
To take a test →	• Read the directions and test items aloud in a quiet whisper. • Read your answers aloud in a quiet whisper.

Read/Write

Read/write learners learn best by reading and writing throughout a course.

Using Your Learning Style	
To read/study →	• Read headings, summaries, and questions in books. • Put what you read into your own words. • Take careful notes from books and lectures, and read them later. • Keep and read all handouts. • Highlight when you read. • Describe charts, diagrams, maps, and other visuals in writing.
To write →	• Freewrite or brainstorm to get ideas. (See p. 52.) • Keep a journal. (See p. 55.)

- Read and reread what you write, making notes for revision.
- Revise your writing several times.

To take a test →
- Read and highlight the directions.
- Write an outline for essay questions, or write quickly and revise.
- Reread your answers carefully.

Kinesthetic (Movement)

Kinesthetic learners learn by doing and by moving around.

Using Your Learning Style

To read/study →
- Stand up when you read or study.
- Take short breaks and walk around.
- Underline or highlight readings, or make notes — do something.
- Make flash cards to study course material.
- Make puzzles, like crosswords, to help you remember important concepts.
- Make your own study guides.
- Relate information to your own experiences.
- Mark examples in texts that are relevant to you.
- Write out questions that you have, and ask them.
- Work with other students to prepare for class and complete activities.

To write →
- Imagine your topic as a movie to get ideas.
- Think of ideas for writing as you walk.
- Imagine what pictures could express your ideas.
- Write ideas or details for a paper on sticky notes, and move the notes around.
- Create a writing notebook with different pockets for different kinds of ideas or writing.
- Write and ask questions about your topic.

To take a test →
- Breathe deeply and regularly throughout the test.
- Stand up and walk to a different part of the room (after asking your instructor for permission).
- Calculate the time you will spend on each part of the test, and time yourself.
- Stand and take a deep breath as you review your answers.

Writing Assignments

. . . .

ASSIGNMENT 1

Choose one of the services you found on your college's Web site, and make an appointment to interview someone who works there. Ask what services are provided, to whom, and how a student can make use of the service. Pick up handouts or brochures. Then, write about that student service, including what you found out in your interview, what useful material you got, and how the service helps students.

. . . .

ASSIGNMENT 2

Write about your life plan for yourself: What do you want to do and how will you do it?

. . . .

ASSIGNMENT 3

Write about one or two of your interests. Then, go to your college Web site and find the page for Student Clubs and Activities. Choose one club and find out more about it by going to the office and talking to someone who is involved in that club. Ask what the club does, when it meets, and who its members are. Write about what you found out.

. . . .

ASSIGNMENT 4

Take the learning styles questionnaire to find out what your learning style is. Write about your reaction to the results: Were you surprised? As you think about how you have learned things (or had trouble learning things), how does knowing your learning style help you adjust your approach to learning in the future? How can knowing more about your learning style help you in college?

. . . .

Chapter Review

1. What are five course basics that can help you succeed in this course and others? *take the course seriously, manage your time, connect to the class, identify your course goals and needs, hang in there*

2. What are some college basics? *know your resources, make a plan, connect to the college, know your learning style*

3.   How can you connect to your college? *Answers will vary.*

_____

_____

> **reflect** Using what you have learned from this chapter, revise your response to
> the "think" question on page 3.

2

Reading Basics

How to Understand What You Read

YOU KNOW THIS

Every day you read and understand what you read.

- You read text messages from your friends.
- You read signs, get information online, read about people or things that interest you, and follow the instructions in manuals and recipes.

think When you read for yourself, do you read differently than when you read for a class? How?

Understand How to Read Actively and Critically

Reading well increases your chances of success not only in college but also at work and in your everyday life. Good readers can find helpful, practical information about anything they are interested in: starting a business, finding a job, treating an illness, protecting themselves from unfair practices, and so on.

Understanding what you read in college—so that you don't finish an assignment without having a clue what it was all about—requires active, critical reading. The steps on the next few pages describe how to read for maximum understanding.

RESOURCES For tips on how to get your students to *do* the reading assignments, see *Practical Suggestions*.

Preview the Reading

Before you begin to read, look ahead. Go quickly through whatever you are reading (essay, chapter, article, and so on) to get an idea of what it contains. Many books, especially textbooks, help you figure out what is important by using headings (separate lines in larger type, like "Preview the Reading" above). They may also have words in **boldface**. In textbooks, magazines, and journals, words may be defined in the margin, or quotations may be pulled out in larger type. When you are reading a textbook or an essay or article in a college course, look through the chapter or piece for headings, boldface type, definitions in the margin, and quotations.

Read Actively

Reading actively means *doing* something with the reading instead of just looking at the words. Here are a few ideas on how to be actively involved with what you are reading.

Reading Actively

- Underline or highlight the main idea.
- Use another highlighter to show ideas that support the main idea.
- Put a checkmark (✓) in the margin in places where you find important information, and go back to review those places when you finish reading.
- Put a question mark (?) next to things you do not understand. Go back to these places later to see if their meaning is clearer after you have read the whole piece.
- Put an exclamation mark (!) next to ideas or points you do not agree with or find surprising.
- Write your reactions in the margin.

As you read, the two most important questions to keep in mind are:

BASIC READING QUESTIONS

1. What is the author's main point?
2. How does he or she support that point?

Find the Main Point

The main point is usually introduced early in a selection, so read the first few sentences or paragraphs with special care. If the writer has stated the main point in a single sentence or a couple of sentences, highlight or underline these words.

• •

PRACTICE 1 Finding the Main Point

Underline the main point in the following paragraphs. Then, write the main point in your own words in the space provided.

1. Psychologists have for some time noted the difference in problem-solving styles of Americans and Chinese, and new research underscores that difference. Psychologists say that Americans are specific problem solvers, focusing on one problem at a time. In contrast, Chinese consider the broader context of a problem before acting. Researchers at the

University of Michigan recently charted the eye movements of two groups of people when they were shown photographs. Americans focused on the foreground with only brief sweeps of the background. Chinese people focused on the background, with many eye movements back and forth and limited stops at a particular object. It appears that eye movements parallel problem-solving styles.

MAIN POINT: _Answers will vary._ _____

2. Many people look at me blankly when I say I am a vegan. They think maybe it is a religion or some unusual ethnic background. But a vegan is a normal person, a vegetarian who eats only plant products. Vegans do not eat meat (including fowl), fish, eggs, or milk products. That means I do not eat cheese, yogurt, or ice cream, among many other milk products. I do not eat anything that comes from a living creature. But that does not make me weird, or even a difficult dinner guest. I eat all kinds of vegetables, fruits, and beans. And I am one of a growing number of people who believe that it is healthier and more humane to eat only plant products. Because my diet does have restrictions, I have learned a lot about nutrition, and I eat no junk food. I am healthy, and I am a vegan.

MAIN POINT: _Answers will vary._ _____

3. The classroom is noisy, with loud voices bouncing off the walls. No one pays attention to the teacher who moves around the room, saying little. Students' desks are arranged in circles of four, but many students are not in their seats: They strain over sheets of paper at the center of each cluster of desks. They point and gesture. They argue. "No, that's not right. Listen to me!" says one student as she leans toward another. Is this the stereotypical chaos of an unruly, unengaged urban high school? No, it is indeed an urban high school classroom, and it indeed seems chaotic. But this is Mr. Brown's algebra class, and Mr. Brown's students are working on solving a problem. An engaged classroom looks and sounds alive, like Mr. Brown's class. A classroom of success is active, not passive.

MAIN POINT: _Answers will vary._ _____

4. The most destructive force in our social relations is aggression. In psychology, aggression has a more precise meaning than it does in every-

day usage. The assertive, persistent salesperson is not aggressive, nor is the dentist who makes you wince in pain. But the person who passes along a vicious rumor about you, the person who verbally assaults you, and the attacker who mugs you are aggressive. <u>In psychology, aggression is any physical or verbal behavior intended to hurt or destroy.</u> Murders and assaults that occurred as hostile outbursts are aggression. So were the 110 million war-related deaths that took place during the last century.

—David G. Myers, *Exploring Psychology,* Sixth Edition (NY: Worth, 2005)

MAIN POINT: *Answers will vary.*

Find the Support for the Main Point

Support—the details that show, explain, or prove the main point—takes different forms, depending on what you are reading. When you read assigned selections in college, you need to be aware of how the author is supporting or proving his or her main point. Ask yourself, "How is the author trying to get me to remember, believe, and agree with the main point being made here?" Sometimes the author uses statistics, facts, definitions, and scientific results to support the main point, and at other times the author uses memories, stories, comparisons, quotations from experts, and personal observations.

In tests and writing assignments, you are often asked to respond to reading selections. For example, you may be asked to consider an author's main point and to explain whether you agree or disagree with it. In your response, you would explain *why* you agree or disagree by referring to the author's support.

PRACTICE 2 Finding the Main Point and Support

The following excerpt is taken from a book about science by Bill Bryson. Double-underline the main idea, and place a checkmark in the margin next to sentences that support the main idea.

<u>The scariest, most out-of-control bacterial disorder of the moment</u> <u>is a disease called *necrotizing fasciitis* in which bacteria essentially eat the</u> <u>victim from the inside out, devouring internal tissue and leaving behind</u> <u>a pulpy, noxious residue.</u> Patients often come in with comparatively mild ✓ complaints—a skin rash and fever typically—but then dramatically deteriorate. When they are opened up it is often found that they are ✓ simply being consumed. The only treatment is what is known as "radical ✓

TIP For more practice identifying the main point and support, visit **bedfordstmartins.com/ realwriting**.

excisional surgery"—cutting out every bit of infected area. Seventy   ✓

percent of victims die; many of the rest are left terribly disfigured. The   ✓

source of the infection is a mundane family of bacteria called Group A

Streptococcus, which normally do no more than cause strep throat. Very   ✓

occasionally, for reasons unknown, some of these bacteria get through

the lining of the throat and into the body proper, where they wreak the

most devastating havoc. They are completely resistant to antibiotics.   ✓

About a thousand cases a year occur in the United States, and no one   ✓

can say that it won't get worse.

—Bill Bryson, *A Short History of Nearly Everything* (New York: Broadway Books, 2003), p. 314.

TIP For more information on support in writing, see Chapter 6.

Now practice reading actively by completing Practice 3. Make sure that you identify the main idea and support.

PRACTICE 3   **Reading Actively**

Look back at the "Reading Actively" box on page 23. Using the techniques listed there, read the following paragraphs actively. (They are from a longer paper written by a student in the Washington, D.C., area.)

The Right to Bear Arms

Sometimes a single sentence can carry great historical weight. In 2008, the United States Supreme Court considered the question of whether two Washington, D.C., laws regarding individual ownership of guns violated the Second Amendment of the Constitution. The laws banned registration of handguns by individuals, carrying a pistol without a license, and keeping firearms loaded and assembled. These laws were enacted in Washington, known at one time as "the murder capital," as a reaction to violence and the city's alarming number of deaths by shooting. The challenge to those laws, however, revolved upon the Court's interpretation of a single sentence in the Second Amendment to the Constitution.

The sentence in question was part of the Bill of Rights, adopted in 1791, when the English that people spoke and wrote was somewhat different than the language we use today. Interpreting the language of 1791 made the decision in 2008 extremely difficult. Legal scholars pored over the sentence: "A well-regulated Militia, being necessary to the security of a free State, the right of the people to keep and bear Arms, shall not be infringed."

Did it mean that the government could not abolish the use of weapons by the military, or could not abolish a military that exists to protect Americans' rights? People in favor of this interpretation point to the historical context: The country had just won independence from the government of England, and it did so because it formed its own militias (military units), which England opposed and wanted to disband. In this reading of the sentence, individual rights to have guns are not protected by the Second Amendment.

Or did the sentence mean people have a right to have guns, individuals as well as military personnel? A decision hinged on nine Supreme Court judges' understanding of that one sentence.

. . . .

What do you think the sentence in the Second Amendment really means? If you do not know how the case was decided, find out. Beyond the specific outcome, this case proves that language and punctuation are important, especially when the writer is not there to explain his or her intention.

TEACHING TIP The Supreme Court ruled that individuals have the right to own guns.

Read Critically

Reading critically means *thinking* about what you read while you read it. Many people believe what they read without questioning it: If it is in print, it must be true, right? Actually, *no*, particularly with material you read on the Internet or in advertisements. You need to examine ideas carefully and question them before accepting what you read as truth.

Critical Reading Questions

- What is the purpose?
- What is the main point?
- What evidence, explanations, or claims does the writer use?
- Does the writer show evidence of bias? How?
- If there is fine print (like in a credit card offer or an advertisement), do I know what it says and what I am agreeing to?
- What do I think of what I have read? Why, specifically?
- How does what I have learned connect to other things I know? How does it relate to experiences I have had?
- What questions do I have about either the writer or the information presented? (In college, these are questions to raise in class.)

• •

PRACTICE 4 Reading Critically

Use your notes on "The Right to Bear Arms" to respond to the questions in the "Reading Critically" box. Use this box as you read other selections, both in this chapter and in other coursework.

• •

PRACTICE 5 Reading Critically

Working by yourself or with other students, read the following documents from college, work, and everyday life, and answer the critical reading questions. *Answers may vary. Possible answers are shown.*

1. What is the writer's purpose? *Excepting the drug label, the documents' purpose is to make money for the people who created them.*

2. Is the writer biased? *Yes; the purpose is to sell something.*

3. What are the key words or major claims? *Answers could include any words in headlines or boldface type.*

4. What is in the fine print? *See "for those who qualify" in the e-mailed advertisement, "Some supply purchases may be required" in the telephone pole posting, and "faux" in the advertisement.*

5. What do you think of what you have read? Why? Does anything seem odd, unrealistic, or unreliable? Give specific examples. *None of the information is reliable: The college and work documents' claims can't possibly be true; the everyday life documents contain errors or misleading information. (Note excessively high dosage on drug label.)*

COLLEGE: AN E-MAILED ADVERTISEMENT

GET A COLLEGE DEGREE IN *TWO* WEEKS!

Are a few letters after your name the only thing that's keeping you from your dream job? Degree Services International will grant you a B.A., M.A., M.S., M.B.A., or Ph.D. from a prestigious nonaccredited institution based on what you already know!

NO CLASSES, EXAMS, OR TEXTBOOKS ARE REQUIRED
for those who qualify

If you order now, you'll receive your degree within two weeks.

CALL 1-800-555-0021

HURRY! Qualified institutions can grant these diplomas only because of a legal loophole that may be closed within weeks.

WORK: A POSTING ON A TELEPHONE POLE

Earn Thousands of Dollars a Week Working at Home!

Flexible Hours ♦ No Experience Needed

The health-care system is in crisis because of the millions of medical claims that have to be processed each day. You can benefit from this situation now by becoming an at-home medical claims processor. Work as much or as little as you like for great pay!

CALL 1-800-555-5831

for your starter kit

Some supply purchases may be required.

EVERYDAY LIFE: ADVERTISEMENT

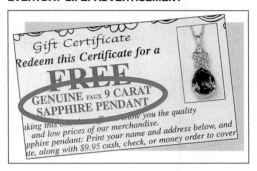

Gift Certificate
Redeem this Certificate for a
FREE
GENUINE ꜰᴀᴜx 9 CARAT
SAPPHIRE PENDANT
̶̶̶̶̶̶̶̶̶ you the quality
aking this ̶̶̶̶ ̶̶̶̶̶̶̶̶̶̶̶̶
and low prices of our merchandise.
pphire pendant: Print your name and address below, and
te, along with $9.95 cash, check, or money order to cover

EVERYDAY LIFE: PART OF A DRUG LABEL

Drug Facts	
Directions	
■ Do not take more than directed.	
Adults and children 12 years and over	■ Take 4 to 6 caplets every 2 hours as needed. ■ Do not take more than 8 caplets in 24 hours.
Children under 12 years	Do not use this product in children under 12 years of age. This could cause serious health problems.

TIP Pay attention to the dosage for adults.

Review and Reflect

When you have finished an article, an essay, a chapter, or a book, take some time to go back and look at your highlighting, marks, and notes to yourself. To help you remember the reading and your reaction to it, you may want to make more notes as you reflect. Reread things you did not understand, and try to answer the following questions.

TIP For tools to build your vocabulary, visit the *Real Writing Student Center* at **bedfordstmartins.com/ realwriting**.

- How would you summarize what you have read in a few sentences?
- What is your overall reaction to what you have read? Why do you have this reaction? (Note: If you answer, "It's boring," you need to give some specific reasons why.)
- What do you think your teacher wants you to get from the reading?

Now we will move to reading documents that are part of every college course: course syllabi and textbooks.

Understand Your Syllabus

It is important to understand your syllabus so that you know what your instructor expects from you. Read it the first day of class, and ask your instructor any questions you have. Check it regularly to make sure you are on course. Syllabi often include headings in **boldface** to help you find important information. The following example notes some critical features.

English 098 — Tuesday / Thursday, 8:30–10

Professor Murphy

Phone: 708-555-1113 / E-mail: murphy@sssc.edu

Office hours: T/Th, 11–12:30 and by appointment

COURSE DESCRIPTION: Students will use the writing process and will read, write, and edit effectively as well as use and document online and library sources.

Read carefully: Your grade will depend on how well you achieve these objectives.

COURSE OBJECTIVES:

- Use a variety of writing strategies.
- Recognize and correct grammar errors.
- Read and think critically and apply information.
- Develop ideas in paragraphs and essays with clear theses.

COURSE MATERIALS: Susan Anker, *Real Writing with Readings,* Fifth Edition

Explanation of grading policies

GRADING POLICIES (PERCENTAGE OF GRADE):

Papers	60%	Homework	10%
Tests	25%	Class participation	5%

Explanation of grading scale

GRADING SCALE FOR TESTS AND PAPERS:

A	90–100%	C	70–79%
B	80–89%	D	60–69%

Explanation of course policies

COURSE POLICIES:

- **Attendance:** Class attendance is required. Students who miss more than three classes must schedule an appointment with me to avoid penalty.
- **Classroom rules:** Arrive on time. Turn off cell phones.
- **Late or missed work:** No late work is accepted without my consent.
- **Academic integrity:** This course adheres to the college handbook.

PRACTICE 6   Reviewing Your Syllabus

Read your syllabus for this course. (1) What are the course goals? (2) What is the absentee policy? (3) Where is your teacher's office, and when are office hours?

Understand Textbook Features

Textbooks have features to help you understand content, such as headings, words in **boldface**, charts, boxes, bulleted and numbered lists, chapter reviews, and checklists. Following is an excerpt from a college psychology textbook explaining the ways in which we encode, or take in, information.

CHAPTER 9 : MEMORY **347**
Chapter number and title

Encoding: Getting Information In

Preview: How does sensory information, once registered, get encoded and transferred into the memory system? What types of information do we absorb incidentally? What types require intentional effort?

Major heading introduces main concept: encoding

How We Encode

Some encoding occurs automatically, freeing your attention to simultaneously process information that requires effort. Thus, your memory for the route you walked to your last class is handled by **automatic processing**. Your learning of this chapter's concepts requires **effortful processing** (FIGURE 9.2).

Minor heading introduces two types of encoding

Boldface type highlights key terms

Automatic Processing

Often with little or no effort, you encode an enormous amount of information about *space*, *time*, and *frequency*: During an exam, you may recall the place on the textbook page where forgotten material appears. To guess where you left your coat, you can re-create a sequence of the day's events. Passing a classmate, you may realize that "this is the third time I've run into you this afternoon." Effort may help us retain such memories, yet they form almost automatically. Not only does *automatic processing* occur effortlessly, it is difficult to shut off. When you hear or read a familiar word in your native language, whether an insult or a compliment, it is virtually impossible not to register its meaning automatically.

Subheading 1: Introduces one way of encoding

Some types of automatic processing we learn. For example, learning to read reversed sentences at first requires effort:

.citamotua emoceb nac gnissecorp luftroffE

After practice, some *effortful processing* becomes more automatic, much as reading from right to left becomes easy for students of Hebrew (Kolers, 1975).

Automatic processing occurs with little or no effort, without our awareness, and without interfering with our thinking about other things. (This is another example of our brain's capacity for parallel processing of multiple information streams.) What then would happen if we asked people to attend to information they encode automatically, such as judging the frequency of words presented during an experiment? Lynn Hasher and Rose Zacks (1979, 1984) found that this extra attention is of little benefit. Although memory for such material may be modestly boosted by effort, our encoding is mostly automatic: We cannot switch it on and off at will.

Effortful Processing

We encode and retain vast amounts of information automatically, but we remember other types of information only with effort and attention. When learning novel information such as names, we can boost our memory through **rehearsal**, or conscious repetition. This was shown long ago by the pioneering researcher of verbal memory, German philosopher Hermann Ebbinghaus (1850–1909). Ebbinghaus was to the study of memory what Ivan Pavlov was to the study of conditioning. Ebbinghaus became impatient with philosophical speculations about memory and decided to study it scientifically. To do so, he chose to study his own learning and forgetting of novel verbal materials.

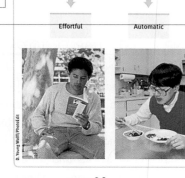

Encoding
Effortful   Automatic

O. Young Wolff/PhotoEdit   Robert Brenner/PhotoEdit

FIGURE 9.2
Automatic versus effortful processing
Some information, such as this chapter's concepts, requires effort to encode and remember. Other information, such as where you ate dinner yesterday, you process automatically.

Diagram shows and illustrates types of encoding

Caption explains diagrams and illustrations

Definitions explain key terms

- **automatic processing** unconscious encoding of incidental information, such as space, time, and frequency, and of well-learned information, such as word meanings.

- **effortful processing** encoding that requires attention and conscious effort.

- **rehearsal** the conscious repetition of information, either to maintain it in consciousness or to encode it for storage.

Subheading 2: Introduces another way of encoding

• •

PRACTICE 7   Reviewing This Textbook

Working by yourself or with another student, find the special features in one chapter of this book: Chapter 22 (on sentence fragments). Use the following questions to guide you. *Answers will vary. Possible answers are shown.*

1.   If you wanted to remember the five fragment trouble spots, what headings would you highlight? *the headings on the five kinds of fragments*

2.   What kind of information is boxed in the chapter? *lists or important words*

3.   What kinds of reviews do you find in the chapter? *A chapter review. Students may cite other reviews as well, such as practices and "Finding and Fixing" charts.*

• •

Highlighting a Textbook Chapter

As you read a textbook chapter, use brightly colored highlighters to mark important headings and information that explains the headings and that will help you review information later.

If you do not want to mark up your book, write the important information in a review notebook, as in the following setup:

IMPORTANT CHAPTER INFORMATION

Chapter number and title
Important headings
     Headings and page numbers
Locations of important definitions
     Terms and page numbers
Locations of boxes and other key extras
     Titles and page numbers
Review items
     Page numbers

• •

PRACTICE 8   Highlighting This Textbook

Look at Chapter 23 (on run-ons) or one that your instructor chooses, and highlight the important information. Use the active reading techniques in the box on page 23. Or, record key information on a separate piece of paper as shown in the previous example.

After you have read and highlighted a textbook chapter, go back and review your highlighting. In the margin or in your review notebook, write a few notes, in your own words, that will remind you of what is important. Also, note what you do not understand so that you can ask your instructor about it. This kind of reading and reviewing takes a little time, but it will save you time later when you are studying for a test. Also, highlighting and making notes will definitely improve your test results, making information "stick" in your memory better than reading alone will.

• •

Reviewing for a Test on a Textbook Chapter

To study for a test on a textbook chapter or chapters, set aside at least two different study sessions (more if it is a test on a whole unit). Allow extra review time the night before the test if you can, and also on the day of the test.

In addition to reviewing what you highlighted and made notes about, try one or more of the following techniques to firmly store the information in your brain:

TIP For a complete guide to test-taking, see Appendix A at the back of this book.

- Read your highlighting and notes aloud, especially standing up. Repeat this technique several times, in both study sessions.

- In both study sessions, rewrite your notes and the information you highlighted.

- Create a study guide for each chapter. To make a study guide, think about what will probably be on the test based on the course syllabus and on what your instructor has emphasized in class.

STUDY GUIDE

Chapter _____
1.   The most important information in this chapter is _____.
2.   The test is likely to have questions about _____.
3.   The most important thing(s) to know about the topics I listed in question 2 are
         Topic
               What I need to know
         Topic
               What I need to know
         Topic
               What I need to know
         Etc.
4.   What are some specific questions the instructor might ask?
5.   Is the test likely to be multiple choice or essay?
6.   The pages I want to review right before the test are _____.

Instructors might answer some of the study guide questions. For instance, they might tell you whether a test will be multiple choice or essay. However, do not expect them to tell you exactly what will be on a test. In college, you will be expected to know the material well enough to be prepared.

· ·

PRACTICE 9 Making a Study Guide

Working with another student or a group of students, assume that you are going to be tested on Chapter 24 (on subject-verb agreement) or on a chapter that your instructor assigns. Create a study guide that you could use to study for the test.

· ·

Chapter Review

1. What are the four ways to understand what you read? *preview the reading, read actively, read critically, review and reflect*

2. What are three techniques of active reading? *any of the six listed in the box on page 23*

3. How can you help yourself find and remember the main point and support? *Mark them with different colored highlighters (or other technique students want to use).*

4. As you read a textbook, what features should you pay attention to? *Answers will vary but may include boldface type, headings, charts, boxes, lists, chapter reviews, and summaries.*

5. Without looking back in the book, what are some questions you should ask yourself when you are practicing critical reading? *any of the questions in the box on page 27*

reflect How will you read differently after having read this chapter?

Writing Basics

Audience, Purpose, and Process

Four elements are key to good writing. Keep them in mind whenever you write.

■■ Four Basics of Good Writing
■■■

1 It considers what the audience knows and needs.

2 It fulfills the writer's purpose.

3 It includes a clear, definite point.

4 It provides support that explains or proves the main point.

This chapter discusses audience and purpose first because they are key to effective writing. Purpose determines a writer's main point, and audience determines how a writer best connects to his or her readers and makes the main point.

The chapter then discusses how to structure writing to meet the four basics and outlines the writing process, previewing steps that will be covered in more detail in the next six chapters. Finally, it gives you some typical grading criteria and shows how they are applied to assess unsatisfactory, satisfactory, and excellent paragraphs.

Understand Audience and Purpose

Your **audience** is the person or people who will read what you write. In college, your audience is usually your instructors. Whenever you write, always have at least one real person in mind as a reader. Think about what that person already knows and what he or she will need to know to understand your main point. In most cases, assume that readers know only what you write about your topic.

Your **purpose** is your reason for writing. Often in college, your purpose for writing will be to describe, explain, or argue. Your writing will vary depending on your audiences and purposes. Read the following two notes, which describe the same situation but are written for different audiences and purposes. Notice the tone and content of each note.

SITUATION: Marta woke up one morning with a fever. When she went into the bathroom, she saw in the mirror that her face was swollen and red. Then, she was hit with a violent attack of nausea. Marta immediately called her doctor, who said she could come right in. Marta's mother was coming to stay with Marta's children in a few minutes, so Marta asked a neighbor to watch her children until her mother got there. Marta then left a note for her mother telling her why she had already left. When she got to the doctor's office, the nurse asked her to write a brief description of her symptoms for the doctor.

MARTA'S NOTE TO HER MOTHER

Ma,
Not feeling very well this morning. Stopping by doctor's office before work. Don't worry, I'm okay, just checking it out. Can't miss any more work. See you after.

MARTA'S NOTE TO THE DOCTOR

When I woke up this morning, I had a fever. When I looked in the mirror, my face was swollen, especially around the eyes, which were almost shut. My lips and skin were red and dry, and my face was itchy. Within a few minutes, I vomited several times.

· ·

PRACTICE 1   Comparing Marta's Notes

Read Marta's two notes and answer the following questions. *Answers will vary. Possible answers are shown.*

1. How does Marta's note to her mother differ from the one to the doctor?
The note to the doctor is more specific and more formal.

2. How do the different audiences and purposes affect what the notes say (the content) and how they say it (the tone)? *Marta doesn't want to worry her mother, so she is general, and she is also informal. Marta wants the doctor to know exactly what happened, so she provides more specifics. She also writes more formally.*

3. Which note has more detail, and why? *the one to the doctor because Marta wants the doctor to know the symptoms she had*

· ·

As these examples show, we communicate with family members and friends differently than we communicate with people in authority (like employers, instructors, or other professionals) — or we should. Marta's note to her mother uses informal English and incomplete sentences, because the two women know each other well and are used to speaking casually to other. Because Marta's purpose is to get quick information to her mother and to reassure her, she doesn't need to provide a lot of details. On the other hand, Marta's note to her doctor is more formal, with complete sentences, because the relationship is more formal. Also, the note to the doctor is more detailed because the doctor will be making treatment decisions based on it.

In college, at work, and in your everyday life, when you are speaking or writing to someone in authority for a serious purpose, use formal English; people will take you seriously.

TIP For more practice with writing for a formal audience, see some of the problem-solving assignments in Part 2 and the "Using Formal English" practices in Chapters 22–25. Or, visit Exercise Central at **bedfordstmartins.com/ realwriting.**

• •

PRACTICE 2   **Writing for a Formal Audience**

A student, Terri Travers, sent the following e-mail to a friend to complain about not getting into a criminal justice course. Rewrite the e-mail as if you were Terri and you were writing to Professor Widener. The purpose is to ask whether the professor would consider allowing you into the class, given that you signed up early and have the necessary grades.

> To: Miles Rona
>
> Fr: Terri Travers
>
> Subject: Bummin
>
> Seriously bummin that I didn't get into Prof Widener's CJ class. U and
> Luis said it's the best ever, lol. Wonder why I didn't . . . I signed up early
> and I have the grades. Sup w/that?
>
> C ya,
> TT

• •

Understand Paragraph and Essay Form

In this course (and in the rest of college), you will write paragraphs and essays. Each of these has a basic structure.

Paragraph Form

A **paragraph** has three necessary parts: the topic sentence, the body, and the concluding sentence.

PARAGRAPH PART	PURPOSE OF THE PARAGRAPH PART
1. The **topic sentence**	states the **main point**. The topic sentence is often the first sentence of the paragraph.

2.	The **body**	supports (shows, explains, or proves) the main point with **support sentences** that contain facts and details.
3.	The **concluding sentence**	reminds readers of the main point and often makes an observation.

Read the paragraph that follows with the paragraph parts labeled.

Topic sentence ————

      Gambling is a growing addiction in this country. As more casinos open and more online gambling sites are created, more people have the opportunity to try gambling. For most people, a casino is simply a fun place to visit, filled with people, lights, noise, food, and a feeling of excitement as patrons try to beat the odds and win. Most people set a limit on how much money they are willing to lose, and when they reach that amount, they stop. Addicts, however, can't stop. They always want to play just one more game to get back what they lost. If they do make up for their losses, they feel lucky and don't want to end their winning streak. Win or lose, they keep playing, and the vast majority lose, returning repeatedly to the cash machine to replenish their funds, or getting cash advances on their credit cards. People have been known to spend their entire savings because they are caught up in the frenzy of trying to win. Because there are more casinos and online gambling sites, more addicts are surfacing, and the casinos and sites encourage the addiction: It means more money for them. The gamblers' support group,[1] Gamblers Anonymous, based on the principles of Alcoholics Anonymous, has seen vastly increased membership in the last few years as more potential addicts are introduced to gambling, fall into its clutches, and struggle to get free. Clearly, gambling needs to be taken as seriously as any other addiction.

Body
(with support sentences) ————

Concluding sentence ————

Essay Form

An **essay** is a piece of writing that examines a topic in more depth than a paragraph. A short essay may have four or five paragraphs, totaling three hundred to six hundred words. A long essay is six paragraphs or more, depending on what the essay needs to accomplish—persuading someone to do something, using research to make a point, or explaining a complex concept.

    An essay has three necessary parts: the introduction, the body, and the conclusion.

TEACHING TIP Have students interview a second- or third-year student in their major to find out what kind of writing that person does for his or her classes.

TEACHING TIP For some students, it helps to present visual analogies. Explain that just as a skyscraper needs more substantial support than a three-story apartment building, an essay needs more detailed support than a paragraph.

	ESSAY PART	PURPOSE OF THE ESSAY PART
1.	The **introduction**	states the **main point**, or **thesis**, generally in a single, strong statement. The introduction may be a single paragraph or multiple paragraphs.
2.	The **body**	supports (shows, explains, or proves) the main point. It generally has at least three **support paragraphs**, each containing facts and details

1. support group: A group of people who meet regularly to talk about, and try to overcome, a difficulty.

that develop the main point. Each support paragraph has a **topic sentence** that supports the thesis statement.

3. The **conclusion**   reminds readers of the main point. It may summarize and reinforce the support, or it may make an observation based on that support. Whether it is a single paragraph or more, the conclusion should relate back to the main point of the essay.

PARAGRAPH		ESSAY
Topic sentence	→	Thesis statement
Support sentences	→	Support paragraphs
Concluding sentence	→	Conclusion

The diagram that follows shows how the parts of an essay correspond to the parts of a paragraph.

RESOURCES *Additional Resources* contains reproducible forms that students can use to plan their paragraphs and essays. These forms are also available online at **bedford stmartins.com/realwriting**.

RELATIONSHIP BETWEEN PARAGRAPHS AND ESSAYS

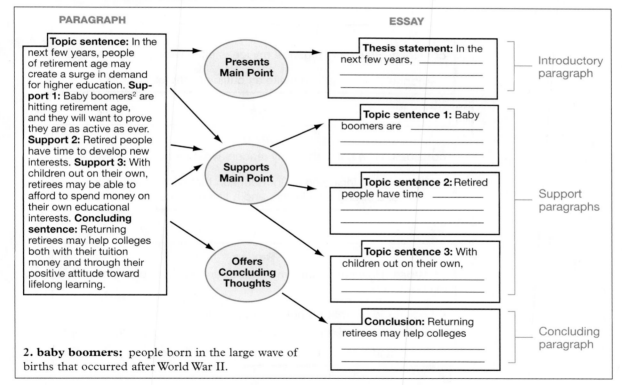

2. **baby boomers:** people born in the large wave of births that occurred after World War II.

Understand the Writing Process

With writing, as with tying a shoe, you have to learn many steps. But once you know the steps, you do them automatically, and they seem to blend together. The process gets a lot easier.

TEACHING TIP Ask students to describe a process related to their college experience, such as registering for classes, buying books, or applying for financial aid.

The chart that follows shows the five stages of the **writing process**: the steps you will follow to write well. The rest of the chapters in Part One cover every stage except editing (presented later in the book). You will practice each stage, see how another student completed the process, and write your own paragraph or essay. While you may not always go in a straight line through the five stages (you might circle back to earlier stages in the process), it helps to have these steps in mind.

The Writing Process

Generate ideas

CONSIDER: What is my purpose in writing? Given this purpose, what interests me? Who will read this? What do they need to know?

- Find and explore your topic (Chapter 4).
- Make your point (Chapter 5).
- Support your point (Chapter 6).

Plan

CONSIDER: How can I organize my ideas effectively for my readers?

- Arrange your ideas and make an outline (Chapter 7).

Draft

CONSIDER: How can I show my readers what I mean?

- Write a draft, including an introduction that will interest your readers, a strong conclusion, and a title (Chapter 8).

Revise

CONSIDER: How can I make my draft clearer or more convincing to my readers?

- Look for ideas that do not fit (Chapter 9).
- Look for ideas that could use more detailed support (Chapter 9).
- Connect ideas with transitional words and sentences (Chapter 9).

Edit

CONSIDER: What errors could confuse my readers and weaken my point?

- Find and correct errors in grammar (Chapters 22–33).
- Look for errors in word use (Chapters 34–35), spelling (Chapter 36), and punctuation and capitalization (Chapters 37–41).

Note: Avoiding Plagiarism

In all the writing you do, it is important to avoid plagiarism—using other people's words as your own or handing in information you gather from another source as your own. Your instructors are very aware of plagiarism and know how to look for it. Writers who plagiarize, either on purpose or by accident, risk failing a course or losing their jobs and damaging their reputations.

To avoid plagiarism, take careful notes on every source (books, interviews, television shows, Web sites, and so on) you might use in your writing. When recording information from sources, take notes in your own words, unless you plan to use direct quotations. In that case, make sure to record the quotation word for word and include quotation marks around it, both in your notes and in your paper.

When you use material from other sources—whether you directly quote or paraphrase—you must name and give citation information about these sources. See Chapter 20 for more about citing sources.

TIP For more information on avoiding plagiarism, and citing and documenting outside sources, see Chapter 20. Visit the Bedford/St. Martin's Workshop on Plagiarism at **http://bcs.bedfordstmartins.com/plagiarism** for online resources on avoiding plagiarism.

Understand Grading Criteria

Your instructor may use a **rubric**, which is a list of the elements or qualities that your papers will be graded on. If your instructor uses a rubric, it may be included in the course syllabus, and you should refer to it each time you write. Also, use the rubric to revise your writing.

The following sample rubric shows you some of the elements you may be graded on. Instructors use different rubrics, so the one here is just one example. Many rubrics include how each element is weighted; because that differs among instructors and courses, the example does not include percentages of importance or points.

Sample Rubric

ELEMENT	GRADING CRITERIA	POINT RANGE
Appropriateness	• Did the student follow the assignment directions?	0–5
Main idea	• Does the paper clearly state a strong main point, written in a complete sentence?	0–10
Support	• Is the main idea developed with specific support, including specific details and examples? • Is enough support presented to effectively make the main point evident to the reader? • Is all of the support directly related to the main point?	0–10
Organization	• Is the writing logically organized? • Does the student use transitions (*also*, *for example*, *sometimes*, and so on) to move the reader from one point to another?	0–10

(continued)

ELEMENT	GRADING CRITERIA	POINT RANGE
Conclusion	• Does the conclusion remind the reader of the main point? • Does the conclusion make an observation based on the support?	0–5
Grammar	• Is the writing free of the four most serious errors? (See Chapters 22–25.) • Is the sentence structure clear? • Does the student choose words that clearly express his or her meaning? • Are the words spelled correctly? • Is the punctuation correct?	0–10

The paragraphs that follow show how rubrics are applied to a piece of writing. For a key to the correction symbols used, see the chart at the back of this book.

ASSIGNMENT: Write a paragraph about something you enjoy doing. Make sure you give enough details about the activity so that a reader who knows little about it will have an idea of why you enjoy it.

PARAGRAPH 1

In my spare time, enjoy talking with friends. Talk about everything like problems fun things we have to do or nothing important. One friend Karen especial. She really understands me we been frends since ten. Without her, I need a shrink to help me thru tings.

ANALYSIS OF PARAGRAPH 1: This paragraph would receive a low grade, for these reasons.

Sample Rubric

ELEMENT	GRADING CRITERIA	POINT: COMMENT
Appropriateness	• Did the student follow the assignment directions?	**2/5:** Generally, yes, though without providing the details the assignment required.
Main idea	• Does the paper clearly state a strong main point, written in a complete sentence?	**0/10:** No. The topic sentence is not a complete sentence (it is missing a subject).

ELEMENT	GRADING CRITERIA	POINT: COMMENT
Support	• Is the main idea developed with specific support, including specific details and examples? • Is enough support presented to effectively make the main point evident to the reader? • Is all of the support directly related to the main point?	**0/10:** No. Few details included is the major problem with the paragraph.
Organization	• Is the writing logically organized? • Does the student use transitions (*also*, *for example*, *sometimes*, and so on) to move the reader from one point to another?	**2/10:** No transitions.
Conclusion	• Does the conclusion remind the reader of the main point? • Does it make an observation based on the support?	**3/5:** No reminder of the main point, but the last sentence has the start of an observation.
Grammar	• Is the writing free of the four most serious errors? (See Chapters 22–25.) • Is the sentence structure clear? • Does the student choose words that clearly express his or her meaning? • Are the words spelled correctly? • Is the punctuation correct?	**2/10:** No, the writing has many errors of all kinds. **TOTAL POINTS: 9/50**

• •

PRACTICE 3 Adding Detail

Rewrite the paragraph, adding detail about the second and fourth sentences. If you know how to correct the grammar (including spelling and punctuation), make the corrections.

TEACHING TIP Have students work in pairs to do Practice 3.

PARAGRAPH 2

In my spare time, I enjoy talking with my friend Karen. I know *(tense)* Karen since we ten, *(tense)* so we have growed *(tense)* up together and been through many things. Like a sister. *(frag)* We can talk about anything.

Sometimes we talk about problems. Money problems, problems with men. *(frag)* When I was in an abusive relationship, for example. *(frag)* Now we both have children and we talk about how to raise them. Things are diffrent (sp) then (sp) when we kids (tense). Talking with a good friend helps me make good decisions and patience (wc). Especially now that my son is a teenager (frag). We also talk about fun things, like what were going to do (punc) on the weekend, what clothes we buy (run-on). We tell each other good jokes and make each other laugh. These conversations are as important as talking about problems.

ANALYSIS OF PARAGRAPH 2: This paragraph would receive a higher grade (but still not an A or B) for the following reasons.

Sample Rubric

ELEMENT	GRADING CRITERIA	POINT: COMMENT
Appropriateness	• Did the student follow the assignment directions?	**5/5:** Yes.
Main idea	• Does the paper clearly state a strong main point, written in a complete sentence?	**10/10:** Yes.
Support	• Is the main idea developed with specific support, including specific details and examples? • Is there enough support to effectively make the main point evident to the reader? • Is all of the support directly related to the main point?	**5/10:** The paragraph has more support and detail than Paragraph 1 does, but it could use more.
Organization	• Is the writing logically organized? • Does the student use transitions (*also, for example, sometimes,* and so on) to move the reader from one point to another?	**6/10:** The student uses a few transitions (*sometimes, when, for example, now*).
Conclusion	• Does the conclusion remind the reader of the main point? • Does it make an observation based on the support?	**5/10:** The conclusion is better than the one in Paragraph 1. It relates back to the main point, but the observation is weak.
Grammar	• Is the writing free of the four most serious errors? (See Chapters 22–25.) • Is the sentence structure clear? • Does the student choose words that clearly express his or her meaning? • Are the words spelled correctly? • Is the punctuation correct?	**6/10:** Compared to Paragraph 1, the writing has fewer grammar errors but still has some major ones. **TOTAL POINTS: 37/50**

● ●

PRACTICE 4   Making Corrections

Correct any of the errors in Paragraph 2 that you can.

RESOURCES If you are interested in having your students keep writing portfolios, see *Practical Suggestions*.

● ●

PRACTICE 5   Writing a Concluding Sentence

Try writing a concluding sentence to Paragraph 2. (Several answers are possible.)

PARAGRAPH 3

In my spare time, I enjoy talking with my friend Karen. We have been friends since we were ten, so we have grown up together. We have been through many things, both good and bad, in our lives, and we understand each other without having to explain the background of any situation. We have talked about our various problems throughout the years. Long ago, most of our problems were with our parents, who tried to control us too much. We would plan how to get around the rules we didn't like. Over the years, we have often talked about our relationships with men, which we call "the good, the bad, and the ugly." When I was in an abusive relationship, Karen helped me see that it wasn't good for me. She helped me get out of and over it. She helped me move on and value myself when I felt low. Now we talk often about our children and how to raise them right. For example, my son is now a teenager, and sometimes I can't control him, just as my parents couldn't control me. Karen helps me think of ways to get through to him without losing my temper. Also, we have always been able to make each other see the humor in whatever is going on. We tell each other good jokes, we make fun of people who are unfair to us, and we have a whole language of fun. These conversations are as important as the ones that help solve problems. Throughout my life, talking with Karen has helped keep me on a good path, and I truly enjoy talking with her.

ANALYSIS OF PARAGRAPH 3: This is an excellent paragraph, for the following reasons.

Sample Rubric

ELEMENT	GRADING CRITERIA	POINT: COMMENT
Appropriateness	• Did the student follow the assignment directions?	**5/5:** Yes.
Main idea	• Does the paper clearly state a strong main point, written in a complete sentence?	**10/10:** Yes.

(continued)

ELEMENT	GRADING CRITERIA	POINT: COMMENT
Support	• Is the main idea developed with specific support, including specific details and examples? • Is there enough support to effectively make the main point evident to the reader? • Is all of the support directly related to the main point?	**10/10:** Good support with lots of details.
Organization	• Is the writing logically organized? • Does the student use transitions (*also, for example, sometimes,* and so on) to move the reader from one point to another?	**10/10:** Good use of transitions (*long ago, over the years, when, now, for example, throughout*).
Conclusion	• Does the conclusion remind the reader of the main point? • Does the conclusion make an observation based on the support?	**10/10:** Strong concluding sentence with good observation.
Grammar	• Is the writing free of the four most serious errors? (See Chapters 22–25.) • Is the sentence structure clear? • Does the student choose words that clearly express his or her meaning? • Are the words spelled correctly? • Is the punctuation correct?	**10/10:** No errors. **TOTAL POINTS: 50/50**

TEACHING TIP Tell students that they will be learning about topic sentences, support, transitions, and conclusions. The practice is to show them that they already know some of what makes for good writing.

PRACTICE 6   Analyzing the Paragraph

Referring to Paragraph 3, answer the following questions. *Some answers will vary. Possible answers are shown.*

1. Which sentence is the topic sentence? *sentence 1*

2. Underline some of the added details that make Paragraph 3 stronger than the first two paragraphs, and note those details here. *Answers will vary.*

3. Circle the transitions and write them here. *long ago, over the years, when, now, for example, throughout*

4. In what way is the last sentence a good concluding sentence? *It refers back to the topic sentence with the phrase "talking with Karen," and it makes an observation: "has helped keep me on a good path."*

RESOURCES For advice about using writing portfolios, including how to structure and evaluate them, see *Practical Suggestions*.

5. What are rubrics? What are four of the elements often evaluated in
rubrics? *grading criteria; appropriateness, main idea, support,*
organization, conclusion, grammar

• •

Chapter Review

1. Go back and highlight important terms in this chapter. Make a list of
them, noting what page they appear on. *Answers will vary.*

2. In your own words, define *audience*. *the person or people who will read*
what I write

3. In college, who is your audience likely to be? *my instructors*

4. What are the stages of the writing process? *generating ideas, planning,*
drafting, revising, editing

5. Think of other courses in which you have written papers or taken tests.
What purposes has that writing had? *showing knowledge of the material,*
arguing for my point of view

6. What did you know about the stages of the writing process before you
read this chapter? _____

_____

7. How do audience and purpose affect how you write? *tone and content*

> **reflect** Having read this chapter, would you change your response to the
> "think" question on p. 35?

Finding, Narrowing, and Exploring Your Topic

Choosing Something to Write About

STUDENT VOICES

Chelsea Wilson exchanged messages with her friend Nick Brown about an assignment she had received. Nick had taken the same writing course a semester earlier.

Message—Chelsea to Nick (9:15 a.m.)

I've got a writing assignment where we choose our own topic.

I can't think of anything to write about.

Message—Nick to Chelsea (9:18 a.m.)

Try asking yourself a few questions.

Like, what are you interested in?

What's been going on in your life lately? How's your job going?

think of a topic you have written about in the past. Was it a good topic? Why or why not?

Understand What a Topic Is

A **topic** is who or what you are writing about, the subject of your paragraph or essay. A good topic is one that interests you, that you can say something about, and that you can get involved in.

QUESTIONS FOR FINDING A GOOD TOPIC

- Does this topic interest me? If so, why do I care about it?
- Do I know something about the topic? Do I want to know more?
- Can I get involved with some part of the topic? Is it relevant to my life in some way?
- Is the topic specific enough for the assignment (a paragraph or a short essay)?

TIP For help finding topic ideas, visit **www.plinky.com**.

Choose one of the following topics or one of your own and focus on one part of it with which you are familiar. (For example, focus on one personal goal or a specific aspect of romantic relationships that interests you.)

- Music/group I like
- Problems of working students
- An activity/group I'm involved in
- Something I can do well
- Reality television
- Relationships
- Sports
- An essential survival skill
- A personal goal
- A time when I took a big risk
- A time when I was lucky/unlucky

PRACTICE 1   Finding a Good Topic

Ask the "Questions for Finding a Good Topic" about the topic you have chosen. If you answer "no" to any of them, keep looking for another topic or modify the topic.

MY TOPIC: _Answers will vary._

With the general topic you have chosen in mind, read this chapter and complete all the practices. When you finish the chapter, you will have found a good topic to write about and explored ideas related to that topic.

Practice Narrowing a Topic

If your instructor assigns a general topic, it may at first seem uninteresting, unfamiliar, or too general. It is up to you to find a good, specific topic based on the general one. Whether the topic is your own or assigned, you next need to narrow and explore it. To **narrow** a general topic, focus on the smaller parts of it until you find one that is interesting and specific.

TEACHING TIP To give students an example of what narrowing a topic is like, use a camera analogy. The general topic is similar to using a wide-angle lens. Narrowing it is like zooming in closer so that you can examine or focus on smaller elements of your subject.

There are many ways to narrow a topic. For example, you can try dividing a general category into smaller subcategories. Or you can think of specific examples from your life or from current events.

Divide It into Smaller Categories

Think of Specific Examples from Your Life

GENERAL TOPIC   **Crime**
Stolen identities (how does it happen?)
When I had my wallet stolen by two kids (how? what happened?)
The telemarketing scam that my grandmother lost money in (how did it work?)

GENERAL TOPIC   **Web sites**
Shopping online (for what, and where?)
Music (what kind? what can I get?)
My favorite sites (why do I like them?)

Think of Specific Examples from Current Events

GENERAL TOPIC   **Economic recession**
Loss of jobs
Foreclosures
Loans becoming harder to get

GENERAL TOPIC   **Heroism**
The guy who pulled a stranger from a burning car
The people who stopped a robbery downtown

A topic for an essay can be a little broader than one for a paragraph, because essays are longer than paragraphs and allow you to develop more ideas. But be careful: Most of the extra length in an essay should come from developing ideas in more depth (giving more examples and details, explaining what you mean), not from covering a broader topic.

When you have found a promising topic for a paragraph or essay, be sure to test it by using the "Questions for Finding a Good Topic" at the beginning of this chapter. You may need to narrow and test several times before you find a topic that will work for the assignment. Read the following examples of how a general topic was narrowed to a more specific topic for an essay, and an even more specific topic for a paragraph.

GENERAL TOPIC		NARROWED ESSAY TOPIC		NARROWED PARAGRAPH TOPIC
Drug abuse	→	How alcoholism affects family life	→	How alcoholism affects a family's budget
Public service opportunities	→	Volunteering at a homeless shelter	→	My first impression of the homeless shelter
A personal goal	→	Getting healthy	→	Eating the right foods
A great vacation	→	A family camping trip	→	What I learned on our family camping trip to Michigan

TEACHING TIP Give students examples of questions they might be asked that are too "big" to answer in a paragraph or essay. Have them figure out how to narrow the question or assignment.

- -

PRACTICE 2   Narrowing a General Topic

Use one of the three methods above to narrow your topic. Then, ask yourself the "Questions for Finding a Good Topic." Write your narrowed topic below.

MY NARROWED TOPIC: *Answers will vary.* _____

- -

Practice Exploring Your Topic

Use **prewriting techniques** to explore your narrowed topic and to generate ideas that you can use in a paragraph or an essay.

Prewriting techniques can give you ideas at any time during your writing: to find a topic, to get ideas for what you want to say about it, and to support your ideas. Ask yourself: What interests me about this topic? What do I know? What do I want to say? Then, use one or more of the prewriting techniques to find the answers. No one uses all of those techniques; writers choose the ones that work best for them. To find out which ones work best for you, though, you will need to try out all of them.

PREWRITING TECHNIQUES

- Freewriting
- Listing/brainstorming
- Discussing
- Clustering/mapping
- Using the Internet
- Keeping a journal

When prewriting, do not judge your ideas. At this point, your goal is to come up with as many ideas as possible, so do not say, "Oh, that's stupid" or "That won't work." Just get your brain working by writing down all the possibilities.

A student, Chelsea Wilson, was assigned to write a short essay. She chose to write on the general topic of a personal goal, which she narrowed to "Getting a college degree." The following pages show how she used the first five prewriting techniques to explore her topic.

Freewriting

TIP If you are writing on a computer, try a kind of freewriting called "invisible writing." Turn the monitor off, or adjust the screen so that you cannot see what you are typing. Then, write quickly for five minutes without stopping. After five minutes, read what you have written. You may be surprised by the ideas that you can generate this way.

Freewriting is like having a conversation with yourself, on paper. To free-write, just start writing everything you can think of about your topic. Write nonstop for five minutes. Do not go back and cross anything out, and don't worry about using correct grammar or spelling; just write. Here is Chelsea's freewriting:

> So I know I want to get a college degree even though sometimes I wonder if I ever can make it because it's so hard with work and my two-year-old daughter and no money and a car that needs work. I can't take more than two courses at a time and even then I hardly get a chance to sleep if I want to do any of the assignments or study. But I have to think I'll get a better job because this one at the restaurant is driving me nuts and doesn't pay much so I have to work a lot with a boss I can't stand and still wonder how I'm gonna pay the bills. I know life can be better if I can just manage to become a nurse. I'll make more money and can live anywhere I want because everyplace needs nurses. I won't have to work at a job where I am not respected by anyone. I want respect, I know I'm hardworking and smart and good with people and deserve better than this. So does my daughter. No one in my family has ever graduated from college even though my sister took two courses, but then she stopped. I know I can do this, I just have to make a commitment to do it and not look away.

Listing/Brainstorming

List all of the ideas about your topic that you can think of. Write as many as you can in five minutes without stopping.

> <u>GETTING A COLLEGE DEGREE</u>
>
> want a better life for myself and my daughter
> want to be a nurse and help care for people
> make more money
> not have to work so many hours
> could live where I want in a nicer place
> good future and benefits like health
> get respect
> proud of myself, achieve, show everyone
> be a professional, work in a clean place

Discussing

Many people find it helpful to discuss ideas with another person before they write. As they talk, they get more ideas, and they get immediate feedback from the other person.

Team up with another person. If you both have writing assignments, first explore one person's topic, then the other's. The person whose topic is being explored is the interviewee; the other person is the interviewer. The interviewer should ask questions about anything that seems unclear and should let the interviewee know what sounds interesting. The interviewee should give thoughtful answers and keep an open mind. It is a good idea to take notes when you are the interviewee. Here is Chelsea's discussion with Nick, a friend who had taken this writing course a semester before.

Nick: How's work?

Chelsea: It's OK except for lots of hours, a sleazy, stingy boss, dirty work with weird hours. Actually, I can't stand it. I want better.

Nick: Like what?

Chelsea: Getting a degree and becoming a nurse. They make good money and can live wherever they want because everyone needs nurses.

Nick: Isn't a personal goal one of the topics the instructor gave you to choose from? How about "getting a degree and becoming a nurse"?

Chelsea: Yeah, I could write about getting a nursing degree, but I'm not sure I know enough about it. And I didn't leave lots of time to find out. The draft is due in two days, and I have work.

Nick: So, other than being a nurse, why else do you want a degree? Write about that.

TIP If you find that talking about your ideas with someone is a good way to get going, you might want to ask another student to be your regular partner and discuss ideas before beginning any paragraph or essay assignment.

RESOURCES Advice for students about giving and getting feedback is available (along with the Peer Factor skills-building game) at the *Re: Writing Plus* site, at **bedford stmartins.com/rewritingplus**.

• •

PRACTICE 3   Exploring Your Narrowed Topic

Use two or three prewriting techniques to explore your narrowed topic.

• •

Clustering / Mapping

Clustering, also called mapping, is like listing except that you arrange your ideas visually. Start by writing your narrowed topic in the center. Then, write the questions Why? What interests me? and What do I want to say? around the narrowed topic. Circle these questions and draw lines to connect them to the narrowed topic. Next, write three answers to these questions. Circle these ideas and connect them to the questions. Keep branching out from the ideas until you feel you have fully explored your topic. On the next page is an example of Chelsea's clustering. Note that when Chelsea filled in "What do I want to say?", "What interests me?", and "Why I want a degree," she had lots of reasons and ideas that she could use in her writing assignment.

TIP For online mapping tools, visit **http://bubbl.us**.

RESOURCES It is helpful to provide students with a form they can use for clustering. A form is provided in *Additional Resources*.

RESOURCES For an animation demonstrating clustering, see the *Make-a-Paragraph Kit* CD-ROM.

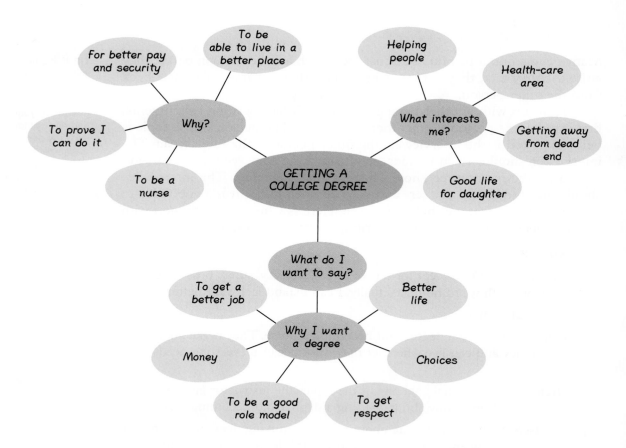

Using the Internet

Go to www.google.com, and type in specific key words about your topic. The search will provide more results than you can use, but it will help you with ideas for your paper. For example, Chelsea typed in "reasons to get a college degree" and got lots of information about aspects of her topic that she didn't know much about, such as what a college degree is worth. Make notes about important or useful ideas you get from the Internet.

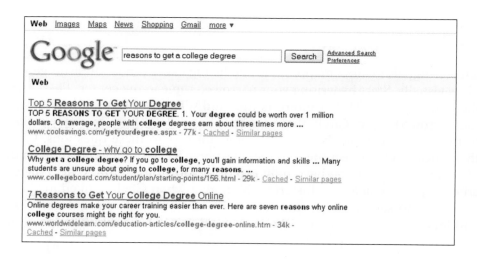

Keeping a Journal

Setting aside a few minutes on a regular schedule to write in a journal will give you a great source of ideas when you need them. What you write does not need to be long or formal. You can use a journal in several ways:

- To record and explore your personal thoughts and feelings
- To comment on things that happen, either to you, or in politics, in your neighborhood, at work, in college, and so on
- To explore situations you don't understand (as you write, you may figure them out)

One student, Jack, was assigned to write in his journal, and at first he didn't like the idea. But as he got used to writing in one, he found that it not only gave him ideas he could use in writing assignments but also helped him understand his own behaviors.

> I've been really stressed lately and kind of depressed about whether I can really make it in college. Might fail my math class and might just skip the test Thursday so I don't have to face another bad grade. I just can't seem to keep up, and my teacher doesn't seem very interested in helping me, maybe because I'm afraid to ask questions and just shrug when he calls on me and I don't know the answer. I don't want to ask him for extra help but I don't think I can pass on my own. Should I just drop the course and try again later? But I'm halfway through already. What can I do? Someone said there's a tutoring center at the college but I wasn't paying attention. Maybe I should find out where it is and what it does and when it's open. I hate asking for help but I don't know if I can make it without understanding things better. I think some of the tutors are other students, so maybe they won't laugh.

TIP Look for the "Idea Journal" and "Learning Journal" assignments throughout this book.

RESOURCES For tips on helping students keep journals, see *Practical Suggestions*.

TEACHING TIP Some students may feel uncomfortable with journal writing. Emphasize that journal entries will not be graded, are confidential, and do not have to be written in polished prose.

Write Your Own Topic and Ideas

If you have worked through this chapter, you should have both your narrowed topic (recorded in Practice 2) and ideas from your prewriting. Now is the time to make sure your topic and ideas about it are clear. Use the checklist that follows to make sure that you have completed this step of the writing process.

CHECKLIST

Evaluating your narrowed topic

- ☐ This topic interests me.
- ☐ My narrowed topic is specific.
- ☐ I can write about it in a paragraph or an essay (whichever you have been assigned).
- ☐ I have generated some things to say about this topic.

Now that you know what you are going to write about, you are ready to move on to the next chapter, which shows you how to express what is important to you about your narrowed topic.

Chapter Review

1.   Highlight important terms from this chapter (for example, *topic, narrow,* and *prewriting techniques*), and list them with their page numbers.

2.   What are four questions that can help you find a good topic? <u>*Does it*</u> <u>*interest me? Do I know something about it? Can I get involved with*</u> <u>*some part of it? Is it specific enough for the assignment?*</u>

3.   What are some prewriting techniques? <u>*freewriting, listing/brainstorming,*</u> <u>*discussing, clustering/mapping, using the Internet, keeping a journal*</u>

4.   What are two kinds of journals? <u>*idea journal, learning journal*</u>

5.   Write for one minute about "What questions I should ask my professor."

STUDENT VOICES

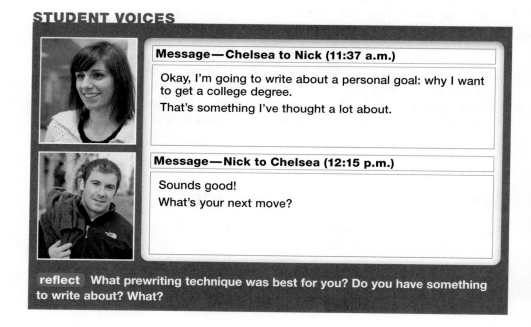

Message—Chelsea to Nick (11:37 a.m.)

Okay, I'm going to write about a personal goal: why I want to get a college degree.

That's something I've thought a lot about.

Message—Nick to Chelsea (12:15 p.m.)

Sounds good!

What's your next move?

reflect   What prewriting technique was best for you? Do you have something to write about? What?

Writing Your Topic Sentence or Thesis Statement

Making Your Point

STUDENT VOICES

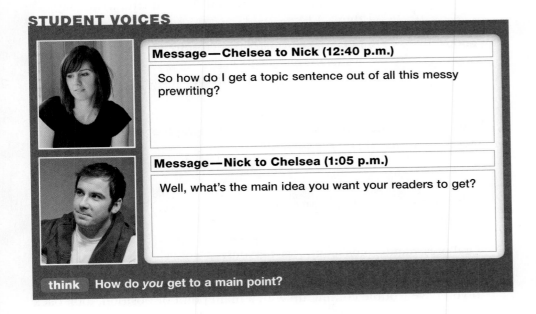

Message—Chelsea to Nick (12:40 p.m.)

So how do I get a topic sentence out of all this messy prewriting?

Message—Nick to Chelsea (1:05 p.m.)

Well, what's the main idea you want your readers to get?

think How do *you* get to a main point?

Chelsea Wilson exchanged messages with her friend Nick Brown about an assignment she had received. Nick had taken the same writing course a semester earlier.

Understand What a Topic Sentence and a Thesis Statement Are

Every good piece of writing has a **main point**—what the writer wants to get across to the readers about the topic, or the writer's position on that topic. A **topic sentence** (for a paragraph) and a **thesis statement** (for an

RESOURCES For an animated demonstration of writing topic sentences, see the Extreme Paragraph Makeover on the *Make-a-Paragraph Kit* CD-ROM.

57

essay) express the writer's main point. To see the relationship between the thesis statement of an essay and the topic sentences of paragraphs that support this thesis statement, see the diagram on page 61.

In many paragraphs, the main point is expressed in either the first or last sentence. In essays, the thesis statement is usually one sentence (often the first or last) in an introductory paragraph that contains several other sentences related to the main point.

A good topic sentence or thesis statement has several basic features.

ESL Some cultures (particularly Asian ones) avoid making direct points in writing. You may need to explain that in English the rhetorical convention is that the writer make a clear, direct point. Ask students if writing conventions in their countries approach the main point differently.

BASICS OF A GOOD TOPIC SENTENCE OR THESIS STATEMENT

- It fits the size of the assignment.
- It states a single main point or position about a topic.
- It is specific.
- It is something you can show, explain, or prove.
- It is a forceful statement.

WEAK   Bill Gates, chairman of Microsoft, started programming computers when he was thirteen, and I think he does a lot of good.
[This statement does not follow the basics for three reasons: It has more than one point (Gates's age and his doing good), it is not specific (what is the good that he does?), and it is not forceful (the writer says, "I think").]

IDEA JOURNAL What are your strongest communication skills? What other skills or talents do you have?

GOOD   Bill Gates, chairman of Microsoft, is a computing genius who showed his talents early.
Bill Gates, chairman of Microsoft, uses his vast wealth for the good of society.

One way to write a topic sentence for a paragraph or a thesis statement for an essay is to use this basic formula as a start:

| Narrowed topic | + | Main point/position | = | Topic sentence Thesis statement |

Oral presentations make me very nervous.

If you have trouble coming up with a main point or position, look back over the prewriting you did. For example, when the student Chelsea Wilson looked over her prewriting about getting a college degree (see p. 52), she realized that several times she had mentioned the idea of more options for employment, living places, and chances to go on and be a nurse. She could also have chosen to focus on the topic of respect or on issues relating to her young daughter, but she was most drawn to write about the idea of *options*. Here is how she stated her main point:

Narrowed topic	+	Main point/position	=	Topic sentence Thesis statement

Getting a college degree would give me more job and life options.

PRACTICE 1   Finding the Topic Sentence and Main Point

Read the paragraph that follows, and underline the topic sentence. In the spaces below the paragraph, identify the narrowed topic and the main point.

A recent survey reported that employers consider communication skills more critical to success than technical skills. Employees can learn technical skills on the job and practice them every day. But they need to bring well-developed communication skills to the job. They need to be able to make themselves understood to colleagues, both in speech and in writing. They need to be able to work cooperatively as part of a team. Employers can't take time to teach communication skills, but without them an employee will have a hard time.

NARROWED TOPIC: *communication skills*

MAIN POINT: *Employers consider communication skills more critical to success than technical skills.*

PRACTICE 2   Identifying Topics and Main Points

In each of the following sentences, underline the topic and double-underline the main point about the topic.

EXAMPLE: Rosie the Riveter was the symbol of working women during World War II.

1. Discrimination in the workplace is alive and well.

2. The oldest child in the family is often the most independent and ambitious child.

3. Gadgets created for left-handed people are sometimes poorly designed.

4. Presidential campaigns bring out dirty politics.

5. Companies that default on their employees' pensions should be taken to court.

6. The magazine *Consumer Reports* can help you decide which brands or models are the best value.

TEACHING TIP Ask students to bring in newspaper or magazine articles in which they have highlighted thesis statements or topic sentences. They should also label the topic and main point or position about that topic. Read and discuss some of these examples in class.

7. Of all the fast-food burgers, Burger King's Whopper is the best buy.

8. Status symbols are for insecure people.

9. Some song lyrics have serious messages about important social issues.

10. The Puritans came to America to escape religious intolerance, but they were intolerant themselves.

• •

Your first try at your topic sentence or thesis statement will probably need some changes to make it better. As you get further along in your writing, you may go back several times to revise the topic sentence or thesis statement, based on what you learn as you develop your ideas. Look at how one student revised the example sentence on page 58 to make it more detailed:

Oral presentations make me so nervous that I freeze and forget what I want to say.

Although a topic sentence or thesis statement states a single main point or position, this main point or position may include more than one idea; however, the ideas should be closely related. For example:

Health-care costs are out of control and must be lowered.

Practice Developing a Good Topic Sentence or Thesis Statement

The explanations and practices in this section, organized according to the "basics" described previously, will help you write good topic sentences and thesis statements.

It Fits the Size of the Assignment

As you develop a topic sentence or thesis statement, think carefully about the length of the assignment.

Sometimes, a main-point statement can be the same for a paragraph or essay.

Topic   Main point

In the next few years, people of retirement age may create a surge in the demand for higher education.

If the writer had been assigned a paragraph, she might write sentences that included the following support points:

SUPPORT 1:   Baby boomers[1] are hitting retirement age, and they will want to prove that they are as active as ever.

SUPPORT 2:   Retired people have time to develop new interests.

SUPPORT 3:   With children out on their own, retirees may be able to afford to spend money on their own educational interests.

CONCLUDING SENTENCE: Returning retirees may help colleges both with their tuition money and through their positive attitude toward lifelong learning.

If the writer had been assigned an essay, she might develop the same support, but instead of writing single sentences to support her main idea, she would develop each support point into a paragraph. The support sentences she wrote in a paragraph might be topic sentences for support paragraphs. (For more on providing support, see Chapter 6.)

Other times, however, a topic sentence for a paragraph is much narrower than a thesis statement for an essay, simply because a paragraph is shorter and allows less development of ideas.

RELATIONSHIP BETWEEN PARAGRAPHS AND ESSAYS

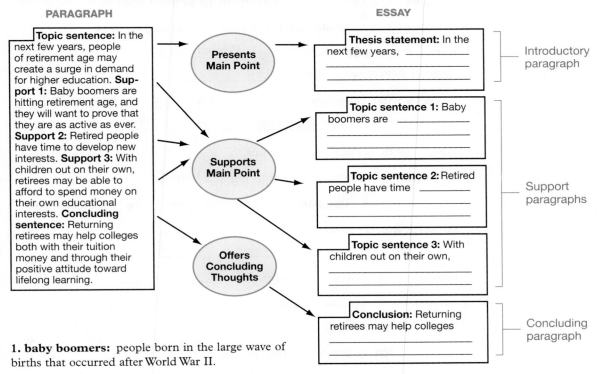

1. baby boomers: people born in the large wave of births that occurred after World War II.

Consider how one general topic could be narrowed into an essay topic, and into an even more specific paragraph topic.

GENERAL TOPIC	NARROWED ESSAY TOPIC	NARROWED PARAGRAPH TOPIC
Drug abuse →	How alcoholism affects family life →	How alcoholism affects a family's budget

POSSIBLE THESIS STATEMENT (ESSAY) Alcoholism can destroy family life.

[The essay might go on to give several ways in which alcoholism negatively affects the family.]

POSSIBLE TOPIC SENTENCE (PARAGRAPH) Alcoholism can drain a family's budget, adding money problems to drinking problems.

[The paragraph focuses on one way alcoholism can affect family life—by creating financial hardships. The paragraph might go on to give examples of how budget pressures hurt the family.]

· ·

PRACTICE 3 Writing Sentences to Fit the Assignment

Using the following example as a guide, write a thesis statement for the narrowed essay topic and a topic sentence for the narrowed paragraph topic.

RESOURCES To test students on choosing effective thesis statements and topic sentences, see the *Testing Tool Kit* CD-ROM available with this book.

EXAMPLE:

TOPIC: Sports

NARROWED FOR AN ESSAY: Competition in school sports

NARROWED FOR A PARAGRAPH: User fees for school sports

POSSIBLE THESIS STATEMENT (essay): *Competition in school sports has reached dangerous levels.*

POSSIBLE TOPIC SENTENCE (paragraph): *This year's user fees for participation in school sports are too high.*

1. **TOPIC:** Public service opportunities

   NARROWED FOR AN ESSAY: Volunteering at a homeless shelter

   NARROWED FOR A PARAGRAPH: My first impression of the homeless shelter

   POSSIBLE THESIS STATEMENT (essay): *Answers will vary.*

   _____

   POSSIBLE TOPIC SENTENCE (paragraph): _____

   _____

2. **TOPIC:** A personal goal

   NARROWED FOR AN ESSAY: Getting healthy

NARROWED FOR A PARAGRAPH: Eating the right foods

POSSIBLE THESIS STATEMENT (essay): _____

_____

POSSIBLE TOPIC SENTENCE (paragraph): _____

_____

3. **TOPIC:** A great vacation

NARROWED FOR AN ESSAY: A family camping trip

NARROWED FOR A PARAGRAPH: A lesson I learned on our family camping trip

POSSIBLE THESIS STATEMENT (essay): _____

_____

POSSIBLE TOPIC SENTENCE (paragraph): _____

_____

TEACHING TIP When students write on the computer, have them use bold type for their topic sentence or thesis statement. This helps you see what they consider their main point and helps them stay focused as they provide support.

. . . .

Some topic sentences or thesis statements are too broad for either a short essay or a paragraph. A main idea that is too broad is impossible to show, explain, or prove within the space of a paragraph or short essay.

TOO BROAD   Art is important.
                   [How could a writer possibly support such a broad concept in a paragraph or essay?]

NARROWER   Art instruction for young children has surprising benefits.

A topic sentence or thesis that is too narrow leaves the writer with little to write about. There is little to show, explain, or prove.

TOO NARROW   Buy rechargeable batteries.
                   [Okay, so now what?]

BROADER   Choosing rechargeable batteries over conventional batteries is one effective action you can take to save the environment.

. . . .

PRACTICE 4 Writing Topic Sentences That Are Neither Too Broad Nor Too Narrow

In the following five practice items, three of the topic sentences are either too broad or too narrow, and two of them are OK. In the space to the left of the item, write either "B" for too broad, "N" for too narrow, or "OK" for just right. Rewrite the three weak sentences to make them broader or narrower as needed.

EXAMPLE: _B_ Life can be tough for soldiers when they come home.

We are not providing our returning soldiers with enough help in
readjusting to civilian life.

_____

1.   _N_ I take public transportation to work.
   Answers will vary.
   _____

2.   _OK_ Because of state and national education budget cuts, schools are having to lay off teachers and cut important programs.
   _____
   _____

3.   _B_ College is challenging.
   _____
   _____

4.   _B_ I would like to be successful in life.
   _____
   _____

5.   _OK_ Having a positive attitude improves people's ability to function, improves their interactions with others, and reduces stress.
   _____
   _____

• •

It Contains a Single Main Point

Your topic sentence or thesis statement should focus on only one main point. Two main points can split and weaken the focus of the writing.

Main Idea with Two Main Points

High schools should sell healthy food instead of junk food, and they should start later in the morning.

The two main points are underlined. Although both are good main points, together they split both the writer's and the readers' focus. The writer would need to give reasons to support each point, and they are completely different ideas.

Main Idea with a Single Main Point

High schools <u>should sell healthy food instead of junk food.</u>

OR

High schools <u>should start later in the morning.</u>

The main point may contain more than one idea, but these ideas should be closely related and serve an overall main point you want to make. For example, some writers use a three-point topic sentence (for a paragraph) or thesis statement (for an essay) that includes the main point and previews three support points that will be explored in the rest of the paragraph or essay.

Three-Point Thesis

High schools should sell healthy food instead of junk food because (1) it is better for students, (2) it is often less expensive, and (3) it can boost levels of energy and attention.

• •

PRACTICE 5   Writing Sentences with a Single Main Point

In each of the following sentences, underline the main point(s). Identify the sentences that have more than a single main point by marking an X in the space provided to the left of that item. Put a checkmark (✓) next to sentences that have a single main point.

> **EXAMPLE:** <u>X</u> Shopping at secondhand stores is <u>a fun way to save</u> <u>money,</u> and <u>you can meet all kinds of interesting people</u> <u>as you shop</u>.

1. <u>✓</u> My younger sister, the baby of the family, <u>was the most adventurous</u> <u>of my four siblings</u>.

2. <u>X</u> Political campaigns are <u>often nasty,</u> and <u>the voting ballots are difficult</u> <u>to understand</u>.

3. <u>X</u> My brother, Bobby, is <u>incredibly creative,</u> and <u>he takes in stray animals</u>.

4. <u>X</u> Pets can actually <u>bring families together,</u> and <u>they require lots of care</u>.

5. <u>✓</u> Unless people conserve voluntarily, we will <u>deplete our supply of water</u>.

• •

It Is Specific

A good topic sentence or thesis statement gives readers specific information so that they know exactly what the writer's main point is.

GENERAL	Students are often overwhelmed.
	[How are students overwhelmed?]
SPECIFIC	Working college students have to learn how to juggle many responsibilities.

One way to make sure that your topic sentence or thesis statement is specific is to make it a preview of what you are planning to say in the rest of the paragraph or essay.

PREVIEW: Working college students have to learn how to juggle many responsibilities: doing a good job at work, getting to class regularly and on time, being alert in class, and doing the homework assignments.

PREVIEW: I have a set routine every Saturday morning that includes sleeping late, going to the gym, and shopping for food.

· ·

PRACTICE 6   Writing Sentences That Are Specific

In the space below each item, revise the sentence to make it more specific. There is no one correct answer. As you read the sentences, think about what would make them more understandable to you if you were about to read a paragraph or essay on the topic.

EXAMPLE: Marriage can be a wonderful thing.

Marriage to the right person can add love, companionship, and support

to life.

1. My job is horrible.

Answers will vary.

2. Working with others is rewarding.

3. I am a good worker.

4. This place could use a lot of improvement.

5. Getting my driver's license was challenging.

· ·

It Is an Idea That You Can Show, Explain, or Prove

If a main point is so obvious that it does not need support, or if it states a simple fact, you will not have much to say about it.

OBVIOUS   Models are thin.

The Honda Accord is a popular car model.

Many people like to take vacations in the summer.

REVISED   In order to be thin, many models have to starve themselves.

Japanese cars became popular because they appealed to customers in ways that American car makers had missed.

The vast and incredible beauty of the Grand Canyon[2] draws crowds of visitors each summer.

FACT   Guns can kill people.

Violent crime was up 10 percent this summer.

More than 60 percent of Americans aged twenty and older are overweight.

REVISED   More than twenty thousand youths under age twenty are killed or injured by firearms each year in the United States.

Summer, a time of vacations, is also a time of increased violent crime.

The obesity rate in the United States is so high that reduction of it is now a national priority.

· ·

PRACTICE 7   Writing Sentences with Ideas That You Can Show, Explain, or Prove

Revise the following sentences so that they contain an idea that you could show, explain, or prove.

    EXAMPLE: Leasing a car is popular.

Leasing a car has many advantages over buying one. _____

1.   I wear my hair long.
    Answers will vary. _____

2.   My monthly rent is $750.

    _____

3.   Health insurance rates rise every year.

    _____

2. Grand Canyon (in Arizona): one of the most popular tourist attractions in the United States.

4. Many people in this country work for minimum wage.

_____

5. Technology is becoming increasingly important.

_____

It Is Forceful

A good topic sentence or thesis is forceful. Do not say you *will* make a point. Just make it. Do not say "I think." Just state your point.

WEAK	In my opinion, everyone should exercise.
FORCEFUL	Everyone should exercise to reduce stress, maintain a healthy weight, and feel better overall.
WEAK	I think student fees are much too high.
FORCEFUL	Student fees need to be explained and justified.

PRACTICE 8   Writing Forceful Sentences

Rewrite each of the following sentences to make them more forceful. Also, add details to make the sentences more specific. *Answers will vary. Possible answers given.*

> **EXAMPLE:** Jason's Market is the best.

Jason's Market is clean, organized, and filled with quality products.

1. I will prove that drug testing in the workplace is an invasion of privacy.
Drug testing in the workplace is an invasion of privacy.

2. This school does not allow cell phones in class. *Because cell phones are disruptive, this school does not allow them in class.*

3. I strongly think that I deserve a raise. *I deserve a raise based on my strong performance over the past year.*

4. Nancy should be the head of the Students' Association.
Because she is hardworking and concerned about campus issues, Nancy should be the head of the Students' Association.

5. I think my neighborhood is nice. *My neighborhood is safe, close to stores, and diverse.*

Write Your Own Topic Sentence or Thesis Statement

If you have worked through this chapter, you should have a good sense of how to write a topic sentence or thesis statement that includes the five features of a good one (see p. 58).

Before writing your own topic sentence or thesis statement, consider the process that Chelsea Wilson used. First, she narrowed her topic.

> **GENERAL TOPIC:** *a personal goal*
>
> **NARROWED TOPIC (FOR A PARAGRAPH):** *why I want to get a college degree*
>
> **NARROWED TOPIC (FOR AN ESSAY):** *the many benefits of getting a college degree*

Then, she did prewriting (see Ch. 4) to get ideas about her topic.

> **FOR A PARAGRAPH:** *why I want to get a college degree*
> *make more money*
> *better job*
> *professional*
> *can live where I want*
>
> **FOR AN ESSAY:** *the many benefits of getting a college degree*
> *get a job as a nurse*
> *make more money*
> *be a good role model for my daughter*
> *be proud of myself*

Next, she decided on the point she wanted to make about her topic—in other words, her position on it.

> **FOR A PARAGRAPH:** *I want to be a nurse, and that means getting a college degree.*
>
> **FOR AN ESSAY:** *Getting a college degree will give me more options to get a nursing degree, find a job, and move.*

Then, she was ready to write the statement of her main point.

> **TOPIC SENTENCE (PARAGRAPH):** *My goal is to get a degree in nursing.*
>
> **THESIS STATEMENT (ESSAY):** *I am committed to getting a college degree.*

TIP For tools to use in getting a job, visit the *Real Writing Student Center* at **bedfordstmartins.com/ realwriting**.

Finally, Chelsea revised this statement to make it more forceful.

> **TOPIC SENTENCE:** *My long-term goal is to become a registered murse.*
>
> **THESIS STATEMENT:** *I am committed to getting a college degree because it will give me many good job and life options.*

You may want to change the wording of your topic sentence or thesis statement later, but following a sequence like Chelsea's should start you off with a good basic statement of your main point.

● ●

TEACHING TIP Even if you aren't reading a student's entire first draft, it always helps to check the topic sentence or thesis statement, because you can clear up numerous potential problems before you have to give a grade.

WRITING ASSIGNMENT

Write a topic sentence or thesis statement using the narrowed topic you developed in Chapter 4, your response to the idea journal prompt on page 58, or one of the following topics (which you will have to narrow).

Community service	Holiday traditions
A controversial issue	A strong belief
Dressing for success	Snitching
Movies	Exciting experiences
Good/bad neighbors	Juggling many responsibilities
Interviewing for jobs	Friendship
Music	Fast food

● ●

After writing your topic sentence or thesis statement, complete the checklist that follows.

> **CHECKLIST**
> **Evaluating your main point**
> ☐ It is a complete sentence.
> ☐ It fits the assignment.
> ☐ It includes my topic and the main point I want to make about it.
> ☐ It states a single main point.
> ☐ It is specific.
> ☐ It is something I can show, explain, or prove.
> ☐ It is forceful.

LEARNING JOURNAL How would you help someone who said, "I have some ideas about my topic, but how do I write a good topic sentence or thesis statement?"

Coming up with a good working topic sentence or thesis statement is the foundation of the writing you will do. Now that you know what you want to say, you are ready to learn more about how to show, explain, or prove it to others. That is covered in the next chapter: Supporting Your Point.

Chapter Review

1. Highlight important terms from this chapter (for example, *topic sentence*, *thesis statement*, and *main point*), and list them with their page numbers.

2. The **main point** of a piece of writing is *what the writer wants to get across to the readers about the topic.*

3. One way to write a **topic sentence** or a **thesis statement** is to include the narrowed topic and *the main point/position about the topic.*

4. The basics of a good topic sentence or thesis statement are

    It fits the size of the assignment.

    It states a single main point or position about a topic.

    It is specific.

    It is something you can show, explain, or prove.

    It is a forceful statement.

5. Write for one minute about "What questions I should ask my professor."

STUDENT VOICES

Message—Chelsea to Nick (2:33 p.m.)

I feel good about my topic sentence!

It tells my readers why I want to get a degree and be a nurse.

Plus, it's specific enough, I know about it, AND it could be interesting to readers.

Message—Nick to Chelsea (2:48 p.m.)

Hey, you've got me wanting to read it!
That's something!

reflect What do you think of Chelsea's topic sentence? Does it fit the basics of a good topic sentence?

6

Supporting Your Point

Finding Details, Examples, and Facts

Chelsea Wilson exchanged messages with her friend Nick Brown about an assignment she had received. Nick had taken the same writing course a semester earlier.

STUDENT VOICES

Message—Chelsea to Nick (3:06 p.m.)

There's something more I don't get.
How do I support my main point?
You know, the one I've stated in my topic sentence?

Message—Nick to Chelsea (3:10 p.m.)

Think specifics. Your main point is that you want a degree, right?
So start with your first reason, and give hard facts to show it's a GOOD reason.

think What is the purpose of support in writing?

RESOURCES For more on support, see the Extreme Paragraph Makeover feature on the *Make-a-Paragraph Kit* CD-ROM.

Understand What Support Is

Support is the collection of examples, facts, or evidence that shows, explains, or proves your main point. **Primary support points** are the major ideas that back up your main point, and **secondary support** gives details to back up your primary support.

72

Without support, you *state* the main point, but you don't *make* the main point. Consider these unsupported statements:

The amount shown on my bill is incorrect.
I deserve a raise.
I am innocent of the crime.

The statements may be true, but without good support, they are not convincing. If you sometimes get papers back with the comment "You need to support/develop your ideas," the suggestions in this chapter will help you.

Writers sometimes confuse repetition with support. The same point repeated several times is not support. It is just repetition.

REPETITION, NOT SUPPORT	The amount shown on my bill is incorrect. You over-charged me. It didn't cost that much. The total is wrong.
SUPPORT	The amount shown on my bill is incorrect. I ordered the bacon-cheeseburger plate, which is $6.99 on the menu. On the bill, the order is correct, but the amount is $16.99.

IDEA JOURNAL Write about a time that you were overcharged for something. How did you handle it?

As you develop support for your main point, make sure that it has these three features.

BASICS OF GOOD SUPPORT

- It relates to your main point. The purpose of support is to show, explain, or prove your main point, so the support you use must be directly related to that main point.

- It considers your readers. Create support that will show your readers what you mean.

- It is detailed and specific. Give readers enough detail, particularly through examples, so that they can see what you mean.

TIP Showing involves providing visual details or other supporting observations. Explaining involves offering specific examples or illustrating aspects of the main point. Proving involves providing specific evidence, sometimes from outside sources.

Read the following two paragraphs. The first paragraph provides some support for the main point but does not give many details about it. The second paragraph has added details (secondary support) to help readers see the main point. The supporting details are underlined; in both paragraphs, the topic sentence is in **bold**.

PARAGRAPH WITH PRIMARY SUPPORT

Training for success in a marathon demands several important steps. Runners should first get a schedule developed by a professional running organization. They should commit to carefully following the schedule. On the night before and the morning of the big day, runners should take special steps to make sure they are prepared for the race.

PARAGRAPH WITH SECONDARY SUPPORT ADDED

> Training for success in a marathon demands several important steps. Runners should first get a schedule developed by a professional running organization. These schedules are available in bookstores or on the Web. A good one is available at www.runnersworld.com. All of the training schedules suggest starting training three to six months before the marathon. Runners should commit to carefully following the schedule. If they cannot stick to it exactly, they need to come as close as they possibly can. The schedules include a mixture of long and short runs at specified intervals. Carefully following the training schedule builds up endurance a little at a time so that by the time of the race, runners are less likely to hurt themselves. The training continues right up until the start of the marathon. On the night before and the morning of the big day, runners should take special steps to make sure they are prepared for the race. The night before the race, they should eat carbohydrates, drink plenty of water, and get a good night's sleep. On the day of the marathon, runners should eat a light breakfast, dress for the weather, and consider doing a brief warm-up before the race's start. Before and during the race, they should drink plenty of water. Running a marathon without completing the essential steps will not bring success; instead it may bring pain and injury.

Practice Supporting a Main Point

Generate Support

To generate support for the main point of a paragraph or essay, try one or more of these three strategies:

THREE QUICK STRATEGIES FOR GENERATING SUPPORT

1. *Circle an important word or phrase* in your topic sentence (for a paragraph) or thesis statement (for an essay) and write about it for a minute or two. Reread your main point to make sure you're on the right track. Keep writing about the word or phrase.

2. *Reread your topic sentence or thesis statement and write down the first thought you have.* Then, write down your next thought. Keep going.

3. *Use a prewriting technique* (freewriting, listing, discussing, clustering, and so on) while thinking about your main point and your audience. Write for three to five minutes without stopping.

TEACHING TIP Emphasize to students that prewriting can help them at every stage of the writing process, whenever they need to develop ideas further or provide more detail.

• •

PRACTICE 1   Generating Supporting Ideas

Choose one of the following sentences, or your own topic sentence or thesis statement, and use one of the three strategies just mentioned to generate support. Because you will need a good supply of ideas to support your main point, try to find at least a dozen possible supporting ideas. Keep your answers because you will use them in later practices in this chapter. *Answers will vary.*

1. The new reality TV programs are stranger than ever.

2. Today there is no such thing as a "typical" college student.

3. Learning happens not only in school but throughout a person's life.

4. Practical intelligence can't be measured by grades.

5. I deserve a raise.

IDEA JOURNAL Write about any of the sentences you don't choose for Practice 1.

Select the Best Primary Support

After you have generated possible support, review your ideas and select the best ones to use as primary support. Here you get to take control of your topic. By choosing the support you give your readers, you are shaping the way they will see your topic and main point. These are *your* ideas, and you need to sell them to your readers.

The following steps can help:

1. Carefully read the ideas you have generated.

2. Select three to five primary support points that will best get your main point across to readers. If you are writing a paragraph, these will become the primary support for your topic sentence. If you are writing an essay, they will become topic sentences of paragraphs that support your thesis statement.

3. Choose the support that will be clearest and most convincing to your readers, providing the best examples, facts, and observations to support your main point.

4. Cross out ideas that are not closely related to your main point.

5. If you find that you have crossed out most of your ideas and do not have enough left to support your main point, use a prewriting technique to find more.

As you review your ideas, you may also come up with new ones that would be good support. If you come up with a new idea, jot it down.

TIP For a diagram showing the relationship between topic sentences and support in paragraphs, and thesis statements and support in essays, see page 61 of Chapter 5.

TEACHING TIP Remind students that just because they find a point interesting doesn't necessarily mean they should include it in their writing. It must support their main point.

PRACTICE 2 Selecting the Best Support

Refer to your response to Practice 1 (p. 74). Of your possible primary support points, choose three to five that you think will best show, explain, or prove your main point to your readers. Write your three to five points in the space provided.

Answers will vary. _____

_____

_____

_____

Add Secondary Support

Once you have selected your best primary support points, you need to flesh them out for your readers. Do this by adding **secondary support**, specific examples, facts, and observations to back up your primary support points.

. . . .

PRACTICE 3   Adding Secondary Support

Using your answers to Practice 3, choose three primary support points and write them in the spaces indicated. Then, read each of them carefully and write down at least three supporting details (secondary support) for each one. For examples of secondary support, see the example paragraph on page 74. *Answers will vary.*

TEACHING TIP Tell students to ask themselves the kinds of questions their readers will ask: Such as? In what way? For example? If their support points answer those questions, readers should understand their main point.

PRIMARY SUPPORT POINT 1:

_____

    SUPPORTING DETAILS: _____

_____

_____

PRIMARY SUPPORT POINT 2:

_____

    SUPPORTING DETAILS: _____

_____

_____

PRIMARY SUPPORT POINT 3:

_____

    SUPPORTING DETAILS: _____

_____

_____

. . . .

Write Your Own Support

Before developing your own support for a main point, look at how Chelsea developed support for hers.

TOPIC SENTENCE: *My goal is to get a degree in nursing and work in that wonderful profession.*

First, she did some prewriting (using the listing technique) and selected the best primary support points, while eliminating ones she didn't think she would use.

PRIMARY SUPPORT POINTS

> *GETTING AN L.P.N. DEGREE*
>
> *nurses help people and I want to do that*
> *jobs all over the country*
> *good jobs with decent pay*
> ~~*good setting, clean*~~
> *a profession, not just a job*
> *opportunity, like R.N.*
> *bigger place, more money*
> *treated with respect*
> *role model*
> *pride in myself and my work, what I've done*
> ~~*good benefits*~~
> ~~*nice people to work with*~~
> *may get paid to take more classes—chance for further professional development*
> ~~*uniform so not lots of money for clothes*~~
> ~~*I'll be something*~~

Chelsea noticed that some of her notes were related to the same subject, so she arranged them into related clusters, with the smaller points indented under the larger ones.

COMPUTER: Have students first type in possible support and then cut and paste to group it. They can easily move the points around to try new groupings.

ORGANIZED LIST OF SUPPORT POINTS

> *good job*
>   *decent pay*
>   *jobs all over the country*
>
> *a profession, not just a job*
>   *treated with respect*
>   *opportunity for the future (like R.N.)*
>   *maybe get paid to take more classes?*
>
> *pride/achievement*
>   *a job that helps people*
>   *I had to work hard*
>   *a role model*
>   *I'm doing something important*

Then she took the notes she made and organized them into primary support and supporting details. Notice how she changed some of her smaller points.

> **PRIMARY SUPPORT:** *Being an L.P.N. is an excellent job.*
> **SUPPORTING DETAILS:** *The pay is regular and averages about $40,000 a year.*
> *I could afford to move to a bigger and better place with more room for my daughter and work fewer hours.*
>
> **PRIMARY SUPPORT:** *Nursing is a profession, not just a job.*
> **SUPPORTING DETAILS:** *Nurses help care for people, an important job, giving to the world.*
> *Future opportunities, like becoming an R.N. with more money and responsibility.*
> *People respect nurses.*
>
> **PRIMARY SUPPORT:** *Being a nurse will be a great achievement for me.*
> **SUPPORTING DETAILS:** *I will have worked hard and met my goal.*
> *I will respect myself and be proud of what I do.*
> *I will be a good role model for my daughter.*

WRITING ASSIGNMENT

Develop primary support points and supporting details using your topic sentence or thesis statement from Chapter 5, your response to the idea journal prompt on page 75, or one of the following topic sentences/thesis statements.

Same-sex marriages should/should not be legal in all fifty states.

The drinking age should/should not be lowered.

All families have some unique family traditions.

People who do not speak "proper" English are discriminated against.

Many movies have important messages for viewers.

After developing your support, complete the following checklist.

LEARNING JOURNAL In your own words, explain what good support points are and why they are important.

> **CHECKLIST**
> **Evaluating your support**
> ☐ It is related to my main point.
> ☐ It uses examples, facts, and observations that will make sense to my readers.
> ☐ It includes enough specific details to show my readers exactly what I mean.

Once you have pulled together your primary support points and secondary supporting details, you're ready for the next step: arranging them into a plan for a draft of a paragraph or essay. For information on making a plan, go on to the next chapter.

Chapter Review

1. Highlight important terms from this chapter (such as *support*, *primary support*, and *secondary support*), and list them with their page numbers.

2. Support points are examples, facts, or evidence that _____*show*_____, _____*explain*_____, or _____*prove*_____ your main point.

3. Three basics of good support are: *It relates to your main point.*
It considers your readers.
It is detailed and specific.

4. To generate support, try these three strategies:
Circle an important word or phrase in your topic sentence or thesis
statement and write about it.
Reread your topic sentence or thesis statement and write down the first
thought you have, then your second, and so on.
Use a prewriting technique.

5. When you have selected your primary support points, what should you then add? *secondary support (or supporting details)*

6. Write for one minute about "What questions I should ask my professor."

STUDENT VOICES

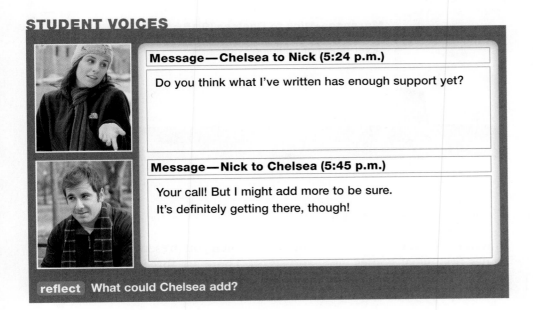

Message—Chelsea to Nick (5:24 p.m.)

Do you think what I've written has enough support yet?

Message—Nick to Chelsea (5:45 p.m.)

Your call! But I might add more to be sure.
It's definitely getting there, though!

reflect What could Chelsea add?

7

Making a Plan

Arranging Your Ideas

YOU KNOW THIS

You make plans every day:

- You arrange dishes, utensils, and cookware in a certain way so that it's easy to work in your kitchen.
- You write a shopping list based on the layout of the supermarket where you shop.
- You make a list of things you need to do, putting the most important first.

Chelsea Wilson exchanged messages with her friend Nick Brown about an assignment she had received. Nick had taken the same writing course a semester earlier.

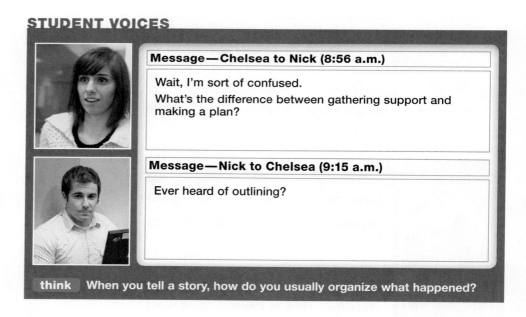

STUDENT VOICES

Message—Chelsea to Nick (8:56 a.m.)

Wait, I'm sort of confused.
What's the difference between gathering support and making a plan?

Message—Nick to Chelsea (9:15 a.m.)

Ever heard of outlining?

think When you tell a story, how do you usually organize what happened?

Understand What a Logical Order Is

In writing, **order** means the sequence in which you present your ideas: what comes first, what comes next, and so on. There are three common ways of ordering—arranging—your ideas: **time order** (also called chronological order), **space order**, and **order of importance**.

80

Read the paragraph examples that follow. In each paragraph, the primary support points are underlined, and the secondary support is in italics.

IDEA JOURNAL Write about a plan you came up with recently. How well did it work?

Use Time Order to Write about Events

Use **time order** (chronological order) to arrange points according to when they happened. Time order works best when you are writing about events. You can go from

- First to last/last to first
- Most recent to least recent/least recent to most recent

EXAMPLE USING TIME ORDER

Because I'm not a morning person, I have to follow the same routine every morning or I'll just go back to bed. First, I allow myself three "snooze" cycles on the alarm. *That gives me an extra fifteen minutes to sleep.* Then, I count to three and haul myself out of bed. *I have to do this quickly or I may just sink back onto the welcoming mattress.* Next, I head to the shower. *I run the water for a minute so it will be warm when I step in. While waiting for it to warm up, I wash my face with cold water. It's a shock, but it jolts me awake.* After showering and dressing, I'm ready for the two cups of coffee *that are necessary to get me moving out of the house.*

What kind of time order does the author use? *first to last*

Use Space Order to Describe Objects, Places, or People

Use **space order** to arrange ideas so that your readers picture your topic the way you see it. Space order usually works best when you are writing about a physical object or place, or a person's appearance. You can move from

- Top to bottom/bottom to top
- Near to far/far to near
- Left to right/right to left
- Back to front/front to back

EXAMPLE USING SPACE ORDER

Donna looked professional for her interview. Her long, dark, curly hair was held back with a gold clip. *No stray wisps escaped. Normally wild and unruly, her hair was smooth, shiny, and neat.* She wore a white silk blouse *with just the top button open at her throat. Donna had made sure to leave time to iron it so it wouldn't be wrinkled. The blouse was neatly tucked into her* black A-line skirt, *which came just to the top of her knee.* She wore black stockings *that she had checked for runs* and black low-heeled shoes. Altogether, her appearance marked her as serious and professional, and she was sure to make a good first impression.

What type of space order does the example use? *top to bottom*

IDEA JOURNAL What would you wear to look professional?

Use Order of Importance to Emphasize a Particular Point

Use **order of importance** to arrange points according to their importance, interest, or surprise value. Usually, save the most important for last.

EXAMPLE USING ORDER OF IMPORTANCE

IDEA JOURNAL What do you think about keeping guns in your house? Does it guard against robberies? Is there risk involved?

People who keep guns in their houses risk endangering both themselves and others. Many accidental injuries occur when a weapon is improperly stored or handled. *For example, someone cleaning a closet where a loaded gun is stored may handle the gun in a way that causes it to go off and injure him or her.* Guns also feature in many reports of "crimes of passion." *A couple with a violent history has a fight, and in a fit of rage one gets the gun and shoots the other, wounding or killing the other person.* Most common and most tragic are incidents in which children find loaded guns and play with them, accidentally killing themselves or their playmates. Considering these factors, the risks of keeping guns in the home outweigh the advantages, for many people.

What is the writer's most important point? *that children sometimes find loaded guns and accidentally kill themselves or their playmates*

Practice Arranging Ideas in a Logical Order

Choose an Order

After you have chosen support for your main point, you need to decide how to arrange your ideas. You might not always want to use one of the orders of time, space, or importance, but they help you to begin organizing your ideas.

• •

PRACTICE 1   Choosing an Order

Read each of the three topic sentences and the support points that follow them, and decide which order you would use to arrange the support in a paragraph. Indicate which point would come first, second, and so on by writing the number in the blank at the left. Then, indicate the type of order you used (time, space, or importance).

RESOURCES To test students on ordering support effectively, see the *Testing Tool Kit* CD-ROM available with this book.

EXAMPLE: Many grocery stores share the same basic layout so that shoppers will have a sense of where to find what they want. *Answers may vary. Possible answers are shown.*

_2_   juices and teas to the left of the produce

_3_   medicines and home goods in the middle

_1_   produce section (fruits and vegetables) on the far right

_4_   refrigerated foods on the far left

Type of order: *space right to left (These items could also be ordered left to right; 3, 2, 4, 1.)*

1.   It was one of those days when everything went wrong.

   _4_   My boss was waiting for me.

   _2_   I had no hot water for a shower.

   _6_   I got sick at lunch and had to go home.

   _3_   I missed the regular bus to work.

   _1_   My alarm didn't go off.

   _5_   I forgot to save work on my computer and lost it.

   Type of order: _time: first to last_

2.   For his fiftieth birthday, Elton John threw himself a huge party and dressed like a king from the eighteenth century.

   _4_   a powdered white wig of long curls

   _2_   tight white satin pants that came only to the knee

   _5_   a headdress made of feathers and long plumes

   _3_   a blue satin jacket with a high neck and diamonds sewn into it

   _1_   blue satin high-heeled shoes studded with diamonds

   Type of order: _space: bottom to top (could also be top to bottom)_

3.   Properly extinguishing a campfire is every camper's duty.

   _3_   You can even get a fine.

   _1_   It cuts down on the smell of smoke, which can bother other campers.

   _2_   If you don't extinguish well, you can get a citation.

   _4_   Partially doused fires can ignite and burn wild.

   Type of order: _importance_

Make a Written Plan

When you have decided how to order your primary support points, it's time to make a more detailed plan for your paragraph or essay. A good, visual way to plan a draft is to arrange your ideas in an outline. An **outline** lists the topic sentence (for a paragraph) or thesis statement (for an essay), the primary support points for the topic sentence or thesis statement, and secondary supporting details for each of the support points. It provides a map of your ideas that you can follow as you write. Sample outlines for a paragraph and for an essay are shown on the next page.

TIP Try using the cut-and-paste function on your computer to experiment with different ways to order support for your main point. Doing so will give you a good sense of how your final paragraph or final essay will look.

Outlining Paragraphs

SAMPLE OUTLINE FOR A PARAGRAPH

Topic sentence
  Primary support point 1
    Supporting details for point 1
  Primary support point 2
    Supporting details for point 2
  Primary support point 3
    Supporting details for point 3
  Concluding sentence

Outlining Essays

If you are writing an essay, the primary support points for your thesis statement will become topic sentences for paragraphs that will make up the body of the essay. These paragraphs will consist of details that support the topic sentences. To remind yourself of the differences between paragraph and essay structure, see the diagram on page 61.

The outline below is for a typical five-paragraph essay, in which three body paragraphs support a thesis statement, which is included in an introductory paragraph; the fifth paragraph is the conclusion. However, essays may include more or fewer than five paragraphs, depending on the size and complexity of the topic.

The example below is a "formal" outline form, with letters and numbers to distinguish between primary supporting and secondary supporting details. Some instructors prefer this format. If you are making an outline just for yourself, you do not have to use the formal system—but you do need a plan to order the points you want to make. In an informal outline, you might want to simply indent the secondary supporting details under each primary support.

TIP For an example of a five-paragraph essay, see Chapter 8.

SAMPLE OUTLINE FOR A FIVE-PARAGRAPH ESSAY

Thesis statement (part of introductory paragraph 1)
  A. **Topic sentence for support point 1** (paragraph 2)
    1. Supporting detail 1 for support point 1
    2. Supporting detail 2 for support point 1 (and so on)
  B. **Topic sentence for support point 2** (paragraph 3)
    1. Supporting detail 1 for support point 2
    2. Supporting detail 2 for support point 2 (and so on)
  C. **Topic sentence for support point 3** (paragraph 4)
    1. Supporting detail 1 for support point 3
    2. Supporting detail 2 for support point 3 (and so on)
Concluding paragraph (paragraph 5)

• •

PRACTICE 2   Making an Outline

The paragraph in this practice appeared earlier in this chapter to illustrate time order of organization. Read it and make an outline for it in the space provided.

> Because I am not a morning person, I have to follow the same routine every morning or I will just go back to bed. First, I allow myself three "snooze" cycles on the alarm. That gives me an extra fifteen minutes to sleep. Then, I count to three and haul myself out of bed. I have to do this quickly or I may just sink back onto the welcoming mattress. Next, I head to the shower. I run the water for a minute so it will be warm when I step in. While waiting for it to warm up, I wash my face with cold water. It is a shock, but it jolts me awake. After showering and dressing, I am ready for the two cups of coffee that are necessary to get me moving out of the house.

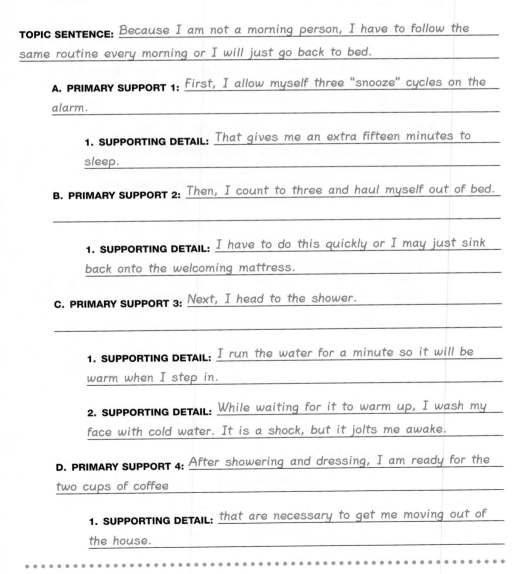

TOPIC SENTENCE: *Because I am not a morning person, I have to follow the same routine every morning or I will just go back to bed.*

A. PRIMARY SUPPORT 1: *First, I allow myself three "snooze" cycles on the alarm.*

    1. SUPPORTING DETAIL: *That gives me an extra fifteen minutes to sleep.*

B. PRIMARY SUPPORT 2: *Then, I count to three and haul myself out of bed.*

    1. SUPPORTING DETAIL: *I have to do this quickly or I may just sink back onto the welcoming mattress.*

C. PRIMARY SUPPORT 3: *Next, I head to the shower.*

    1. SUPPORTING DETAIL: *I run the water for a minute so it will be warm when I step in.*

    2. SUPPORTING DETAIL: *While waiting for it to warm up, I wash my face with cold water. It is a shock, but it jolts me awake.*

D. PRIMARY SUPPORT 4: *After showering and dressing, I am ready for the two cups of coffee*

    1. SUPPORTING DETAIL: *that are necessary to get me moving out of the house.*

• •

Make Your Own Plan

RESOURCES A reproducible blank outline for essays is in *Additional Resources*.

Before making your own plan, look at what Chelsea Wilson did with the support she wrote. She had already grouped together similar points and put the more specific details under the primary support (see p. 78). When she thought about how to order her ideas, the only way that made sense to her was by importance. If she had been telling the steps she would take to become a nurse, time order would have worked well. If she had been describing a setting where nurses work, space order would be a good choice. But since she was writing about why she wanted to get a college degree and become a nurse, she decided to arrange her reasons in order of importance. Notice that Chelsea also made changes in her primary and secondary support. At each stage, her ideas and the way she expressed them changed as she got closer to what she wanted to say.

TEACHING TIP You might point out to students that Chelsea has added a concluding sentence. It might change, but she is beginning to think about possible endings.

TOPIC SENTENCE: *Becoming a nurse is a longtime goal of mine because it offers so much that I value.*

> **PRIMARY SUPPORT 1:** *It is a good and practical job.*
>
>> **SUPPORTING DETAILS:** *Licensed practical nurses make an average of $40,000 per year. That amount is much more than I make now. With that salary, I could move to a better place with my daughter and give her more, including more time.*
>
> **PRIMARY SUPPORT 2:** *Nursing is a profession, not just a job.*
>
>> **SUPPORTING DETAILS:** *It helps people who are sick and in need. It gives people great opportunities, like the chance to go on and become a registered nurse, with more money and responsibility. People respect nurses.*
>
> **PRIMARY SUPPORT 3:** *I will respect and be proud of myself for achieving my goal through hard work.*
>
>> **SUPPORTING DETAILS:** *I will be a good role model for my daughter. I will help her and others, but I will also be helping myself by knowing I can accomplish good things.*

CONCLUSION: *Reaching my goal is important to me and worth the work.*

WRITING ASSIGNMENT

Make a plan for a paragraph or essay using support you generated in Chapter 6, your responses to the idea journal prompts, or one of the following.

The teacher I remember best is _____.

This school would make students happier/more successful if _____.

Work to live, don't live to work.

If I could make one change in my life, it would be _____.

Most people are poor listeners.

After writing your plan, complete the following checklist.

CHECKLIST

Evaluating your plan

☐ It follows a logical order of organization.

☐ It includes all of my ideas, arranged in the order I want to present them.

Now that you have a plan, you are ready to write a complete draft of your paragraph or essay, so move on to the next chapter.

LEARNING JOURNAL In your own words, explain why making a written plan for your writing is helpful.

Chapter Review

1. Highlight the important terms from this chapter (such as *time order*, *space order*, and *order of importance*), and list them with their page numbers.

2. In writing, what does *order* mean? _the sequence in which you present_ _your ideas_

3. Three ways to order ideas are _____time_____, _____space_____, and ____importance____.

4. Making ____an outline____ is a useful way to plan your draft.

5. Write for one minute about "What questions I should ask my professor."

STUDENT VOICES

Message—Chelsea to Nick (9:42 a.m.)

Not so bad—you were right about the outline!

Message—Nick to Chelsea (9:50 a.m.)

What can I say? I guess I'm just smart.

reflect **Did you know what making a plan was? How often do you actually write one?**

8

Drafting

Putting Your Ideas Together

STUDENT VOICES

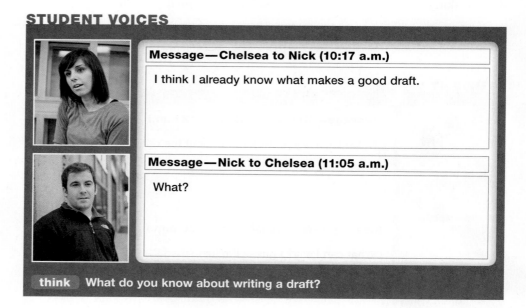

Chelsea Wilson exchanged messages with her friend Nick Brown about an assignment she had received. Nick had taken the same writing course a semester earlier.

Message—Chelsea to Nick (10:17 a.m.)

I think I already know what makes a good draft.

Message—Nick to Chelsea (11:05 a.m.)

What?

think What do you know about writing a draft?

Understand What a Draft Is

IDEA JOURNAL Write about a time when you had a trial run before doing something.

A **draft** is the first whole version of all your ideas put together in a piece of writing. Do the best job you can in drafting, but know that you can make changes later.

Practice Writing a Draft Paragraph

The draft of a paragraph needs to have the following characteristics:

BASICS OF A GOOD DRAFT PARAGRAPH

- It has a topic sentence that makes a clear main point.
- It has primary and secondary support that shows, explains, or proves the main point.
- It has ideas arranged in a logical order.
- It has a concluding sentence that makes an observation about the main point.
- It follows standard paragraph form (see p. 92).

TEACHING TIP Students can refer to these characteristics of a good draft in evaluating one another's papers in peer review.

Write a Draft Using Complete Sentences

When you begin to write a draft, work with your outline in front of you. Be sure to include your topic sentence, and express each point in a complete sentence. As you write, you may want to add support or change the order. It is okay to make changes from your outline as you write—an outline is only a plan.

Read the following paragraph, annotated to show the various parts of the paragraph.

Narcolepsy: A Misunderstood Problem ——— Title

——— Topic sentence

Narcolepsy, a disorder that causes people to fall asleep suddenly and uncontrollably, is often misunderstood. Narcoleptics may be in the middle of a meal or a conversation or almost any other activity, and they just nod off, usually for only a minute or so. Because most of us associate falling asleep with boredom or a lack of interest, people are often offended when someone falls asleep in the middle of something. We don't look kindly on someone whose face falls into his or her plate during a dinner conversation, for example. Students with narcolepsy are often criticized, or even ridiculed, for falling asleep in the middle of a class. On the job, narcolepsy can be even more of a problem. No one looks favorably on an employee who falls asleep in the middle of an important meeting or is found sleeping on the job. However, narcoleptics have no control over this disorder; when they suddenly fall asleep, it is not from boredom, rudeness, or lack of a good night's sleep.

——— Support

Although paragraphs typically begin with topic sentences, they may also begin with a quote, an example, or a surprising fact or idea. The topic sentence is then presented later in the paragraph. For examples of various introductory techniques, see pages 95–96.

TIP For more on topic sentences, see Chapter 5.

Write a Concluding Sentence

A **concluding sentence** refers back to the main point and makes an observation based on what you have written. The concluding sentence does not just repeat the topic sentence.

TEACHING TIP Tell students that the concluding sentence gives them an opportunity to express a personal opinion based on the support they have provided, but they should not use it to introduce new, unrelated ideas.

In the paragraph above, the main point, expressed in the topic sentence, is "Narcolepsy, a disorder that causes people to fall asleep suddenly and uncontrollably, is often misunderstood."

A good concluding sentence might be "Narcolepsy is a legitimate physical disorder, and narcoleptics do not deserve the harsh reactions they often receive." This sentence **refers back to the main point** by repeating the word *narcolepsy* and by restating that it is a real disorder. It **makes an observation** by stating, ". . . narcoleptics do not deserve the harsh reactions they often receive."

Concluding paragraphs for essays are discussed on pages 97–99.

• •

PRACTICE 1 Choosing a Concluding Sentence

Each of the following paragraphs has three possible concluding sentences. Circle the letter of the one you prefer, and be prepared to say why you chose it.

1. Have you ever noticed that people often obey minor rules while they ignore major ones? For example, most people cringe at the thought of ripping off the "Do not remove under penalty of law" tag from a new pillow. This rule is meant for the seller so that the buyer knows what the pillow is made of. The owner of the pillow is allowed to remove the tag, but people hesitate to do so. Another minor rule that people obey is the waiting-line procedure in a bank. Ropes often mark off where a line should form, and a sign says "enter here." Customers then zigzag through the rope lines even when no one is waiting in line. The same people who tremble at the thought of removing a tag or ignoring the rope lines may think nothing of exceeding the speed limit, even at the risk of a possible accident.

a. This behavior doesn't make sense to me.

b. What is it about those minor rules that makes people follow them?

(c.) Apparently "under penalty of law" is a greater deterrent than "endangering your life."

2. Student fees should not be increased without explanation. These fees are a mystery to most students. Are the fees for campus improvements? Do they support student activities, and if so, which ones? What exactly do we get for these mysterious fees? We are taught in classes to think critically, to look for answers, and to challenge accepted wisdom. We are encouraged to be responsible citizens. As responsible citizens and consumers, we should not blindly accept increases until we know what they are for.

(a.) We should let the administration know that we have learned our lessons well.

b. Student fees should be abolished.

c. Only fees that go directly to education should be approved.

• •

PRACTICE 2 **Writing Concluding Sentences**

Read the following paragraphs, and write a concluding sentence for each one.

     1. One of the most valuable ways that parents can help children is to read to them. Reading together is a good way for parents and children to relax, and it is sometimes the only "quality" time they spend together during a busy day. Reading develops children's vocabulary. They understand more words and are likely to learn new words more easily. Also, hearing the words aloud helps children's pronunciation and makes them more confident with oral language. Additionally, reading at home increases children's chances of success in school because reading is required in every course in every grade.

Possible Concluding Sentence: *Answers will vary but should include*
the idea that reading helps children in many ways and/or that it is an
important activity for parents and children to share.

     2. Almost everyone uses certain memory devices, called *mnemonics*. One of them is the alphabet song. If you want to remember what letter comes after *j*, you will probably sing the alphabet song in your head. Another is the "Thirty days hath September" rhyme that people use when they want to know how many days are in a certain month. Another mnemonic device is the rhyme "In 1492, Columbus sailed the ocean blue."

Possible Concluding Sentence: *Answers will vary but should refer to*
the memory devices and how commonly they are used.

Title Your Paragraph

The title is the first thing readers see, so it should give them a good idea of what your paragraph is about. Decide on a title by rereading your draft, especially your topic sentence. A paragraph title should not repeat your topic sentence.

     Look at the title of the paragraph on page 89. It includes the topic (narcolepsy) and the main point (that this condition is misunderstood). It lets readers know what the paragraph is about, but it does not repeat the topic sentence.

     Titles for essays are discussed on pages 99–100.

PRACTICE 3 **Writing Titles**

Write possible titles for the paragraphs in Practice 2.

1.   *Answers will vary.*

2.   _____

DISCUSSION Ask students to name favorite TV shows, movies, or songs, and write them on the board. Then, invite students to discuss what makes these titles interesting or dull, topic-appropriate or irrelevant. Can they think of better alternatives?

Write Your Own Draft Paragraph

Before you draft your own paragraph, read Chelsea Wilson's annotated draft below.

Chelsea Wilson

Professor Holmes

EN 099

September 8, 2010

My Career Goal

Title

Topic sentence (indented first line)

Support point 1

Supporting details

My longtime career goal is to become a nurse because it offers so much that I value. Being a nurse is a good and practical job. Licensed practical nurses make an average of $39,000 per year. That amount is much more than I make now working long hours at a minimum-wage job in a restaurant. Working as a nurse, I could be a better provider for my daughter. I could also spend more

Support point 2

Supporting details

time with her. Also, nursing is more than just a job; it is a profession. As a nurse, I will help people who are sick, and helping people is important to me. With time, I will be able to grow within the profession, like becoming a registered nurse who makes more money and has more responsibility. Because nursing is a profession, nurses are respected. When I become a nurse, I will

Support point 3

Supporting details

respect myself and be proud of myself for reaching my goal, even though I know it will take a lot of hard work. The most important thing about becoming a nurse is that it will be good for my young daughter. I will be a good role model for her. For all of these reasons, my goal is to become a nurse. Reaching

Concluding sentence (refers back to main point)

this goal is important to me and worth the work.

WRITING ASSIGNMENT   **Paragraph**

COMPUTER Suggest to students that they highlight (using boldface or underlining) the support points in their drafts. This keeps them on track and also helps peer editors focus on the support points.

Write a draft paragraph, using what you have developed in previous chapters, your response to the idea journal prompt on page 88, or one of the following topic sentences. If you use one of the topic sentences below, you may want to revise it to fit what you want to say.

Being a good _____ requires _____.

I can find any number of ways to waste my time.

People tell me I'm _____, and I guess I have to agree.

So many decisions are involved in going to college.

The most important thing to me in life is _____.

After writing your draft, complete the following checklist.

CHECKLIST

Evaluating your draft paragraph

☐   It has a clear, confident topic sentence that states my main point.

☐   Each primary support point is backed up with supporting details, examples, or facts.

(continued)

> ☐ The support is arranged in a logical order.
> ☐ The concluding sentence reminds readers of my main point and makes an observation.
> ☐ The title reinforces the main point.
> ☐ All of the sentences are complete, consisting of a subject and verb, and expressing a complete thought.
> ☐ The draft is properly formatted:
>   • My name, my instructor's name, the course, and the date appear in the upper left corner.
>   • The first sentence of the paragraph is indented, and the text is double-spaced (for easier revision).
> ☐ I have followed any other formatting guidelines provided by my instructor.

Practice Writing a Draft Essay

The draft of an essay needs to have the following characteristics:

BASICS OF A GOOD DRAFT ESSAY

- It has a thesis statement that makes a clear main point.
- It has primary and secondary support that shows, explains, or proves the main point.
- Each of its primary support points is a topic sentence for a paragraph.
- It has ideas arranged in a logical order.
- It has an introductory paragraph that draws readers in.
- It has a concluding paragraph that reminds readers of the main point and makes an observation about this point.
- It follows standard essay form (see p. 100).

Write Topic Sentences and Draft the Body of the Essay

When you start to draft your essay, use your outline to write complete sentences for your primary support points. These will serve as the topic sentences for the body paragraphs of your essay.

· ·

PRACTICE 4   Writing Topic Sentences

Each thesis statement that follows has support points that could be topic sentences for the body paragraphs of an essay. For each support point, write a topic sentence.

EXAMPLE

THESIS STATEMENT: My daughter is showing definite signs of becoming a teenager.

SUPPORT POINT: constantly texting friends

> **TOPIC SENTENCE:** *She texts friends constantly, even when they are sitting with her while I'm driving them.*

SUPPORT POINT: a new style of clothes

> **TOPIC SENTENCE:** *She used to like really cute clothing, but now she has a new style.*

SUPPORT POINT: doesn't want me to know what's going on

> **TOPIC SENTENCE:** *While she used to tell me everything, now she is secretive and private.*

SUPPORT POINT: developing an "attitude"

> **TOPIC SENTENCE:** *The surest and most annoying sign that she is becoming a teenager is that she has developed a definite "attitude."*

1. **THESIS STATEMENT:** Rhonda acts as if she is trying to fail this course.

   SUPPORT POINT: misses most classes

   > **TOPIC SENTENCE:** *Answers will vary.* _____

   SUPPORT POINT: is always late whenever she does come to class

   > **TOPIC SENTENCE:** _____

   SUPPORT POINT: never has her book or does any homework

   > **TOPIC SENTENCE:** _____

2. **THESIS STATEMENT:** The Latin American influence is evident in many areas of U.S. culture.

   SUPPORT POINT: Spanish language used in lots of places

   > **TOPIC SENTENCE:** _____

   SUPPORT POINT: lots of different kinds of foods

   > **TOPIC SENTENCE:** _____

   SUPPORT POINT: new kinds of music and popular musicians

   > **TOPIC SENTENCE:** _____

• •

Drafting topic sentences for your essay is a good way to start drafting the body of the essay (the paragraphs that support each of these topic sentences). As you write support for your topic sentences, refer back to your outline, where you listed supporting details. (For an example, see Chelsea Wilson's outline on page 86 of Chapter 7.) Turn these supporting details into complete sentences, and add additional support if necessary. (Prewriting techniques can help here; see Chapter 4.) Don't let yourself get stalled if you are having trouble with one word or sentence. Just keep writing. If you are writing by hand, use every other line to leave space for changes. Remember, a draft is a first try; you will have time later to improve it.

Write an Introduction for Your Essay

The introduction to your essay captures your readers' interest and presents the main point. Ask yourself: How can I sell my essay to readers? You need to market your main point.

The thesis statement is usually either the first or the last sentence in an introductory paragraph.

BASICS OF A GOOD INTRODUCTION

- It should catch readers' attention.
- It should present the thesis statement of the essay.
- It should give readers a clear idea of what the essay will cover.

Here are some common kinds of introductions that spark readers' interest. In each one, the introductory technique is in boldface. These are not the only ways to start essays, but they should give you some useful models.

Open with a Quotation

A good short quotation definitely gets people interested. It must lead naturally into your main point, however, and not be there just for effect. If you start with a quotation, make sure that you tell the reader who the speaker is.

> **George Farquhar once said that necessity was the mother of invention, but we know that to be nonsense, really:** Who needs an iPod that holds 10,000 songs? There is, however, one area of life in which technology keeps step with nature—the size of things. As we Americans are getting bigger (the Centers for Disease Control and Prevention in Atlanta estimate that roughly a third of Americans are overweight, with 20 percent of us qualifying as obese), so, too, is our stuff.
>
> —James Verini, "Supersize It"

Give an Example or Tell a Story

People like stories, so opening an essay with a brief story or example often draws them in.

> **Something snapped inside Jerry Sola during his evening commute through the Chicago suburbs two years ago.** When the driver in front of the fifty-one-year-old salesman suddenly slammed on his brakes, Sola got so incensed that he gunned his engine to cut in front of the man. Still steaming when both cars stopped at a red light, Sola grabbed a golf club from the backseat and got out.
>
> —Dianne Hales, "Why Are We So Angry?"

Start with a Surprising Fact or Idea

Surprises capture people's interest. The more unexpected and surprising something is, the more likely people are to take notice of it.

IDEA JOURNAL Write about the ways that advertising attracts people's attention.

ESL Remind nonnative speakers that it is a convention of English to present the main point in the first paragraph, stated explicitly.

TEACHING TIP Verini's and Hales's complete essays are in Chapter 44.

TEACHING TIP In the inverted-pyramid strategy, the introductory paragraph starts with a general statement and narrows to a thesis statement.

Now here is something to bear in mind should you ever find yourself using a changing room in a department store or retail establishment. **It is perfectly legal—indeed, it is evidently routine—for the store to spy on you while you are trying on their clothes.**

—Bill Bryson, "Snoopers at Work"

Offer a Strong Opinion or Position

The stronger the opinion, the more likely it is that people will pay attention. Don't write wimpy introductions. Make your point and shout it!

RESOURCES Maxwell's complete essay is in Chapter 50.

Cedric "C. J." Mills. Isaiah Brooks. Tedric Maynor. Felicia Hines. Vinson Phillips. Kurt Anthony Bryant. Amuel Murph. Alfonso Williams. These names are forever inscribed on my private "Wall of Black Death." My wall contains the names of black people killed by other black people, along with those believed to have been killed by fellow blacks, in the Tampa Bay area since May. I will update the roster as new deaths are reported. More are sure to follow. I do not have answers as to how to stop blacks from killing their brethren. **But I do have an answer for catching some, if not all, of these murderers. Snitch.**

—Bill Maxwell, "Start Snitching"

Ask a Question

A question needs an answer, so if you start your introduction with a question, your readers will need to read on to get the answer.

TIP If you get stuck while writing your introductory statement, try one or more of the prewriting techniques described in Chapter 4, pages 51–55.

RESOURCES You can read Wood's complete essay in Chapter 13.

Have you ever noticed how many gym membership advertisements appear on television right after the New Year? Many people overindulge through the holiday season, beginning with Halloween candy and ending with the last sip of eggnog on Christmas evening. On average, Americans gain seven pounds in that six-week period. That weight gain does not include the other forty-six weeks of the year when people typically overeat and quit going to the gym. Do not despair; there is hope! Instead of dreading the inevitable holiday weight gain and spending money on expensive exercise clubs, you can instead resign yourself to starting a new exercise routine at home. Exercise is the best way to combat the "battle of the bulge." One of the most effective ways to lose weight and get into shape is aerobic exercise. I am living proof that beginning a home workout regimen will become a positive, life-altering experience that quickly balances your physical and emotional health, has a maximum gain for minimum pain, and can lead you to improve other aspects of your life as well.

—Michele Wood, "My Home Exercise Program"

. . . .

PRACTICE 5   **Marketing Your Main Point**

As you know from advertisements, a good writer can make just about anything sound interesting. For each of the following topics, write an introductory statement using the technique indicated. Some of these topics are purposely dull to show you that you can make an interesting statement about almost any subject if you put your mind to it.

EXAMPLE

TOPIC: Reality TV

TECHNIQUE: Question

Exactly how many recent hits have been recorded by former contestants of reality TV singing contests?

1. **TOPIC:** Smoking cigarettes

   TECHNIQUE: Strong opinion

   Answers will vary.

2. **TOPIC:** Food in the cafeteria

   TECHNIQUE: Example or story

3. **TOPIC:** Credit cards

   TECHNIQUE: Surprising fact or idea

4. **TOPIC:** Role of the elderly in society

   TECHNIQUE: Question

5. **TOPIC:** Stress

   TECHNIQUE: Quote (You can make up a good one.)

TEACHING TIP Remind students that since the introduction should catch readers' attention, they should consider who their readers are and what those readers would find interesting.

PRACTICE 6 Identifying Strong Introductions

In a newspaper, a magazine, an advertising flier—anything written—find a strong introduction. Bring it to class to explain why you chose it as an example.

Write a Conclusion

Conclusions too often just fade out because writers feel they're near the end and think the task is over—but it isn't *quite* over. Remember, people usually remember best what they see, hear, or read last. Use your conclusion to drive your main point home one final time. Make sure your conclusion has the same energy as the rest of the essay, if not more.

BASICS OF A GOOD ESSAY CONCLUSION

- It refers back to the main point.

- It sums up what has been covered in the essay.

- It makes a further observation or point.

In general, a good conclusion creates a sense of completion: It brings readers back to where they started, but it also shows them how far they have come.

One of the best ways to end an essay is to refer directly to something in the introduction. If you asked a question, re-ask it and answer it. If you started a story, finish it. If you used a quote, use another one—maybe a quote by the same person or maybe one by another person on the same topic. Or, use some of the same words you used in your introduction. Look again at two of the introductions you read earlier, and note how the writers conclude their essays. Pay special attention to the text in bold.

HALES'S INTRODUCTION

Something snapped inside Jerry Sola during his evening commute through the Chicago suburbs two years ago. When the driver in front of the fifty-one-year-old salesman suddenly slammed on his brakes, Sola got so incensed that he gunned his engine to cut in front of the man. Still steaming when both cars stopped at a red light, Sola grabbed a golf club from the backseat and got out.

—Dianne Hales, "Why Are We So Angry?"

HALES'S CONCLUSION

Since his roadside epiphany, Jerry Sola has conscientiously worked to rein in his rage. "I am a changed person," he says, "especially behind the wheel. I don't have to listen to the news on the car radio. Instead, I put on nice, soothing music. I force myself to smile at rude drivers. And if I feel myself getting angry, I ask a simple question: 'Why should I let a person I'm never going to see again control my mood and ruin my whole day?'"

—Dianne Hales, "Why Are We So Angry?"

MAXWELL'S INTRODUCTION

Cedric "C. J." Mills. Isaiah Brooks. Tedric Maynor. Felicia Hines. Vinson Phillips. Kurt Anthony Bryant. Amuel Murph. Alfonso Williams. These names are forever inscribed on my private "Wall of Black Death." My wall contains the names of black people killed by other black people, along with those believed to have been killed by fellow blacks, in the Tampa Bay area since May. I will update the roster as new deaths are reported. More are sure to follow. I do not have answers as to how to stop blacks from killing their brethren. **But I do have an answer for catching some, if not all, of these murderers. Snitch.**

—Bill Maxwell, "Start Snitching"

MAXWELL'S CONCLUSION

Because I regularly write about this issue, I receive a lot of hate mail from both blacks and whites. White letter-writers remind me that blacks are "animals" and "cause all of America's social problems." Black letter-writers see me as the "enemy of people" and a "sell-out" because I condemn blacks for killing one another without taking into account the nation's history of racism. To whites, I have nothing to say. **To blacks, I have one message: We need to start snitching. Only we can stop black-on-black murders. Until then, I will be adding names to the Wall of Black Death.**

—Bill Maxwell, "Start Snitching"

• •

PRACTICE 7   Analyzing Conclusions

How is the conclusion to the essay "Why Are We So Angry?" linked to the introduction (p. 98)? How does it refer back to the introduction? Make some notes about these questions and be prepared to discuss your answers in class.

Answers will vary, but students might point out that the writer

concludes the "story" begun in the introduction by revisiting Jerry Sola.

_____

_____

• •

PRACTICE 8   Finding Good Introductions and Conclusions

In a newspaper or magazine or anything written, find a piece of writing that has a strong introduction and conclusion. (You may want to use what you found for Practice 6.) Answer the questions that follow.

1. What method of introduction is used? *Answers will vary.* _____

2. What does the conclusion do? Restate the main idea? Sum up the support? Make a further observation? _____

_____

3. How are the introduction and the conclusion linked? _____

_____

TEAMWORK Cut out the introductions and conclusions that students bring in, scramble them, and have the students work in small groups to match introductions and conclusions.

RESOURCES To test students on choosing effective introductions and conclusions, see the *Testing Tool Kit* CD-ROM available with this book.

• •

Title Your Essay

Even if your title is the *last* part of the essay you write, it is the *first* thing readers read. Use your title to get your readers' attention and to tell them, in a brief way, what your paper is about. Use vivid, strong, specific words.

BASICS OF A GOOD ESSAY TITLE

- It makes people want to read the essay.
- It does not merely repeat the thesis statement.
- It may hint at the main point but does not state it outright.

TIP Center your title at the top of the page before the first paragraph. Do not put quotation marks around it or underline it.

One way to find a good title is to consider the type of essay you are writing. If you are writing an argument (as you will in Chapter 18), state your position in your title. If you are telling your readers how to do something (as you will in Chapter 13), try using the term *steps* or *how to* in the title. This way, your readers will know immediately not only what you are writing about but how you will discuss it.

• •

PRACTICE 9   Titling an Essay

Reread the paired paragraphs on pages 98–99, and write alternate titles for the essays that they belong to.

Hales's introduction/conclusion: *Answers will vary.* _____

Maxwell's introduction/conclusion: _____

• •

Write Your Own Draft Essay

Before you draft your own essay, read Chelsea Wilson's annotated draft of her essay below. (You saw her developing her thesis statement in Chapter 5. Here she develops her paragraph into an essay.)

Chelsea Wilson
Professor Holmes
EN 099
September 14, 2010

Title indicates main point —————— **The Benefits of Getting a College Degree**

Introduction —————— My goal is to get a college degree. I have been taking college courses for two years, and it has been difficult for me. Many times I have wondered if getting a college degree is really worth the struggle. However, there are many benefits of getting a college degree.

Thesis statement ——————

Topic sentence/Support point 1 —————— I can work as a nurse, something I have always wanted to do. As a nurse, I can make decent money: The average salary for a licensed practical nurse is $39,000 per year. That amount is substantially more than I make now working at a restaurant job that pays minimum wage and tips. With the economy so bad, people are tipping less. It has been hard to pay my bills, even though I work more than forty hours a week. Without a degree, I don't see how that situation will change. I have almost no time to see my daughter, who is in preschool.

Supporting details ——————

I didn't get serious about getting a degree until I became a mother. Then, I realized I wanted more for my daughter than I had growing up. I also wanted to have time to raise her properly and keep her safe. She is a good girl, but she sees crime and violence around her. I want to get her away from danger, and I want to show her that there are better ways to live. Getting a college degree will help me do that.

The most important benefit of getting a college degree is that it will show me that I can achieve something hard. My life is moving in a good direction, and I am proud of myself. My daughter will be proud of me, too. I want to be a good role model for her as she grows up.

Because of these benefits, I want to get a college degree. It pays well, it will give my daughter and me a better life, and I will be proud of myself.

Topic sentence/Support point 2

Supporting details

Topic sentence/Support point 3

Supporting details

Conclusion

WRITING ASSIGNMENT Essay

Write a draft essay using what you have developed in previous chapters, your response to the idea journal prompt on page 88, or one of the following thesis statements. If you choose one of the thesis statements below, you may want to modify it to fit what you want to say.

Taking care of a sick (child/parent/spouse/friend) can test even the most patient person.

Being a good _____ requires _____ .

Doing _____ gave me a great deal of pride in myself.

A good long-term relationship involves flexibility and compromise.

Some of the differences between men and women create misunderstandings.

After you have finished writing your draft, complete the following checklist.

CHECKLIST

Evaluating your draft essay

- ☐ A clear, confident thesis statement states my main point.
- ☐ The primary support points are now topic sentences that support the main point.
- ☐ Each topic sentence is part of a paragraph, and the other sentences in the paragraph support the topic sentence.
- ☐ The support is arranged in a logical order.
- ☐ The introduction will interest readers.
- ☐ The conclusion reinforces my main point and makes an additional observation.
- ☐ The title reinforces the main point.

(continued)

> ☐ All of the sentences are complete, consisting of a subject and verb, and expressing a complete thought.
> ☐ The draft is properly formatted:
>   • My name, my instructor's name, the course, and the date appear in the upper left corner.
>   • The first sentence of each paragraph is indented, and the text is double-spaced (for easier revision).
>   • The pages are numbered.
> ☐ I have followed any other formatting guidelines provided by my instructor.

LEARNING JOURNAL In your own words, explain how you write a draft.

Don't think about your draft anymore—for the moment. Give yourself some time away from it—at least a few hours and preferably a day. Taking a break will allow you to return to your writing later with a fresher eye and more energy for revision, resulting in a better piece of writing—and a better grade. After your break, you will be ready to take the next step: revising your draft.

Chapter Review

1. Highlight important terms from this chapter (such as *draft*, *concluding sentence*, and *title*), and list them with their page numbers.

2. A draft is *the first whole version of all your ideas put together in a piece of writing.*

3. List the basic features of a good draft paragraph *or* essay: *(Lists should include features on page 89 or page 93.)*

4. Five ways to start an essay are

     Open with a quotation.

     Give an example or tell a story.

     Start with a surprising fact or idea.

     Offer a strong opinion or position.

     Ask a question.

5. Three features of a good essay conclusion are

     It refers back to the main point.

     It sums up what has been covered in the essay.

     It makes a further observation or point.

6. Three basic features of a good essay title are

It makes people want to read the essay.

It does not merely repeat the thesis statement.

It may hint at the main point but does not state it outright.

7. Write for one minute about "What questions I should ask my professor."

STUDENT VOICES

Message—Chelsea to Nick (5:38 p.m.)

Okay, I think I'm done!

Message—Nick to Chelsea (5:50 p.m.)

Are you totally sure?

I used to think I was done with a paper, but then I would set it down for a while and come back to it.

And I always found things I wanted to fix!

reflect   What two changes could Chelsea make to improve her paragraph or her essay?

9

Revising

Improving Your Paragraph or Essay

Chelsea Wilson exchanged messages with her friend Nick Brown about an assignment she had received. Nick had taken the same writing course a semester earlier.

STUDENT VOICES

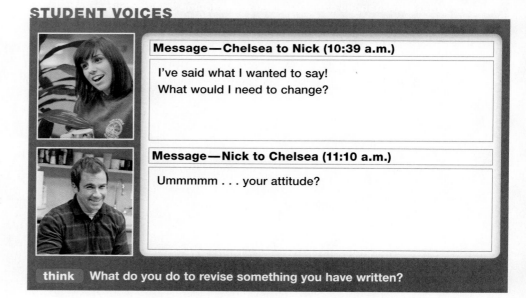

Message—Chelsea to Nick (10:39 a.m.)

I've said what I wanted to say!
What would I need to change?

Message—Nick to Chelsea (11:10 a.m.)

Ummmmm . . . your attitude?

think   What do you do to revise something you have written?

Understand What Revision Is

When you finish a draft, you probably wish that that were the end: You don't want to have to look at it again. But a draft is just the first whole version, a rough cut, not the best you can do to represent yourself and your ideas. After taking a break, you need to look at the draft with fresh eyes to revise and edit it.

Revising is taking another look at your ideas to make them clearer, stronger, and more convincing. When revising, you are evaluating how well you have made your point.

Editing is finding and correcting problems with grammar style, word choice and usage, and punctuation. When editing, you are evaluating the words and phrases you have used.

Most writers find it difficult to revise and edit well if they try to do both at once. It is easier to solve idea-level problems first (by revising) and then to correct smaller, word-level ones (by editing). This chapter focuses on revising. For editing help, use Chapters 21–41.

Here are some basic tips for revising your writing.

TIPS FOR REVISING YOUR WRITING

- Wait a few hours or a couple of days before starting to revise.

- Read your draft aloud and listen to what you are saying.

- Read critically and ask yourself questions, as if you were reading through someone else's eyes.

- Make notes about changes to make. For small things, like adding a transition, you can make the change on the draft. For other things, like adding or getting rid of an idea or reordering your ideas, make a note in the margin.

- Get help from a tutor at the writing center or get feedback from a friend (see p. 106 for information on peer review).

If you finish reading your draft and have not found anything that could be better, you are not reading carefully enough or are not asking the right questions. Even the best writers do not get it right the first time. Use the following checklist to help you make your writing better. As you ask the questions, really think.

CHECKLIST

Revising your writing

- ☐ If I read just my topic sentence or thesis statement, what do I think the paper is about? Does it make any impression on me? What would I need to do to make it more interesting?

- ☐ If I read each support point separately, do I find that each one really relates to my main point? What more could I say about the idea so that someone else will see it my way? Is any of what I have written weak? If so, should I delete it?

- ☐ What about the way the ideas are arranged? Should I change the order to make more sense or have more effect on a reader?

- ☐ What about the ending? Does it just droop and fade away? This is my last chance to make my point: How could I make it better?

- ☐ If I knew nothing about the topic or disagreed with the position, would what I have written be enough for me to understand or be convinced?

TIP Add transitions as you read to help move from one idea to the next.

Understand What Peer Review Is

Peer review—exchanging drafts with other students and commenting on the drafts—is one of the best ways to get help with revising your writing. Other students can often see things that you might not—parts that are good and parts that need to be strengthened or clarified.

If you are working with one other student, read each other's papers and write down a few comments. If you are working in a small group, you may want to have writers take turns reading their papers aloud. Group members can make notes while listening and then offer comments to the writer that will help improve the paper. The first time someone comments on what you have written, you may feel a little awkward or embarrassed, but you will get over it.

BASICS OF USEFUL FEEDBACK

- It is given in a positive way.
- It is specific.
- It offers suggestions.
- It may be given in writing or orally.

Often, it is useful for the writer to give the person or people providing feedback a few questions to focus on as they read or listen.

TEAMWORK Try modeling peer review. Bring in a short paragraph or essay, and have students answer the Questions for Peer Reviewers in small groups, with one person acting as a recorder. You can join each group for a few minutes to make sure students understand the process. Then, discuss the comments as a class.

RESOURCES *Practical Suggestions* contains a discussion of peer feedback. The Peer Factor skills-building online game is also available, at **bedfordstmartins.com/ rewritingplus**.

CHECKLIST

Questions for peer reviewers

- [ ] What is the main point?
- [ ] Can I do anything to make my opening more interesting?
- [ ] Do I have enough support for my main point? Where could I use more?
- [ ] Where could I use more details?
- [ ] Are there places where you have to stop and reread something to understand it? If so, where?
- [ ] Do I give my reader clues as to where a new point starts? Does one point "flow" smoothly to the next?
- [ ] What about my conclusion? Does it just fade out? How could I make my point more forcefully?
- [ ] Where could the paper be better? What would you do if it were your paper?
- [ ] If you were getting a grade on this paper, would you turn it in as is?
- [ ] What other comments or suggestions do you have?

Practice Revising for Unity, Detail, and Coherence

You may need to read what you have written several times before deciding what changes would improve it. Remember to consider your audience and your purpose and to focus on three areas: unity, detail, and coherence.

Revise for Unity

Unity in writing means that all the points you make are related to your main point; they are *unified* in support of your main point. As you draft a paragraph or an essay, you may detour from your main point without even being aware of it, as the writer of the following paragraph did with the underlined sentences. The diagram after the paragraph shows what happens when readers read the paragraph.

First, double-underline the main point in the paragraph that follows. This will help you see where the writer got off-track.

If you want to drive like an elderly person, use a cell phone while driving. A group of researchers from the University of Utah tested the reaction times of two groups of people—those between the ages of sixty-five to seventy-four and those who were eighteen to twenty-five—in a variety of driving tasks. All tasks were done with hands-free cell phones. That part of the study surprised me because I thought the main problem was using only one hand to drive. I hardly ever drive with two hands, even when I'm not talking to anyone. Among other results, braking time for both groups slowed by 18 percent. A related result is that the number of rear-end collisions doubled. The study determined that the younger drivers were paying as much—or more—attention to their phone conversations as they were to what was going on around them on the road. The elderly drivers also experienced longer reaction times and more accidents, pushing most of them into the category of dangerous driver. This study makes a good case for turning off the phone when you buckle up.

TEACHING TIP Read the paragraph aloud to the class, and ask students to stop you as soon as they hear it detouring from the main point.

IDEA JOURNAL Write about your reactions to this study, including your own experiences with cell phones and driving.

TOPIC SENTENCE: If you want to drive like an elderly person, use a cell phone while driving.

Group of researchers studied reaction times of two groups of people

DETOUR

That part of the study . . .

Braking time for both groups slowed by 18 percent

Number of rear-end collisions doubled

Younger drivers paid too much attention to talking on the phone

```
          ↓
┌─────────────────────────────────────────┐
│  Elderly drivers also got worse          │
└─────────────────────────────────────────┘
          ↓
```

> **CONCLUDING SENTENCE:** This study makes a good case for turning off the phone when you buckle up.

Detours weaken your writing because readers' focus is shifted from your main point. As you revise, check to make sure that your paragraph or essay has unity.

• •

PRACTICE 1 Revising for Unity

Each of the following paragraphs contains a sentence that detours from the main point. First double-underline the main point. Then, underline the detour in each paragraph.

EXAMPLE:

IDEA JOURNAL Write about the statement "Education is one of the few things people are willing to pay for and not get." Do you agree? How does this statement apply to you?

"Education is one of the few things people are willing to pay for and not get." When we buy something expensive, we make sure we take it home and use it. For example, we wouldn't think of spending a couple of hundred dollars on a new coat and shoes only to hide them away in a closet never to be worn. And we certainly wouldn't pay for those items and then decide to leave them at the store. I once left a bag with three new shirts in it at the cash register, and I never got it back. People pay a lot for education, but sometimes they look for ways to leave the "purchase" behind. They cheat themselves by not attending class, not paying attention, not studying, or not doing assignments. At the end of the term, they have a grade but didn't get what they paid for: education and knowledge. They have wasted money, just as if they had bought an expensive sound system and had never taken it out of the box.

1. One way to manage time is to keep a calendar or schedule. It should have an hour-by-hour breakdown of the day and evening, with space for you to write next to the time. As appointments or responsibilities come up, add them on the right day and time. Before the end of the day, consult your calendar to see what's going on the next day.

For example, tomorrow I have to meet Kara at noon, and if I forget, she will be furious with me. Using a calendar saves you trouble, because once you have noted the appointment or activity, you don't have to think about it anymore. Once you are in the habit of using a calendar, you will see that it frees your mind because you are not always trying to think about what you're supposed to do, where you're supposed to be, or what you might have forgotten.

2. As you use a calendar to manage your time, think about how long certain activities will take. A common mistake is to underestimate the time needed to do something, even something simple. For example, when you are planning the time needed to get money from the cash machine, remember that a line of people may be ahead of you. Last week in the line I met a woman I went to high school with. When you are estimating time for a more complex activity, such as reading a chapter in a textbook, block out more time than you think you will need. If you finish in less time than you have allotted, so much the better. Allow for interruptions. It is better to allow too much time than too little.

TIP For more advice on managing your time, see Chapter 1, pages 4–5.

3. Effective time management means allowing time for various "life" activities. For example, it is important to budget time for paying bills, buying food, picking up a child, or going to the doctor. My doctor is always an hour behind schedule. A daily schedule should also account for communication with other people, such as family members, friends, service people, and others. It is important to allow time for relaxation. Allow yourself a little unscheduled time when possible. Finally, leave time for unexpected events that are a huge part of life, like last-minute phone calls, a car that won't start, or a bus that is late.

Revise for Detail and Support

When you revise a paper, look carefully at the support you have developed, and imagine yourself as your reader: Do you have enough information to understand the main point? Are you convinced of the main point?

In the margin or between the lines of your draft (which should be double-spaced), note ideas that seem weak or unclear. As you revise, build up your support by adding more details.

• •

PRACTICE 2   Revising for Detail and Support

Read the following paragraph, double-underline the main point, and add at least three additional support points or supporting details to it. Write them in the spaces provided under the paragraph, and indicate where they should go in the paragraph by writing in a caret (ˆ) and the number.

EXAMPLE:

Sojourner Truth was a brave woman who helped educate people about the evils of slavery. She was a slave herself in New York. 1 2After she had a religious vision, she traveled from place to place giving speeches about how terrible it was to be a slave. 3But even after the Emancipation Proclamation was signed in 1863, slave owners did not follow the laws. Sojourner Truth was active in the Civil War, nursing soldiers and continuing to give speeches. She was active in the fight for racial equality until her death in 1883.

1.   *and was not allowed to learn to read or write.*

2.   *Sojourner Truth ran away from her owner because of his cruelty.*

3.   *Although she was beaten for her beliefs, she continued her work and was part of the force that caused Abraham Lincoln to sign the Emancipation Proclamation freeing the slaves.*

1. Sports fans can turn from normal people into maniacs. After big wins, fans sometimes riot. Police have to be brought in. Even in school sports, parents of the players can become violent. People get so involved that they lose control of themselves and are dangerous.

1.   *Answers will vary.*

2.   _____

3.   _____

2. If you make your own pizza, you can add all the toppings you want. Just start with dough you buy in the supermarket. Then, think about what toppings you want to use and put lots on. You can add

different toppings to each half, making it the most delicious pizza you can imagine.

1. _____

2. _____

3. _____

Revise for Coherence

Coherence in writing means that all of your support connects to form a whole. In other words, even when the points and details are assembled in an order that makes sense, they still need "glue" to connect them.

Coherence in writing helps readers see how one point leads to another. Individual ideas should be connected to make a clear whole. A good way to improve coherence is to use transitions.

Transitions are words, phrases, and sentences that connect your ideas so that your writing moves smoothly from one point to the next. Use transitions when moving from one main support point to another. Also use them wherever you want to improve the flow of your writing. The table on page 112 shows some common transitions and what they are used for.

Here are two paragraphs, one that does not use transitions and one that does. Read them and notice how much easier the second paragraph is to follow. Both paragraphs make the same points, but the transitions (underlined) in the second paragraph help "hold it together."

NO TRANSITIONS

It is not difficult to get organized—it takes discipline to stay organized. All you need to do is follow a few simple ideas. You must decide what your priorities are and do these tasks first. You should ask yourself every day: What is the most important task I have to accomplish? Make the time to do it. To be organized, you need a personal system for keeping track of things. Making lists, keeping records, and using a schedule help you remember what tasks you need to do. It is a good idea not to let belongings and obligations stack up. Get rid of possessions you don't need, put items away every time you use them, and do not take on more responsibilities than you can handle. Getting organized is not a mystery; it is just good sense.

TRANSITIONS ADDED

It is not difficult to get organized—<u>even though</u> it takes discipline to stay organized. All you need to do is follow a few simple ideas. You must decide what your priorities are and do these tasks first. <u>For example</u>, you should ask yourself every day: What is the most important task I have to accomplish? <u>Then</u>, make the time to do it. To be organized, you <u>also</u> need a personal system for keeping track of things. Making lists, keeping records, and using a schedule help you remember what tasks you need to do. <u>Finally</u>, it is a good idea not to let belongings and obligations stack up. Get rid of possessions you do not need, put items away every time you use them, and do not take on more responsibilities than you can handle. Getting organized is not a mystery; it is just good sense.

Common Transitional Words and Phrases

INDICATING SPACE

above	below	near	to the right
across	beside	next to	to the side
at the bottom	beyond	opposite	under
at the top	farther/further	over	where
behind	inside	to the left	

INDICATING TIME

after	eventually	meanwhile	soon
as	finally	next	then
at last	first	now	when
before	last	second	while
during	later	since	

INDICATING IMPORTANCE

above all	in fact	more important	most
best	in particular	most important	worst
especially			

SIGNALING EXAMPLES

for example	for instance	for one thing	one reason

SIGNALING ADDITIONS

additionally	and	as well as	in addition
also	another	furthermore	moreover

SIGNALING CONTRAST

although	in contrast	nevertheless	still
but	instead	on the other hand	yet
however			

SIGNALING CAUSES OR RESULTS

as a result	finally	so	therefore
because			

● ●

PRACTICE 3 Adding Transitions

Read the following paragraphs. In each blank, add a transition that would smoothly connect the ideas. In each case, there is more than one right answer.

EXAMPLE:

Life Gem, a Chicago company, has announced that it can turn cremated human ashes into high-quality diamonds. _____*After*_____ cremation, the ashes are heated to convert their carbon to graphite. _____*Then*_____, a lab wraps the graphite around a tiny diamond piece and again heats it and pressurizes it. _____*After*_____ about a week of crystallizing, the result is a diamond. _____*Because of*_____ the time and labor involved, this process costs about $20,000. _____*Although*_____ the idea is very creative, many people will think it is also very weird. *Answers will vary.*

1. Selena Quintanilla's story is both inspiring and tragic. _____*When*_____ she was very young, Selena sang in English in her father's band. _____*As*_____ a teenager, she started singing Tejano music in Spanish. Tejano literally means "Texan," but it has come to represent a culture of Mexican Americans. Selena's new Tejano music became very popular and successful, and she was ready to release an album in English. _____*However*_____, she was murdered right before the album's release. _____*After*_____ it was released, her album sold 175,000 copies in a single day, becoming one of the best-selling albums in history. Selena's death and stardom occurred almost simultaneously, when she was only twenty-four.

2. Many fast-food restaurants are adding healthier foods to their menus. _____*For example*_____, several kinds of salads are now on most menus. These salads offer fresh vegetables and roasted, rather than fried, chicken. _____*However*_____, be careful of the dressings, which can be very high in calories. _____*Also*_____, avoid the huge soft drinks that have large amounts of sugar. _____*Finally*_____, avoid the french fries. They are high in fat and calories and do not have much nutritional value.

LEARNING JOURNAL How would you explain the terms *unity*, *support*, and *coherence* to someone who had never heard them?

● ●

Another way to give your writing coherence is to repeat a **key word**, a word that is directly related to your main point. For example, look back at the paragraph on pages 111–112, the example with transitions added. The main point of the paragraph is that it's not difficult to get organized. Note that the writer repeats the word *organized* several times throughout the paragraph. Repetition of a key word is a good way to keep your readers focused on your main point, but make sure that you don't overdo the repetition.

Revise Your Own Paragraph

In the last chapter, you read Chelsea's draft paragraph (p. 92). Reread that now as if it were your own, asking yourself the questions in the Checklist for Revising Your Writing on page 105. Work either by yourself or with a partner or a small group to answer the questions about Chelsea's draft. Then, read Chelsea's revised paragraph that follows and discuss the changes you suggested with those that she made. Make notes on the similarities and differences to discuss with the rest of the class.

TEACHING TIP If you are working with paragraphs only, ask students to read this section and then move on to the Chapter Review, page 118. If you are working with essays, skip this section and go to "Revise Your Own Essay," page 115.

TEACHING TIP You might challenge teams of students to find the most revisions to the paragraph.

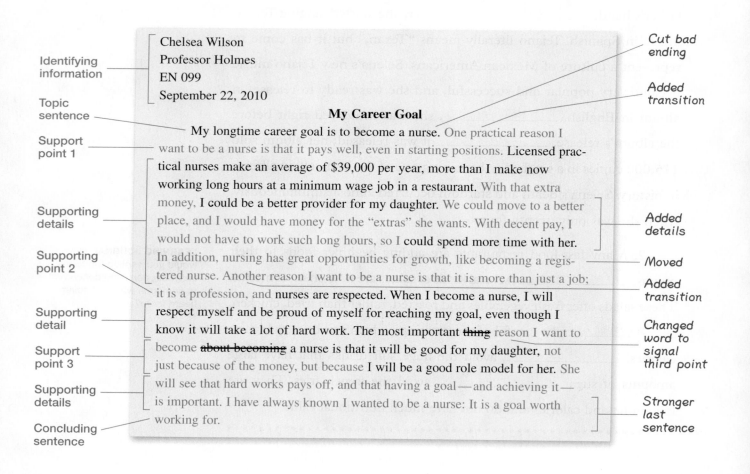

Identifying information

Chelsea Wilson
Professor Holmes
EN 099
September 22, 2010

Cut bad ending

My Career Goal

Topic sentence

My longtime career goal is to become a nurse. One practical reason I

Added transition

Support point 1

want to be a nurse is that it pays well, even in starting positions. Licensed practical nurses make an average of $39,000 per year, more than I make now working long hours at a minimum wage job in a restaurant. With that extra

Supporting details

money, I could be a better provider for my daughter. We could move to a better place, and I would have money for the "extras" she wants. With decent pay, I would not have to work such long hours, so I could spend more time with her.

Added details

Supporting point 2

In addition, nursing has great opportunities for growth, like becoming a registered nurse. Another reason I want to be a nurse is that it is more than just a job; it is a profession, and nurses are respected. When I become a nurse, I will

Moved

Added transition

Supporting detail

respect myself and be proud of myself for reaching my goal, even though I know it will take a lot of hard work. The most important ~~thing~~ reason I want to

Changed word to signal third point

Support point 3

become ~~about becoming~~ a nurse is that it will be good for my daughter, not just because of the money, but because I will be a good role model for her. She

Supporting details

will see that hard works pays off, and that having a goal—and achieving it— is important. I have always known I wanted to be a nurse: It is a goal worth

Stronger last sentence

Concluding sentence

working for.

• •

PRACTICE 4   Revising a Paragraph

1.   What major changes were suggested in response to the Checklist for
Revising Your Writing?

_____

_____

_____

2.   Did Chelsea make any of the suggested changes? Which ones?

_____

_____

3.   Did Chelsea make any changes that were not suggested? Which ones?
Were they good changes?

_____

_____

_____

• •

WRITING ASSIGNMENT   Paragraph

Revise the draft paragraph you wrote in Chapter 8. After revising your draft, complete the following checklist.

• •

CHECKLIST

Evaluating your revised paragraph

☐   My topic sentence is confident, and my main point is clear.
☐   My ideas are detailed, specific, and organized logically.
☐   My ideas flow smoothly from one to the next.
☐   This paragraph fulfills the original assignment.
☐   I am ready to turn in this paragraph for a grade.
☐   This is the best I can do.

After you have finished revising your paragraph, you are ready to edit it. See
the Important Note about this on page 117.

Revise Your Own Essay

In the last chapter, you read Chelsea's draft essay (pp. 100–01). Reread that
now as if it were your own, asking yourself the questions in the Checklist for
Revising Your Writing on page 105. Work either by yourself or with a partner
or a small group to answer the questions about Chelsea's draft. Then, read
Chelsea's revised essay that follows and compare the changes you suggested
with those that she made. Make notes on the similarities and differences to
discuss with the rest of the class.

TEACHING TIP You might challenge teams of students to find
the most revisions in the essay.

Identifying information

Title, centered

First line indented

Introduction question

Details

Thesis statement

Topic sentence support point 1

Supporting details

Transition to next point

Topic sentence support point 2

Supporting details

Topic sentence support point 3

Supporting details

Repeats introductory question

Conclusion answers question and makes an observation

Chelsea Wilson

Professor Holmes

EN 099

September 29, 2010

The Benefits of Getting a College Degree

Why am I practically killing myself to get a college degree? I have been taking college courses for two years, and it has been difficult for me because I have a full-time job, a young daughter, and a car that breaks down often. Many times as I have sat, late at night, struggling to stay awake to do homework or to study, I have wondered if getting a college degree is really worth the struggle. That is when I remind myself why getting a degree is so important: It will benefit every aspect of my life.

One benefit of getting a degree is that I can work as a nurse, something I have always wanted to do. Even as a child, I enjoyed helping my mother care for my grandmother or take care of my younger brothers and sisters when they were sick. I enjoy helping others, and nursing will allow me to do that while making good money. The average salary for a licensed practical nurse is $39,000 per year, substantially more than I make now working at a restaurant. Without a degree, I don't see how that situation will change. Meanwhile, I have almost no time to spend with my daughter.

Another benefit of getting a college degree is that it will allow me to be a better mother. In fact, I didn't get serious about getting a degree until I became a mother. Then, I realized I wanted more for my daughter than I had had: a safer place to live, a bigger apartment, some nice clothes, and birthday presents. I also wanted to have time to raise her properly and keep her safe. She is a good girl, but she sees crime and violence around her. I want to get her away from danger, and I want to show her that there are better ways to live. The job opportunities I will have with a college degree will enable me to do that.

The most important benefit of getting a college degree is that it will show me that I can achieve something hard. In the past, I have often given up and taken the easy way, which has led to nothing good. The easy way has led to a hard life. Now, however, working toward a goal has moved my life in a good direction. I have confidence and self-respect. I can honestly say that I am proud of myself, and my daughter will be proud of me, too. I will be a good role model as she grows up, not only for her but also for her friends. She will go to college, just like her mother.

So why am I practically killing myself to get a degree? I am doing it because I see in that degree the kind of life I want to live on this earth and the kind of human being I want to be. That is worth all the struggles.

PRACTICE 5   Revising an Essay

1. What major changes were suggested in response to the questions in the Checklist for Revising Your Writing?

_____

_____

_____

2. Did Chelsea make any of the suggested changes? Which ones?

_____

_____

_____

3. Did Chelsea make any changes that were not suggested? Which ones? Were they good changes?

_____

_____

_____

RESOURCES For suggestions on having students keep writing portfolios, see *Practical Suggestions*.

WRITING ASSIGNMENT   Essay

Revise the draft essay you wrote in Chapter 8. After revising your draft, complete the following checklist.

CHECKLIST

Evaluating your revised essay

- ☐ My thesis statement is confident, and my main point is clear.
- ☐ My ideas are detailed, specific, and organized logically.
- ☐ My ideas flow smoothly from one to the next.
- ☐ This essay fulfills the original assignment.
- ☐ I am ready to turn in this essay for a grade.
- ☐ This is the best I can do.

TEACHING TIP Ask students to write you an informal letter and attach it to their papers. In the letter, they should comment on the assignment: whether it was easy or hard, interesting or not. They should also indicate what they might change about their own writing process if they were to do the assignment again.

IMPORTANT NOTE: Editing—making changes in grammar, word use, punctuation, and capitalization—follows revising and is the final stage in the writing process. After you have revised your writing to make the ideas clear and strong, you need to edit it to eliminate any errors or distractions that could prevent readers from understanding your message. When you are ready to edit your writing, turn to Part Four, the beginning of the editing chapters.

LEARNING JOURNAL In your own words, summarize what you have learned about the writing process.

Chapter Review

1. Highlight the important terms from this chapter (for example, *revising* and *editing*), and list them with their page numbers.

2. Revising is *taking another look at your ideas to make them clearer, stronger, and more convincing.*

3. Why is revision important? (See p. 105.)
   A draft is a rough cut, not the best you can. Revision is critical to good writing.

4. Four basic features of useful feedback are
   It is given in a positive way. It is specific. It offers suggestions. It may be given in writing or orally.

5. As you revise, make sure that your paragraph or essay has these three things: *unity*, *detail/support*, and *coherence*.

6. *Unity* means that all the points you make are related to your main point.

7. Coherence means *that all of your support connects to form a whole.*

8. An important way to ensure coherence in your writing is to *use transitions.*

9. Transitions are *words, phrases, and sentences that connect your ideas so that your writing moves smoothly from one point to the next.*

10. Write for one minute about "What questions I should ask my instructor."

STUDENT VOICES

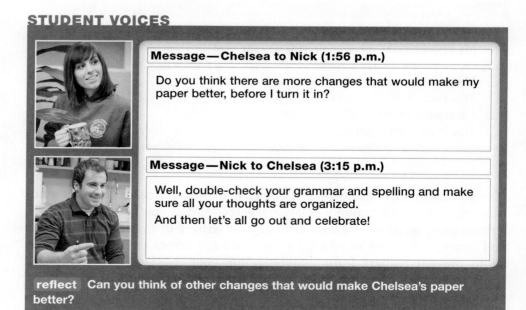

Message—Chelsea to Nick (1:56 p.m.)

Do you think there are more changes that would make my paper better, before I turn it in?

Message—Nick to Chelsea (3:15 p.m.)

Well, double-check your grammar and spelling and make sure all your thoughts are organized.
And then let's all go out and celebrate!

reflect   Can you think of other changes that would make Chelsea's paper better?

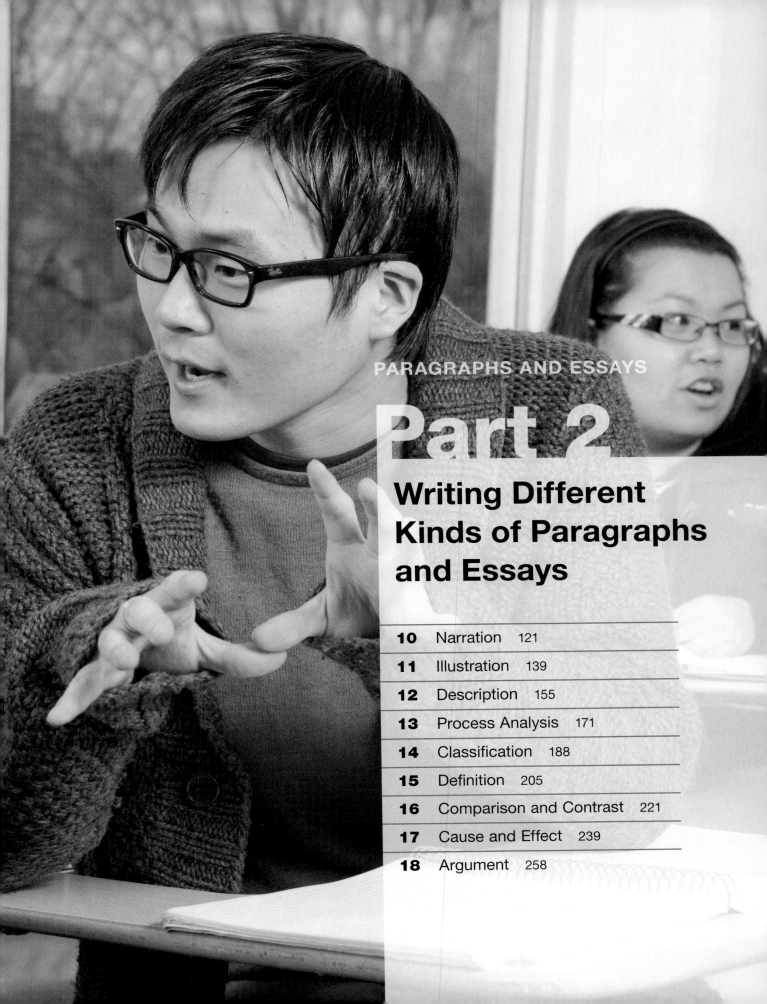

Part 2

Writing Different Kinds of Paragraphs and Essays

YOU KNOW THIS

You often use narration:

- You explain a TV episode to a friend who missed it.
- You say, "You won't believe what happened." Then, you tell the story.

write for two minutes about what makes a good story or a good telling of events.

10

Narration

Writing That Tells Important Stories

Understand What Narration Is

Narration is writing that tells the story of an event or an experience.

■■
■■ **Four Basics of Good Narration**

1 It reveals something of importance to you (your main point).

2 It includes all of the major events of the story (primary support).

3 It brings the story to life with details about the major events (secondary support).

4 It presents the events in a clear order, usually according to when they happened.

In the following paragraph, each number and color corresponds to one of the Four Basics of Good Narration.

1 Last year, a writing assignment that I hated produced the best writing I have done. 2 When my English teacher told us that one of our assignments would be to do a few hours of community service and write about it, I was furious. 3 I am a single mother, I work full-time, and I am going to school: Isn't that enough? 2 The next day, I went to talk with my teacher during her office hours and told her that I was already so busy that I could hardly make any time for homework, never mind housework. My own life was too full to help with anyone else's life. She understood that, right? 3 She said that she understood perfectly and that

4 Events in chronological order

the majority of the students at the college had lives as full as mine. Then, she went on to explain that the service assignment was just for four hours and that her students in the past had enjoyed both doing the assignment and writing about their experiences. She said they were all surprised and that I would be, too. **2** After talking with her, I decided I did not really have a choice because I needed to pass the course before taking others, so I accepted my fate. The next week, I went to the office of the Community Service Club, and a student there set me up to spend a few hours at an adult day-care center that is near where I live. A few weeks later, I went to the Creative Care Center in Cocoa Beach, not knowing what to expect. **3** What I found were friendly, approachable people who had so many stories to tell. They all had long, full lives, and they were eager to talk with me about them. **2** The next thing I knew, I was taking notes because I was interested in these people: **3** their marriages, life during the Depression, the wars they fought in, their children, their joys and sorrows. I felt as if I was traveling with them to the past and experiencing everything they lived while they shared their history with me. **2** When it came time to write about my experience, I had more than enough to write about: **3** I wrote the stories of the many wonderful elderly people I had talked with. **2** I got an A on the paper, and beyond that accomplishment, I made friends whom I will visit on my own, not because of an assignment, but because I value them. I never would have guessed that what started as an annoying assignment would turn out to be the best thing I did that semester.

STUDENT PHOTO

Photograph by student Andrew Dillon Bustin, taken during a walk in the woods with friends.

write **What is the story here?**

You can use narration in many practical situations:

COLLEGE   In a lab course, you are asked to tell what happened in an experiment. In a reading or English course, you are asked to tell, in your own words, the basic story of a piece of literature.

WORK   Something goes wrong at work, and you are asked to explain to your boss—in writing—what happened.

EVERYDAY   In a letter of complaint about service you received, you
LIFE   need to tell what happened that upset you.

Main Point in Narration

In narration, the **main point** is what is important about the story—to you and to your readers. To help you discover the main point for your own narration, complete the following sentence:

MAIN POINT   **What is important to me about the experience is. . . .**
IN NARRATION

Then, ask yourself, "So what?" until you know your readers would not have to ask that question to understand your main point. Notice the difference between the following two opening sentences in a narration:

IMPORTANCE   My child plays soccer. [So what?]
NOT CLEAR

IMPORTANCE   Soccer takes up all of my child's free time.
CLEAR

The topic sentence (paragraph) or thesis statement (essay) usually includes the topic and the main point the writer wants to make about the topic.

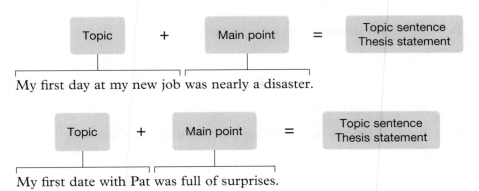

Writers usually reveal the main point either at the beginning or at the end of their narration. You will most likely want to start off with your main point and remind readers of that main point at the end of your paragraph or essay.

IDEA JOURNAL Write about something that happened to you this week.

• •

PRACTICE 1   **Writing a Main Point**

Look at the example narration paragraph on pages 121–122. Fill in the diagram with the paragraph's topic sentence.

A writing assignment produced the best writing I have done.

• •

PRACTICE 2   **Deciding on a Main Point**

For each of the following topics, write what main point you might make in a narration. Then, write a sentence that includes your topic and your main point. The sentence you write would be your topic sentence (paragraph) or thesis statement (essay). There is no one correct answer; you are practicing how to decide on a main point about a topic. Before writing your answer, you may need to make some notes about the topic.

EXAMPLE:

Topic: A fight I had with my sister

Important because: *it taught me something* _____

Main point: *learned it's better to stay cool* _____

Topic sentence/Thesis: *After a horrible fight with my sister, I learned the value of staying calm.*

1.   Topic: A commute to work or school

Important because: *Answers will vary.* _____

Main point: *Answers will vary.* _____

Topic sentence/Thesis: *Answers will vary.* _____

2.   Topic: An embarrassing experience

Important because: _____

Main point: _____

Topic sentence/Thesis: _____

3.   Topic: A strange or interesting incident that you witnessed

Important because: _____

Main point: _____

Topic sentence/Thesis: _____

4.   Topic: A typical evening at home

Important because: _____

Main point: _____

Topic sentence / Thesis: _____

5.   Topic: A funny or frightening dream

Important because: _____

Main point: _____

Topic sentence / Thesis: _____

· ·

Support in Narration

In narration, **support** consists of the major events you include (primary support) and the details (secondary support) you give the reader about those events. Your support should demonstrate your main point—what's important about the story.

The way you describe events creates a story with a certain point of view. For example, two people who witness or participate in the same series of events may give different accounts of it because they either focused on different events and details or saw them differently. The stories Charlene and Daryl tell in the following two paragraphs reflect different points of view. Read these two accounts of the same experience.

TIP In an essay, the major events may form the topic sentences of paragraphs. The details supporting the major events then make up the body of these paragraphs.

CHARLENE'S STORY

This morning, I got upset with my husband. While I was running around yelling at the kids, trying to get them fed and off to school, he just sat there having breakfast. When I finally sat down, he just kept on eating and daydreaming, even though I needed to talk to him. After several attempts to get through to him, I finally barked out, "Daryl! I have a few things I need to say!" He looked up, smiled, got another cup of coffee, and said, "What?" But as I began talking, he zoned out again. Does he live in another world?

TIP In writing a narration, you may use direct quotations (as this writer did) or indirect quotations. For more information on how to incorporate and punctuate quotations, see Chapter 20, pages 297–300.

DARYL'S STORY

This morning my family enjoyed some "quality time" together. The children were all in the kitchen eating and talking with each other. After they left for school, my wife and I were able to sit and share some quiet time. It really started the day out right.

As you can see, the events are the same, but the stories are not; they are told from two different points of view. Be careful to describe events in a way that will tell the story you want to tell.

ESL Ask students if they have seen certain events differently than other people have because of language or cultural differences.

Choosing Major Events

When you tell a story to a friend in person or on the phone, you can include events that are not essential to the story or go back and fill in any gaps in the story. When you are talking, keeping your story focused and advancing in a straight line is not overly important. However, when you are writing a

TEACHING TIP Ask students to write a narrative joke they have heard—then, examine the structure of one or two of these jokes.

narration, you need to give more careful thought to which events to include, selecting only those that most clearly demonstrate your main point. If you find out later that you have left out something important, you can add it when you are revising.

• •

PRACTICE 3   Choosing Major Events

This practice uses three items from Practice 2, where you wrote topic sentences/thesis statements. Using three sentences from that practice, write three events for each that would help you make your main point. Remember, there is no one correct answer. What you want to do is to think logically about three essential events that will demonstrate your main point to readers.

EXAMPLE:

Topic: A fight I had with my sister

Topic sentence/Thesis: _After a horrible fight with my sister, I learned_ _the value of staying calm._

Events: _We disagreed about who was going to have the family party._ _She made me so mad that I started yelling at her, and I got nasty._ _I hung up on her, and now we're not talking._

1.   Topic: A commute to work or school

Topic sentence/Thesis: _Answers will vary._

_____

Events: _Answers will vary._

_____

_____

2.   Topic: An embarrassing experience

Topic sentence/Thesis: _____

_____

Events: _____

_____

_____

3.   Topic: A typical evening at home

Topic sentence/Thesis: _____

_____

Events: _____

_____

_____

• •

Giving Details about the Events

When you write a narration, include examples and details that will make each event more realistic and specific to your audience. You want your readers to share your point of view and see the same message in the story that you do. Give your readers helpful information by adding details that make each event easier to visualize and understand.

. . . .

PRACTICE 4   Giving Details about the Events

Choose two of the items in Practice 3, and write your topic sentence or thesis statement for each. Then, write the major events in the spaces provided. Give a detail about each event.

EXAMPLE:

Topic sentence/Thesis: *After a horrible fight with my sister, I learned the value of staying calm.*

Event: *We disagreed about who was going to have the family party.*

    Detail: *Even though we both work, she said she was too busy and that I would have to do it.*

Event: *She made me so mad I started yelling at her, and I got nasty.*

    Detail: *I brought up times in the past when she had tried to pass responsibilities off on me, and I told her I was sick of being the one who did everything.*

Event: *I hung up on her, and now we are not talking.*

    Detail: *I feel bad, and I know I will have to call her sooner or later because she is my sister. I do love her, even though she's a pain sometimes.*

1. Topic sentence/Thesis: *Answers will vary.*

    Event: *Answers will vary.*

        Detail: _____

    Event: _____

        Detail: _____

    Event: _____

        Detail: _____

2. Topic sentence / Thesis: _____

_____

Event: _____

    Detail: _____

_____

Event: _____

    Detail: _____

_____

Event: _____

    Detail: _____

_____

Organization in Narration

TIP For more on time order, see page 81.

Narration usually presents events in the order in which they happened, known as **time order**. A narration starts at the beginning of the story and describes events as they unfolded. Then, after the main point is explored or resolved, the narration draws to a close ("the end").

Common Time Transitions

after	eventually	meanwhile	soon
as	finally	next	then
at last	first	now	when
before	last	second	while
during	later	since	

PRACTICE 5   Using Transitions in Narration

Read the paragraph that follows, and fill in the blanks with time transitions.
Answers may vary. Possible answers are shown.

_____After_____ a horrible fight with my sister, I learned the value

of staying calm. The fight started over who was going to have the family

party. _____First_____, she said that she was too busy, even though

we both work. _____Then_____, I got mad and started yelling at her.

I brought up times in the past when she had tried to pass responsibilities off on me, and I told her I was sick of being the one who did everything. _____*Finally*_____ , I hung up on her, and _____*now*_____ we are not talking. I feel bad because she's my sister, and I do love her. _____*Eventually*_____ , I know that I will have to call her.

Read and Analyze Narration

Reading examples of narration will help you write your own. The first example in this section is a Profile of Success from the real world of nursing. Kelly Layland found that she was not prepared for college work, but she stuck with it in order to reach her goal of becoming a nurse. Her Profile of Success shows how she uses writing in her work and gives an example of how she uses narration. Whatever your goals, you, too, will need to be able to write accurate accounts of what happened in certain situations.

The second and third examples—first a narration paragraph and then an essay—are both written by students. As you read these selections, pay attention to the vocabulary, and answer the questions in the margin. They will help you read the pieces critically.

READING SELECTIONS For more examples of and activities for narration, see Chapter 42.

PROFILE OF SUCCESS

Narration in the Real World

The following profile shows how a nurse uses narration on the job.

Background   In high school, I was not a good student. I had a lot of other things to do, like having fun. I am a very social person; I loved my friends, and we had a great time. But when I decided I wanted to go to college, I had to pay the price. I had to take lots of noncredit courses to get my skills up to college level because I had fooled around during high school. The noncredit English course I took was very beneficial to me. After I passed it, I took English 101 and felt prepared for it.

Degrees/College(s)   A.S., Monroe Community College; L.P.N., Isabella Graham Hart School of Nursing; R.N., Monroe Community College

Employer   Rochester General Hospital

Writing at work   I write nursing notes that are narratives of patients' changing conditions and the level of care required. When I describe physical conditions, I have to support my descriptions with detailed examples. When I recommend medication for treatment, I have to justify it by explaining the patient's condition and the reasons I am making the recommendation. I also have to write notes that

Kelly Layland
Registered Nurse

integrate care with Medicare documentation. Basically, I have to write about everything I recommend and all that I do.

How Kelly uses narration   Every day I write brief narratives that recount all that went on with the patient during the day: things that went wrong and things about his or her treatment that need to be changed.

Kelly's Narration

The following paragraph is an example of the daily reports that Kelly writes on each patient.

RESOURCES For a discussion of how to use the profiles in Part Two, see *Practical Suggestions*.

> <u><u>Karella Lehmanoff, a two-month-old female infant, is improving steadily.</u></u> When she was born, her birth weight was 1.3 pounds, but <u>it has increased to 3.1 pounds.</u> <u>Her jaundice has completely disappeared</u>, and her skin has begun to look rosy. Karella's pulse rate is normal for her development, and <u>her resting heart rate has stabilized at about 150 beats per minute.</u> Lung development was a big concern because of Karella's premature birth, but <u>her lungs are now fully developed and largely functional.</u> <u>Dr. Lansing saw Karella at 1 p.m. and pronounced her in good condition.</u> The parents were encouraged, and so am I. The prognosis for little Karella gets better with each day.

1. Double-underline the **main point** of the narration.

2. Underline the **major events**.

3. What order of organization does Kelly use? _____*time order*_____

Student Narration Paragraph

Jelani Lynch
My Turnaround

Vocabulary development
Underline these words as you read Jelani's paragraph.

integrity: honesty; having a sound moral code
mentor: a counselor, a teacher, an adviser

Jelani Lynch expects to graduate from Cambridge College/Year Up in 2009 with a degree in information technology. As a writer, he says he is interested in exploring "issues that affect the community and the disparities that continue to affect the world." Reflecting on what motivated him to begin this essay, Jelani comments that he viewed his writing as a means of helping those around him: "I wrote this essay after I had just begun to get my life on track. I felt that the struggles that I have encountered needed to be publicized so my mistakes are not repeated by the people who read this essay."

PREDICT What will Jelani's paragraph explain?

_____

_____

_____

Before my big turnaround, my life was headed in the wrong direction.[1] I grew up in the city and had a typical sad story: broken home, not much money, gangs, and drugs. In this world, few positive male role models are available.[2] I played the game "Street Life": running the streets, stealing bikes, robbing people, carrying a gun, and selling drugs. The men in my neighborhood did not have regular jobs; they got their money outside the system. No one except my mother thought school was worth much.[3] I had a history of poor school performance, a combination of not showing up and not doing any work when I did. My pattern of failure in that area was pretty strong. When I was seventeen, though, things got really bad.[4] I was arrested for possession of crack cocaine. I was kicked out of school for good.[5] During this time, I realized that my life was not going the way I wanted it to be. I was headed nowhere, except a life of crime, violence, and possibly early death. I knew that way of life, because I was surrounded by people who had chosen that direction. I did not want to go there anymore.[6] When I made that decision, my life started to change.[7] First, I met Shawn Brown, a man who had had the same kind of life I did. He got out of that life, though, by graduating from high school and college and getting a good job. He has a house, a wife, and children, along with great clothes. Shawn became my role model, showing me that with honesty, integrity, and hard work I could live a much better life. Since meeting Shawn, I have turned my life around.[8] I started taking school seriously and graduated from high school, something I thought I would never do. Working with Shawn, I have read books and learned I enjoy writing. I have met the mayor of Boston and got a summer job at the State House. I have been part of an educational video and had many opportunities to meet and work with people who are successful. Now, I am a mentor with Diamond Educators, and I work with other young, urban males to give them a role model and help them make good choices. Now, I have a bright future with goals and plans. I have turned my life around and know I will be a success.

REFLECT Have you ever made a decision that changed your life?

_____

_____

_____

SUMMARIZE How did meeting Shawn change Jelani's life?

_____

_____

_____

1. Underline the **topic sentence**.

2. What is important about the story? _Answers will vary. Possible answer:_
    People can take control of their lives with the help of a mentor.

3. Number the **major events**.

4. Circle the transitions.

5. Does Jelani's paragraph follow the Four Basics of Good Narration
    (p. 121)? Be ready to give specific reasons for your answer. _Answers will_
    vary. Possible answer: Yes. The story is important. It describes events
    and details in a clear time order.

Student Narration Essay

Dale Hill, a student at Kaskaskia College in Centralia, Illinois, wrote the following essay, which received an honorable mention in the Paul Simon Student Essay Contest sponsored by the Illinois Community College Trustees Association.

Dale Hill

How Community College Has Changed My Life

After graduating from Kaskaskia College, Dale Hill went on to receive an M.A. in English from Southern Illinois University in 2008 and currently teaches English at Kaskaskia, his community college alma mater. Hill most enjoys reading "short stories and essays, since the work must be done with precision and power," and he aims to achieve a similar level of conciseness in his own writing. He encourages other aspiring writers "to read widely in order to absorb the beauty of the language, to write constantly even if your writing seems inadequate at first, and to set realistic goals that you never give up on."

PREDICT Read the title and the first paragraph. How do you think the writer's attitude might have changed?

_____

_____

REFLECT How does your family feel about your going to college?

_____

_____

REFLECT Do you share any of Dale's feelings?

_____

_____

Grandpa was a sharecropper. With only a second-grade education, he 1
planted his seeds and raised his family of seven sons and three daughters. My father, third eldest of the sons, broke new ground when he became the first person ever in the family to graduate from high school. Although Dad was very bright, it never occurred to him to go on to college. He and Grandpa shared the attitude that college was only for rich people and that you cannot change a sow's ear into a silk purse. Dad was expected to work to help support his younger brothers and sisters, and that is what he did. And that is what I did, too, for a long while. Now, however, my attitude has changed, and I have learned that there are other ways to seed future growth. The change did not happen overnight.

While I was growing up in the same small farming town and attending 2
Dad's same high school, people still thought that college was only for the rich. College was my dream deferred. Like my father before me, I was expected to work after graduation to help support the family, and like my father before me, that is what I did. What followed was twenty wasted and fruitless years of unfulfilling factory and retail jobs. Only last year, faced with the prospect of starting over again with a son of my own to set an example for, did I return to my dream.

The prospect of attending college, leaving old attitudes and beliefs 3
behind, was daunting. The world I knew was greatly different from the

academic world, and I was unsure that I would fit in. I was twenty years older than traditional students and was not confident that I could compete. Going to a university full-time would require a commitment of time and money that would cause hardship for my family. My wife suggested that I enroll at my local community college first, which I did.

I discovered that community college acts as the perfect stepping stone   4
between the mundane life that I wished to leave behind and the new one I wished to begin. The proximity, affordability, and flexibility offered by my local community college lessen the sacrifices my family is called upon to make. Community college allows me to test the waters of an academic environment without fear of plunging in over my head. It encourages me to challenge myself and build my confidence even as it expands my horizons. My community college nourishes me and helps me to grow.

I have discovered that my father's and grandfather's attitudes about   5
college were right. College education *is* for the rich: the rich in mind and spirit, the rich in wonder and curiosity. How has community college changed my life? It has shown me how rich I am. I am planting a new seed for my family now, a crop that will bear fruit for generations to come.

CRITICAL THINKING: READING

TIP For reading advice, see Chapter 2.

1.   What is Dale's purpose for writing? *Answers will vary. Possible answers:*
to explain how his attitude about college changed; to win the essay contest

Does he achieve it? *Answers will vary.*

2.   In your own words, state his main point.
Answers will vary. Possible answer: that breaking with family tradition
is sometimes important

TIP For tools to build your vocabulary, visit the *Real Writing Student Center* at **bedfordstmartins.com/ realwriting.**

3.   Double-underline the **thesis statement**, and underline the **topic sentences** that support the thesis.

4.   How has Dale organized his essay? ____*time order*____ Circle the **transitional words and phrases** that indicate this order.

5.   Double-underline the sentence in the last paragraph that reminds readers of the main point and makes an observation.

6.   What do you think of this essay? Why? *Answers will vary.*

CRITICAL THINKING: WRITING

Choose one of the following questions and respond in a paragraph or essay.

1.   Have you broken with family tradition in some way? How, and why?

2.   What are your dreams for your life?

3. What expectations does your family have for you? Are they the same as or different from those you have for yourself?

4. How did becoming a parent change your life?

5. Dale writes, "College education *is* for the rich: the rich in mind and spirit, the rich in wonder and curiosity." In what ways is your life rich?

Write Your Own Narration

Narration at a Glance

↓

Topic sentence (paragraph) or thesis statement (essay)
Says what's important about the experience

↓

First major event
Details about the event

↓

Second major event
Details about the event

↓

Third major event
Details about the event

↓

Conclusion
Reminds readers of the main point and makes an observation based on it

In this section, you will write your own narration paragraph or essay based on one of the following assignments. Use the following tools to help you:

1. Review the Four Basics of Good Narration (p. 121).
2. Use "Narration at a Glance" as a basic organizer.
3. Use the Checklist: How to Write Narration (pp. 136–37) as you write and revise.

• •

ASSIGNMENT 1   Writing about College, Work, and Everyday Life

Write a narration paragraph or essay on one of the following topics or on one of your own choice. Look back at your written responses to the photograph on page 122 and the idea journal on page 123.

COLLEGE
- A time when you experienced success
- Your best school year
- How a teacher made a difference

WORK
- A work achievement that you are proud of
- Your worst job
- A funny work story

EVERYDAY LIFE
- A mistake that you learned from
- An experience that triggered a strong emotion: happiness, sadness, fear, anger, regret
- Your biography or a story to post on MySpace or Facebook

RESOURCES Reproducible peer-review guides for different kinds of papers are available in *Additional Resources*, and online at **bedfordstmartins .com/realwriting**.

• •

ASSIGNMENT 2   Writing about Connections

Read the following account of Jenny Haun before doing the assignment.

COMMUNITY MATTERS

Jenny Haun

The color-coded example of the Four Basics of Good Narration (pp. 121–22) is the story of Jenny Haun's experience.

Jenny was born in Peru but moved to the United States, where she had her first child at age fourteen. She escaped from an abusive marriage and moved to Florida, where she met and married her true love. Tragically, he was one of nineteen soldiers killed in Saudi Arabia in 1996 (the story is told in the 2007 movie *The Kingdom*). Jenny went back to school in 2006 and plans to get her A.A. in 2010. She has returned to the adult day-care center and has made many friends there; she feels a part of that community.

Here is part of the narration she wrote for her class assignment.

Mackie has led a hard but happy life. Adopted at two years old, Mackie loved her adopted mother very, very much. She was sad when she told me, "My real mom did not want me or maybe could not keep me; she was only sixteen when she gave me up for adoption." Then, she smiled as she said, "I was so lucky my adopted parents picked me out." Her adopted mom could not have any children, but she was wonderful, caring, and loving to Mackie. Mackie met her late husband at a bus stop, and after a year, they got married and were happy together. As an adult, Mackie worked as an X-ray technician and raised four children, the youngest of whom has serious disabilities. Now her daughter who is disabled is in love with and married to another person with a disability, and they are doing well. Mackie feels the hard work was worth it, and she believes her life is a lucky one.

RESOURCES For advice on "Writing about Connections," see *Practical Suggestions*.

ASSIGNMENT: Choose one of the following and write a narration paragraph or essay. Work either on your own or with a partner.

- Interview an older person and write his or her story.
- Interview someone in your class.

TIP For more on connecting to community, visit **bedfordstmartins.com/ realwriting**.

WRITING DIFFERENT KINDS OF PARAGRAPHS AND ESSAYS

- Go to the student government office and find out if there is a community service club that offers short-term assignments. Take one of these short-term assignments. Write about your experience.

- Write about a time when you helped someone else.

- Write about a time when someone helped you.

- Write about how you made a difference in someone else's life. (Focus on one way you made a difference, so that you can tell the story in a paragraph or short essay.)

· ·

ASSIGNMENT 3   Writing in the Real World/Solving a Problem

Read Appendix B, "Solving Problems."

PROBLEM: You have learned that a generous scholarship is available for low-income, first-generation college students. You really need the money to cover day-care expenses while you are taking classes (in fact, you had thought you would have to stop going to college for a while). Many people have been applying. Part of the application is to write about yourself and why you deserve the scholarship.

TIP Such scholarships really do exist. Go online or to the college financial aid office to find out about them. If you are pleased with what you have written for this assignment, you could use it as part of your application.

ASSIGNMENT: Write a paragraph or essay that tells your story and why you should be considered for the scholarship. Think about how you can make your story stand out. You might start with the following sentence:

Even though you will be reading applications from many first-generation college students, my story is a little different because

_____ .

CHECKLIST: HOW TO WRITE NARRATION	
STEPS IN NARRATION	**HOW TO DO THE STEPS**
☐ Focus.	• Think about your story and what is important about it.
☐ Narrow and explore your topic. See Chapter 4.	• Make the topic more specific. • Prewrite, recalling what happened. As you prewrite, ask: Why is the story important?
☐ Write a topic sentence (paragraph) or thesis statement (essay) that includes your main point about the story. See Chapter 5.	• Say what is important about the story—how it affected you and others.

CHECKLIST: HOW TO WRITE NARRATION

STEPS IN NARRATION	HOW TO DO THE STEPS
☐ Support your point. See Chapter 6.	• Recall the major events, and choose the essential ones. • Provide any background information that your readers will need. • Describe the events with specific details.
☐ Make a plan. See Chapter 7.	• Arrange the events in time order.
☐ Write a draft. See Chapter 8.	**FOR A PARAGRAPH** • Write a paragraph with your topic sentence, major events, and details about the events. Use complete sentences. **FOR AN ESSAY** • Consider using one of the introduction types in Chapter 8. Include your thesis statement in your introduction. • Using your plan, write topic sentences for the major events. • Write paragraphs for each topic sentence with event details. **FOR PARAGRAPHS AND ESSAYS** • Write a conclusion that reminds readers of your main point and makes an observation based on what you have written. • Write a title that previews your main point but does not repeat it. • Get feedback from others using the peer-review guide for narration at **bedfordstmartins.com/realwriting**.
☐ Revise your draft, making at least four improvements. See Chapter 9.	• Read to make sure that all events and details about them show, explain, or prove your main point about the story. • Add events and/or details that help make your main point. • Add time transitions to move your readers from one event to another.
☐ Edit your revised draft. See Parts 4 through 7.	• Correct errors in grammar, spelling, word use, and punctuation.
☐ Ask yourself:	• Does my paper have the Four Basics of Good Narration (p. 121)? • What is the best sentence in my paper? Why? • Is this the best I can do?

Chapter Review

1. Narration is writing that _tells the story of an event or experience._

2. List the Four Basics of Good Narration. _It reveals something of_ _importance to you. It includes all of the major events of the story. It_

brings the story to life with details about the major events. It presents
the events in a clear order, usually according to when they happened.

3. The topic sentence in a narration paragraph or the thesis statement in a narration essay usually includes what two things?

your narrowed topic; your main point

4. What type of organization do writers of narration usually use?

time order, also known as chronological order

5. List five common transitions for this type of organization.

Answers will vary.

LEARNING JOURNAL Reread your idea journal entry about an event that happened to you this week (p. 123), then rewrite it using what you now know about narration.

6. Write sentences using the following vocabulary words: *integrity, defer, mundane, proximity.*

Answers will vary.

_____

_____

_____

---

reflect Write for two minutes about how to tell a good story. Then, compare what you have written to what you wrote in response to the "write" prompt on page 121.

Spot and Start Narration Assignments in Other Courses

↓

Spot

In college, at work, and in your everyday life, you use narration in many situations (see p. 123), but the word *narration* probably will not appear in those situations. Instead, the assignment might ask you to *describe* the events, *report* what happened, or *retell* what happened. Words or phrases that call for an *account of events* are situations that require narration.

↓

Start

Ask yourself:

1. What is important about the story or event? If a reader asked, "*So what?*" what would I say?
2. What background information will my readers need to know?
3. What happened, first, next, later? What is the sequence of the events that make up the story?

YOU KNOW THIS

You use examples to illustrate your point in daily communication:

- You answer the question "Like what?"
- You give a friend some examples of fun things to do this weekend.

write for two minutes on what you know about writing description.

11

Illustration

Writing That Gives Examples

Understand What Illustration Is

Illustration is writing that uses examples to show, explain, or prove a point. Giving examples is the basis of all good writing and speaking: You make a statement, and then you give an example that shows (illustrates) what you mean.

Four Basics of Good Illustration

1 It has a point.

2 It gives specific examples that show, explain, or prove the point.

3 It gives details to support the examples.

4 It uses enough examples to get the point across to the reader.

In the following paragraph, each number and color corresponds to one of the Four Basics of Good Illustration.

1 Many people would like to serve their communities or help with causes that they believe in, but they do not have much time and do not know what to do. Now, the Internet provides people with ways to help that do not take much time or money. 2 Web sites now make it convenient to donate online. With a few clicks, an organization of your choice can receive your donation or money from a sponsoring advertiser. For example, if you are interested in helping to rescue unwanted and abandoned animals, you can go to www.theanimalrescuesite.com, and

139

4 Enough examples to get the point across to the reader

3 just by clicking as instructed, a sponsor advertiser, not you, will make a donation to help provide food and care for the 27 million animals in shelters. At the same site, an online store allows you to shop, and a portion of the money you spend will go to providing animal care. **2** If you want to help fight world hunger, go to www.thehungersite.com **3** and click daily to have sponsor fees directed to hungry people in more than seventy countries via the Mercy Corps and America's Second Harvest. Each year, hundreds of millions of cups of food are distributed to the one billion hungry people around the world. With just a click, you can help some of the 24,000 people who die every day from hunger. **2** Other examples of click-to-give sites are the child health site at www.thechild healthsite.com, the literacy site at www.theliteracysite.com, the breast cancer site at www.breastcancersite.com, and many others. **3** Also on these sites are information about organizations and other ways to help, great online stores that direct a percentage of the purchase price of what you buy to charity, and links to help you learn about causes you are interested in. One hundred percent of the sponsors' donations go to the charities, and you can give with a click every single day. Since I have found out about these sites, I go to at least one of them every day. **1** I have learned a lot about various problems, and every day, I feel as if I have helped a little.

STUDENT PHOTO

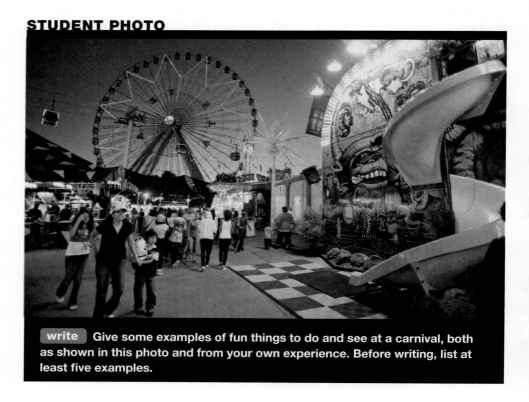

This photograph was taken by student Caleb Miller, at the State Fair of Texas.

write   Give some examples of fun things to do and see at a carnival, both as shown in this photo and from your own experience. Before writing, list at least five examples.

It is hard to explain anything without using examples, so you use illustration in almost every communication situation:

COLLEGE   An exam question asks you to explain and give examples of a concept.

WORK   Your boss asks you to tell her what office equipment needs to be replaced and why.

EVERYDAY   You complain to your landlord that the building super-
LIFE   intendent is not doing his job. The landlord asks for examples.

Main Point in Illustration

In illustration, the **main point** is the message you want your readers to receive and understand. To help you discover your main point, complete the following sentence:

MAIN POINT IN   **What I want readers to know about this topic is. . . .**
ILLUSTRATION

The topic sentence (in a paragraph) or thesis statement (in an essay) usually include the topic and the main point the writer wants to make about the topic.

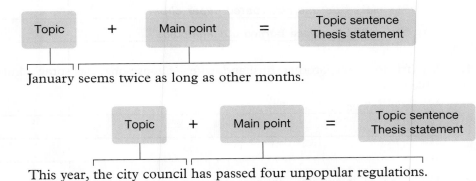

| Topic | + | Main point | = | Topic sentence Thesis statement |

January seems twice as long as other months.

| Topic | + | Main point | = | Topic sentence Thesis statement |

This year, the city council has passed four unpopular regulations.

• •

PRACTICE 1 Making a Main Point

Each of the items in this practice is a narrowed topic. Think about each of them, and in the space provided, write a main point about each topic.

EXAMPLE: The words to songs I like *relate closely to experiences I have had.*

1. A few moments alone *Answers will vary.*

2. A course I am taking _____

3.   The busiest time at work _____

4.   Being a parent of a newborn baby _____

5.   Working with other people _____

Support in Illustration

In illustration, **support** consists of examples and details that explain your main point to readers.

The best way to generate good detailed examples (if you do not already have some in mind) is to use one or more of the prewriting techniques discussed in Chapter 4. First, write down all of the examples that come into your mind. Then, review your examples and choose the ones that will best communicate your point to your readers.

PRACTICE 2   Supporting Your Main Point with Examples

Read the following main points, and give three examples you might use to support each one.

EXAMPLE: My boss's cheapness is unprofessional.

makes us bring in our own calculators

makes us use old, rusted paper clips

will not replace burned-out lightbulbs

1.   My (friend, sister, brother, husband, wife—choose one) has some admirable traits.

Answers will vary.

_____

_____

2.   My boss is (fair, unfair—choose one).

_____

_____

_____

3.   This weekend is particularly busy.

_____

_____

_____

ESL Tell students that if they are writing about something from their native country's culture, they have to think about what their readers may not be familiar with. They may need to give more details than they would need to provide for people from their native culture.

PRACTICE 3   Giving Details about the Examples

Choose two of the items from Practice 2, where you wrote specific examples to support main points. In the spaces provided, first copy the main point you are using and your examples from Practice 2. Then, write a detail that further shows, explains, or proves what you mean.

EXAMPLE:

Main point: My boss's cheapness is unprofessional.

Example: *makes us bring in our own calculators*

    Detail: *Some people do not have a calculator.*

Example: *makes us use old, rusted paper clips*

    Detail: *They leave rust marks on important documents.*

Example: *will not replace burned-out lightbulbs*

    Detail: *The dim light leads to more errors.*

1. Main point: *Answers will vary.*

Example: *Answers will vary.*

    Detail: *Answers will vary.*

Example: _____

    Detail: _____

Example: _____

    Detail: _____

2. Main point: _____

Example: _____

    Detail: _____

Example: _____

    Detail: _____

Example: _____

    Detail: _____

Organization in Illustration

Illustration often uses **order of importance**, saving the most powerful example for last. Or, it might be organized by **time order** if the examples are given according to when they happened.

TIP For more on order of importance and time order, see pages 81–82.

Transitions in illustration let readers know that you are introducing an example or moving from one example to another.

Common Illustration Transitions			
also	first, second, and so on	for instance	in addition
another		for one thing/	one example/
finally	for example	for another	another example

- -

PRACTICE 4   Using Transitions in Illustration

Read the paragraph that follows, and fill in the blanks with transitions.
Answers may vary. Possible answers are shown.

    My computer was working against me today. _____*First*_____, I had to try several times just to turn it on. _____*Second*_____, after I finally turned it on, it froze. I turned the computer off and on again, and it worked for a few minutes, but then it crashed yet again. When I restarted the computer, the work I had done was lost. _____*Another*_____ problem with my computer today was that it would not accept a disk to save my work. _____*For example*_____, when I inserted the disk into the disk drive, the computer froze. I think I need a new computer. _____*For one thing*_____, a new computer will work better than my old one. _____*For another*_____, it will make life much less stressful for me.

- -

Read and Analyze Illustration

READING SELECTIONS
For further examples of and activities for illustration, see Chapter 43.

Reading examples of illustration will help you write your own. The first example in this section is a Profile of Success from the real world of business. Karen Upright started and dropped out of college several times, but she credits her college English teacher for her ultimate success. Her profile shows how she uses writing in her work and gives an example of how she uses illustration to communicate with her colleagues at Procter & Gamble. She says of her writing, "I am particular about the words and structure I choose when I communicate either in writing or in speech."

    The second and third examples are both student writing, first an illustration paragraph and then an illustration essay. As you read, pay attention to the vocabulary, and answer the questions in the margin. They will help you read the piece critically.

Illustration in the Real World

The following profile shows how a business manager uses writing and includes an example of how she uses illustration in her work.

Karen Upright
Systems Manager

Background   I started college a couple of times but failed most of my courses, mainly because I did not go to class and was not motivated. I was not involved and did not have a particular reason to go to college. I enrolled at FCCJ and took classes irregularly—sometimes full-time, sometimes part-time. I did well in some of the classes and poorly in others.

During this time, I got a job at CityStreet, a global benefits provider, and I realized that I really liked business. I also realized that I would not go far without a college degree. So I decided to try college one more time. My first course then was English, and my teacher, Marian Beaman, was great. I did well in that course and from then on. From FCCJ, I went to Florida State and Purdue University, where I have recently completed an M.B.A. Later, I wrote Professor Beaman to thank her for setting me on a good course; it changed my life.

I now have a great job with lots of potential for advancement.

Degrees / College(s)   A.A., Florida Community College, Jacksonville; B.S., Florida State University; M.B.A., Purdue University

Employer   Procter & Gamble

Writing at work   I write many kinds of documents, like memos, work and development plans, and speeches for presentations. We have structured meetings at P&G, so before meetings we prepare and distribute talk sheets, which provide the necessary background for what will be discussed at the meeting. I write technical design documents with precision analyses of systems. I also write e-mail that is read by senior management. I always make sure that those e-mails are correct because I do not want the executives to be distracted by errors. If I make careless mistakes in writing, I will not get far in the company. I also write about human resources issues. Whenever you manage people, you have to be aware of issues and situations that might offend employees.

I was surprised by how much writing I do as an essential part of the job. I am a computer scientist, but my writing has to be good.

Karen's Illustration

The following memo is an example of the illustration that Karen writes as part of her job. It details the objectives of a workplace initiative to help women already employed by Procter & Gamble to plan careers within the company.

Vocabulary development

Underline the following words as you read Karen's memo.

retain: to keep
matrix: a grid, or table
aspects: parts of
align: to be in line or parallel (in this case, to agree)
objectives: goals

From: Upright, Karen

Subject: Women's Network: Assignment Planning Matrix

As you know, we have an enrollment goal for 30 percent of our employees to be women, but we are currently at 20 percent. We need to grow our enrollment, but we also need to retain the women currently in the organization. Greg and I met a few weeks ago to determine how to improve assignment planning for the women in our organization. We agreed to use the Assignment Planning Matrix as a starting point. The matrix is a good career-planning tool, with a section on career interests, rated from "highly desirable" to "undesirable." It also contains a section on specific P&G career interests, with sections to describe aspects that make a particular choice desirable or undesirable and a place to give weight to the various career choices. Completing the matrix requires thought as to what course an individual wants to pursue and why. I have reviewed a sample with and provided training to the women in our organization. Each of them has been asked to complete the matrix, meet with her manager to align on content, and submit a final version to her manager. This information can be shared at the next Leadership Team meeting.

This initiative has several objectives:

- Have each member of the network start a long-term plan for her career.
- Use the long-term plan to develop a short-term plan for assignments and competency development.
- Share this information in written form with the immediate manager and section manager of each member of the network, enabling the manager to speak for each woman's career interests, and providing a reference point for each member's career goals.
- Enable the Leadership Team to plan assignments within the organization for each member of the network, matching individual goals and interests to organizational goals and needs.

I encourage you to support the women on your teams as they work through the Assignment Planning Matrix over the next few weeks. Please let me know if you have any questions.

1. Double-underline the **main point** of the memo.

2. Karen gives examples about two topics. What are the two topics? _the Assignment Planning Matrix and the objectives_

3. What is the purpose of the memo? _Answers will vary but should say to describe what action is being taken to meet a goal and what Karen thinks the action will achieve._

Student Illustration Paragraph

Casandra Palmer
Gifts from the Heart

Casandra Palmer is majoring in accounting and expects to graduate from the University of Akron/Wayne College in 2009. After completing her essay "Gifts from the Heart," Casandra went on to seek publication in her campus paper at the encouragement of her instructor. She spent a few days revising the essay and looked to feedback from others to help strengthen the clarity of her points. With plans to continue writing for publication when time allows, Casandra enjoys reading inspirational novels and offers this advice to other student writers: "Learn all you can and never give up. Follow your dreams!"

PREDICT After reading the title, what do you think the paragraph will be about?

_____

_____

_____

In our home, gift exchanges have always been meaningful items to us. We do not just give things so that everyone has lots of presents. Each item has a purpose, such as a need or something that someone has desired for a long time. Some things have been given that may have made the other person laugh or cry. I remember one Christmas, our daughter Hannah had her boyfriend, who looked a lot like Harry Potter, join us. We wanted to include him, but we did not know him well, so it was hard to know what to give him. We decided to get Hannah a Harry Potter poster and crossed out the name Harry Potter. In place of Harry Potter, we put her boyfriend's name. Everyone thought it was funny, and we were all laughing, including Hannah's boyfriend. It was a personal gift that he knew we had thought about. For some reason, Hannah did not think it was so funny, but she will still remember it. (Another) meaningful gift came from watching the movie *Titanic* with my other daughter, Tabitha. We both cried hard and hugged each other. She surprised me by getting a necklace that resembled the gem known as "Heart of the Ocean." I was so touched that she gave me something to remind me of the experience we shared. These special moments have left lasting impressions on my heart.

REFLECT Have you ever received a gift that made you laugh or cry?

_____

_____

_____

1.   Double-underline the **topic sentence**.

2.   Underline the **examples** that support the main point.

3.   Circle the **transitions**.

4.   Does the paragraph have the Four Basics of Good Illustration (p. 139)? Why or why not? *Answers will vary but might say that the writer could have said more about Hannah's reaction or about what the necklace looked like.*

5. Does the paragraph use a particular kind of organization, like time, space, or importance? Does that choice help the paragraph or not? _No._ _The paragraph might have been more effective if the examples had been presented in order of increasing importance._

Student Illustration Essay

Kathleen Aharonian

Does Anyone Want Some More Calories with That?

Kathleen Aharonian expects to graduate from Pasadena City College (PCC) in 2011 or 2012. She was inspired to write this piece for her journalism class after noticing how hard it was to maintain a healthy diet while attending school. After submitting her piece to the school newspaper, she revised it with the help of the newspaper's editor to make sure that it was "as good as it could be for readers' eyes." Kathleen advises others who are interested in writing for publication, "The more time you have to gather information, the better you can make your writing, and you may even find out fun little facts."

Vocabulary development
Underline these words as you read the essay.
fundamental: basic, essential
speech pathology: the study of various speech and language disorders
mind-set: a way of thinking and making decisions

REFLECT What does your cafeteria offer?

_____

_____

_____

Obesity is one of the biggest problems in California. Every other commercial on TV is trying to promote some kind of diet product. News reports are full of statistics about how fat our country has grown and how dangerous obesity is. We all know that two things are fundamental to avoid getting fat or to lose weight: exercise and healthy eating habits. Yet, staying healthy on the campus of PCC can be a bit of a challenge because of the lack of healthy food products.   1

"All I ever see are cookies and doughnuts," complains Lisa Estrada, a twenty-two-year-old majoring to be a speech language pathology assistant.   2

You might go into the school cafeteria with the mind-set of picking something healthy to eat, but you are soon going to realize you don't have many choices and the very few you do have are expensive. Eating healthy here on campus is an expensive business.   3

"I just think their healthy selections are too expensive, like a fruit cup is four dollars compared to a corn dog that's one dollar. It is ridiculous," agrees Estrada. "Why is it so hard for them to order a couple of extra healthy products over the regular fatty ones?"   4

Eating healthy is also hard here because there are a lot more unhealthy choices. For example, there are fifteen or more different regular potato chip products, while there is just one choice of the healthier baked brand. What happens when it runs out? Yes, we could just skip the chips altogether, but   5 many people like chips with their lunch. Even if the cafeteria stocked just one brand, it should at least have a good supply of them.

"I do not think they have a lot of healthy food considering the cafeteria only has one refrigerator full of it," said Monica Lina, a nineteen-year-old pre-nursing student.   6

"I think having more healthy products would be good, so I could choose healthier food," said Courtney Boomsma, twenty, major undecided.   7

The pizzas and hot dogs are right in front of us, along with the other unhealthy foods, while the few salads are stuck in the fridge and are not labeled, so you do not know what kind of salad they are. People who want to make the right choices are basically stuck eating snacks or just not being able to eat at all.   8   **REFLECT** What would you change about your cafeteria?

_____

_____

_____

"I find the fact they do not label the products troubling. I think everything needs to be labeled," said Lina.   9

Students tend to have busy schedules with work and school, which can make eating right complicated and finding time to exercise impossible. So sometimes we just have to grab anything we can find and go, which is hard if the school you attend does not offer any healthier products.   10

All PCC has to do in order to solve this problem is order less fatty items, which is not that complicated.   11   **EVALUATE** Is the conclusion accurate?

_____

_____

_____

CRITICAL THINKING: READING

1. Double-underline the **thesis statement**.

2. Rewrite the thesis statement to make it stronger. _Answers will vary._

_____

3. Underline three examples of Kathleen's main point.

4. Why do you think Kathleen includes quotes from other students?   **TIP** For reading advice, see Chapter 2.
Answers will vary. _____

5. Where could you add transitions? _Answers will vary._ _____

6. How could the conclusion be stronger? _Answers will vary._ _____

7. What do you think of this essay? Do you have enough information to tell whether the food choices at PCC are similar to those at your college cafeteria? _Answers will vary._ _____

_____

CRITICAL THINKING: WRITING

Choose one of the following topics, and respond in a paragraph or an essay.

1. Write about whether your college cafeteria offers healthy eating choices, giving specific examples supporting your point.

2. Write about healthy behaviors, giving examples of why they are healthful.

3. Write a letter to the director of your college cafeteria, giving suggestions for making it a more health-friendly place.

4. Write about the foods you like, giving examples and describing why you like them.

5. Interview the person who orders food for the cafeteria, asking that person to agree or disagree with the last statement in the essay.

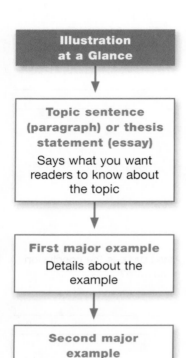

Illustration at a Glance

↓

Topic sentence (paragraph) or thesis statement (essay)
Says what you want readers to know about the topic

↓

First major example
Details about the example

↓

Second major example
Details about the example

↓

Third major example (often the most powerful)
Details about the example

↓

Conclusion
Reminds readers of the main point and makes an observation based on it

Write Your Own Illustration

In this section, you will write your own illustration paragraph or essay based on one of the following assignments. Use the following tools to help you:

1. Review the Four Basics of Good Illustration (p. 139).

2. Use "Illustration at a Glance" as a basic organizer.

3. Use the Checklist: How to Write Illustration (pp. 152–53) as you write and revise.

· ·

ASSIGNMENT 1   Writing about College, Work, and Everyday Life

Write an illustration paragraph or essay on one of the following topics or one of your own choice. For writing ideas, look back at your idea-journal entry (p. 141) or revise your writing about the photograph on page 140.

COLLEGE
- Your goals for this course
- Obstacles to coming to college
- Student resources on your campus

WORK
- Skills you bring to any job
- Things that made a job either the worst or the best job you ever had
- Examples of jobs you would like to have

EVERYDAY LIFE
- Stresses in your life
- Things you like about your life
- Important memories

· ·

ASSIGNMENT 2   Writing about Connections

Read the following account of Evelka Rankins before doing the assignment below.

COMMUNITY MATTERS

Evelka Rankins

Evelka Rankins works full-time, has four children, and takes classes from 6:00 to 9:00 three evenings a week. She has a busy life. Still, when Jessica Felizardo, one of Evelka's teachers, asked for a volunteer to put together a weekly, one-page student newsletter that would list college and community events, Evelka signed on for one semester. The newsletter includes both practical information—important dates and times for registration, advising, ID-photo-taking, and graduation—and listings for interesting and enjoyable events such as "Poem in Your Pocket" Day and a talent show. Community events mentioned in the newsletter include music, theater, fairs, volunteer opportunities, and conferences.

Evelka volunteered to work on "Urban Events," thinking it would not take much time. She found out otherwise, and it takes her about five hours every week to research and write. She talks with people at the college, reads newspaper event listings, looks for postings on bulletin boards, listens to the radio, and pays attention when people tell her about something that is coming up.

Although it took more time than she had thought it would, Evelka volunteered for another semester as editor. She enjoys finding out what is going on in her community, has met lots of people at the college, and is proud of the newsletter, which other students love (copies often run out on the first day). Here is part of one issue.

Urban Events April 14ᵗʰ – April 20ᵗʰ

*Instructor, please read at the beginning of class. Thank you.

Inside Urban

*Urban College Photo IDs will be available starting Monday April 14, 2008 through April 17, 2008 from 3pm to 6pm, on the 7ᵗʰ floor.

*April is National Poetry Month! To help spread the word, we are going to participate in Poem in Your Pocket Day, which is April 17. The idea is to carry with you that day a *poem in your pocket*. Here is a link to the event's website: **poets.org/pocket**. In anticipation of this day, a large pocket billboard will be placed in the LRC where staff, faculty and students can post their poems to share with the college. These can be any poems, from any author, from any period and in any language. The idea is to share works to inspire or to delight others. Please participate in this event by bringing in a poem beginning on Wednesday, April 2, and running for two weeks through April 17.

RESOURCES For advice on "Writing about Connections," see *Practical Suggestions*.

TIP For more on connecting to community, visit **bedfordstmartins.com/ realwriting**.

ASSIGNMENT: Produce a one- or two-page newsletter for other students in your class on one of the following topics:

- Student clubs, with descriptions of their activities and relevant contact information

- Volunteer opportunities

- Sports opportunities

- Upcoming campus events

- Upcoming local community events of interest

. . . .

ASSIGNMENT 3   Writing in the Real World/Solving a Problem

Read Appendix B, "Solving Problems."

RESOURCES Reproducible peer-review guides for different kinds of papers are available in *Additional Resources*.

PROBLEM: Your college is increasing its tuition by $500 next year, and you do not think that you can continue. You have done well so far, and you really want to get a college degree.

ASSIGNMENT: Rather than just giving up and dropping out next year, as many students do, working in a small group or on your own, make a list of resources you could consult to help you, and explain how they might help. You might want to start with the following sentence:

Before dropping out of school for financial reasons, students should

consult _____ because _____ .

For a paragraph: Name your best resource and give examples of how this person or office might help you.

For an essay: Name your three best resources and give examples of how they might help you.

. . . .

CHECKLIST: HOW TO WRITE ILLUSTRATION

STEPS IN ILLUSTRATION	HOW TO DO THE STEPS
☐ Focus.	• Think about your topic and what point you want to make about it.
☐ Narrow and explore your topic. See Chapter 4.	• Make the topic more specific. • Prewrite to get ideas about that narrowed topic.
☐ Write a topic sentence (paragraph) or thesis statement (essay) that includes your main point about the topic. See Chapter 5.	• Decide what is most important to you about the topic and what you want your readers to understand.

CHECKLIST: HOW TO WRITE ILLUSTRATION

STEPS IN ILLUSTRATION	HOW TO DO THE STEPS
☐ Support your point. See Chapter 6.	• Choose examples to show, explain, or prove what is important about your topic. • Give specific details that will make your examples clear to your readers.
☐ Make a plan. See Chapter 7.	• Put the examples in a logical order.
☐ Write a draft. See Chapter 8.	**FOR A PARAGRAPH** • Write a paragraph with your topic sentence, major examples, and details about the examples. Use complete sentences. **FOR AN ESSAY** • Consider using one of the introduction types in Chapter 8. Include your thesis statement in your introduction. • Using your plan, write topic sentences for the major examples. • Write paragraphs for each topic sentence with details about the examples. **FOR PARAGRAPHS AND ESSAYS** • Write a conclusion that reminds readers of your main point and makes an observation based on what you have written. • Write a title that previews your main point but does not repeat it.
☐ Revise your draft, making at least four improvements. See Chapter 9.	• Get feedback from others using the peer-review guide for illustration at **bedfordstmartins.com/realwriting**. • Read to make sure that all examples show, explain, or prove your main point. • Add examples and/or details that help make your main point. • Add transitions to move your readers from one example to another.
☐ Edit your revised draft. See Parts 4 through 7.	• Correct errors in grammar, spelling, word use, and punctuation.
☐ Ask yourself:	• Does my paper have the Four Basics of Good Illustration (p. 139)? • What is the best part of my paper? • Is this the best I can do?

Chapter Review

LEARNING JOURNAL Reread your idea journal entry from page 141. Write another entry on the same topic, using what you have learned about illustration.

1. Illustration is writing that *uses examples to show, explain, or prove a point.*

2. What are the Four Basics of Good Illustration? *It has a point. It gives specific examples that show, explain, or prove the point. It gives details to support the examples. It uses enough examples to get the point across to the reader.*

> **reflect** Write for two minutes on what you have learned about writing illustration.

Spot and Start Illustration Assignments in Other Courses

↓

Spot

In college, at work, and in your everyday life, you use illustration in many situations (see p. 141), but the word *illustration* may not appear in the assignment. Instead, the assignment might ask you to *give examples of*, or *be specific about* _____. Actually, all writing and speaking requires that you give examples, so even if you are writing a narration or a description, you will still use what you know about illustration to give examples.

↓

Start

Ask yourself

1. What examples will show my reader what I mean? If a reader asks, "*Like what?*" what would I say?

2. How can I make the examples "real" to readers?

3. How should I arrange the examples so readers understand my point?

YOU KNOW THIS

You use description every day:

- You describe what someone looks like.
- You describe an item you want to buy.

write for two minutes on what you know about writing description.

12

Description

Writing That Creates Pictures in Words

Understand What Description Is

Description is writing that creates a clear and vivid impression of the topic. Description translates your experience of a person, place, or thing into words, often by appealing to the physical senses: sight, hearing, smell, taste, and touch.

Four Basics of Good Description

1 It creates a main impression—an overall effect, feeling, or image— about the topic.

2 It uses specific examples to support the main impression.

3 It supports those examples with details that appeal to the five senses: sight, hearing, smell, taste, and touch.

4 It brings a person, place, or physical object to life for the reader.

In the following paragraph, each number and color corresponds to one of the Four Basics of Good Description. A student sent this paragraph to helium.com, a Web site for writing, sharing information, contributing to organizations, writing contests, and much more.

> Scars are stories written on a person's skin and sometimes on his heart. 1 My scar is not very big or very visible. 2 It is only about three inches long and an inch wide. It is on my knee, so it is usually covered, unseen. 3 It puckers the skin around it, and the texture of the scar itself

TIP Check out the Web site **www.helium.com** for more information on just about anything.

TEACHING TIP If you have done narration, point out to students that this description also uses narration.

155

is smoother than my real skin. It is flesh-colored, almost like a raggedy bandage. The story on my skin is a small one. **1** The story on my heart, though, is much deeper. **2** It was night, very cold, **3** my breath pluming into the frigid air. I took deep breaths that smelled like winter, piercing through my nasal passages and into my lungs as I walked to my car. I saw a couple making out against the wall of a building I was nearing. **2** I smiled and thought about them making their own heat. **3** I thought I saw steam coming from them, but maybe I imagined that. As I got near, I heard a familiar giggle: my girlfriend's. Then I saw her scarlet scarf, one I had given her, along with soft red leather gloves. I turned and ran, before they could see me. There was loud pounding in my ears, from the inside, sounding and feeling as if my brain had just become the loudest bass I had ever heard. My head throbbed, and slipping on some ice, I crashed to the ground, landing on my hands and knees, ripping my pants. I knew my knee was bleeding, even in the dark. I didn't care: That scar would heal. The other one would take a lot longer.

STUDENT PHOTO

This photograph was taken by a student photographer at the University of Texas at Austin.

write   Describe this photograph in detail. First, look at the photograph and write ten words you want to use in your description.

Being able to describe something or someone accurately and in detail is important in many situations:

COLLEGE   On a physical therapy test, you describe the symptoms you observed in a patient.

| WORK | You write a memo to your boss describing how the office could be arranged for increased efficiency. |
| EVERYDAY LIFE | You have to describe something you lost to the lost-and-found clerk at a store. |

Main Point in Description

In description, the **main point** is the main impression you want to create for your readers. If you do not have a main impression about your topic, it usually helps to think about how it smells, sounds, looks, tastes, or feels. To help you discover the main point for your description, complete the following sentence:

| MAIN POINT IN DESCRIPTION | **What is most vivid and important to me about this topic is. . . .** |

IDEA JOURNAL Describe what you are wearing.

• •

PRACTICE 1   Finding a Main Impression

For the following general topics, jot down four impressions that appeal to you, and circle the one you would use as a main impression. Base your choice on what is most interesting, vivid, and important to you.

EXAMPLE:

Topic: A vandalized car

    Impressions: *wrecked, smashed, damaged, battered* _____

1. Topic: A movie-theater lobby

    Impressions: *Answers will vary.* _____

2. Topic: A fireworks display

    Impressions: _____

3. Topic: A pizza place

    Impressions: _____

4. Topic: An old person

    Impressions: _____

5. Topic: The room you are in

    Impressions: _____

• •

The topic sentence (paragraph) or thesis statement (essay) in description usually contains both your narrowed topic and your main impression.

New York City is always noisy.

My van has all the comforts of a studio apartment.

To be effective, your topic sentence or thesis statement should be specific. You can make it specific by adding details and using descriptive words that appeal to the senses. Here is a more specific version of the preceding statement about New York City.

MORE SPECIFIC: Even in the middle of the night, New York City is alive with the noises of people at work and at play.

. . . .

PRACTICE 2   Writing a Statement of Your Main Impression

Choose three of the items from Practice 1 to use in this practice. In the spaces below, write the topic and the main impression you chose. Then, write a statement of your main impression. Finally, revise the sentence to make the main impression sharper and more specific.

EXAMPLE:

Topic/Main impression: *A vandalized car/battered*

Statement: *The vandalized car on the side of the highway was battered.*

More specific: *The shell of a car on the side of the road was dented all over, apparently from a bat or club, and surrounded by broken glass.*

1.   Topic/Main impression: *Answers will vary.* _____

Statement: _____

More specific: _____

_____

2.   Topic/Main impression: _____

Statement: _____

More specific: _____

_____

3.   Topic/Main impression: _____

Statement: _____

More specific: _____

_____

. . . .

Support in Description

In description, **support** is the specific, concrete details that show the sights, sounds, smells, tastes, and textures of your topic. Your description should show your readers what you mean, not just tell them. Sensory details can bring your description to life. Here are some qualities to consider.

TEAMWORK Put students in small groups, and give each group an object to describe using the questions in the text.

TIP For tools to build your vocabulary, visit the *Real Writing Student Center* at **bedfordstmartins.com/ realwriting**.

SIGHT	SOUND	SMELL
Colors?	Loud/soft?	Sweet/sour?
Shapes?	Piercing/soothing?	Sharp/mild?
Sizes?	Continuous/off and on?	Good? (Like what?)
Patterns?		Bad? (Rotten?)
Shiny/dull?	Pleasant/unpleasant? (How?)	New? (New what? Leather? Plastic?)
Does it look like anything else?	Does it sound like anything else?	Old?
		Does it smell like anything else?

TASTE	TOUCH
Good? (What does "good" taste like?)	Hard/soft?
	Liquid/solid?
Bad? (What does "bad" taste like?)	Rough/smooth?
	Hot/cold?
Bitter/sugary? Metallic?	Dry/oily?
Burning? Spicy?	Textures?
Does it taste like anything else?	Does it feel like anything else?

. . . .

PRACTICE 3   Finding Details to Support a Main Impression

Read the statements below, and write four sensory details you might use to support the main impression.

EXAMPLE:

Even at night, New York City echoes with noise.

a. *police and fire sirens*

b. *people on the street*

    c. *sounds of music from clubs*

    d. *car horns*

1. My favorite meal smells as good as it tastes.

    a. *Possible answers: sweetness of sweet potatoes*

    b. *sage in stuffing*

    c. *buttery roasting turkey*

    d. *apple pie with cinnamon*

2. The new office building has a contemporary look.

    a. *Possible answers: lots of glass*

    b. *concrete*

    c. *steel*

    d. *tall*

3. A classroom during an exam echoes with the "sounds of silence."

    a. *Possible answers: people coughing*

    b. *rustle of papers*

    c. *radiator hissing*

    d. *sounds of pens scratching paper*

Organization in Description

TIP For more on these orders of organization, see pages 80–82.

Description can use any of the orders of organization—**time**, **space**, or **importance**—depending on the purpose of the description. If you are writing to create a main impression of an event (for example, a description of fireworks, an explosion, or a storm), you might use time order. If you are describing what someone or something looks like, you might use space order, the most common way to organize description. If one detail about your topic is the strongest, you could use order of importance and leave that detail for last.

ORDER	SEQUENCE
Time	first to last/last to first, most recent to least recent/least recent to most recent
Space	top to bottom/bottom to top, right to left/left to right, near to far/far to near
Importance	end with detail that will make the strongest impression

Use **transitions** to move your readers from one sensory detail to the next. Usually, use transitions that match your order of organization.

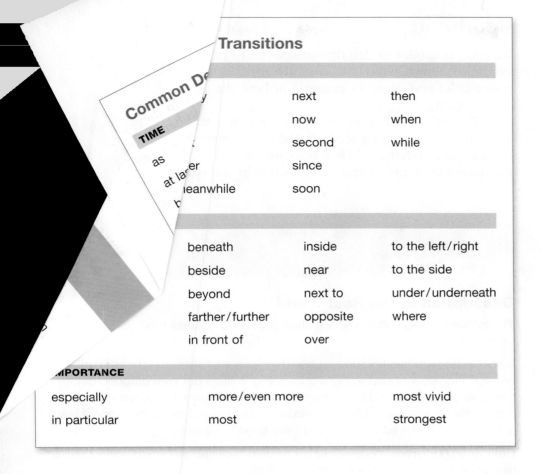

Transitions

next	then	
now	when	
second	while	
since		
meanwhile	soon	

beneath	inside	to the left/right
beside	near	to the side
beyond	next to	under/underneath
farther/further	opposite	where
in front of	over	

IMPORTANCE

especially	more/even more	most vivid
in particular	most	strongest

Common De...

TIME

as
at la...er
...eanwhile

· ·

PRACTICE 4   Using Transitions in Description

Read the paragraph that follows, and fill in the blanks with transitions.
Answers may vary. Possible answers are shown.

     As I walked into the airport terminal, I knew something had to be

wrong. Just ___*inside, beyond*___ the doors, people were packed about

forty deep. I heard a loud, harsh buzzing that was actually the noise

of people's voices. The room was steamy, the result of many people

in winter clothing jammed into an overheated space. Looking

_____*over*_____ the heads of the crowd, I could see the ticket

counter far in the distance. A young woman spoke quickly as a man

waved his arms angrily, punching air. *Behind, In front of* her, two armed

guards stood solemnly, eyes straight ahead, stony. ____*Over, Above*____

their heads, the flight board read, "All flights canceled." Unable to do

anything else, I joined the helpless mob, waiting for someone to give us

information.

· ·

Read and Analyze Description

Reading examples of description will help you write
example below, Celia Hyde talks about how she uses
police chief and gives an example of how she uses de
scene report.

The other examples are a description paragraph a *first*
essay, both by the same student and on the same subject. *ns*
larities and differences. As you read, pay attention to vocabula
the questions in the margin. They will help you read the piece

PROFILE OF SUCCESS

Celia Hyde
Chief of Police

RESOURCES For a discussion of how to use the profiles in Part Two, see *Practical Suggestions.*

Description in the Real World

The following profile shows how a chief of police in a small town uses description
on the job.

Background   When I graduated from high school, I was not interested in academics. I took some courses at a community college but then dropped out to travel. After traveling and trying several different colleges, I returned home. The police chief in town was a family friend and encouraged me to think about law enforcement. I entered that field and have been there since.

College(s)/Degrees   Greenfield Community College, Mt. Wachusett Community College, Fort Lauderdale Community College

Employer   Town of Bolton, Massachusetts

Writing at work   As chief of police, I do many kinds of writing: policies and procedures for the officers to follow; responses to attorneys' requests for information; letters, reports, and budgets; interviews with witnesses; statements from victims and criminals; accident reports. In all of the writing I do, detail, clarity, and precision are essential. I have to choose my words carefully to avoid any confusion or misunderstanding.

How Celia uses description   When I am called to a crime scene, I have to write a report that describes precisely and in detail what the scene looks like.

Celia's Description

The following report is one example of the descriptive reports Celia writes every day. The name of the homeowner has been changed.

> **Report, breaking and entering scene**
> **Response to burglar alarm, 17:00 hours**
>   The house at 123 Main Street is situated off the road with a <u>long, narrow</u> <u>driveway</u> and no visible neighbors. The dense fir trees along the drive block

natural light, though it was almost dusk and getting dark. There was snow on the driveway from a recent storm. I observed one set of fresh tire marks entering the driveway and a set of footprints exiting it.

The homeowner, Mr. Smith, had been awakened by the sounds of smashing glass and the squeaking of the door as it opened. He felt a cold draft from the stairway and heard a soft shuffle of feet crossing the dining room. Smith descended the stairs to investigate and was met at the bottom by the intruder, who shoved him against the wall and ran out the front door.

While awaiting backup, I obtained a description of the intruder from Mr. Smith. The subject was a white male, approximately 25–30 years of age and 5'9"–5'11" in height. He had jet-black hair of medium length, and it was worn slicked back from his forehead. He wore a salt-and-pepper, closely shaved beard and had a birthmark on his neck the size of a dime. The subject was wearing a black nylon jacket with some logo on it in large white letters, a blue plaid shirt, and blue jeans.

1. What is your **main impression** of the scene and of the intruder?
   a dark, isolated crime scene/an ordinary-looking man

2. Underline the **details** that support the main impression.

3. What senses do the details appeal to? _sight, hearing, touch_

4. How is the description organized? _time order_

Student Description Paragraph

Cathy Vittoria
The Peach Tree

When I reminisce about my childhood, the fondest memories I have revolve around food. Our family often went on picnics to the beach. There at the water's edge, my father would struggle to light the charcoal in the gusty wind. My mother's anise-flavored bread was the perfect match for ham on Easter morning and the days that followed. On my birthday we always had gnocchi, fluffy pillows of pasta that melted in my mouth, tossed with a heavenly tomato sauce. In August we had peaches, not just any peaches, but the peaches from our own peach tree. I loved our peach tree; it produced the sweetest, most succulent peaches I've ever eaten. When I think about my past, that peach tree plays an integral part in my childhood memories.

—Diablo Valley Community College Web site (Brian McKinney, instructor)

Vocabulary development
Underline these words as you read the description paragraph.
reminisce: to recall past experiences
anise: an herb that tastes like licorice
succulent: juicy
integral: essential; necessary

READING SELECTIONS For further examples of and activities for description, see Chapter 44.

1. Double-underline the **topic sentence**.

2. What main impression does Cathy create?

3. Underline the **sensory details** (sight, taste, smell, sound, texture) that create the main impression.

4. What order of organization does Cathy use? *importance order*
    Circle the **transitions**.

5. Does the paragraph have the Four Basics of Good Description (p. 155)? Why or why not?
    Yes. Specific answers will vary, but students should be able to give examples of the Four Basics.

Student Description Essay

Cathy Vittoria
The Peach Tree

PREDICT What do you think this essay will be about?

_____

_____

IDENTIFY Circle details that appeal to the senses.

Vocabulary development
Underline these words as you read the description essay.
flecks: small marks; dots
vibrant: bright
excesses: extra amounts
summon: to call
runt: small (refers to an under-size animal)
barren: empty
nostalgia: longing for the past
luscious: delicious

Although it may seem an odd childhood memory, a peach tree was an   1
important part of my childhood. The peach tree was special to my sisters and me. It was, in fact, the only tree in our small yard. We grew through the seasons with it. Every February, the first bits of pink showed through the tightly closed flower buds. By March, it was covered in pink, like overgrown cotton candy. In April little flecks of green accented the pink blossoms and slowly pushed out the pink until a fresh, vibrant green blanketed the crown of the tree. During this transition, the lawn became a carpet of pink. Then slowly the fruit came, growing from little nubs like pumpkin seeds to the size of walnuts. In June, the tree dropped its excesses, and green fruit, hard as golf balls, would bomb us as we played in the yard. After that, it was just a matter of waiting. Being children, we put the time to good use. We climbed and swung on the tree's branches. We played house and frontier fort in the tree. We were pirates, Tarzan,[1] Jane,[2] and George of the Jungle.[3]

By mid-August, the fragrance perfumed the air. The fruit, the size of   2
softballs, bent the branches. Not heeding our parents' advice, we would sneak a peach, unable to resist. We were usually greeted by a tasteless, crunchy disappointment. One day, Mom and Dad would summon us to tell us it was time. We picked baskets full of peaches, more than we could eat. We stood on the lawn eating while leaning forward to keep the juice from dripping onto our clothing. The juice still ran down our faces and arms onto everything. We

---

1. Tarzan: a fictional man who lived in the jungle.   **2. Jane:** Tarzan's mate.
3. George of the Jungle: a Tarzan-like cartoon character.

were sticky but satisfied. Mom would make the best peach pies, but my father's favorite dessert was peaches and red wine. We would have peaches on pancakes, peaches on ice cream, peaches on cereal, and peaches on peaches. After that, the canning began. Mom would peel, slice, and carefully cut away any of the bad parts of the peach before canning. The jars would be lined up on the kitchen counter under the open window, waiting to cool before being stored in the basement. Knowing that there would be peaches for us during the other eleven months of the year was always great comfort.

The peach tree declined in health as we grew up. Peach leaf curl was a   3
chronic problem. Winter storms caused some damage; limbs cracked and broke off. Eventually, the old tree was producing only a few runt-sized fruit. One winter, my parents cut down the tree. It left a scar on the lawn and a barren space in the yard. I hadn't thought much about that old tree for some time, even though it was the peach tree that planted the seed, so to speak, of my passion for gardening. The first fruit trees I planted in my own backyard were peaches. When I told my sisters that I was writing about the peach tree, they both smiled a familiar smile. For a moment, they were transported to another place and time. And I knew that it was not simply nostalgia; it was real. In the years that have followed, I have never found a peach as large, juicy, and luscious as the ones from our tree.

—Diablo Valley Community College Web site (Brian McKinney, instructor)

REFLECT How do you think the author felt when the peach tree was cut down?

_____

_____

CRITICAL THINKING: READING

TIP For reading advice, see Chapter 2.

1. The paragraph on page 163, also written by Cathy, is another part of this essay. Where do you think the paragraph would fit in the essay?
    It is the introductory paragraph.

    _____

2. Double-underline the **thesis statement**.

3. Underline the **transitions**.

4. Why do you think that Cathy has never found a peach that was as good as the ones from her family's tree? _Answers will vary._

5. Do you think Cathy's description of the peach tree would be different if she were writing about a tree she had never seen before? Why or why not?
    Answers will vary. Possible answer: The new tree would not have the

    fond memories attached to it.

CRITICAL THINKING: WRITING

Choose one of the following topics, and respond in a paragraph or essay.

1. Describe a tradition, family or otherwise, that is important to you.

2. Describe an object or a place that was important to you or your family when you were a child.

3. How did you and your sisters, brothers, or friends play as children?

4. Think about your childhood. What experiences did you have that you hope your own children could have?

Write Your Own Description

In this section, you will write your own description based on one of the three assignments that follow. Use the following tools to help you:

1. Review the Four Basics of Good Description (p. 155).

2. Use "Description at a Glance" as a basic organizer.

3. Use the Checklist: How to Write Description (pp. 168–69) as you write and revise.

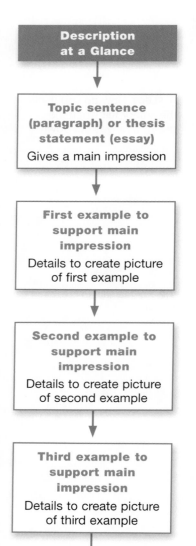

Description at a Glance

↓

Topic sentence (paragraph) or thesis statement (essay)
Gives a main impression

↓

First example to support main impression
Details to create picture of first example

↓

Second example to support main impression
Details to create picture of second example

↓

Third example to support main impression
Details to create picture of third example

↓

Conclusion
Reminds readers of the main impression

ESL Have students describe a famous place or popular meal in their native countries.

ASSIGNMENT 1 Writing about College, Work, and Everyday Life

Write a description on one of the following topics or on one of your own choice. For other ideas, look back at your responses to the photograph on p. 156 or the idea journal on p. 157.

COLLEGE
- Sounds in the cafeteria
- The entrance to the student center
- An art display on campus

WORK
- A coworker or boss
- The place where you work
- The products your workplace produces

EVERYDAY LIFE
- A favorite photograph
- A season
- Your favorite piece of clothing

ASSIGNMENT 2 Writing about Connections

Read the following account of Alessandra Cepeda before doing the assignment below.

COMMUNITY MATTERS

Alessandra Cepeda
Arriving in the United States from Brazil with no English, Alessandra Cepeda enrolled at Bunker Hill Community College in Boston, but she had to drop out for a variety of reasons. When she later returned to BHCC, she became

involved with Phi Theta Kappa. There, she expanded the organization's community work to include animal welfare. She had always cared deeply about animals, and she wanted to find ways to help them. During college, she worked with the Humane Society to improve conditions for many types of animals and was involved in several rescue efforts. As Alessandra became more involved in her work with Phi Theta Kappa, her grades got better, and her language improved because she had to use good English to work on her causes. She says, "Volunteering makes me feel good; I want to do more. Students who come to the United States from other countries think college is just classes and books, but it can be so much more than that: It is a chance to get involved in the community and the culture, too."

Alessandra rescued a group of birds that had been abandoned in a storage unit. Here is a description of where Alessandra found Sammy, the bird in the picture with her.

> When the owner opened the empty storage unit, we could not believe that any living creature could have survived under such horrible conditions. The inside was complete darkness, with no windows and no ventilation. The air hit us with the smell of rot and decay. A flashlight revealed three birds, quiet and huddled in the back corner. They were quivering and looked sickly. Two of the birds had injured wings, hanging from them uselessly at odd angles, obviously broken. They were exotic birds who should have had bright and colorful feathers, but the floor of the unit was covered in the feathers they had molted. We entered slowly and retrieved the abused birds. I cried at how such beautiful and helpless creatures had been mistreated. We adopted two of them, and our Samantha is now eight years old, with beautiful green feathers topped off with a brilliant blue and red head. She talks, flies, and is a wonderful pet who is dearly loved and, I admit, very spoiled. She deserves it after such a rough start to her life.

RESOURCES For advice on "Writing about Connections," see *Practical Suggestions*.

TIP For more on connecting to community, visit **bedfordstmartins.com/ realwriting**.

ASSIGNMENT: Choose one of the following and write a description paragraph or essay. Work either on your own or with a partner.

■ Visit a local animal shelter, and describe one or two of the animals.

■ Go to an art exhibit, and write about one piece of art in the exhibit.

■ Arrange to visit an art class, and describe what you see there.

■ Look at some family photographs, and describe one you like.

■ Describe a particular place in your community, and explain why you chose it.

ASSIGNMENT 3 Writing in the Real World: Solving a Problem

Read Appendix B, "Solving Problems."

PROBLEM: An abandoned house on your street is a safety hazard for the children in the neighborhood. Although you and some of your neighbors have called the local Board of Health, nothing has been done. Finally, you and your neighbors decide to write the mayor.

ASSIGNMENT: Working in a small group or on your own, write a letter to the mayor describing why this abandoned house is a safety hazard. To do this, you will need to describe the house (outside, inside, or both). Imagine a place that is not just ugly; it must also pose safety problems to children. Be as colorful as you can in describing this horrible place to the mayor. You might start with the following sentence:

Not only is the abandoned house at 45 Main Street an eyesore, but

it is also _____.

For a paragraph: Describe in detail one room on the first floor of the house, or just the exterior you can see from the street.

RESOURCES Reproducible peer-review guides for different kinds of papers are available in *Additional Resources*.

For an essay: Describe in detail at least three rooms in the house, or the exterior you can see if you walk entirely around the house.

CHECKLIST: HOW TO WRITE DESCRIPTION	
STEPS IN DESCRIPTION	**HOW TO DO THE STEPS**
☐ Focus.	• Think about what you want to describe and what picture you want to create for your readers.
☐ Narrow and explore your topic. See Chapter 4.	• Prewrite, thinking of the senses you could use to describe your topic.

CHECKLIST: HOW TO WRITE DESCRIPTION

STEPS IN DESCRIPTION	HOW TO DO THE STEPS
☐ Write a topic sentence (paragraph) or a thesis statement (essay) that includes your narrowed topic and the main impression you want to give. See Chapter 5.	• Review your prewriting. Then, close your eyes and try to experience your topic as you first did. • Decide what is most important to you about the experience.
☐ Support your main impression. See Chapter 6.	• Prewrite for details and images that bring your topic to life. • Read the details and add more to fill in the picture.
☐ Make a plan. See Chapter 7.	• Arrange your details in a logical order (time, space, or importance).
☐ Write a draft. See Chapter 8.	**FOR A PARAGRAPH** • Write a paragraph with your topic sentence, major examples/images, and supporting sensory details. Use complete sentences. **FOR AN ESSAY** • Consider using one of the introduction types in Chapter 8. Include your thesis statement in your introduction. • Using your plan, write topic sentences for the major examples/images. In each paragraph, include sensory details that bring the examples/images to life. **FOR PARAGRAPHS AND ESSAYS** • Write a conclusion that reminds your readers of the topic and main impression and makes an observation based on what you have written. • Write a title that previews your main impression but does not repeat it.
☐ Revise your draft, making at least four improvements. See Chapter 9.	• Get feedback from others using the peer-review guide for description at **bedfordstmartins.com/realwriting**. • Read to make sure that all examples and details serve to create your main impression. • Add more sensory details that make the description stronger. • Add transitions to move your readers from one detail to another.
☐ Edit your revised draft. See Parts 4 through 7.	• Correct errors in grammar, spelling, word use, and punctuation.
☐ Ask yourself:	• Does my paper have the Four Basics of Good Description (p. 155)? • What is the best part of my paper? • Is this the best I can do?

Chapter Review

LEARNING JOURNAL Reread your idea journal entry from page 157. Write another entry on the same topic, using what you have learned about good description.

1. Description is writing that *creates a clear and vivid impression of the topic.*

2. What are the Four Basics of Good Description?

   It creates a main impression about the topic.

   It uses specific examples to support the main impression.

   It supports those examples with details that appeal to the five senses.

   It brings a person, place, or physical object to life for the reader.

3. The topic sentence in a description paragraph or the thesis statement in a description essay includes what two elements? *a narrowed topic and main impression about that topic*

4. Write sentences using the following vocabulary words: *reminisce, integral, vibrant, barren, nostalgia.* *Answers will vary.*

---

reflect Write for two minutes on what you have learned about writing description.

Spot and Start Description Assignments in Other Courses

Spot

In college, at work, and in your everyday life, you use description in many situations (see pp. 156–57). Often, the word *describe* may mean *tell about* or *report*. However, when an assignment asks you actually to describe a place, a person, or an emotion, you will need to use the kinds of concrete, specific descriptive details you used in this chapter. Try to see and experience the images in your mind, using specific colors, shapes, sizes, smells, textures, or tastes.

Start

Ask yourself

1. What overall, intense impression do I want to create? This impression might be your starting point.

2. What will make my readers really see or feel what I do? For example, if the bathrooms at work are disgusting, what about them makes them that way? The look, the smell, the colors, what?

3. How should I organize the details so that my readers can see or feel them as I do?

YOU KNOW THIS

You often use process analysis:

- You teach a friend or a family member how to do something.
- You learn how to make or do something.

write for two minutes on how to do something you know about.

13

Process Analysis

*Writing That Explains
How Things Happen*

Understand What Process Analysis Is

Process analysis either explains how to do something (so your readers can do it) or explains how something works (so your readers can understand it). Both types of process analysis present the steps involved in the process.

Four Basics of Good Process Analysis

1 It tells readers what process you want them to know about and makes a point about it.

2 It presents the essential steps in the process.

3 It explains the steps in detail.

4 It presents the steps in a logical order (usually time order).

In the following paragraph, which a student sent to **http://ehow.com**, each number and color corresponds to one of the Four Basics of Good Process Analysis.

1 All of us have to buy food, but many people do not understand that there are certain steps that they can follow to save money at the grocery store. 2 The first step to saving is to make a list of the items you need. 3 If you are familiar with the layout of the store, save time at the store by organizing your list according to what items you come to as you go through the store. So, for example, if your store has the produce section first, list the fruits and vegetables first on your list. Sticking to

4 Time order is used.

171

your list will save money because you will get what you need rather than buying items on impulse. **2** Second, use coupons for items you need. **3** You can find many coupons online at many different sites, such as www.coupons.com. To find coupons, use a search engine and type in "grocery store coupons." Remember, though, do not buy an item just because you have a good coupon. Buy only what you need and will use. **2** Third, look at the store's weekly flier for items that are on sale that week. **3** Check your list to see what you need that is on sale. Also, make sure the price is really a sale price. Sometimes, grocery stores will advertise "2 for $5," which is the regular price of $2.50 each, but the stores try to make people think that "2 for $5" is a sale price. **2** Next, try to avoid going to the grocery store when you are hungry. **3** Many studies have shown that people buy more when they are hungry. Have *something* to eat, or chew gum, before going to the store. **2** Finally, watch while the cashier rings up your groceries. **3** Many times, sale items have not been changed to the sale price. Also, many items are just mismarked, usually at a price that is higher than the real one. If you see a mistake, let the cashier know: It is not his or her fault, and most cashiers know that many items are mismarked. If you are using coupons, make sure the cashier enters them. Also, check your cash register receipt for accuracy. These simple steps are sure to save you money on your grocery bill.

STUDENT PHOTO

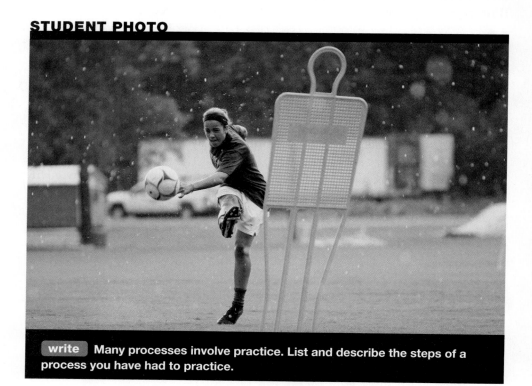

This photograph by student Kate Napier shows a member of the University of North Carolina women's soccer team at practice.

write Many processes involve practice. List and describe the steps of a process you have had to practice.

You use process analysis in many situations:

COLLEGE   In a science course, you explain how photosynthesis works.

WORK   You write instructions to explain how to operate something (the copier, the fax machine).

EVERYDAY LIFE You write out a recipe for an aunt.

Main Point in Process Analysis

In process analysis, your **purpose** is to explain how to do something or how something works by presenting the steps in the process. Your **main point** should tell readers what about the process you want them to know. Your topic sentence (paragraph) or thesis statement (essay) should not simply state the process: It should make a point about it.

NO MAIN POINT Please follow these directions exactly.

WITH A MAIN POINT Please follow these directions exactly to make sure that we exit the building safely.

To help you discover the main point for your process analysis, complete the following sentence:

MAIN POINT IN PROCESS ANALYSIS **What I want readers to know about this process is that. . . .**

Here are more examples of effective topic sentences / thesis statements:

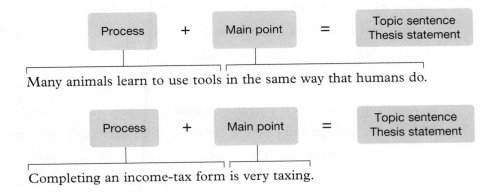

Many animals learn to use tools in the same way that humans do.

Completing an income-tax form is very taxing.

Support in Process Analysis

To perform or understand a process, your readers must know all of its essential steps; those steps are the **support** for your main point in a process analysis.

Because you are describing a familiar process, you may not think about each individual step. For example, as you tie your shoes, you probably are not aware of the steps involved; you just do them. But when you explain a process in writing, you need to think carefully about what the individual steps are so that you do not leave out any essential ones.

Your readers may also need to know details, facts, or examples that will help them understand each step. As you describe the process, think about what you would need to know about each step in order to understand it or perform it.

· ·

PRACTICE 1   Finding the Main Point and Supplying Missing Steps

In each of the following process analysis paragraphs, an essential step is missing. In real life, the writer would naturally do that essential step, but he or she left it out of the paragraph.

Either by yourself, with a partner, or in a small group, first identify the main point, and then underline it. Next, supply the missing step in each paragraph. Indicate with a caret sign (∧) where it should appear in the paragraph. *Placement of carets may vary.*

1. <u>Getting myself ready for work in the morning is a mad dash.</u>

First, I shut off the alarm clock and drag myself out of bed. I turn on the shower and splash cold water on my face while waiting for the shower to get hot. Then, I jump into the shower for a quick shampoo and lather up with soap. After rinsing myself off and shutting off the water, I grab the towel and dry myself off.∧Blow-drying my hair takes just two minutes. Then, I go down to the kitchen for coffee that my roommate has already made. I gulp down one cup at the table and then walk around with a second one, gathering up what I need to take with me to work. After running a comb through my hair, I am out the door. I run down to the bus stop, and I am off to another fast-paced day. From beginning to end, the whole process takes only twenty minutes.

WHAT'S MISSING? *getting dressed*

2. <u>Anyone can make a cake from a packaged cake mix; it is easy.</u>

First, get the package and read the directions.∧Then, assemble the ingredients you will need to add. These usually include water, eggs, and sometimes oil. If the instructions say so, grease and flour the cake pan or pans you will use to bake the cake. Next, mix the ingredients together in a bowl and stir or beat as directed. Then, transfer the batter into the right-size cake pans. Put the pans into the oven and set the timer for the baking time indicated. It is hard to go wrong.

WHAT'S MISSING? *turning on the oven*

● ●

PRACTICE 2   Finding and Choosing the Essential Steps

For each of the following topics, write the essential steps in the order you would perform them.

1.   Making (your favorite food) is simple.
   Answers will vary. _____

   _____

2.   I think I could teach anyone how to _____ .

   _____

3.   Operating a _____ is _____ .

   _____

   _____

● ●

PRACTICE 3   Adding Details to Essential Steps

Choose one of the topics from Practice 2. In the spaces that follow, first copy down that topic and the steps you wrote for it in Practice 2. Then, add a detail to each of the steps. If the process has more than four steps, you might want to use a separate sheet of paper.

TIP If you have written a narration paragraph already, you will notice that narration and process analysis are alike in that they both usually present events or steps in time order— the order in which they occur. The difference is that narration reports what happened, whereas process analysis describes how to do something or how something works.

   Topic: _Answers will vary._ _____

   Step 1: _____

      Detail: _____

   Step 2: _____

      Detail: _____

   Step 3: _____

      Detail: _____

   Step 4: _____

      Detail: _____

● ●

Organization in Process Analysis

Process analysis is usually organized by **time (chronological) order** because it explains the steps of the process in the order in which they occur, starting with the first step.

   Process analysis uses **time transitions** to move readers smoothly from one step to the next.

TIP For more on time order, see page 81.

Common Transitions in Process Analysis

after	eventually	meanwhile	soon
as	finally	next	then
at last	first	now	when
before	last	second	while
during	later	since	

• •

PRACTICE 4   Using Transitions in Process Analysis

Read the paragraph that follows, and fill in the blanks with transitions.
Answers may vary. Possible answers are shown.

Starting a club on campus is easier than most students realize.
_____*First*_____, ask other students you know or who are in your class
if they are interested in being a member of the kind of club you want to
start. _____*When*_____ you have a group of at least ten people, talk
about what you would like the club to be or do. _____*Next*_____, talk
to one of your instructors or your adviser about being a faculty adviser.
_____*Then*_____, work with that person to write up a short description
of the club: what it does, why it is valuable, what its purpose is.
_____*Next*_____, contact the student government or student activities
office, and ask how you should proceed. You might be asked how much
funding you will need. If you are asked, prepare a simple budget. Make
an appointment to attend a student government meeting where you will
talk about the club. _____*Finally*_____, get started. You will meet other
people with similar interests, and you will learn more than you ever
thought. Best of all, you will have a surprising amount of fun.

• •

Read and Analyze Process Analysis

READING SELECTIONS For
further examples of and activities for other process analysis
paragraphs and essays, see
Chapter 45.

Reading examples of process analysis will help you write your own. The first
example in this section is a Profile of Success from the real world of teaching. Rocío Murillo talks about how she uses writing in her job as a teacher.
She gives an example of how she used process analysis with her students in
a successful class project in which she asked students to commit to using a
simple process.

The second and third examples are both student writing, first a process analysis paragraph and then a process analysis essay. As you read, pay attention to the vocabulary, and answer the questions in the margin. They will help you read the piece critically.

TIP For advice on building your vocabulary, visit the *Real Writing Student Center* at **bedfordstmartins.com/ realwriting**.

PROFILE OF SUCCESS

Process Analysis in the Real World

The following profile shows how a teacher uses process analysis on the job.

Background   I grew up speaking only Spanish because my father didn't want us to forget our native language. My high-school counselor insisted that I did not have what it takes to go to college. Fortunately, I didn't listen to him, but I wasn't confident about my abilities.

After high school, I went to El Camino College and found out about the Puente Project. In this program, I was blessed with a caring Latino counselor, a gifted English teacher, and an inspiring mentor. I blossomed and realized that I was good enough to be accepted as a University of California, Irvine, student.

My first quarter at UC Irvine was incredibly difficult. I was working three jobs, and I received a letter of probation that stated that if I did not better my grades by the next quarter, I would be kicked out. I remember sitting on the outside steps of a building one lonely afternoon and crying. But I was determined to go on and did better the next quarter.

Now I have a master's degree, a job I love, a wonderful husband, and twins. I am a survivor.

Degrees / College(s)   A.A., El Camino College; B.A., University of California, Irvine; M.Ed., Pepperdine University

Employer   Lennox (California) School District

Writing at work   Regular lesson plans; materials for classroom use; letters to parents, administrators, and businesses; memos to other teachers; grant proposals.

How Rocío uses process analysis   I give students directions for assignments and activities, explaining, step-by-step, how to do something.

Rocío Murillo
Teacher

RESOURCES For a discussion of how to use the profiles in Part 2, see *Practical Suggestions*.

Rocío's Process Analysis

Rocío wrote the following paragraph about reading for her students. After they had read it together in class, she asked her students to make a commitment to follow the process, at least for one term. They agreed, and their reading skills and scores improved. Also, their writing improved, as did their self-esteem.

> We are not all born good readers, but you can take steps to become good readers. The steps are not hard, but they require practice, as learning anything
>
> *(continued)*

TIP For tools to build your vocabulary, visit the Student Center at **bedfordstmartins.com/ realwriting.**

new does. Learning and practicing the steps will help you in so many ways, such as improving your grades and understanding. You will do better and be better students. Once you have learned the steps, you will not even have to think about them anymore: They will come naturally, just as when you first learned to tie your shoe, it was hard, but now it is easy. The (first step) to becoming a better reader is to read. Even though you might not enjoy reading right now, to read better you have to read. Find magazines or Web sites you are interested in, and READ. Read even comic books, anything you can get your little hands on. The (second step) is to read every day. You do not have to spend a lot of time, but spend at least fifteen minutes reading every day, all at one time. If you have to, turn your television to mute, and read the captions that come on for people with hearing difficulties. Just do it, every day. The (third step) is to think while and after you read; don't just turn the pages without knowing what is on them and what you think about what is on them. In class, we will have reading partners. Outside of class, talk with someone about what you have read, even if you talk to just yourself. The more you talk about what you have read, the more you will understand it. These three steps are the three golden rules of reading, and practicing them will definitely make you a better reader. They will also help you write.

1. What **process** is being analyzed? _how to be a better reader_

2. How many steps does Rocío give? _three_

3. Circle the words that move you from one step to the next one.

4. In your own words, what are the steps to becoming a better reader?
   Answers will vary.

Student Process Analysis Paragraph

Charlton Brown

Buying a Car at an Auction

PREDICT What do you think Charlton will say buyers need to be prepared about?

Buying a car at an auction is a good way to get a cheap car, but buyers need to be prepared. (First), decide what kind of vehicle you want to buy. (Then), find a local auction. Scams are common, though, so be careful. Three top sites that are legitimate are www.gov-auctions.org, www.carauctioninc .com, and www.seizecars.com. (When) you have found an auction and a vehicle you are interested in, become a savvy buyer. Make sure you know the car's actual market value. You can find this out from Edmunds.com, Kelly bluebook.com, or NADA (the National Automobile Dealers Association). Because bidding can become like a competition, decide on the highest bid you will make, and stick to that. Do not get drawn into the competition. On the day of the auction, get to the auction early so that you can look at the actual cars. If you do not know about cars yourself, bring someone who does with you to the auction so that he or she can examine the car. Next, begin your thorough examination. Check the exterior; especially look for any signs that the car has been in an accident. Also, check the windshield because many states will not give an inspection sticker to cars with any damage to the windshield. Check the interior and try the brakes. Start the engine and listen to how it sounds. Check the heat and air conditioning, the CD player, and all other functions. As a final check before the bidding, look at the car's engine and transmission. Finally, get ready to place your bid, and remember, do not go beyond the amount you settled on earlier. Good luck!

1. Double-underline the **topic sentence**.

2. What is Charlton's **main point**? _Buyers should be prepared before buying a car at an auction._

3. Underline the **major steps**.

4. Circle the words that signal when Charlton moves from one step to the next.

5. Does Charlton's paragraph follow the Four Basics of Good Process Analysis (p. 171)? Why or why not? _Yes. Answers will vary._

SUMMARIZE What steps are necessary to buy a car at auction?

_____

_____

_____

Student Process Analysis Essay

Michele Wood
My Home Exercise Program

Michele Wood is currently pursuing a degree in sociology at Florida Community College in Jacksonville, Florida. Her interests as a writer include health, fitness, cooking, baking, and nutrition. Michele's essay, "My Home Exercise Program," stems from her personal connection to the topic. She writes, "Fitness and living a healthy lifestyle is my passion. I have been taught that the best writing comes from personal experiences, especially those that spark enthusiasm or passion." When giving advice to other student writers, Michele says, "Be patient. Writing . . . is a skill that one has to develop. Like most things, practice, practice, practice! Don't give up. . . . Write from your heart."

Have you ever noticed how many gym membership advertisements are   1
on television right after the New Year? Many people overindulge through the
holiday season, beginning with Halloween candy and ending with the last
sip of eggnog on Christmas evening. On average, Americans gain seven
pounds in that six-week period. That weight gain does not include the other
forty-six weeks of the year when people typically overeat and quit going to
the gym. Do not despair; there is hope! Instead of dreading the inevitable
holiday weight gain and spending money on expensive exercise clubs, you
can instead resign yourself to starting a new exercise routine at home. Exercise is the best way to combat "the battle of the bulge." One of the most effective ways to lose weight and get into shape is aerobic exercise. I am living
proof that beginning a home workout regimen will become a positive, life-
altering experience that quickly balances your physical and emotional health,
has a maximum gain for minimal pain, and can lead you to improve other
aspects of your life as well.

(When) I wake up in the morning, the first thing I reach for is my work-   2
out clothing. Loose-fitting and comfortable, these clothes are ones that I do
not mind soaking with sweat. Exercise apparel does not require investing a
large sum of money on name brands like Nike, Adidas, or Reebok. In fact,
an old T-shirt and baggy nylon pants work just as well. However, wearing
good shoes is important and possibly expensive. Your shoes need to be specifically designed for aerobics or cross-training. They should be supportive,
sturdy, and well constructed. During aerobic activity, your feet are subjected
to constant pounding from jumping and bouncing as well as the repeated
start-and-stop of the exercises.

SUMMARIZE Why are shoes
important?

_____

_____

_____

My preferred shoes are Brooks, Ryka, or New Balance. If you are using   3
your aerobic shoes three or more times a week, replace them every six
months to a year. Your feet are essential body parts—after all, they have to
hold you up all day long. The best shoes are constructed to withstand the
sustained beating your feet endure during aerobic exercise and have the
necessary support required for such a high-impact activity.

(After) I am properly dressed, I grab a large (32-ounce) bottle of water.   4
It is crucial to maintain hydration during a workout. While you sweat, your
body loses water and essential electrolytes. Without water, your organs cannot function properly. Also, not drinking enough water can lead to hospital-
ization. Trust me, going to a hospital for dehydration is definitely not fun.
The nurse puts a needle in your arm, and it is attached to an IV that ever-
so-slowly drips, drips, drips into your veins. It is one of the most uncomfortable experiences I have had. To avoid dehydration, try to drink at least
32 ounces of water before, during, and after your workout, taking moderate

sips regularly. The recommended daily water consumption—in ounces—is an amount equal to your weight in pounds. If you weigh 150 pounds, you should drink 150 ounces of water each day. The easiest way to do this is to buy a few inexpensive water bottles and keep them filled in the refrigerator.

(The next step) of my routine is to select a DVD from my collection of exercise DVDs and videos. I own several terrific videos that I use regularly. *I Want That Body*, *Tighter Assets: Cardio Blast*, and *Tighter Assets: Weight Loss* by Tamilee Webb are my favorites. I also use the Firm's *Maximum Cardio Burn Plus Abs* and *Complete Aerobics and Weight Training*. When I'm not in the mood for any of those, I use prerecorded exercise programs from FitTv, part of the regular cable service on television. I highly recommend that you start with *I Want That Body*, which is educational as well as fun. Tamilee Webb is a phenomenal instructor: She has a great personality, her workout music is upbeat, and the routines are clearly structured. She has a master's degree in exercise science and has been part of the fitness industry for well over twenty years. When choosing a DVD or video, three elements are important: (1) The instructor should be enjoyable; (2) the music should be motivational; and (3) the moves should be relatively comfortable for you. These three things are fundamental to a good home workout regimen.

You may be wondering, "How long should I exercise in order to see results?" Experts generally recommend that people exercise for at least thirty minutes at least three times a week. During those thirty minutes, your heart rate should be elevated for twenty minutes, allowing for warm-up and cool-down. Once you have mastered a thirty-minute aerobic exercise routine, it is time to increase the duration and frequency of your workout. Expect to see visible results in as few as four weeks, or as many as twelve weeks, depending on your individual metabolism.

Weight loss puts people on a path to a healthier life, but the emotional changes outweigh the physical ones. On my journey, I have expanded my own education about health, nutrition, and fitness. I have increased energy, brighter eyes, and more restful sleep in addition to smaller thighs. Regular aerobic exercise has encouraged me to assess my overall nutrition and health, positively changing my life. In the wise words of Tamilee Webb, "You get only one body. If you don't take care of it, no one else will."

5   **SUMMARIZE** What are the basic steps in Michele's routine?

_____

_____

_____

6

7   **REFLECT** Does Michele convince you?

_____

_____

_____

TIP For reading advice, see Chapter 2.

CRITICAL THINKING: READING

1.   Double-underline the **thesis statement**. In your own words, what is Michele's main point? *Answers will vary but should say that home exercise has lots of benefits.*

2.   Circle the transitions Michele uses to move from one step to the next.

3. Underline the major steps in Michele's process.

4. What are some essential elements to an exercise program? *Answers will vary but might include choosing good shoes, drinking water, and using a DVD or video you like.*

5. Michele gives many good reasons to exercise. Could you commit to an exercise program of just thirty minutes three times a week? If not, why? *Answers will vary.*

6. Does Michele's essay follow the Four Basics of Good Process Analysis (p. 171)? Why or why not? *Yes. Answers will vary.*

CRITICAL THINKING: WRITING

Choose one of the following topics, and respond in a paragraph or an essay.

1. Discuss a process that you have learned that has improved your life.

2. What are the steps to making a commitment to something?

3. Describe to a beginner how to do something you do well.

4. Describe something that you do for your health or well-being.

Write Your Own Process Analysis

In this section, you will write your own process analysis based on one of the three assignments that follow. Use the following tools to help you:

1. Review the Four Basics of Good Process Analysis (p. 171).
2. Use "Process Analysis at a Glance" (p. 183) as a basic organizer.
3. Use the Checklist: How to Write Process Analysis (pp. 185–86) as you write and revise.

ASSIGNMENT 1   Writing about College, Work, and Everyday Life

Write a process analysis paragraph or essay on one of the following topics or one of your own choice. Look back at your responses to the photograph on page 172 and idea journal on page 173.

COLLEGE
How to
- Be a successful student
- Use the writing center
- Study for an exam

WORK

How to

- Get information about a company you want to work for
- Perform a specific task at work
- Make a positive impression in a job interview

EVERYDAY LIFE

How to

- Get ready in the morning
- Do something you are good at (dance, cook, play video games, and so on)

ASSIGNMENT 2   Writing about Connections

Read the following account of Robin Wyant before doing the assignment below.

COMMUNITY MATTERS

Robin Wyant

Robin Wyant is a single mother of two young daughters, works as a home health-care aide, and is a full-time student at Ivy Tech. She hopes to become a nurse. In an English class, her teacher assigned a writing project that was linked to a short community service experience. Robin chose to spend eight hours at the community crisis center in her city, spread out over four weeks (about two hours a week). There, she worked on preparing to mail a pamphlet for families affected by suicide. Although Robin has little spare time, she was glad to have the opportunity to help others. She says, "It was like 'paying it forward.' I needed and received help myself when I was having trouble."

Here, Robin describes the process of preparing the pamphlets for mailing.

The Lafayette Crisis Center had just finished a pamphlet for families affected by suicide when I volunteered to help for a few hours. My job was to prepare the pamphlet for mailing. The first step in my assignment was to run off copies using the center's color copy machine. Before doing that, I had to have someone show me how to use the machine, including how to do double-sided copies and how to get them to come out collated, folded, and stapled. As she was talking, I took notes on the steps because I did not want to have to ask again. I asked if she would go a little more slowly so that I could get

(continued)

Process Analysis at a Glance

↓

Topic sentence (paragraph) or thesis statement (essay)

Includes the process you are describing

↓

First step in process

Details about the first step (how to do it or how it works)

↓

Second step in process

Details about the second step

↓

Third step in process

Details about the third step

↓

Conclusion

Reminds readers of the process and makes an observation related to your main point

ESL Suggest that students write about a process that they used in their native country or culture but don't use where they live now.

RESOURCES For advice on "Writing about Connections," see *Practical Suggestions*.

everything right. When the copy came out, she explained how to check to make sure the color was correct. She then left me alone with the big machine, on my own. I made a test copy to make sure I had all the steps down, and I was happy that it came out correctly. Then, I had to print out mailing labels and put them in exactly the right place on the pamphlet. My third step was to separate the pamphlets by zip code. Because it was a bulk mailing, you have to follow special rules, and bundling by zip code is an important one. Then, I put rubber bands around the pamphlets. The final step was to address some pamphlets by hand and then enter the addresses into the mailing label program. As I worked, I felt part of something important—not just mailing junk. Because I have at times needed help, I was happy to be able to give back to others.

TIP For more on connecting to community, visit **bedfordstmartins.com/realwriting**.

ASSIGNMENT: Choose one of the following, and write a process analysis paragraph or essay. Work either on your own or with a partner.

- Describe how everyone in the class could communicate and help one another by using Facebook or MySpace.

- Visit one of the following Web sites that help people get involved, and write about what it is and how some of the programs work: www.squidoo.com, www.idealist.org, www.helium.com, http://coolpeoplecare.org, http://ehope.nu, http://charityguide.org, http://one.org, www.rootsandshoots.org/collegestudents, or some of the links you find on these sites.

- Describe an activity or event you have participated in as part of a community you are involved in, such as your religious community, neighbors, coworkers, fellow students, or a sports organization. If you have not had such an experience, visit a local soup kitchen and watch what goes on there. Then, write about it.

· ·

ASSIGNMENT 3 Writing in the Real World/Solving a Problem

Read Appendix B, "Solving Problems."

PROBLEM: Midway through a course you are taking, your instructor asks the class to tell her how she could improve the course. You have not been happy with the class because the instructor is always late and comes in seeming rushed and tense. She then lectures for most of the class before giving you an assignment that you start on while she sits at her desk, busily grading papers. You are afraid to ask questions about the lecture or assignment. You want to tell the instructor how the course could be better, but you do not want to offend her.

TEAMWORK For more detailed guidance on group work, see *Practical Suggestions*.

ASSIGNMENT: Working in a small group or on your own, write to your instructor about how she could improve the course. Think of how the class could be structured differently so that you could learn more. Begin with how the class could start, and then describe how the rest of the class period could go, suggesting specific activities if you can. State your suggestions in positive terms. For example, instead of telling the instructor what *not* to do, make suggestions using phrases like *you could*, *we could*, or *the class could*. Be sure to use formal English.

You might start in this way:

Several simple changes might improve our learning. At the start of each class, _____ .

At the end, remember to thank your instructor for asking for students' suggestions.

RESOURCES Reproducible peer-review guides for different kinds of papers are available in *Additional Resources*.

• •

CHECKLIST: HOW TO WRITE PROCESS ANALYSIS

STEPS IN PROCESS	HOW TO DO THE STEPS
☐ Focus.	• Think about a process that interests you or that you need to describe for others.
☐ Narrow and explore your topic. See Chapter 4.	• Make sure the process is specific/narrow enough to be described in a paragraph or an essay. • Prewrite to get ideas about the narrowed topic.
☐ Write a topic sentence (paragraph) or thesis statement (essay) that includes your main point about the process. See Chapter 5.	• Ask: What do you want your readers to know about the process, other than how to do it or how it works?
☐ Support your point. See Chapter 6.	• Include all of the steps in the process. • Give specific details about how to do the steps or about how they work so that your readers will understand them.
☐ Make a plan. See Chapter 7.	• Arrange the steps in time order.
☐ Write a draft. See Chapter 8.	**FOR A PARAGRAPH** • Write a paragraph with your topic sentence, essential steps, and details about the steps. Use complete sentences. **FOR AN ESSAY** • Consider using one of the introduction types in Chapter 8. Include your thesis statement in your introduction. • Using your plan, write topic sentences for the essential steps. • For each topic sentence, write paragraphs with details about the steps. *(continued)*

CHECKLIST: HOW TO WRITE PROCESS ANALYSIS

STEPS IN PROCESS	HOW TO DO THE STEPS
☐ Write a draft. See Chapter 8.	**FOR PARAGRAPHS AND ESSAYS** • Write a conclusion that reminds your readers of your main point and makes an observation based on what you have written. • Write a title that previews your main point but does not repeat it. • Get feedback from others using the peer-review guide for process analysis at **bedfordstmartins.com/realwriting**.
☐ Revise your draft, making at least four improvements. See Chapter 9.	• Read to make sure that you have included all of the essential steps in the process. • Add more details about the steps. • Add time transitions to move your readers from one step to another.
☐ Edit your revised draft. See Parts 4 through 7.	• Correct errors in grammar, spelling, word use, and punctuation.
☐ Ask yourself:	• Does my paper have the Four Basics of Good Process Analysis (see p. 171)? • What is the best part of my paper? • Is this the best I can do?

Chapter Review

1. Process analysis is writing that *either explains how to do something or explains how something works.*

2. What are the Four Basics of Good Process Analysis?

    It tells readers what process you want them to know about and makes a point about it.

    It presents the essential steps in the process.

    It explains the steps in detail.

    It presents the steps in a logical order (usually time order).

LEARNING JOURNAL Reread your idea journal entry on how to do something you recently learned (p. 173). Make another entry on the same process, using what you have learned about process analysis. Assume you are teaching someone else this process.

3. Write sentences using the following vocabulary words: *legitimate, savvy, inevitable, phenomenal, metabolism.* *Answers will vary.*

reflect Write for two minutes on what you have learned about writing process analysis.

Spot and Start Process Analysis Assignments in Other Courses

Spot

In college, at work, and in your everyday life, you use process analysis in many situations (see p. 173). The assignment may ask you to *describe the process of*, but it might also use phrases such as *describe the stages of*, *how does _____ work*, or *explain how _____ works*. Whenever you need to identify and explain the steps or stages of anything, you will use process analysis.

Start

Ask yourself

1. What are the steps in the process? Think it through: If I knew nothing about the process, would I know how to do it or how it works by carefully reading the steps?

2. What details and examples do readers need in order to do (or understand) the step?

3. Have I left anything out in this round of thinking?

14

YOU KNOW THIS

You have had experience classifying various items:

- You see how movies in a video store are arranged.
- You sort items for recycling.

write for two minutes about the kinds of responsibilities you have.

Classification

Writing That Sorts Things into Groups

Understand What Classification Is

Classification is writing that organizes, or sorts, people or items into categories. It uses an **organizing principle**: *how* the people or items are sorted. The organizing principle is directly related to the purpose for classifying. For example, you might sort clean laundry (your purpose) using one of the following organizing principles: by ownership (yours, your roommate's) or by where it goes (the bedroom, the bathroom).

■■ Four Basics of Good Classification

1 It makes sense of a group of people or items by organizing them into categories.

2 It has a purpose for sorting the people or items.

3 It categorizes using a single organizing principle.

4 It gives detailed examples or explanations of what fits into each category.

In the following paragraph, each number and color corresponds to one of the Four Basics of Good Classification. A student wrote this for an English assignment.

1 Since I have been working as a cashier at Wal-Mart, I have discovered there are several kinds of customers 2 who drive me crazy. 3 First are the openly rude ones. 4 They frown and make loud, sarcastic

comments about how long the line is and how long they have been waiting. They throw their money on the counter and never say hello or acknowledge me as anything but human scum. They are just plain rude. I am embarrassed for myself, but I'm also embarrassed for them. **3** Second are the silent but obviously impatient customers. **4** Although they do not say anything, I am aware of them from the time they get in line. They make faces, roll their eyes, and look at their watches every ten seconds. What do they expect? This is Wal-Mart; there are always lines. **3** The third kind is really my least favorite: suspicious customers who watch my every move as if my goal in life is to overcharge them. **4** They turn the monitor so they can see every price, but that is not enough. After looking at the price there, they lean over the counter toward me and look at what price comes up on the register. Then, their heads snap back to look at the monitor. They clearly do not trust me and are just waiting for me to make a mistake, at which point they will jump all over me. This kind of customer makes me nervous and a lot more likely to mess up. If you are one of these three kinds of customers, remember me next time you are at Wal-Mart; I'm the one just trying to do my job, and you are driving me crazy!

—Joyce Kenneally

TIP For tools to use in getting a job, visit the Student Center at **bedfordstmartins.com/ realwriting**.

STUDENT PHOTO

write about the two kinds of footwear in this picture, and what they tell you about the people.

Jasmine Sodergren dangles in the arms of her husband, Tim, on his return from deployment in Afghanistan. This photograph, taken by student Jenn Ackerman, won an Award of Excellence in the General News category in the 63rd College Photographer of the Year contest.

NICOLE DAY: As an office manager, my whole job is organizing.

(See Nicole Day's **PROFILE OF SUCCESS** on p. 196.)

IDEA JOURNAL Write about the different kinds of students in this class or the different kinds of friends you have.

You use classification anytime you want to organize people or items.

COLLEGE   In a criminal justice course, you are asked to discuss the most common types of chronic offenders.

WORK   For a sales presentation, your boss asks you to classify the kinds of products your company produces.

EVERYDAY LIFE   You classify your typical monthly expenses to make a budget.

Main Point in Classification

The **main point** in classification uses a single **organizing principle** to sort items in a way that serves your purpose. The categories should help you achieve your purpose.

To help you discover the organizing principle for your classification, complete the following sentences:

MAIN POINT IN CLASSIFICATION

My purpose for classifying my topic is to explain _____ to readers.

It would make most sense to my readers if I sorted this topic by. . . .

Sometimes, it helps to think of classification in diagram form. Here is a diagram of the Four Basics of Good Classification paragraph on pages 188–89.

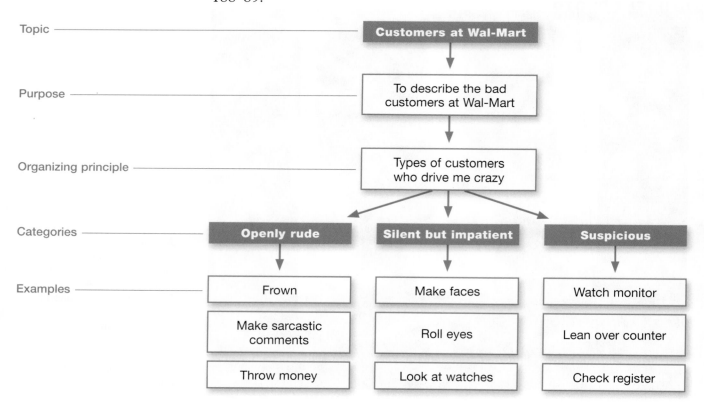

Imagine the following situation in your college bookstore. The purpose of sorting textbooks is to help students find them. The best way to organize the books is by subject area or course number. But not in this bookstore:

> You walk into the bookstore looking for an algebra text and expect to find it in the math textbook area, classified according to its subject area. Instead, the books on the shelves are not classified in any logical way.
>
> When you ask the salesclerk how to find the book, he says, "What color is it? The right half of the store has books arranged by color: blue over there, green in the middle, and so on. The left half of the store has them arranged by author."

This new arrangement is confusing for three reasons:

1. It does not serve the purpose of helping students find textbooks.
2. It does not sort the books into useful categories. (You probably do not know what color the book is.)
3. It does not have a single organizing principle. (It has two principles: color and author.)

The following diagram shows how you would expect textbooks to be classified.

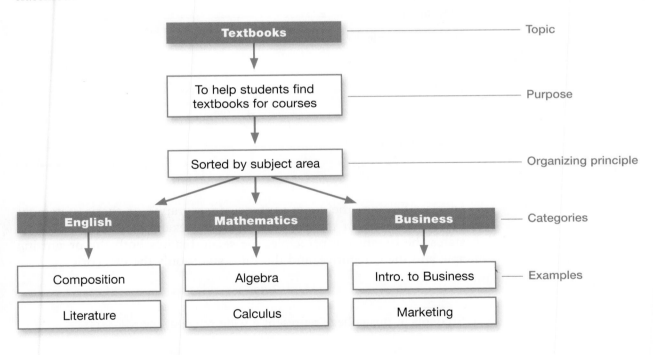

* * *

PRACTICE 1   Using a Single Organizing Principle

For each topic that follows, one of the categories does not fit the same organizing principle as the rest. Circle the letter of the category that does not fit, and in the space provided write the organizing principle that the rest follow.

Answers may vary. Possible answers are shown.

EXAMPLE:

Topic: Shoes

Categories:

a. Running   c. Golf

(b.) Leather   d. Bowling

Organizing principle: *by type of activity*

1. Topic: Relatives

Categories:

a. Aunts   c. Sisters

(b.) Uncles   d. Nieces

Organizing principle: *female relatives*

2. Topic: Jobs

Categories:

a. Weekly   c. Monthly

b. Hourly   (d.) Summer

Organizing principle: *pay period*

3. Topic: Animals

Categories:

a. Dogs   c. Rabbits

b. Cats   (d.) Whales

Organizing principle: *pets; four legs*

• •

In classification, the topic sentence (paragraph) or thesis statement (essay) can take one of three forms. Read the examples that follow: The first states the organizing principle, the second states both the organizing principle and the categories, and the third states only the categories.

      Topic   Organizing principle

Students at this college represent a wide range of races.

      Topic   Organizing principle

Students at this college represent a wide range of races, including Caucasian, African American, Asian American, and Hispanic American.

                         Categories

Topic   Categories

This college has a diverse student body composed of Caucasian, African American, Asian American, Hispanic American, and Portuguese American students.

Support in Classification

In classification, **support** consists of the categories you sort information into and the examples of things that fit into each category. First, you need to choose useful categories; then, you need to find the best examples and explanations for these categories.

The **categories** you choose for your classification tell your readers how you are organizing your topic. First, find useful categories. Then, give **examples** of things that fit into each category.

· ·

PRACTICE 2   Choosing Useful Categories

In the items that follow, you are given a topic and a purpose for sorting. For each item, list three useful categories. (There are more than three correct categories for each item.)

EXAMPLE:

Topic: Pieces of paper in my wallet

Purpose for sorting: To get rid of what I do not need

Categories:

a. *Things I need to keep in my wallet*

b. *Things I can throw away*

c. *Things I need to keep, but not in my wallet*

1. Topic: Animals in a pet shop

Purpose for sorting: To decide what kind of pet to get

Categories: *Answers will vary. Possible answers:*

a. *Dogs*

b. *Birds*

c. *Fish*

2. Topic: College courses

Purpose for sorting: To decide what I will register for

Categories: *Answers will vary. Possible answers:*

a. *English*

TEACHING TIP Walk students through this step. Use a simple topic (stores in town or at a local mall, clothing students are wearing, courses offered at the college) and demonstrate how you would classify it. Or break the class into small groups and give each group a topic. Then, call on students from each group to tell what they did.

    b. *Accounting*

    c. *Math*

3.   Topic: Stuff in my notebook

    Purpose for sorting: To organize my schoolwork

    Categories: *Answers will vary. Possible answers:*

    a. *Homework*

    b. *Notes*

    c. *Class handouts*

4.   Topic: Wedding guests

    Purpose for sorting: To arrange seating at tables

    Categories: *Answers will vary. Possible answers:*

    a. *Family members*

    b. *Neighbors*

    c. *Friends*

5.   Topic: Clothing

    Purpose for sorting: To get rid of some clothes

    Categories: *Answers will vary. Possible answers:*

    a. *Out of style*

    b. *Do not fit*

    c. *Good*

Organization in Classification

Classification can be organized in different ways (**time order**, **space order**, or **order of importance**) depending on its purpose.

PURPOSE	LIKELY ORGANIZATION
to explain changes or events over time	time
to describe the arrangement of people / items in physical space	space
to discuss parts of an issue or problem	importance

PRACTICE 3 Organizing Classification

TIP For more on the orders of organization, see pages 80–82.

For each of the three items, read the topic sentence/thesis statement and purpose. Then, fill in the likely type of organization.

EXAMPLE:

Topic sentence/Thesis: **Richmond Forest attracts three different types of campers, each one preferring a particular campsite.**

Purpose: **To describe the different types of campers and where they like to camp**

Likely organization: *space order*

1. Topic sentence/Thesis: Three kinds of crime are committed in this neighborhood.

    Purpose: To describe the kinds of crime

    Likely organization: *order of importance*

2. Topic sentence/Thesis: Clothes selling at 60 percent off were all over the store.

    Purpose: To tell about where the clothes on sale are located

    Likely organization: *space order*

3. Topic sentence/Thesis: In the last ten years, many styles of jeans have been popular.

    Purpose: To describe jean styles over the last ten years

    Likely organization: *time order*

As you write your classification, use **transitions** to move your readers smoothly from one category to another.

Common Transitions in Classification

another	for example
another kind	for instance
first, second, third, and so on	last
	one example/another example

PRACTICE 4 Using Transitions in Classification

Read the paragraph that follows, and fill in the blanks with transitions. You are not limited to the ones listed in the preceding box.
Answers may vary. Possible answers are shown.

Every day, I get three kinds of e-mail: work, personal, and junk. The _____*first kind*_____ of e-mail, work, I have to read carefully and promptly.

Sometimes, the messages are important ones directed to me, but mostly they are group messages about meetings, policies, or procedures. _For example, For instance_ , it seems as if the procedure for leaving the building during a fire alarm is always changing. ___The second kind,___ ___Another kind___ of e-mail, personal, is from friends or my mother. These I read when I get a chance, but I read them quickly and delete any that are jokes or messages that have to be sent to ten friends for good luck. _The third kind, The last kind_ of e-mail is the most common and most annoying: junk. I get at least thirty junk e-mails a day, advertising all kinds of things that I do not want, such as life insurance or baby products. Even when I reply asking that the company stop sending me these messages, they keep coming. Sometimes, I wish e-mail did not exist.

Read and Analyze Classification

READING SELECTIONS For further examples of and activities for classification, see Chapter 46.

Reading examples of classification will help you write your own. The first example in this section is a Profile of Success from the real world of business. Nicole Day is an office manager and a student. An interesting note: When Nicole had just completed her first college writing course, she was part of a group of students that the author interviewed to give advice on how to be successful to students just starting the course (see Chapter 1).

The second and third examples are both student writing, first a classification paragraph and then a classification essay. As you read, pay attention to the vocabulary, and answer the questions in the margin. They will help you read the piece critically.

PROFILE OF SUCCESS

Nicole Day
Office Manager

Classification in the Real World

The following profile shows how an office manager uses writing and includes an example of how she uses classification in her work.

Background   I did not pay much attention in high school, and I also did not take the placement tests seriously. When I got to college, I took a developmental English writing course, and even now, years later, I ask my former teacher, Karen Eisenhauer, for advice about papers I write and reports I have to prepare.

Right before I was going to start college at Brevard CC, I was diagnosed with breast cancer. I had chemo on days I was not in class. Then, my mother became sick with advanced colon cancer, and I dropped out of college to be her primary caretaker and guardian. One of the things that got me through that time was keeping a journal, where I wrote to my mother.

After my mother had died, I eventually returned to college at Brevard and went on to graduate.

Degrees/College(s) A.A., Brevard Community College; B.A., University of Central Florida; now applying to graduate school

Employer Maker Millwork

Writing at work Letters to homebuilders, correspondence with customers, directions about legal documents, sales information, e-mails, other. I have to write a lot, and a lot of different things.

Nicole's Classification

The following is part of an updated job description that Nicole wrote.

Position: Office Manager

Types of responsibilities: The Office Manager oversees all office operations, including administrative, customer communication, and internal sales information.

Specific duties:

Administrative: order all office supplies, prepare tracking reports, coordinate document maintenance and retention, interface with management team

Customer communication: respond to telephone, e-mail, and written inquiries from homebuilders and individuals; provide information on specific Maker Millwork products; advise on issues such as liens

Internal sales information: prepare mailings and brochures, compile monthly sales reports, communicate with sales team

Vocabulary development

Underline the following words as you read Nicole's job description.

administrative: managing business affairs
retention: keeping (something)
interface: to interact with, communicate with
lien: a legal term meaning the right to take or sell property as payment for a debt
compile: to gather together, collect

1. Double-underline the **main point** of the job description.

2. What categories does Nicole break her job responsibilities into?
   administrative, customer communication, internal sales information

3. What is her purpose, and who is her audience? *to describe the responsibilities of her job for someone new on the job*

Student Classification Paragraph

Lorenza Mattazi

All My Music

From the time I was young, I have always loved music, all kinds of music. My first experience of music was the opera that both of my parents always had playing in our house. I learned to understand the drama and

TIP For advice on building your vocabulary, visit the *Real Writing Student Center* at **bedfordstmartins.com/realwriting.**

197

emotion of operas. My parents both spoke Italian, and they told me the stories of the operas and translated the words sung in Italian to English so that I could understand. Because hearing opera made my parents happy, and they taught me about it, I loved it, too. Many of my friends think I am weird when I say I love opera, but to me it is very emotional and beautiful. (When) I was in my early teens, I found rock music and listened to it no matter what I was doing. I like the music with words that tell a story that I can relate to. In that way, rock can be like opera, with stories that everyone can relate to, about love, heartbreak, happiness, and pain. The best rock has powerful guitars and bass, and a good, strong drumbeat. I love it when I can feel the bass in my chest. Rock has good energy and power. (Now,) I love rap music, too, not the rap with words that are violent or disrespectful of women, but the rest. The words are poetry, and the energy is so high that I feel as if I just have to move my body in the beat. That rhythm is so steady. I have even written some good rap, which my friends say is really good. Maybe I will try to get it published, even on something like Helium, or I could start a blog. I will always love music because it is a good way to communicate feelings and stories, and it makes people feel good.

1. Double-underline the **topic sentence**.

2. What **categories** of music does Lorenza write about? _opera, rock music, rap_

3. Circle the **transitions**.

4. Does the paragraph have the Four Basics of Good Classification (p. 188)? Why or why not? _Answers will vary, but the paragraph could use some more detailed examples._

5. What kind of organization does Lorenza use? _time_

Vocabulary development

Underline these words as you read the classification essay.

skeptical: doubtful
validity: worth
trendsetter: one who starts a new style or movement
ruthless: without pity
compassionate: sympathetic
adaptable: able to adjust to a variety of situations
tactful: polite
procrastinate: to delay doing something

Student Classification Essay

Danny Fitzgerald

Blood Type and Personality

PREDICT What do you think this essay will discuss?

_____

_____

In Japan, the question "What's your blood type?" is as common as   1
"What's your sign?" in the United States. Some Japanese researchers claim that people's personalities can be classified by their blood types. You may be skeptical about this method of classification, but don't judge its validity before you read the descriptions the researchers have put together. Do you see yourself?

If you have blood type O, you are a leader. (When) you see something
you want, you strive to achieve your goal. You are passionate, loyal, and self-
confident, and you are often a trendsetter. Your enthusiasm for projects and
goals spreads to others who happily follow your lead. (When) you want something, you may be ruthless about getting it or blind to how your actions affect others.

(Another) blood type, A, is a social, "people" person. You like people
and work well with them. You are sensitive, patient, compassionate, and affectionate. You are a good peacekeeper because you want everyone to be
happy. In a team situation, you resolve conflicts and keep things on a smooth
course. (Sometimes), type A's are stubborn and find it difficult to relax. They
may also find it uncomfortable to do things alone.

People with type B blood are usually individualists who like to do things
on their own. You may be creative and adaptable, and you usually say exactly
what you mean. Although you can adapt to situations, you may not choose
to do so because of your strong independent streak. You may prefer working
on your own to being part of a team.

(The final) blood type is type AB. If you have AB blood, you are a natural
entertainer. You draw people to you because of your charm and easygoing
nature. AB's are usually calm and controlled, tactful and fair. On the down-
side, though, they may take too long to make decisions. And they may procrastinate, putting off tasks until the last minute.

Classifying people's personalities by blood type seems very unusual
until you examine what researchers have found. Most people find the descriptions fairly accurate. (When) you think about it, classification by blood
type isn't any more far-fetched than classification by horoscope sign. What
will they think of next? Classification by hair color?

2   **TEAMWORK** If most students
know their blood type, form
groups according to blood
type and have students determine if they have the traits
discussed in the essay. They
could then write a classification
essay on their own blood type's
characteristics.

3

4

5   **IDENTIFY** What are the four
blood types?

_____

_____

6

TIP For reading advice, see
Chapter 2.

CRITICAL THINKING: READING

1. Double-underline the **thesis statement**.

2. What are the categories Danny uses? _blood types (O, A, B, AB)_

3. Underline the sentences where he introduces each category.

4. Circle the **transitions**.

5. Each paragraph describes not only the general characteristics of a blood
    type but also _each type's positive and negative traits._

6. In most of the final paragraph, Danny seems to believe in the blood
    type/personality connection. However, two sentences give a different im-
    pression. Underline them. Do you think these sentences help or hurt his
    conclusion? _Answers will vary. Possible answer: The last two sentences_
    seem to contradict the rest of the paragraph.

Classification at a Glance

Topic sentence (paragraph) or thesis statement (essay)
- the topic + organizing principle
  OR
- the topic + organizing principle + categories
  OR
- the topic + categories

↓

First category
Examples/explanations of first category

↓

Second category
Examples/explanations of second category

↓

Third category
Examples/explanations of third category

↓

Conclusion
Refers back to the classification's purpose/categories and makes an observation

TEACHING TIP Suggest to students that they make journal entries on some of the topics that they don't write about for this assignment.

ESL Suggest to students that they write about something unique to their native cultures: foods, holidays, stores, vacation spots, housing, and so on.

CRITICAL THINKING: WRITING

Choose one of the following topics, and respond in a paragraph or essay.

1. If you know your blood type, write about whether the Japanese system describes you and how it does or does not. If you do not know your type, write about what category you *think* you are and why.

2. Would you describe yourself as skeptical of this essay's ideas, or open to them? Why? Give examples.

3. Describe a time when you were skeptical about something you heard or read. What made you skeptical and why?

Write Your Own Classification

In this section, you will write your own classification based on one of the three assignments that follow. Use the following tools to help you:

1. Review the Four Basics of Good Classification (p. 188).
2. Use "Classification at a Glance" as a basic organizer.
3. Use the Checklist: How to Write Classification (pp. 202–03) as you write and revise.

• •

ASSIGNMENT 1   Writing about College, Work, and Everyday Life

Write a classification on one of the following topics or one of your own. For ideas, see your responses to the photograph (p. 189) and the idea journal (p. 190).

COLLEGE
Types of
- Teachers
- Assignments in this class
- Resources in a college library

WORK
Types of
- Bosses
- Work you like (or dislike)
- Skills needed to do your job

EVERYDAY LIFE
Types of
- Challenges you face
- Stress
- Music you like

• •

ASSIGNMENT 2   Writing about Connections

Read the following account of Caroline Powers before doing the assignment below.

COMMUNITY MATTERS

Caroline Powers

Caroline Powers first got involved with community service when she took a course in college in which, for 20 percent of their final grade, students had the option of doing either a research paper or a shorter paper based on community service work. Caroline chose the service work option, working in the Girlfriends program at Girls, Inc., with girls from five to seventeen years old, most of whom were poor and living in unstable family environments. She had always liked the idea of helping people but had not had an opportunity before taking this course. Caroline so enjoyed her work at Girls, Inc., that she became a volunteer coordinator at the college, connecting community experience with class assignments. She said that the students always liked the experience: "Some of the jocks signed up for service projects because they thought it would be easy, but then they got really excited—like a couple of guys set up a basketball clinic for boys and girls in the community." Caroline was involved with a different project each semester, including spending a summer at the Pine Ridge Reservation in South Dakota.

Here, Caroline classifies the kinds of work she did at the local welfare office.

Student volunteers are involved in various types of work at the welfare office: There is plenty to do, and all of it directly helps people with a variety of needs. One type of work involves working with homeless teenagers. Unfortunately, there are more of them than most people realize. We provide the teenagers with information, mainly, such as where they can have free, nutritious meals and hot showers. We also refer them to local shelters. Another type of service that we provide for homeless teenagers is information about birth control and where they can receive medical services. We want the teenagers to have all the information that will keep them safe and healthy, but we do not force choices upon them. A third type of work we provide is homework help for children of refugee parents who do not speak English. Of course, we offer help to their parents as well, including referring them to free or low-cost English language courses, but as a student volunteer, I worked primarily with children and teenagers. I enjoyed all the work I have done as part of the college program, but I also continued my work at Girls, Inc., after the course ended. I truly enjoy helping others and realize that I can make a difference in the world.

RESOURCES For advice on "Writing about Connections," see *Practical Suggestions*.

ASSIGNMENT: Choose one of the following, and write a classification paragraph or essay. Work either on your own or with a partner.

■   Find out about social service volunteer opportunities in your community. Either write about the types of opportunities or research an organization you are interested in and write about the kinds of things it does.

TIP For more on connecting to community, visit **bedfordstmartins.com/ realwriting**.

- Visit one of the following Web sites and write about the types of activities you find there: www.coolpeoplecare.org, www.idealist.org, www.helium.org, www.charityguide.org, and www.ehope.org.

- Write about ways in which you have helped people or have received help.

- Write about the ways that social networks, such as Facebook or MySpace, connect people.

- Write about ways to get involved in your college community.

RESOURCES Reproducible peer-review guides for different kinds of papers are available in *Additional Resources*.

TEAMWORK For more detailed guidance on group work, see *Practical Suggestions*.

ASSIGNMENT 3   Writing in the Real World/Solving a Problem

Read Appendix B, "Solving Problems."

PROBLEM: You need a car loan. The loan officer gives you an application that asks for your monthly income and expenses. Since every month you find yourself short on money, you realize that you need to see how you spend your money. You decide to make a monthly budget that categorizes the kinds of expenses you have.

ASSIGNMENT: Working with a group or on your own, break your monthly expenses into categories, thinking of everything that you spend money on. Then, review the expenses carefully to see which ones might be reduced. Next, write a classification paragraph or essay for the loan officer that classifies your monthly expenses, with examples, and ends with one or two suggestions about how you might reduce your monthly spending. You might start with this sentence:

My monthly expenses fall into _____ *(number)* _____ basic categories: _____ , _____ , and _____ .

CHECKLIST: HOW TO WRITE CLASSIFICATION	
STEPS IN CLASSIFICATION	**HOW TO DO THE STEPS**
☐ Focus.	• Think about what you want to classify and your purpose for classifying.
☐ Narrow and explore your topic. See Chapter 4.	• Prewrite to get ideas for categories and for things that fit into those categories. • Review your prewriting and choose the categories that best serve your purpose.
☐ Write a topic sentence (paragraph) or thesis statement (essay). See Chapter 5.	• State your topic, the categories you are using to sort it, and/or your organizing principle.

CHECKLIST: HOW TO WRITE CLASSIFICATION

STEPS IN CLASSIFICATION	HOW TO DO THE STEPS
☐ Support your point. See Chapter 6.	• Prewrite to find examples or explanations of things that fit into your categories.
☐ Make a plan. See Chapter 7.	• Arrange your categories to best suit your purpose and help your readers understand the topic.
☐ Write a draft. See Chapter 8.	**FOR A PARAGRAPH** • Write a paragraph with your topic sentence, categories, and examples or explanations of things that fit into those categories. Use complete sentences. **FOR AN ESSAY** • Consider using one of the introduction types in Chapter 8. Include your thesis statement in your introduction. • Using your plan, write topic sentences for each of the categories. • Write paragraphs that give examples or explanations of what is in each category. **FOR PARAGRAPHS AND ESSAYS** • Write a conclusion that reminds your readers of your topic and makes an observation based on what you have written. • Write a title that previews your main point but does not repeat it.
☐ Revise your draft, making at least four improvements. See Chapter 9.	• Get feedback from others using the peer-review guide for classification at **bedfordstmartins.com/realwriting**. • Read to make sure that the categories all follow the same organizing principle. • Add any other examples or explanations that come to your mind. • Add transitions to move readers from one category to the next.
☐ Edit your revised draft. See Parts 4 through 7.	• Correct errors in grammar, spelling, word use, and punctuation.
☐ Ask yourself:	• Does my paper have the Four Basics of Good Classification (see p. 188)? • What is the best part of my paper? • Is this the best I can do?

Chapter Review

1. Classification is writing that *organizes/sorts people or items into categories.*

2. The organizing principle is *how you sort the people or items.*

3. What are the Four Basics of Good Classification?

   It makes sense of a group of people or items by organizing them into categories.

   It has a purpose for sorting the people or items.

   It categorizes using a single organizing principle.

   It gives detailed examples or explanations of what fits into each category.

LEARNING JOURNAL Reread your idea journal entry (p. 190) on the kinds of students in this class or the kinds of friends you have. Make another entry on the same topic, using what you have learned about classification.

4. Write sentences using the following vocabulary words: *skeptical, valid, ruthless, tactful, polite. Answers will vary.*

> **reflect** Write for two minutes on the kinds of responsibilities you have. Then, compare what you have written to what you wrote in response to the "write" prompt on page 188.

Spot and Start Classification Assignments in Other Courses

Spot

In college, at work, and in your everyday life, you will use classification in many situations (see p. 190), but the assignment probably will not use the word *classification*. Instead, it may use words and phrases such as *describe the types of _____*, or *explain the types or kinds of _____*. It might also use words such as *how is _____ organized?* or *what are the parts of _____?* Words and phrases that signal that you need to sort things into categories require classification.

Start

Ask yourself

1. If I were actually sorting my subject, what categories would I sort them into?

2. What items or events would fit into each category?

3. How should I describe those items or events to my readers?

Definition

Writing That Tells What Something Means

Understand What Definition Is

Definition is writing that explains what a term or concept means.

Four Basics of Good Definition

1 It tells readers what is being defined.

2 It presents a clear basic definition.

3 It uses examples to show what the writer means.

4 It gives details about the examples that readers will understand.

In the following paragraph, each number and color corresponds to one of the Four Basics of Good Definition.

A 1 stereotype 2 is a conventional idea or image that is simplistic—and often wrong, particularly when it is applied to people or groups of people. Stereotypes can prevent us from seeing people as they really are because stereotypes blind us with preconceived notions about what a certain type of person is like. 3 For example, I had a stereotyped notion of Native Americans until I met my friend Daniel, a Chippewa Indian. 4 I thought all Indians wore feathers and beads, had long black hair, and avoided all contact with non–Native Americans because they resented their land being taken away. Daniel, however, wears jeans and T-shirts, and we talk about everything—even our different ancestries.

After meeting him, I understood that my stereotype of Native Americans was completely wrong. **3** Not only was it wrong, but it set up an us–them concept in my mind that made me feel that I, as a non–Native American, would never have anything in common with Native Americans. My stereotype would not have allowed me to see any Native American as an individual: I would have seen him or her as part of a group that I thought was all alike, and all different from me. From now on, I won't assume that any individual fits my stereotype; I will try to see that person as I would like them to see me: as myself, not a stereotyped image.

STUDENT PHOTO

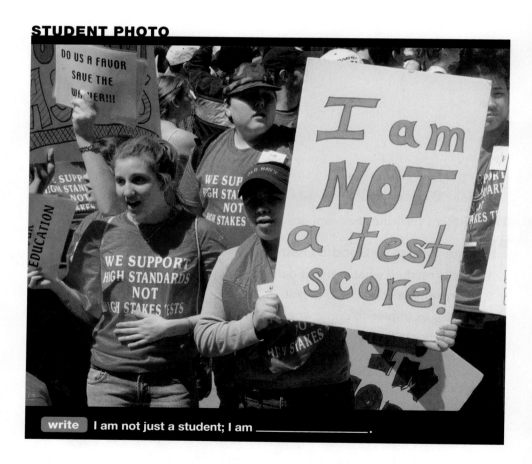

This photo was taken by David Jennings.

write   I am not just a student; I am _____.

You can use definition in many practical situations:

COLLEGE   On a math exam, you are asked to define *exponential notation.*

WORK   On an application that says, "Choose one word that describes you," you must define yourself in a word and give examples that support this definition. (This is also a common interview question.)

EVERYDAY LIFE   In a relationship, you define for your partner what you mean by *commitment* or *communication*.

Main Point in Definition

In definition, the **main point** usually defines a term or concept. The main point is related to your purpose: to help your readers understand the term or concept as you are using it.

When you write your definition, do not just copy the dictionary definition; write it in your own words as you want your readers to understand it. To help you, you might first complete the following sentence:

MAIN POINT IN DEFINITION   **I want readers to understand that this term means. . . .**

Then, based on your response, write a topic sentence (paragraph) or thesis statement (essay). These sentences can follow several different patterns.

"Class" is the larger group the term belongs to.

WALTER SCANLON: I take my writing seriously because I know that is how people will judge me.

(See Walter Scanlon's **PROFILE OF SUCCESS** on p. 210.)

TIP For tools to build your vocabulary, visit the *Real Writing Student Center* at **bedfordstmartins.com/ realwriting**.

TIP Once you have a basic statement of your definition, try revising it to make it stronger, clearer, or more interesting.

- -

PRACTICE 1   Writing a Statement of Your Definition

For each of the following terms, write a definition statement using the pattern indicated in brackets. You may need to use a dictionary.

EXAMPLE:

Cirrhosis [term + class + detail]:

Cirrhosis is a liver disease often caused by alcohol abuse.

Answers will vary. Possible answers are shown.

1.   Stress [term + class + detail]: *Stress is an emotionally upsetting condition that can have physical effects.*

IDEA JOURNAL Write about what success means.

2.   Vacation [term + *means/is* + basic definition]: <u>Vacation means taking</u>
     <u>time off to relax.</u>

3.   Confidence [term + class + detail]: <u>Confidence is a feeling of trust or</u>
     <u>faith.</u>

4.   Conservation [term + *means/is* + basic definition]: <u>Conservation means</u>
     <u>preserving something from damage, loss, or neglect.</u>

5.   Marriage [term + *means/is* + basic definition]: <u>Marriage is a union that</u>
     <u>requires respect, communication, and the ability to compromise.</u>

Support in Definition

Support in definition explains what a term or concept means by providing specific examples and giving details about the examples so that your readers understand what you mean.

If a friend says, "Don't take that class; it's terrible," you will not really know what she means by *terrible* until she explains it. Let us say she adds, "The teacher sometimes falls asleep, his lectures put the students to sleep, and the bathroom next door floods the room." These examples support her definition so that you have no doubt about what she means.

PRACTICE 2   Selecting Examples and Details to Explain the Definition

COMPUTER In computer class-rooms, have students type one example into their computers and then move to the next computer, add an example for the topic there, and continue until there are three examples for each definition.

List three examples or pieces of information that you could use to explain each of the following definitions.

   EXAMPLE:

   Insomnia means sleeplessness.

   a. <u>hard to fall asleep</u>

   b. <u>wake up in the middle of the night</u>

   c. <u>wake up without feeling rested in the morning</u>

Answers will vary. Possible answers are shown.

1.   Confidence is feeling that you can conquer any obstacle.

   a. <u>You focus on chances of success.</u>

   b. <u>You know you have the needed skills.</u>

   c. <u>You let others know you are optimistic.</u>

2.   A real friend is not just someone for the fun times.

   a. <u>sticks up for you</u>

b. *helps when you need it* _____

c. *likes you for who you are* _____

DISCUSSION Ask students, "How has the definition of *family* changed in the last decade?"

3. A family is a group you always belong to, no matter what.

a. *You can always count on family.* _____

b. *Distance, divorce, even death will not change it.* _____

c. *Sometimes you might want to escape, but you cannot.* _____

Organization in Definition

The examples in definition are often organized by **order of importance**, meaning that the example that will have the most impact on readers is saved for last.

TIP For more on order of importance, see page 82.

  Transitions in definition move readers from one example to the next. Use transitions within a paragraph and also to move from one paragraph to another to link the paragraphs. Here are some transitions you might use in definition, though many others are possible, too.

Common Definition Transitions

another; one/another	for example
another kind	for instance
first, second, third, and so on	

PRACTICE 3   Using Transitions in Definition

Read the paragraph that follows, and fill in the blanks with transitions. You are not limited to the ones listed in the preceding box.
Answers may vary. Possible answers are shown.

  Each year, *Business Week* publishes a list of the most family-friendly companies to work for. The magazine uses several factors to define the organizations as family-friendly. _____ *One* _____ factor is whether the company has flextime, allowing employees to schedule work hours that better fit family needs. _____ *For example* _____, a parent might choose to work from 6:30 A.M. to 2:30 P.M. to be able to spend time with children. *Another, A second* factor is whether family leave programs are encouraged. In addition to maternity leaves, _____ *for example* _____, does the company encourage paternity leaves and leaves for care of elderly parents? A final factor is whether the company makes allowances for one-day or part-day absences for a child's illness, parent-teacher conferences, and other important family duties. Increasingly, companies are trying to become more family-friendly to attract and keep good employees.

Read and Analyze Definition

READING SELECTIONS For further examples of and activities for definition, see Chapter 47.

Reading examples of definition will help you write your own. The first example in this section is a Profile of Success from the real world of business. Walter Scanlon has an inspiring personal story, and in his work now, he says that when he is not face-to-face with someone, his writing represents him. Walter's profile shows how he uses writing in his work and gives an example of how he uses definition in his work as a program and workplace consultant.

TIP For advice on building your vocabulary, visit the *Real Writing Student Center* at **bedfordstmartins.com/ realwriting**.

The second and third examples—first a definition paragraph and then a definition essay—are both by students. As you read, pay attention to the vocabulary, and answer the questions in the margin. They will help you read the piece critically.

PROFILE OF SUCCESS

Walter Scanlon
Program and Workplace
Consultant

RESOURCES For a discussion of how to use the profiles in Part 2, see *Practical Suggestions*.

Definition in the Real World

The following profile shows how a business consultant uses definition on the job.

Background   I grew up in a working-class neighborhood in New York City, in a family with a long history of alcohol problems. From my earliest days in grammar school, I assumed the role of class clown, somehow managing to just get by academically. By the time I reached high school, I was using drugs and alcohol, and I soon dropped out of school. For the next ten years, I was in and out of hospitals and prisons. When I was not in an institution, I lived on the streets—in abandoned buildings and deserted cars.

At one point after being released from yet another prison, I knew I had to do something different if I were to survive. Instead of looking for a drink or a drug this time out of jail, I joined Alcoholics Anonymous.[1] That was the beginning of a new life for me.

I earned a GED, and took a pre-college reading course to improve my reading skills. Then, I took one college-level course, never intending to earn a degree but

1. **Alcoholics Anonymous:** an organization in which people support each other to stay sober.

READING SELECTIONS
Students might also be interested in Walter Scanlon's "It's Time I Shed My Ex-Convict Status," which appears in Chapter 42 of the Readings section.

just to say I went to college. I did not do all that well in the first course, but I kept taking courses and got a bachelor's degree. I then went on for a master's and, finally, a Ph.D. Now, I run my own successful consulting business in which I work with companies' employee assistance programs, private individual clients, and families with a wide range of complex problems. I have also published two books and professional articles.

Degrees/College(s) B.A., Pace University; M.B.A., New York Institute of Technology; Ph.D., Columbus University

Employer Self

Writing at work I do all kinds of writing in my job: letters, proposals, presentations, articles, books, training programs, e-mails, memos, and more. I take my writing seriously because I know that is how people will judge me. Often I have only a few minutes to present myself, so I work hard to make my point early on, and very clearly. I believe that if you write clearly, you think clearly. In most situations, there are many factors that I cannot control, but I can always control my writing and the message it gives people.

I sometimes get e-mails that have all kinds of grammar mistakes in them, and believe me, I notice them and form opinions about the sender. (For an example of an e-mail that Walter received and his reaction to it, see Chapter 24, p. 361.)

How Walter uses definition As I work with clients, I often have to define a term so that they can understand it before I explain its relevance to the situation within which we are working.

Walter's Definition

In the following paragraph, Walter defines *employee assistance program* for a client.

Employee Assistance Program

The "employee assistance program" (EAP) is a confidential, early-intervention workplace counseling service designed to help employees who are experiencing personal problems. It is a social service within a work environment that can be found in most major corporations, associations, and government organizations. EAP services are always free to the employee and benefit the organization as much as the employee. Employees who are free of emotional problems are far more productive than those who are not. An employee whose productivity is negatively affected by a drinking problem, for example, might seek help through the EAP. He/she would be assessed by a counselor and then referred to an appropriate community resource for additional services. The *employee* is helped through the EAP while the *employer* is rewarded with improved productivity. An EAP is a win-win program for all involved.

---

1. Double-underline the **topic sentence**.

2. Fill in the blanks with the term defined in the paragraph and the definition.

   Term: _employee assistance program_

   Definition: _a confidential, early-intervention workplace counseling service designed to help employees who are experiencing personal problems_

3. Underline an **example** of what an EAP might do.

4. Double-underline the sentence that makes a final observation about the topic.

Student Definition Paragraph

This paragraph is an excerpt from a longer piece that won first place in the *Composition Merit Awards Journal* online competition in 2006.

Abigail Klatt graduated from Minnesota State University, Mankato, in 2008 with a degree in nursing. She wrote this piece for a composition course after her cousin was diagnosed with multiple sclerosis, and Klatt became interested in learning about alternative medical treatments for this condition. While Klatt prefers not to show her work to anyone before submitting it, she went through four drafts on her own before she was satisfied with this essay. Klatt notes that although she originally thought nursing would not be a writing-intensive career, "We do write a lot of notes and grammar is important, as are spelling and punctuation, and I never realized how important citations would be!"

PREDICT What do you think the paragraph will be about?

_____

_____

_____

Vocabulary development

Underline these words as you read Abigail's paragraph.

scam: a phony scheme
alternative: in a medical sense, nontraditional; otherwise, a choice or possibility
electrotherapy: therapy using electrical currents
neurologists: doctors specializing in the brain and nervous system
spasticity: a condition characterized by sudden, involuntary muscle contractions
cannabis: marijuana
spasms: sudden, involuntary muscle contractions
pursue: to follow
complementary: in a medical sense, used along with traditional medicine
hoaxes: deceitful acts
gimmicks: in this sense, information or devices designed to trick or mislead

Abigail Klatt

Not All CAM Is a Scam

Alternative medicine is a system based on belief, and sometimes long-standing historical and cultural practices rather than science. In the nineteenth and twentieth centuries, medical practices resembled present-day alternative medicine. Patients were treated with arsenic, strychnine, potassium iodide, mercury, and belladonna in addition to herbs, minerals, baths, massage, various electrotherapies, and complex diets. While neurologists struggled to find better drugs for spasticity, increasing numbers of patients were quietly using cannabis, which gave them better relief from pain and spasms, even if it impaired alertness and balance. People who pursue alternative treatments need to be knowledgeable about the therapy they choose. CAM (complementary and alternative medicine) therapies can sometimes interact with each other, and the patient needs to be aware of this fact. Some treatments can also cause an allergic response, while others can be hoaxes; therefore, it is critical to understand the risks and benefits of treatments. When considering which option to choose, the best option is to be informed and aware of what gimmicks are out there.

1. Double-underline the **topic sentence**.

2. What term is Abigail defining? *alternative medicine* _____

3. After reading Abigail's paragraph, how would you define *alternative medicine*, in your own words? *Answers will vary.* _____
_____

4. What is CAM? *complementary and alternative medicine* _____

5. What does the title mean? *that CAM is a legitimate form of medicine* _____

6. Why is it important for people to be knowledgeable about CAM? *Answers will vary.* _____

Student Definition Essay

Kelli Whitehead
"Oh, You're a College Student"

Kelli Whitehead is a student at the University of Colorado, where she is majoring in business. She works part-time at Chili's and American Eagle. When she is not working, going to classes, or doing homework she enjoys playing soccer and hanging out with friends. And each Thanksgiving for the past fourteen years, she and her younger sister, Kate, have made personalized Christmas ornaments that they give to members of their large, extended family. Each year, Kelli and Kate try to outdo themselves with their creations.

Vocabulary development

Underline these words as you read.

accurate: correct
portrays: describes
perception: a way of understanding something
sensationalistic: shocking or exciting
binger: a person who does something to excess
dole: give
brainwashed: pressured someone to change their beliefs

It seems sometimes as if everyone has a definite opinion of what a college student is, and those people assume I fit their definition. Well, I am one, and much of what people say is not accurate, at least from what I—a real college student—have seen. The news media portrays one image of college students, people I know who are *not* in college have another perception, but neither of them defines what I am or how I behave.

News and entertainment media focus on the students who make great, sensationalistic stories: We all go to Mexico and drink. We all go to parties and drink. Then we pass out or damage property or ourselves. Sometimes

1 **PREDICT** What do you think Kelli's essay will be about?

_____
_____
_____

2

REFLECT Do you agree with what Kelli says about media coverage?

_____

_____

_____

we die from drinking. Sometimes we are dangerous. Mostly, we are out-of-control bingers who live to drink, and sometimes die from our excesses.

The media also love the students who cheat, and otherwise do not earn our success. We plagiarize, we buy student papers online, or we organize cheating rings to pass tests. We are spoiled by our parents, who endlessly dole out money and help. We arrive in the workplace without the necessary skills, and we are not ready for hard work and responsibility. We are losers, falling far short of the character needed to be a productive citizen.   3

To some others, college students are full of themselves. Now that we are in college, whatever we were like before, we think we are too good for friends who aren't in college. We are set apart, apparently by choice, from "regular" people. We read things that have changed us, and our professors have brainwashed us with radical ideas. We look down on anyone who hasn't been to college. We are stuck-up jerks.   4

No, we really are not all those things. Yes, like individuals who are part of any population, some college students drink too much, commit crimes, cheat, and behave badly. That doesn't mean that the whole group is made up of drunks, cheats, and losers. I am a college student, I also have to work, so I have a job in a restaurant, and not a fancy one. I can't get drunk all the time (even if I wanted to) because I have classes I have to attend, homework I have to do, and a job with as many hours as I can get. I don't cheat, and if anyone doesn't believe me, some of my grades are proof. I work a lot harder than I did in high school. Life was a lot easier then: I lived at home for free, I worked for spending money, and I breezed through high school classes with good grades.   5

SUMMARIZE How does Kelli define a "college student"?

_____

_____

_____

I know that I am privileged to have the chance to go to college, and I am glad to be challenged to learn and to work as hard as I can. I believe that all of it is making me a better human being, and an adult who can contribute to our world. Many of my friends (other college students) and I not only work and go to school, we are also involved in college activities and in volunteering in the community—at soup kitchens, churches, recycling centers, and shelters, among other places. We try to be good members of our community. So, please, when you see me, don't think of me as a "college student." I am Kelli, no more, no less, and I am pleased to meet you.   6

TIP For reading advice, see Chapter 2.

CRITICAL THINKING: READING

1. According to Kelli, how does the media portray college students?
    as drunkards and cheats

2. What are some other misperceptions about college students? _that they_
    think they are better than other people

3. Why does Kelli first say what media and others think before saying what she thinks? *Answers will vary, but because she wants to end with her own definition.*

4. When Kelli writes, "I am Kelli, no more, no less," what does she mean? *Answers will vary.*

5. What is her purpose for writing this essay, and who is her audience? *to defend college students against wrong perceptions. The audience is the general reader.*

CRITICAL THINKING: WRITING

Choose one of the following topics and respond in a paragraph or essay.

1. Choose a label for yourself ("I am a _____") and define and give examples of what you mean.

2. Write about how you have been stereotyped and why you don't fit that stereotype.

3. If you had to define "college student," what would you write?

4. How have your looks defined you?

Write Your Own Definition

In this section, you will write your own definition based on one of the three assignments that follow. Use the following tools to help you:

1. Review the Four Basics of Good Definition (p. 205).

2. Use "Definition at a Glance" as a basic organizer.

3. Use the Checklist: How to Write Definition (pp. 218–19) as you write and revise.

. . . .

ASSIGNMENT 1   Writing about College, Work, and Everyday Life

Write a definition for one of the following terms (in italics) or topics or one of your own. For other ideas, see your responses to the photograph (p. 206) or the idea journal (p. 207).

COLLEGE
- *Good student* or *bad student*
- *Cheating*
- *Learning*

WORK
- A satisfying job (or unsatisfying job)
- A term used in your work
- *Self-starter*

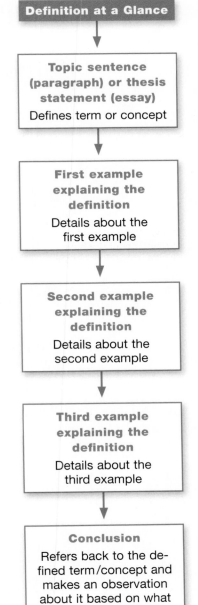

Definition at a Glance

↓

Topic sentence (paragraph) or thesis statement (essay)
Defines term or concept

↓

First example explaining the definition
Details about the first example

↓

Second example explaining the definition
Details about the second example

↓

Third example explaining the definition
Details about the third example

↓

Conclusion
Refers back to the defined term/concept and makes an observation about it based on what you have written

ESL Suggest that students define a common term in their language that has no direct counterpart in English.

EVERYDAY LIFE
- *Common sense*
- *Success*
- A nurturing relationship

· ·

ASSIGNMENT 2 Writing about Connections

Read the following account of Corin Costas before doing the assignment below.

COMMUNITY MATTERS

RESOURCES For advice on "Writing about Connections," see *Practical Suggestions*.

Corin Costas

Corin Costas had some significant medical issues as a teenager, including surgery to remove his pituitary gland, an organ that affects growth. The operation left him blind in his left eye and without a sense of smell. Then, he had more surgery to remedy the effects of losing his pituitary gland. When he started at Bunker Hill Community College, he took basic English and math and was not involved much with the college community.

After a couple of years, a friend asked if he was interested in starting a business club on campus. He and his friend collected the signatures of twenty other students who were interested in joining the club, and Corin ran it for two years. Now, he runs SHOCWAVES (Students Helping Our Community with Activities). This club has a budget from the college of $2,000–$5,000, which he manages, an experience he considers to be "good business training." The club is engaged in many community service projects. Corin initiated several, including Light One Little Candle, which asked students at BHCC to give $1 to have their names put on a paper candle. The money raised was donated to Dana-Farber Cancer Center to buy books for children with cancer.

Through his service and connection to the college and outside community, Corin has met lots of people, practiced his business skills, and learned much. He feels good about himself and what he does. He also believes that these connections and his work were crucial to his educational success: He stayed in school to graduate and transferred to the University of Massachusetts, Boston, with a $14,000 scholarship.

The following is part of a piece Corin wrote about his work. He defines SHOCWAVES and what it does.

SHOCWAVES is a student organization at Bunker Hill Community College. SHOCWAVES stands for Students Helping Our Community with Activities, and its mission is to get students involved with the community—to become part of it by actively working in it in positive ways. Each year, SHOCWAVES is assigned a budget by the Student Activities Office, and it spends that budget in activities that help the community in a variety of ways. Some of the money is spent, for example, in fund-raising events for community causes. We have money to plan and launch a fund-raiser, which raises far more than we spend. In the process, other students and members of the community also become involved in the helping effort. We get to know lots of people, and we usually have a lot of fun—all while helping others. Recently, we have worked as part of the Charles River Cleanup, the Walk for Hunger, collecting toys for sick and needy children, and Light One Little Candle. While SHOCWAVES's mission is to help the community, it also benefits its members. Working in the community, I have learned so many valuable skills, and I always have something I care about to write about for my classes. I have learned about budgeting, advertising, organizing, and managing. I have also developed my creativity by coming up with new ways to do things. I have networked with many people, including people who are important in the business world. SHOCWAVES has greatly improved my life, and my chances for future success.

ASSIGNMENT: Choose one of the following topics, and write a definition paragraph or essay. Work either on your own or with a partner.

- Ask three (or more) people to tell you what they think *community service* means. Take notes on their responses, and then write a paragraph or an essay combining their definitions with your own.

- If there is a community service or service learning club on campus, interview some students in the club about how they define *community service*, *service learning*, or *volunteerism*, giving examples of what they mean. Then, write a definition.

- If you play a team sport, define *teamwork*.

- If you belong to a community of any sort (religious, neighborhood, social), define what makes it a community.

- Are social networks communities?

TIP For more on connecting to community, visit **bedfordstmartins.com/ realwriting**.

ASSIGNMENT 3 Writing in the Real World/Solving a Problem

Read Appendix B, "Solving Problems."

RESOURCES Reproducible peer-review guides for different kinds of papers are available in *Additional Resources*.

PROBLEM: A recent survey asked business managers what skills or traits they value most in employees. The top five responses were (1) motivation, (2) interpersonal skills, (3) initiative, (4) communication skills, and (5) maturity.

You have a job interview next week, and you want to be able to present yourself well. Before you can do that, though, you need to have a better understanding of the five skills and traits noted above and what examples you might be able to give to demonstrate that you have them.

TIP For tools to use in getting a job, visit the *Real Writing Student Center* at **bedfordstmartins.com/ realwriting**.

ASSIGNMENT: Working in a group or on your own, come up with definitions of three of the five terms, and think of some examples of how the skills or traits could be used at work. Then, do one of the following assignments. You might begin with the following sentence:

I am a person who is (or has) _____.

TEAMWORK For more detailed guidance on group work, see *Practical Suggestions*.

For a paragraph: Choose one of the terms, and give examples of how you have demonstrated the trait.

For an essay: Write about how you have demonstrated the three traits.

CHECKLIST: HOW TO WRITE DEFINITION

STEPS IN DEFINITION	HOW TO DO THE STEPS
☐ Focus.	• Think about the term or concept you want to define and the meaning you want to give your readers.
☐ Explore your topic. See Chapter 4.	• Prewrite about the term or concept and its definition as you are using it. • Review your prewriting and choose a definition.
☐ Write a topic sentence (paragraph) or thesis statement (essay). See Chapter 5.	• Write a sentence using one of the patterns on page 207.
☐ Support your definition. See Chapter 6.	• Prewrite to get examples that will show what you mean by the term or concept.
☐ Make a plan. See Chapter 7.	• Organize your examples, saving for last the one that you think will have the most impact on readers.

CHECKLIST: HOW TO WRITE DEFINITION

STEPS IN DEFINITION	HOW TO DO THE STEPS
☐ Write a draft. See Chapter 8.	**FOR A PARAGRAPH** • Write a paragraph that includes a topic sentence and defines your term or concept, showing what you mean through examples. Use complete sentences. **FOR AN ESSAY** • Consider using one of the introduction types in Chapter 8. Include your thesis statement in your introduction. • Using your plan, write topic sentences for each of the examples. • Write paragraphs that give details about the examples. **FOR PARAGRAPHS AND ESSAYS** • Write a conclusion that restates the term or concept and makes an observation about it based on what you have written. • Write a title that previews your main point but does not repeat it.
☐ Revise your draft, making at least four improvements. See Chapter 9.	• Get feedback from others using the peer-review guide for definition at **bedfordstmartins.com/realwriting**. • Reread your definition of the term or concept to make sure that it clearly states your meaning. • Add any other examples that come to mind, and delete any that do not clearly show the meaning of the term or concept. • Add transitions to move readers from one example to the next.
☐ Edit your revised draft. See Parts 4 through 7.	• Correct errors in grammar, spelling, word use, and punctuation.
☐ Ask yourself:	• Does my paper include the Four Basics of Good Definition (p. 205)? • What is the best part of my paper? • Is this the best I can do?

Chapter Review

1. Definition is writing that *explains what a term or concept means.*

2. What are the Four Basics of Good Definition?

It tells readers what is being defined.

It presents a clear basic definition.

It uses examples to show what the writer means.

It gives details about the examples that readers will understand.

LEARNING JOURNAL Reread your idea journal entry from page 207. Write another entry on the same topic, using what you have learned about definition.

3. Write sentences using the following vocabulary words: *alternative, pursue, trivial, predominantly, inevitable.* <u>Answers will vary.</u>

_____

_____

---

reflect Write for two minutes about how you would define a term for someone who is not familiar with it. Compare what you have written with your response to the "write" prompt on page 205.

Spot and Start Definition Assignments in Other Courses

Spot

In college, at work, and in your everyday life, you use definition in many situations (see pp. 206–07). The assignment or question may use the word *define*, but it might also use words such as *explain the meaning of _____,* and *discuss the meaning of _____.* In these cases, you should use what you know about definition to define and explain the term.

Start

Ask yourself

1. What do I need to define? In a college course, it might be, for example, a term you have learned.
2. What is the simplest basic definition that my readers will understand?
3. What examples will clarify the basic definition for my readers?

16

Comparison and Contrast

Writing That Shows Similarities and Differences

Understand What Comparison and Contrast Are

Comparison is writing that shows the similarities among subjects—people, ideas, situations, or items; **contrast** shows the differences. In conversation, people often use the word *compare* to mean either compare or contrast, but as you work through this chapter, the terms will be separated.

Compare	=	Similarities

Contrast	=	Differences

■■ ■ Four Basics of Good Comparison and Contrast

1 It uses subjects that have enough in common to be compared/ contrasted in a useful way.

2 It serves a purpose—either to help readers make a decision or to help them understand the subjects.

3 It presents several important, parallel points of comparison/contrast.

4 It arranges points in a logical order.

In the following paragraph each number and color corresponds to one of the Four Basics of Good Comparison and Contrast.

4 Organized by order of importance

TEACHING TIP Point out to students that some professors in other disciplines ask for comparison when they really mean *both* comparison and contrast. Suggest that they ask professors to clarify questions that ask for comparisons.

1 Grocery stores in wealthy suburbs are **2** much better than the **1** ones in poor, inner-city neighborhoods. **3** Suburban stores are large, bright, and stocked with many varieties of each food. In contrast, inner-city stores are often cramped, dark, and limited in choice. For example, the cereal section in suburban stores often runs for an entire aisle, with hundreds of choices, ranging from the sugary types to the organic, healthy brands. The inner-city stores often stock only the very sugary cereals. Another way in which suburban stores are better is in the quality and freshness of the produce. The fruits and vegetables are plentiful and fresh in typical suburban markets. In inner-city neighborhoods, the choices are again limited, fruits are bruised, and vegetables are often limp and soft. A more important difference between the suburban and inner-city stores is in the prices. You might expect that the prices in wealthy suburban groceries would be high and that those in the poor neighborhoods would be lower. However, the reverse is true: Wealthy suburban shoppers actually pay less for a nicer environment, more choice, and higher-quality food than shoppers at inner-city stores do. Grocery stores are just one example of how "the rich get richer, and the poor get poorer."

STUDENT PHOTO

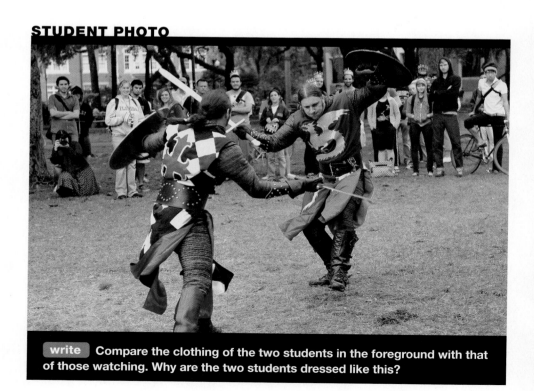

This photograph taken by student Harrison Diamond shows two University of Florida students sword fighting.

write   Compare the clothing of the two students in the foreground with that of those watching. Why are the two students dressed like this?

Many situations require you to understand similarities and differences:

COLLEGE	In a pharmacy course, you compare and contrast the side effects of two drugs prescribed for the same illness.
WORK	You are asked to contrast this year's sales with last year's.
EVERYDAY LIFE	At the supermarket, you contrast brands of the same food to decide which to buy.

Main Point in Comparison and Contrast

The **main point** in a comparison/contrast paragraph or essay is related to your **purpose**. Comparing or contrasting subjects can serve different purposes:

- to help readers make a decision about the subjects
- to help readers understand the subjects
- to show your understanding of the subjects

To help you discover your main point, complete the following sentence:

MAIN POINT IN COMPARISON AND CONTRAST

I want my readers to _____ after reading my comparison or contrast.

Then, write a topic sentence (paragraph) or thesis statement (essay) that identifies the subjects and states the main point you want to make about them.

Leasing a car and buying one are different arrangements.

[Purpose: to help readers decide whether to lease or buy]

My two sons have completely different personalities.

[Purpose: to help readers understand the sons' personalities and how they differ]

The Vietnam and Iraq wars have several significant similarities.

[Purpose: to demonstrate your understanding of the wars and their similarities]

Support in Comparison and Contrast

The **support** in comparison/contrast demonstrates your main point by showing how your subjects are the same or different. To find support, many people make a list with two columns, one for each subject, with parallel points of comparison or contrast.

TOPIC SENTENCE/THESIS STATEMENT: The two credit cards I am considering offer different financial terms.

BIG CARD	MEGA CARD
no annual fee	$35 annual fee
$1 fee per cash advance	$1.50 fee per cash advance
30 days before interest charges begin	25 days before interest charges begin
15.5% finance charge	17.9% finance charge

Choose points that will be convincing and understandable to your readers. Explain your points with facts, details, or examples.

● ●

PRACTICE 1   Finding Points of Contrast

Each of the following items lists some points of contrast. Fill in the blanks with more.

EXAMPLE:

Contrast hair lengths

Long hair	**Short hair**
takes a long time to dry	dries quickly
can be worn a lot of ways	_only one way to wear it_
does not need to be cut often	needs to be cut every five weeks
gets tangled, needs brushing	_low maintenance_

1. Contrast snack foods

Potato chips	**Pretzels**
high fat	low fat
Answers will vary but should	twists or sticks
focus on differences.	_____

2. Contrast pets

Dogs	**Cats**
bark	_____

_____   independent

_____   _____

3. Contrast buildings

The most modern one in town   **An older building**

lots of glass   _____

_____   only a few stories tall

_____   _____

4. Contrast dancing and other forms of exercise

Dancing   **Other forms of exercise**

purpose: social, for fun   _____

_____   done at a gym

_____   _____

· ·

PRACTICE 2   Finding Points of Comparison

Each of the following items lists some points of comparison. Fill in the blanks with
more.

1. Compare sports

Basketball   **Soccer**

team sport   team sport

Answers will vary but should   _____

focus on similarities.   _____

2. Compare pets

Dogs   **Cats**

shed fur   _____

common household pet   _____

_____   _____

3. Compare dancing and other forms of exercise

Dancing   **Other forms of exercise**

done to music   done to music

_____   _____

_____   _____

· ·

Organization in Comparison and Contrast

Comparison/contrast can be organized in two ways: A **point-by-point** organization presents one point of comparison or contrast between the subjects and then moves to the next point. A **whole-to-whole** organization presents all the points of comparison or contrast for one subject and then all the points for the next subject. (For charts illustrating these two methods, see pp. 233–234.) Consider which organization will best explain the similarities or differences to your readers. Whichever organization you choose, stay with it throughout your writing.

• •

PRACTICE 3   Organizing a Comparison/Contrast

The first outline that follows is for a comparison paper using a whole-to-whole organization. Reorganize the ideas and create a new outline (#2) using a point-by-point organization. The first blank has been filled in for you.

The third outline is for a contrast paper using a point-by-point organization. Reorganize the ideas and create a new outline (outline 4) using a whole-to-whole organization. The first blank has been filled in for you.

TEACHING TIP Point out that in a whole-to-whole essay, there usually needs to be a strong transition when the essay moves from subject 1 to subject 2.

1.   Comparison paper using whole-to-whole organization

Main point: My daughter is a lot like I was at her age.

   a. Me

   Not interested in school

   Good at sports

   Hard on myself

   b. My daughter

   Does well in school but doesn't study much or do more than the minimum

   Plays in a different sport each season

   When she thinks she has made a mistake, she gets upset with herself

2.   Comparison paper using point-by-point organization

Main point: My daughter is a lot like I was at her age.

   a. Interest in school

   Me: _Not interested in school_____

   My daughter: _____

   b. _____

   Me: _____

   My daughter: _____

   c. _____

   Me: _____

   My daughter: _____

3. Contrast paper using point-by-point organization

Main point: My new computer is a great improvement over my old one.

a. Weight and portability

New computer: _small and light_

Old computer: _heavy, not portable_

b. _Speed_

New computer: _fast_

Old computer: _slow_

c. _Cost_

New computer: _inexpensive_

Old computer: _expensive_

4. Contrast paper using whole-to-whole organization

Main point: My new computer is a great improvement over my old one.

a. New computer

small and light

_____

_____

b. Old computer

_____

_____

_____

· ·

Comparison/contrast is often organized by **order of importance**, meaning that the most important point is saved for last.

Using **transitions** in comparison/contrast is important, to move readers from one subject to another and from one point of comparison or contrast to the next.

TIP For more on order of importance, see page 82.

· ·

PRACTICE 4   Using Transitions in Comparison and Contrast

Read the paragraph that follows, and fill in the blanks with transitions. You are not limited to the ones listed in the preceding box.

Answers may vary. Possible answers are shown.

College is much more difficult than high school. ___One difference___

is that students have to pay for college classes, while high school is free.

As a result, many college students have to work, take out loans, or both,

Common Comparison/Contrast Transitions

COMPARISON	CONTRAST
both	in contrast
like	most important difference
most important similarity	now/then
one similarity/another similarity	one difference/another difference
similarly	unlike
	while

making staying in school much more of a challenge. *Another difference* is that there is a lot more work in college than in high school. College students have to spend more time out of class doing schoolwork than they had to in high school. Also, _____ *in contrast* _____ to the content of high school classes, college courses are much more difficult. Often, students have to get help from their instructors during office hours. *The most important* difference between college and high school is that college instructors expect students to do the assignments without being reminded. In high school, teachers remind students to do their homework and ask why if students do not do it. In college, students have to take responsibility for their own success or failure.

Read and Analyze Comparison and Contrast

READING SELECTIONS For further examples of and activities for comparison and contrast, see Chapter 48.

Reading examples of comparison and contrast will help you write your own. The first example in this section is a Profile of Success from the real world of business. Brad Leibov started his own company, which helps to revitalize urban areas, and he writes about one project, contrasting how it looked before and after.

The second and third examples are both student writing, first a comparison/contrast paragraph and then a comparison/contrast essay. As you read, pay attention to the vocabulary, and answer the questions in the margin. They will help you read the piece critically.

PROFILE OF SUCCESS

Comparison and Contrast in the Real World

The following profile shows how a company president uses comparison and contrast in his job.

Background   In high school, I put very little effort into completing my coursework. When I first enrolled at Oakton Community College, I was not motivated and soon dropped all my courses. An instructor from Project Succeed contacted me after my first year, and this program helped me recognize that I really wanted to put in the effort necessary to succeed.

A few years later, I earned a B.A. degree from a four-year university. After working for a few years in community development, I was accepted into a top-tier graduate program in urban planning and policy, from which I graduated with a perfect grade-point average. Later, I started my own urban planning and development company to help revitalize inner-city commercial areas.

Degrees/College(s)   B.A., DePaul University; M.A., University of Illinois, Chicago

Writing at work   I write contracts, proposals, marketing materials, etc.

How Brad uses comparison and contrast   I often give examples of how my company can improve a community—kind of before-and-after contrasts.

Brad Leibov
President,
New Chicago Fund, Inc.

Brad's Comparison and Contrast

The following paragraph describes how Brad's company restored a special service area (SSA), a declining community targeted for improvements.

RESOURCES For a discussion of how to use the profiles in Part 2, see *Practical Suggestions*.

New Chicago Fund, Inc., is an expert at advising and leading organizations through all the steps necessary to establish an SSA with strong local support. Our experience acting as liaison among various neighborhood groups and individuals affected by an SSA helps us plan for and address the concerns of residents and property owners. In 2005, New Chicago Fund assisted the Uptown Community Development Corporation with establishing an SSA in Uptown, Chicago. Uptown's commercial area was estimated to lose approximately $506 million annually in consumer expenditures to neighboring commercial districts and suburban shopping centers. Community leaders recognized that Uptown's sidewalks were uninviting with litter, hazardous with unshoveled snow, and unappealing in the lack of pedestrian-friendly amenities found in neighboring commercial districts. The Uptown SSA programs funded the transformation of the commercial area. The sidewalks are regularly cleaned and are litter-free. People no longer have to walk around uncleared snow mounds and risk slipping on the ice because maintenance programs provide full-service clearing. Additionally, SSA funds provided new pedestrian-friendly amenities such as benches, trash receptacles, flower planters, and street-pole banners. The Uptown area is now poised for commercial success.

Vocabulary development
Underline these words as you read.

liaison: someone who acts as a communication link
hazardous: dangerous
amenities: attractive features
receptacles: containers
poised: in this sense, ready; also means natural and balanced, relaxed

1. Double-underline the **topic sentence**.

2. What subjects are being contrasted and what are the points of contrast? _an area before and after SSA improvements; sidewalk features_

3. What is the purpose of the statement? _to sell services of the New Chicago Fund_

4. What are the points of contrast? _buildings, street activities, feelings of residents_

Student Comparison/Contrast Paragraph

Samson Green

Men and Women Getting Lost

When they get lost while driving, women and men have different ways to find the right route. As soon as a woman thinks she might be lost, she will pull into a store or gas station and ask for directions. As she continues on, if she's still not sure of the directions,[2] she will stop again and ask someone else for help. Until they know they are on the right track,[3] women will continue to ask for directions.[1] In contrast, men would rather turn around and go home than stop and ask for directions. First, a man does not readily admit he is lost.[2] When it is clear that he is, he will pull over and consult a map. If he still finds himself lost, he will again pull out that map. Either the map will finally put the man on the right route, or—[3]as a last resort—he will reluctantly stop at a store or gas station and let his wife go in and ask for directions. Many battles of the sexes have raged over what to do when lost while driving.

Vocabulary development

Underline these words as you read.

consult: look at
last resort: final step
reluctantly: with hesitation; unwillingly

TIP For tools to build your vocabulary, visit the *Real Writing Student Center* at **bedfordstmartins .com/realwriting**.

1. Double-underline the **topic sentence**.

2. Is the **purpose** of the paragraph to help readers make a decision or to help them understand the subjects better? _to help them understand_

3. Underline **each point of contrast** in the sample paragraph. Give each parallel, or matched, point the same number.

4. Which organization (point-by-point or whole-to-whole) does Samson use? _whole-to-whole_

5. Circle the **transitions** in the paragraph.

Student Comparison/Contrast Essay

Lou Enrico

Target and Wal-Mart: Not as Different as You Think

Keep Wal-Mart Out! That slogan is what you hear from a lot of people who think Wal-Mart is just plain bad, while Target is good. Communities organize to prevent Wal-Mart from building new stores, and groups promote boycotts of the whole chain. In contrast, Target, the fourth-biggest retailer in the United States, is welcome anywhere. However, the two stores are more alike than different; the biggest difference is in people's perceptions about them.

One perceived difference is in the quality of the merchandise of the two chains. Many people think that low quality comes with Wal-Mart's low prices. They believe that the store's clothing will fall apart because of poor workmanship and inferior fabrics. They think its electronics will fail just after the warranty expires. Target, on the other hand, is perceived as carrying stylish, high-quality merchandise at affordable prices. People think that the clothing and shoes are as durable as they are hip and that the furniture could be found in expensive department stores. However, there is no proof at all that the clothing, electronics, furniture, food—anything—at Target is higher quality than anything at Wal-Mart.

Another perceived difference is in the business practices of the two chains. The media are always running reports that make Wal-Mart look like a villain: Wal-Mart employees are poorly paid. Wal-Mart buys from sweatshops in third-world countries. Wal-Mart discourages unions (Borosage and Peters). Recently, the American Federation of Teachers urged a boycott of Wal-Mart because of its "dismal record" on worker pay, benefits, and rights ("Join"). In contrast, Target is rarely in the news, so we assume that its practices are better. However, there is no proof that Target employees make any more than Wal-Mart workers, and Target discourages unionization (Bhatnagar; Jones). Target also buys products from foreign sources that may not pay and treat their workers fairly. In reality, Wal-Mart has made many positive changes to its business practices, while Target has not, probably because it has not been criticized by the media. Wal-Mart has changed sources of foreign suppliers, for one thing. Also, it was recently named one of the thirty best companies for diversity by *Black Enterprise*.

One of the biggest perceived differences concerns Wal-Mart's effect on local economies. People accuse Wal-Mart of putting small retailers out of

1

2

3

4

PREDICT What do you think this essay will discuss?

_____

_____

IDENTIFY Outside sources are in parentheses. Put a check-mark by these.

business and destroying downtowns that once had many family businesses (Borosage and Peters). It is said to be personally responsible for changing the U.S. economy for the worse. In contrast, people are happy to hear that Target is opening a new store. It is true that some Wal-Marts do put local retailers out of business. The stores are big, they are not located in downtown areas, and they carry a whole range of merchandise that used to be spread throughout many smaller businesses. However, Target also takes business away from smaller stores. Yet Wal-Mart, in contrast to Target, often helps rural towns by opening stores where people previously had to drive long distances to shop. You will not find many Targets in these kinds of areas. Target wants to locate in richer communities.

The fact that Wal-Mart is the largest retailer has led to a lot of the   5 negative publicity it is getting. This negative publicity makes me wonder how else the media changes people's perceptions. Is perception reality?

Works Cited

Bhatnagar, Parija. "Just Call It 'Teflon' Target." CNN/*Money*. 20 Apr. 2005. Cable News Network, 2005. Web. 6 Dec. 2005.

Borosage, Robert L., and Troy Peters. "Target Wal-Mart." TomPaine.com, 14 Nov. 2005. Web. 5 Dec. 2005.

"Join the 'Send Wal-Mart Back to School' Campaign." American Federation of Teachers, 2005. Web. 6 Dec. 2005.

Jones, Sandra. "Target's Image Trumps Wal-Mart's." Crain Communications, 11 Apr. 2005. Web. 6 Dec. 2005.

TIP For reading advice, see Chapter 2.

CRITICAL THINKING: READING

1. Double-underline the **thesis statement**. Put Lou's main point in your own words. *Answers will vary. Possible answer: Wal-Mart and Target have much in common, but people think of them differently.*

2. Underline the **points of contrast** in the essay.

3. Why does Lou think that people have certain perceptions of the two chains? *Answers will vary but should include the media's negative reports on Wal-Mart.*

4. What larger point does Lou make at the end of the essay? *Answers will vary but could refer to how much the media influences people.*

5. Lou has cited four outside sources. What other sources or outside information might have been useful? *Answers will vary but could include sources with quotes from Wal-Mart officials, quotes from Target officials, or quotes from employees of either chain.*

CRITICAL THINKING: WRITING

Choose one of the following topics, and respond in a paragraph or essay.

1. Go to a Wal-Mart and a Target, and compare or contrast three things about them.

2. Listen to the news or read an online news story. Choose one story and write about how its observations may be perception rather than fact.

3. Look at an advertisement and write about how it creates a certain perception of a product or service.

4. Write about how the media shape people's beliefs. Include at least three specific examples.

Write Your Own Comparison and Contrast

In this section, you will write your own comparison and contrast based on one of the three assignments that follow. Use the following tools to help you:

1. Review the Four Basics of Good Comparison and Contrast (p. 221).
2. Use either the Comparison/Contrast "Point-by-Point" or "Whole-to-Whole" (p. 234) flowchart as a basic organizer.
3. Use the Checklist: How to Write Comparison and Contrast (pp. 236–37) as you write and revise.

ASSIGNMENT 1   Writing about College, Work, and Everyday Life

Write a comparison/contrast on one of the following topics or one of your own. For other ideas, see your responses to the photograph (p. 222) and the idea journal (p. 223).

COLLEGE
- Two teachers
- High school and college
- Successful versus unsuccessful student behaviors

WORK
- A job you liked versus one you did not like
- Good employee behavior versus bad employee behavior
- The job you have versus the job you would like to have

EVERYDAY LIFE
- Two friends or family members
- Two types of music
- Your life now versus how you would like your life to be in five years

ASSIGNMENT 2   Writing about Connections

Read the following account of Lynze Schiller before doing the assignment below.

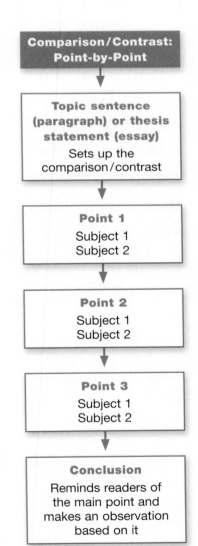

Comparison/Contrast: Point-by-Point

↓

Topic sentence (paragraph) or thesis statement (essay)
Sets up the comparison/contrast

↓

Point 1
Subject 1
Subject 2

↓

Point 2
Subject 1
Subject 2

↓

Point 3
Subject 1
Subject 2

↓

Conclusion
Reminds readers of the main point and makes an observation based on it

Comparison/Contrast: Whole-to-Whole

↓

Topic sentence (paragraph) or thesis statement (essay)
Sets up the comparison/contrast

↓

Subject 1
Point 1
Point 2
Point 3

↓

Subject 2
Point 1
Point 2
Point 3

↓

Conclusion
Reminds readers of the main point and makes an observation based on it

RESOURCES For advice on "Writing about Connections," see *Practical Suggestions*.

COMMUNITY MATTERS

Lynze Schiller

Lynze Schiller started out at Middlesex County College and then transferred to Marymount College. A friend invited her to an event sponsored by Personal Dynamics, an organization that promotes community service projects. She was inspired by the event and started attending their trainings: "They show you how to *be* the change you want in the world." One project she was involved in was the transformation of a couple of storage rooms at a church in the Bronx, New York, that does work in the community with battered women, homeless people, AIDS patients, victims of violence, and other groups needing help. A crew went to work to make two rooms—a library and the Empowerment Room—safe spaces for people. The crew cleaned out the rooms, painted them, collected donated furniture, and painted a mural of helping hands in the Empowerment Room (see photo). All the work and materials were donated.

Here, Lynze describes the transformation of the storage space into the Empowerment Room.

The room was used for storage and was full of stuff from floor to ceiling. It was filthy and musty. All of the contents were covered in thick layers of dust and grime, and most of what was in there was just junk. A large heating pipe stretched across the top of the room, covered in cobwebs and with strips of dust just hanging from it. It was a dingy gray, formerly some type of white. The parts of the walls that were visible behind the junk were an ugly green and badly scuffed, scratched, and scraped. Once we could see the floors, we realized that they were hardwood, but full of gouges with any finish completely worn away. We had a big job in front of us, but we were up to it.

We got to work, emptying the room and scrubbing it from top to bottom. We resanded the floor and applied several coats of polyethylene to it. Cleaning and sanding were the worst parts of the job, and we were all covered in dust and grime, sneezing constantly. Next, we used spackle to smoothe the wall surfaces, and then painted them a calming blue. We repaired the woodwork and painted it. We decided on a mural image, and one volunteer brought in a screen to project the image on the wall. We painted the image. As a final step, an electrician came and installed donated computers that people can use to communicate, find out about resources, find jobs, and so on.

When we were done, the storage room was truly transformed. All clutter and junk were gone, leaving a clean, open space. The walls were sky blue, perfectly clean, and the ugly pipe, painted the same blue, blended in with the walls. The red oak floors gleamed and were covered with a beautiful brown and beige Oriental carpet donated to our effort. Tables were set up for computers and conversations. We were proudest of the wonderful and comforting mural, which looked as if it had been painted by a professional. Transforming this room gave me a lot in return for my effort: a sense of contribution beyond myself, teamwork, pride, paying it forward, and a chance to help others. It helped me as a person and connected me with people who are great.

ASSIGNMENT: Choose one of the following topics, and write a comparison/contrast paragraph or essay. Work either on your own or with a partner.

- Participate in a cleanup effort in your community and then compare and contrast how the area looked before the cleanup with how it looked afterward.

- Help a friend paint a room or decorate a space. Compare and contrast the appearance before and after.

- Contact a hospital or nursing home about decorating for an upcoming holiday. Compare and contrast how the place looks with and without decorations.

TIP For more on connecting to community, visit **bedfordstmartins.com/ realwriting**.

. . . .

ASSIGNMENT 3 Writing in the Real World / Solving a Problem

Read Appendix B, "Solving Problems."

> **PROBLEM:** You need a new smart phone, and you want the best one for your money. Before ordering, you do some research.

ASSIGNMENT: Working with a group or on your own, consult the rating chart on page 236 or an online one. Identify three points that are contrasted in the chart (or that you identify on your own) and make notes about why each point is important to you. Then, choose a model based on these points. Finally, write a contrast paragraph or essay that explains your decision and contrasts your choice versus another model. Make sure to support your choice based on the three points you considered.

TEAMWORK For more detailed guidance on group work, see *Practical Suggestions*.

RESOURCES Reproducible peer-review guides for different kinds of papers are available in *Additional Resources*.

. . . .

1 Samsung   3 Motorola   5 Pantech   7 Palm   10 Apple   11 T-Mobile

Ratings Smart phones

In performance order.

Legend: ● Excellent | ◔ Very good | ○ Good | ◑ Fair | ● Poor

Recommendation	Rank	Brand & model	Price	Size	Operating system	Overall score	Listening	Talking	Phone	PDA	Talk time (hr.)	Sensitivity	Editing	Keyboard	Touch screen	Broadband speed	Wi-Fi	Voice command	Memory-card slot	GPS navigation	Camera (MP)	Bluetooth, data	Bluetooth, stereo
✓	1	**Samsung** Blackjack II (AT&T)	$100	M	W	69	○	○	◔	●	8	◔	•	F		high			•	•	1.9	•	•
	2	**T-Mobile** Wing	300	M	W	66	◑	○	◔	●	7¾	◔	•	F	•	low			•		1.9	•	•
✓	3	**Motorola** Moto Q 9c (Verizon) Alltel $80, Sprint-Nextel $100	150	M	W	65	○	○	◔	●	5¼	◔	•	F		high			•	•	1.3f	•	•
✓	4	**T-Mobile** Shadow	100	S	W	65	◑	◔	◔	●	6¾	○	•	C		low			•		1.9	•	•
✓	5	**Pantech** Duo (AT&T)	80	S	W	63	◑	○	◔	●	5½	○	•	F		high			•		1.3	•	•
	6	**AT&T** Tilt	200	M	W	62	○	○	◔	●	5¼	◔	•	F	•	high			•	•	3.1	•	•
✓	7	**Palm** Centro 685 (AT&T)	100	S	P	61	○	○	◔	◔	4	◔	•	F	•	low			•		1.3	•	•
	8	**Palm** Treo 800w (Sprint-Nextel)	250	M	W	61	○	○	◔	●	3¾	◔	•	F	•	high	•		•	•	1.9	•	•
	9	**Palm** Treo 755P (Sprint-Nextel) Alltel $100	200	M	P	61	○	○	◔	◔	4¾	○	•	F	•	high			•		1.3	•	•
✓	10	**Apple** iPhone 3G (8 GB) (AT&T) Apple iPhone 3G (16 GB) $300	200	M	M	61	◑	◔	◔	◔	6¼	◔		V	•	high	•			•	1.9	•	
✓	11	**T-Mobile** G1	180	M	A	61	◑	◔	◔	◔	6	◔		F	•	high	•	•	•	•	3.1	•	
	12	**T-Mobile** Sidekick LX	200	L	D	59	◑	◔	◔	○	7¼	◔		F		low				•	1.3f		
✓	13	**BlackBerry** Pearl 8120 (T-Mobile) AT&T $200	150	S	B	58	○	○	◔	◔	5½	◔	•	C		low			•	•	1.9f	•	•
	14	**Palm** Treo 700 WX (Sprint-Nextel) ① Alltel $100, Verizon $300	–	M	W	58	○	○	◔	●	4¼	○	•	F	•	high			•		1.3	•	•
	15	**T-Mobile** Dash	100	M	W	58	◑	○	◔	○	6	◔		F		low	•			•	1.3	•	•
	16	**BlackBerry** Curve 8330 (Sprint-Nextel) Alltel $200, Verizon $100	100	M	B	56	◑	◔	◔	○	4½	◔		F		high	•	•	•	•	1.9f	•	
✓	17	**Palm** Centro 690 (Sprint-Nextel) Verizon $100	100	S	P	56	○	○	◔	●	3¾	◔	•	F	•	high			•		1.3	•	
	18	**HTC** Touch Diamond (Sprint-Nextel)	250	S	W	56	○	◔	◔	●	3¾	◔		V	•	high	•		•	•	3.1	•	•
	19	**HTC** Touch (Sprint-Nextel) Alltel $130	100	S	W	56	○	○	◔	●	3¾	○	•	V	•	high			•	•	1.9	•	•
✓	20	**BlackBerry** Pearl 8130 (Sprint-Nextel) Alltel $80	130	S	B	52	○	○	◔	○	3¾	◔		C		high	•	•	•	•	1.9f	•	
	21	**BlackBerry** 8830 (Verizon) Alltel $250	150	M	B	52	○	○	○	◔	4½	○		F		high	•	•			•	•	

① Discontinued by Sprint-Nextel, though still available from the other listed carriers.

CHECKLIST: HOW TO WRITE COMPARISON AND CONTRAST	
STEPS	**HOW TO DO THE STEPS**
	• Think about what you want to compare or contrast and your purpose for doing so.
...lore your	• Choose specific subjects to compare/contrast, making sure they have enough in common to result in a meaningful paper. • Write down some ideas about the subjects.

CHECKLIST: HOW TO WRITE COMPARISON AND CONTRAST

STEPS	HOW TO DO THE STEPS
☐ Write a topic sentence (paragraph) or thesis statement (essay). See Chapter 5.	• Include the subjects and your main point about them. • Make sure the sentence serves your purpose.
☐ Support your main point. See Chapter 6.	• Prewrite to find similarities or differences. Try making a two-column list (see p. 224). • Add details that will help your readers see the similarity or difference in each point of comparison or contrast.
☐ Make a plan. See Chapter 7.	• Decide whether to use point-by-point or whole-to-whole organization. • Make an outline with the points of comparison or contrast in the order you want to present them.
☐ Write a draft. See Chapter 8.	**FOR A PARAGRAPH** • Write a paragraph that includes a topic sentence and detailed points of comparison or contrast. Use complete sentences. **FOR AN ESSAY** • Consider using one of the introduction types in Chapter 8. Include your thesis statement in your introduction. • Using your plan, write topic sentences for each of the points of comparison or contrast. • Write paragraphs with details on each point of comparison/contrast. **FOR PARAGRAPHS AND ESSAYS** • Write a conclusion that reminds readers of your main point and makes an observation based on what you have written. • Write a title that previews your main point but does not repeat it.
☐ Revise your draft, making at least four improvements. See Chapter 9.	• Get feedback from others using the peer-review guide for comparison and contrast at **bedfordstmartins.com/realwriting**. • Reread to make sure that all points of comparison or contrast are parallel and relate to your main point. • Add details to show readers similarities or differences. • Add transitions to move readers from one point or subject to the next.
☐ Edit your revised draft. See Parts 4 through 7.	• Correct errors in grammar, spelling, word use, and punctuation.
☐ Ask yourself:	• Does my paper include the Four Basics of Good Comparison and Contrast (p. 221)? • What is the best part of my paper? • Is this the best I can do?

Chapter Review

1. What are the Four Basics of Good Comparison and Contrast?
It uses subjects that have enough in common to be compared/ contrasted in a useful way. It serves a purpose—either to help readers make a decision or to help them understand the subjects. It presents several important, parallel points of comparison/contrast. It arranges points in a logical order.

2. The topic sentence (paragraph) or thesis statement (essay) in comparison/ contrast should include what two basic parts? *the subjects being compared or contrasted and the main point of the comparison/contrast*

3. What are the two ways to organize comparison/contrast? *point-by-point and whole-to-whole*

4. In your own words, explain what these organizations are. *Answers will vary.*

5. Write sentences using the following vocabulary words: *liaison, amenities, poised, perceptions, durable. Answers will vary.*

LEARNING JOURNAL Reread your idea journal entry (p. 224) on the differences between men and women. Make another entry on the same topic, using what you have learned about comparison and contrast.

> **reflect** Write for two minutes about the elements of a good comparison/contrast.

**Spot and Start
Comparison Assignments in Other Courses**

Spot

In college, at work, and in your everyday life, you use comparison and contrast in many situations (see p. 223). The assignment or question might use the words *compare and contrast*, but it might also use words such as *discuss similarities and differences, how is X like (or unlike) Y?*, or *what do X and Y have in common?* Also, assignments may use only the word *compare*.

Start

Ask yourself

1. How are the subjects alike or different? Make a list.
2. What examples will show readers similarities or differences?
3. Should I use point-by-point or whole-to-whole organization?

YOU KNOW THIS

You consider causes and effects every day:

- You explain to your boss what caused you to be late.
- You consider the possible effects of calling in sick.

write for two minutes about what a cause is and what an effect is.

17

Cause and Effect

Writing That Explains Reasons or Results

Understand What Cause and Effect Are

A **cause** is what made an event happen. An **effect** is what happens as a result of the event.

■■ Four Basics of Good Cause and Effect
■■

1 The main point reflects the writer's purpose: to explain causes, effects, or both.

2 If the purpose is to explain causes, it presents real causes.

3 If the purpose is to explain effects, it presents real effects.

4 It gives readers detailed examples or explanations of the causes or effects.

TEACHING TIP Explain to students the differences between *effect* (noun) and *affect* (verb).

In the following paragraph, each number and color corresponds to one of the Four Basics of Good Cause and Effect.

1 Although the thought of writing may be a source of stress for college students, researchers have recently found that it can also be a potent stress reliever. In the winter of 2008, during a time when many people catch colds or the flu or experience other symptoms of ill health, two psychologists conducted an experiment with college students to find out if writing could have positive effects on their minds and/or their bodies. After gathering a large group of college students, a mix of ages, genders, and backgrounds, the psychologists explained the task. The students were asked to write for only two minutes, on two consecutive

days, about their choice of three different kinds of experiences: a traumatic experience, a positive experience, or a neutral experience (something routine that happened). The psychologists did not give more detailed directions about the kinds of experiences, basically just a bad one, a good one, or one neither good nor bad. A month after collecting the students' writing, the psychologists interviewed each of the students and asked them to report any symptoms of ill health, such as colds, flu, headaches, or lack of sleep. 3 What the psychologists found was quite surprising. 4 Those students who had written about emotionally charged topics, either traumatic or positive, all reported that they had been in excellent health, avoiding the various illnesses that had been circulating in the college and the larger community. The students who had chosen to write about routine, day-to-day things that didn't matter to them reported the ill health effects that were typical of the season, such as colds, flu, poor sleep, or coughing. From these findings, the two psychologists reported that writing about things that are important to people actually has a positive impact on their health. Their experiment suggests the value to people of regularly recording their reactions to experiences, in a journal of some sort. If writing can keep you well, it is worth a good try. The mind-body connection continues to be studied because clearly each affects the other.

TEACHING TIP Have students try the experiment, or just have them write about either negative or positive experiences.

STUDENT PHOTO

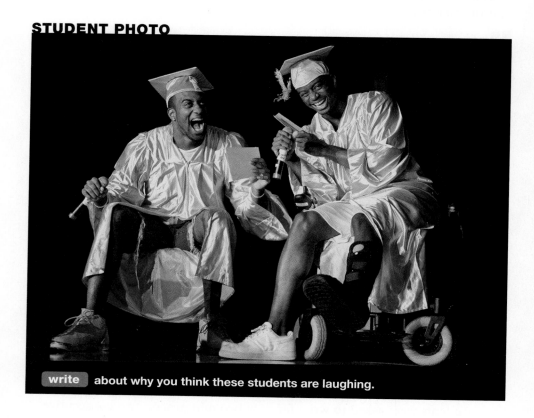

This photograph was taken by student Kate Napier of two senior University of North Carolina basketball players watching a video of a game.

write   about why you think these students are laughing.

When you are writing about causes and effects, make sure that you do not confuse something that happened before an event with a real cause or something that happened after an event with a real effect. For example, if you have pizza on Monday and get the flu on Tuesday, eating the pizza is not the cause of the flu just because it happened before you got the flu, nor is the flu the effect of eating pizza—you just happened to get the flu the next day.

Jim Rice of Quinsigamond Community College helps his students visualize the cause/effect relationship by suggesting that they think of three linked rings:

POSSIBLE CAUSES

Not studying

Not going to class

Not doing assignments

Not taking quizzes and tests

Not getting help with problems and questions

Not asking questions if material is not understood

EVENT/SITUATION

Failing a course

POSSIBLE EFFECTS

Losing value of tuition already paid

Losing student aid

Getting discouraged

Dropping out

Feeling angry or depressed

Staying in same rut

You use cause and effect in many situations:

COLLEGE   In a nutrition course, you are asked to identify the consequences (effects) of poor nutrition.

WORK   Sales are down in your group, and you have to explain the cause.

EVERYDAY   You explain to your child why a certain behavior is not
LIFE   acceptable by warning him or her about the negative effects of that behavior.

Main Point in Cause and Effect

The **main point** in cause and effect reflects your purpose. For example, your purpose might be to explain the effects of Hurricane Katrina on the nation's economy.

Hurricane Katrina had devastating effects on the national economy.

To help you discover your main point, complete the following sentence:

MAIN POINT IN   **(Your topic) causes (or caused)....**
CAUSE AND EFFECT   **(Your topic) resulted in (or results in)....**

IDEA JOURNAL Write about a time when something you did caused someone to be happy or unhappy.

The topic sentence (paragraph) or thesis statement (essay) usually includes the topic and an indication of whether you will present causes, effects, or both.

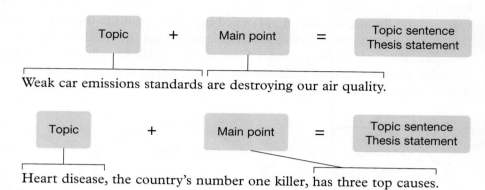

Weak car emissions standards are destroying our air quality.

Heart disease, the country's number one killer, has three top causes.

PRACTICE 1   Choosing Direct Causes and Effects

For each of the situations that follow, create a ring diagram. Write three possible causes in the left ring and three possible effects in the right one. There is no one correct set of answers, but your choices should be logical, and you should be prepared to explain how your answers were direct causes and effects. *Answers will vary.*

EXAMPLE:

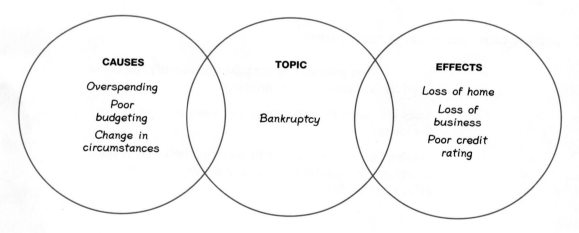

1. Topic: A fire in someone's home

2. Topic: An "A" in this course

3. Topic: A car accident

PRACTICE 2   Stating Your Main Point

For each of the topics in Practice 1, review your causes and effects, and write a sentence that states a main point. First, look at the following example and at the list of causes for the topic (bankruptcy) in the example in Practice 1.

EXAMPLE:

Topic: Bankruptcy

Main point: *Although many different kinds of people declare bankruptcy each year, the causes of bankruptcy are often the same.*

1.   Topic: A fire in someone's home

Main point: *Answers will vary.*

2.   Topic: An "A" in this course

Main point: _____

3.   Topic: A car accident

Main point: _____

. . . .

Support in Cause and Effect

In cause/effect writing, **support** consists of detailed examples or explanations of the causes or effects.

Your reader may not immediately understand how one event or situation caused another or what particular effects resulted from a certain event or situation. You need to give specific examples and details to explain the relationship.

. . . .

PRACTICE 3   Giving Examples and Details

Look at your answers to Practices 1 and 2. Choose two causes or two effects for each of the three items and give an example or detail that explains each cause or effect.

EXAMPLE:

Topic: Bankruptcy

Cause 1: *Overspending* _____

   Example/Detail: *bought a leather jacket I liked and charged it*

Cause 2: *Poor budgeting* _____

   Example/Detail: *never tracking monthly expenses versus monthly income*

1.   Topic: A fire in someone's home

Cause/Effect 1: *Answers will vary.* _____

   Example/Detail: _____

         Cause/Effect 2: _____

           Example/Detail: _____

2.   Topic: An "A" in this course

         Cause/Effect 1: _____

           Example/Detail: _____

         Cause/Effect 2: _____

           Example/Detail: _____

3.   Topic: A car accident

         Cause/Effect 1: _____

           Example/Detail: _____

         Cause/Effect 2: _____

           Example/Detail: _____

Organization in Cause and Effect

TIP For more on the different orders of organization, see pages 80–82.

Cause and effect can be organized in a variety of ways, depending on your purpose.

MAIN POINT	PURPOSE	ORGANIZATION
Hurricane Katrina had devastating effects on the national economy.	to explain Katrina's effects on the U.S. economy	order of importance, saving the most important effect for last
Hurricane Katrina caused devastation throughout New Orleans.	to describe the destruction	space order
Hurricane Katrina destroyed New Orleans in two distinct stages, first as the storm ripped through the city and then when the levees broke.	to describe the effects of the storm over time	time order

NOTE: If you are explaining both causes and effects, you would present the causes first and the effects later.

    Use **transitions** to move readers smoothly from one cause to another, from one effect to another, or from causes to effects. Because cause and effect can use any method of organization depending on your purpose, the following list shows just a few of the transitions that you might use.

Common Cause and Effect Transitions

also	more important/serious cause/effect
as a result	most important/serious cause/effect
because	one cause/effect; another cause/effect
the final cause/effect	a primary cause; a secondary cause
the first, second, third cause/effect	a short-term effect; a long-term effect

PRACTICE 4 Using Transitions in Cause and Effect

Read the paragraph that follows, and fill in the blanks with transitions.
Answers may vary. Possible answers are shown.

Recently, neuroscientists, who have long been skeptical about meditation,[1] confirm that it has numerous positive outcomes. _One, The first_ is that people who meditate can maintain their focus and attention longer than people who do not. This ability to stay "on task" was demonstrated among students who had been practicing meditation for several weeks. They reported more effective studying and learning because they were able to pay attention. _Another, A second_ positive outcome was the ability to relax on command. While meditating, people learned how to reduce their heart rates and blood pressure so that they could relax more easily in all kinds of situations. _A third, The most important_ outcome was a thickening of the brain's cortex. Meditators' cortexes were uniformly thicker than nonmeditators'. Because the cortex enables memorization and the production of new ideas, this last outcome is especially exciting, particularly in fighting Alzheimer's disease and other dementias.

Read and Analyze Cause and Effect

Reading examples of cause and effect will help you write your own. The first example in this section is a Profile of Success from the real world of teaching and entertainment. La Q Booker is a rap singer. Her profile shows an example of her early rap, written for her students while she was a teacher. She

READING SELECTIONS For further examples of and activities for cause and effect, see Chapter 49.

1. **meditation:** the practice of focusing the mind through exercises or other means.

found that sometimes her students would listen more carefully to rap than to spoken advice.

The second and third examples are both student writing, first a cause/effect paragraph and then a cause/effect essay. As you read, pay attention to the vocabulary, and answer the questions in the margin. They will help you read the piece critically.

PROFILE OF SUCCESS

Mary LaCue Booker
Singer, Actor
(stage name: La Q)

Cause and Effect in the Real World

The following profile shows how a rap singer uses cause and effect in her work.

Background   I grew up in a small town in Georgia but always had big dreams that I followed. Those dreams included becoming a nurse, a teacher, and then a singer and an actor. Before becoming a nurse and teacher, I went to college, studying both nursing and psychology. Later, I followed my dream of performing and left Georgia to attend the competitive American Academy of Dramatic Arts in Los Angeles.

I returned to Georgia and combined teaching and performance as chair of the Fine Arts Department at Columbia Middle School. I wrote rap songs for my students, and my first one, "School Rules," was an immediate hit in Atlanta. I now have three CDs and acted in the movie *We Must Go Forward*, about African American history. In addition to performing, I also am busy giving motivational speeches.

Degrees/College(s)   A.A., DeKalb College; B.S., Brenau Women's College; M.Ed., Cambridge College

Writing at work   When I taught, I wrote lesson plans, reports for students, and communications with parents. Now, I write song lyrics, speeches, and screenplays. I believe writing is critical. I write from the heart, and it is a good outlet for my emotions. Sometimes, I freewrite around one word, like *mischievous*, which is the name of my new CD.

RESOURCES For a discussion of how to use the profiles in Part 2, see *Practical Suggestions*.

How La Q uses cause and effect   Many of my songs and speeches are about causes and effects, like the effects of how we act or love or what causes pain or happiness. I wrote "School Rules" for my students, who did not listen to regular rules but would listen to a rap song about them.

La Q's Cause and Effect

Following are some lyrics from "School Rules."

> *Now get this, now get this, now get this.*
> If ya wanna be cool, obey the rules
> Cause if ya don't, it's your future you lose.

I'm a school teacher from a rough school.
I see students every day breakin' the rules.
Here comes a new boy with a platinum grill
Makin' trouble, ringin' the fire drill.

There goes anotha' fool wanna run the school,
Breakin' all the damn school rules.
Runnin' in the halls, writin' graffiti on the walls,
Tellin' a lie without blinkin' an eye,
Usin' profanity, pleadin' insanity,
Callin' names, causin' pain,
Joinin' gangs like it's fame,
Dissin' the teacha and each otha.
Regardless of color, they're all sistas and brothas.

Now get this, now get this, now get this, now get this.
Boys and girls are skippin' class,
Cause they late with no hall pass.
They wanna have their say, and that's okay,
But they're outta their minds if they wanna have their way.

Now get this, now get this, now get this.
If ya wanna be free, school's not the place ta be.
But if ya wanna degree, you gotta feel me.
So if you wanna be cool, obey the rules
Cause if ya don't, it's your future you lose.

---

1. What is La Q's **purpose**? *to tell students that breaking the rules will prevent them from getting a degree*

2. What are the **effects** of breaking the rules? *not getting a degree, losing your future*

3. Underline the **causes** that lead to these effects.

4. With a partner, or as a class, translate this rap into formal English.

TIP For more on using formal English, see Chapter 3.

Student Cause / Effect Paragraph

Caitlin Prokop

A Difficult Decision with a Positive Outcome

Caitlin Prokop is currently pursuing a degree in elementary education at the University of Hawaii. She is interested in writing about politics, family, and personal experience and was inspired to write her essay by her parents and their life choices. Caitlin often produces several drafts of her work and understands the balance between inspiration and revision in writing. Of writing, she says, "Follow what the brain is telling the hand. Let it flow. If you cannot write about the topic that is given, put yourself in someone else's shoes and then write. Let your thoughts flow; then, revise and edit to get the finished copy."

Vocabulary development

Underline these words as you read Caitlin's paragraph.

accompany: to be with; to go with

cherish: to value highly

When my mother made the decision to move back to New York, I made the choice to move in with my dad so that I could finish high school. This decision affected me in a positive way because I graduated with my friends, built a better relationship with my father, and had the chance to go to college without leaving home. Graduating with my friends was very important to me because I have known most of them since we were in kindergarten. It was a journey through childhood that we had shared, and I wanted to finish it with them. Accomplishing the goal of graduating from high school with my close friends, those who accompanied me through school, made me a stronger and more confident person. Another good outcome of my difficult decision was the relationship I built with my dad. We never saw eye-to-eye when I lived with both of my parents. For example, we stopped talking for five months because I always sided against him with my mom. Living together for the past five years has made us closer, and I cherish that closeness we have developed. Every Thursday is our day, a day when we talk to each other about what is going on in our lives, so that we will never again have a distant relationship. A third good outcome of my decision is that I can go to Brevard Community College, which is right down the street. In high school, I had thought I would want to go away to college, but then I realized I would miss my home. By staying here, I have the opportunity to attend a wonderful college that is preparing me for transferring to a four-year college and finding a good career. I have done some research and believe I would like to become a police officer, a nurse, or a teacher. Through the school, I can do volunteer work in each of these areas. Right now, I am leaning toward becoming a teacher, based on my volunteer work in a kindergarten class. There,

I can explore what grades I want to teach. In every way, I believe that my difficult decision was the right one, giving me many opportunities that I would not have had if I had moved to a new and unfamiliar place.

1. Double-underline the **topic sentence**.

2. Does Caitlin write about causes or effects? _____*effects*_____ How many does she present? _____*three*_____

3. Circle the **transitions** Caitlin uses to move readers from one point to the next.

4. Does Caitlin's paragraph include the Four Basics of Good Cause and Effect? Why or why not? *Yes. Answers will vary.* _____

5. Have you made a difficult decision that turned out to be a good one? Why and how? *Answers will vary.* _____

Student Cause / Effect Essay

Kimberly Sharpe

Graduation Day: A Life-Changing Experience

Kimberly Sharpe is currently working toward a degree in hospitality management from Owens Community College in Ohio and plans to attend Le Cordon Bleu in Las Vegas, one of the best culinary arts schools in the world. As a writer, she enjoys "writing about what I know best—my life and interests," which in her case include topics relating to food. She often reads cookbooks, food magazines, and restaurant critic articles and hopes to one day write about food and restaurants for a newspaper. In advice to other student writers, Kimberly says, "Have confidence in your own abilities, and repeatedly read your essay to yourself and others to find any mistakes or ideas that are unclear."

When I was in high school, I never realized how important it was for me to graduate. So, when I found myself pregnant at seventeen, I chose to drop out of school and raise my child. It was not until I turned thirty that I realized I should have stayed in school and graduated. With that thought, and my boyfriend constantly nagging me to get a GED, I decided to go back to school. After a lot of studying and taking the overwhelming two-day GED test, I received my diploma in the mail. That day changed my life forever. It was then that I realized that I was finally going to receive my diploma in

TIP For advice on building your vocabulary, visit the *Real Writing Student Center* at **bedfordstmartins.com/realwriting**.

Vocabulary development

Underline these words as you read Kimberly's essay.

GED: general equivalency diploma
obtaining: receiving; getting
deafening: overly loud
tradition: a custom; something that is handed from generation to generation
abundance: plenty
impact: effect
plead: to beg

1

PREDICT From the title, do you predict that Kimberly will write about causes, effects, or both?

_____

_____

front of my family and friends. In addition to obtaining a GED, I could also obtain a better job. Furthermore, having a GED permitted me to start attending college, something that I have always wanted to do. Another wonderful thing that happened was how differently people looked at me. However, the best part of achieving my diploma is the inspiration that it gave to my children. Passing the GED test and graduating have changed the way I view the importance of a good education.

TEACHING TIP Point out to students how this essay combines both cause/effect and narration.

A few days after I received my GED diploma in the mail, I received a   2
phone call from my GED teacher. She said, "We are having a graduation ceremony for the 2004 GED graduates on December 17 at 5:00 P.M." I hung up the phone feeling as if I was on top of the world. I sent invitations announcing the day of my graduation to all of my family and close friends. The day I had been waiting for finally arrived. I felt both excited and nervous while I waited for the announcer to call my name. I peeked around the corner and could see the excitement on my family's and friends' faces. When the announcer called my name, I felt extremely proud of myself. As I walked across the stage, I could hear my family and friends screaming, "Go Kim!" My eyes filled with tears when the superintendent of the Toledo Public Schools placed the long-awaited diploma in my hand. The audience applause was deafening as all of us graduates walked out of the room. Tears of joy streamed down my cheeks as we walked into the hallway. We threw our caps up with pride, in the tradition of all graduates.

TIP For tools to use in getting a job, visit the *Real Writing Student Center* at **bedfordstmartins.com/ realwriting**.

A few days after my graduation ceremony, I drove around town filling   3
out applications for better jobs. When I returned home that evening, I was pleasantly surprised to find three messages from employers wanting to interview me. I returned each of the calls and set up interviews. I felt relieved each time an employer asked if I had a diploma, and I could proudly respond, "Yes, I do!" I found myself for the first time being able to pick which job I wanted, rather than taking any job I could get. I started a job with better pay just a few short weeks after my graduation.

One month after my graduation, I drove to Owens Community College. I walked into College Hall feeling scared and confused. After asking a woman in the hall where to sign up, I headed for the Student Services office. A nice young woman behind the desk told me what I needed to do to finally start my college career. My confidence grew as I went through the steps of enrolling in college. Four weeks after I started college, I passed my math class twelve weeks ahead of time. I felt an abundance of pride when I told my family of my accomplishment. I am almost through the first semester now, and college is sometimes very difficult. However, I have found that college is also very rewarding.

Getting more respect from the people around me is another thing I **5** have noticed. Friends and coworkers around me appreciate the goals I am working so hard on. Each time we talk, my friends ask, "How is school?" I would reply, "School is great!" They would follow by expressing their pride in me. The day my boyfriend asked me to marry him was yet another dream come true. I have never been married, and I am deeply in love with my boyfriend, so his proposal was wonderful. Even though I was completely shocked by his proposal, I leaped into his arms with excitement and said, "YES!" When I asked him later what changed his earlier negative opinion of marriage, he replied, "I want to marry a woman who cares about our future and will work hard to have a better life."

A few months after my graduation, I learned the enormous impact it **6** had on my children. My son, who had all failing grades and terrible behavior in school, was suddenly doing better. He now has all passing grades and has not been in any trouble for months. My daughter brought up her failing grades enough to be on the honor roll at her school. And my stepdaughter, who was considering dropping out of college, decided to stay in school. My children have all expressed to me how proud of me they are. I am very proud of myself for setting a good example for my children. They see that education is important because of the example that I set for them.

I learned and accomplished so much when I finally walked into the **7** GED class for the first time. I am a 2004 Toledo Public Schools Adult Education Graduate. I now have a better-paying job, and I am finally attending college as I always wanted to. I am also planning my wedding to the man of my dreams. My children are proud of me and are inspired to do better in their own studies. My education has made my life so much better. I have more confidence and pride in myself than I ever had before. I have learned that a good education is very important. I would plead with anyone who has quit school to return and graduate, because when I reflect back on how I used to feel about myself and my education, I know I was wrong. The best decision I ever made was going back to school; it has changed my life forever.

CRITICAL THINKING: READING

1. Double-underline the **thesis statement**.

2. Does Kimberly's essay follow the Four Basics of Good Cause and Effect? Why or why not? _Answers will vary._

3. Which of Kimberly's examples has the most impact on you? Why? _Answers will vary._

REFLECT Write about a time when people were respectful of you, and why.

SUMMARIZE What are three effects of Kimberly's getting a GED?

_____

_____

_____

TIP For reading advice, see Chapter 2.

4. In your own words, summarize some of the major effects of Kimberly's choice to go back to school. *Answers will vary but might include GED, college, respect, children and boyfriend being proud of her.*

Cause and Effect at a Glance

↓

Topic sentence (paragraph) or thesis statement (essay)
Indicates causes, effects, or both

↓

Cause 1 or effect 1
Detailed explanation or example of the first cause or effect

↓

Cause 2 or effect 2
Detailed explanation or example of the second cause or effect

↓

Cause 3 or effect 3
Detailed explanation or example of the third cause or effect

↓

Conclusion
Reminds readers of your main point and makes an observation about it based on what you have written

ESL Suggest that students write about the cause or effect of a cultural misunderstanding.

CRITICAL THINKING: WRITING

Choose one of the following topics, and respond in a paragraph or an essay.

1. What effects does being a student have on your life right now?

2. What do you think the future effects of having a college education will be?

3. Write about a major event in your life and either the causes or effects of it.

4. What made you decide to come to college?

Write Your Own Cause and Effect

In this section, you will write your own cause and effect based on one of the three assignments that follow. Use the following tools to help you:

1. Review the Four Basics of Good Cause and Effect (p. 239).

2. Use "Cause and Effect at a Glance" as a basic organizer.

3. Use the Checklist: How to Write Cause and Effect (pp. 255–56) as you write and revise.

ASSIGNMENT 1   Writing about College, Work, and Everyday Life

Write a cause/effect paper on one of the following topics or one of your own. For ideas, see your responses to the photograph (p. 240) and the idea journal (p. 241).

COLLEGE
- Causes/effects of not studying for an exam
- Effects of getting a college degree
- Causes of your interest in a particular course or major

WORK
- Causes of frequent absences
- Causes/effects of stress at work
- Causes of job satisfaction/dissatisfaction

EVERYDAY LIFE
- Causes/effects of not getting enough sleep
- Causes/effects of a difficult decision
- Causes/effects of a major change in your life

ASSIGNMENT 2   Writing about Connections

Read the following account of Shawn Elswick before doing the assignment below.

COMMUNITY MATTERS

Shawn Elswick

Shawn was the victim of an abusive relationship with her husband. On a cold winter night, when she was pregnant with her first child at seventeen, Shawn's husband dumped scalding coffee on her head and threw her out of the house. Then, he kicked her in the stomach, causing her to go into premature labor. The abuse, both verbal and physical, continued, but like many women, she did not leave right away. Most of the abuse was a constant verbal attack, which she did not even recognize as abuse. She left him once after a physical attack and went to a shelter, but returned, not sure she could make it on her own. Finally, after her husband attacked her with a sledgehammer and she was certain she would die, she took her three children and again escaped to the shelter.

At the shelter, she realized she had to put together a life for herself and her children. She started taking classes at Mott Community College and wrote a paper for her English class about the abuse that her grandmother had been a victim of and that she herself had experienced. Her teacher put Shawn in touch with a person at the college who, through a grant, wanted to start an on-campus organization for abuse victims. With that person, Shawn began the 3P Club, named after the national program "Prevent, Protect, and Prosecute Violence against Women." The interest was immediate, and the club meets weekly, providing a safe environment to talk and learn about abuse, its causes and effects, and how to help women. The club also organizes fund-raising events for domestic abuse causes and shelters. In the photo on page 254, Shawn is shown with T-shirts about abuse that members made and sold. Shawn recently graduated from Mott CC with a degree in psychology and plans to attend the University of Michigan at Flint, where she will start another 3P Club.

Shawn now gives many presentations to educate people about abuse, and sometimes the police even call her for advice. She started 3P because she wanted to help people like herself survive and because she wanted to give back to the community. In the process, she has raised her own self-esteem and restored the confidence that was taken from her by years of abuse.

The following is part of a piece Shawn wrote, titled "The Causes of Abuse."

Boom! All I could see were stars flashing through every ray of light that hit my eyes. My husband had just punched me in the head so hard that my neck was sprained. Then, the verbal attacks started. Who could I turn to for help? I had three children and no family support. I was a prisoner in my home. My ex-husband, Jon, controlled every aspect of my life, including timing my visits to the grocery store and telling me where I must park. I could not understand: How could Jon say he loved me, yet hurt me so badly, again and again? Now, I have come to understand some of what caused the torment that permanently scarred his children and me.

One cause of abuse is that the abuser often has unrealistic expectations of his partner. The partner should always be happy and attentive, keep a neat home, and so on. When the reality differs from the abuser's expectation, he is enraged, furious, and the violence follows. The rage explodes without reason or proportion; the abuser is out of control.

(continued)

RESOURCES For advice on "Writing about Connections," see *Practical Suggestions*.

Another cause of abuse is that the abuser needs to feel in control. If I did not follow my husband's directions, there would be severe consequences. Or if something happened at work that Jon did not like and could not control, he would find a reason to be furious at me. There was really nothing I did or could do to prevent the abuse: It did not have much to do with me. However, I put myself and my children in danger by staying, and it took patience and careful planning to escape — we were risking our lives if he caught us.

The most common cause of abuse is that it runs in families, and those who abuse were often abused themselves. . . .

No one deserves abuse. The effects are long-term and painful. It takes a lot of patience and strength to break free from the chains. Therefore, I have dedicated my life to helping victims become knowledgeable, safe, and healthy. Using the tragic events that have occurred in my life, along with my education, I hope to give back what was given to us: freedom from abuse.

TIP For more on connecting to community, visit **bedfordstmartins.com/ realwriting**.

ASSIGNMENT: Choose one of the following topics, and write a cause/effect paragraph or essay. Work either on your own or with a partner.

- Either go online and research the causes and effects of domestic abuse, or interview someone knowledgeable or someone you know who has been abused, either physically or verbally. Some Web sites you might consult are www.TheresNoExcuse.com, www.endabuse.org, and www.EndDomestic Abuse.org. Then, write about your findings.

- Arrange to spend a few hours at a local soup kitchen or food pantry or some other program that you have some interest in. (You can use a search engine to find volunteer opportunities in your area.) Write about how the experience affected you.

- Interview a student involved in the college community. What caused the student to get involved? How has the involvement affected him or her?

- Write about a time that you joined a group, or quit one. Explain why.

ASSIGNMENT 3   Writing in the Real World/Solving a Problem

Read Appendix B, "Solving Problems."

PROBLEM: You have learned of a cheating ring at school that uses cell phones to give test answers to students taking the test. A few students in your math class, who are also friends of yours, think this is a great idea and are planning to cheat on a test you will be taking next week. You decide not to participate, partly because you fear getting caught, but also because you think cheating is wrong. Now you want to convince your friends not to cheat, because you don't want them to get caught and possibly kicked out of school. How do you make your case?

ASSIGNMENT: Working in a group or on your own, list the various effects of cheating—both immediate and long-term—that you could use to convince your friends. Then, write a cause/effect paragraph or essay that identifies and explains some possible effects of cheating. You might start with this sentence:

RESOURCES Reproducible peer-review guides for different kinds of papers are available in *Additional Resources*.

TEAMWORK For more detailed guidance on group work, see *Practical Suggestions*.

Cheating on tests or papers is not worth the risks.

CHECKLIST: HOW TO WRITE CAUSE AND EFFECT	
STEPS	**HOW TO DO THE STEPS**
☐ Focus.	• Think about your topic and whether you want to describe what caused it or what resulted from it.
☐ Narrow and explore your topic. See Chapter 4.	• Choose a topic that is narrow enough that you can present all important causes and/or effects. • Prewrite to get ideas about the narrowed topic.
☐ Write a topic sentence (paragraph) or thesis statement (essay). See Chapter 5.	• Include your topic and an indication of whether you will discuss causes, effects, or both. *(continued)*

CHECKLIST: HOW TO WRITE CAUSE AND EFFECT

STEPS	HOW TO DO THE STEPS
☐ Support your main point. See Chapter 6.	• Prewrite to find causes and/or effects. • Choose the most significant causes and/or effects. • Explain the causes/effects with detailed examples.
☐ Make a plan. See Chapter 7.	• Arrange the causes/effects in a logical order (space, time, or importance).
☐ Write a draft. See Chapter 8.	**FOR A PARAGRAPH** • Write a paragraph that includes a topic sentence, your cause(s), effect(s), and detailed examples. Use complete sentences.
	FOR AN ESSAY • Consider using one of the introduction types in Chapter 8. Include your thesis statement in your introduction. • Using your plan, write topic sentences for each of the causes or effects. • Write paragraphs with detailed examples of the causes or effects.
	FOR PARAGRAPHS AND ESSAYS • Write a conclusion that reminds readers of your main point and makes an observation based on what you have written. • Write a title that previews your main point but does not repeat it.
☐ Revise your draft, making at least four improvements. See Chapter 9.	• Get feedback from others using the peer-review guide for cause and effect at **bedfordstmartins.com/realwriting**. • Cut anything that does not directly explain what caused or resulted from the situation or event. • Add examples and details that help readers understand the causes and/or effects. • Add transitions to move readers from one cause or effect to the next or from causes to effects.
☐ Edit your revised draft. See Parts 4 through 7.	• Correct errors in grammar, spelling, word use, and punctuation.
☐ Ask yourself:	• Does my paper include the Four Basics of Good Cause and Effect (p. 239)? • What is the weakest part of my paper? • Is this the best I can do?

Chapter Review

1. A cause is *what made an event happen.*

2. An effect is *what happens as a result of the event.*

3. What are the Four Basics of Good Cause and Effect?

   The main point reflects the writer's purpose: to explain causes, effects,
   or both.

   If the purpose is to explain causes, it presents real causes.

   If the purpose is to explain effects, it presents real effects.

   It gives readers detailed examples or explanations of the causes or
   effects.

4. Write sentences using the following vocabulary words: *cherish, obtain,*
   abundant, impact, plead. *Answers will vary.*

LEARNING JOURNAL Reread your idea journal entry (p. 241) on a time you caused someone to be happy or unhappy. Make another entry on this topic, using what you have learned about cause and effect.

reflect Write for two minutes about what you have learned about cause and effect writing.

**Spot and Start Cause and Effect Assignments
in Other Courses**

Spot

In college, at work, and in your everyday life, you need to explain causes and effects in many situations (see p. 241). A cause and effect assignment might use the words *discuss the causes (or effects) of*, but it might also use words such as *explain the results of*, *discuss the impact of*, and *how did X affect Y?*

Start

Ask yourself

1. Am I being asked to write about causes, effects, or both? List the causes, effects, or both, based on your answer.

2. Are my causes or effects really direct causes or effects, or are they just things that happened before or after the event or situation?

3. What examples of the causes and effects will show my readers how one event caused or affected another?

18

Argument

Writing That Persuades

YOU KNOW THIS

You often try to persuade others or make your opinion known:

- You convince your partner that it's better to save some money than to buy a new television.
- You persuade someone to lend you money or let you borrow a car.

write for two minutes about how you convince others to see something your way.

Understand What Argument Is

Argument is writing that takes a position on an issue and gives supporting evidence to persuade someone else to accept, or at least consider, the position. Argument is also used to convince someone to take (or not take) an action.

Argument helps you persuade people to see things your way, or at least to understand your position. Most of us have experienced the feeling of being a helpless victim—just standing by while something that we do not want to happen does occur. Although knowing how to argue will not eliminate all such situations, it will help you to stand up for what you want. You may not always win, but you will sometimes, and you will at least be able to put up a good fight.

■■ Four Basics of Good Argument
■■

1 It takes a strong and definite position.

2 It gives good reasons and supporting evidence to defend the position.

3 It considers opposing views.

4 It has enthusiasm and energy from start to finish.

In the following paragraph, each number and color corresponds to one of the Four Basics of Good Argument.

TEACHING TIP Explain to students that argument is not like bickering or fighting. It is a reasonable defense of a position.

4 Argument is enthusiastic and energetic.

1 The government should not require all citizens, particularly young people, to have health insurance. I am a recent college graduate and have

a decent job, but my company does not provide health insurance. To require me to buy an individual policy is not fair or reasonable. **2** One reason is that such a policy would be expensive and would take most of my income. As someone just starting out in life, my income barely covers my rent and food. If I had to buy health insurance, I would have to take another job, find another roommate, or try to find a cheaper apartment. Another reason is that any policy I could buy would have such a high deductible that I would have to pay most of my own expenses anyway. Most inexpensive policies have deductibles of $250 to $1,000, so I would be paying that on top of a high monthly premium. The most important reason that young people should not be required to buy individual health insurance is that, statistically, we are not likely to need expensive medical treatment. So why should we be expected to pay for it? **3** Although the people who want everyone to have insurance hope that the government plan will provide lower rates for low-income families and children, they haven't considered how such a requirement will penalize the many young people who are just getting started. A new system may be needed, but not one that is unfair to a whole generation of citizens.

STUDENT CARTOON

write Using this picture, write a paragraph or essay starting with the sentence, "The costs of an education are too high."

This drawing is by Josh Ferrin, a student at the University of Utah and winner of the MSNBC Best College Cartoonist of the Year, 2008.

REGGIE HARRIS: As a district recruiter, I give students good reasons to come to Hinds.

(See Reggie Harris's **PROFILE OF SUCCESS** on page 267.)

IDEA JOURNAL Persuade a friend who has lost his job to take a course at your college.

Knowing how to make a good argument is one of the most useful skills you can develop. Consider the following examples:

COLLEGE   You argue for or against makeup exams for students who do not do well the first time.

WORK   You need to leave work an hour early one day a week for twelve weeks to take a course. You persuade your boss to allow you to do so.

EVERYDAY LIFE   You try to negotiate a better price on an item you want to buy.

Main Point in Argument

Your **main point** in argument is the position you take on the issue (or topic) about which you are writing. When you are free to choose an issue, choose something that matters to you. When you are assigned an issue, try to find some part of it that matters to you. You might try starting with a "should" or "should not" sentence:

MAIN POINT IN ARGUMENT   **Young people should/should not be required to buy health insurance.**

If you have trouble seeing how an issue matters, talk about it with a partner or write down ideas about it using the following tips.

TIPS FOR BUILDING ENTHUSIASM AND ENERGY

- Imagine yourself arguing your position with someone who disagrees.
- Imagine that your whole grade rests on persuading your instructor to agree with your position.
- Imagine how this issue could affect you or your family personally.
- Imagine that you are representing a large group of people who care about the issue very much and whose lives will be forever changed by it. It is up to you to win their case.

In argument, the topic sentence (in a paragraph) or thesis statement (in an essay) usually includes the issue/topic and your position about it.

Day-care facilities should be provided at a low cost to employees.

Many good topic sentences or thesis statements in argument use words such as these:

could (not)	must have	ought (not)	should (not)
must (not)	needs	requires	would or may

When you have a statement of your position, try revising it to make it sound stronger, clearer, or more interesting. Here are progressively stronger revisions:

TIP For more on revising, see Chapter 9.

1. Day-care facilities should be provided for employees.
2. Companies should provide day-care facilities at a low cost to employees.
3. Employees are entitled to low-cost, company-sponsored day care.

- -

PRACTICE 1 Writing a Statement of Your Position

Write a statement of your position for each item. *Answers will vary. Possible answers are shown.*

EXAMPLE:

Issue: Prisoners' rights

Position statement: <u>*Prisoners should not have more rights and privileges than law-abiding citizens.*</u>

1. Issue: Lab testing on animals

Position statement: <u>*Animals should continue to be used for lab testing.*</u>

2. Issue: Use of cell phones while driving

Position statement: <u>*Using a cell phone while driving is an individual's decision.*</u>

3. Issue: Athletes' salaries

Position statement: <u>*Limits should be placed on major league baseball players' salaries.*</u>

- -

TEACHING TIP Have students type some keywords about their topic into a search engine (e.g., **www.google.com**)—for instance, *animal testing* and *pros and cons*. Seeing the points others have raised about an issue can help them consider the various sides.

Support in Argument

A strong position must be **supported** with convincing reasons and evidence. Remember that you want to persuade readers that your position is the right one. Use strong reasons and supporting evidence that will be convincing to your audience, consider opposing views, and end on a strong note.

Reasons and Evidence

The primary support for your position is the **reasons** you give. Your reasons need to be supported by **evidence**, such as *facts*, *examples*, and *expert opinions*.

TEACHING TIP Go over the concept of evidence carefully. Students' arguments are often weak because of poor evidence or lack of evidence.

- **FACTS:** Statements or observations that can be proved. Statistics—real numbers from actual studies—can be persuasive factual evidence.

- **EXAMPLES:** Specific information or experiences that support your position.

- **EXPERT OPINIONS:** The opinion of someone who is considered an expert in the area or topic you are exploring in your paper. The person must be known for his or her expertise in your topic. For example, the opinion of the head of the FBI about the benefits of a low-fat diet is not strong evidence. The FBI director is not an expert in the field of nutrition.

In the following examples, a reason and appropriate evidence support each position.

POSITION: It pays to stay in college.

REASON: College graduates generally earn more than people without degrees.

EVIDENCE/FACT: Community-college graduates earn 58 percent more than high-school graduates and 320 percent more than high-school dropouts.

POSITION: Genetically modified foods should be banned until they have been thoroughly tested for safety.

REASON: Currently, nobody is certain about the effects of such foods on humans and animals.

EVIDENCE/EXAMPLE: The government and the biotech industry have not produced convincing evidence that such foods are as safe or nutritious as foods that have not been genetically modified.

POSITION: The drug Ritalin is overprescribed for attention-deficit/hyperactivity disorder (ADHD) in children.

REASON: It is too often considered a "wonder drug."

EVIDENCE/EXPERT OPINION: Dr. Peter Jensen, a pediatric specialist, warns, "I fear that ADHD is suffering from the 'disease of the month' syndrome, and Ritalin is its 'cure.'"

TIP To find good reasons and strong evidence, you may want to consult outside sources, either at the library or on the Internet. For more on using outside sources, see Chapter 20.

As you choose reasons and evidence to support your position, consider what your audience is likely to think about your view of the issue. Are they likely to agree with you, to be uncommitted, or to be hostile? Think about what kinds of reasons and evidence would be most convincing to a typical member of your audience.

When writing an argument, it is tempting to cite as evidence something that "everyone" knows or believes or does. But be careful of "everyone" evidence; everyone usually doesn't know or believe it. It is better to use facts (including statistics), specific examples, and expert opinions.

. . . .

PRACTICE 2   Finding Evidence

For each of the following positions, give the type of evidence indicated (you may have to make up the evidence).

EXAMPLE:

Position: Pesticides should not be sprayed from planes.

Reason: They can cause more damage than they prevent.

Evidence/Fact: *Scientific studies prove that both plant life and people are harmed.*

1. Position: The parking situation on this campus is impossible.

   Reason: Too few spaces exist for the number of students.

   Evidence/Example: *Answers will vary.*

2. Position: People should be careful when dieting.

   Reason: Losing weight quickly is unhealthy.

   Evidence/Fact: _____

3. Position: Smoking is harmful to smokers and nonsmokers alike.

   Reason: Even secondhand smoke can cause lung damage.

   Evidence/Expert opinion: _____

Your reasons and evidence may be convincing to you, but will they persuade your readers? Review the support for your argument by using these strategies.

TESTING YOUR REASONS AND EVIDENCE

- Reread your reasons and evidence from your opponent's perspective, looking for ways to knock them down. Anticipate your opponent's objections and include evidence to answer them.

- Ask someone else to cross-examine your reasons, trying to knock them down.

- Do not overgeneralize. Statements about what everyone else does or what always happens are easy to disprove.

- Make sure that you have considered every important angle of the issue. Take the time to present good support for your position; your argument depends on the quality of your reasons and evidence.

- Reread your reasons and evidence to make sure that they support your position. They must be relevant to your argument.

PRACTICE 3   Reviewing the Evidence

For each of the following positions, one piece of evidence is weak: It does not support the position. Circle the letter of the weak evidence, and in the space provided, state why it is weak.

COMPUTER If you are working in a lab setting, have each student list the evidence for his or her topic on the computer. Then, have each student move to another student's computer and write down opposition to the evidence that is listed. Students should then return to their own computers and try to answer the objections.

DISCUSSION Model the opponent's perspective in class. Put a topic and some evidence on the board. Ask for ideas about how the opposition would try to knock down the evidence.

EXAMPLE:

Position: Advertisements should not use skinny models.

Reason: Skinny should not be promoted as ideal.

a. Three friends of mine became anorexic trying to get skinny.

(b.) Everyone knows that most people are not that thin.

c. A survey of young girls shows that they think they should be as thin as models.

d. People can endanger their health trying to fit the skinny "ideal" promoted in advertisements.

Not strong evidence because *"everyone knows" is not strong evidence; everyone obviously doesn't know that.*

1. Position: People who own guns should not be allowed to keep them at home.

   Reason: It is dangerous to keep a gun in the house.

   a. Guns can go off by accident.

   b. Keeping guns at home has been found to increase the risk of home suicides and adolescent suicides.

   c. Just last week a story in the newspaper told about a man who, in a fit of rage, took his gun out of the drawer and shot his wife.

   (d.) Guns can be purchased easily.

   Not strong evidence because *it is irrelevant; it doesn't support the position.*

2. Position: Schoolchildren in the United States should go to school all year.

   Reason: Year-round schooling promotes better learning.

   (a.) All of my friends have agreed that we would like to end the long summer break.

   b. A survey of teachers across the country showed that children's learning improved when they had multiple shorter vacations rather than entire summers off.

   c. Many children are bored and restless after three weeks of vacation and would be better off returning to school.

   d. Test scores improved when a school system in Colorado went to year-round school sessions.

   Not strong evidence because *wanting it doesn't mean it should happen; also this is a personal preference, not evidence.*

3. Position: The "three strikes and you're out" law that forces judges to send people to jail after three convictions should be revised.

   Reason: Basing decisions about sentencing on numbers alone is neither reasonable nor fair.

a. A week ago, a man who stole a slice of pizza was sentenced to eight to ten years in prison because it was his third conviction.

b. The law makes prison overcrowding even worse.

(**c.**) Judges always give the longest sentence possible anyway.

d. The law too often results in people getting major prison sentences for minor crimes.

Not strong evidence because _it is a generality; not all judges do this._

- -

The Conclusion

Your conclusion is your last opportunity to convince readers of your position. Make it memorable and dramatic. Remind your readers of the issue, your position, and the rightness of your position.

Before writing your conclusion, build up your enthusiasm again. Then, reread what you have written. As soon as you finish reading, write a forceful ending. Aim for power; you can tone it down later.

Organization in Argument

TIP For more on order of importance, see page 82.

Most arguments are organized by **order of importance**, starting with the least important evidence, and saving the most convincing reason and evidence for last.

Use **transitions** to move your readers smoothly from one supporting reason to another. Here are some of the transitions you might use in your argument.

Common Argument Transitions

above all	more important
also	most important
best of all	one fact/another fact
especially	one reason/another reason
for example	one thing/another thing
in addition	remember
in fact	the first (second, third) point
in particular	worst of all
in the first (second, third) place	

· ·

PRACTICE 4   Using Transitions in Argument

Read the paragraph that follows, and fill in the blanks with transitions. You are not limited to the ones in the preceding box. *Answers may vary. Possible answers are shown.*

Daylight saving time should not be extended for an additional two months. Supporters of this change believe that it will save energy, but the savings are doubtful, and there are definite disadvantages. _For one thing, In the first place_, while it would be light later into the evening, the morning hours would be darker. Many experts do not believe that there will be much difference in the amount of energy used. _Also, In the second place, One important disadvantage is that_ the cost of the change could be extremely high. For example, computers are now set to change with the usual schedule of daylight saving. These computers run hospitals, transportation systems, and a whole range of operations, and updating them would be expensive. _The biggest disadvantage is that, Worst of all,_ children would be placed at risk. They would be going to school in darkness, increasing the chance of crime or accidents. I support changes that make sense, but changing the schedule of daylight saving is not one of them.

· ·

Read and Analyze Argument

READING SELECTIONS For further examples of and activities for argument, see Chapter 50.

Reading examples of argument will help you write your own. The first example in this section is a Profile of Success from the real world of college recruiting. Reggie Harris gives presentations to high-school students to show that Hinds Community College would be a good choice for them. He also writes letters for the same purpose.

The second and third examples are student writing, both short essays on the topic of the fairness of a national gas tax. As you read, pay attention to the vocabulary, and answer the questions in the margin. They will help you read the piece critically.

PROFILE OF SUCCESS

Argument in the Real World

The following profile shows how Reggie uses writing and includes an example of how he uses argument in his work.

Background I grew up in a family of six brothers and sisters, raised by a single mother. I was an athlete and in high school was voted Most Valuable Player in both football and baseball. When I arrived at Hinds Community College, I realized that my reading skills were weak, so I took developmental reading with a teacher, Vashti Muse, who became my mentor. In the supportive environment of Hinds, I thrived. I was a member of the Fellowship of Christian Athletes on campus, a group that meets to share ideals and find ways to help the campus and other communities. I became a big brother to a local high-school student and have been rewarded by helping others.

After getting a B.A. from Delta State, I returned to be a college recruiter for Hinds, where I now oversee recruitment, supervising three other recruiters and enrollment specialists. I visit local high schools to give presentations and talk about the many advantages Hinds offers students. I encourage students who are not confident in their academic skills to try Hinds, and I tell them that if I could do it, they can too.

Degrees/College(s) B.A., Delta State University; M.Ed., Jackson State University

Employer Hinds Community College

Writing at work After campus visits, I write visit summaries. After students have visited our campus, I write thank-you letters as a follow-up. I also write letters to students who have made inquiries about Hinds, telling them about what we offer and why we are such a good place to come to college. I also write a big year-end report that summarizes the whole year's activities, along with other reports, e-mails, and other things. Writing is a big part of my job.

Reggie Harris
District Recruiting Coordinator

Reggie's Argument

This is part of a presentation that Reggie gives to high-school students. His purpose is to convince them of what a good choice Hinds is. If you have studied comparison and contrast, note as you read that to make his argument, he uses elements of comparison and contrast.

> As a former student at Hinds Community College, I can honestly tell you that it is a wonderful place to go to college, for a whole range of reasons. One obvious reason is that it is more affordable than many other colleges. Most of us do not have a lot of extra money to throw around, so attending a college that allows you not to have such high student loans to repay is important. Students can get a great education and not be so burdened. With lower loan payments to make, you will be more able to live the kind of life you strive for. Another good reason is the class size. At Hinds, the student-faculty ratio is 17:1, a much better

(continued)

TIP For advice on building your vocabulary, visit the *Real Writing Student Center* at bedfordstmartins.com/realwriting.

Vocabulary development

Underline these words as you read Reggie's argument.

burdened: carrying a heavy load
strive: to work for
ratio: a numerical relation between two things
proportion: a numerical relation between two things

proportion of students to faculty than at many other local colleges. This ratio makes getting individual attention easier than at a larger place. With smaller classes, faculty can work one-on-one with students to make sure that they succeed. This point leads me to (the most important reason) to attend Hinds: Students receive an excellent, high-quality education. Some people say that community colleges aren't as good as four-year colleges and universities, but I am living proof that Hinds Community College provides a first-rate educational experience. Students at Hinds are diverse, with ACT scores ranging from low to very high. The professors at Hinds are great teachers, and teaching is their primary focus. At four-year colleges, some professors are more interested in research than in teaching. Here, teaching is the most important faculty responsibility. Here, you will not find yourself in a huge class run by a graduate student who is not a good teacher. The instructors at Hinds go above and beyond in their efforts to help students learn and succeed in college. When I transferred from Hinds to Delta State, I was able to make the academic transition easily because of all the support and attention available to all Hinds students. When you add it all up—low cost, good ratio of teachers to students, and devotion to academic excellence—Hinds is a great choice for college. It set me on the path to success and a great life, and it can do that for you, too.

1. Double-underline Reggie's **topic sentence**.

2. How many reasons does Reggie use to support his main point? _three_

3. Underline the primary support/reasons.

4. Circle the **transitions** Reggie uses to move readers from one reason to the next.

5. Does Reggie consider an opposing view? _yes, after his third reason_

6. Does Reggie's argument follow the Four Basics of Good Argument? Why or why not? _Yes. Answers will vary._

The next two student essays argue about the fairness of a national gas tax. The first is in favor; the second is against. Read both, and answer the questions at the end of the second essay.

Student Argument Essay in Favor of the Gas Tax

Rollina Lowe

The Gas Tax Is Fair

Many people feel that a national gas tax is unfair and that we should find other ways to raise revenues. They say that people who live in the suburbs and rural areas are unfairly paying a tax that people who live in cities do not share. They say that they need the gas to get to work and that the tax basically means a cut in salary. While I understand why people are against the tax, I believe that this country will never kick its gasoline addiction unless gas prices are high. Our historical driving habits prove my point. **1**

When the price of gas is high, people think about their driving habits. They cluster their errands to be more efficient. This planning ahead saves both time and gas. People do not make four trips out when they can make one. **2**

People also share driving. When gas is expensive, more people form carpools to get to work, school, and social occasions. This behavior is good not only because it saves gas but also because it cuts down on traffic congestion and parking problems. Ride-sharing and carpooling make sense. **3**

With high gas prices, people do less driving. Statistics show that more people use public transportation when the cost of driving gets expensive. People also walk more and ride bicycles. If people were more active, it could also help with our national obesity problem. Families spend more time together, too, because they walk more, drive together more, and have more time because they are not all running around in their separate cars. Most important is that with people driving less, we help reduce global warming. **4**

Historically, when the cost of gas drops, most people go back to their old habits. Once again, we drive to work and school alone. We never walk or bike if we can drive. We continue to pollute our environment. For all of these reasons, we need a gas tax: It helps much more than it hurts. **5**

Student Argument Essay against the Gas Tax

Jim Green

Unequal Taxation

The gas tax is unfair because it is not shared equally among the country's citizens. It penalizes people who have to drive, most of them because they have no other options. Especially in a weak economy, a gas tax is a **1** terrible idea. Some people say that people will never stop wasting gas unless it is expensive because of a tax, but I believe these people are not the ones who are unfairly bearing the burden of it.

Many people have to drive to work. If you live in the city, maybe you   2 can use public transportation, and that option is great. But what about those of us who live where there is not any public transportation. For example, I live in a semi-rural place. It does not have buses or trains, and businesses are spread far apart. I have to drive a long distance to get to my job, whatever job that is. With gas prices high, I am losing money while people in cities are not affected at all, and people in suburbs have choices.

With companies cutting back, fewer jobs are available, and many people   3 have to take whatever they can get, whether a job is far away or not. They do not have a choice. If the only job they can get is fifty miles away, they have to drive that far and use that much gas. For some people, the gas tax will make paying bills even harder and may make them lose their homes.

When people lose their homes, the bad effects can go on for years.   4 Families might have nowhere to go and end up in homeless shelters and on welfare. Welfare costs everyone, and no one likes to be on welfare, especially if they are working and trying as hard as they can. Families also might have to split up, living with different relatives. Children's educations are interrupted, and the health of family members can take a downturn.

Meanwhile, some people are not affected by the tax at all because they   5 have other options. Rich people do not care because they can afford it. People in cities can take other kinds of transportation or even walk. People in suburbs with lots of companies close by can ride together and share the cost. But people like me are stuck, and the gas tax might rip my life apart. It is not fair.

TIP For reading advice, see Chapter 2.

CRITICAL THINKING: READING

Read both essays before answering the questions that follow.

1.   Double-underline the **thesis statement** in each essay.

2.   Underline the **reasons** in each essay.

3.   Do both essays consider the opposing view? _yes_

4.   Do both of the essays give good reasons that relate to the thesis? _Answers will vary, but the second essay gets off topic with the third reason._

5.   Read the Four Basics of Good Argument (p. 258), and consider whether each essay includes them. Reread the essays with the four basics in mind, and have specific examples to support your answer. _Answers will vary._

6.   Which of the essays is a better argument? Why? _Answers will vary._

_____

_____

CRITICAL THINKING: WRITING

Choose one of the following, and respond in a paragraph or essay.

1.   Argue for or against a national gas tax.

2.   Write a letter to your state senator or representative making your argument.

3.   Write about another policy or law (it can be national or local) that you think is unfair.

4.   Write a letter to either Rollina or Jim, either in support of or against their argument.

Write Your Own Argument

In this section, you will write your own argument based on one of the three assignments that follow. Use the following tools to help you:

1.   Review the Four Basics of Good Argument (p. 258).

2.   Use "Argument at a Glance" as a basic organizer.

3.   Use the Checklist: How to Write Argument (pp. 274–75) as you write and revise.

· ·

ASSIGNMENT 1   Writing about College, Work, and Everyday Life

Write an argument paragraph or essay on one of the following topics or one of your own. For other ideas, see your responses to the cartoon (p. 259) and the idea journal (p. 260).

COLLEGE
- Take a position on a controversial issue on your campus.
- Persuade your instructor to raise your grade.
- Argue for or against standardized or placement tests.
- Argue for or against the writing requirements for students.
- Argue for or against affirmative action in college admissions.

WORK
- Take a position on a controversial issue in your workplace.
- Persuade your boss to give you a raise.
- Argue for a change at work.
- Persuade someone to buy your company's product or service.
- Argue that a company policy is not fair.

EVERYDAY LIFE
- Take a position on a controversial issue in your community.
- Argue for or against smoking restrictions.
- Convince your landlord not to raise your rent.

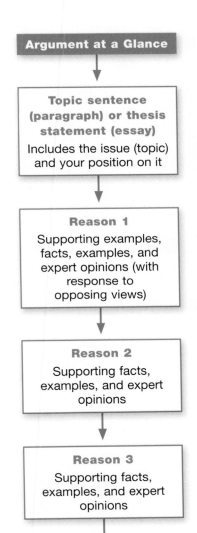

Argument at a Glance

Topic sentence (paragraph) or thesis statement (essay)
Includes the issue (topic) and your position on it

Reason 1
Supporting examples, facts, examples, and expert opinions (with response to opposing views)

Reason 2
Supporting facts, examples, and expert opinions

Reason 3
Supporting facts, examples, and expert opinions

Conclusion
Reminds readers of your position and makes a strong last attempt to convince them of that position, based on the reasons you have presented

• •

ASSIGNMENT 2   Writing about Connections

Read the following account of Jorge Roque before doing the assignment below.

COMMUNITY MATTERS

RESOURCES For advice on "Writing about Connections," see *Practical Suggestions*.

Jorge Roque

Jorge Roque is a veteran of the Iraq War, where he served in the Marine Corps and was partially disabled. When he returned after his tour ended, he had trouble finding work and ended up living in his car. He was referred to Veteran Love, an organization that helps soldiers returning from the war.

He started at Miami-Dade Community College in 2007, taking developmental reading, writing, and math. On his own, he organized students to write letters to soldiers in Iraq because he knew how much letters helped morale. Then, he made fliers on how people could help and posted them around the campus. He also gives presentations to classes about Veteran Love. Billie Jones, the faculty adviser for Omicron Delta Alpha, a service fraternity, heard of Jorge's work and asked him to join. He did, and his first project was to organize a food drive for the homeless. He is vice president of Omicron Delta Alpha and has since created and served in many community events while still taking classes and working at the financial aid office. He is also active in the Student Government Association.

Here is part of an argument Jorge presents for getting involved in service work while you are a student.

Even for the busiest student, getting involved in service organizations is worth the time and effort it takes. At one point, after I had returned from Iraq, was homeless, and was experiencing post-traumatic stress disorder, I was referred to Veteran Love, a nonprofit organization that helps disabled ex-soldiers, and they helped when I needed it most. When I was back on track, I knew that I wanted to help others. I was working and going to school with very little extra time, but getting involved has been important in ways I had not expected.

One reason to get involved is that you meet many new people and form a new and larger network of friends and colleagues. You also learn new skills, like organization, project management, communication, teamwork, and public speaking, among others. I have learned many skills that will be great for what I want to do: run a nonprofit organization. The practical experience I have now is more than I could have gotten from a class, and I have met people who want to help me in my career.

Another reason for doing service work is that you help other people and learn about them. You feel as if you have something to give that is valuable. You also feel part of something larger than yourself. So often students are not connected to meaningful communities and work, and service helps you while you help others.

The most important reason to get involved is that the work makes you feel better about yourself and your abilities. I have developed confidence and know that I am a competent person. I have passed all of my classes and am getting great recommendations from instructors. What I am doing is important and real, and I feel better than I ever have because of my service involvement. If you get involved with community service of any kind, you will become addicted to it. You get more than you could ever give.

ASSIGNMENT: Choose one of the following, and write an argument paragraph or essay. Work either on your own or with a partner.

TIP For more on connecting to community, visit **bedfordstmartins.com/ realwriting**.

- Find out if there are organizations in your community or on campus for veterans of the war in Iraq. Arrange to visit one, and write an argument about why the veterans organization is important.

- Write a response to an opinion piece in your campus newspaper, either agreeing or disagreeing. Send it to the paper after getting some feedback.

- Your school or town is about to cut funding for a program you value. Write a letter to the editor of the local paper arguing that the program is worthwhile.

- Go to www.helium.com/debate, and read a couple of the debates on topics you are interested in. Then, write your own opinion on the topic, and send it to www.helium.com, or to the author of one side of the debate.

- Choose a community or organization you belong to, and write about why it is important. Try to persuade your readers to join.

. . . .

ASSIGNMENT 3 Writing in the Real World / Solving a Problem

Read Appendix B, "Solving Problems."

PROBLEM: Your friend / child / relative has just turned sixteen and is planning to drop out of high school. He has always done poorly, and if he drops out, he can increase his hours at the restaurant where he works. You think this is a terrible idea for many reasons.

ASSIGNMENT: In a group or on your own, come up with various reasons in support of your decision. Consider, too, your friend's / child's / relative's possible objections to your argument and account for those. Then, write an argument paragraph or essay to persuade him to complete high school. Give at least three solid reasons and support your reasons with good evidence or examples. You might start with the following sentence:

There are so many important reasons to stay in school.

TEACHING TIP Suggest to students that they make journal entries on some of the topics that they don't write about for this assignment.

TEAMWORK For more detailed guidance on group work, see *Practical Suggestions*.

ASSIGNMENT 4   Writing Argument for a Writing Test

Many states and colleges require students to take a writing test. Often, the test calls for an argument paragraph or essay on an assigned topic, and students must argue for or against something, as directed. To practice, choose one of the following topics, and come up with reasons and evidence to support both sides of the issue, writing a paragraph or essay defending each side. If you have a time limit, budget your time carefully: Allow enough time to decide on your position for each side, write a topic sentence (for a paragraph) or thesis statement (for an essay), and develop strong reasons and evidence to support your position.

DISCUSSION Organize debates on some of these topics. Poll the class on the issues, divide students into groups to develop arguments, and suggest using the library to gather evidence. Devote a class period to the debates and a discussion of the effectiveness of the arguments.

1. People convicted of drunk driving should lose their licenses forever.

2. Recently a well-respected high-school teacher in Illinois was dismissed from his position because people found out that when he was a high-school student, he had been convicted of marijuana possession (two joints). The law in the state says that no one convicted of any drug crime may serve as a teacher in a public school, so the principal had to dismiss the teacher despite his superb record. Argue for and against this law.

3. A conviction for first-degree murder should carry a mandatory death penalty.

CHECKLIST: HOW TO WRITE ARGUMENT

STEPS	HOW TO DO THE STEPS
☐ Focus.	• Think about topics/issues that interest you.
☐ Narrow and explore your topic. See Chapter 4.	• Choose a particular issue that is meaningful to you. (If your topic has been assigned, think of an angle that interests you.) • Write down some ideas about the issue.
☐ Write a topic sentence (paragraph) or thesis statement (essay). See Chapter 5.	• Build energy by thinking how you are personally affected by the issue. • Write your topic sentence or thesis statement, including your position. • Rewrite the topic sentence or thesis statement to make it more definite and confident.
☐ Support your position. See Chapter 6.	• Prewrite to come up with reasons and evidence. • Use facts, examples, and expert opinions. • Consider what your readers' position on the issue might be and what types of reasons and evidence will most likely convince them. • Consider opposing views and anticipate objections.
☐ Make a plan. See Chapter 7.	• Arrange the reasons in order of importance, saving the most important for last.

CHECKLIST: HOW TO WRITE ARGUMENT

STEPS	HOW TO DO THE STEPS
☐ Write a draft. See Chapter 8.	**FOR A PARAGRAPH** • Write a paragraph that includes a topic sentence, the reasons for your position, and supporting evidence. Use complete sentences. **FOR AN ESSAY** • Consider using one of the introduction types in Chapter 8. Include your thesis statement in your introduction. • Write topic sentences for each reason that supports your position. • Write paragraphs with supporting evidence for each of the reasons. **FOR PARAGRAPHS AND ESSAYS** • Write a conclusion that reminds readers of your position and makes a strong last attempt to convince them, based on the reasons presented. • Write a title that previews your main point but does not repeat it.
☐ Revise your draft, making at least four improvements. See Chapter 9.	• Get feedback from others using the peer-review guide for argument at **bedfordstmartins.com/realwriting**. • Cut reasons that do not directly support your position or that are weak. • Add reasons and evidence to help readers understand your position. Read your argument as if you hold the opposing view, and try to anticipate any criticisms. • Check to make sure the essay is organized by order of importance, with the most convincing reason presented last. • Add transitions to move readers from one point or subject to the next.
☐ Edit your revised draft. See Parts 4 through 7.	• Correct errors in grammar, spelling, word use, and punctuation.
☐ Ask yourself:	• Does my paper include the Four Basics of Good Argument (p. 258)? • What is the strongest reason in my paper? The weakest? • Is this the best I can do?

Chapter Review

1. Argument is writing *that takes a position on an issue and gives*
   evidence to support it.

2. What are the Four Basics of Good Argument?
   It takes a strong and definite position.
   It gives good reasons and supporting evidence to defend the position.
   It considers opposing views.
   It has enthusiasm and energy from start to finish.

3. The topic sentence (paragraph) or thesis statement (essay) in an argument should include what two elements? <u>an issue and the writer's</u> <u>position on that issue</u>

RESOURCES Reproducible peer-review guides for different kinds of papers are available in *Additional Resources*.

4. What three types of information make good evidence? <u>facts, examples,</u> <u>expert opinions</u>

5. Why do you need to be aware of opposing views? <u>to anticipate attacks</u> <u>that may damage the strength of your argument</u>

LEARNING JOURNAL Reread your idea journal entry (p. 260) on why your friend should take a college course. Make another entry on this topic, using what you have learned about argument.

6. Write sentences using the following vocabulary words: *strive, errand, pollute, burden, rural.* <u>Answers will vary.</u>

> **reflect** Write for two minutes on what you have learned about writing a good argument.

Spot and Start Argument Assignments in Other Courses

↓

Spot
In college, at work, and in your everyday life, you need to present and defend your position in many situations (see p. 260). An argument assignment or question might use the words *do you agree with* _____, *defend or refute* _____, or *is* _____ *fair and just?* Argument assignments require you to take a stand on a position and defend it with good reasons.

↓

Start
Ask yourself

1. What is my position on the issue or topic?
2. Why? What are my reasons?
3. How can I explain my reasons to readers who do not share my position? What will convince them?

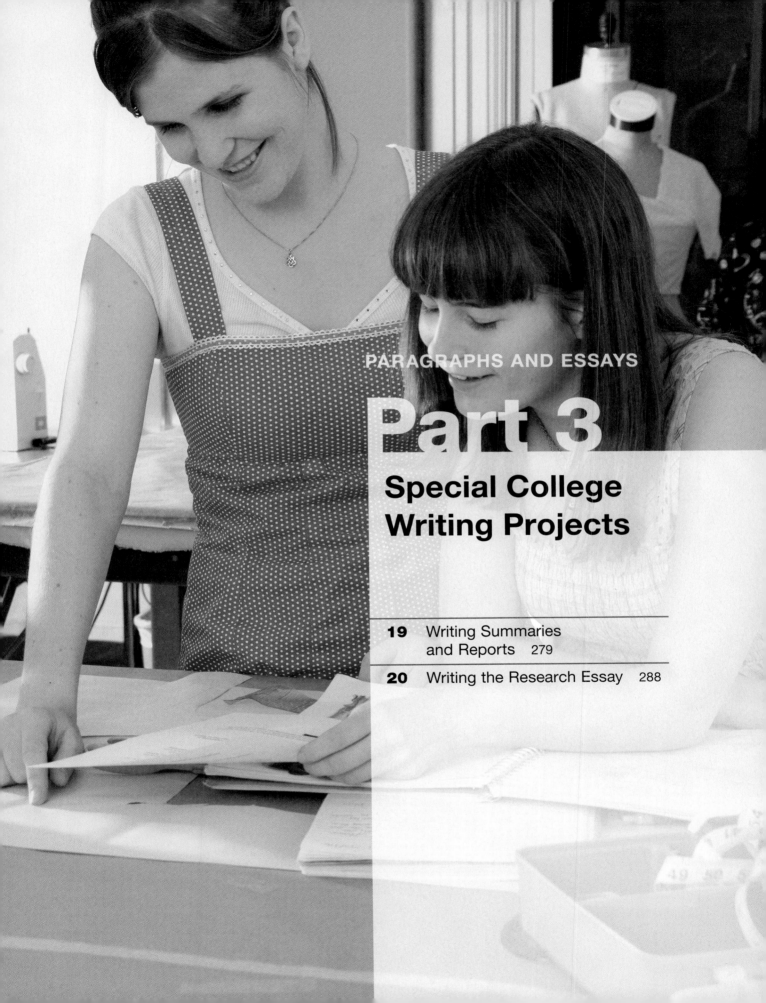

PARAGRAPHS AND ESSAYS

Part 3

Special College Writing Projects

19

Writing Summaries and Reports

Condensing Important Information

Write a Summary

A **summary** is a condensed, or shortened, version of a longer piece of writing, a conversation, or a situation. It presents the main ideas and major support, stripping down the information to its essential elements.

■■ Four Basics of a Good Summary
■■

1 It has a topic sentence (in a paragraph) or a thesis statement (in an essay) that states what is being summarized and its main idea.

2 It identifies the major support points.

3 It includes any final observations or recommendations made in the original piece.

4 It is written in your own words and presents information without your opinions.

1 The essay "Target and Wal-Mart: Not as Different as You Think" states that while Wal-Mart is often villainized, and Target is welcomed, the two large chains are more similar than different. **2** The first similarity the author presents is the quality of the merchandise, which, he says, is perceived as poor at Wal-Mart and high at Target. However, there is no proof for this perception, he notes. The second similarity concerns the business practices of the two chains. While Wal-Mart is often criticized for its low pay and anti-union activities, Target is not blamed for its

TIP The essay "Target and Wal-Mart: Not as Different as You Think" is on pages 231–32.

279

4 Summary is in the writer's own words.

negative business practices. The author cites improvements Wal-Mart has made in its practices. The third similarity is the effect on local economies. Both chain stores can have a negative effect on small businesses, but Wal-Mart, not Target, is fought by local communities. The author gives examples of how Wal-Mart has helped local economies, while Target has not. **3** The author concludes by saying that Wal-Mart is singled out for bad publicity because of its large size. He wonders about other ways in which the media shape people's views.

There are many uses for summarizing.

COLLEGE	A test question asks you to summarize a particular procedure or finding.
WORK	You write a summary of a telephone conversation to send to a client and your boss.
EVERYDAY LIFE	You summarize a car accident for your insurance company.

The Reading Process for Summaries

To write a summary, you must first understand what you are reading. To note what is important as you read, you might follow this process:

READING TO SUMMARIZE

1. Double-underline the main point and write "main point" in the margin next to it.
2. Underline each major support point. This support may be a sentence or a group of sentences. For each major support point, write "major support" in the margin.
3. Underline the final observations, recommendations, or conclusions, and write "conclusion" in the margin.
4. After you finish reading, write a sentence or two, in your own words, about what is important about the piece.

NOTE: Instead of underlining, you could use two different-colored highlighters for steps 1 and 2.

Here is the paragraph from the Four Basics of a Good Summary, underlined and annotated using the steps of the reading process.

Main point ——————

Major support ——————

The essay "Target and Wal-Mart: Not as Different as You Think" states that while Wal-Mart is often villainized, and Target is welcomed, the two large chains are more similar than different. The first similarity the author presents is the quality of the merchandise, which, he says, is perceived as poor at Wal-Mart and high at Target. However, there is no proof for this perception, he notes. The second similarity concerns the business practices of the two chains. While Wal-Mart is often criticized for its low pay and anti-union activities, Target is not blamed for its negative business practices. The author cites improvements Wal-Mart has made in its practices. The third similarity is the effect on local economies. Both chain stores can have a negative effect on small businesses, but Wal-Mart, not Target, is fought by local communities. The author gives examples of how Wal-Mart has helped local economies, while Target has not. The author concludes by saying that Wal-Mart is singled out for bad publicity because of its large size. He wonders about other ways in which the media shape people's views.

— Major support

— Major support

— Conclusion

WHAT'S IMPORTANT: The writer argues that Wal-Mart is really no worse than Target, yet Wal-Mart has been criticized even as it has tried to improve its business practices.

· ·

PRACTICE 1   Reading to Summarize

Read the following essay, and mark it according to the four steps of Reading to Summarize.

In 2009, Wall Street met Main Street, as financial institutions received billions of dollars of taxpayer money to rescue them. After receiving huge infusions of cash from the government, many financial institutions continued business as usual, with excessive spending and a reluctance to account for how they spent the bailout money. Only when a specific practice was discovered did the institutions agree to modify their behavior. On Friday, January 30, 2009, Missouri Senator Claire McCaskill captured the public feeling when she said, "They don't get it. These people are idiots. You can't use taxpayer money to pay out $18 billion in bonuses. . . . What planet are these people on?" ("McCaskill")

— Main point

One example of excess was the bonuses paid to Merrill Lynch executives after it had been acquired by Bank of America. Despite massive losses, Merrill Lynch decided to pay some of its employees nearly $5 billion in bonuses, even *after* Bank of America had already received one payment from Washington and had requested a second. Upon learning of this, the attorney general of New York issued a subpoena to the executives responsible for this highly irresponsible action. Other companies were exposed for similar bonuses paid to executives who helped to destroy the economy.

— Major support

Major support ——————

Major support ——————

Major support ——————

As daily examples of corporate excess were exposed, the public out-cry was loud and sustained. Citigroup outraged people repeatedly. First, the media discovered that after receiving public funds, the company planned to purchase a $5 million luxury corporate jet. Only with intense pressure did it cancel the order. A few weeks later, its plans to spend $400 million for naming rights to the New York Mets Shea Stadium were revealed. Meanwhile, other recipients of bailout money continued to plan luxurious, all-expenses-paid trips to reward employees, to places like Monte Carlo and Las Vegas. Such trips were canceled only when they were exposed by the press.

New to office, President Barack Obama expressed shock at the prac-tices of these institutions and moved to limit the pay of senior executives (who were being so lavishly rewarded with salary and bonuses while their companies bled money). Few believed, however, that Wall Street would change its practices to accommodate Main Street opinion. Most believed that the companies would somehow find ways to hide their excesses and continue their traditional practices.

Conclusion ——————

Work Cited

"McCaskill Proposes Compensation Cap for Private Companies Getting Federal Dollars," *Senate Newsroom*, 30 Jan. 2009. Web. 9 Feb. 2009.

WHAT'S IMPORTANT: *Answers will vary but should indicate the excesses and the public response to them.*

· ·

PRACTICE 2   Reading to Summarize

Read Kelli Whitehead's essay on pages 213–14 and mark it according to the four steps of Reading to Summarize.

· ·

The Writing Process for Summaries

Use the following checklist to help you write summaries.

CHECKLIST: HOW TO WRITE A SUMMARY

STEPS	HOW TO DO THE STEPS
☐ Focus.	• Think about why you are writing the summary and for whom. How much information will your audience need?
☐ Read the selection carefully.	• Underline the main idea, the major support, and the conclusion(s), noting each in the margin.
☐ Write a short statement about what you have read.	• In your own words, write what is important about the piece.
☐ Reread the sections you underlined and annotated, along with your written statement.	• Make additional notes or annotations.
☐ For an essay-length summary, make an outline.	• Include a thesis statement with the name of what you are summarizing. • Arrange the support points in the order you will mention them.
☐ Draft the summary.	• Refer to the original piece, but use your own words. • Work in the points you have annotated, using your outline if you wrote one.
☐ Revise the summary.	• Read your draft, making sure it includes the main point and major support. • Add transitions to move readers smoothly from one point to another. • Make sure the summary is all in your own words.
☐ Edit your work. (See Parts 4 through 7 of this book.)	• Check for errors in grammar, spelling, and punctuation.
☐ Ask yourself:	• Does my paper have the Four Basics of a Good Summary (p. 279)?

Summary Assignments

Choose one of the following assignments, and complete it using the previous checklist.

- Using your notes from Practice 1, write a summary of the piece in Practice 1.
- Summarize a section of a textbook from one of your other courses.
- Summarize an editorial from a print or online magazine or newspaper.

- Summarize an entry from a blog that you have read.
- Summarize the plot of a movie or television program.
- Summarize one of the essays in Chapters 10–18 under "Read and Analyze."

Write a Report

A **report** usually begins with a short summary of a piece of writing, a conversation, or a situation. Then, it analyzes the information, providing reactions, opinions, or recommendations. Unlike a summary, a report often includes the writer's opinions.

TIP Note that the present tense is used to describe the action in essays and literary works.

■■ Four Basics of a Good Report

1 It states the title and author of the piece in the first sentence or paragraph.

2 It summarizes the original piece, conversation, or event, including the main idea and major support points.

3 It then moves to the writer's reactions to the piece and reasons for those reactions.

4 It has a conclusion that usually includes a general comment from the writer. The writer may give an opinion (such as whether the piece is good or bad) or make a general observation.

NOTE: Reports often use specific passages or quotations from a piece. For more information on citing and documenting source material, see Chapter 20.

"A Brother's Murder": A Painful Story That Is as True as Ever

Main point

1 In the essay "A Brother's Murder," Brent Staples writes about his younger brother, Blake, who took a different path in life than Staples did. 2 The essay starts with a phone call in which Staples learns that Blake has been murdered, shot six times by a former friend (517). The essay goes on to tell about the conditions in which Blake grew up. The neighborhood in which the brothers lived was violent, and young men grew into dangerous adults. Staples recalls a conversation he overheard there between two Vietnam veterans, in which one of them said how much he preferred to fight with young men from the inner city, who wear "their manhood on their sleeves." They weren't afraid to fight, believing that violence proved they were *real* men (518).

Summary with major events/support

Direct reference

The author leaves the neighborhood to go to college, and he never returns. Blake, however, stays, and the author recalls a visit home when he sees that his brother has been transformed and now hangs out with drug dealers and gangs (518). When Staples notices a wound on his brother's hand, Blake shrugs it off as "kickback from a shotgun" (519). The author wants to help his brother and makes a date to see him the next night (519). Blake does not show up, and the author returns to Chicago, where he lives. Sometime later, he gets the phone call that announces Blake's death, and he regrets that he had not done something to help his brother.

— Direct reference

Summary with major events/support

3 "A Brother's Murder" is a moving and sad story about how men growing up in the inner city are destroyed. Although the essay was written in 1986, its message is at least as true today as it was more than twenty years ago. Staples shows how his brother is sucked into the routine violence of the streets, shooting and being shot because that is what he knows and that is how a man shows he is a man.

4 Today, thousands of young men live this life and die before they are thirty. This essay makes me wonder why this continues, but it also makes me wonder how two brothers could go such different ways. What happened to save Brent Staples? Could he have saved Blake? What can we do to stop the violence? "A Brother's Murder" is an excellent and thought-provoking essay about a dangerous and growing societal problem.

Writer's reaction in conclusion

Work Cited

Staples, Brent. "A Brother's Murder." *Outlooks and Insights: A Reader for College Writers*. Ed. Paul Eschholz and Alfred Rosa. 4th ed. Bedford/ St. Martin's: 1995. 284–87. Print.

You may need to write a report in a number of situations:

COLLEGE	You are assigned to write a book report.
WORK	You have to write a report on a patient's condition. You are asked to report on a product or service your company is considering.
EVERYDAY LIFE	You write an e-mail to a friend reporting on how your first months of college are going.

The Reading Process for Reports

Reading to write a report is like reading to write a summary except that, in the last step, you write your response to the piece instead of just noting what is important about it.

READING TO REPORT

1. Double-underline the main point and write "main point" in the margin next to it.

2. Underline each major support point (may be a sentence or a group of sentences). For each, write "major support" in the margin.

3. Underline the final observations, recommendations, or conclusions, and write "conclusion" in the margin.

4. After you finish reading, write a sentence or two, in your own words, about how you responded to the piece and why.

PRACTICE 3   Reading to Report

Read the essay "Blood Type and Personality" on pages 200–01. Then, mark whichever essay you select according to the four steps of Reading to Report.

The Writing Process for Reports

Use the following checklist to help you write reports.

CHECKLIST: HOW TO WRITE A REPORT	
STEPS	**HOW TO DO THE STEPS**
☐ Focus.	• Think about why you are writing the report and for whom. What do you think of the piece, and how can you get that view across to readers?
☐ Read the selection carefully.	• Underline the main idea, the major support, and the conclusion(s), noting each in the margin.
☐ Write a short statement about what you have read.	• In your own words, write your reactions to the piece and reasons for those reactions.
☐ Reread your underlinings, marginal notes, and reactions.	• Make additional notes, and look for specific statements from the piece you might use in your report.
☐ For an essay-length report, make an outline.	• Include a thesis statement with the name of what you are reporting on. • Arrange the support points in the order you will mention them. • Put your reactions last.
☐ Draft the report.	• Refer to the original piece, but use your own words. • Start with a summary, including the major support points. • Work from your outline if you wrote one, including your reactions.

CHECKLIST: HOW TO WRITE A REPORT	
STEPS	**HOW TO DO THE STEPS**
☐ Revise the report.	• Make sure your draft includes a main point and major support. • Make sure that your response is clear and that you give reasons for your response. • Add transitions to move readers smoothly from one point to another. • Make sure the report (aside from quotations) is all in your own words.
☐ Edit your work. (See Parts 4 through 7 of this book.)	• Check for errors in grammar, spelling, and punctuation.
☐ Ask yourself:	• Does my paper have the Four Basics of a Good Report (p. 284)?

Report Assignments

Complete one of the following assignments, using the checklist above.

- Using your notes from Practice 3, write a report on "Blood Type and Personality."
- Report on a movie or a concert you have seen recently.
- Report on an event in your community.
- Report on an article in a print or online magazine or news source.
- Report on one of the essays in Chapters 10–18.

Chapter Review

1. How is a summary different from a report? *A summary is objective, while a report includes the writer's responses.*

2. What are the Four Basics of a Good Summary?
It has a topic sentence (paragraph) or a thesis statement (essay) that states what is being summarized and its main idea. It identifies the major support points. It includes any final observations or recommendations made in the original piece. It is written in your own words and presents information without your opinions.

3. How do the Four Basics of a Good Report differ from the basics in question 2? *The fourth basic calls for the writer's opinion/response.*

20

Writing the Research Essay

Using Outside Sources in Your Writing

In all areas of your life, doing research makes you better informed and strengthens any point you want to make. In college, you will need to use outside sources to write papers in many different courses. Here are some situations in which you might use research skills:

COLLEGE	In a criminal justice course, you are asked to write about whether the death penalty deters crime.
WORK	You are asked to do some research about a major office product (such as a phone or computer system) that your company wants to purchase.
EVERYDAY LIFE	Your child's doctor has prescribed a certain medication, and you want information about it.

This chapter explains the major steps of writing a college research essay: how to make a schedule; choose a topic and guiding research question; and find, evaluate, and document sources. A checklist guides you through the process of writing a research essay.

Make a Schedule

Writing a college research essay takes time: It cannot be started and finished in a day or two. To make sure you allow enough time, make a schedule, and stick to it.

You can use the following schedule as a model for making your own.

SAMPLE RESEARCH ESSAY SCHEDULE

Assignment: (Write out what your instructor has assigned.) _____

_____

Number of outside sources required: _____

Length (if specified): _____

Draft due date: _____

Final due date: _____

My general topic: _____

TIP For detailed information about writing a research essay, visit **bedfordstmartins.com/researchroom**.

DO BY	STEP
_____	Choose a topic.
_____	Find and evaluate sources; decide which ones to use.
_____	Take notes, keeping publication information for each source.
_____	Write a working thesis statement by answering a research question.
_____	Review all notes; choose the best support for your working thesis.
_____	Make an outline that includes your thesis statement and support.
_____	Write a draft, including a title.
_____	Revise the draft.
_____	Prepare a list of works cited using correct documentation form.
_____	Edit the revised draft.
_____	Submit the final copy.

Choose a Topic

Your instructor may assign a topic or want you to think of your own topic for a research paper assignment. If you are free to choose your own topic, find a subject that personally interests you and that you feel curious to explore. Ask yourself some questions such as the following:

1. What is going on in my own life that I want to know more about?

2. What do I daydream about? What frightens me? What do I see as a threat to me or my family? What inspires or encourages me?

3. What am I interested in doing in the future, either personally or professionally, that I could investigate?

4. What famous person or people interest me?

5. What current issue do I care about?

TEACHING TIP Have students write an "I-search" paper—a proposal in which they report on what they are interested in learning and explain why they are interested in it. In the I-search papers, have students tell you what they know about their topics already and the specific questions they want answers to.

TEACHING TIP Have students choose three of these topics to write about in their journals.

Here are some current topics that you might want to research:

Assisted suicide	Obesity in the United States
Behavior disorders	Online dating services
A career you are interested in	Privacy and the Internet
Environmental issues	Road rage
Gay/lesbian marriage	School issues
Health issues	Travel
Medical issues	Violence in the media
Music/musical groups	Volunteer opportunities

When you have an idea for a general topic, write answers to these questions:

1. Why is this topic of interest to me?
2. What do I know about the topic? What do I want to find out?

Before writing a working thesis statement, you need to learn more about your topic. It helps to come up with a **guiding research question** about your narrowed topic. This question—often a variation of "What do I want to find out?"—will help to guide and focus your research. Following is one student's research question.

> **MARCUS SHANKS'S GUIDING RESEARCH QUESTION:** Marcus chose the topic of the mandatory registration of sex offenders. He asked this guiding research question:
>
> **Should registration of sex offenders be mandatory?**

Find Sources

With both libraries and the Internet available to you, finding information is not a problem. Knowing how to find good, reliable sources of information, however, can be a challenge. The following strategies will help you.

Consult a Reference Librarian

TEACHING TIP If the library offers group training on library resources, schedule such a session for the class since many students will have the same questions.

RESOURCES For reproducible research handouts, see *Additional Resources*.

The Internet does not reduce the need for reference librarians, who are essential resources in helping to find appropriate information in both print and electronic forms. In fact, with all of the information available to you, librarians are a more important resource than ever, saving you time and possible frustration in your search for relevant material.

If your library allows, schedule an appointment with a librarian. Before your appointment, write down some questions to ask, such as the following. Begin your conversation by telling the librarian your research topic.

QUESTIONS FOR THE LIBRARIAN

- How do I use an online catalog? What information will the library's catalog give me?

- Can I access the library catalog and article databases from home or other locations?

- What other reference tools would you recommend as a good starting place for research on my topic?

- Once I identify a source that might be useful, how do I find it?

- Can you recommend an Internet search engine that will help me find information on my topic? Can you also recommend some useful keywords?

- Does the college have a research database, such as *EBSCO*, *InfoTrac*, or *LexisNexis*?

- How can I tell whether a Web site is reliable?

- I have already found some articles related to my topic. Can you suggest some other places to look for sources?

- I have found good online sources, but how can I find some good print sources on my topic?

Use the Online Catalog

Most libraries now list their holdings online rather than in a card catalog. You can search by keyword, title, author, subject, publication data, and call number. Online catalog help is usually easy to find (generally on the screen or in a Help menu) and easy to follow. If you are just beginning your research, use the keyword search.

Marcus Shanks, who wrote a research essay on mandatory registration of sex offenders (see the excerpt on pages 305–06), searched his library's online catalog using the keywords *sex offender registration*. Here is one source he found:

TIP For more on conducting keyword searches, see page 293.

Author:	Illinois State Police
Title:	A Guide to Sex Offender Registration and Community Notification in Illinois
Published:	Springfield: Illinois State Police, ©1997
Location:	State Library Stacks
Call #:	HQ72.U53 G843 1997
Status:	Available
Description:	1 v.; 28 cm.
Contents:	History of sex offender registration in Illinois, 730 ILCS 150—Qualifying sex offenses—Court/probation—Illinois Department of Corrections facility or other penal institution—Penalty for failure to register—Access to sex offender registration records.
OCLC #:	ocm40706307

A call number is a book's identification number. Knowing the call number will help you locate a source in the library. Once you do locate the source, browse the nearby shelves. Since a library's holdings are organized by subject, you may find other sources related to your topic.

If the book is available only at another library, ask a librarian to have the book sent to your library, or request it at your library's Web site.

Look at Your Library's Web Site

Most libraries have Web sites and databases that can help researchers find useful information. The home page may have links to electronic research sources that the library subscribes to and that are free to library users. These databases are usually reliable and legitimate sources of information. The library home page will also list the library's hours and resources, and it may offer research tips and other valuable information.

Use Your Library's Online Databases and Other Reference Materials

Magazines, journals, and newspapers are called *periodicals*. Periodical indexes help you locate information published in these sources. Online periodical indexes are called *periodical databases* and often include the full text of magazine, journal, or newspaper articles. Libraries often subscribe to these online services. Here are some of the most popular periodical indexes and databases:

- *InfoTrac*
- *JSTOR*
- *LexisNexis*
- *NewsBank*
- *New York Times Index*
- *ProQuest*
- *Readers' Guide to Periodical Literature*

Use the Internet

The Internet provides access to all kinds of information. This section will offer some basics on finding what you need. To start, visit sites that categorize information on the Web, such as the Internet Public Library at www.ipl.org or the Librarians' Internet Index at http://lii.org.

A WORD OF CAUTION: Many instructors do not consider Wikipedia a good reference source. You might ask your instructor whether you may use Wikipedia for your research paper.

NOTE: Some Internet sites charge fees for information (such as archived newspaper or magazine articles). Before using any of these, check to see whether the sources are available free through your library's database.

TEAMWORK Send groups of students on a collaborative research trip to the library, asking each group to find and report to the rest of the class on one of the reference sources listed here. (First make sure that the library has these sources.) Students should be able to explain how the source they reported on could be relevant to their classmates' research projects.

TIP Visit **www.census.gov**, the official Web site of the U.S. Census Bureau, for current state and national statistical data related to population, economics, and geography.

Uniform Resource Locator (URL)

Every Web site has an address, called a uniform resource locator (URL). If you know the URL of a Web site that you think would be helpful, enter it into the address field of your Web browser. If you do not know the URL of a particular site you want to visit, or if you want to look at multiple Web sites related to your topic, use a search engine.

Search Engines and Keyword Searches

Google (www.google.com) is the most commonly used search engine. Others include Yahoo! at www.yahoo.com, www.dmoz.com, and Lycos at www.lycos.com.

To use a search engine, type in keywords from your subject. Adding more specific keywords or phrases and using an Advanced Search option may narrow the number of entries (called *hits*) you have to sift through to find relevant information. Adding additional search terms can narrow a search even more.

When you discover a Web site to which you might want to return, save the URL so that you do not have to remember it each time you want to go to the site. Different browsers have different ways of saving URLs; use the Bookmarks menu in Netscape or Firefox, or the Favorites menu in Microsoft Internet Explorer.

TEACHING TIP Ask students to test three different search engines by typing in keywords related to their research paper. Which search engine seemed most effective for their research needs? Why?

Other Helpful Online Research Sites

Go to the following sites for guided tutorials on research processes; advice on finding, evaluating, and documenting sources; tips on avoiding plagiarism; and more.

- **bedfordstmartins.com/researchroom**
- **Citing Electronic Information** (from the Internet Public Library) at www.ipl.org/div/farq/netciteFARQ.html. This site contains links to various sources that explain how to document information found online.
- **Evaluating Web Pages** (from Cornell University) at www.library.cornell.edu/olinuris/ref/research/webcrit.html. This site gives five ways to evaluate Internet sources. Your own college library may also have a similar Web site.

Interview People

Personal interviews can be excellent sources of information. Before interviewing anyone, however, plan carefully. First, consider what kind of person to interview. Do you want information from an expert on the subject, or from someone directly affected by the issue? The person should be knowledgeable about the subject and have firsthand experience. When you have decided whom to interview, schedule an appointment.

TEAMWORK Have students interview each other on their research topics. They can write a short summary of the interview using both direct quotations and paraphrases.

Next, to get ready for the interview, prepare a list of five to ten questions. Ask more open-ended questions (What do you think of the proposal to build a new library?) than closed ones that require only a simple "yes" or "no" response (Are you in favor of building a new library?). Leave space for notes about the person's responses and for additional questions that may occur to you during the interview. Include the person's full name and qualifications and the date of the interview in your research notes.

As you conduct the interview, listen carefully and write down any important ideas. If you plan to use any of the person's exact words, put them in quotation marks in your notes. Doing so will help you remember if your notes are the exact words of the person you interviewed. For more on using direct quotations, see page 300 of this chapter and Chapter 39.

Using a small recorder during the interview can be helpful. If you want to do this, make sure you ask the person for permission to record the interview.

Evaluate Sources

Evaluating sources means determining how reliable and appropriate they are. Reliable sources present accurate, up-to-date information written by authors with appropriate credentials for the subject matter. Research materials found in a college library (books, journals, and newspapers, for example) are generally considered reliable sources.

Site sponsored by the makers of Hoodia Maxx to promote the product

No names are supplied, and there are no actual endorsements.

Unrealistic claims

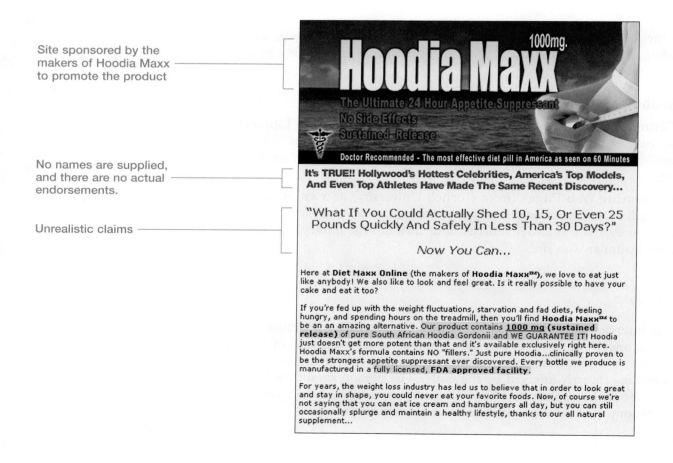

Do not assume that an Internet source is reliable just because it exists online; anyone can create a Web site and put whatever he or she wants on it. If you are searching the Web for information about drugs for migraine headaches, for example, you will find a range of sources. These include reliable ones, such as an article published by the *Journal of the American Medical Association*, and questionable ones sponsored by manufacturers of migraine drugs. Whether you are doing research for a college course, a work assignment, or personal reasons, make sure that the sources you use are reliable.

When you are viewing a Web site, try to determine its purpose. A Web site set up solely to provide information might be more reliable than an online product advertisement. A keyword search on "how to lose weight," for example, would point a researcher to thousands of sites; the two shown on page 294 and below are just samples. Which do you think contains more reliable information?

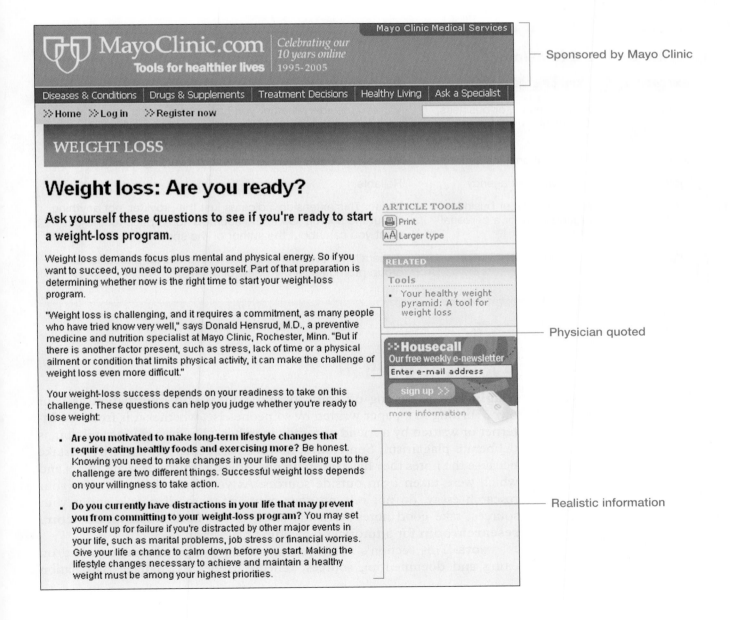

Here are some questions you can ask to evaluate a source. If you answer "no" to any of these questions, think twice about using the source.

TIP For more information on evaluating sources, visit **bedfordstmartins.com/ researchroom**.

QUESTIONS FOR EVALUATING A PRINT OR ELECTRONIC SOURCE

- Is the source reliable? Is it from a well-known magazine or publisher or from a reputable Web site? (For Web sites, also consider the URL extension; see the box on page 296 for guidance.)

- Is the author qualified to write reliably about the subject? If there is no biographical information, try an online search using the author's name.

TEACHING TIP Evaluating Internet sources is difficult for students. Have them apply these questions to an article or Web site printout that you (or they) bring to class. Decide as a class whether the source is reliable.

- Who sponsored the publication or Web site? Be aware of the sponsor's motives (for example, to market a product) and how they might affect the type of information presented.

- Does the author provide adequate support for key points, and does he or she cite the sources of this support?

Guide to URL Extensions

EXTENSION	TYPE OF SITE	HOW RELIABLE?
.com	A commercial, or business, organization	Varies. Consider whether you have heard of the organization, and be sure to read its home page or "About us" link carefully.
.edu	An educational institution	Reliable, but may include materials of varying quality.
.gov	A government agency	Reliable.
.net	A commercial or business organization, or a personal site	Varies. This extension indicates just the provider, not anything about the source. Go to the source's home page to find out what you can about the author or the sponsor.
.org	A nonprofit organization	Generally reliable, although each volunteer or professional group promotes its own view or interests.

Avoid Plagiarism

ESL In some cultures, copying someone else's work is a gesture of respect. Be very clear with students about what constitutes plagiarism.

Plagiarism is passing off someone else's ideas and information as your own. Turning in a paper written by someone else, whether it is from the Internet or written by a friend or family member who gives you permission, is deliberate plagiarism. Sometimes, however, students plagiarize by mistake because the notes they have taken do not indicate which ideas are theirs and which were taken from outside sources. As you find information for your research essay, do not rely on your memory to recall details about your sources; take good notes from the start. Go to **bedfordstmartins.com/ researchroom** for a tutorial on avoiding plagiarism.

NOTE: This section's advice on recording source information, and on citing and documenting sources, reflects Modern Language Association

(MLA) style, the preferred style for English classes and other humanities courses.

Keep a Running Bibliography

A **bibliography** is a complete list, alphabetized by author, of the outside sources you consult. A **Works Cited** list is a complete list, alphabetized by author, of the outside sources that you actually use in your essay. Most instructors require a list of Works Cited at the end of a research essay. Some may require a bibliography as well.

You can keep information for your bibliography and Works Cited list on notecards or on your computer. Whatever method you use, be sure to record complete publication information for each source at the time you consult it, even if you are not sure you will use it; this will save you from having to look up this information again when you are preparing your list of Works Cited.

Following is a list of information to record for each source. For Marcus Shanks's Works Cited list, see page 306.

TEACHING TIP Have students practice citing and documenting sources throughout the semester. For example, if they write summaries of readings from this textbook, articles, or Web sites, ask them to use in-text citations and to include a list of Works Cited at the end of each summary.

TIP Go to **bedfordstmartins .com/researchroom**, and click on "The Bedford Bibliographer" for help with your bibliography.

BOOKS	ARTICLES	WEB SITES
Author name(s)	Author name(s)	Author name(s) (if any)
Title and subtitle	Title of article and page number(s)	Title of page or site
Publisher and location of publisher	Title of magazine, journal, or newspaper	Date of publication or latest update (if available)
Year of publication	Year, month, day of publication (2009 Jan. 4)	Name of sponsoring organization
	Print or Web	Date on which you accessed the source
		Optional: URL (online address) in angle brackets (</>)k

You will probably integrate source material by summary, paraphrase, and direct quotation. As you take notes, record which method you are using so that you do not accidentally plagiarize. Following are tips for summarizing, paraphrasing, and using direct quotations.

Indirect Quotation: Summary

Be careful if you choose to summarize (or paraphrase). It is easy to think you are using your own words when you are actually using only some of your own and some of the author's or speaker's words. When you summarize, follow these guidelines:

- Check your summary against the original source to make sure you have not used the author's words or copied the author's sentence structure.

- Make sure to introduce the outside source when it is first mentioned—for example, "In an article in *Psychological Bulletin*, Lita Furby stated that sex offenders are more likely. . . ."

- Include in parentheses the page number(s), if available, of the entire section you have summarized. (You will need to provide full publication information later, in the Works Cited list.)

SUMMARY OF AN ARTICLE

Identifying information ⎯⎯⎯⎯⎯⎯⎯⎯⎯⎯⎯⎯

Page reference ⎯⎯⎯⎯⎯⎯⎯⎯⎯⎯⎯⎯⎯⎯

In their article in *Psychological Bulletin* titled "Sex Offender Recidivism[1]: A Review," Lita Furby, Mark Weinrott, and Lyn Blackshaw present data on the repeat offenses of sex offenders (3–4). They collected data from all fifty states, documenting the type of offense, type of punishment, whether upon release the sex offender returned to the same area or a new one, how many offenders repeated a sexual crime, the time lapsed between the first crime and the next one, and whether the nature of the repeat crime episode was similar to or different from the first. They also compared the repeat rate of sex-offender crime with the rate of other types of crime. While the authors report that fewer than half of all convicted sex offenders repeat their crimes, they note that the rate is higher than most kinds of crime and that methods of tracking the whereabouts of sex offenders are essential to curb recidivism.

TIP For more on writing summaries, see Chapter 19.

Indirect Quotation: Paraphrase

To paraphrase responsibly, use these guidelines:

RESOURCES *Additional Resources* contains exercises on integrating and citing sources within a research essay.

- Check your paraphrase against the original source to make sure you have not used too many of the author's words or copied the author's sentence structure.

- Make sure to introduce the outside source—for example, "District Attorney Joseph P. Conti stated that. . . ."

- Include in parentheses the page number, if available, of the section you have paraphrased.

TEACHING TIP Remind students that they must cite sources even when they summarize and paraphrase. Students often think they need to cite only when quoting directly.

Following are examples of unacceptable and acceptable paraphrases.

ORIGINAL SOURCE

Reliance on measures of repeat crimes as reflected through official criminal justice system data obviously omits offenses that are not cleared through an arrest or those that are never reported to the police. This dis-

---

1. recidivism: repeating of crimes.

tinction is critical in the measurement of the frequency of repeated crimes among sex offenders. For a variety of reasons, sexual assault is a vastly underreported crime. The National Crime Victimization Survey (Bureau of Justice Statistics) conducted in 2000 indicates that only 32 percent (one out of three) of sexual assaults against persons 12 or older are reported to law enforcement. No current studies indicate the rate of reporting for child sexual assault, although it is generally assumed that these assaults are equally underreported. Many victims are afraid to report sexual assault to the police. They may fear that reporting will lead to further trauma.

—Center for Sex Offender Management (CSOM),
"Recidivism of Sex Offenders," May 2001

UNACCEPTABLE PARAPHRASE, TOO CLOSE TO ORIGINAL

Relying on reports of repeated crimes based on the official police data clearly does not show unreported offenses. In the case of sex offenders, this is an important distinction because sexual assault is often not reported. A survey by the Bureau of Justice Statistics in 2000 showed that only 32 percent of victims of sexual assault aged 12 or over report the crime. It is likely that assaults on children also are underreported for fear of more stress on the child.

This paraphrase is unacceptable for several reasons:

- The first sentence uses the same structure and some of the same words as the first sentence of the original.
- The paraphrase too closely follows the sentences and ideas of the original source.
- The writer has not included the page numbers of the source.
- The writer has not expressed the ideas in his or her own words.

ACCEPTABLE PARAPHRASE

The Center for Sex Offender Management cautions that using police data to assess the rate of repeated sex offenses may not be accurate because many sexual assaults go unreported (CSOM 3–4). The report cites the National Crime Victimization Survey (2000), which found that 32 percent of sexual assaults on adolescents and adults are not reported, and assaults on children probably have a similar percentage of unreported crimes.

— Identifying phrase

— Publication and page reference

The acceptable paraphrase presents the basic ideas, but in the writer's own words and structures. It also includes a parenthetical reference.

Direct Quotation

Use these guidelines when you write direct quotations:

- Record the exact words of the source.
- Include the name of the writer or speaker. If there is more than one author or speaker, record all names.

RESOURCES To gauge students' skills in summarizing, paraphrasing, and using direct quotations, and with citing and documenting sources, use the *Testing Tool Kit* CD-ROM available with this book.

- Enclose the writer's or speaker's words in quotation marks.

- For print sources, include the page number, if available, on which the quotation appeared in the original source. The page number should go in parentheses after the end quotation mark but before the period. If the person quoted is not the author of the book or the article, write "qtd. in," then give the author's name in parentheses along with the page number. If there are two or three authors, give all names.

- If a direct quotation is more than five typed lines, indent the whole quotation and do not use quotation marks.

DIRECT QUOTATION

Identifying phrase ——————————— According to Erie County, Pennsylvania, District Attorney Joseph P. Conti, "I believe strongly in mandatory registration of sex offenders.

Quotation in quotation marks ——————— Because sex offenders may repeat their heinous crimes, our citizens need a means of protecting themselves" (qtd. in Schmitz 5).

Page reference ———————————

Cite and Document Your Sources

TIP For more information on documenting sources, visit **bedfordstmartins.com/ researchroom**.

You need to document your sources at the end of your research essay in a Works Cited list; your instructor may also require a bibliography. Also, you need to include in-text citations of sources as you use them in the essay.

No one can remember the specifics of correct citation and documentation, so be sure to refer to this section or a reference that your instructor directs you to. Include all of the correct information, and pay attention to where punctuation marks such as commas, periods, and quotation marks should go.

There are several different systems of documentation. Most English instructors prefer the Modern Language Association (MLA) system, which is used in this chapter. However, when you are writing a research paper in another course, you may be required to use another system.

Use In-Text Citations within Your Essay

In-text citations such as the ones shown below are used for books and periodicals. For Web sites and other electronic sources, you typically will not be able to include page numbers, although you can note any screen or paragraph numbers used in place of page numbers.

When you refer to the author (or authors) in an introductory phrase, write just the relevant page number(s), if available, in parentheses at the end of the quotation.

> **DIRECT QUOTATION:** In an article by Jon Schmitz, Erie County, Pennsylvania, District Attorney Joseph P. Conti was quoted as saying, "I believe strongly in mandatory registration of sex offenders. Because sex offenders may repeat their heinous crimes, our citizens need a means of protecting themselves" (5).

INDIRECT QUOTATION: In an article by Jon Schmitz, Erie County, Pennsylvania, District Attorney Joseph P. Conti stated that citizens needed special protection from sex offenders, who may again commit crimes (5).

When you do not refer to the author(s) in an introductory phrase, write the author's name followed by the page number(s), if available, at the end of the quotation. If an author is not named, use the title of the source.

DIRECT QUOTATION: "Many victims are afraid to report sexual assault to the police. They may fear that reporting will lead to further trauma" (CSOM 3–4).

INDIRECT QUOTATION: Fear of being harmed further may prevent sexual-assault victims from telling police what happened to them (CSOM 3–4).

For personal interviews, include the name of the person interviewed unless the speaker does not want his or her name used, in which case write "anonymous."

PERSONAL INTERVIEW CITATION

Tarisha Moldovado and her three children lived next door to a child molester for two years without knowing of his offense. She said the neighbor kept to himself and was not a problem, but she wishes she had known so that she could have kept closer watch over her children (personal interview).

Use a Works Cited List at the End of Your Essay

Following are model Works Cited entries for major types of sources. At the end of your paper, you will need to include such entries for each source you cite in the body of the paper.

TIP If you have additional questions about MLA style—especially on how to cite electronic sources—visit the MLA Web site at **www.mla.org**.

Books

1. Book with one author

Full title

Anker, Susan. *Real Writing: Paragraphs and Essays for College, Work, and Everyday Life.* 5th ed. Boston: Bedford/St. Martin's, 2010. Print.

Author, last name first · Edition number · Place of publication · Publisher · Publication date

All lines after first line of entry are indented.

2. Book with two or three authors

Levitt, Steven D., and Stephen J. Dubner. *Freakonomics: A Rogue Economist Explores the Hidden Side of Everything.* New York: Morrow, 2005. Print.

Quigley, Sharon, Gloria Florez, and Thomas McCann. *You Can Clean Almost Anything.* New York: Sutton, 1999. Print.

3. **Book with four or more authors (*et al.* means "and others")**

    Henretta, James A., et al. *America: A Concise History*. 4th ed. Boston: Bedford/
    St. Martin's, 2009. Print.

4. **Book with an editor**

    Price, Steven D., ed. *The Best Advice Ever Given*. Guilford: The Lyons Press,
    2006. Print.

5. **Work in an anthology**

    Wilson, Kathy. "Dude Looks Like a Lady." *ReMix: Reading and Composing
    Culture*. 2nd ed. Ed. Catherine G. Latterell. Boston: Bedford/St. Martin's,
    2009. 21–23. Print.

6. **Encyclopedia article**

    "Boston Common." *The Encyclopedia of New England*. 2005. Print.

Periodicals

7. **Magazine article**

    Date

    Tuttle, Steve. "The Frugal Family Guide." *Newsweek* 16 March 2009: 17–18. Print.

    Author   Title   Name of periodical   Inclusive
    page numbers

8. **Newspaper article**

    Riley, Kathryn. "Garden Is Place for Healing." *Bolton Common* 20 Oct. 2008: 3.
    Print.

9. **Editorial in a magazine or newspaper**

    Dubner, Stephen J. "The Cost of Fearing Strangers." Opinion. *New York Times*
    7 Jan. 2009: A22. Print.

Electronic Sources

Electronic sources include Web sites; databases or subscription services such
as *ERIC, InfoTrac, LexisNexis*, and *ProQuest*; and electronic communications
such as e-mail. Because electronic sources change often, always note the
date you accessed or read the source as well as the date on which the source
was posted or updated online, if this information is available.

10. **An entire Web site**

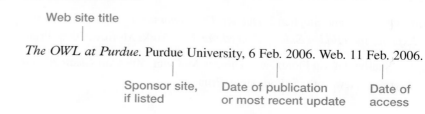

Web site title

The OWL at Purdue. Purdue University, 6 Feb. 2006. Web. 11 Feb. 2006.

Sponsor site,   Date of publication   Date of
if listed   or most recent update   access

11. **Part of a larger Web site**

"How to Evaluate Sources: Introduction." *The Bedford Research Room*. Bedford/
St. Martin's, n.d. Web. 9 Feb. 2009.

12. **Article from a database**

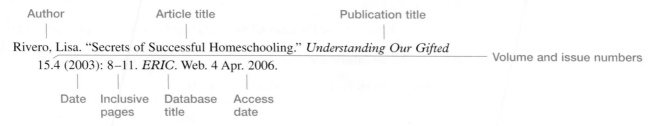

13. **Article in an online magazine or newspaper**

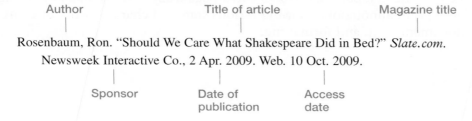

14. **Government publication**

United States. Department of Education. *Go to College*. U.S. Department of
Education, Apr. 2009. Web. 14 May 2009.

15. **Weblog (blog)**

16. **E-mail**

Bustin, Martha. "Note on MLA." Message to Susan Anker. 4 Feb. 2009. E-mail.

Multimedia

17. **Film/video**

Gran Torino. Dir. Clint Eastwood. Warner Bros., 2008. Film.

18. **Radio/television**

"The High Holiday." *ER*. NBC. 11 Dec. 2008. Television.

19. **Podcast**

Brady-Myerov, Monica. "Warning Signs Can Portend a Dropout Years in Advance." Host Monica Brady-Myerov. *Project Dropout*. WBUR, 23 Feb. 2009. MP3 file. 2 Apr. 2009.

20. **Recording**

West, Kanye. "Love Lockdown." *808s & Heartbreak*. Roc-a-Fella, 2008. CD.

21. **Personal interview**

Cirillo, Todd. Personal interview. 11 Mar. 2009.

Excerpt from a Student Research Essay

Here is the first page and Works Cited page from Marcus Shanks's research essay, with annotations showing various standard characteristics of content, documentation, and formatting.

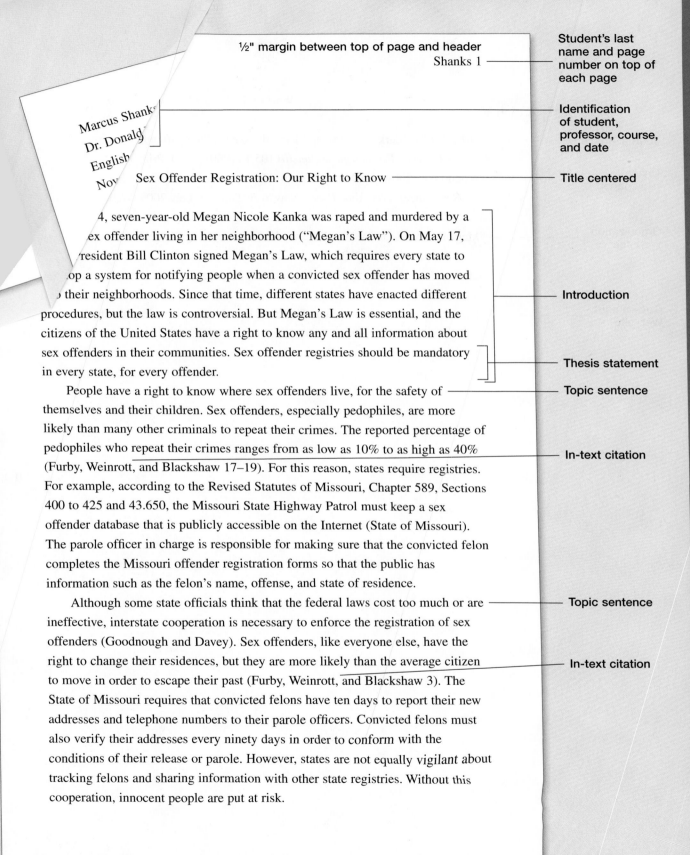

½" margin between top of page and header

Shanks 1 —————————— Student's last name and page number on top of each page

Marcus Shanks ———————————— Identification of student, professor, course, and date

Dr. Donald

English

Nov   Sex Offender Registration: Our Right to Know ——————— Title centered

4, seven-year-old Megan Nicole Kanka was raped and murdered by a
ex offender living in her neighborhood ("Megan's Law"). On May 17,
resident Bill Clinton signed Megan's Law, which requires every state to
op a system for notifying people when a convicted sex offender has moved
their neighborhoods. Since that time, different states have enacted different ——————— Introduction
procedures, but the law is controversial. But Megan's Law is essential, and the
citizens of the United States have a right to know any and all information about
sex offenders in their communities. Sex offender registries should be mandatory ——————— Thesis statement
in every state, for every offender.

People have a right to know where sex offenders live, for the safety of ——————— Topic sentence
themselves and their children. Sex offenders, especially pedophiles, are more
likely than many other criminals to repeat their crimes. The reported percentage of
pedophiles who repeat their crimes ranges from as low as 10% to as high as 40% ——————— In-text citation
(Furby, Weinrott, and Blackshaw 17–19). For this reason, states require registries.
For example, according to the Revised Statutes of Missouri, Chapter 589, Sections
400 to 425 and 43.650, the Missouri State Highway Patrol must keep a sex
offender database that is publicly accessible on the Internet (State of Missouri).
The parole officer in charge is responsible for making sure that the convicted felon
completes the Missouri offender registration forms so that the public has
information such as the felon's name, offense, and state of residence.

Although some state officials think that the federal laws cost too much or are ——————— Topic sentence
ineffective, interstate cooperation is necessary to enforce the registration of sex
offenders (Goodnough and Davey). Sex offenders, like everyone else, have the
right to change their residences, but they are more likely than the average citizen ——————— In-text citation
to move in order to escape their past (Furby, Weinrott, and Blackshaw 3). The
State of Missouri requires that convicted felons have ten days to report their new
addresses and telephone numbers to their parole officers. Convicted felons must
also verify their addresses every ninety days in order to conform with the
conditions of their release or parole. However, states are not equally vigilant about
tracking felons and sharing information with other state registries. Without this
cooperation, innocent people are put at risk.

Works Cited   Shanks 2

Journal article — Furby, Lucas, Mark Weinrott, and Lyn Blackshaw. "Sex Offender Recid[...]
A Review." *Psychological Bulletin* 105.1 (1989): 3–30. Print.

Online
newspaper — Goodnough, Abby, and Monica Davey. "Effort to Track Sex Offenders Draw[...]
Resistance." *New York Times*. New York Times, 9 Feb. 2009. Web. 16 Sept.
2009.

Organization
Web site — "Megan's Law State by State." *Klaas Kids Foundation*. Klaas Kids Foundation,
9 Feb. 2009. Web. 2 Oct. 2009.

Schmitz, Jon. "Megan's Law Debated before High Court." *Post-Gazette.com*.
Post-Gazette, 17 Sept. 1998. Web. 8 Sept. 2009.

Government
Web site — State of Missouri. Missouri State Highway Patrol. "Sex Offender Registry."
Missouri State Highway Patrol, 13 Nov. 2005. Web. 9 Sept. 2009.

To write a research essay, use the checklist below.

CHECKLIST: HOW TO WRITE A RESEARCH ESSAY

STEPS	HOW TO DO THE STEPS
☐ Make a schedule. (See the model on p. 289.)	• Include the due date and dates for doing the research, finishing a draft, and revising.
☐ Choose a topic. (See pp. 289–90.)	• Ask yourself the five questions on page 289. • Choose a topic that interests you. • Make sure the topic is narrow enough to cover in a paper of the assigned length.
☐ Ask a guiding research question. (See p. 290.)	• Ask a question about your topic that you will begin to answer as you do your initial research.
☐ Find sources. (See pp. 290–94.)	• Go to the library and find out what resources are available to you, both in print and online.
☐ Evaluate your sources. (See pp. 294–303.)	• Particularly for Web sites, look for the sponsor and judge whether the site is reliable and accurate.
☐ Avoid plagiarism. (See pp. 297–300.)	• As you make notes from your sources, write down the publication information you will need.
☐ Write a thesis statement. (For more on writing a thesis statement, see Chapter 5.)	• Based on what you have read so far, write a thesis statement that includes the main idea of your research essay. • Try turning your guiding research question into a statement: **Research question:** Should registration of sex offenders be mandatory? **Thesis statement:** Sex offender registries should be mandatory. **Revised:** Sex offender registries should be mandatory in every state, for every offender.
☐ Support your thesis statement. (For more on supporting your point, see Chapter 6.)	• Review all of your notes, and choose the points that best support your thesis statement. • If you do not have enough support to make your point, do a little more reading.
☐ Make an outline. (For more on making an outline, see Chapter 7.)	• Include your thesis statement and the major support, arranged by order of importance. *(continued)*

CHECKLIST: HOW TO WRITE A RESEARCH ESSAY

STEPS	HOW TO DO THE STEPS
☐ Write a draft essay. (For more on writing a draft, see Chapter 8.)	• Write an introduction that includes your thesis statement. • Write topic sentences for each major support, and include supporting evidence. • Write a conclusion that reminds readers of your thesis statement, reviews the evidence you have provided, and makes a final observation in support of your main point.
☐ Cite and document your sources. (See pp. 300–04.)	• Cite sources in the body of your essay, and provide full publication information at the end, in the list of Works Cited.
☐ Revise your draft. (For more on revising, see Chapter 9.) Consider getting comments from a peer first. For more information, see page 106.	Ask yourself: • Does each topic sentence support my thesis statement? • Does the support in each of my body paragraphs directly support the thesis statement? • Do I have enough support that my readers are likely to understand my position on my topic? • Have I included transitions that will help readers move smoothly from one point to the next? • Does my conclusion make my point again, strongly? • Have I integrated source material smoothly into the essay? Do I need to smooth out any parts that have a "dumped in" quality? • Are all sources documented correctly? • What else can I do to make the essay stronger?
☐ Edit your essay.	• Reread your essay, looking for errors in grammar, spelling, and punctuation.
☐ Ask yourself:	• Is this the best I can do?

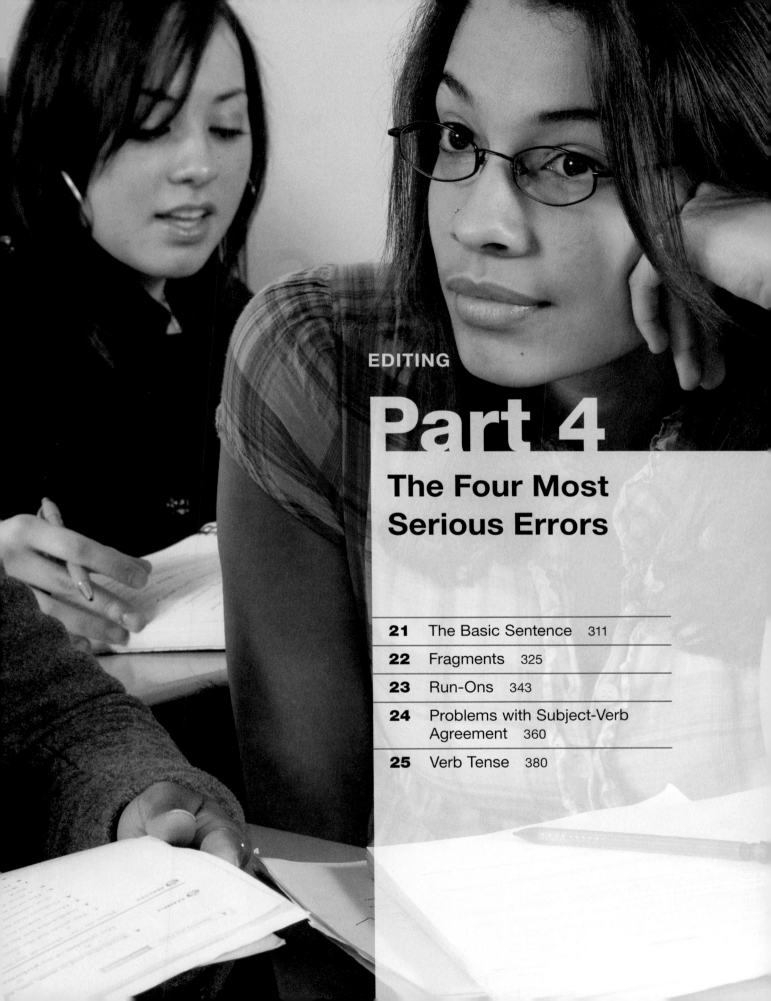

EDITING

Part 4

The Four Most Serious Errors

21

The Basic Sentence

An Overview

The Four Most Serious Errors

This book focuses first on four grammar errors that people most often notice.

THE FOUR MOST SERIOUS ERRORS

1. Fragments (Chapter 22)
2. Run-ons (Chapter 23)
3. Problems with subject-verb agreement (Chapter 24)
4. Problems with verb form and tense (Chapter 25)

If you can edit your writing to correct these four errors, your grades will improve.

This chapter reviews the basic sentence elements that you will need to understand before starting the chapters covering the four most serious errors.

TIP In the examples in this chapter, subjects are underlined once, and verbs are underlined twice.

TIP For fun podcasts with tips on grammar and usage, check out Grammar Girl's Quick and Dirty Tips for Better Writing at **bedfordstmartins.com/realwriting**.

The Parts of Speech

There are seven basic parts of speech:

1. **Noun:** names a person, place, thing, or idea.

   Jaime dances.

TEACHING TIP Make a list of your ten top grammar pet peeves and give it to your students to use.

2.   **Pronoun:** replaces a noun in a sentence. *He, she, it, we,* and *they* are pronouns.

She dances.

3.   **Verb:** tells what action the subject does or links a subject to another word that describes it.

Jaime **dances**.   [The verb *dances* is what the subject, Jaime, does.]

She **is** a dancer.   [The verb *is* links the subject, Jaime, to a word that describes her, *dancer*.]

4.   **Adjective:** describes a noun or a pronoun.

Jaime is **skinny**.   [The adjective *skinny* describes the noun *Jaime*.]

She is **thin**.   [The adjective *thin* describes the pronoun *She*.]

5.   **Adverb:** describes an adjective, a verb, or another adverb. Adverbs often end in *-ly*.

Jaime is **extremely** thin.   [The adverb *extremely* describes the adjective *thin*.]

She practices **often**.   [The adverb *often* describes the verb *practices*.]

Jaime dances **quite** beautifully.   [The adverb *quite* describes another adverb, *beautifully*.]

6.   **Preposition:** connects a noun, pronoun, or verb with some other information about it. *Across, around, at, in, of, on,* and *out* are prepositions (there are many others).

Jaime practices **at** the studio.   [The preposition *at* connects the verb *practices* with the noun *studio*.]

TIP For more practice with the parts of speech, visit Exercise Central at **bedfordstmartins .com/realwriting**.

7.   **Conjunction:** connects words to each other. *And, but, for, nor, or, so,* and *yet* are conjunctions. An easy way to remember the seven common conjunctions is to remember **FANBOYS**: *for, and, nor, but, or, yet, so*.

The studio is expensive **but** good.

LANGUAGE NOTE: Any idea that ends with a period needs a subject and a verb to be a complete sentence. For a review of subjects and verbs, see pages 312–19.

If you are not sure about how to order the parts of speech, see Chapter 33.

Common Prepositions

about	before	for	on	until
above	behind	from	out	up
across	below	in	outside	upon
after	beneath	inside	over	with
against	beside	into	past	within
along	between	like	since	without
among	by	near	through	
around	down	next to	to	
at	during	of	toward	
because of	except	off	under	

TIP For common prepositional phrases, see Chapter 33.

Subject   Preposition

One of my best friends races cars.

Prepositional phrase

Although you might think the word *friends* is the subject of the sentence, it isn't. *One* is the subject. The word *friends* cannot be the subject because it is in the prepositional phrase *of my best friends*. When you are looking for the subject of a sentence, cross out the prepositional phrase.

PREPOSITIONAL PHRASE CROSSED OUT

One ~~of the students~~ won the science prize.

The rules ~~about the dress code~~ are very specific.

The sound ~~of water dripping~~ drives me crazy.

LANGUAGE NOTE: The example sentences use the word *the* before the noun (*the rules*, *the dress code*, *the sound*). *The*, *a*, and *an* are called *articles*. If you have trouble deciding which article to use with which nouns, see Chapter 33.

· ·

PRACTICE 2   Identifying Subjects and Prepositional Phrases

In each of the following sentences, cross out any prepositional phrases, and underline the subject of the sentence.

    EXAMPLE: The head ~~of the company~~ earned a high salary.

TIP For more practices on sentence basics, visit Exercise Central at **bedfordstmartins .com/realwriting**.

1. A company ~~without a chief executive officer~~ conducted a search to find a new leader.

2. The policy ~~of the corporate board~~ was to find an experienced CEO.

3. The people ~~on the short list of candidates~~ had all run other companies.

4. Their work ~~at other businesses~~ had not always made the companies more successful.

5. One man ~~from a bankrupt firm~~ had earned a ten-million-dollar salary.

6. His payments ~~in stock options~~ had been even higher.

7. His appearance ~~before the members of the board~~ did not convince them.

8. One member ~~of the board~~ suggested looking further.

9. The workforce ~~within the company~~ included many talented executives.

10. A vice president ~~from the marketing division~~ became the company's new CEO.

Verbs

Every sentence has a **main verb,** the word or words that tell what the subject does or that link the subject to another word that describes it. Verbs do not always immediately follow the subject: Other words may come between the subject and the verb. There are three kinds of verbs: action verbs, linking verbs, and helping verbs.

Action Verbs

An **action verb** tells what action the subject performs.

To find the main action verb in a sentence, ask yourself: **What action does the subject perform?**

ACTION VERBS   The band played all night.

The alarm rings loudly.

Linking Verbs

A **linking verb** connects (links) the subject to another word or group of words that describes the subject. Linking verbs show no action. The most common linking verb is *be* (*am, is, are,* and so on). Other linking verbs, such as *seem* and *become,* can usually be replaced by a form of the verb *be,* and the sentence will still make sense.

To find linking verbs, ask yourself: **What word joins the subject and the words that describe the subject?**

LINKING VERBS   The bus is late.

I feel great today. (I am great today.)

My new shoes look shiny. (My new shoes are shiny.)

The milk tastes sour. (The milk is sour.)

Some words can be used as either action verbs or linking verbs, depending on how the verb is used in a particular sentence.

ACTION VERB   Justine smelled the flowers.

LINKING VERB   The flowers smelled wonderful.

Common Linking Verbs

FORMS OF BE	FORMS OF SEEM AND BECOME	FORMS OF SENSE VERBS
am	seem, seems, seemed	look, looks, looked
are		appear, appears, appeared
is	become, becomes, became	
was		smell, smells, smelled
were		taste, tastes, tasted
		feel, feels, felt

LANGUAGE NOTE: The verb *be* cannot be left out of sentences in English.

INCORRECT   Tonya well now.

CORRECT   Tonya **is** well now.

Helping Verbs

A **helping verb** joins the main verb in a sentence to form the **complete verb.** The helping verb is often a form of the verbs *be*, *have*, or *do*. A sentence may have more than one helping verb along with the main verb.

Helping verb	+	Main verb	=	Complete verb

Sharon was listening to the radio as she was studying for the test.

[The helping verb is *was*; the complete verbs are *was listening* and *was studying*.]

<u>I</u> <u>am saving</u> my money for a car.

<u>Colleen</u> <u>might have borrowed</u> my sweater.

<u>You</u> <u>must pass</u> this course before taking the next one.

<u>You</u> <u>should stop</u> smoking.

Common Helping Verbs

FORMS OF *BE*	FORMS OF *HAVE*	FORMS OF *DO*	OTHER
am	have	do	can
are	has	does	could
been	had	did	may
being			might
is			must
was			should
were			will
			would

Before you begin Practice 3, look at these examples to see how action, linking, and helping verbs are different.

ACTION VERB	<u>Kara</u> <u>graduated</u> last year. [The verb *graduated* is an action that Kara performed.]
LINKING VERB	<u>Kara</u> <u>is</u> a graduate. [The verb *is* links Kara to the word that describes her: *graduate.* No action is performed.]
HELPING VERB	<u>Kara</u> <u>is graduating</u> next spring. [The helping verb *is* joins the main verb *graduating* to make the complete verb *is graduating*, which tells what action the subject is taking.]

• •

PRACTICE 3   Identifying the Verb (Action, Linking, or Helping Verb + Main Verb)

In the following sentences, underline each subject and double-underline each verb. Then, identify each verb as an action verb, a linking verb, or a helping verb + a main verb.

Helping verb + main verb

EXAMPLE: <u>Bowling</u> <u>was created</u> a long time ago.

1. The ancient Egyptians invented bowling.
   Action verb

2. Dutch settlers were responsible for bowling's introduction to North
   Linking verb

   America.

3. They bowled outdoors on fields of grass.
   Action verb

4. One area in New York City is called Bowling Green because the Dutch
   Helping verb + main verb
   bowled there in the 1600s.
   Action verb

5. The first indoor bowling alley in the United States opened in 1840 in
   Action verb

   New York.

6. Indoor bowling soon became popular across the country.
   Linking verb

7. The largest bowling alley in the United States offers more than a hun-
   Action verb

   dred lanes.

8. Visitors to Las Vegas can bowl there.
   Helping verb + main verb

9. Most people would not think of bowling as more popular than
   Helping verb + main verb

   basketball.

10. However, more Americans participate in bowling than in any other sport.
    Action verb

Complete Thoughts

A **complete thought** is an idea, expressed in a sentence, that makes sense by itself, without other sentences. An incomplete thought leaves readers wondering what's going on.

INCOMPLETE THOUGHT	because my alarm didn't go off
COMPLETE THOUGHT	I was late because my alarm didn't go off.
INCOMPLETE THOUGHT	the people who won the lottery
COMPLETE THOUGHT	The people who won the lottery were old.

To determine whether a thought is complete, ask yourself: **Do I have to ask a question to understand?**

INCOMPLETE THOUGHT	in my wallet
	[You would have to ask a question to understand, so this is not a complete thought.]
COMPLETE THOUGHT	My ticket is in my wallet.

. . . .

PRACTICE 4   Identifying Complete Thoughts

Some of the following items contain complete thoughts, and others do not. In the space to the left of each item, write either "C" for complete thought or "I" for incomplete thought. If you write "I," add words to make a sentence.

EXAMPLE: _I_   My limited cooking skills. *are well known* ^

Answers will vary. Possible edits are shown. ^

TEAMWORK Have students read the items in this practice aloud to each other and decide if the items are sentences or incomplete thoughts.

_C_   **1.** Last week, I wanted to cook dinner for my new roommate.

_I_   **2.** ~~Decided~~ to fix spaghetti and a salad. *I decided* ^

_I_   **3.** Because mother had taught me to cook spaghetti, *I felt I could do this.* ^

_C_   **4.** I bought the ingredients and decided to buy dessert.

_I_   **5.** A luscious cherry pie from the bakery. *I chose a* ^

_C_   **6.** Walking into the kitchen, I tripped and fell.

_I_   **7.** Landing face down in the cherry pie. *was messy* ^

_C_   **8.** At that moment, my roommate walked in and stared at the mess.

_I_   **9.** And then started to laugh at the ridiculous sight. *she* ^

_C_   **10.** Together, we cleaned up the mess and then went out for hamburgers.

. . . .

Six Basic English Sentence Patterns

In English, there are six basic sentence patterns, some of which you have just worked through in this chapter. Although there are other patterns, they build on these six.

1. **Subject-Verb (S-V).** This is the most basic pattern, as you have already seen.

   $\quad$ S $\quad$ V

   <u>Babies</u> <u><u>cry</u></u>.

2. **Subject-Linking Verb-Noun (S-LV-N)**

   $\quad$ S $\quad$ LV $\quad$ N

   <u>They</u> <u><u>are</u></u> children.

3. **Subject-Linking Verb-Adjective (S-LV-ADJ)**

   $\quad$ S $\quad$ LV $\quad$ ADJ

   <u>Parents</u> <u><u>are</u></u> tired.

4. **Subject-Verb-Adverb (S-V-ADV)**

   $\quad$ S $\quad$ V $\quad$ ADV

   <u>They</u> <u><u>sleep</u></u> poorly.

5. **Subject-Verb-Direct Object (S-V-DO).** A *direct object* directly receives the action of the verb.

        S   V   DO

Teachers give tests.   [The *tests* are given.]

6. **Subject-Verb-Direct Object-Indirect Object.** An *indirect object* does not directly receive the action of the verb.

        S   V   DO   IO

Teachers give tests to students.   [The *tests* are given; the *students* are not.]

This pattern can also have the indirect object before the direct object.

        S   V   IO   DO

Teachers give students tests.

- -

PRACTICE 5   Identifying Basic Sentence Patterns

Using the sentence pattern indicated, write a sentence for each of the following items.

Answers will vary.

1. (Subject-verb-direct object) _____

_____

2. (Subject-linking verb-noun) _____

_____

3. (Subject-verb-adverb) _____

_____

4. (Subject-verb-direct object-indirect object) _____

_____

5. (Subject-verb-indirect object-direct object) _____

_____

- -

PRACTICE 6   Identifying Complete Sentences

In this essay, underline the subject of each sentence, and double-underline the verb. Correct five incomplete thoughts.

Answers may vary. Possible edits are shown.

    (1) Space travel fascinates my grandpa Bill. (2) He watches every space movie at least a dozen times. (3) Before 1996, he never even thought about the moon, Mars, or beyond. (4) He was too old to be an astronaut. (5) Now, however, he is on board a satellite. (6) It analyzes particles in the atmosphere. (7) He has the company of millions of other people, (8) ~~And~~ *and* me, too. (9) Truthfully, only our names travel to Mars or beyond. (10) We are happy with that.

(11) In 1996, the Planetary Society flew the names of members into
space (12) ~~Using~~ *using* the Mars *Pathfinder*. (13) At first, individuals signed
a paper. (14) Then, Planetary Society members put the signatures into
electronic form. (15) Now, people submit names on the Internet
(16) ~~By~~ *by* filling out a form. (17) The names go on a microchip. (18) The
next spacecraft to the moon will have more than a million names on
board. (19) Some people have placed their names on a spacecraft going
past Pluto and out of our solar system. (20) Their names are on a CD
(21) ~~Which~~ *which* could survive for billions of years.

(22) Grandpa and I feel good about our journey into space. (23) In
a way, we will travel to places only dreamed about. (24) After signing
up, we received colorful certificates to print out (25) ~~To~~ *to* tell about our
mission. (26) My certificate hangs on my wall. (27) My grandpa and I
travel proudly into space.

• •

PRACTICE 7   Using the Parts of Speech

Fill in the blanks with the specified part of speech.
Answers may vary. Possible answers are shown.

(1) Last week, I forgot to take my notebook and my ____*pen*____
(noun) to class. (2) I blame it on all the ____*work*____ (noun) we
have to do in school. (3) Yesterday, I ____*walked*____ (verb) to the car,
____*tossed*____ (verb) my backpack ____*on*____ (preposition)
the seat, and was ready to go. (4) Then, I realized my car keys were in
the house. (5) This seems to happen often: For example, today, when
____*class*____ (noun) was over, I stopped at the ____*new*____
(adjective) supermarket. (6) I arrived home ____*and*____ (conjunction) ____*dropped*____ (verb) my books on the table. (7) The ice
cream I had bought was melting ____*quickly*____ (adverb), so I shoved
it in the freezer while my roommate put the ____*groceries*____ (plural
noun) on the shelf. (8) Then, ____*she*____ (pronoun) asked to
borrow my car to go to a lecture, where a famous writer was going to
speak. (9) I looked on the table, ____*but*____ (conjunction) I
could not find my keys. (10) We ____*searched*____ (verb) my backpack.
(11) "What did you do when you came in?" my roommate asked
____*hopefully*____ (adverb). (12) I knew ____*immediately*____ (adverb)
where my car keys were. (13) We found them next to the ice cream
____*in*____ (preposition) the freezer.

• •

Chapter Review

1. List the seven parts of speech. _nouns, pronouns, verbs, adjectives,_
   adverbs, prepositions, and conjunctions

2. Write three sentences using all the parts of speech. Label the parts.
   Answers will vary.

3. A sentence must have three things: _a subject, a verb, and a complete_
   thought.

4. A _____subject_____ is the person, place, or thing that a sentence is
   about.

5. A noun is a word that _names a person, place, thing, or idea._

6. A prepositional phrase is _a word group that begins with a preposition_
   and ends with a noun or a pronoun.

7. What are five common prepositions? _Answers will vary._

8. Write an example of a prepositional phrase (not from one of the examples presented earlier): _Answers will vary._

9. An action verb tells _what action the subject performs._

10. A linking verb _connects the subject to another word or group of words_
    that describe the subject.

11. A helping verb _joins the main verb in a sentence to form the complete_
    verb.

LEARNING JOURNAL What is
the main thing you learned from
this chapter? What is one thing
that is unclear to you?

TEACHING TIP You can collect
students' learning journals to
find out what the class or individuals need more work on.

Chapter Test

Circle the correct choice for each of the following items.

TIP For advice on taking tests,
see Appendix A.

1. Identify the underlined part of speech in this sentence.

   Devon <u>walks</u> so fast that I can never keep up with him.

   a. Noun   **(b.)** Verb   **c.** Preposition   **d.** Adjective

2. Identify the underlined part of speech in this sentence.

   When you sent Gita a birthday present, did <u>she</u> send you a
   thank-you note?

   a. Noun   **b.** Verb   **(c.)** Pronoun   **d.** Conjunction

RESOURCES *Testing Tool Kit*,
a CD-ROM available with this
book, has even more tests.

3. Identify the underlined part of speech in this sentence.

In spring, the trees around our house are a <u>beautiful</u> shade of green.

(a.) Adjective   **b.** Adverb   **c.** Preposition   **d.** Verb

4. Identify the underlined part of speech in this sentence.

I ran for the bus, <u>but</u> it drove away before I reached it.

a. Noun   **b.** Verb   **c.** Pronoun   **(d.)** Conjunction

5. Identify the underlined part of speech in this sentence.

<u>Shopping</u> is Jerimiah's favorite hobby.

(a.) Noun   **b.** Verb   **c.** Adjective   **d.** Adverb

6. Identify the type of verb in this sentence.

The baby always <u>seems</u> tired after lunch.

a. Action verb   **(b.)** Linking verb   **c.** Helping verb

7. Identify the type of verb in this sentence.

Katarina <u>swims</u> five miles every day.

(a.) Action verb   **b.** Linking verb   **c.** Helping verb

8. Identify the type of verb in this sentence.

He <u>has</u> flown small planes in several countries.

a. Action verb   **b.** Linking verb   **(c.)** Helping verb

9. Choose the item that is a complete sentence.
  a. Driving to the store.
  (b.) Driving to the store, I hit a squirrel.
  c. Driving to the grocery store last Wednesday.

10. Choose the item that is a complete sentence.
  (a.) Whenever I feel sick, I take aspirin.
  b. Whenever I feel sick.
  c. Takes me to the doctor whenever I feel sick.

22

Fragments

Incomplete Sentences

Understand What Fragments Are

A **fragment** is a group of words that is missing one or more parts of a complete sentence: a subject, a verb, or a complete thought.

SENTENCE   I was late, so I ate some cold pizza and drank a soda.

FRAGMENT   I was late, so I ate some cold pizza. *And drank a soda.*
            [*And drank a soda* contains a verb (*drank*) but no subject.]

LANGUAGE NOTE: Remember that any idea that ends with a period needs a subject and verb to be complete. For a review of subjects and verbs, see pages 313–19.

TIP In the examples in this chapter, subjects are underlined once, and verbs are underlined twice.

IDEA JOURNAL Write about a pet peeve.

In the Real World, Why Is It Important to Correct Fragments?

SITUATION: Irene is applying for the position of administrative assistant for a small business. She sends her résumé and a cover letter to the office manager. Although she really wants the job, her cover letter hurts her chances.

TEACHING TIP Students should underline the fragments for Practice 1 (on p. 326), and correct them for Practice 10 (on p. 339).

I have an A.A. from Central Community College, where I took classes in business. Because I am interested in someday owning my own company. While going to school, I worked part-time in an office. After classes and some evenings and weekends. In that position, I did typing, filing, and lots of copying. Especially of financial reports for the president of the company. I am organized and work hard. I believe I would be a good addition to your organization, and hope. <u>To get a chance to meet with you.</u>

People outside the English classroom notice major grammar errors, and though they may not assign you a course grade, they do judge you by your communication skills.

STUDENT VOICES

NICOLE DAY'S RESPONSE: Nicole Day, office manager, responded to Irene's letter:

Irene might have good experience, but after reading her letter, I did not even look at her résumé. Writing and communicating well are big parts of any job in this office. When we write to customers, our writing represents us. Unfortunately, Irene's letter has some mistakes that tell me she is not a good writer. Even though writing is not the only part of the job, it is an important part. So many people are looking for jobs that I would not even interview Irene.

(See Nicole's **PROFILE OF SUCCESS** on p. 196.)

Find and Correct Fragments

To find fragments in your own writing, look for the five trouble spots in this chapter. They often signal fragments.

When you find a fragment in your own writing, you can usually correct it in one of two ways.

BASIC WAYS TO CORRECT A FRAGMENT

TEACHING TIP Consider having students use different-colored highlighters to indicate subjects and verbs.

- Add what is missing (a subject, a verb, or both).
- Attach the fragment to the sentence before or after it.

· ·

PRACTICE 1   Finding Fragments

Find and underline the four fragments in Irene's letter above.

· ·

TIP Remember, the subject of a sentence is *never* in a prepositional phrase (see p. 322).

1.   Fragments That Start with Prepositions

Whenever a preposition starts what you think is a sentence, check for a subject, a verb, and a complete thought. If the group of words is missing any of these three elements, it is a fragment.

FRAGMENT   I pounded as hard as I could. *Against the door.*

[*Against the door* lacks both a subject and a verb.]

Correct a fragment that starts with a preposition by connecting it to the sentence either before or after it. If you connect such a fragment to the sentence after it, put a comma after the fragment to join it to the next sentence.

Finding and Fixing Fragments:
Fragments That Start with a Preposition

Find

I pounded as hard as I could. (Against) the door.

1. **Circle** any preposition that starts a word group.
2. **Ask:** Does the word group have a subject? *No.* A verb? *No.* **Underline** any subject, and **double-underline** any verb.
3. **Ask:** Does the word group express a complete thought? *No.*
4. If the word group is missing a subject or verb or does not express a complete thought, it is a fragment. *This word group is a fragment.*

Fix

I pounded as hard as I could/ Against the door.
                                    a

5. **Correct the fragment** by joining it to the sentence before or after it.

Common Prepositions

about	before	for	on	until
above	behind	from	out	up
across	below	in	outside	upon
after	beneath	inside	over	with
against	beside	into	past	within
along	between	like	since	without
among	by	near	through	
around	down	next to	to	
at	during	of	toward	
because of	except	off	under	

TIP For more practice correcting fragments, visit Exercise Central at **bedfordstmartins .com/realwriting**.

RESOURCES To gauge students' skills in correcting fragments, use the *Testing Tool Kit* CD-ROM available with this book.

DISCUSSION Ask students to jot down what they think the word *dependent* means in the real world and to give an example. After getting some responses, ask how *dependent* in *dependent clause* is similar to *dependent* in the real world.

COMPUTER Suggest that students become aware of the dependent words they use most by doing a computer search for them as they edit their own writing. They can then make sure that dependent clauses are attached to sentences.

2. Fragments That Start with Dependent Words

A **dependent word** (also called a **subordinating conjunction**) is the first word in a dependent clause.

SENTENCE WITH A DEPENDENT WORD   We arrived early *because* we left early.

[*Because* is a dependent word introducing the dependent clause *because we left early.*]

A dependent clause cannot be a sentence because it does not express a complete thought, even though it has a subject and a verb. Whenever a dependent word starts what you think is a sentence, stop to check for a subject, a verb, and a complete thought.

FRAGMENT   *Since I moved.* I have eaten out every day.

[*Since I moved* has a subject (*I*) and a verb (*moved*), but it does not express a complete thought.]

Common Dependent Words

after	if/if only	until
although	now that	what (whatever)
as/as if/as though	once	when (whenever)
as long as/as soon as	since	where (wherever)
because	so that	whether
before	that	which
even if/even though	though	while
how	unless	who/whose

When a word group starts with *who*, *whose*, or *which*, it is not a complete sentence unless it is a question.

FRAGMENT   That woman is the police officer. *Who gave me a ticket last week.*

QUESTION   *Who* gave you a ticket last week?

FRAGMENT   He is the goalie. *Whose team is so bad.*

QUESTION   *Whose* team are you on?

FRAGMENT   Sherlene went to the HiHo Club. *Which does not serve alcohol.*

QUESTION   *Which* club serves alcohol?

Correct a fragment that starts with a dependent word by connecting it to the sentence before or after it. If the dependent clause is joined to the sentence before it, you do not usually need to put a comma in front of it. If the dependent clause is joined to the sentence after it, put a comma after the dependent clause.

PRACTICE 2 Correcting Fragments That Start with Prepositions or Dependent Words

In the following items, circle any prepositions or dependent words that start a word group. Then, correct each fragment by connecting it to the sentence before or after it. *Answers may vary. Possible edits are shown.*

EXAMPLE: I have a bowl of stones, On my desk.

TIP Answers to odd-numbered practice items are on pp. AK-1–10 at the back of the book.

1. (Because) I have gathered these stones from different places, They each have a special meaning for me.

2. My collection started many years ago, When I was a child visiting my grandparents.

3. I was taking a long walk with my grandfather, In the neighborhood park near his house.

4. He stopped suddenly and bent down to pick up a brown rock, Which was in the middle of the path.

5. (When) he showed me the rock, We both smiled because it had marks that made it look like a smiley face.

6. I found another special rock, At a gem and mineral show when I was a teenager.

7. (Although) the rock is brown and gray on one side, The other side is made up of beautiful purple amethyst crystals.

8. (Even though) those rocks are special, Another one is my favorite because I have had it for a long time.

9. It is a flat tan rock, With a picture of a horse sketched on it with a Magic Marker.

10. This rock is my favorite, Because my son drew the picture when he was eight years old.

Finding and Fixing Fragments: Fragments That Start with a Dependent Word

Find

(Because) a job search is important. People should take the time to do it right.

1. **Circle** any dependent word that starts either word group.
2. **Ask:** Does the word group have a subject? *Yes.* A verb? *Yes.* **Underline** any subject, and **double-underline** any verb.
3. **Ask:** Does the word group express a complete thought? *No.*
4. If the word group is missing a subject or verb or does not express a complete thought, it is a fragment. *This word group is a fragment.*

Fix

Because a job search is important, People should take the time to do it right.

5. **Correct the fragment** by joining it to the sentence before or after it. Add a comma if the dependent word group comes first.

TIP For more on commas with dependent clauses, see Chapters 30 and 37.

. . . .

PRACTICE 3 **Correcting Fragments That Start with Prepositions or Dependent Words**

Read the following paragraph, and circle the ten fragments that start with prepositions or dependent words. Then, correct the fragments. *Answers may vary. Possible edits are shown.*

(For many hundreds of years,) People have used natural remedies to heal an illness. They eat chicken soup. (Because it is healthy and helps the immune system.) People are not the only ones (Who like chicken soup.) Two pandas are fed chicken soup to help maintain their health. (In the Wuhan Zoo in central China.) The animals had been moved in June, (Because their habitat had been damaged by an earthquake.) They faced a challenge adjusting to their new home. Then, during a national holiday, many visitors came. (To the zoo to see the pandas.) The animals got tired and stressed. (When so many people crowded around their area.) Zoo-keepers cooked up chicken soup. (Because colder weather was on the way.) They boiled the chicken for twelve hours, (Which seems like a long time but helped increase the flavor.) The keepers were not sure the pandas would enjoy the soup. Each panda ate over two pounds of soup. In giant

dishes along with their regular diet.

. . . .

3. Fragments That Start with *-ing* Verb Forms

An **-ing verb form** (also called a **gerund**) is the form of a verb that ends in
-ing: *walking, writing, running*. Unless it has a helping verb (**was** *walking*, **was**
writing, **was** *running*), it cannot be a complete verb in a sentence. Sometimes,
an *-ing* verb form is used at the beginning of a complete sentence.

> **SENTENCE**   Walking is good exercise.
>
> [The *-ing* verb form *walking* is the subject; *is* is the verb. The sen-
> tence expresses a complete thought.]

Sometimes, an *-ing* verb form introduces a fragment. When an *-ing*
verb form starts what you think is a sentence, stop and check for a subject,
a verb, and a complete thought.

> **FRAGMENT**   I ran as fast as I could. *Hoping to get there on time.*
>
> [*Hoping to get there on time* lacks a subject and a verb.]

LANGUAGE NOTE: English uses *-ing* verb forms (*Han loves* **running**) and *infinitives* (*to* before the verb) (*Han loves* **to run**). If these forms confuse you,
pay special attention to this section. See also Chapter 33.

Correct a fragment that starts with an *-ing* verb form either by adding
whatever sentence elements are missing (usually a subject and a helping
verb) or by connecting the fragment to the sentence before or after it. Usually, you will need to put a comma before or after the fragment to join it to
the complete sentence.

Finding and Fixing Fragments:
Fragments That Start with *-ing* Verb Forms

Find

I was running as fast as I could. Hoping to get there on time.

1. **Circle** any *-ing* verb that starts a word group.
2. **Ask:** Does the word group have a subject? *No.* A verb? *Yes.* **Underline**
   any subject, and **double-underline** any verb.
3. **Ask:** Does the word group express a complete thought? *No.*
4. If the word group is missing a subject or a verb or does not express a complete thought, it is a fragment. *This word group is a fragment.*

↓

```
                          Fix

                        , h
    I was running as fast as I could. Hoping to get there on time.
                              ^

                             I was still hoping
    I was running as fast as I could. Hoping to get there on time.
                                     ^
```

5. **Correct the fragment** by joining it to the sentence before or after it. **Alternative:** Add the missing sentence elements.

· ·

PRACTICE 4   Correcting Fragments That Start with *-ing* Verb Forms

Circle any *-ing* verb that appears at the beginning of a word group in the paragraph. Then, read the word group to see if it has a subject and a verb and expresses a complete thought. Not *all* of the word groups that start with an *-ing* verb are fragments, so read carefully. In the space provided, record the number of the items that are fragments. Then, on a separate piece of paper, correct the fragment either by adding the missing sentence elements or by connecting it to the sentence before or after it. *Answers will vary. Possible edits are shown.*

Which numbers are fragments?   _____4, 7, 9, 11_____

    (1) People sometimes travel long distances in unusual ways trying to set new world records. (2) (Walking) is one unusual way to set records. (3) In 1931, Plennie Wingo set out on an ambitious journey, (4) (Walking) backward around the world. (5) (Wearing) sunglasses with rearview mirrors, he started his trip early one morning. (6) After eight thousand miles, Wingo's journey was interrupted by a war in Pakistan, (7) (Ending) his ambitious journey. (8) Hans Mullikan spent more than two years in the late 1970s traveling to the White House by crawling from Texas to Washington, D.C. (9) (Taking) time out to earn money as a logger and a Baptist minister. (10) Alvin Straight, suffering from poor eyesight, traveled across the Midwest on a lawnmower, (11) (Looking) for his long-lost brother.

· ·

4.   Fragments That Start with *to* and a Verb

When what you think is a sentence begins with *to* and a verb (called the *infinitive* form of the verb), you need to make sure that it is not a fragment.

FRAGMENT   Each day, I check freecycle.com. *To see if it has anything I need.*

CORRECTED   Each day, I check freecycle.com to see if it has anything
                      I need.

If a word group begins with *to* and a verb, it must have another verb, or it is not a complete sentence. When you see a word group that begins with *to* and a verb, first check to see if there is another verb. If there is no other verb, the word group is a fragment.

SENTENCE   *To run* a complete marathon was my goal.
                      [*To run* is the subject; *was* is the verb.]

FRAGMENT   Cheri got underneath the car. *To change the oil.*
                      [No other verb appears in the word group that begins with *to change.*]

LANGUAGE NOTE: Do not confuse the infinitive (*to* before the verb) with *that.*

INCORRECT   My brother wants *that* his girlfriend cook.

CORRECT   My brother wants his girlfriend *to cook.*

To correct a fragment that starts with *to* and a verb, join it to the sentence before or after it, or add the missing sentence elements.

Finding and Fixing Fragments:
Fragments That Start with *to* and a Verb

Find

Cheri got underneath the car. (To change) the oil.

1. **Circle** any *to*-plus-verb combination that starts a word group.
2. **Ask:** Does the word group have a subject? *No.* A verb? *Yes.* **Underline** any subject, and **double-underline** any verb.
3. **Ask:** Does the word group express a complete thought? *No.*
4. If the word group is missing a subject or verb or does not express a complete thought, it is a fragment. *This word group is a fragment.*

Fix

                                   t
Cheri got underneath the car. To change the oil.
                              ^

To change the oil,
Cheri got underneath the car. ~~To change the oil.~~
^

                              She needed to
Cheri got underneath the car. ~~To~~ change the oil.
                              ^

5. **Correct the fragment** by joining it to the sentence before or after it. If you put the *to*-plus-verb word group first, put a comma after it. **Alternative:** Add the missing sentence elements.

. . . .

PRACTICE 5   Correcting Fragments That Start with *to* and a Verb

Circle any *to*-plus-verb combination that appears at the beginning of a sentence in the paragraph. Then, read the word group to see if it has a subject and a verb and expresses a complete thought. Not *all* of the word groups that start with *to* and a verb are fragments, so read carefully. In the space provided, record the number of the items that are fragments. Then, on a separate piece of paper, correct the fragment either by adding the missing sentence elements or by connecting it to the sentence before or after it. *Answers may vary. Possible edits are shown.*

Which numbers are fragments?   ___4, 7, 9, 14___

(1) In the past, someone had to be famous to appear on a postage stamp. (2) Now, though, it is easy to put any face or image on a stamp. (3) Many Web sites show you how. (4) To make personalized stamps. (5) To be on a stamp, the photo must be in digital format. (6) Many parents use the sites after their children are born. (7) To make stamps to put on birth announcements. (8) Photo stamps of grandchildren are great gifts. (9) To give to grandparents. (10) Some people put photos of their pets on stamps. (11) To people who are used to seeing only famous people or objects on stamps, personalized stamps are still surprising. (12) Personalized stamps are not cheap, though. (13) It costs more than twice as much as regular stamps. (14) To order stamps with personal photos.

. . . .

5.   Fragments That Are Examples or Explanations

As you edit your writing, pay special attention to groups of words that are examples or explanations of information you presented in the previous sentence. They may be fragments.

FRAGMENT	People have different kinds of learning styles. *For example, visual or auditory.*
FRAGMENT	I learn best by performing an action. *Such as an experiment.*
	[*For example, visual and auditory* and *Such as an experiment* are not complete thoughts.]

This last type of fragment is harder to recognize because there is no single word or kind of word to look for. The following words may signal a fragment, but fragments that are examples or explanations do not always start with these words.

especially   for example   like   such as

When a group of words gives an example of information in the previous sentence, stop to check it for a subject, a verb, and a complete thought.

FRAGMENT   I have found great things at freecycle.com. *Like a nearly new computer.*

FRAGMENT   Freecycle.com is a good site. *Especially for household items.*

FRAGMENT   It lists many gently used appliances. *Such as DVD players.*

> [*Like a nearly new computer, Especially for household items,* and *Such as DVD players* are not complete thoughts.]

TIP *Such as* and *like* do not often begin complete sentences.

Correct a fragment that starts with an example or explanation by connecting it to the sentence before or after it. Sometimes, you can add whatever sentence elements are missing (a subject or a verb or both) instead. When you connect the fragment to a sentence, you may need to change some punctuation. For example, fragments that are examples and fragments that are negatives are often set off by a comma.

Finding and Fixing Fragments:
Fragments That Are Examples or Explanations

Find

Freecycle.com recycles usable items. (Such as clothing.)

1. **Circle** the word group that is an example or explanation.
2. **Ask:** Does the word group have a subject, a verb, and a complete thought? *No.*
3. If the word group is missing a subject or a verb or does not express a complete thought, it is a fragment. *This word group is a fragment.*

Fix

                                          , s
Freecycle.com recycles usable items. Such as clothing.
                                     ^ ^

You may need to add some words to correct fragments:

> I should list some things on freecycle.com. The sweaters I never
> wear. *could keep others warm*
>   ^

4. **Correct the fragment** by joining it to the sentence before or after it or by adding the missing sentence elements.

PRACTICE 6   Correcting Fragments That Are Examples or Explanations

Circle word groups that are examples or explanations. Then, read the word group to see if it has a subject and verb and expresses a complete thought. In the space provided, record the numbers of the items that are fragments. Then, on a separate piece of paper, correct the fragment either by adding the missing sentence elements or by connecting it to the sentence before or after it. *Answers may vary. Possible edits are shown.*

Which numbers are fragments?   *2, 4, 6, 8, 10*

(1) Being a smart consumer can be difficult. (2) Especially when making a major purchase. (3) At car dealerships, for example, important information is often in small type. (4) Like finance charges or preparation charges. (5) Advertisements also put negative information in small type. (6) Such as a drug's side effects. (7) Credit card offers often use tiny, hard-to-read print for the terms of the card. (8) Like interest charges and late fees, which can really add up. (9) Phone service charges can also be hidden in small print. (10) Like limits on text messaging and other functions. (11) Especially now, as businesses try to make it seem as if you are getting a good deal, it is important to read any offer carefully.

Edit for Fragments

Use the chart, Finding and Fixing Fragments, on page 342, to help you complete the practices in this section and edit your own writing.

PRACTICE 7   Editing Fragments

TEAMWORK Divide the class into small groups, and have each group present a corrected paragraph. Compare the different ways that the groups correct the fragments.

In the following items, circle each word group that is a fragment. Then, correct fragments by connecting them to the previous or the next sentence or by adding the missing sentence elements. *Answers will vary. Possible edits are shown.*

EXAMPLE: (With the high cost of producing video games) ~~Game~~ **, game** publishers are turning to a new source of revenue.

1. (To add to their income) ~~Publishers~~ **, publishers** are placing advertisements in their games.

2. Sometimes, the ads show a character using a product. (For example, **a character might be shown** drinking a specific brand of soda to earn health points.)

3. One character, a racecar driver, drove his ad-covered car. ~~Across~~ the
across

finish line.

4. When a warrior character picked up a sword decorated with an athletic-
shoe logo. ~~Some~~ players complained.
, some

5. Worrying that ads are distracting. ~~Some~~ publishers are trying to limit the
, some
number of ads per game.

6. But most players do not seem to mind seeing ads in video games. ~~If~~
if
there are not too many of them.

7. These players are used to seeing ads in all kinds of places. ~~Like~~ grocery
, like
carts and restroom walls.

8. For video game publishers. ~~The~~ goal is making a profit, but most pub-
, the
lishers also care about the product.

9. To strike a balance between profitable advertising and high game quality.
~~That~~ is what publishers want.

10. Doing market research. ~~Will~~ help publishers find that balance.
will

• •

PRACTICE 8   Editing Fragments

Find and correct ten fragments in the following paragraphs.

1. Ida Lewis was born on February 25, 1842, in Newport, Rhode
Island. Her father, Hosea, had been a coast pilot but was transferred to
the Lighthouse Service. Although he was in failing health. ~~In~~ 1853, he
i
was appointed lighthouse keeper at Lime Rock in Newport. Many lighthouse keepers were forced to leave family behind when they assumed
their duties. ~~Because~~ the lighthouses were in remote locations and the
b
living situations were poor. At first, Lime Rock had only a shed. ~~For~~ the
f
keeper and a temporary lantern for light. Appropriate housing was constructed in 1857, and Hosea moved his family to Lime Rock.

2. Hosea was completely disabled by a stroke. ~~In~~ only a few months.
i
Ida, who was already caring for an ill sister, took care of her father and
the lighthouse as well. ~~Keeping~~ the lighthouse lamp lit. At sunset, the
, k
lamp had to be filled with oil and refilled at midnight. The reflectors
needed constant polishing, and the light had to be extinguished in the
morning. Since schools were on the mainland, Ida rowed her brothers

and sisters to school every day, Strengthening her rowing ability, which ultimately saved many lives. In 1872, Hosea died, and Ida's mother was appointed keeper. Even though Ida did all the work. Finally, in 1879, Ida became the keeper and received a salary of $500 a year.

3. She was the best-known lighthouse keeper because of her many rescues. Some called her "The Bravest Woman in America." Saving eighteen lives during her time of service. In 1867, during a storm, sheepherders had gone into the water after a lost sheep. Ida saved both the sheep and the sheepherders. She became famous, and many important people came to see her, For example, President Ulysses S. Grant. All the ships anchored in the harbor tolled their bells, To honor her after her death. Later, the Rhode Island legislature changed the name of Lime Rock to Ida Lewis Rock, the first and only time this honor was awarded.

- -

PRACTICE 9 Editing Fragments and Using Formal English

TIP For more advice on using formal English, see Chapter 3. For advice on choosing appropriate words, see Chapter 34.

Your friend wants to send this thank-you note to an employer who interviewed her for a job. She knows the note has problems and has asked for your help. Correct the fragments in the note. Then, edit the informal English in it. *Answers will vary. Possible edits are shown.*

Dear Ms. Hernandez,

(1) Thank you so much for taking the time. (2) To meet with me this
past Wednesday. (3) I am more ~~psyched~~ *excited* than ever about the administrative assistant position at Fields Corporation. (4) Learning more
about the ~~stuff I would need to do. Was very cool.~~ *challenges and requirements of the job was valuable to me.* (5) Also, I enjoyed
meeting you and the other managers. (6) With my strong organizational
skills, professional experience, and friendly personality, (7) I'm sure
that I would be ~~awesome for the job.~~ *an asset to the company.* (8) Because ~~I'm totally jazzed~~ *of my strong interest in the position,*
~~about the position.~~ (9) I hope you will keep me in mind. (10) Please let
me know if you need any other ~~info.~~ *information, like* (11) ~~Like~~ references or a writing
sample.
(12) ~~Thank U much,~~ *Thanks again for your time.*

Sincerely,

Terri Hammons

● ●

PRACTICE 10   Editing Irene's Letter

Look back at Irene's letter on page 321. You may have already underlined the fragments in her letter; if not, do so now. Next, using what you have learned in this chapter, correct each fragment in the letter.

● ●

PRACTICE 11   Editing Your Own Writing for Fragments

As a final practice, edit fragments in a piece of your own writing—a paper you are working on for this class, a paper for another course, or your idea journal (p. 325) response. Use the chart on page 342 to help you.

● ●

Chapter Review

1.   A *sentence* is a group of words that has three elements: a
_____*subject*_____ , a _____*verb*_____ , and a *complete thought* .

2.   A _____*fragment*_____ seems to be a complete sentence but is only a piece of one. It lacks a _____*subject*_____ , a _____*verb*_____ , or a *complete thought* .

3.   What are the five trouble spots that signal possible fragments?
A word group that starts with a preposition
A word group that starts with a dependent word
A word group that starts with an "-ing" verb form
A word group that starts with "to" and a verb
A word group that is an example or explanation

4.   What are the two basic ways to correct fragments?
Add what is missing (a subject, a verb, or both).
Attach the fragment to the sentence before or after it.

LEARNING JOURNAL What kind of fragments do you find in your writing? What is the main thing you have learned about fragments that will help you? What is unclear to you?

TEACHING TIP You can collect students' learning journals to find out what the class or individual students need more work on.

RESOURCES For Cumulative Editing Review Tests, see pages 601–10.

Chapter Test

TIP For advice on taking tests, see Appendix A.

Circle the correct choice for each of the following items. Use the Finding and Fixing Fragments chart on page 342 to help you.

1. If an underlined portion of this sentence is incorrect, select the revision that fixes it. If the sentence is correct as written, choose d.

   Natalie did not <u>go on</u> our bike <u>trip. Because</u> she could not <u>ride a</u> bike.
   A$$B$$C

   a. go. On

   b. trip because ⃝

   c. ride; a

   d. No change is necessary.

RESOURCES The *Testing Tool Kit* CD-ROM available with this book has even more tests.

2. Choose the item that has no errors.

   a. Since Gary is the most experienced hiker here, he should lead the way. ⃝

   b. Since Gary is the most experienced hiker here. He should lead the way.

   c. Since Gary is the most experienced hiker here; he should lead the way.

3. If an underlined portion of this sentence is incorrect, select the revision that fixes it. If the sentence is correct as written, choose d.

   <u>Planting fragrant flowers will</u> attract <u>wildlife. Such</u> as butterflies.
   A$$B$$C

   a. When planting

   b. flowers; will

   c. wildlife, such ⃝

   d. No change is necessary.

4. Choose the item that has no errors.

   a. To get to the concert hall; take exit 5 and drive for three miles.

   b. To get to the concert hall. Take exit 5 and drive for three miles.

   c. To get to the concert hall, take exit 5 and drive for three miles. ⃝

5. If an underlined portion of this sentence is incorrect, select the revision that fixes it. If the sentence is correct as written, choose d.

   Buying many unnecessary <u>groceries. Shows</u> that you felt <u>deprived as</u>
   ABC
   a child.

   a. groceries shows ⃝

   b. that: you

   c. deprived. As

   d. No change is necessary.

6. If an underlined portion of this sentence is incorrect, select the revision that fixes it. If the sentence is correct as written, choose d.

Some scientists <u>predict that</u> people will <u>soon take</u> vacation
$\qquad$ A $\qquad\qquad\qquad$ B

<u>cruises. Into</u> space.
$\qquad$ C

   a. predict, that   **(c.)** cruises into

   b. soon; take   **d.** No change is necessary.

7. Choose the item that has no errors.

   a. Walking for ten miles after her car broke down. Pearl became tired and frustrated.

   b. Walking for ten miles after her car broke down; Pearl became tired and frustrated.

   (c.) Walking for ten miles after her car broke down, Pearl became tired and frustrated.

8. Choose the item that has no errors.

   a. Many people find it hard. To concentrate during stressful times.

   (b.) Many people find it hard to concentrate during stressful times.

   c. Many people find it hard, to concentrate during stressful times.

9. If an underlined portion of this sentence is incorrect, select the revision that fixes it. If the sentence is correct as written, choose d.

<u>Growing suspicious,</u> the secret <u>agent discovered</u> a tiny recording
$\qquad$ A $\qquad\qquad\qquad\qquad$ B

device <u>inside a flower vase.</u>
$\qquad$ C

   a. Growing, suspicious   **c.** inside, a flower vase

   b. agent. Discovered   **(d.)** No change is necessary.

10. If an underlined portion of this sentence is incorrect, select the revision that fixes it. If the sentence is correct as written, choose d.

<u>Early in their training,</u> <u>doctors learn</u> there is a fine <u>line. Between</u>
$\qquad$ A $\qquad\qquad\qquad$ B $\qquad\qquad\qquad\qquad$ C

life and death.

   a. Early, in   **(c.)** line between

   b. doctors. Learn   **d.** No change is necessary.

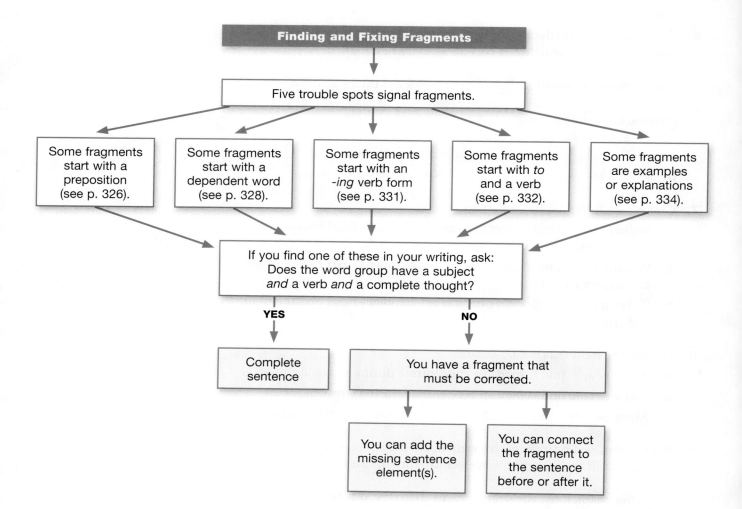

Finding and Fixing Fragments

Five trouble spots signal fragments.

Some fragments start with a preposition (see p. 326).

Some fragments start with a dependent word (see p. 328).

Some fragments start with an *-ing* verb form (see p. 331).

Some fragments start with *to* and a verb (see p. 332).

Some fragments are examples or explanations (see p. 334).

If you find one of these in your writing, ask: Does the word group have a subject *and* a verb *and* a complete thought?

YES

NO

Complete sentence

You have a fragment that must be corrected.

You can add the missing sentence element(s).

You can connect the fragment to the sentence before or after it.

Run-Ons

Two Sentences Joined Incorrectly

Understand What Run-Ons Are

A sentence is also called an **independent clause**, a group of words with a subject and a verb that expresses a complete thought. Sometimes, two independent clauses can be joined to form one larger sentence.

TIP In the examples throughout this chapter, subjects are underlined once, and verbs are underlined twice.

SENTENCE WITH TWO INDEPENDENT CLAUSES

The college offers financial aid, and it encourages students to apply.

There are two kinds of run-ons: **fused sentences** and **comma splices**. A **run-on** is two complete sentences joined incorrectly as one sentence.

A **fused sentence** is two complete sentences joined without any punctuation.

FUSED SENTENCE

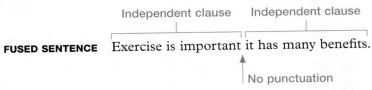

Exercise is important it has many benefits.

No punctuation

A **comma splice** is two complete sentences joined by only a comma.

TIP To find and correct run-ons, you need to be able to identify a complete sentence. For a review, see Chapter 21.

COMMA SPLICE

My mother jogs every morning, she runs three miles.

Comma

When you join two sentences, use the proper punctuation.

CORRECTIONS Exercise is important; it has many benefits.

My mother jogs every morning; she runs three miles.

In the Real World, Why Is It Important to Correct Run-Ons?

Run-ons are errors that people notice and consider major mistakes.

SITUATION: Naomi is applying to a special program for returning students at Cambridge College. Here is one of the essay questions on the application, followed by a paragraph from Naomi's response.

STATEMENT OF PURPOSE: In two hundred words or less, describe your intellectual and professional goals and how a Cambridge College education will assist you in achieving them.

For many years, I did not take control of my life; I just drifted without any goals. I realized one day as I met with my daughter's guidance counselor that I hoped my daughter would not turn out like me. From that moment, I decided to do something to help myself and others. I set a goal of becoming a teacher. To begin on that path, I took a math course at night school, then I took another in science. I passed both courses with hard work, I know I can do well in the Cambridge College program. I am committed to the professional goal I finally found it has given new purpose to my whole life.

STUDENT VOICES

MARY LACUE BOOKER'S RESPONSE: Mary LaCue Booker, a master's degree recipient from Cambridge College, read Naomi's answer and commented:

Cambridge College wants students who are thoughtful, hardworking, and mature. Although Naomi's essay indicates that she has some of these qualities, her writing gives another impression. She makes several noticeable errors; I wonder if she took the time to really think about this essay. If she is careless on a document that represents her for college admission, will she be careless in other areas as well? It is too bad, because her qualifications are quite good otherwise.

• (See Mary's **PROFILE OF SUCCESS** on page 246.)

Find and Correct Run-Ons

To find run-ons, focus on each sentence in your writing, one at a time. Until you get used to finding them (or until you do not make the errors anymore), this step will take extra time. But if you spend the extra time, your writing will improve.

. . . .

PRACTICE 1   Finding Run-Ons

Find and underline the four run-ons in Naomi's writing on page 345.

. . . .

Once you have found a run-on, there are five ways to correct it.

FIVE WAYS TO CORRECT RUN-ONS

1. **Add a period.**

   He
   I saw the man. ~~he~~ was running home.
   ^

2. **Add a semicolon.**

   I saw the man; he was running home.

3. **Add a semicolon, a conjunctive adverb, and a comma.**

   however,
   I saw the man; he was running home.
   ^

4. **Add a comma and a coordinating conjunction.**

   but
   I saw the man, he was running home.
   ^

5. **Add a dependent word.**

   When
   I saw the man, he was running home.
   ^

Add a Period

You can correct run-ons by adding a period to make two separate sentences. After adding the period, capitalize the letter that begins the new sentence. Reread your two sentences to make sure they each contain a subject, a verb, and a complete thought.

S + V . S + V .

Independent clause   Independent clause

FUSED SENTENCE   . *S*
(CORRECTED)   I interviewed a candidate for a job ~~s~~he gave me the
                                                        ^
     "dead fish" handshake.

| **COMMA SPLICE (CORRECTED)** | The "dead fish" is a limp handshake ̣T the person plops her hand into yours. |

Add a Semicolon

A second way to correct run-ons is to use a semicolon (;) to join the two sentences. Use a semicolon only when the two sentences express closely related ideas and the words on each side of the semicolon can stand alone as a complete sentence. Do not capitalize the word that follows a semicolon unless it is the name of a specific person, place, or thing that is usually capitalized—for example, Mary, New York, or Eiffel Tower.

| **FUSED SENTENCE (CORRECTED)** | Slouching creates a terrible impression ; it makes a person seem uninterested, bored, or lacking in self-confidence. |

| **COMMA SPLICE (CORRECTED)** | It is important in an interview to hold your head up ; it is just as important to sit up straight. |

Add a Semicolon and a Conjunctive Adverb

A third way to correct run-ons is to add a semicolon followed by a **conjunctive adverb** and a comma.

Common Conjunctive Adverbs

consequently	indeed	moreover	still
finally	instead	nevertheless	then
furthermore	likewise	otherwise	therefore
however	meanwhile	similarly	

> ## Finding and Fixing Run-Ons:
> ## Adding a Period or Semicolon

> ### Find
>
> Few <u>people</u> <u>know</u> the history of many popular holidays <u>Valentine's Day</u> <u>is</u> one of these holidays.
>
> 1. To see if there are two independent clauses in a sentence, **underline** the subjects, and **double-underline** the verbs.
> 2. **Ask:** If the sentence has two independent clauses, are they separated by either a period or a semicolon? *No. It is a run-on.*

> ### Fix
>
> Few people know the history of many popular holidays.
> Valentine's Day is one of these holidays.
>
> Few people know the history of many popular holidays;
> Valentine's Day is one of these holidays.
>
> Few people know the history of many popular holidays; *indeed,*
> Valentine's Day is one of these holidays.
>
> 3. **Correct** the error by adding a period, a semicolon, or a semicolon and a conjunctive adverb.

TEACHING TIP You may want to warn students that if they have written a sentence that is longer than two lines, they should look at it closely to see if it has errors.

PRACTICE 2 Correcting a Run-On by Adding a Period or a Semicolon

TIP For more practices on run-ons, visit Exercise Central at **bedfordstmartins.com/realwriting**.

For each of the following items, indicate in the space to the left whether it is a fused sentence ("FS") or a comma splice ("CS"). Then, correct the error by adding a period or a semicolon. Capitalize the letters as necessary to make two sentences. *Answers will vary. Possible answers are shown.*

> **EXAMPLE:** _FS_ Being a farmer can mean dealing with all types of challenges; one of the biggest ones comes from the sky.

RESOURCES To gauge students' skills in correcting run-ons, use the *Testing Tool Kit* CD-ROM available with this book.

_CS_ **1.** Farmers have been trying to keep hungry birds out of their crops for centuries; the first scarecrow was invented for this reason.

_CS_ **2.** Some farmers have used a variety of chemicals. Other farmers have tried noise, such as small cannons.

_FS_ **3.** Recently, a group of berry farmers tried something new. They brought in bigger birds called falcons.

_FS_   **4.** Small birds such as starlings love munching on berries ⌃; each year they destroy thousands of dollars' worth of farmers' berry crops.

_FS_   **5.** Because these starlings are frightened of falcons, they fly away when they see these birds of prey in the fields ~~they~~ . They ⌃ need to get to where they feel safe.

_CS_   **6.** Using falcons to protect their crops saves farmers money, . It it ⌃ does not damage the environment either.

_FS_   **7.** A falconer, or a person who raises and trains falcons, keeps an eye on the birds during the day . He ~~he~~ ⌃ makes sure they only chase away the starlings instead of killing them.

_CS_   **8.** Falcons are used for protection in other places as well, . They ~~they~~ ⌃ are used in vineyards to keep pests from eating the grapes.

_FS_   **9.** In recent years, the falcons have also been used in landfills to scatter birds and other wildlife . Some ~~some~~ ⌃ have even been used at large airports to keep flocks of birds away from landing airplanes.

_FS_   **10.** Although a falconer's services are not cheap, they cost less than some other methods that farmers have tried . for ~~for~~ ⌃ example, putting nets over a berry field can often cost more than $200,000.

Add a Comma and a Coordinating Conjunction

A fourth way to correct run-ons is to add a comma and a **coordinating conjunction**: a link that joins independent clauses to form one sentence. The seven coordinating conjunctions are *and, but, for, nor, or, so, yet*. Some people remember these words by thinking of them as *fanboys: for, and, nor, but, or, yet, so*.

To correct a fused sentence, add a comma and a coordinating conjunction. A comma splice already has a comma, so just add a coordinating conjunction that makes sense in the sentence.

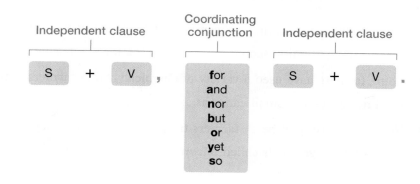

TIP Notice that the comma does not follow the conjunction. The comma follows the word before the conjunction.

**FUSED SENTENCE
(CORRECTED)**   Nakeisha was qualified for the job ~~,~~ *but* she hurt her chances by mumbling.

**COMMA SPLICE
(CORRECTED)**   The candidate smiled, *and* she waved to the crowd.

Coordinating conjunctions need to connect two independent clauses. They are not used to join a dependent and an independent clause.

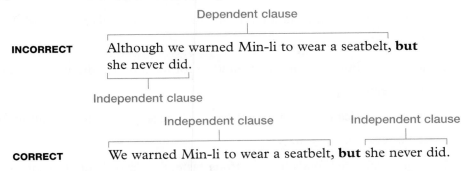

Dependent clause

INCORRECT   Although we warned Min-li to wear a seatbelt, **but** she never did.

Independent clause

Independent clause   Independent clause

CORRECT   We warned Min-li to wear a seatbelt, **but** she never did.

Finding and Fixing Run-Ons:
Using a Comma and a Coordinating Conjunction

Find

Foods differ from place to place your favorite treat might disgust someone from another culture.

1. To see if there are two independent clauses in a sentence, **underline** the subjects, and **double-underline** the verbs.

2. **Ask:** If the sentence has two independent clauses, are they separated by either a period or a semicolon? *No. It is a run-on.*

Fix

Foods differ from place to place *, and* your favorite treat might disgust someone from another culture.

3. **Correct** a fused sentence by adding a comma and a coordinating conjunction between the two independent clauses. Correct a comma splice by adding just a coordinating conjunction.

**PRACTICE 3   Correcting Run-Ons by Adding a Comma
and/or a Coordinating Conjunction**

Correct each of the following run-ons by adding a comma, if necessary, and an appropriate coordinating conjunction. First, underline the subjects, and double-underline the verbs. *Answers will vary. Possible edits are shown.*

> **EXAMPLE:** Most <u>Americans</u> <u>do</u> not <u>like</u> the idea of eating certain kinds
> of food, *and* most of us <u>would</u> probably <u>reject</u> horse meat.
>   ^

1. In most cultures, popular <u>foods</u> <u>depend</u> on availability and tradition *, so*
   <u>people</u> <u>tend</u> to eat old familiar favorites.
                                       ^

2. <u>Sushi</u> <u>shocked</u> many Americans twenty years ago, *but* today some young
   <u>people</u> in the United States <u>have grown up</u> eating raw fish.
                              ^

3. In many societies, certain <u>foods</u> <u>are allowed</u> to age *, for* this <u>process</u> <u>adds</u>
   flavor.
                                                         ^

4. <u>Icelanders</u> <u>bury</u> eggs in the ground to rot for months, *and* these aged <u>eggs</u> <u>are</u>
   <u>considered</u> a special treat.
                                                       ^

5. As an American, <u>you</u> <u>might</u> not like such eggs *, or* the <u>thought</u> of eating them
   <u>might</u> even <u>revolt</u> you.
                                       ^

6. In general, aged <u>foods</u> <u>have</u> a strong taste, *so* the <u>flavor</u> <u>is</u> unpleasant to
   someone unaccustomed to those foods.
                                    ^

7. Many <u>Koreans</u> <u>love</u> to eat kimchee, a spicy aged cabbage, *but* <u>Americans</u>
   often <u>find</u> the taste odd and the smell overpowering.
                                                  ^

8. <u>Herders</u> in Kyrgyzstan <u>drink</u> kumiss *, and* this <u>beverage</u> <u>is made</u> of aged
   horse's milk.
                                          ^

9. <u>Americans</u> on a visit to Kyrgyzstan <u>consider</u> themselves brave for tasting
   kumiss, *but* local <u>children</u> <u>drink</u> it regularly.
          ^

10. We <u>think</u> of familiar foods as normal, *yet* favorite American <u>foods</u> <u>might</u>
    <u>horrify</u> people in other parts of the world.
                                    ^

Add a Dependent Word

A fifth way to correct run-ons is to make one of the complete sentences a dependent clause by adding a dependent word (a **subordinating conjunction** or a **relative pronoun**), such as *after, because, before, even though, if, that, though, unless, when, who,* and *which.* (For a more complete list of these words, see the graphic on p. 351.) Choose the dependent word that best expresses the relationship between the two clauses.

Use a dependent word when the clause it begins is less important than the other clause or explains the other clause, as in the following sentence.

> *When* <u>I</u> <u>get</u> to the train station, <u>I</u> <u>will call</u> Josh.

The italicized clause is dependent (subordinate) because it just explains when the most important part of the sentence—calling Josh—will happen. It begins with the dependent word *when.*

Because a dependent clause is not a complete sentence (it has a subject and verb but does not express a complete thought), it can be joined to a sentence without creating a run-on. When the dependent clause is the second clause in a sentence, you usually do not need to put a comma before it unless it is showing contrast.

TWO SENTENCES

Halloween was originally a religious holiday. People worshiped the saints.

DEPENDENT CLAUSE: NO COMMA NEEDED

Halloween was originally a religious holiday *when people worshiped the saints.*

DEPENDENT CLAUSE SHOWING CONTRAST: COMMA NEEDED

Many holidays have religious origins, *though the celebrations have moved away from their religious roots.*

TIP For more on using commas with dependent clauses, see Chapters 30 and 37.

after	if/if only	until
although	now that	what(ever)
as	once	when(ever)
because	since	where
before	so that	whether
even if/though	that	which(ever)
how	though	while
	unless	who

FUSED SENTENCE (CORRECTED) Your final statement should express your interest in , although the position you do not want to sound desperate.
[The dependent clause *although you do not want to sound desperate* shows contrast, so a comma comes before it.]

COMMA SPLICE (CORRECTED) It is important to end an interview on a positive note, because that final impression is what the interviewer will remember.

You can also put the dependent clause first. When the dependent clause comes first, be sure to put a comma after it.

FUSED SENTENCE (CORRECTED) When the The interviewer stands, the candidate should shake hands firmly.

After the

COMMA SPLICE   ~~The~~ interview is over, the candidate should stand and
(CORRECTED)

smile politely.

**Finding and Fixing Run-Ons:
Making a Dependent Clause**

Find

Alzheimer's disease is a heartbreaking illness, it causes a steady

decrease in brain capacity.

1. To see if there are two independent clauses in a sentence, **underline** the
   subjects, and **double-underline** the verbs.
2. **Ask:** If the sentence has two independent clauses, are they separated by a
   period, a semicolon, or a comma and a coordinating conjunction? *No. It is
   a comma splice.*

Fix

because

Alzheimer's disease is a heartbreaking illness, it causes a steady

decrease in brain capacity.

3. If one part of the sentence is less important than the other, or if you want to
   make it so, add a dependent word to the less important part.

PRACTICE 4   Correcting a Run-On by Adding a Dependent Word

Correct run-ons by adding a dependent word to make a dependent clause. First,
underline the subjects, and double-underline the verbs. Although these run-ons
can be corrected in different ways, in this exercise correct by adding dependent
words. You may want to refer to the chart on page 351.

, although

EXAMPLE: Fans like basketball's many rules and traditions they

sometimes forget about the actual ball's history.

Answers will vary. Possible edits are shown.

1. The National Basketball Association (NBA) has used basketballs made

   although

   out of leather for decades, it recently decided to use ones made out of a

   synthetic material instead.

2. The NBA decided to make this change in 2006, *when* it wanted every basket-

   ball it produced to feel and bounce exactly the same.

3. ~~This~~ *While this* was a reasonable idea, it did not work as planned.

4. ~~Players~~ *When players* began complaining immediately about the synthetic basketballs, the NBA knew something was wrong and began investigating.

5. To find out what was not working with the basketballs, the NBA talked to several scientists *since* they know a great deal about how everyday items work.

6. ~~The~~ *As the* scientists studied the friction of synthetic basketballs versus leather ones, they quickly discovered that friction determined how well players could hold onto a ball.

7. ~~The~~ *Though the* plastic ball was easier to grip when it was dry, it lost friction and was harder to hold once it got wet.

8. ~~Players~~ *When players* who have been in the game for a long time begin to perspire, leather basketballs absorb the sweat, while plastic ones cannot.

9. ~~The~~ *Until the* researchers analyzed the differences between the leather and synthetic basketballs, they did not realize that the logo printed on the plastic ones also made them bounce improperly.

10. ~~The~~ *Although the* traditional leather basketballs are not perfect, they will continue to be used until something more reliable comes along.

. . . .

A Word That Can Cause Run-Ons: *Then*

Many run-ons are caused by the word *then*. You can use *then* to join two sentences, but if you add it without the correct punctuation or added words, your sentence will be a run-on. Often, writers use just a comma before *then*, but that makes a comma splice.

COMMA SPLICE   I picked up my laundry, then I went home.

Use any of the methods you have just practiced to correct errors caused by *then*. These methods are shown in the following examples.

I picked up my laundry; *T*hen I went home.

I picked up my laundry; then I went home.

I picked up my laundry, *and* then I went home.

I picked up my laundry, *before* ~~then~~ I went home.

Edit Run-Ons

Use the chart on page 359, Finding and Fixing Run-Ons, to help you complete the practices in this section and edit your own writing.

· ·

PRACTICE 5   Editing Run-Ons

In the following items, correct any run-ons. Use each method of correcting such errors—adding a period, adding a semicolon, adding a semicolon and a conjunctive adverb, adding a comma and a coordinating conjunction, or adding a dependent word—at least once. *Answers will vary. Possible edits are shown.*

> **EXAMPLE:** Most people expect to be cramped in an airplane seat *, but* more spacious seating is on the way.

1. *Even though jumbo* ~~Jumbo~~-sized airplanes can hold up to 500 people, they are now being designed with only 300 seats.

2. This design allows space for onboard lounges *; moreover,* it provides room for passengers to walk around.

3. Another way to add room is to eliminate the phones on the seatbacks *since* hardly anyone uses those phones anyway.

4. This change moves the upper seatback two inches farther from the person behind it *;* that will make a surprising difference in comfort.

5. New design features will also make passengers feel more comfortable *.* *T* these include softer lighting and larger overhead luggage bins.

6. Also, the bathrooms will be bigger *;* this change will be welcomed by many passengers.

7. The most noticeable difference in the new planes will be the large windows *. T* they will be 19 inches high and 11 inches wide.

8. This new dimension is twice the size of normal airplane portholes *, so* passengers will get better views of the sky and land.

9. Something about being able to see more of our surroundings puts us at ease *;* at least, that is what the airlines hope.

10. Nevertheless, added spaciousness will not matter to some travelers *because* many people will never fly for any reason.

PRACTICE 6   Editing for Run-Ons

Find and correct the six run-ons in the following paragraphs. *More than one correct response is possible.*

TEACHING TIP Have students read the paragraphs aloud to listen for errors.

(1) For the first time, monster-size squids were filmed while still in the wild. (2) The images were caught on camera in the North Pacific Ocean ; the site is located just off the coast of southeastern Japan. (3) A team of Japanese scientists followed a group of sperm whales to locate the rare squids . The the whales like to eat the eight-legged creatures. (4) Wherever the whales went, the squids were likely to be found as well.

(5) From aboard their research ship, the team located the squids thousands of feet under the water , . The the scientists lowered bait over the side to attract them. (6) Next, they sent down cameras alongside the bait to catch images of these bizarre animals as soon as they appeared.

(7) The Dana octopus squid, also known as *Taningia danae*, often grows to the size of a human being or even larger. (8) Their eight arms are covered in suckers, as most squid species are , ; however, these particular types end in catlike claws. (9) Two of the arms contain special organs on the ends called photophores. (10) These photophores produce flashing bursts of light . They they are designed to lure and capture prey. (11) The burst of light stuns other creatures, giving the squid a chance to capture and eat its victim. (12) When the squid isn't hunting, it still glows. (13) Experts believe that squids remain lighted as a way of communicating with other squids about potential dangers or as a way of attracting mates. (14) These lights appear eerie , but the scientists were glad for them, as the lights made the giant squid slightly easier to find and finally film.

PRACTICE 7   Editing Run-Ons and Using Formal English

Your brother has been overcharged for an MP3 reader he ordered online, and he is about to send this e-mail to the seller's customer-service department. Help him by correcting the run-ons. Then, edit the informal English. *Answers will vary. Possible edits are shown.*

TIP For more advice on using formal English, see Chapter 3. For advice on choosing appropriate words, see Chapter 34.

(1) I'm writing 2U cuz *to you because* I was seriously ripped off *overcharged* for the Star 3 MP3 player I ordered from your Web site last week. (2) U *You* listed the price as $150 , but $250 was charged to my credit card. (3) Check *If you check* out any

competitors' sites, ~~U~~ *you* will see that no one expects people ~~2 cough up~~ *to pay that much money for the Star model. The* ~~that much cash for the Star model,~~ the prices are never higher than $165. (4) I overpaid ~~big bucks on this,~~ *Because a large amount for this product,* I want my money back as soon as possible.

(5) ~~Seriously bummin',~~ *Sincerely,*

Chris Langley

- -

PRACTICE 8   Editing Naomi's Application Answer

Look back at Naomi's writing on page 344. You may have already underlined the run-ons; if not, underline them now. Then, correct each error.

- -

PRACTICE 9   Editing Your Own Writing for Run-Ons

As a final practice, edit a piece of your own writing—a paper you are working on for this course or a paper for another course. Use the chart on page 359 to help you.

- -

Chapter Review

LEARNING JOURNAL If you found run-ons in your writing, how did you correct them? What is the main thing you have learned about run-ons that you will use? What is one thing that remains unclear?

1. A sentence can also be called an <u>independent clause</u>.

2. A <u>fused sentence</u> is two complete sentences joined without any punctuation.

3. A <u>comma splice</u> is two complete sentences joined by only a comma.

4. What are the five ways to correct run-ons?

   <u>Add a period.</u>

   <u>Add a semicolon.</u>

   <u>Add a semicolon, a conjunctive adverb, and a comma.</u>

   <u>Add a comma and a coordinating conjunction.</u>

   <u>Add a dependent word.</u>

5. What word in the middle of a sentence may signal a run-on?

   <u>then</u>

TEACHING TIP You can collect students' learning journals to find out what the class or individual students need more work on.

Chapter Test

Circle the correct choice for each of the following items. Use the Finding and Fixing Run-Ons chart on page 359 to help you.

1. Choose the item that has no errors.
   a. Please fill this prescription for me, it is for my allergies.
   (b.) Please fill this prescription for me. It is for my allergies.
   c. Please fill this prescription for me it is for my allergies.

2. If an underlined portion of this sentence is incorrect, select the revision that fixes it. If the sentence is correct as written, choose d.

   Harlan is busy <u>now ask him if</u> he can do his <u>report next</u> week.
   A   B   C

   (a.) now, so   c. report; next
   b. him, if   d. No change is necessary.

3. Choose the item that has no errors.
   a. You cut all the onion slices to the same thickness, they will finish cooking at the same time.
   b. You cut all the onion slices to the same thickness they will finish cooking at the same time.
   (c.) If you cut all the onion slices to the same thickness, they will finish cooking at the same time.

4. Choose the correct answer to fill in the blank.

   I have told Jervis several times not to tease the baby

   _____ he never listens.

   a. ,   c. No word or punctuation is
   (b.) , but   necessary.

5. Choose the item that has no errors.
   a. I am in no hurry to get a book I order it online.
   b. I am in no hurry to get a book, I order it online.
   (c.) When I am in no hurry to get a book, I order it online.

6. If an underlined portion of this sentence is incorrect, select the revision that fixes it. If the sentence is correct as written, choose d.

   <u>Many people</u> think a tomato is a <u>vegetable it is</u> <u>really a</u> fruit.
       A   B   C

TIP For advice on taking tests, see Appendix A.

RESOURCES For Cumulative Editing Review Tests, see pages 600–10.

RESOURCES The *Testing Tool Kit* CD-ROM available with this book has even more tests.

a. Many, people   **c.** really; a

b. vegetable; it   **d.** No change is necessary.

7. Choose the item that has no errors.

   a. Although air conditioning makes hot days more comfortable, it will increase your energy bills.

   b. Air conditioning makes hot days more comfortable it will increase your energy bills.

   c. Air conditioning makes hot days more comfortable, it will increase your energy bills.

8. If an underlined portion of this sentence is incorrect, select the revision that fixes it. If the sentence is correct as written, choose d.

   In northern Europe, bodies that are thousands of years <u>old have</u>
   A

   been found in <u>swamps, some</u> bodies are so well preserved that they
   B

   <u>look like</u> sleeping people.
   C

   a. old, have   **c.** look, like

   b. swamps. Some   **d.** No change is necessary.

9. Choose the item that has no errors.

   a. Do not be shy about opening doors for strangers, courtesy is always appreciated.

   b. Do not be shy about opening doors for strangers; courtesy is always appreciated.

   c. Do not be shy about opening doors for strangers courtesy is always appreciated.

10. Choose the correct answer to fill in the blank.

    You can ride with me to work _____ you can take the train.

    a. , or   **c.** No word or punctuation is

    b. if   necessary.

24

Problems with Subject-Verb Agreement

When Subjects and Verbs Don't Match

EVER THOUGHT THIS?

"I know sometimes the verb is supposed to end with -*s* and sometimes it isn't, but I always get confused."
—Mayerlin Fana, Student

This chapter

- explains what *agreement* between subjects and verbs is
- explains the simple rules for *regular verbs*
- identifies five trouble spots that can cause confusion
- gives you practice finding and fixing errors in subject-verb agreement

Understand What Subject-Verb Agreement Is

TIP In the examples throughout this chapter, subjects are underlined, and verbs are double-underlined.

In any sentence, the **subject and the verb must match—or agree—**in number. If the subject is singular (one person, place, or thing), then the verb must also be singular. If the subject is plural (more than one), the verb must also be plural.

SINGULAR	The skydiver jumps out of the airplane.
PLURAL	The skydivers jump out of the airplane.

Regular verbs (with forms that follow standard English patterns) have two forms in the present tense: one that ends in -*s* and one that has no end-

Regular Verbs, Present Tense

	SINGULAR		PLURAL
First person	I walk.	} no -*s*	We walk.
Second person	You walk.		You walk.
Third person	He (she, it) walks.	} all end in -*s*	They walk.
	Joe walks.		Joe and Alice walk.
	The student walks.		The students walk.

ing. The third-person subjects *he*, *she*, *it*, and singular nouns always use the form that ends in *-s*. First-person subjects (*I*), second-person subjects (*you*), and plural subjects use the form with no ending.

> **LANGUAGE NOTE:** Some nouns that do not end in *-s* are plural and thus need plural verbs. For example, *children* and *people* do not end in *-s*, but they indicate more than one child or person, so they are plural.

INCORRECT	These <u>children</u> <u>is making</u> me crazy.
CORRECT	These <u>children</u> <u>are making</u> me crazy.

In the Real World, Why Is It Important to Correct Errors in Subject-Verb Agreement?

SITUATION: Regina Toms (name changed) wrote the following brief report about a company employee whom she was sending to the employee assistance program. (These programs help workers with various problems, such as alcoholism or mental illness, that may affect their job performance.)

Mr. XXX, who has been a model employee of the company for five years, ~~have~~ *has* recently behaved in ways that ~~is~~ *are* inappropriate. For example, last week he was rude when a colleague asked him a question. He has been late to work several times and has missed work more often than usual. When I spoke to him about his behavior and asked if he ~~have~~ *has* problems, he admitted that he had been drinking more than usual. I would like him to speak to someone who ~~understand~~ *understands* more about this than I do.

TEACHING TIP Students should underline the errors for Practice 1 (on p. 364), and correct them for Practice 12 (on p. 376).

STUDENT VOICES

WALTER SCANLON'S RESPONSE: When Walter Scanlon, program and workplace consultant, received Regina's report, he responded in this way:

I immediately formed an opinion of her based on this short piece of correspondence: that she was either not well educated or not considerate of the addressee. Ms. Toms may indeed be intelligent and considerate, but those qualities are not reflected in this report. In this fast-paced world we live in, rapid-fire faxes, e-mails, and brief telephone conversations are likely to be our first mode of contact. Since one never gets a second chance to make a first impression, make the first one count!

(See Walter's **PROFILE OF SUCCESS** on p. 210.)

Find and Correct Errors in Subject-Verb Agreement

To find problems with subject-verb agreement in your own writing, look for five trouble spots that often signal these problems.

1.   The Verb Is a Form of *Be*, *Have*, or *Do*

The verbs *be*, *have*, and *do* do not follow the rules for forming singular and plural forms; they are **irregular verbs**.

Forms of the Verb *Be*

PRESENT TENSE	SINGULAR	PLURAL
First person	I am	we are
Second person	you are	you are
Third person	she, he, it is	they are
	the student is	the students are
PAST TENSE		
First person	I was	we were
Second person	you were	you were
Third person	she, he, it was	they were
	the student was	the students were

Forms of the Verb *Have*, Present Tense

	SINGULAR	PLURAL
First person	I have	we have
Second person	you have	you have
Third person	she, he, it has	they have
	the student has	the students have

Forms of the Verb *Do*, Present Tense

	SINGULAR	**PLURAL**
First person	I do	we do
Second person	you do	you do
Third person	she, he, it does	they do
	the student does	the students do

These verbs cause problems for writers who in conversation use the same form in all cases (*He do the cleaning; they do the cleaning*). People also sometimes use the word *be* instead of the correct form of *be* (*She be on vacation*).

In college and at work, use the correct forms of the verbs *be*, *have*, and *do* as shown in the charts above.

are
They ~~is~~ sick today.

is
She ~~be~~ at the library every morning.

does
Carlos ~~do~~ the laundry every Wednesday.

has
Joan ~~have~~ the best jewelry.

Finding and Fixing Problems with Subject-Verb Agreement:
Making Subjects and Verbs Agree When the Verb Is *Be*, *Have*, or *Do*

↓

Find

I (am / is / are) a true believer in naps.

1. **Underline** the subject.
2. **Ask:** Is the subject in the first (*I*), second (*you*), or third person (*he/she*)? *First person.*
3. **Ask:** Is the subject singular or plural? *Singular.*

↓

Fix

I (am)/ is / are) a true believer in naps.

4. **Choose** the verb by matching it to the form of the subject (first person, singular).

• •

PRACTICE 1   Identifying Problems with Subject-Verb Agreement

Find and underline the four problems with subject-verb agreement in Regina Toms's paragraph on page 361.

• •

PRACTICE 2   Choosing the Correct Form of *Be*, *Have*, or *Do*

TIP For more practices on subject-verb agreement, visit Exercise Central at **bedfordstmartins.com/ realwriting.**

In each sentence, underline the subject of the verb *be*, *have*, or *do*, and circle the correct form of the verb.

> **EXAMPLE:** Most people (does /do) not get enough sleep.

1. Sleep (is/ are) necessary for people to function well.

2. Most people (has /have) to get eight hours or more of sleep to be completely alert.

3. Electric lights (was /were) once uncommon, so people usually went to bed when the sun went down.

4. Today, darkness (does/ do) not make us go to sleep.

5. Almost every home (has / have) electricity, so people stay up long after sundown.

6. Modern Americans (has /have) such busy lives that they often sleep less than they should.

7. Often, a working college student (does/ do) not have time to get eight hours of sleep.

8. Job duties (has /have) to be done, but schoolwork is equally important.

9. If you study when you (be /are) tired, you remember less information.

10. Busy people today try to get by on little sleep, but it (is/ are) unhealthy to be sleep-deprived.

• •

PRACTICE 3   Using the Correct Form of *Be*, *Have*, or *Do*

RESOURCES To gauge students' understanding of subject-verb agreement, use the *Testing Tool Kit* CD-ROM available with this book.

In each sentence, underline the subject of the verb *be*, *have*, or *do*, and fill in the correct form of the verb indicated in parentheses.

> **EXAMPLE:** She _____has_____ (*have*) often looked at the stars on
> clear, dark nights.

1. Stars _____are_____ (*be*) clustered together in constellations.

2. Every constellation _____has_____ (*have*) a name.

3. I _____do_____ (*do*) not know how they got their names.

4. Most constellations _____*do*_____ (*do*) not look much like the people or creatures they represent.

5. You _____*have*_____ (*have*) to use your imagination to see the pictures in the stars.

6. Twelve constellations _____*are*_____ (*be*) signs of the zodiac.

7. One _____*is*_____ (*be*) supposed to look like a crab.

8. Other star clusters _____*have*_____ (*have*) the names of characters from ancient myths.

9. Orion, the hunter, _____*is*_____ (*be*) the only one I can recognize.

10. He _____*does*_____ (*do*) not look like a hunter to me.

. . . .

2. Words Come between the Subject and the Verb

When the subject and verb are not right next to each other, it is more difficult to find them to make sure they agree. Most often, either a prepositional phrase or a dependent clause comes between the subject and the verb.

Prepositional Phrase between the Subject and the Verb

A **prepositional phrase** starts with a preposition and ends with a noun or pronoun: I took my bag *of books* and threw it *across the room*.

    The subject of a sentence is never in a prepositional phrase. When you are looking for the subject of a sentence, you can cross out any prepositional phrases.

TIP For a list of common prepositions, see page 315.

COMPUTER Have students highlight prepositional phrases in their writing and read only the nonhighlighted parts of their sentences.

A <u>volunteer</u> ~~in the Peace Corps~~ (serve / <u>serves</u>) two years.

The <u>speaker</u> ~~of the U.S. House of Representatives~~ (give / <u>gives</u>) many interviews.

> **Finding and Fixing Problems with Subject-Verb Agreement:**
> **Making Subjects and Verbs Agree When They Are**
> **Separated by a Prepositional Phrase**

↓

Find

<u>Learners</u> ~~with dyslexia~~ (face / <u>faces</u>) many challenges.

1. **Underline** the subject.
2. **Cross out** any prepositional phrase that follows the subject.
3. **Ask:** Is the subject singular or plural? *Plural.*

↓

> **Fix**
>
> Learners with dyslexia (face)/ faces) many challenges.
>
> 4. **Choose** the form of the verb that matches the subject.

PRACTICE 4   Making Subjects and Verbs Agree When They Are Separated By a Prepositional Phrase

In each of the following sentences, cross out the prepositional phrase between the subject and the verb, and circle the correct form of the verb. Remember, the subject of a sentence is never in a prepositional phrase.

   EXAMPLE: Life ~~in these fast-paced times~~ ((does)/ do) not leave much time for rest.

1. Stress ~~from a job or family commitments~~ ((makes)/ make) sleeping diffi-cult for some.

2. Crying fits ~~after midnight~~ (wakes /(wake)) parents of small children, giving the parents little rest.

3. Also, people ~~with cable television~~ often (wants /(want)) to stay up to see their favorite shows.

4. A recent report ~~on sleeping habits~~ ((is)/ are) revealing.

5. People ~~from all parts of our society~~ (is /(are)) going to bed late.

6. One ~~out of every three adult Americans~~ ((gets)/ get) to bed after midnight during the week.

7. Adults ~~across America~~ also (sleeps /(sleep)) less than people from many other countries.

8. The report ~~on sleeping habits~~ ((shows)/ show) that 19 percent of Ameri-cans sleep six or fewer hours a night.

9. But most ~~of us~~ (needs /(need)) about eight hours of sleep a night to function well.

10. Even a nap ~~during afternoon hours~~ ((helps)/ help) a person feel refreshed.

Dependent Clause between the Subject and the Verb

A **dependent clause** has a subject and a verb, but it does not express a complete thought. When a dependent clause comes between the subject and the verb, it usually starts with the word *who, whose, whom, that,* or *which.*

The subject of a sentence is never in a dependent clause. When you are looking for the subject of a sentence, you can cross out any dependent clauses.

The <u>coins</u> ~~that I found last week~~ (<u>seem</u> / seems) valuable.

The <u>person</u> ~~who delivers our street's newspapers~~ (throw / <u>throws</u>) them everywhere but on people's porches.

> **Finding and Fixing Problems with Subject-Verb Agreement:**
> **Making Subjects and Verbs Agree When They**
> **Are Separated by a Dependent Clause**

Find

The security <u>systems</u> ~~that shopping sites on the Internet provide~~ (is / are) surprisingly effective.

1. **Underline** the subject.
2. **Cross out** any dependent clause that follows the subject. (Look for the words *who*, *whose*, *whom*, *that*, or *which* because they can signal such a clause.)
3. **Ask:** Is the subject singular or plural? *Plural.*

Fix

The security systems that shopping sites on the Internet provide (is /(are)) surprisingly effective.

4. **Choose** the form of the verb that matches the subject.

· ·

PRACTICE 5   Making Subjects and Verbs Agree When They Are Separated by a Dependent Clause

In each of the following sentences, cross out any dependent clauses. Then, correct any problems with subject-verb agreement. If the subject and the verb agree, write "OK" next to the sentence.

EXAMPLE: My cousins ~~who immigrated to this country from Ecuador~~
            have
            ~~has~~ jobs in a fast-food restaurant.

1. The restaurant ~~that hired my cousins~~ *is* ~~are~~ not treating them fairly.

2. People ~~who work in the kitchen~~ *have* ~~has~~ to report to work at 7:00 A.M.

3. The boss ~~who supervises the morning shift~~ tells the workers not to punch in until 9:00 A.M. *OK*

4. The benefits ~~that full-time workers earn~~ have not been offered to my cousins. *OK*

5. Ramón, ~~whose hand was injured slicing potatoes~~, need^s to have physical therapy.

6. No one ~~who works with him~~ has helped him file for worker's compensation. *OK*

7. The doctors ~~who cleaned his wound and put in his stitches at the hospital~~ expect*s* him to pay for the medical treatment.

8. The managers ~~who run the restaurant~~ insist*s* that he is not eligible for medical coverage.

9. My cousins, ~~whose English is not yet perfect~~, feel*s* unable to leave their jobs.

10. The restaurant ~~that treats them so badly~~ offers the only opportunity for them to earn a living. *OK*

. . . .

3.   The Sentence Has a Compound Subject

A **compound subject** is two (or more) subjects joined by *and*, *or*, or *nor*.

And/Or Rule: If two subjects are joined by *and*, use a plural verb. If two subjects are joined by *or* (or *nor*), the verb should agree with whatever subject it is closer to.

Plural subject = Plural verb

The teacher *and* her aide grade all of the exams.

If two subjects are separated by the word *or* or *nor*, they are not combined. The verb should agree with whichever subject is closer to it.

Subject *or* Singular subject = Singular verb

Either the teacher *or* her aide grades all of the exams.

Subject *or* Plural subject = Plural verb

The teacher *or* her aides grade all of the exams.

Subject *nor* Plural subject = Plural verb

Neither the teacher *nor* her aides grade all of the exams.

TIP Whenever you see a compound subject joined by *and*, try replacing it in your mind with *they*.

> **Finding and Fixing Problems with Subject-Verb Agreement:**
> **Making Subjects and Verbs Agree in a Sentence**
> **with a Compound Subject**

Find

Watermelon (or) cantaloupe (makes / make) a delicious and
healthy snack.

1. **Underline** the subjects.
2. **Circle** the word between the subjects.
3. **Ask:** Does that word join the subjects to make them plural or keep them separate? *Keeps them separate.*
4. **Ask:** Is the subject that is closer to the verb singular or plural? *Singular.*

Fix

Watermelon or cantaloupe ((makes) / make) a delicious and
healthy snack.

5. **Choose** the verb form that agrees with the subject that is closer to the verb.

PRACTICE 6   Choosing the Correct Verb in a Sentence with a Compound Subject

In each of the following sentences, underline the word (*and* or *or*) that joins the parts of the compound subject. Then, circle the correct form of the verb.

> **EXAMPLE:** My mother <u>and</u> my sister (has / (have)) asked a nutritionist
> for advice on a healthy diet.

1. A tomato <u>and</u> a watermelon (shares / (share)) more than just red-colored flesh.

2. A cooked tomato <u>or</u> a slice of watermelon ((contains) / contain) a nutrient called lycopene that seems to protect the human body from some diseases.

3. Fruits <u>and</u> vegetables (is / (are)) an important part of a healthy diet, most experts agree.

4. Nutrition experts <u>and</u> dietitians (believes / (believe)) that eating a variety of colors of fruits and vegetables is best for human health.

5. Collard greens <u>or</u> spinach (provides / provide) vitamins, iron, and protection from blindness to those who eat them.

6. Carrots <u>and</u> yellow squash (protects / protect) against cancer and some kinds of skin damage.

7. Too often, a busy college student <u>or</u> worker (finds / find) it hard to eat the recommended five to nine servings of fruits and vegetables a day.

8. A fast-food restaurant <u>or</u> vending machine (is / are) unlikely to have many fresh vegetable and fruit selections.

9. A salad <u>or</u> fresh fruit (costs / cost) more than a hamburger in many places where hurried people eat.

10. Nevertheless, a brightly colored vegetable <u>and</u> fruit (adds / add) vitamins and healthy fiber to any meal.

4.   The Subject Is an Indefinite Pronoun

An **indefinite pronoun** replaces a general person, place, or thing or a general group of people, places, or things. Indefinite pronouns are often singular, though there are some exceptions, as shown in the chart on page 371.

SINGULAR	<u>Everyone</u> <u><u>wants</u></u> the semester to end.
PLURAL	<u>Many</u> <u><u>want</u></u> the semester to end.
SINGULAR	<u>Either</u> of the meals <u><u>is</u></u> good.

Often, an indefinite pronoun is followed by a prepositional phrase or dependent clause. Remember that the verb of a sentence must agree with the subject of the sentence, and the subject of a sentence is *never in a prepositional phrase or dependent clause*. To choose the correct verb, focus on the indefinite pronoun—you can cross out the prepositional phrase or dependent clause.

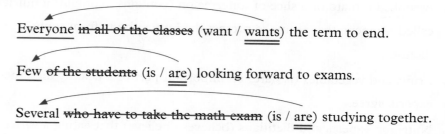

<u>Everyone</u> ~~in all of the classes~~ (want / <u><u>wants</u></u>) the term to end.

<u>Few</u> ~~of the students~~ (is / <u><u>are</u></u>) looking forward to exams.

<u>Several</u> ~~who have to take the math exam~~ (is / <u><u>are</u></u>) studying together.

Indefinite Pronouns

ALWAYS SINGULAR			MAY BE SINGULAR OR PLURAL
another	everybody	no one	all
anybody	everyone	nothing	any
anyone	everything	one (of)	none
anything	much	somebody	some
each (of)*	neither (of)*	someone	
either (of)*	nobody	something	

*When one of these words is the subject, mentally replace it with *one*. *One* is singular and takes a singular verb.

> **Finding and Fixing Problems with Subject-Verb Agreement: Making Subjects and Verbs Agree When the Subject Is an Indefinite Pronoun**

Find

One ~~of my best friends~~ (lives / live) in California.

1. **Underline** the subject.
2. **Cross out** any prepositional phrase or dependent clause that follows the subject.
3. **Ask:** Is the subject singular or plural? *Singular.*

Fix

One of my best friends (lives) / live) in California.

4. **Choose** the verb form that agrees with the subject.

- -

PRACTICE 7 Choosing the Correct Verb When the Subject Is an Indefinite Pronoun

In each of the following sentences, cross out any prepositional phrase or dependent clause that comes between the subject and the verb. Then, underline the subject, and circle the correct verb.

> **EXAMPLE:** One ~~of the strangest human experiences~~ (results / result)
> from the "small-world" phenomenon.

1. Everyone (remembers / remember) an example of a "small-world" phenomenon.

2. Someone ~~whom you have just met~~ (tells / tell) you a story.

3. During the story, one ~~of you~~ (realizes / realize) that you are connected somehow.

4. One ~~of your friends~~ (lives / live) next door to the person.

5. Someone ~~in your family~~ (knows / know) someone in the person's family.

6. Each ~~of your families~~ (owns / own) a home in the same place.

7. One ~~of your relatives~~ (plans / plan) to marry his cousin.

8. Some (believes / believe) that if you know one hundred people and talk to someone who knows one hundred people, together you are linked to one million people through friends and acquaintances.

9. Someone ~~in this class~~ probably (connects / connect) to you in one way or another.

10. Each ~~of you~~ probably (knows / know) a good "small-world" story of your own.

· ·

5. The Verb Comes before the Subject

In most sentences, the subject comes before the verb. Two kinds of sentences often reverse the usual subject-verb order: questions and sentences that begin with *here* or *there*. In these two types of sentences, check carefully for errors in subject-verb agreement.

Questions

In questions, the verb or part of the verb comes before the subject. To find the subject and verb, you can turn the question around as if you were going to answer it.

Where is the bookstore? / The bookstore is . . .

Are you excited? / You are excited.

When is the bus going to leave? / The bus is going to leave . . .

TEAMWORK Divide the class down the middle. One side asks questions (students go in turns according to where they are sitting). The other side turns the questions around (anyone can answer by raising his or her hand or calling out the answer). Keep a fairly fast pace.

LANGUAGE NOTE: For reference charts showing how to form questions, see pages 504–05 and pages 507–10, in Chapter 33.

Sentences That Begin with *Here* or *There*

When a sentence begins with *here* or *there*, the subject often follows the verb. Turn the sentence around to find the subject and verb.

Here is your key to the apartment. / Your key to the apartment is here.

There are four keys on the table. / Four keys are on the table.

LANGUAGE NOTE: *There is* and *there are* are common in English. These expressions have the general meaning of *have/has.*

There is time to finish = We have time to finish.

Finding and Fixing Problems with Subject-Verb Agreement:
Making Subjects and Verbs Agree When
the Verb Comes before the Subject

Find

What classes (is / are) the professor teaching?

1. If the sentence is a question, **turn the question into a statement**: *The professor (is/are) teaching the classes.*

   There (is / are) two good classes in the music department.

2. If the sentence begins with *here* or *there*, **turn it around**: *Two good classes (is/are) in the music department.*

3. **Identify** the subject in each of the two new sentences. *It is "professor" in the first sentence and "classes" in the second.*

4. **Ask:** Is the subject singular or plural? *"Professor" is singular; "classes" is plural.*

Fix

The professor (is)/ are) teaching the classes.

Two good classes (is / are) in the music department.

5. **Choose** the form of the verb in each sentence that matches the subject.

• •

PRACTICE 8 Correcting a Sentence When the Verb Comes before the Subject

Correct any problem with subject-verb agreement in the following sentences. If a sentence is already correct, write "OK" next to it.

does
EXAMPLE: What electives ~~do~~ the school offer?

is
1. What ~~are~~ the best reason to study music?

are
2. There ~~is~~ several good reasons.

3. There is evidence that music helps students with math. *OK*

4. What is your favorite musical instrument? *OK*

are
5. Here ~~is~~ a guitar, a saxophone, and a piano.

are
6. There ~~is~~ very few people with natural musical ability.

do
7. What time of day ~~does~~ you usually practice?

8. There is no particular time. *OK*

do
9. What musician ~~does~~ you admire most?

is
10. Here ~~are~~ some information about the importance of regular practice.

• •

Edit for Subject-Verb Agreement

Use the chart, Finding and Fixing Problems with Subject-Verb Agreement, on page 379, to help you complete the practices in this section and edit your own writing.

• •

PRACTICE 9 Correcting Various Problems with Subject-Verb Agreement

In the following sentences, identify any verb that does not agree with its subject. Then, correct the sentence using the correct form of the verb.

are
EXAMPLE: Thousands of people ~~is~~ actually being paid to go shopping.

earn
1. The shoppers who take on this work ~~earns~~ money for checking on a store's quality of service.

are
2. There ~~is~~ two names for them: mystery shoppers and secret shoppers.

hire
3. Chain stores across the nation ~~hires~~ mystery shoppers.

4. Fast-food restaurants and retail stores ~~uses~~ *use* these shoppers the most.

5. What reasons ~~motivates~~ *motivate* a person to become a mystery shopper?

6. Mystery shoppers with a sense of justice ~~says~~ *say* they do their work to make sure consumers are treated well.

7. Others say they ~~has~~ *have* only one reason: the money they are paid.

8. The pay and benefits ~~appeals~~ *appeal* to many mystery shoppers; they typically get $7 to $30 per store visit, plus money to cover purchases.

9. One ~~do~~ *does* not have to pay a fee to become a mystery shopper.

10. Anybody who likes the idea of getting paid to visit stores ~~are~~ *is* advised to visit www.mysteryshop.org.

. . . .

PRACTICE 10   Editing Paragraphs for Subject-Verb Agreement

Find and correct six problems with subject-verb agreement in the following paragraphs.

(1) You probably ~~does~~ *do* not have a mirror at your computer desk, but if you did, you might notice something about yourself you had not been aware of before. (2) As you sit there, hour after hour, your shoulders are rounded, your back is slumped, and your posture ~~are~~ *is* awful.

(3) Do not worry; you are not alone. (4) Most students spend hours in front of a computer monitor with terrible posture. (5) Then, they make things worse by getting up and heading off to school with painfully heavy backpacks on their backs. (6) Young people who carry a heavy burden ~~is~~ *are* forced to hunch forward even more to balance the weight, adding strain to already seriously fatigued muscles. (7) Everyone who studies these trends ~~are~~ *is* concerned.

(8) The study of people and their surroundings is known as ergonomics. (9) Improperly slouching at the computer and toting around a heavy backpack are both examples of poor ergonomics. (10) These bad habits ~~is~~ *are* two causes of chronic back pain that can interfere with school, work, and sports. (11) Everyone, according to experts, ~~need~~ *needs* to sit up straight while at the computer, take frequent breaks to get up and walk around, and carry less in his or her backpack.

• •

PRACTICE 11   Editing Subject-Verb Agreement Errors and Using Formal English

A friend of yours has been turned down for a course because of high enrollment, even though she registered early. She knows that her e-mail to the instructor teaching the course has a few problems in it. Help her by correcting any subject-verb agreement errors. Then, edit the informal English in the e-mail. *Answers will vary. Possible answers are shown.*

TIP For more advice on using formal English, see Chapter 3. For advice on choosing appropriate words, see Chapter 34.

(1) ~~Hey Prof~~ *Dear Professor* Connors,

(2) I am e-mailing you to make sure you ~~gets~~ *got* the e-mail I sent before about registering for your Business Writing course this semester.

(3) ~~IMHO,~~ *In my humble opinion,* it is one of the best classes this college offers. (4) I ~~does~~ *did* not miss the deadline; I signed up on the first day, in fact. (5) I ~~plans~~ *plan* to graduate with a degree in business and economics, so your class is important to me. (6) Could you please check ~~yur~~ *your* class roster to see if I was somehow skipped or missed? (7) I would sure appreciate it ~~a ton,~~ ~~LOL.~~ (8) ~~Plz~~ *Please* let me know what you ~~finds~~ *find* out. (9) If I cannot get into your class this semester, I will have to rearrange my schedule so that I can ~~takes~~ *take* it next semester instead. (10) I look forward to taking your class and learning all about business writing. (11) ~~You rocks, prof.~~ *You are great, professor.*

(11) Sincerely,

Cameron Taylor

• •

PRACTICE 12   Editing Regina's Report

Look back at Regina Toms's report on page 361. You may have already underlined the subject-verb agreement errors; if not, do so now. Next, using what you have learned in this chapter, correct each error.

• •

PRACTICE 13   Editing Your Own Writing for Subject-Verb Agreement

Use your new skill at editing for subject-verb agreement on a piece of your own writing—a paper you are working on for this class, a paper you have already finished, a paper for another course, or a recent piece of writing from your work or everyday life. Use the chart on page 379 to help you.

• •

Chapter Review

1. The ___subject___ and the ___verb___ in a sentence must agree (match) in terms of number. They must both be ___singular___, or they must both be plural.

2. Five trouble spots can cause errors in subject-verb agreement:

   - When the verb is a form of ___be___, ___have___, or ___do___.

   - When a _prepositional phrase_ or a _dependent clause_ comes between the subject and the verb.

   - When the sentence has a ___compound___ subject joined by *and, or,* or *nor.*

   - When the subject is an ___indefinite___ pronoun.

   - When the ___verb___ comes ___before___ the subject.

Chapter Test

Circle the correct choice for each of the following items. Use the Finding and Fixing Problems with Subject-Verb Agreement chart on page 379 to help you.

1. If an underlined portion of this sentence is incorrect, select the revision that fixes it. If the sentence is correct as written, choose d.

   There is only certain times when you can call to get technical
     A   B   C
   support for this computer.

   (a.) There are   **c.** getting
   b. you could   **d.** No change is necessary.

2. Choose the correct word to fill in the blank.

   Dana's dog Bernard _____ just a puppy, but he moves so slowly that he seems old.

   a. be   **c.** being
   b. am   **(d.)** is

3. If an underlined portion of this sentence is incorrect, select the revision that fixes it. If the sentence is correct as written, choose d.

The <u>umpire was</u> not happy to see that <u>everyone were</u> watching him
      A   B

<u>argue with</u> the baseball player.
      C

   a. umpire were   **c.** argues with

   (b.) everyone was   **d.** No change is necessary.

4. Choose the correct word to fill in the blank.

The woman who rented us our kayaks _____ now paddling her own kayak down the river.

   a. are   **b.** be   **(c.)** is

5. Choose the item that has no errors.

   a. Alex and Dane likes to travel now that they have retired from their jobs.

   b. Alex and Dane liking to travel now that they have retired from their jobs.

   (c.) Alex and Dane like to travel now that they have retired from their jobs.

6. Choose the correct word to fill in the blank.

The builders of this house _____ used the best materials they could find.

   (a.) have   **b.** having   **c.** has

7. Choose the correct word to fill in the blank.

The calm before hurricanes _____ most people with anxiety.

   a. fill   **b.** filling   **(c.)** fills

8. Choose the item that has no errors.

   (a.) Sheryl and her sons go to the beach whenever they can find the time.

   b. Sheryl and her sons goes to the beach whenever they can find the time.

   c. Sheryl and her sons is going to the beach whenever they can find the time.

9. Choose the correct word to fill in the blank.

Where _____ the children's wet swimsuits?

   (a.) are   **b.** is   **c.** be

10. If an underlined portion of this sentence is incorrect, select the revision
that fixes it. If the sentence is correct as written, choose d.

Anybody who <u>can</u> speak several languages <u>are</u> in great demand to
          A   B

<u>work</u> for the government, especially in foreign embassies.
  C

  a. could

  b. is

  c. working

  d. No change is necessary.

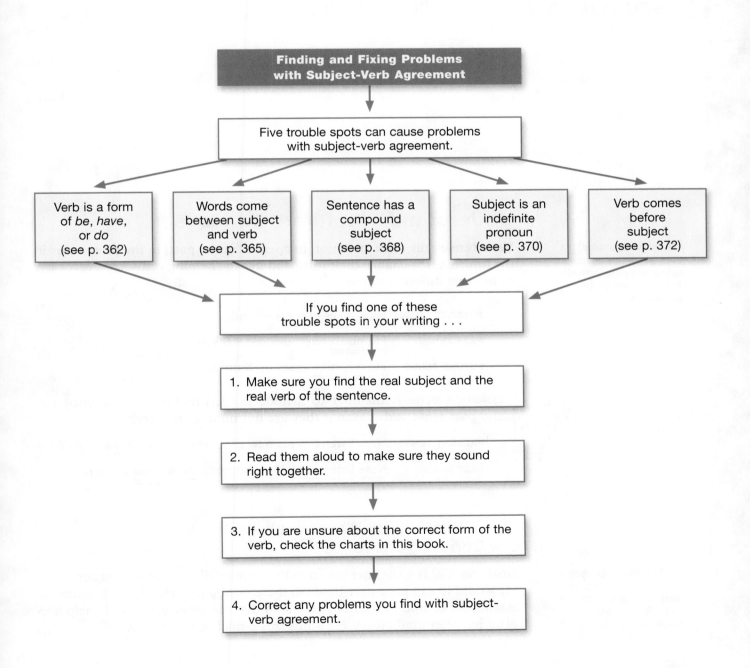

Verb Tense

Using Verbs to Express Different Times

Understand What Verb Tense Is

TIP In the examples throughout this chapter, subjects are underlined, and verbs are double-underlined.

Verb tense tells *when* an action happened: in the past, in the present, or in the future. Verbs change their form and use the helping verbs *have*, *be*, or *will* to indicate different tenses.

PRESENT TENSE	Rick hikes every weekend.
PAST TENSE	He hiked ten miles last weekend.
FUTURE TENSE	He will hike again on Saturday.

LANGUAGE NOTE: Remember to include needed endings on present-tense and past-tense verbs, even if they are not noticed in speech.

PRESENT TENSE	Nate listens to his new iPod wherever he goes.
PAST TENSE	Nate listened to his iPod while he walked the dog.

In the Real World, Why Is It Important to Use the Correct Verb Tense?

TIP To find and correct problems with verbs, you need to be able to identify subjects and verbs. For a review, see Chapter 21.

SITUATION: Cal is a summer intern in the systems division of a large company. He would like to get a part-time job there during the school year because he is studying computer science and knows that the experience would help him get a job after graduation. He sends this e-mail to his supervisor.

I have work hard since coming to Technotron and learn many new things. I enjoy learning about systems analysis and know that it help me in the future. Mr. Joseph tell me he like my work and that I shown good motivation and teamwork. I been working part-time while in school and would like to continue my work here beyond the summer. I would like an opportunity to discuss this with you and hope that you considers me.

Sincerely,

Cal Troppo

TEACHING TIP Students should underline the verb errors for Practice 1, below, and correct them for Practice 17, on page 400.

STUDENT VOICES

KAREN UPRIGHT'S RESPONSE: Karen Upright, systems manager, read Cal's e-mail, and made the following comments:

I would probably not hire him because of the many errors in his writing. While he is in school, he should take a writing course and learn more about using correct verbs and verb tenses. Otherwise, his writing will be a barrier to his employment, not just at Procter & Gamble, but anywhere.

(See Karen's **PROFILE OF SUCCESS** on p. 145.)

Using verbs incorrectly is an error that people notice.

Practice Using Correct Verbs

This section will teach you about verb tenses and give you practice with using them. The best way to learn how to use the various verb tenses correctly, however, is to read, write, and speak them as often as possible.

- -

PRACTICE 1   Identifying Verb Errors

Find and underline the eight verb errors in Cal's e-mail above.

- -

RESOURCES *Additional Resources* contains tests and supplemental practice exercises for this chapter as well as a transparency master for the summary chart at the end of the chapter.

Regular Verbs

Most verbs in English are **regular verbs** that follow standard rules about what endings to use to express time.

Present-Tense Endings: -s and No Ending

The **present tense** is used for actions that are happening at the same time that they are being written about (the present) and for things that happen all the time. Present-tense, regular verbs either end in *-s* or have no ending added.

-S ENDING	NO ENDING
jumps	jump
walks	walk
lives	live

Use the *-s* ending when the subject is *he, she, it,* or the name of one person or thing. Use no ending for all other subjects.

TIP For more about making verbs match subjects, see Chapter 24.

Regular Verbs in the Present Tense

	SINGULAR	PLURAL
First person	I jump.	We jump.
Second person	You jump.	You jump.
Third person	She (he, it) jumps.	They jump.
	The child jumps.	The children jump.

Do not confuse the simple present tense with the **present progressive**, which is used with a form of the helping verb *be* to describe actions that are in progress right now.

SIMPLE PRESENT	I eat a banana every day.
PRESENT PROGRESSIVE	I am eating a banana.

LANGUAGE NOTE: Some languages do not use the progressive tense. If you have trouble using the present progressive, see Chapter 34.

PRACTICE 2 Using Present-Tense Regular Verbs Correctly

In each of the following sentences, first underline the subject, and then circle the correct verb form.

TIP For more practices on verb problems, visit Exercise Central at **bedfordstmartins.com/realwriting**.

EXAMPLE: I (tries / (try)) to keep to my budget.

1. My classes (requires / (require)) much of my time these days.

2. In addition to attending school, I (works / (work)) twenty hours a week in the college library.

3. The other <u>employees</u> (agrees / (agree)) that the work atmosphere is pleasant.

4. Sometimes, <u>we</u> even (manages / (manage)) to do homework at the library.

5. The <u>job</u> ((pays) / pay) a fairly low wage, however.

6. My <u>roommate</u> ((helps) / help) with the rent on the apartment.

7. Because he is not in school, <u>he</u> often ((wonders) / wonder) how I get by.

8. <u>I</u> (uses / (use)) my bicycle to get everywhere I need to go.

9. The <u>bicycle</u> ((allows) / allow) me to stay in shape both physically and financially.

10. I know that I will not be in school forever, so for now, <u>life</u> on a budget ((satisfies) / satisfy) me.

RESOURCES To gauge students' skills in using verbs, use the *Testing Tool Kit* CD-ROM available with this book. See also the Extreme Paragraph Makeover in the *Make-a-Paragraph Kit.*

DISCUSSION A common error is using only the present tense in writing. If your students do this, ask why. A common answer is that they know the present form and are less certain about others. Point out that using the present-tense form of a verb where the past tense is correct is as serious an error as using an incorrect past form.

One Regular Past-Tense Ending: -ed

The **past tense** is used for actions that have already happened. An *-ed* ending is needed on all regular verbs in the past tense.

	PRESENT TENSE	PAST TENSE
First person	I <u>avoid</u> her.	I <u>avoided</u> her.
Second person	You <u>help</u> me.	You <u>helped</u> me.
Third person	He <u>walks</u> fast.	He <u>walked</u> fast.

TIP If a verb already ends in *-e*, just add *-d*: dance/danced. If a verb ends in *-y*, usually the *-y* changes to *-i* when *-ed* is added: *spy/spied*; *try/tried*.

PRACTICE 3   Using the Past Tense of Regular Verbs Correctly

In each of the following sentences, fill in the correct past-tense forms of the verbs in parentheses.

(1) Last winter, I ____displayed____ (*display*) the clear signs of a cold. (2) I ____sneezed____ (*sneeze*) often, and I ____developed____ (*develop*) a sore throat. (3) The congestion in my nose and throat ____annoyed____ (*annoy*) me, and it ____seemed____ (*seem*) that blowing my nose was useless. (4) However, I ____visited____ (*visit*) with my friends and ____attended____ (*attend*) classes at college. (5) I ____assumed____ (*assume*) that I could not give anyone else my cold once I showed the symptoms. (6) Unfortunately, many people ____joined____ (*join*) me in my misery because of my ignorance. (7) Later, I ____learned____ (*learn*) that I ____remained____ (*remain*) contagious for several days after I first showed symptoms. (8) My

doctor ____explained____ (*explain*) to me that I ____started____ (*start*) spreading my cold about one day after I became infected with it. (9) However, after my symptoms ____disappeared____ (*disappear*), I ____passed____ (*pass*) on my cold to others for up to three days more. (10) I ____wanted____ (*want*) to apologize to everyone I had infected, but I also ____realized____ (*realize*) that others had given me their colds as well.

● ●

One Regular Past-Participle Ending: -ed

The **past participle** is a verb that is used with a helping verb, such as *have* or *be*. For all regular verbs, the past-participle form is the same as the past-tense form: It uses an *-ed* ending. (To learn about when past participles are used, see pp. 392–97.)

PAST TENSE	PAST PARTICIPLE
My <u>kids</u> <u><u>watched</u></u> cartoons.	<u>They</u> <u>have</u> <u>watched</u> cartoons before.
<u>George</u> <u><u>visited</u></u> his cousins.	<u>He</u> <u>has</u> <u>visited</u> them every year.

● ●

PRACTICE 4   Using the Past Participle of Regular Verbs Correctly

In each of the following sentences, underline the helping verb (a form of *have*), and fill in the correct form of the verb in parentheses.

EXAMPLE: Because of pressure to keep up with others, families <u>have</u> ____started____ (*start*) to give fancier and fancier birthday parties.

1. We <u>have</u> all ____received____ (*receive*) invitations to simple birthday parties where children played games and had cake, but those days are gone.

2. Kids' birthday parties <u>have</u> ____turned____ (*turn*) into complicated and expensive events.

3. Price tags for some of these parties <u>have</u> ____climbed____ (*climb*) to $1,000 or more.

4. By the time she had finished planning her daughter's birthday, one mother <u>had</u> ____devoted____ (*devote*) hundreds of dollars to the event.

5. She discovered that she <u>had</u> ____handed____ (*hand*) out $50 for a clubhouse rental, $200 for a cotton-candy maker, and $300 for an actor dressed as the Little Mermaid.

6. The money spent on gifts <u>has</u> ____increased____ (*increase*) as well.

7. At the end of each year, many parents find that they <u>have</u>
_____<u>purchased</u>_____ (*purchase*) an average of twenty gifts costing $20
each—$400 total.

8. However, some families <u>have</u> _____<u>decided</u>_____ (*decide*) to go against the
trend.

9. My best friend <u>has</u> _____<u>saved</u>_____ (*save*) money and effort by having
small birthday parties for her son.

10. The savings <u>have</u> _____<u>reached</u>_____ (*reach*) $500, and she is putting the
money toward his college education.

Irregular Verbs

Irregular verbs do not follow the simple rules of regular verbs, which have
just two present-tense endings (*-s* or *-es*) and two past-tense endings (*-d* or
-ed). Irregular verbs show past tense with a change in spelling, although
some irregular verbs, such as *cost*, *hit*, and *put*, do not change their spelling.
The most common irregular verbs are *be* and *have* (see p. 388). As you write
and edit, use the following chart to make sure you use the correct form of
irregular verbs.

Irregular Verbs

PRESENT TENSE	PAST TENSE	PAST PARTICIPLE (USED WITH HELPING VERB)
be (am/are/is)	was/were	been
become	became	become
begin	began	begun
bite	bit	bitten
blow	blew	blown
break	broke	broken
bring	brought	brought
build	built	built
buy	bought	bought
catch	caught	caught
choose	chose	chosen
come	came	come
cost	cost	cost

(continued)

ESL It is helpful for students to *hear* the verb forms, particularly for irregular verbs. If you have access to a language lab, you might have them listen to verb tapes. If students can record, have them record examples for each other, using personalized examples.

See also the Extreme Paragraph Makeover in the *Make-a-Paragraph Kit*.

PRESENT TENSE	PAST TENSE	PAST PARTICIPLE (USED WITH HELPING VERB)
dive	dived, dove	dived
do	did	done
draw	drew	drawn
drink	drank	drunk
drive	drove	driven
eat	ate	eaten
fall	fell	fallen
feed	fed	fed
feel	felt	felt
fight	fought	fought
find	found	found
fly	flew	flown
forget	forgot	forgotten
get	got	gotten
give	gave	given
go	went	gone
grow	grew	grown
have/has	had	had
hear	heard	heard
hide	hid	hidden
hit	hit	hit
hold	held	held
hurt	hurt	hurt
keep	kept	kept
know	knew	known
lay	laid	laid
lead	led	led
leave	left	left
let	let	let
lie	lay	lain
light	lit	lit
lose	lost	lost

TEACHING TIP Give students a few minutes in class, or ask them, as a homework assignment, to review the list of irregular verbs and underline the fifteen verbs they use most frequently.

PRESENT TENSE	PAST TENSE	PAST PARTICIPLE (USED WITH HELPING VERB)
make	made	made
mean	meant	meant
meet	met	met
pay	paid	paid
put	put	put
quit	quit	quit
read	read	read
ride	rode	ridden
ring	rang	rung
rise	rose	risen
run	ran	run
say	said	said
see	saw	seen
seek	sought	sought
sell	sold	sold
send	sent	sent
shake	shook	shaken
show	showed	shown
shrink	shrank	shrunk
shut	shut	shut
sing	sang	sung
sink	sank	sunk
sit	sat	sat
sleep	slept	slept
speak	spoke	spoken
spend	spent	spent
stand	stood	stood
steal	stole	stolen
stick	stuck	stuck
sting	stung	stung
strike	struck	struck, stricken
swim	swam	swum

(continued)

PRESENT TENSE	PAST TENSE	PAST PARTICIPLE (USED WITH HELPING VERB)
take	took	taken
teach	taught	taught
tear	tore	torn
tell	told	told
think	thought	thought
throw	threw	thrown
understand	understood	understood
wake	woke	woken
wear	wore	worn
win	won	won
write	wrote	written

Present Tense of Be and Have

The present tense of the verbs *be* and *have* is very irregular, as shown in the chart.

Present Tense of *Be* and *Have*

BE		HAVE	
I am	we are	I have	we have
you are	you are	you have	you have
he, she, it is	they are	he, she, it has	they have
the editor is	the editors are		
Beth is	Beth and Christina are		

PRACTICE 5   Using *Be* and *Have* in the Present Tense

In each of the following sentences, fill in the correct form of the verb indicated in parentheses.

EXAMPLE: Because of my university's internship program, I ___am___

(*be*) able to receive academic credit for my summer job.

1. I _____*have*_____ (*have*) a job lined up with a company that provides private security to businesses and residential developments.

2. The company _____*has*_____ (*have*) a good record of keeping its clients safe from crime.

3. The company _____*is*_____ (*be*) part of a fast-growing industry.

4. Many people no longer _____*have*_____ (*have*) faith in the ability of the police to protect them.

5. People with lots of money _____*are*_____ (*be*) willing to pay for their own protection.

6. Concern about crime _____*is*_____ (*be*) especially noticeable in so-called gated communities.

7. In these private residential areas, no one _____*has*_____ (*have*) the right to enter without permission.

8. If you _____*are*_____ (*be*) a visitor, you must obtain a special pass.

9. Once you _____*have*_____ (*have*) the pass, you show it to the security guard when you reach the gate.

10. In a gated community, the residents _____*are*_____ (*be*) likely to appreciate the security.

• •

Past Tense of Be

The past tense of the verb *be* is tricky because it has two different forms: *was* and *were*.

Past Tense of *Be*

	SINGULAR	**PLURAL**
First person	I was	we were
Second person	you were	you were
Third person	she, he, it was	they were
	the student was	the students were

• •

PRACTICE 6   Using *Be* in the Past Tense

In the paragraph that follows, fill in each blank with the correct past tense of the verb *be*.

> **EXAMPLE:** During college, my sister _____was_____ excited about a
> big decision she had made.

(1) My sister _____was_____ always afraid of visits to the doctor. (2) Therefore, my parents and I _____were_____ surprised when she announced that she wanted to become a doctor herself. (3) We thought that medicine _____was_____ a strange choice for her. (4) "Since you _____were_____ a little girl, you have disliked doctors," I reminded her. (5) I _____was_____ sure she would quickly change her mind. (6) She admitted that she _____was_____ still afraid, but she hoped that understanding medicine would help her overcome her fears. (7) Her premedical courses in college _____were_____ difficult, but finally she was accepted into medical school. (8) We _____were_____ very proud of her that day, and we knew that she would be a great doctor.

• •

PRACTICE 7   Using Irregular Verbs in the Past Tense

In each of the following sentences, fill in the past tense of the irregular verb in parentheses. If you do not know the answer, find the word in the chart of irregular verb forms on pages 385–88.

> **EXAMPLE:** It _____took_____ (*take*) many years for baseball players
> in the Negro Leagues to get recognized for their abilities.

1. The Negro Leagues _____began_____ (*begin*) in 1920, founded by pitcher Andrew "Rube" Foster.

2. Segregation _____made_____ (*make*) it impossible for black players to play on the all-white major league teams at that time.

3. The Negro Leagues _____gave_____ (*give*) black athletes the opportunity to play professional baseball.

4. Some Negro League players _____became_____ (*become*) legendary.

5. People across the country _____knew_____ (*know*) the name of Satchel Paige, the pitcher for the Kansas City Monarchs.

6. The Kansas City Monarchs' infielder, Jackie Robinson, _____laid_____ (*lay*) the groundwork for all future black baseball players.

7. Robinson _____*left*_____ (*leave*) the Negro Leagues in 1947 to become the first black player to join a major league team, the Brooklyn Dodgers.

8. Other Negro League players _____*hit*_____ (*hit*) home runs and _____*stole*_____ (*steal*) bases but did not become famous.

9. The Negro Leagues _____*shut*_____ (*shut*) down in 1960.

10. Supporters _____*built*_____ (*build*) the Negro Leagues Baseball Museum in Kansas City, Missouri.

· ·

PRACTICE 8   Using Irregular Verbs in the Past Tense

In the following paragraph, replace any incorrect present-tense verbs with the correct past tense of the verb.

(1) In 1900, my great-grandfather ~~grows~~ *grew* wheat and raised a few cattle on his farm in Wyoming. (2) When my grandmother and her brothers were young, they ~~go~~ *went* to the fields every day to help their father. (3) The family ~~does~~ *did* not have much money, and they hoped for good weather every year. (4) Droughts and damaging storms often cost them a lot. (5) One year, high winds ~~blow~~ *blew* down the barn, and hailstones ~~break~~ *broke* their windows. (6) Another year, very little rain ~~falls~~ *fell*, and they almost ~~lose~~ *lost* the farm. (7) Somehow, they ~~keep~~ *kept* going in spite of their difficulties. (8) Their life was hard, but the whole family ~~understands~~ *understood* that the rewards of owning their own land were worthwhile.

· ·

For irregular verbs, the past participle is often different from the past tense.

	PAST TENSE	PAST PARTICIPLE
REGULAR VERB	I walked home.	I have walked home before.
IRREGULAR VERB	I drove home.	I have driven home before.

It is difficult to predict how irregular verbs form the past participle. Until you are familiar with them, find them in the chart on pages 385–88.

· ·

PRACTICE 9   Using the Past Participle of Irregular Verbs

In each of the following sentences, fill in the correct helping verb (a form of *have*) and the correct past-participle form of the verb in parentheses. If you do not know the correct form, find the word in the chart on pages 385–88.

EXAMPLE: For some time, Rob Wrubel and George Lichter
_____had known_____ (*know*) that their stressful jobs were
damaging their health.

1. They were top executives of an Internet search engine company, and
   their lives _____had become_____ (*become*) full of work and travel.

2. For a long time, their bodies _____had been_____ (*be*) telling them that
   they were paying a high price for their busy schedules.

3. Lichter _____had begun_____ (*begin*) to feel pain in his back and legs, and
   Wrubel had gained a lot of weight and had high blood pressure.

4. By the time the two executives met, each of them _____had found_____
   (*find*) relief in practicing yoga.

5. Late in 2001, the two men discussed new business opportunities, saying
   how they _____had grown_____ (*grow*) tired of stressful work.

6. By this time, they _____had left_____ (*leave*) their companies.

7. Now, they _____have put_____ (*put*) their business skills and passion for
   yoga to work in creating a new corporation.

8. They _____have built_____ (*build*) a small chain of yoga studios and hope
   to open locations nationwide.

9. For several years now, their company, Yoga Works, _____has run_____
   (*run*) fourteen studios in California and New York.

10. Wrubel and Lichter _____have shown_____ (*show*) that hard work and a little
    imagination can turn a negative situation into a positive one.

Past Participles

TEACHING TIP As you introduce this section, remind students that the purpose of this chapter is not to memorize the terms but to use verbs correctly in writing.

A **past participle**, by itself, cannot be the main verb of a sentence. But when a past participle is combined with another verb, called a **helping verb**, it can be used to make the present perfect tense and the past perfect tense.

| *Have / Has* | + | Past participle | = | Present perfect tense |

The **present perfect** tense is used for an action that began in the past and either continues into the present or was completed at some unknown time in the past.

Present tense of
have (helping verb)   Past participle

PRESENT PERFECT TENSE   My car has stalled several times recently.
[This sentence says the stalling began in the past but
may continue into the present.]

PAST TENSE My <u>car</u> <u>stalled</u>.

[This sentence says that the car stalled once and that it's over.]

Past   Present (now)   Future

Present Perfect

My car stalled.   My car has stalled. . . .

Present Perfect Tense

	SINGULAR	PLURAL
First person	I have laughed.	We have laughed.
Second person	You have laughed.	You have laughed.
Third person	She/he/it has laughed.	They have laughed.
	The baby has laughed.	The babies have laughed.

LANGUAGE NOTE: Be careful not to leave out *have* when it is needed for the present perfect. Time-signal words like *since* and *for* may mean that the present perfect is required.

INCORRECT	I <u>drive</u> since 1985.	We <u>wait</u> for two hours.
CORRECT	I **have** <u>driven</u> since 1985.	We **have** <u>waited</u> for two hours.

- -

PRACTICE 10 Using the Present Perfect Tense

In each of the following sentences, circle the correct verb tense.

> **EXAMPLE:** For many years now, the laws of most states
> (allowed /(have allowed) only doctors to write prescriptions
> for patients.

1. In the past few years, a number of states (began /(have begun)) to allow physician assistants and nurse practitioners to write prescriptions.

2. Before the changes in the laws, physician assistants and nurse practitioners (saw)/ have seen) patients with common illnesses.

3. However, if the patients (needed)/ have needed) a prescription, a doctor had to write it.

4. Many doctors (said /(have said)) that the changes are a good idea.

5. Physician assistants and nurse practitioners (spent /(have spent)) years in training by the time they get their licenses.

6. Since the new laws took effect, physician assistants and nurse practitioners (wrote /(have written)) many common prescriptions.

7. Recently, some people (expressed /(have expressed)) concern that physician assistants and nurse practitioners might make mistakes in writing prescriptions.

8. However, the possibility of a mistake in a prescription (always existed / (has always existed)).

9. For the past several years, pharmacists (kept /(have kept)) track of prescription errors.

10. Doctors made all but one of the mistakes they (found /(have found)) so far.

Use *had* plus the past participle to make the **past perfect tense**. The past perfect tense is used for an action that began in the past and ended before some other past action.

PAST PERFECT TENSE   My car had stalled several times before I called the mechanic.

[This sentence says that both the *stalling* and *calling the mechanic* happened in the past, but the stalling happened before the calling.]

PRACTICE 11   Using the Past Perfect Tense

In each of the following sentences, circle the correct verb tense.

EXAMPLE: When musician Ray Charles was born in September 1930, the Depression already (caused /(had caused)) many Americans to lose hope.

1. His family (was /(had been)) poor even before the Depression started.

2. Until he was four years old, Ray ((enjoyed)/ had enjoyed) normal vision.

3. However, by the time he was seven, he (became /(had become)) totally blind.

4. When he ((tripped)/ had tripped) over furniture and asked for his mother's help, often she just watched him and remained silent.

5. In this way, she ((encouraged)/ had encouraged) him to learn how to help himself get back up.

6. She (come/(had come)) to recognize how important it was for Ray to find his way on his own.

7. Ray later ((spent)/ had spent) several years in Florida's state school for the deaf and blind.

8. By the time he left the school, he (developed /(had developed)) his unusual gift for playing, composing, and arranging music.

9. By the time he became a star, Ray Charles (refined /(had refined)) his unique musical style.

10. By the time of his death in 2004, Charles understood that he (inspired / (had inspired)) many people.

· ·

| *Be* | + | Past participle | = | Passive voice |

A sentence that is written in the **passive voice** has a subject that does not perform an action. Instead, the subject is acted upon. To create the passive voice, combine a form of the verb *be* with a past participle.

Form of *be*   Past participle
(helping verb)

PASSIVE   The newspaper was thrown onto the porch.
[The subject, *newspaper*, did not throw itself onto the porch. Some unidentified person threw the newspaper.]

Most sentences should be written in the **active voice**, which means that the subject performs the action.

ACTIVE   The delivery person threw the newspaper onto the porch.
[The subject, *delivery person*, performed the action: He or she threw the newspaper.]

Use the passive voice when no one person performed the action, when you do not know who performed the action, or when you want to emphasize the receiver of the action. When you know who performed the action, it is usually preferable to identify the actor.

ACTIVE	The bandleader chose Kelly to do a solo.
PASSIVE	Kelly was chosen to do a solo.
	[If you wanted to emphasize Kelly's being chosen rather than the bandleader's choice, you might decide to use the passive voice.]

Finding and Fixing Verb-Tense Errors:
Changing from Active to Passive Voice

↓

Find

He sent the payment over two weeks ago.

1. **Underline** the subject, and **double-underline** the verb.
2. **Ask:** What word in the sentence is receiving the action? *Payment.*
3. **Cross out** the subject.

↓

Fix

                The payment
He sent ~~the payment~~ over two weeks ago.
        ^

4. Make the word that is receiving the action the subject by moving it to the beginning of the sentence.

                The payment was
He sent ~~the payment~~ over two weeks ago.
        ^

5. Add the correct form of the verb *be* in front of the main verb.

                The payment was   by him
He sent ~~the payment~~ over two weeks ago.
        ^   ^

6. You can either delete the performer of the action or put this information after the verb and the word *by.*

NOTE: If the original sentence uses a form of *have* followed by a past participle, form the passive voice by using a form of *have* + *been* + the past participle:

                The payment   been .
He has sent ~~the payment.~~
        ^   ^   ^

LANGUAGE NOTE: Avoid confusing the passive voice and the present perfect tense, which only uses *been* in sentences with *be* as the main verb.

INCORRECT	My aunt and uncle have been trained the dogs.
CORRECT	My aunt and uncle **have trained** the dogs.
	(present perfect)
CORRECT	The dogs **have been trained** by my aunt and uncle.
	(passive)

PRACTICE 12   Changing the Passive Voice to the Active Voice

Rewrite the following sentences, changing them from the passive voice to the active voice. *Answers will vary. Possible answers are shown.*

> *The legislature cut funding*
> **EXAMPLE:** ~~Funding~~ for animal shelters. ~~was cut by the legislature.~~

The owners were going to close some
1. Some shelters. ~~were going to be closed by the owners.~~

No one knew what
2. ~~What~~ would become of the animals. ~~was unknown.~~

Animal lovers started a
3. A campaign. ~~was started by animal lovers.~~

The owners and volunteers at shelters gave interviews.
4. ~~Interviews were given by the owners and volunteers at shelters.~~

News teams filmed the
5. The animals. ~~were filmed by news teams.~~

All the local television stations aired the
6. The stories. ~~were aired on all the local television stations.~~

Animal lovers across the state staged a
7. A protest. ~~was staged by animal lovers across the state.~~

People held fund-raisers
8. ~~Fund-raisers~~ of all sorts. ~~were held.~~

The legislature restored some
9. Some funds. ~~were restored by the legislature.~~

People raised enough
10. ~~Enough~~ money ~~was raised~~ to keep the shelters open.

Consistency of Verb Tense

Consistency of verb tense means that all actions in a sentence that happen (or happened) at the same time are in the same tense. If all of the actions happen in the present or happen all the time, use the present for all verbs in the sentence. If all of the actions happened in the past, use the past tense for all verbs.

As you edit your writing, make sure that whenever a verb tense changes, it is because the action the verb describes happened at a different time. Otherwise, the shift in tenses causes an inconsistency.

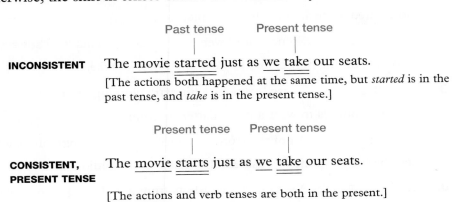

       Past tense   Present tense

INCONSISTENT   The movie started just as we take our seats.

[The actions both happened at the same time, but *started* is in the past tense, and *take* is in the present tense.]

       Present tense   Present tense

CONSISTENT,   The movie starts just as we take our seats.
PRESENT TENSE

[The actions and verb tenses are both in the present.]

		Past tense Past tense
CONSISTENT, PAST TENSE	The <u>movie</u> <u><u>started</u></u> just as <u>we</u> <u><u>took</u></u> our seats.

[The actions *started* and *took* both happened in the past, and both are in the past tense.]

· ·

PRACTICE 13   Using Consistent Verb Tense

In each of the following sentences, double-underline the verbs, and correct any unnecessary shifts in verb tense. Write the correct form of the verb in the blank space provided.

> **EXAMPLE:** _____*have*_____ Although some people <u><u>dream</u></u> of having their picture taken by a famous photographer, not many <u>had</u> the chance.

1. _____*wants*_____ Now, special stores in malls <u><u>take</u></u> magazine-quality photographs of anyone who <u>wanted</u> one.

2. _____*heard*_____ The founder of one business <u><u>got</u></u> the idea when she <u>hear</u> friends complaining about how bad they <u><u>looked</u></u> in family photographs.

3. _____*felt*_____ They <u>feel</u> they <u><u>were</u></u> always blinking or making a funny face.

4. _____*decided*_____ She <u>decide</u> to open a business to take studio-style photographs that <u><u>did</u></u> not cost a lot of money.

5. _____*offered*_____ Her first store <u><u>included</u></u> special lighting and <u>offers</u> different sets, such as colored backgrounds and outdoor scenes.

6. _____*want*_____ Now, her stores even <u><u>have</u></u> makeup studios for people who <u>wanted</u> a special look for their pictures.

7. _____*advise*_____ Some stores even <u><u>provide</u></u> consultants who <u>advised</u> customers on the best colors to wear and poses to take.

8. _____*keep*_____ These locations <u>kept</u> extra clothing on hand in case a customer <u><u>chooses</u></u> to wear a more flattering color.

9. _____*like*_____ All of the stores <u><u>use</u></u> professional photographers who <u>liked</u> the high volume of business they <u><u>get</u></u> at mall studios.

10. _____*charges*_____ A set of ten headshots from a mall studio <u><u>costs</u></u> about $50, while a typical professional photographer <u>charged</u> hundreds of dollars for this type of package.

· ·

TIP For answers to odd-numbered practice items, see pp. AK-1–10 at the back of the book.

Edit for Verb Problems

Use the chart on page 403, Finding and Fixing Verb-Tense Errors, to help you complete the practices in this section and edit your own writing.

• •

PRACTICE 14   Correcting Various Verb Problems

In the following sentences, find and correct any verb problems.

> *is*
> **EXAMPLE:** Sheena ~~be~~ tired of the tattoo on her left shoulder.

1. Many of Sheena's friends ~~was~~ *were* getting tattoos ten years ago.
2. Sheena had never consider *ed* a tattoo until several of her friends got them.
3. Sheena was twenty-two when she ~~goes~~ *went* to the tattoo parlor.
4. After looking at many designs, she ~~choose~~ *chose* a purple rose, which she gave to the tattoo artist.
5. Her sister liked the tattoo, but her mother faint *ed*.
6. Many people who *have* now reached their thirties want to get rid of their old tattoos.
7. Dermatologists have ~~saw~~ *seen* the development of a new trend toward tattoo removal.
8. A few years ago, when a person ~~decides~~ *decided* to have a tattoo removed, doctors had to cut out the design.
9. That technique ~~leaved~~ *left* scars.
10. Today, doctors ~~using~~ *use* laser light to break up the ink molecules in the skin.
11. Six months ago, Sheena start *ed* to have treatments to remove her tattoo.
12. The procedure ~~hurted~~ *hurt* every time she saw the doctor, but she hoped it would be worth the pain.

• •

PRACTICE 15   Editing Paragraphs for Correct Verbs

Find and correct seven problems with verb tense in the following paragraphs.

> *think*
> (1) When you ~~thought~~ about a farm, you probably imagine acres of cornfields and stalls full of noisy animals. (2) Although that is an understandable vision, it may not be a particularly accurate one in the near future. (3) Some experts ~~believes~~ *believe* that farms of the future will be found inside the top floors of a city's tallest skyscrapers. (4) This concept ~~have~~ *has* been referred to as "vertical gardening."

(5) Indoor city gardening not only would help make places become more self-sufficient but also could provide new uses for the variety of abandoned buildings that are ~~finded~~ *found* scattered throughout large cities. (6) Experts ~~has~~ *have* suggested that the water used for these small farms and gardens could be recycled from indoor fish ponds. (7) False sunlight could be created through the use of artificial lights. (8) Thermostats could control the indoor temperatures.

(9) Although this technology is not currently available, architects ~~has~~ *have* been toying with possible designs. (10) In the future, farms will most likely include everything from solar panels and windmills to generators that run on biofuels. (11) It ~~is~~ *will be* about five to ten years before all of these ideas will be commonplace.

. . . .

PRACTICE 16   Editing Verb Problems and Using Formal English

Your sister has a bad case of laryngitis and wants to bring a note about her condition to her doctor. Help her by correcting the verb problems in the note. Then, edit the informal English. *Answers will vary. Possible edits are shown.*

Dear Dr. Kerrigan,
(1) ~~What's up, Doc Kerrigan?~~
(2) Your assistant ~~ask~~ *asked* me to tell you about my symptoms, so I *will* describe them as well as I can. (3) I ~~becomed~~ *became* sick about a day ago. (4) Now, my throat ~~hurt~~ *hurts* every time I ~~swallowed~~, and I cannot speak. (5) Also, I ~~has~~ *have* a high fever, and I ~~be wicked~~ *am very* tired. (6) I do not think I ~~has~~ *have* ever ~~feeled~~ *felt* so ~~crappy~~ *bad* before. (7) I ~~looked~~ *look* forward to seeing you during my appointment.
(8) Thanks ~~mucho,~~ *very much,*
Corrine Evans

. . . .

PRACTICE 17   Editing Cal's E-Mail

Look back at Cal's e-mail on page 381. You may have already underlined the eight verb errors; if not, do so now. Next, using what you have learned in this chapter, correct each error.

. . . .

PRACTICE 18   Editing Your Own Writing for Verb Tense

Edit verbs in a piece of your own writing—a paper you are working on for this class, a paper you have already finished, a paper for another course, or a recent piece of writing from your work or everyday life. Use the chart on page 403 to help you.

. . . .

Chapter Review

1. Verb _____tense_____ indicates when the action in a sentence happens (past, present, or future).

2. What are the two present-tense endings for regular verbs? *-s and no ending*

3. How do regular verbs in the past tense end? *-ed*

4. The past participle is used with a _____helping_____ verb.

5. Verbs that do not follow the regular pattern for verbs are called _____irregular_____ .

6. An action that started in the past but might continue into the present uses the _present perfect tense_ .

7. An action that happened in the past before something else that happened in the past uses the ___past perfect tense___ .

8. You should usually avoid using the _____passive_____ voice, which has a subject that performs no action but is acted upon.

9. Verb tenses are consistent when actions that happen at the same _____time_____ are in the same _____tense_____ .

LEARNING JOURNAL If you found verb errors in your writing, what kind were they? What is the main thing you have learned about verb tense that you will use? What is one thing that remains unclear?

TEACHING TIP You can collect students' learning journals to find out what the class or individual students need more work on.

Chapter Test

Circle the correct choice for each of the following items. Use the Finding and Fixing Verb-Tense Errors chart on page 403 and the Verb Reference charts on pages 404–07.

TIP For advice on taking tests, see Appendix A.

1. If an underlined portion of this sentence is incorrect, select the revision that fixes it. If the sentence is correct as written, choose d.

   It has <u>became</u> difficult to tell whether Trisha <u>is</u> tired of her work or
        A   **B**

   <u>tired</u> of her boss.
    C

   (a.) become   **c.** tiring

   b. be   **d.** No change is necessary.

RESOURCES The *Testing Tool Kit* CD-ROM available with this book has even more tests.

2. Choose the item that has no errors.

   a. By the time we arrived, Michelle already gave her recital.

   (b.) By the time we arrived, Michelle had already given her recital.

   c. By the time we arrived, Michelle has already given her recital.

3. If an underlined portion of this sentence is incorrect, select the revision that fixes it. If the sentence is correct as written, choose d.

I likes Manuel's new car, but I wish he wouldn't park it in my space
  A   B

when he comes home from work.
         C

a. like   **c.** came

b. wishing   **d.** No change is necessary.

4. Choose the item that has no errors.

a. Patrick has such a bad memory that he has to write down everything he is supposed to do.

b. Patrick had such a bad memory that he has to write down everything he is supposed to do.

c. Patrick had such a bad memory that he having to write down everything he is supposed to do.

5. Choose the correct word(s) to fill in the blank.

For many years, Steven _____ the manual typewriter that his grandfather had given to him.

a. keeped   **b.** kept   **c.** was keeping

6. Choose the item that has no errors.

a. I have be cutting back on the amount of coffee I drink.

b. I has been cutting back on the amount of coffee I drink.

c. I have been cutting back on the amount of coffee I drink.

RESOURCES For Cumulative Editing Review Tests, see pages 601–10.

7. Choose the correct word(s) to fill in the blank.

We had intended to visit Marina's parents while we _____ in town, but we did not have time.

a. was   **b.** had were   **c.** were

8. Choose the correct word(s) to fill in the blank.

Each family _____ a dish and brought it to our knitting club's annual dinner.

a. prepares   **b.** prepared   **c.** have prepared

9. If an underlined portion of this sentence is incorrect, select the revision that fixes it. If the sentence is correct as written, choose d.

The boy <u>jumped</u> out of the way just before the car <u>is</u> about to <u>hit</u> him.
       A   B   C

- **a.** jumping
- **(b.)** was
- **c.** hitted
- **d.** No change is necessary.

10. Choose the correct word to fill in the blank.

Who has _____ the train to New York before?

- **(a.)** taken
- **b.** take
- **c.** taked

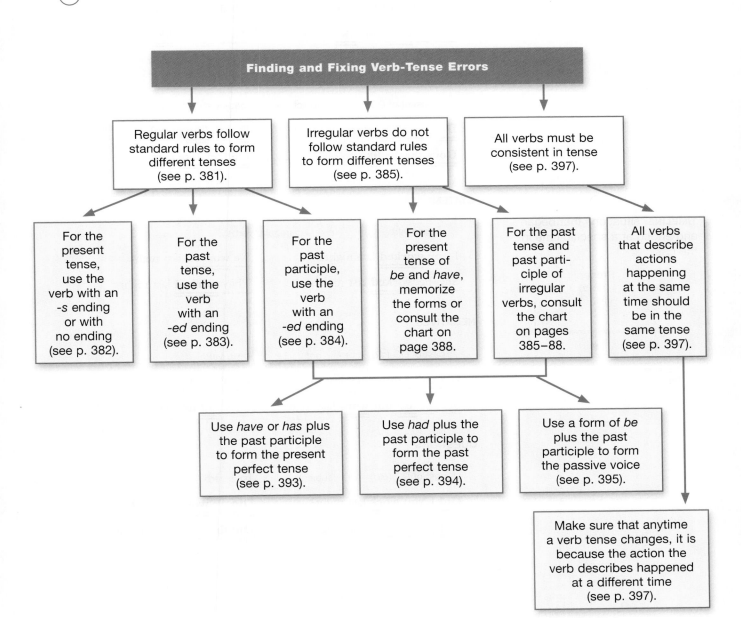

THE SIMPLE TENSES

TENSE

Simple Present

TIMELINE: situations that exist always (now, in the past, and in the future)

STATEMENTS

In the third-person singular, regular verbs end in -s or -es.

I/you **like** pizza.   We **like** pizza.

She/he **likes** pizza.   They **like** pizza.

NEGATIVES

present of *DO* + *not* + base verb

I/you **do not like** pizza.   We **do not like** pizza.

She/he **does not like** pizza.   They **do not like** pizza.

QUESTIONS

present of *DO* + subject + base verb

Do I/you **like** pizza?   **Do** we **like** pizza?

Does she/he **like** pizza?   **Do** they **like** pizza?

Simple Past

TIMELINE: situations that began and ended at a specific time in the past

STATEMENTS

base verb + -d or -ed (regular verbs)

I/you **worked** last night.   We **worked** last night.

She/he **worked** last night.   They **worked** last night.

NEGATIVES

past of *DO* (*did*) + *not* + base verb

I/you **did not work** last night.   We **did not work** last night.

She/he **did not work** last night.   They **did not work** last night.

QUESTIONS

past of *DO* (*did*) + subject + base verb

Did I/you **work** last night?   **Did** we **work** last night?

Did she/he **work** last night?   **Did** they **work** last night?

TENSE	
Simple Future	**STATEMENTS**

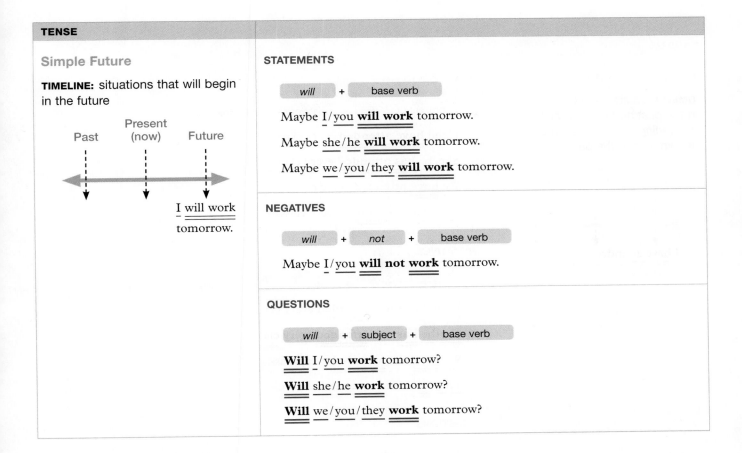

TENSE

Simple Future

TIMELINE: situations that will begin in the future

Past   Present (now)   Future

I will work tomorrow.

STATEMENTS

will + base verb

Maybe I/you **will work** tomorrow.

Maybe she/he **will work** tomorrow.

Maybe we/you/they **will work** tomorrow.

NEGATIVES

will + *not* + base verb

Maybe I/you **will not work** tomorrow.

QUESTIONS

will + subject + base verb

Will I/you **work** tomorrow?

Will she/he **work** tomorrow?

Will we/you/they **work** tomorrow?

THE PERFECT TENSES

TENSE

Present Perfect

TIMELINE: a situation that began in the past and either is *still happening* or ended at an unknown time in the past

Past   Present
              (now)   Future

I have attended
every class.

STATEMENTS

present of *HAVE* + past participle of base verb

I/you **have attended** every class.

She/he **has attended** every class.

We **have attended** every class.

They **have attended** every class.

NEGATIVES

present of *HAVE* + *not* + past participle of base verb

I/you **have not attended** every class.

She/he **has not attended** every class.

We **have not attended** every class.

They **have not attended** every class.

QUESTIONS

present of *HAVE* + subject + past participle of base verb

Have I/you **attended** every class?

Has she/he **attended** every class?

Have we **attended** every class?

Have they **attended** every class?

Past Perfect

TIMELINE: a situation that began and ended before some other past situation occurred

Past   Present
          (now)   Future

(somebody)   Gil's
left   arrival

STATEMENTS

past of *HAVE* (*had*) + past participle of base verb

I/you **had left** before Gil arrived.

She/he **had left** before Gil arrived.

We **had left** before Gil arrived.

They **had left** before Gil arrived.

TENSE	
Past Perfect	**NEGATIVES** past of *HAVE* (*had*) + *not* + past participle of base verb **Usually used for "if" situations** If you **had not left**, you would have seen him. If she/he **had not left**, she/he would have seen him. If we **had not left**, we would have seen him. If they **had not left**, they would have seen him. **QUESTIONS** past of *HAVE* (*had*) + subject + past participle of base verb **Had** I/you **left** before Gil arrived? **Had** we **left** before Gil arrived? **Had** she/he **left** before Gil arrived? **Had** they **left** before Gil arrived?
Future Perfect **TIMELINE:** a situation that will be completed in the future before another future situation Past Present (now) Future graduation moving	**STATEMENTS** *will have* + past participle of base verb I/you **will have graduated** before I/you move. She/he **will have graduated** before you move. We **will have graduated** before you move. They **will have graduated** before you move. **NEGATIVES** *will not have* + past participle of base verb I/you **will not have graduated** before I/you move. She/he **will not have graduated** before you move. We **will not have graduated** before you move. They **will not have graduated** before you move. **QUESTIONS** *will* + subject + *will* + past participle of base verb **Will** I/you **have graduated** before I/you move? **Will** she/he **have graduated** before you move? **Will** we **have graduated** before you move? **Will** they **have graduated** before you move?

Part 5

Other Grammar Concerns

THIS CHAPTER

- explains what the different kinds of pronouns are
- explains how to make your pronouns agree with your nouns
- shows how to avoid pronoun problems
- gives you practice using the different kinds of pronouns correctly

26

Pronouns

Using Substitutes for Nouns

Understand What Pronouns Are

Pronouns replace nouns or other pronouns in a sentence so that you do not have to repeat them.

Sheryl got into ~~Sheryl's~~ *her* car.

I like Mario. ~~Mario~~ *He* is a good dancer.

In most cases, a pronoun refers to a specific noun or pronoun mentioned nearby.

Noun

I picked up my new glasses. They are cool.

Pronoun replacing noun

TIP For fun podcasts with tips on grammar and usage, check out Grammar Girl's Quick and Dirty Tips for Better Writing on **bedfordstmartins.com/ realwriting**.

RESOURCES *Additional Resources* contains tests and supplemental exercises for this chapter as well as a transparency master for the chart at the end.

Practice Using Pronouns Correctly

Identify Pronouns

Before you practice finding and correcting common pronoun errors, it will help you to practice identifying pronouns.

Common Pronouns

PERSONAL PRONOUNS	POSSESSIVE PRONOUNS	INDEFINITE PRONOUNS	
I	my	all	much
me	mine	any	neither (of)
you	your/yours	anybody	nobody
she/he	hers/his	anyone	none (of)
her/him	hers/his	anything	no one
it	its	both	nothing
we	our/ours	each (of)	one (of)
us	our/ours	either (of)	some
they	their/theirs	everybody	somebody
them	their/theirs	everyone	someone
		everything	something
		few (of)	

. . . .

PRACTICE 1   Identifying Pronouns

TIP For more practice with pronoun usage, visit Exercise Central at **bedfordstmartins .com/realwriting.**

In each of the following sentences, circle the pronoun, underline the noun it refers to, and draw an arrow from the pronoun to the noun.

> **EXAMPLE:** People can have a hard time seeing stars at night if (they) live in or near a big city.

1. Each night the stars fill the skies, but in many large cities (they) are impossible to see.

RESOURCES To gauge students' skills in pronoun usage, use the *Testing Tool Kit* CD-ROM available with this book.

2. The huge amount of light coming from homes, businesses, and streets creates a type of pollution, and (it) makes seeing the stars difficult.

3. The average night sky has approximately 2,500 stars in (it), and (they) can be seen with the human eye.

4. In many neighborhoods, however, only two hundred or three hundred stars can be spotted, while in a big city only about a dozen of (them) can be seen.

5. The International Dark Sky Association focuses on reducing light pollution as (its) main goal and has several recommendations.

6. Pointing lights down toward the ground instead of allowing (them) to shine up toward the sky is one suggestion.

7. To help battle light pollution, some cities and towns have passed laws limiting what lights (they) will allow.

8. Experts have been studying light pollution, and (they) have reported that (it) can affect many things, including wildlife and even human health.

9. Migrating birds sometimes fly over brightly lit cities and, confused by the unnatural light, fly in circles until (they) become exhausted.

10. Too much light has also been shown to be harmful to humans, and studies are being done to determine just how this overexposure affects (them).

ESL ESL students may have particular trouble with pronouns and benefit from extra practice exercises.

Check for Pronoun Agreement

A pronoun must agree with (match) the noun or pronoun it refers to in number. It must be either singular (one) or plural (more than one).

If a pronoun is singular, it must also match the noun or pronoun it refers to in gender (*he*, *she*, or *it*).

CONSISTENT	Magda sold *her* old television set. [*Her* agrees with *Magda* because both are singular and feminine.]
CONSISTENT	The Wilsons sold *their* old television set. [*Their* agrees with *the Wilsons* because both are plural.]

Watch out for singular, general nouns. If a noun is singular, the pronoun that refers to it must be singular as well.

INCONSISTENT	Any student can tell you what *their* least favorite course is. [*Student* is singular, but the pronoun *their* is plural.]
CONSISTENT	Any student can tell you what *his* or *her* least favorite course is. [*Student* is singular, and so are the pronouns *his* and *her*.]

To avoid using the awkward phrase *his or her*, make the subject plural when you can.

CONSISTENT	Most students can tell you what *their* least favorite course is.

Two types of words often cause errors in pronoun agreement: indefinite pronouns and collective nouns.

Indefinite Pronouns

An **indefinite pronoun** does not refer to a specific person, place, or thing: It is general. Indefinite pronouns often take singular verbs. Whenever a pronoun refers to an indefinite pronoun, check for agreement.

her
Someone left ~~their~~ purse in the cafeteria.

his
The monks got up at dawn. Everybody had ~~their~~ chores for the day.

Indefinite Pronouns

ALWAYS SINGULAR			MAY BE PLURAL OR SINGULAR
another	everyone	nothing	all
anybody/anyone	everything	one (of)	any
anything	much	somebody	none
each (of)	neither (of)	someone	some
either (of)	nobody	something	
everybody	no one		

NOTE: Many people object to the use of only the masculine pronoun *he* when referring to a singular indefinite pronoun, such as *everyone*. Although grammatically correct, using the masculine form alone to refer to an indefinite pronoun is considered sexist. Here are two ways to avoid this problem:

1.   Use *his or her*.

     Someone posted *his or her* e-mail address to the Web site.

2.   Change the sentence so that the pronoun refers to a plural noun or pronoun.

     Some students posted *their* e-mail addresses to the Web site.

· ·

PRACTICE 2   Using Indefinite Pronouns

Circle the correct pronoun or group of words in parentheses.

(1) Anyone who wants to start (their / his or her) own business had better be prepared to work hard. (2) One may find, for example, that (his or her / their) work is never done. (3) Something is always waiting, with

its) / their) own peculiar demands. (4) Nothing gets done on (their /(its)

own. (5) Anybody who expects to have more freedom now that (he or

she no longer works) / they no longer work) for a boss may be disap-

pointed. (6) After all, when you work as an employee for a company,

someone above you makes decisions as (they see /(he or she sees)) fit.

(7) When you are your own boss, no one else places (themselves /

(himself or herself)) in the position of final responsibility.

(8) Somebody starting a business may also be surprised by how

much tax (they /(he or she)) must pay. (9) Each employee at a company

pays only about half as much toward social security as what (they /

(he or she)) would pay if self-employed. (10) Neither medical nor dental

coverage can be obtained as inexpensively as (it)/ they) can when a

person is an employee at a corporation.

TIP Answers to odd-numbered practice items are on pages AK-1–10 at the back of the book.

Collective Nouns

A **collective noun** names a group that acts as a single unit.

Common Collective Nouns		
audience	company	group
class	crowd	jury
college	family	society
committee	government	team

Collective nouns are usually singular, so when you use a pronoun to refer to a collective noun, it too must usually be singular.

         its
The team had ~~their~~ sixth consecutive win of the season.

         its
The jury returned ~~their~~ verdict.

If the people in a group are acting as individuals, however, the noun is plural and should be used with a plural pronoun.

The class brought *their* papers to read.

> **Finding and Fixing Pronoun Problems:**
> **Using Collective Nouns and Pronouns**

Find

The <u>committee</u> changed (its / their) meeting time.

1. **Underline** any collective nouns.
2. **Ask:** Is the collective noun singular (a group acting as a single unit) or plural (people in a group acting as individuals)? *Singular.*

Fix

The committee changed (its)/ their) meeting time.

3. **Choose** the pronoun that agrees with the subject.

PRACTICE 3   Using Collective Nouns and Pronouns

Fill in the correct pronoun in each of the following sentences.

> **EXAMPLE:** In 1884, a Swiss company called Victorinox began selling a
> new kind of knife that _____*it*_____ had invented.

1. A large group of customers sent _____*their*_____ thanks to Victorinox, in letters praising the knife's quality and the tools included with it.

2. The company had found a way to add a screwdriver, a punch, and a can opener to _____*its*_____ knife.

3. The Swiss military at that time issued plain knives with wooden handles, but many army officers went to Victorinox to buy _____*its*_____ knives.

4. The Swiss army officially began equipping _____*its*_____ soldiers with Victorinox's knives in 1896.

5. In 1908, a committee from a rival company submitted _____*its*_____ bid to sell the company's own knives to the Swiss army.

6. The Swiss government awarded half of _____*its*_____ knife order to this company, called Wenger.

7. Wenger's corporate board raised _____*their*_____ voices in a cheer.

8. Victorinox got the other half of the order, and _____ *it* _____ was
pleased that it kept at least some of the business.

9. Recently, a team of executives from both companies announced
_____ *its* _____ decision to merge the two businesses.

10. My brother's family, all of whom like to hike and hunt, buy
_____ *their* _____ own custom knives from a small manufacturer.

. . . .

Make Pronoun Reference Clear

If the reader isn't sure what noun or pronoun a pronoun refers to, the sentence may be confusing. Look for and edit any sentence that has an ambiguous, vague, or repetitious pronoun reference.

In an **ambiguous pronoun reference**, the pronoun could refer to more than one noun.

AMBIGUOUS	Enrico told Jim *he* needed a better résumé.
	[Did Enrico tell Jim that Enrico himself needed a better résumé? Or did Enrico tell Jim that Jim needed a better résumé?]
EDITED	Enrico advised Jim to revise his résumé.
AMBIGUOUS	I put the glass on the shelf, even though *it* was dirty.
	[Was the glass or the shelf dirty?]
EDITED	I put the dirty glass on the shelf.

In a **vague pronoun reference**, the pronoun does not refer clearly to any particular person, place, or thing. To correct a vague pronoun reference, use a more specific noun instead of the pronoun.

VAGUE	When Tom got to the clinic, *they* told him it was closed.
	[Who told Tom the clinic was closed?]
EDITED	When Tom got to the clinic, the nurse told him it was closed.
VAGUE	Before I finished printing my report, *it* ran out of paper.
	[What was out of paper?]
EDITED	Before I finished printing my report, the printer ran out of paper.

Finding and Fixing Pronoun Problems:
Avoiding Ambiguous or Vague Pronoun References

↓

Find

The <u>cashier</u> said (they) were out of milk.

1. **Underline** the subject.
2. **Circle** the pronoun.
3. **Ask:** Who or what does the pronoun refer to? *No one. "They" does not refer to "cashier."*

↓

Fix

the store was
The cashier said ~~they were~~ out of milk.
          ^

4. **Correct the pronoun reference** by revising the sentence to make the pronoun more specific.

- -

PRACTICE 4   Avoiding Ambiguous or Vague Pronoun References

Edit each sentence to eliminate ambiguous or vague pronoun references. Some sentences may be revised in more than one way. *Answers may vary. Possible edits are shown.*

EXAMPLE: I am always looking for good advice on controlling my
experts
weight, but ~~they~~ have provided little help.
       ^

1. My doctor referred me to a physical therapist, *who*
   ~~and she~~ said I needed to
               ^
   exercise more.

2. I joined a workout group and did exercises with the members, but *exercising*
   ~~it~~ did
                                                                    ^
   not solve my problem.

3. I tried a lower-fat diet along with the exercising, but *this combination*
   ~~it~~ did not really
                                                          ^
   work either.

4. *Some nutritionists*
   ~~They~~ used to say that eliminating carbohydrates is the easiest way to lose
    ^
   weight.

5. Therefore, I started eating fats again and stopped consuming carbs, but
   these methods were
   ~~this was~~ not a permanent solution.
    ^

6. Although I lost weight and loved eating fatty foods, *this low-carb diet*
   ~~it~~ did not keep me
                                                        ^
   from eventually gaining the weight back.

7. Last week, I overheard my Uncle Kevin talking to my brother, and ~~he~~ *my uncle*

explained how he stayed slender even while traveling a lot.

8. Uncle Kevin eats fruit and vegetables instead of junk food while traveling, and ~~it~~ *this diet* has kept off the pounds.

9. He says it is not hard to pack carrots or apples for a trip, so anyone can
~~do this.~~ *plan in advance.*

10. I now try to plan better, eat less at each meal, and ignore all diet books,
and I hope ~~it~~ *these three ideas* works.

· ·

In a **repetitious pronoun reference**, the pronoun repeats a reference
to a noun rather than replacing the noun.

> The nurse at the clinic ~~he~~ told Tom that it was closed.

> The newspaper ~~it~~ says that the new diet therapy is promising.

LANGUAGE NOTE: In some languages, like Spanish, it is correct to repeat a
noun with a pronoun. In formal English, however, a pronoun is used to
replace a noun, not to repeat it.

INCORRECT	My instructor he gives us lots of homework.
CORRECT	My instructor gives us lots of homework.

Finding and Fixing Pronoun Problems: Avoiding Repetitious Pronoun References

Find

Television advertising (it) sometimes has a negative influence on
young viewers.

1. **Underline** the subject, and **double-underline** the verb.
2. **Circle** any pronouns in the sentence.
3. **Ask:** What noun does the pronoun refer to? *Advertising.*
4. **Ask:** Do the noun and the pronoun that refers to it share the same verb? *Yes.*
   Does the pronoun just repeat the noun rather than replace it? *Yes.* If the
   answer to one or both questions is yes, the pronoun is repetitious.

| **Fix** |
| Television advertising ~~it~~ sometimes has a negative influence on young viewers. |
| 5. **Correct the sentence** by crossing out the repetitious pronoun. |

· ·

PRACTICE 5   Avoiding Repetitious Pronoun References

Correct any repetitious pronoun references in the following sentences.

> **EXAMPLE:** Car commercials ~~they~~ want viewers to believe that buying a certain brand of car will bring happiness.

1. Young people ~~they~~ sometimes take advertisements too literally.

2. ~~In a~~ A beer advertisement, ~~it~~ might imply that drinking alcohol makes people more attractive and popular.

3. People who see or hear an advertisement ~~they~~ have to think about the message.

4. Parents should help their children understand why advertisements ~~they~~ do not show the real world.

5. A recent study, ~~it~~ said that parents can help kids overcome the influence of advertising.

· ·

Use the Right Type of Pronoun

Three important types of pronouns are **subject pronouns**, **object pronouns**, and **possessive pronouns**. Notice their uses in the following sentences.

Object   Subject
pronoun   pronoun

The dog barked at *him*, and *he* laughed.

Possessive
pronoun

As Josh walked out, *his* phone started ringing.

TIP Never put an apostrophe in a possessive pronoun.

Pronoun Types

	SUBJECT	OBJECT	POSSESSIVE
First-person singular/plural	I/we	me/us	my, mine/ our, ours
Second-person singular/plural	you/you	you/you	your, yours/ your, yours
Third-person singular	he, she, it	him, her, it	his, her, hers, its
	who	whom	whose
Third-person plural	they	them	their, theirs
	who	whom	whose

LANGUAGE NOTE: Notice that pronouns have gender (*he/she, him/her, his/ her/hers*). The pronoun must agree with the gender of the noun it refers to.

INCORRECT	Carolyn went to see *his* boyfriend.
CORRECT	Carolyn went to see *her* boyfriend.

Also, notice that English has different forms for subject and object pronouns, as shown in the previous chart.

Read the following sentence, and replace the underlined nouns with pronouns. Note that the pronouns are all different.

When Andreas made an A on ~~Andreas's~~ [his] final exam, ~~Andreas~~ [he] was proud of himself, and the teacher congratulated ~~Andreas~~ [him].

Subject Pronouns

Subject pronouns serve as the subject of a verb.

You live next door to a graveyard.

I opened the door too quickly.

LANGUAGE NOTE: Do not use *you* to mean *people*.

INCORRECT	The instructor says that you have to turn in your homework.
CORRECT	The instructor says that **students** have to turn in **their** homework.

LANGUAGE NOTE: Some languages do not use subject pronouns, but English sentences always have a subject noun or pronoun.

INCORRECT	Works every weekend.
CORRECT	*She* works every weekend.

TIP For a list of common prepositions, see page 315.

Object Pronouns

Object pronouns either receive the action of a verb or are part of a prepositional phrase.

OBJECT OF THE VERB	Jay gave *me* his watch.
OBJECT OF THE PREPOSITION	Jay gave his watch to *me*.

Possessive Pronouns

Possessive pronouns show ownership.

Dave is *my* uncle.

That book is *yours*.

Three trouble spots make it difficult to know what type of pronoun to use.

- Compound subjects and objects
- Comparisons
- Sentences that need *who* or *whom*

Pronouns Used with Compound Subjects and Objects

A **compound subject** has more than one subject joined by a conjunction such as *and* or *or*. A **compound object** has more than one object joined by a conjunction. (For a list of conjunctions, see p. 348.)

COMPOUND SUBJECT	Chandler and *I* worked on the project.
COMPOUND OBJECT	My boss gave the assignment to Chandler and *me*.

To decide what type of pronoun to use in a compound construction, try leaving out the other part of the compound and the conjunction. Then, say the sentence aloud to yourself.

TIP When you are writing about yourself and someone else, always put yourself after everyone else. *My friends and I went to a club*, not *I and my friends went to a club*.

Compound subject

~~Joan and~~ (me / **I**) went to the movies last night.
[Think: *I* went to the movies last night.]

Compound object

The car was headed right for ~~Tom and~~ (she / **her**).
[Think: The car was headed right for *her*.]

If a pronoun is part of a compound object in a prepositional phrase, use an object pronoun.

TIP Many people make the mistake of using *I* in the phrase *between you and I*. The correct pronoun with *between* is the object *me*.

Compound object

I will keep that information just between you and (I / **me**).
[*Between you and me* is a prepositional phrase, so an object pronoun, *me*, is required.]

> **Finding and Fixing Pronoun Problems:**
> **Using Pronouns in Compound Constructions**

Find

~~My friend and~~ <u>me</u> <u><u>talk</u></u> at least once a week.

1. **Underline** the subject, **double-underline** the verb, and **circle** any object or objects.
2. **Ask:** Does the sentence have a compound subject or object? *Yes—"friend and me" is a compound subject.*
3. **Ask:** Do the nouns in the compound construction share a verb? *Yes—"talk."*
4. **Cross out** one of the subjects so that only the pronoun remains.
5. **Ask:** Does the sentence sound right with just the pronoun as the subject? *No.*

Fix

My friend and ~~me~~ *I* talk at least once a week.

6. **Correct the sentence** by replacing the incorrect pronoun with the correct one.

. . . .

PRACTICE 6 Editing Pronouns in Compound Constructions

Edit each sentence using the proper type of pronoun. If a sentence is already correct, write a "C" next to it.

> **EXAMPLE:** Don King approached Zaire's President Mobutu, and
> *he*
> Mobutu and ~~him~~ reached an agreement.

1. In 1974, George Foreman was the heavyweight boxing champion, and
he
~~him~~ and Muhammad Ali agreed to a fight for the title.

2. President Mobutu of Zaire wanted to make his country famous, so the
him
financial backing for the fight came from ~~he~~ and the people of Zaire.

3. Because American officials considered Mobutu a strong anticommunist,
they and he
~~them and him~~ were allies, but Mobutu was a dictator who stole money
intended for his impoverished country.

4. According to the agreement with Mobutu, he and Don King guaranteed
Foreman and Ali $5 million each for the championship fight. *C*

5. Foreman angered the people of Zaire immediately when ~~him~~ *he* and his
German shepherd dog were seen getting off the airplane.

6. German shepherds were part of Zaire's unhappy past, when the streets were patrolled by them and the Belgian colonial police; people were afraid of the dogs. *C*

7. The people loved Muhammad Ali, and pictures of he *(him)* and his group in Zaire showed adoring crowds everywhere.

8. Foreman was younger and stronger, so most boxing fans believed that in a fight between him and Ali, Foreman would win an easy victory. *C*

9. Ali may have feared losing the fight, but when him *(he)* and Foreman finally got in the ring, Ali took punch after punch.

10. Foreman became so tired that the end of the fight came for he *(him)* and Ali in the eighth round; Ali knocked out the champion and regained the world heavyweight title.

● ●

TEACHING TIP Have each student write a sentence that uses implied words in a comparison. Then, have the students read the sentences aloud and ask other class members to supply the missing words.

Pronouns Used in Comparisons

Using the right type of pronoun in comparisons is particularly important because using the wrong type changes the meaning of the sentence. Editing comparisons can be tricky because they often imply words that are not actually included in the sentence.

Bob trusts Donna more than *I*.
[This sentence means Bob trusts Donna more than I trust her. The implied words are *trust her*.]

TIP To find comparisons, look for the words *than* or *as*.

Bob trusts Donna more than *me*.
[This sentence means Bob trusts Donna more than he trusts me. The implied words are *he trusts*.]

To decide whether to use a subject or object pronoun in a comparison, try adding the implied words and saying the sentence aloud.

The registrar is much more efficient than (us / (we)).
[Think: The registrar is much more efficient than *we are*.]

TIP Add the additional words to the comparison when you speak and write. Then others will not think you are incorrect.

Susan rides her bicycle more than ((he)/ him).
[Think: Susan rides her bicycle more than *he does*.]

| **Finding and Fixing Pronoun Problems:** |
| **Using Pronouns in Comparisons** |

↓

Find

The other band attracts a bigger audience (than) us on Friday
nights.

1. **Circle** the word that indicates a comparison.

2. **Ask:** What word or words that would come after the comparison word are implied but missing from the sentence? *"Do."*

3. **Ask:** If you add the missing word or words, does the pronoun make sense? *No.*

↓

Fix

                                                        we (do)
The other band attracts a bigger audience than ~~us~~ on Friday
                                                          ^
nights.

4. **Correct the sentence** by replacing the incorrect pronoun with the correct one.

· ·

PRACTICE 7   Editing Pronouns in Comparisons

Edit each sentence using the correct pronoun type. If a sentence is correct, put a "C" next to it.

> **EXAMPLE:** The camping trip we planned did not seem dangerous to
> Hannah, so she was not as nervous about it as ~~me~~.
>   *I*
>   ^

1. In addition, I was nowhere near as well equipped for camping as ~~her~~.
                                                                    she
                                                                     ^

2. In the store, it was Hannah rather than ~~me~~ who did all the talking.
                                            I
                                             ^

3. At the campground, I could see that some of the other camping groups
   were not as prepared as we. *C*

4. The park ranger chatted with the other campers more than ~~we~~.
                                                            us
                                                             ^

5. He seemed to believe that we were more experienced than ~~them~~.
                                                           they
                                                            ^

6. On the hiking trail, the other campers walked faster than we. *C*

7. They all hurried past us, but Hannah kept hiking just as slowly as ~~me~~.
                                                                      I
                                                                       ^

8. Our boots had been crunching on the trail for hours when we suddenly
   heard that a group ahead was being much louder than ~~us~~.
                                                       we
                                                        ^

TEACHING TIP Have students read the sentences aloud, adding the implied words.

9. When Hannah and I saw the group running back toward us, I was more
   alarmed than ~~her~~ she.

10. When we spotted the bear that was chasing the other hikers, Hannah ran
    to hide a lot faster than I. *C*

. . . .

Choosing between *Who and* Whom

Who is always a subject; *whom* is always an object. If a pronoun performs an action, use the subject form *who*. If a pronoun does not perform an action, use the object form *whom*.

> **TIP** In the examples here, subjects are underlined, and verbs are double-underlined.

WHO = SUBJECT	I would like to know *who* delivered this package.
WHOM = OBJECT	He told me to *whom* I should report.

> **TIP** *Whoever* is a subject pronoun; *whomever* is an object pronoun.

In sentences other than questions, when the pronoun (*who* or *whom*) is followed by a verb, use *who*. When the pronoun (*who* or *whom*) is followed by a noun or pronoun, use *whom*.

The pianist (who / whom) played was excellent.
[The pronoun is followed by the verb *played*. Use *who*.]

The pianist (who / whom) I saw was excellent.
[The pronoun is followed by another pronoun: *I*. Use *whom*.]

. . . .

PRACTICE 8   Choosing between *Who* and *Whom*

In each sentence, circle the correct word, *who* or *whom*.

EXAMPLE: Police officers (who / whom) want to solve a crime—or prevent one—are now relying more than ever on technology.

1. Face-recognition software, now being introduced, is supposed to identify possible criminals (who / whom) cameras have photographed in public places.

2. Use of such software, which can compare security-camera images with photos from a criminal database, can help law enforcement officials determine (who / whom) they want to question about a crime.

3. Police will try to detain any person (who / whom) is identified by the software as a criminal.

4. Police know that the software will single out some innocent people (who / whom) resemble criminals.

5. However, police and nervous Americans are hopeful that this method can help to identify terrorists (who / whom) appear in airports or other locations.

· ·

Make Pronouns Consistent in Person

Person is the point of view a writer uses—the perspective from which he or she writes. Pronouns may be in first person (*I, we*), second person (*you*), or third person (*he, she,* or *it*). (See the chart on p. 421.)

INCONSISTENT	*I* wanted to sign up for a computer class, but the person said *you* had to know word processing.
	[The sentence starts in the first person (*I*) but shifts to the second person (*you*).]
CONSISTENT	*I* wanted to sign up for a computer class, but the person said *I* had to know word processing.
	[The sentence stays with the first person, *I*.]
INCONSISTENT	As soon as *a shopper* walks into the store, *you* can tell it is a weird place.
	[The sentence starts with the third person (*a shopper*) but shifts to the second person (*you*).]
CONSISTENT	As soon as *a shopper* walks into the store, *he* or *she* can tell it is a weird place.
CONSISTENT, PLURAL	As soon as *shoppers* walk into the store, *they* can tell it is a weird place.

Finding and Fixing Pronoun Problems:
Making Pronouns Consistent in Person

▼

Find

I had the right answer, but to win the tickets you had to be the ninth caller.

1. **Underline** all of the subject nouns and pronouns in the sentence.
2. **Circle** any pronouns that refer to another subject noun or pronoun in the sentence.
3. **Ask:** Is the subject noun or pronoun that the circled pronoun refers to in the first (*I, we*), second (*you*), or third person (*he, she,* or *it*)? *First person.*
4. **Ask:** What person is the pronoun in? *Second.*

▼

↓

> **Fix**
>
> I had the right answer, but to win the tickets ~~you~~ *I* had to be the
> ninth caller.
>
> 5. **Correct the sentence** by changing the pronoun to be consistent with the
> noun or pronoun it refers to.

. . . .

PRACTICE 9   Making Pronouns Consistent in Person

In the following sentences, correct the shifts in person. There may be more than one
way to correct some sentences. *Answers may vary. Possible edits are shown.*

> **EXAMPLE:** Many college students have access to a writing center
> where ~~you~~ *they* can get tutoring.

1. A writing tutor must know ~~your~~ *his or her* way around college writing assignments.

2. I have gone to the writing center at my school because sometimes ~~you~~ *I*
   need a second pair of eyes to look over a paper.

3. Students signing up for tutoring at the writing center may not be in ~~your~~ *their*
   first semester of college.

4. Even a graduate student may need help with ~~your~~ *his or her* writing at times.

5. The writing-center tutor is careful not to correct ~~their~~ *his or her* students' papers.

6. My tutor told me that ~~you~~ *I* had to learn to edit a paper.

7. Every student has to learn to catch ~~your~~ *his or her* own mistakes.

8. A student's tutor is not like ~~your~~ *his or her* English professor.

9. No student gets ~~their~~ *his or her* grade on a paper from a writing tutor.

10. Tutors do not judge but simply help students with ~~your~~ *their* papers.

. . . .

Edit for Pronoun Use

. . . .

PRACTICE 10   Correcting Various Pronoun Problems

In the following sentences, find and correct problems with pronoun use. You may
be able to revise some sentences in more than one way, and you may need to rewrite some sentences to correct errors. *Answers may vary. Possible edits are
shown.*

EXAMPLE: ~~Everyone with a busy schedule has~~ probably been tempted
Students with busy schedules have

to take shortcuts on their coursework.

1. My class received ~~its~~ term paper grades yesterday.
their

2. My friend Gene and ~~me~~ were shocked to see that he had gotten an F on
I

   his paper.

3. I usually get better grades than ~~him~~, but he does not usually fail.
he

4. Mr. Padilla, the instructor, ~~who~~ most students consider strict but fair,
whom

   scheduled an appointment with Gene.

5. When Gene went to the department office, ~~they~~ told him where to find
the office assistant

   Mr. Padilla.

6. Mr. Padilla ~~told Gene that he did not think he~~ had written the paper.
did not think that Gene

7. The paper ~~it~~ contained language that was unusual for Gene.

8. The instructor said that ~~you~~ could compare Gene's in-class writing with
he

   this paper and see differences.

9. Mr. Padilla, ~~whom~~ had typed some passages from Gene's paper into a

   search engine, found two online papers containing sentences that were

   also in Gene's paper.

10. Gene ~~told Mr. Padilla~~ that he had made a terrible mistake.
admitted

11. Gene told my girlfriend and ~~I~~ later that he did not realize that borrowing
me

    sentences from online sources was plagiarism.

12. We looked at the paper, and ~~you~~ could tell that parts of it did not sound
we

    like Gene's writing.

13. Anyone doing Internet research must be especially careful to document

    ~~their~~ sources, as Gene now knows.
his or her

14. The department decided ~~that they would~~ not suspend Gene from school.
to

15. Mr. Padilla will let Gene take the class again and will help him avoid

    accidental plagiarism, and Gene said that no one had ever been more re-

    lieved than ~~him~~ to hear that news.
he

• •

PRACTICE 11   Editing Paragraphs for Pronoun Use

Find and correct five errors in pronoun use in the following paragraphs.

   (1) Have you ever felt extremely sleepy? (2) Fatigue can really

make a person feel as if ~~they are~~ unable to learn or concentrate. (3) It
he or she is

TEACHING TIP Have students underline every pronoun in their paragraphs and draw an arrow to the word or words each pronoun refers to.

interferes with the ability to focus, and soon you may find your eyes drifting closed when they should stay open. (4) Can your brain do anything to help keep ~~them~~ *you* awake?

(5) In fact, it can. (6) A brain chemical called dopamine often comes to the rescue. (7) Dopamine keeps people awake even though they may still feel quite tired. (8) When the energy is needed, the chemical increases in two different parts of the brain. (9) This burst of dopamine keeps you alert.

(10) A recent study on two groups of women measured how a lack of sleep affected ~~her~~ *their* memory and attention span. (11) One group had gotten a good night's sleep, whereas the other was kept up all night long. (12) When both groups were tested, ~~them~~ *those* suffering from a lack of sleep had the greatest increases in dopamine levels. (13) Sleep researchers will continue to study the effects of exhaustion on the brain. (14) In the process, perhaps ~~it~~ *they* will learn more about how to help others stay awake and pay attention when they most need to.

. . . .

PRACTICE 12   Editing Your Own Writing for Pronoun Use

As a final practice, edit a piece of your own writing for pronoun use. It can be a paper you are working on for this course, a paper you have already finished, a paper for another course, or a recent piece of writing from your work or everyday life. Use the chart on page 433 to help you. Record in your learning journal any problem sentences you find, along with a corrected version of these sentences.

. . . .

Chapter Review

1. Pronouns replace _____*nouns*_____ or other _____*pronouns*_____ in a sentence.

2. A pronoun must agree with (match) the noun or pronoun it replaces in _____*number*_____ and _____*gender*_____ .

3. In an _____*ambiguous*_____ pronoun reference, the pronoun could refer to more than one noun.

4. Subject pronouns serve as the subject of a verb. Write a sentence using a subject pronoun. *Answers will vary. Possible answer: We went to the movies last night.*

5. What are two other types of pronouns? _object pronouns and possessive_
pronouns

6. What are three trouble spots in pronoun use?

compound subjects and objects

comparisons

sentences that need who or whom

Chapter Test

Circle the correct choice for each of the following items.

1. Choose the item that has no errors.

   a. When he skis, Jim never falls down as much as me.

   b. When he skis, Jim never falls down as much as I.

   c. When he skis, Jim never falls down as much as mine.

2. Choose the correct word(s) to fill in the blank.

Everyone hopes the jury will deliver _____ verdict by the end of this week.

   a. his or her   **b.** their   **c.** its

3. If an underlined portion of this sentence is incorrect, select the revision that fixes it. If the sentence is correct as written, choose d.

She is the one <u>who</u> Jake always calls whenever <u>he</u> wants a favor.
  A   B   C

   a. Her   **c.** him

   b. whom   **d.** No change is necessary.

4. If an underlined portion of this sentence is incorrect, select the revision that fixes it. If the sentence is correct as written, choose d.

Somebody has left <u>their</u> camera here, and <u>we</u> do not know to <u>whom</u>
                       A   B   C

it belongs.

   a. his or her   **c.** who

   b. us   **d.** No change is necessary.

5. Choose the item that has no errors.

   a. Becky told Lydia that she needed to help clean up after the party.

   b. Becky told Lydia to help clean up after the party.

   c. Becky told Lydia that she needed to help clean up after it.

6. Choose the item that has no errors.

   a. When I applied for the tour operator job, I was told that you needed a special certificate.

   b. When I applied for the tour operator job, you were told that you needed a special certificate.

   c. When I applied for the tour operator job, I was told that I needed a special certificate.

7. Choose the correct word(s) to fill in the blank.

Nicole's _____ must be lonely because he barks all the time.

   a. dog he   **b.** dog him   **c.** dog

8. Choose the correct words to fill in the blank.

The other players in my soccer club like me because

_____ agree on the importance of teamwork.

   a. they and I   **b.** them and me   **c.** them and I

9. If an underlined portion of this sentence is incorrect, select the revision that fixes it. If the sentence is correct as written, choose d.

I think <u>my next-door</u> neighbor has mice in <u>him house</u> because he
          A   B

keeps asking me to <u>lend him</u> my cat.
                      C

   a. me next-door   **c.** lend he

   b. his house   **d.** No change is necessary.

10. Choose the item that has no errors.

   a. Any lifeguard can tell you about a scary experience they have had on the job.

   b. Any lifeguard can tell you about a scary experience her have had on the job.

   c. Most lifeguards can tell you about a scary experience they have had on the job.

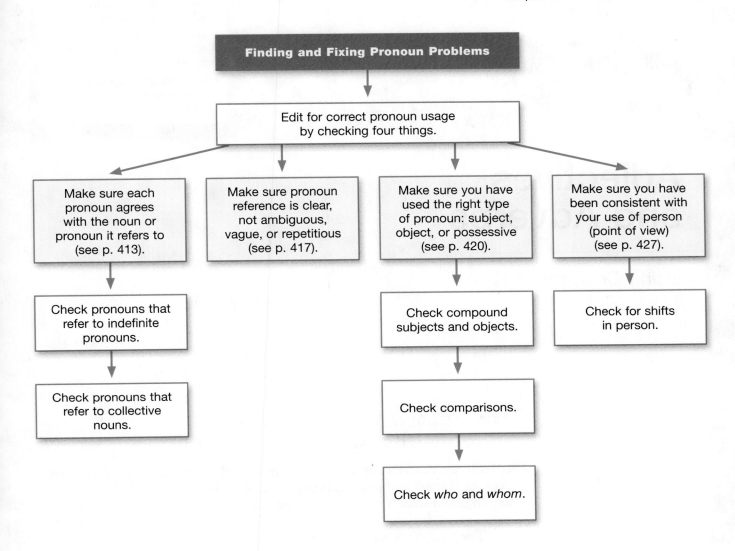

27

Adjectives and Adverbs

Using Descriptive Words

THIS CHAPTER

- explains what adjectives and adverbs are and do
- explains when to use an adjective and when to use an adverb
- gives you practice using adjectives and adverbs correctly

Understand What Adjectives and Adverbs Are

Adjectives describe or modify nouns (words that name people, places, ideas, or things) and pronouns (words that replace nouns). They add information about *what kind*, *which one*, or *how many*.

The *final* exam was today.

It was *long* and *difficult*.

The *three shiny new* coins were on the dresser.

> **TIP** To understand this chapter on adjectives and adverbs, you need to know what nouns and verbs are. For a review, see Chapter 21.

LANGUAGE NOTE: In English, adjectives do not indicate whether the words they describe are singular or plural.

INCORRECT	The three babies are *adorables*.
	[The adjective *adorables* should not end in *-s*.]
CORRECT	The three babies are *adorable*.

Adverbs describe or modify verbs (words that tell what happens in a sentence), adjectives, or other adverbs. They add information about *how*, *how much*, *when*, *where*, *why*, or *to what extent*.

MODIFYING VERB	Sharon *enthusiastically* accepted the job.
MODIFYING ADJECTIVE	The *very* young lawyer handled the case.

MODIFYING ANOTHER ADVERB	The team played *surprisingly* well.

Adjectives usually come before the words they modify; adverbs come before or after. You can use more than one adjective or adverb to modify a word.

> **LANGUAGE NOTE:** The *-ed* and *-ing* forms of adjectives are sometimes confused. Common examples include *bored/boring, confused/confusing, excited/exciting,* and *interested/interesting.*
>   Often, the *-ed* form describes a person's reaction, while the *-ing* form describes the thing to which a person is reacting.
>
> | INCORRECT | Janelle is interesting in ghosts and ghost stories. |
> |---|---|
> | CORRECT | Janelle is interested in ghosts and ghost stories. |
> | CORRECT | Janelle finds ghosts and ghost stories interesting. |

If you are confused about when to use an adjective and when to use an adverb, remember that adverbs modify verbs, adjectives, and other adverbs but not nouns. Adverbs often end in *-ly.*

INCORRECT	José is a *quickly* runner.
	[The adverb *quickly* should not be used to describe the noun *runner.*]
CORRECT	José is a *quick* runner.
	[The adjective *quick* describes the noun *runner.*]
CORRECT	José runs *quickly.*
	[The adverb *quickly* describes the verb *runs.*]

Practice Using Adjectives and Adverbs Correctly

Choosing between Adjectives and Adverbs

Many adverbs are formed by adding *-ly* to the end of an adjective.

ADJECTIVE	ADVERB
She received a *quick* answer.	Her sister answered *quickly.*
The *new* student introduced himself.	The couple is *newly* married.
That is an *honest* answer.	Please answer *honestly.*

DISCUSSION To get students focused on adjectives and adverbs, throw out a few sentences containing adjectives, with students in the class as the subjects (*Dan is wearing a black leather jacket*). Ask the student named in the sentence what the adjectives are.

To decide whether to use an adjective or an adverb, find the word being described. If that word is a noun or pronoun, use an adjective. If it is a verb, adjective, or another adverb, use an adverb.

TIP For more practice with adjective and adverb usage, visit Exercise Central at **bedfordstmartins.com/ realwriting**.

● ●

PRACTICE 1   Choosing between Adjectives and Adverbs

In each sentence, underline the word in the sentence that is being described or modified, and then circle the correct word in parentheses.

EXAMPLE: People are (common /(commonly)) aware that smoking causes health risks.

1. Many smokers are ((stubborn)/ stubbornly) about refusing to quit.

2. Others who are thinking about quitting may decide (sudden /(suddenly)) that the damage from smoking has already been done.

3. In such cases, the ((typical)/ typically) smoker sees no reason to stop.

4. The news about secondhand smoke may have made some smokers stop (quick /(quickly)) to save the health of their families.

5. Research now shows that pet lovers who smoke can have a ((terrible)/ terribly) effect on their cats.

6. Cats who live with smokers (frequent /(frequently)) develop cancer.

7. Veterinarians point out that the cats of smokers may smell (strong / (strongly)) of smoke.

8. Cats like to have their fur ((clean)/ cleanly), and they lick the fur to groom themselves.

9. When they are grooming, cats may inhale a ((large)/ largely) dose of tobacco smoke.

10. Perhaps some smokers who feel that it is too late for their own health will (serious /(seriously)) consider quitting for the sake of their pets.

● ●

Using Adjectives and Adverbs in Comparison

To compare two people, places, or things, use the **comparative** form of adjectives or adverbs. Comparisons often use the word *than*.

> Carol ran *faster* than I did.
> Johan is *more intelligent* than his sister.

To compare three or more people, places, or things, use the **superlative** form of adjectives or adverbs.

> Carol ran the *fastest* of all the women runners.
> Johan is the *most intelligent* of the five children.

If an adjective or adverb is short (one syllable), add the endings *-er* to form the comparative and *-est* to form the superlative. Also use this pattern for adjectives that end in *-y* (but change the *-y* to *-i* before adding *-er* or *-est*).

For all other adjectives and adverbs, add the word *more* to make the comparative and the word *most* to make the superlative.

Forming Comparatives and Superlatives

ADJECTIVE OR ADVERB	COMPARATIVE	SUPERLATIVE
ADJECTIVES AND ADVERBS OF ONE SYLLABLE		
tall	taller	tallest
fast	faster	fastest
ADJECTIVES ENDING IN -Y		
happy	happier	happiest
silly	sillier	silliest
OTHER ADJECTIVES AND ADVERBS		
graceful	more graceful	most graceful
gracefully	more gracefully	most gracefully
intelligent	more intelligent	most intelligent
intelligently	more intelligently	most intelligently

Use either an ending (*-er* or *-est*) or an extra word (more or most) to form a comparative or superlative—not both at once.

Lance Armstrong is the ~~most~~ greatest cyclist in the world.

LANGUAGE NOTE: Some languages, such as Spanish, always use words meaning *more* or *most* in comparisons, even when an adjective or adverb has the equivalent of an *-er* or *-est* ending. English does not. If an adjective or adverb has an *-er* or *-est* ending, do not use *more* or *most*.

INCORRECT	José is *more* rich*er* than I am.
CORRECT	José is *richer* than I am.
CORRECT	José is *more* rich than I am.

TEACHING TIP This is a good practice to do aloud so that students can hear the correct choice.

RESOURCES To gauge students' skills in adjective and adverb usage, use the *Testing Tool Kit* CD-ROM available with this book.

• •

PRACTICE 2   Using Adjectives and Adverbs in Comparisons

In the space provided in each sentence, write the correct form of the adjective or adverb in parentheses. You may need to add *more* or *most* to some adjectives and adverbs.

EXAMPLE: It was one of the _____scariest_____ (scary) experiences of my life.

1. I was driving along Route 17 and was ___more relaxed___ (relaxed) than I ought to have been.

2. Knowing it was a busy highway, I was ___more careful___ (careful) than usual to be sure my cell phone was ready in case of an accident.

3. I had run the cord for the phone's ear bud over my armrest, where it would be in the ___easiest___ (easy) place to reach if the phone rang.

4. I was in the ___heaviest___ (heavy) traffic of my drive when the cell phone rang.

5. I saw that the ear bud was ___harder___ (hard) to reach than before because the cord had fallen between the front seats of the car.

6. When I reached down to get the ear bud, a pickup truck to my right suddenly started going ___faster___ (fast).

7. The truck swerved toward my lane, coming ___closer___ (close) than I wanted it to be.

8. I took the ___quickest___ (quick) action I could think of, shifting to the left lane and just barely avoiding the pickup.

9. ___Calmer___ (Calm) now, I decided to give up on trying to find the ear bud.

10. I wanted the cell phone ready for safety's sake, but I now think that concentrating on my driving is the ___most intelligent___ (intelligent) thing to do.

• •

Using *Good, Well, Bad,* and *Badly*

Four common adjectives and adverbs have irregular forms: *good, well, bad,* and *badly.*

Forming Irregular Comparatives and Superlatives

TIP *Irregular* means not following a standard rule.

	COMPARATIVE	SUPERLATIVE
ADJECTIVE		
good	better	best
bad	worse	worst
ADVERB		
well	better	best
badly	worse	worst

People often get confused about whether to use *good* or *well*. *Good* is an adjective, so use it to describe a noun or pronoun. *Well* is an adverb, so use it to describe a verb or an adjective.

ADJECTIVE She has a *good* job.

ADVERB He works *well* with his colleagues.

Well can also be an adjective to describe someone's health: I am not *well* today.

· ·

PRACTICE 3 Using *Good* and *Well*

Complete each sentence by circling the correct word in parentheses. Underline the word that *good* or *well* modifies.

EXAMPLE: A (good)/ well) <u>pediatrician</u> spends as much time talking with parents as he or she does examining patients.

1. The ability to <u>communicate</u> (good /(well)) is something that many parents look for in a pediatrician.

2. With a firstborn child, parents see a doctor's visit as a (good)/ well) <u>chance</u> to ask questions.

3. Parents can become worried when their infant does not <u>feel</u> (good /(well)) because the child cannot say what the problem is.

4. Doctors today have (good)/ well) diagnostic <u>tools</u>, however.

5. An otoscope helps a doctor <u>see</u> (good /(well)) when he or she looks into a patient's ear.

6. A fever and an inflamed eardrum are (good)/ well) <u>signs</u> of a middle-ear infection.

7. Children who have many ear infections may not <u>hear</u> as (good /(well)) as children who have fewer infections.

8. If the pediatrician presents clear options for treatment, parents can make a (good /(well))-informed decision about treating their child's illness.

9. Some parents decide that ear-tube surgery is a (good)/ well) <u>solution</u> to the problem of frequent ear infections.

10. Within an hour after ear-tube surgery, most <u>children</u> are (good /(well)) enough to go home.

* *

PRACTICE 4   Using Comparative and Superlative Forms of *Good* and *Bad*

Complete each sentence by circling the correct comparative or superlative form of *good* or *bad* in parentheses.

EXAMPLE: Men tend to sleep (better)/ best) than women do.

1. One of the (worse /(worst)) gaps in human knowledge about sleep disorders used to be that little research had been done using female subjects.

2. Until the 1990s, most scientists considered male subjects a (better)/ best) choice than female ones for sleep research.

3. Now that (better)/ best) research on sleep disorders in women is available, scientists know that women suffer more than men from certain kinds of sleep problems.

4. One of the (worse /(worst)) problems for new mothers is loss of sleep.

5. Whether because of habit or some biological cause, women are (better)/ best) than men at hearing the sound of a child crying in the middle of the night.

6. New sleep research shows that women suffer (worse)/ worst) than men do from insomnia, whether or not they are parents.

7. In the past, many women who complained of being tired were diagnosed with depression rather than with sleep disorders; the treatment often failed to help and sometimes made the problems (worse)/ worst).

8. So far, the (better /(best)) explanation that researchers can offer for women's sleep problems is that sleeplessness may be related to levels of hormones.

9. However, hormone therapies, according to some scientists, can create health problems that are (worse) / worst) than the ones they are supposed to solve.

10. No one is certain yet of the (better /(best)) solution for insomnia and sleep problems in women, but the increasing availability of information will probably improve the situation.

Edit for Adjectives and Adverbs

PRACTICE 5 Editing Paragraphs for Correct Adjectives and Adverbs

Find and correct seven adjective and adverb errors in the following paragraphs. *Answers may vary. Possible edits are shown.*

    (1) Every day, many people log on to play one of the ~~popularest~~ *most popular* computer games of all time, *World of Warcraft*. (2) This multiplayer game was first introduced by Blizzard Entertainment in 1994 and has grown ~~quick~~ *quickly* ever since. (3) More than 11 million players participate in the game every month, according to the ~~recentest~~ *most recent* figures.

    (4) Computer game experts call *World of Warcraft* a "massively multi-player online role-playing game," or MMORPG for short. (5) Players of this game select a realm in which to play. (6) They choose from among four ~~differently~~ *different* realms. (7) Each realm has its own set of rules and even its own language. (8) Players also choose if they want to be members of the Alliance or the Horde, which are groups that oppose each other. (9) Each side tends to think it is ~~gooder~~ *better* than the other one.

    (10) In *World of Warcraft*, questing is one of the ~~funnest~~ *most fun* activities. (11) Questing players undertake special missions or tasks in order to earn experience and gold. (12) The goal is to trade these earnings for better skills and equipment. (13) Players must proceed ~~careful~~ *carefully* to stay in the game and increase their overall power and abilities.

TEAMWORK Copy an article from the newspaper or some other source, and have students find all the adjectives and adverbs, drawing arrows from the modifiers to the words they modify. This can be done in small groups in class or as-signed as homework and gone over the next day in class.

PRACTICE 6 Editing Your Own Writing for Correct Adjectives and Adverbs

As a final practice, edit a piece of your own writing for correct use of adjectives and adverbs. It can be a paper you are working on for this course, a paper you have already finished, a paper for another course, or a recent piece of writing from your work or everyday life. Record in your learning journal any problem sentences you find, along with their corrections. You may want to use the chart on page 443 to help you.

• •

Chapter Review

LEARNING JOURNAL Did you find errors in your writing? What is the main thing you have learned about adjectives and adverbs that will help you? What is unclear to you?

1.   Adjectives modify _____*nouns*_____ and _____*pronouns*_____ .

2.   Adverbs modify _____*verbs*_____ , _____*adjectives*_____ , or _____*other adverbs*_____ .

3.   Many adverbs are formed by adding an _____*-ly*_____ ending to an adjective.

4.   The comparative form of an adjective or adverb is used to compare how many people, places, or things? _____*two*_____

TEACHING TIP You can collect students' learning journals to find out what the class or individual students need more work on.

5.   The superlative form of an adjective or adverb is used to compare how many people, places, or things? _____*three or more*_____

6.   What four words have irregular comparative and superlative forms? _____*good, well, bad, badly*_____

Chapter Test

TIP For advice on taking tests, see Appendix A.

Circle the correct choice for each of the following items.

1.   Choose the correct word to fill in the blank.

We performed _____ in the debate, so we will have to be better prepared next time.

RESOURCES The *Testing Tool Kit* CD-ROM available with this book has even more tests.

  a. bad   **b.** worse   **(c.)** badly

2.   If an underlined portion of this sentence is incorrect, select the revision that fixes it. If the sentence is correct as written, choose d.

After the <u>beautiful</u> wedding, the groom danced <u>happy</u> down the
          A   B
church's <u>stone</u> steps.
          C

  a. beautifully   **c.** stonily
  (b.) happily   **d.** No change is necessary.

3.   Choose the item that has no errors.

  a.   Sarah's foot is healing well, and she is making a good recovery.

  b.   Sarah's foot is healing good, and she is making a good recovery.

  c.   Sarah's foot is healing good, and she is making a well recovery.

4.   Choose the correct word(s) to fill in the blank.

With Kenneth's wild imagination, he is a _____ choice than Conor for writing the play's script.

  a.   gooder   **b.**   better   **c.**   more good

5.   If an underlined portion of this sentence is incorrect, select the revision that fixes it. If the sentence is correct as written, choose d.

When asked about the <u>thoughtfulest</u> person I know, I immediately
                              A

gave the name of my <u>best</u> friend, who is <u>kind</u> to everyone.
                       B   C

  a.   most thoughtful   **c.**   kindest

  b.   bestest   **d.**   No change is necessary.

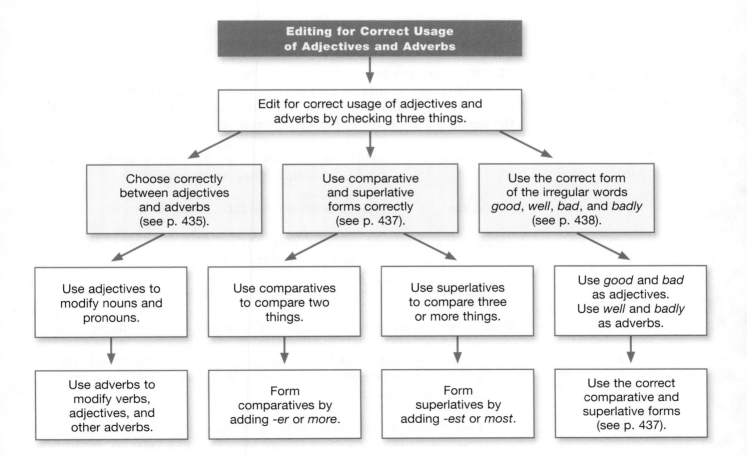

Editing for Correct Usage of Adjectives and Adverbs

Edit for correct usage of adjectives and adverbs by checking three things.

Choose correctly between adjectives and adverbs (see p. 435).

Use comparative and superlative forms correctly (see p. 437).

Use the correct form of the irregular words *good*, *well*, *bad*, and *badly* (see p. 438).

Use adjectives to modify nouns and pronouns.

Use comparatives to compare two things.

Use superlatives to compare three or more things.

Use *good* and *bad* as adjectives. Use *well* and *badly* as adverbs.

Use adverbs to modify verbs, adjectives, and other adverbs.

Form comparatives by adding *-er* or *more*.

Form superlatives by adding *-est* or *most*.

Use the correct comparative and superlative forms (see p. 437).

Misplaced and Dangling Modifiers

Avoiding Confusing Descriptions

THIS CHAPTER

- explains what misplaced and dangling modifiers are
- gives examples of the kinds of modifiers that are often misplaced
- gives you practice correcting misplaced and dangling modifiers

Understand What Misplaced Modifiers Are

TIP For a review of basic sentence elements, see Chapter 21.

Modifiers are words or word groups that describe other words in a sentence. Modifiers should be near the words they modify; otherwise, the sentence can be unintentionally funny. A **misplaced modifier**, because it is in the wrong place, describes the wrong word or words.

> **MISPLACED**   Linda saw the White House *flying over Washington, D.C.*
> [Was the White House flying over Washington?]

> **CLEAR**   *Flying over Washington, D.C.*, Linda saw the White House.

To correct a misplaced modifier, place the modifier as close as possible to the word or words it modifies, often directly before it.

> *Wearing my bathrobe,*
> I went outside to get the paper. ~~wearing my bathrobe.~~

Four constructions in particular often lead to misplaced modifiers.

RESOURCES *Additional Resources* contains tests and supplemental practice exercises for this chapter as well as a transparency master for the chart at the end.

1.   **Modifiers such as *only*, *almost*, *hardly*, *nearly*, and *just*.** These words need to be right before—not just close to—the words or phrases they modify.

> *only*
> I ~~only~~ found two old photos in the drawer.
> [The intended meaning is that just two photos were in the drawer.]

Joanne ~~almost~~ ate _almost_ the whole cake.

[Joanne actually ate; she did not "almost" eat.]

Thomas ~~nearly~~ spent _nearly_ two hours waiting for the bus.

[Thomas spent close to two hours waiting; he did not "nearly" spend them.]

2. Modifiers that are prepositional phrases.

The cashier found money _from the cash register_ on the floor.~~from the cash register.~~

Jen served punch _in plastic cups_ to the seniors.~~in plastic cups.~~

3. Modifiers that start with _-ing_ verbs.

Using jumper cables, Darlene started the car.~~using jumper cables.~~

[The car was not using jumper cables; Darlene was.]

Wearing flip-flops, Javier climbed the mountain.~~wearing flip-flops.~~

[The mountain was not wearing flip-flops; Javier was.]

4. Modifier clauses that start with _who_, _whose_, _that_, or _which_.

Joel found the computer virus _that was infecting my hard drive_ attached to an e-mail message.~~that was infecting my hard drive.~~

[What was infecting the hard drive, the virus or the message?]

The baby _who was crying_ on the bus ~~who was crying~~ had curly hair.

[The bus was not crying; the baby was.]

TEAMWORK As homework, have each student write a sentence that is funny because of a misplaced or dangling modifier. Collect the sentences and read some aloud, asking the class for corrections.

Practice Correcting Misplaced Modifiers

PRACTICE 1   Correcting Misplaced Modifiers

Find and correct misplaced modifiers in the following sentences.

    EXAMPLE: I write things in my blog that I used to ~~only~~ tell _only_ my best friends.

1. I still write _in a diary_ about all kinds of personal things and private observations. ~~in a diary.~~

2. Now, I ~~nearly~~ write _nearly_ the same things in my blog.

3. Any story _that is entertaining_ might show up in my blog.~~that is entertaining.~~

4. The video I was making _of my cousin Tim's birthday_ was definitely something I wanted to write about in my blog.~~of my cousin Tim's birthday.~~

TIP For more practice correcting misplaced and dangling modifiers, visit Exercise Central at **bedfordstmartins.com/ realwriting.**

RESOURCES To gauge students' skills in correcting misplaced and dangling modifiers, use the _Testing Tool Kit_ CD-ROM available with this book.

Wanting the video to be funny,

5. ⌃I had invited to the birthday party my loudest, wildest friends.~~wanting the video to be funny~~.

6. We jumped off tables, had mock swordfights, and ~~almost~~ used ⌃*almost* ten cans of whipped cream in a food fight.

7. Unfortunately, the battery in the video recorder died.⌃*that Tim loaned me* ~~that Tim loaned me~~.

Apologizing to Tim, *him*
8. ⌃I told ~~Tim~~ that I would write a blog about the party anyway.⌃~~apologizing to him~~.

in the blog
9. I explained how I would include ⌃the funny story about the failed video-taping.⌃~~in the blog~~.

hardly
10. Tim ~~hardly~~ said he could ⌃wait until we tried again to make the video.

Understand What Dangling Modifiers Are

COMPUTER Have students highlight introductory phrases in their writing. Then, ask them to look at the first word after the phrase to make sure that it is the noun or pronoun the phrase describes.

A **dangling modifier** "dangles" because the word or words it modifies are not in the sentence. Dangling modifiers usually appear at the beginning of a sentence and seem to modify the noun or pronoun that immediately follows them; however, they are really modifying another word or group of words.

DANGLING	*Rushing to class*, the books fell out of my bag.
	[The books were not rushing to class.]
CLEAR	*Rushing to class*, I dropped my books.

There are two basic ways to correct dangling modifiers. Use the one that makes the most sense. You can add the word being modified right after the opening modifier so that the connection between the two is clear.

I   *on my bike*
Trying to eat a hot dog, ⌃~~my bike~~ swerved⌃.

Or you can add the word being modified in the opening modifier itself.

TEACHING TIP Students sometimes try to correct a dangling modifier by adding a subordinating conjunction (such as *while*) without sufficiently reworking the sentence itself. Point out that adding *while* alone does not correct the problem with this sentence: *While trying to eat a hot dog. . . .*

While I was trying
~~Trying~~ to eat a hot dog, my bike swerved off the path.
⌃

Practice Correcting Dangling Modifiers

PRACTICE 2   **Correcting Dangling Modifiers**

Find and correct any dangling modifiers in the following sentences. If a sentence is correct, write a "C" next to it. It may be necessary to add new words or ideas to some sentences. *Answers may vary. Possible edits are shown.*

Because I had invited
EXAMPLE: ~~Inviting~~ my whole family to dinner, the kitchen was filled
^

with all kinds of food.

While I was preparing
1. ~~Preparing~~ a big family dinner, the oven suddenly stopped working.
^

2. In a panic, we searched for Carmen, who can solve any problem. *C*

With everyone trying
3. ~~Trying~~ to help, the kitchen was crowded.
^

we could see that
4. Looking into the oven, ^ the turkey was not done.

we almost canceled dinner.
5. Discouraged, ~~the dinner was about to be canceled.~~
^

As I was staring
6. ~~Staring~~ out the window, a pizza truck went by.
^

7. Using a credit card, Carmen ordered six pizzas. *C*

One   *and*
8. ~~With one~~ quick phone call, six large pizzas solved our problem.
^

When I returned
9. ~~Returning~~ to the crowd in the kitchen, family members still surrounded
^

the oven.

they cheered.
10. Delighted with Carmen's decision, ~~cheers filled the room.~~
^

Edit for Misplaced and Dangling Modifiers

PRACTICE 3   **Editing Paragraphs for Misplaced
and Dangling Modifiers**

Find and correct any misplaced or dangling modifiers in the following
paragraphs. *Answers may vary. Possible edits are shown.*

(1) Carrying overfilled backpacks is a common habit, but not neces-

sarily a good one. (2) Bulging with books, water bottles, and sports

backpacks can
equipment and weighing an average of 14 to 18 pounds, ~~students' backs~~
gradually damage students' backs.   *students*
~~can gradually become damaged.~~ (3) Because ~~they~~ have to plan ahead for
^   ^

the whole day and often need books, extra clothes, and on-the-go meals,

their
backpacks get heavier and heavier. (4) An increasing number of doctors,
^

primarily physical therapists, are seeing young people with chronic back

problems.
from the University of Pennsylvania and the Marine Biological Laboratory
(5) Researchers have recently invented a new type of backpack. ~~from~~
^   ^

~~the University of Pennsylvania and the Marine Biological Laboratory.~~

(6) Designed with springs, the backpack moves up and down as a person

walks. (7) This new backpack creates energy, which is then collected and

transferred to an electrical generator. (8) Experiencing relief from the
wear and tear on muscles, *wearers of the new pack find that* the springs make the pack more comfortable.

(9) What is the purpose of the electricity generated by these new
backpacks? (10) Needing electricity for their night-vision goggles, ~~the~~
~~backpacks~~ *soldiers* could solve a problem. *use the backpacks to* ~~for soldiers.~~ (11) Soldiers could
benefit from such an efficient energy source to power their global posi-
tioning systems and other electronic gear. (12) ~~Instead of being battery~~
~~operated, the soldiers~~ *They* could use the special backpack and would not have
to carry additional batteries. *for their battery-operated gear* (13) For the average student, these backpacks might one day provide convenient energy for video games,
television, and music players, all at the same time. (14) ~~Designed~~ *Wearing backpacks designed* with
this technology, kids would just have to look both ways before crossing
the street.

• •

PRACTICE 4   Editing Your Own Writing for Misplaced and Dangling Modifiers

As a final practice, edit a piece of your own writing for misplaced and dangling modifiers. It can be a paper you are working on for this course, a paper you have already finished, a paper for another course, or a recent piece of writing from your work or everyday life. Record in your learning journal any problem sentences you find, along with their corrections. You may want to use the chart on page 450.

• •

Chapter Review

LEARNING JOURNAL Do you sometimes write sentences with misplaced or dangling modifiers? What is the main thing you have learned about their correct use? What remains unclear to you?

TEACHING TIP You can collect students' learning journals to find out what the class or individual students need more work on.

1.   _____*Modifiers*_____ are words or word groups that describe other words in a sentence.

2.   A _*misplaced modifier*_ describes the incorrect placement of a modifying word or words within a sentence.

3.   When an opening modifier does not modify any word in the sentence, it is a _*dangling modifier*_ .

4.   Which four constructions often lead to misplaced modifiers?
modifiers such as "only," "almost," "hardly," "nearly," and "just"; that
are prepositional phrases; that start with "-ing" verbs; and modifier
clauses that start with "who," "whose," "that," or "which"

Chapter Test

Circle the correct choice for each of the following items.

TIP For advice on taking tests, see Appendix A.

1. If an underlined portion of this sentence is incorrect, select the revision that fixes it. If the sentence is correct as written, choose d.

    <u>Annoyed</u> by the flashing cameras, <u>the limousine drove the celebrity</u>
       A   B

    away from the crowd <u>in front of the restaurant.</u>
                                    C

RESOURCES The *Testing Tool Kit* CD-ROM available with this book has even more tests.

    a. Annoying
    b. the celebrity got into the limousine, which drove
    c. the restaurant in front of
    d. No change is necessary.

2. Choose the item that has no errors.
    a. The thief found the code in the bank clerk's desk for the alarm system.
    b. The thief found the code for the alarm system in the bank clerk's desk.
    c. For the alarm system, the thief found the code in the bank clerk's desk.

3. If an underlined portion of this sentence is incorrect, select the revision that fixes it. If the sentence is correct as written, choose d.

    <u>Talking on</u> <u>his cell phone,</u> <u>his shopping cart rolled</u> over my foot.
       A   B   C

    a. Talking and concentrating too much
    b. his cell phones
    c. he rolled his shopping cart
    d. No change is necessary.

4. If an underlined portion of this sentence is incorrect, select the revision that fixes it. If the sentence is correct as written, choose d.

    I <u>only bought</u> two tickets to the game, so <u>one</u> <u>of the three of us</u>
          A   B   C

    cannot go.

    a. bought only   c. of the us three of
    b. to go to the game   d. No change is necessary.

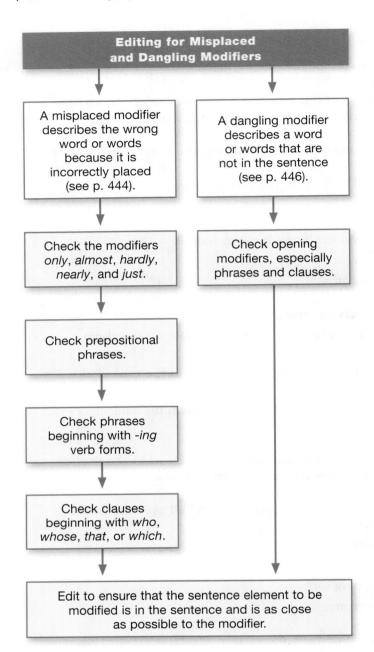

29

Coordination

Joining Sentences with Related Ideas

Understand What Coordination Is

Coordination is used to join two sentences with related ideas, and it can make your writing less choppy. The sentences remain complete and independent, but they are joined with a comma and a coordinating conjunction.

TIP To understand this chapter, you need to be familiar with basic sentence elements. For a review, see Chapter 21.

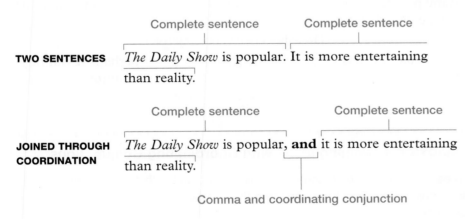

	Complete sentence	Complete sentence
TWO SENTENCES	*The Daily Show* is popular.	It is more entertaining than reality.

	Complete sentence	Complete sentence
JOINED THROUGH COORDINATION	*The Daily Show* is popular, **and** it is more entertaining than reality.	

Comma and coordinating conjunction

Practice Using Coordination

Using Coordinating Conjunctions

Conjunctions join words, phrases, or clauses. **Coordinating conjunctions** (*and, but, for, nor, or, so,* and *yet*) join ideas of equal importance. (You can remember them by thinking of FANBOYS—*for, and, nor, but, or, yet, so.*) To join two sentences through coordination, put a comma and one of

RESOURCES *Additional Resources* contains tests and supplemental practice exercises for this chapter as well as a transparency master for the chart at the end.

451

these conjunctions between the sentences. Choose the conjunction that makes the most sense for the meaning of the two sentences.

TIP For more on the use of commas, see Chapter 37.

TEACHING TIP Emphasize that conjunctions are not inter-changeable (*but* can't fill in for *so*, for example). Write two independent clauses on the board (*Tom was hungry/he had a sandwich*). Ask students which conjunctions would work. Ask how the sentence would have to change to use others.

Complete sentence	, for , and , nor , but , or , yet , so	Complete sentence

Wikipedia is a popular encyclopedia	, for	it is easily available online.

[*For* indicates a reason or cause.]

The encyclopedia is open to all	, and	anyone can add information to it.

[*And* simply joins two ideas.]

Often, inaccurate entries cannot be stopped	, nor	is there any penalty for them.

[*Nor* indicates a negative.]

People have complained about errors	, but	the mistakes may or may not be fixed.

[*But* indicates a contrast.]

Some people delete information	, or	they add their own interpretations.

[*Or* indicates alternatives.]

Many people know Wikipedia is flawed	, yet	they continue to use it.

[*Yet* indicates a contrast or possibility.]

Wikipedia now has trustees	, so	perhaps it will be monitored more closely.

[*So* indicates a result.]

· ·

PRACTICE 1 Joining Ideas with Coordinating Conjunctions

In each of the following sentences, fill in the blank with an appropriate coordinating conjunction. There may be more than one correct answer for some sentences. *Answers may vary. Possible answers are shown.*

TIP For more practice with coordination and subordination, visit Exercise Central at **bedfordstmartins.com/ realwriting.**

EXAMPLE: Companies want workers with diverse skills,

_____ *but* _____ parents may find that child-rearing

experience does not always impress potential employers.

1. Parents who quit work to care for children may worry about making

enough money, _____ *or* _____ they may fear that small children will

be hard to deal with all day long.

2. Those problems can cause people to think twice about leaving their jobs, _____ *yet* _____ the real problem for many people may come when they want to go back to work.

3. Finding a job can be difficult in any circumstances, _____ *so* _____ a job-seeker's résumé needs to be impressive.

4. Résumé experts say that every gap in employment should be explained, _____ *for* _____ employers want to know what a person did during that time.

5. Many parents fear that employers will see that the job-seekers have spent a few years raising children, _____ *and* _____ they worry that their résumés won't receive consideration.

6. Employers may not realize that parenting requires all kinds of skills, _____ *so* _____ a person returning to work after raising young children must make employers see that the experience was valuable.

7. The wrong description can make child care sound like dull, unimaginative work, _____ *but* _____ a good résumé can demonstrate how challenging and diverse the job of raising children can be.

8. Some parents who want to return to careers find ways to fill gaps on their résumés, _____ *and* _____ others come up with ways to get around the problem of résumés altogether.

9. Skills that a worker had before leaving a career can be used in a new business, _____ *so* _____ a person who starts a business does not have to worry about creating a perfect résumé.

10. Parents who leave careers have new challenges to consider, _____ *but* _____ they can get jobs when they decide to return to work.

RESOURCES To gauge students' skills with coordination, use the *Testing Tool Kit* CD-ROM available with this book.

· ·

PRACTICE 2 Combining Sentences with Coordinating Conjunctions

Combine each pair of sentences into a single sentence by using a comma and a coordinating conjunction. In some cases, there may be more than one correct answer. *Answers may vary. Possible edits are shown.*

     EXAMPLE: E-mail has become common in business communication, *so people* ~~People~~ should mind their e-mail manners.

1. Many professionals use e-mail to keep in touch with clients and contacts, *so they* ~~They~~ must be especially careful not to offend anyone with their e-mail messages.

2.   However, anyone who uses e-mail should be cautious, ~~It~~ *, for it* is dangerously easy to send messages to the wrong person.

3.   Employees may have time to send personal messages from work, ~~They~~ *, but they* should remember that employers often have the ability to read their workers' messages.

4.   R-rated language and jokes may be deleted automatically by a company's server, ~~They~~ *, or they* may be read by managers and cause problems for the employee sending or receiving them.

5.   No message should be forwarded to everyone in a sender's address book, ~~Senders~~ *, and senders* should ask permission before adding someone to a mass-mailing list.

6.   People should check the authenticity of mailings about lost children, dreadful diseases, and terrorist threats before passing them on, ~~Most~~ *, for most* such messages are hoaxes.

7.   Typographical errors and misspellings in e-mail make the message appear less professional, ~~Using~~ *, yet using* all capital letters—a practice known as *shouting*—is usually considered even worse.

8.   People who use e-mail for business want to be taken seriously, ~~They~~ *, so they* should make their e-mails as professional as possible.

Using Semicolons

A **semicolon** is a punctuation mark that can join two sentences through coordination. Use semicolons *only* when the ideas in the two sentences are closely related. Do not overuse semicolons.

Complete sentence	;	Complete sentence
Antarctica is a mystery	;	few people know much about it.
Its climate is extreme	;	few people want to endure it.
My cousin went there	;	he loves to explore the unknown.

A semicolon alone does not tell readers much about the relationship between the two ideas. To give more information about the relationship, use a **conjunctive adverb** after the semicolon. Put a comma after the conjunctive adverb.

Complete sentence	; also,	Complete sentence
	; as a result,	
	; besides,	
	; furthermore,	
	; however,	
	; in addition,	
	; in fact,	
	; instead,	
	; moreover,	
	; still,	
	; then,	
	; therefore,	

Antarctica is largely unexplored	; as a result,	it is unpopulated.
It receives little rain	; also,	it is incredibly cold.
It is a huge area	; therefore,	scientists are becoming more interested in it.

PRACTICE 3   Joining Ideas with Semicolons

Join each pair of sentences by using a semicolon alone.

EXAMPLE: Tanning booths can cause skin to age. *; they* ~~They~~ may also pro-

mote cancer.

1.   Too much exposure to the sun can cause skin cancer. *; using* ~~Using~~ tanning

booths has similar risks.

2.   Using a tanning booth does not mean that you will definitely harm your-

self. *; what* ~~What~~ it does mean is that you are taking a chance.

3.   It is easy to ignore long-term health dangers. *; the* ~~The~~ desire to look good is

tempting.

4.   Some people wear no clothes in a tanning booth. *; this* ~~This~~ behavior can

damage skin that is normally covered by a bathing suit.

5.   Ultraviolet light can injure the eyes. *; tanning-* ~~Tanning-~~salon patrons should always

wear protective goggles.

PRACTICE 4   Combining Sentences with Semicolons and Conjunctive Adverbs

Combine each pair of sentences by using a semicolon and a conjunctive adverb.
In some cases, there may be more than one correct answer. *Answers may vary.*
Possible edits are shown.

EXAMPLE: Mermaids are a myth. *; however, some* ~~Some~~ tribes in Asia have fishlike

characteristics.

1. One such group is the sea gypsies, who spend a lot of time swimming
and diving. ~~Their~~ *; therefore, their* eyes have adapted to seeing underwater.

2. Human eyes are not designed to see clearly through water. ~~Images~~ *; as a result, images* tend
to be blurry.

3. Objects often look vague under the surface. ~~People~~ *; also, people* are hard to recognize.

4. The sea gypsies of Southeast Asia have worked and fished in the ocean
for generations. ~~Their~~ *; yet, their* way of life remains a mystery to outsiders.

5. Parents in this culture teach their children to dive deep into the ocean.
~~From~~ *; in fact, from* an early age, the children collect clams, sea cucumbers, and pearls
from the ocean floor.

6. Children practice diving and staying underwater. ~~They~~ *; consequently, they* can find small
bits of food without using masks or goggles.

7. Scientists believe that the sea gypsies' eyes have adapted to an underwater environment. ~~Their~~ *; in addition, their* excellent vision may also have a genetic
component.

8. The divers tie rocks to their waists in order to stay submerged for long
periods. ~~They~~ *; also, they* squint while underwater, which thickens the lenses of their
eyes and brings more objects into focus.

9. Sea gypsies can also make their pupils constrict. ~~They~~ *; as a result, they* can see objects
measuring less than a quarter of an inch.

10. People are not able to live underwater. ~~Sea~~ *; however, sea* gypsies are remarkable for
their underwater powers.

• •

Editing for Coordination:
Joining Sentences with Related Ideas

↓

Find

I go to bed late at night. I get up early in the morning.

1. **Ask:** Should the sentences be joined by a coordinating conjunction (FANBOYS)
or a semicolon and a conjunctive adverb? *These sentences should be joined*
by a coordinating conjunction.

2. **Ask:** What coordinating conjunction or conjunctive adverb best expresses the
relationship between the two sentences? *"And" could join the two ideas;*
"but" could show a contrast.

↓

> **Edit**
>
>   *, and*
> I go to bed late at night ⁄ I get up early in the morning.
>   ^
>   *, but*
> I go to bed late at night ⁄ I get up early in the morning.
>   ^
>
> 3. **Join the two sentences** with a coordinating conjunction or a semicolon and a conjunctive adverb.

Edit for Coordination

PRACTICE 5 **Choosing the Right Coordinating Conjunctions and Conjunctive Adverbs**

Fill in the blanks with a coordinating conjunction or conjunctive adverb that makes sense in the sentence. Make sure to add the correct punctuation.
Answers may vary. Possible answers are shown.

> **EXAMPLE:** Rebates sound like a good deal _____ *, but* _____ they rarely are.

1. Rebate offers are common _____ *, and* _____ you have probably seen many of them on packages for appliances and electronics.

2. These offers may promise to return hundreds of dollars to consumers _____ *; as a result* _____ many people apply for them.

3. Applicants hope to get a lot of money back soon _____ *; however,* _____ they are often disappointed.

4. They might have to wait several months _____ *, or* _____ they might not get their rebate at all.

5. Rebate applications are not short _____ *, nor* _____ are they easy to fill out.

6. One applicant compared completing a rebate form to filling out tax forms _____ *, for* _____ he spent more than an hour on the process.

7. Manufacturers sometimes use rebates to move unpopular products off the shelves _____ *; then,* _____ they can replace these products with newer goods.

8. Only about 10 to 30 percent of people who apply for a rebate eventually get it _____ *; therefore,* _____ consumer groups are warning people to be careful.

9. Problems with rebates are getting more attention _____ *, so* _____ companies that offer them might have to improve their processes for giving refunds.

10. Manufacturers have received a lot of complaints about rebates _____ *; yet,* _____ they will probably never stop making these offers.

• •

PRACTICE 6   Editing Paragraphs for Coordination

In the following paragraphs, join the six pairs of underlined sentences using a co-ordinating conjunction or a semicolon and a conjunctive adverb. Do not forget to punctuate correctly. More than one correct answer is possible. *Answers may vary. Possible edits are shown.*

(1) Identity theft is becoming an increasingly serious problem. *, and teenagers* (2) ~~Teenagers~~ are frequent victims of this crime. (3) Why is this particular group vulnerable to identity theft? (4) <u>Young people are common targets because they are relatively inexperienced, trusting, and disorganized.</u> *; in addition, they* (5) <u>~~They~~ usually have clean credit records.</u> (6) Thieves can do a great deal of damage.

(7) <u>Experts recommend that teens always leave their Social Security cards at home at all times.</u> *; in fact, credit* (8) <u>~~Credit~~ cards and checkbooks should never be taken to parties or other social gatherings.</u> (9) It is too easy to misplace a wallet or purse in these situations, and it may be days before a teen notices that anything is missing. (10) <u>Teenagers make many purchases online and use peer-to-peer file-sharing programs such as LimeWire to download music and movies.</u> *, so they* (11) <u>~~They~~ become especially easy prey for identity thieves who steal bank account numbers and loan information.</u> (12) If young people choose to use a credit card over the Internet, they should make sure the Web sites they use are secure, and they should avoid swapping or downloading anything from peer-to-peer file-sharing services. (13) Having a firewall in place (and not turning it off to download files) can also help to protect personal computers from thieves.

(14) Consumer groups report that as many as 750,000 people a year are victims of identity theft. (15) <u>It can take years to get everything straightened out.</u> *, and the* (16) <u>~~The~~ process can cost more than $1,000.</u> (17) Identity thieves operate from many countries around the world. (18) Through the peer-to-peer file-sharing services, they routinely steal vast amounts of private financial information; they then use this

information for their own gain and resell it to other thieves. (19) <u>Thieves</u> <u>got away with nearly $100 million last year.</u> ; *therefore, people,* (20) ~~People~~, especially <u>teenagers, must protect themselves before they become part of future</u> <u>statistics about this crime.</u>

· ·

PRACTICE 7   **Editing Your Own Writing for Coordination**

As a final practice, edit a piece of your own writing for coordination. It can be a paper you are working on for this course, a paper you have already finished, a paper for another course, or a recent piece of writing from your work or everyday life. Record in your learning journal any choppy sentences you find, along with the edited versions. You may want to use the chart on page 460.

· ·

Chapter Review

1. What word will help you remember what the coordinating conjunctions are? <u>*FANBOYS*</u>

2. What are two ways to join sentences through coordination?
   <u>*Use a comma and a coordinating conjunction.*</u>
   <u>*Use a semicolon alone or a semicolon and a conjunctive adverb.*</u>

3. Use a semicolon *only* when the sentences are <u>*closely related*</u>.

4. List six conjunctive adverbs that you are most likely to use. <u>*Answers*</u> <u>*could include any adverbs from the list on page 455.*</u>

5. If you use a semicolon and a conjunctive adverb to join two sentences, what other punctuation must you use, and where? <u>*a comma after the*</u> <u>*conjunctive adverb*</u>

6. Write two sentences using coordination.

   _____

   _____

LEARNING JOURNAL Did you find errors in your writing? What is the main thing you have learned about coordination that will help you? What is unclear to you?

TEACHING TIP You can collect students' learning journals to find out what the class or individual students need more work on.

Chapter Test

Circle the correct choice to fill in each blank.

TIP For advice on taking tests, see Appendix A.

1. We were delighted when Eva was transferred to our department, _____ she does not seem pleased with the change.

   a. or   **b.** and   **c.** but

RESOURCES The *Testing Tool Kit* CD-ROM available with this book has even more tests.

2. Daniel is very clever _____ he can convince anyone that he is right.

    a. , but   **(b.)** ;   **c.** ,

3. I do not have to pay extra for long-distance cell phone calls;

_____ I use my cell phone for all my out-of-state calls.

    a. besides,   **b.** then,   **(c.)** as a result,

4. I did not like the teacher's criticism of my paper; _____ I must admit that everything she said was right.

    a. as a result,   **b.** in addition,   **(c.)** still,

5. Jenna is the best speaker in the class, _____ she will give the graduation speech.

    a. or   **(b.)** so   **c.** yet

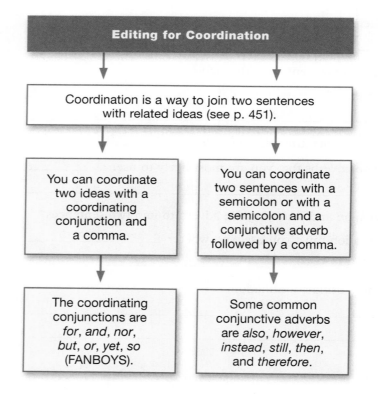

Editing for Coordination

Coordination is a way to join two sentences with related ideas (see p. 451).

You can coordinate two ideas with a coordinating conjunction and a comma.

You can coordinate two sentences with a semicolon or with a semicolon and a conjunctive adverb followed by a comma.

The coordinating conjunctions are *for, and, nor, but, or, yet, so* (FANBOYS).

Some common conjunctive adverbs are *also, however, instead, still, then,* and *therefore.*

Subordination

Joining Sentences with Related Ideas

Understand What Subordination Is

Like coordination, **subordination** is a way to join short, choppy sentences with related ideas into a longer sentence. With subordination, you put a dependent word (such as *after*, *although*, *because*, or *when*) in front of one of the sentences, which then becomes a dependent clause and is no longer a complete sentence.

TIP To understand this chapter, you need to be familiar with basic sentence elements. For a review, see Chapter 21.

	Complete sentence	Complete sentence
TWO SENTENCES	Patti is proud of her son.	He was accepted into the Officer Training Program.

	Complete sentence	Dependent clause
JOINED THROUGH SUBORDINATION	Patti is proud of her son	**because** he was accepted into the Officer Training Program.

Practice Using Subordination

To join two sentences through subordination, use a **subordinating conjunction**. Choose the conjunction that makes the most sense with the two sentences. Here are some of the most common subordinating conjunctions.

TEACHING TIP Write two sentences on the board and have students suggest how the sentences would have to change to accommodate different subordinating conjunctions.

461

TEACHING TIP Point out that unlike the conjunctive adverbs on page 455, these subordinating conjunctions are never used with a semicolon in front of them or a comma after.

Complete sentence	after	now that	Dependent clause
	although	once	
	as	since	
	as if	so that	
	because	unless	
	before	until	
	even if/	when	
	though	whenever	
	if	where	
	if only	while	

I love music	because	it makes me relax.
It is hard to study at home	when	my children want my attention.

When a dependent clause ends a sentence, it usually does not need to be preceded by a comma unless it is showing a contrast.

When the dependent clause begins a sentence, use a comma to separate it from the rest of the sentence.

Subordinating conjunction	Dependent clause	,	Complete sentence
When	I eat out	,	I usually have steak.
Although	it is harmful	,	young people still smoke.

**Editing for Subordination:
Joining Ideas with Related Ideas**

Find

It is hard to sleep in the city. It is always very noisy.

1. **Ask:** What is the relationship between the two complete sentences? *The second sentence explains the first.*

2. **Ask:** What subordinating conjunctions express that relationship? *"Because," "as," or "since."*

Edit

because it
It is hard to sleep in the city. ~~It~~ is always very noisy.

3. **Join the two sentences** with a subordinating conjunction that makes sense.

- -

PRACTICE 1   Joining Ideas through Subordination

In the following sentences, fill in the blank with an appropriate subordinating conjunction. There may be more than one correct choice. *Answers may vary.*
Possible answers are shown.

EXAMPLE: _____*When*_____ the Treasury Department redesigned the
twenty-dollar bill, many people thought that it looked like
play money.

RESOURCES To gauge your
students' skills with subordination, use the *Testing Tool
Kit* CD-ROM available with this
book.

1. The Treasury Department decided to change the design of American
paper money _____*because*_____ it was too easy for criminals to copy.

2. _____*Since*_____ security was the only reason for the change, the basic
elements of each bill remain the same.

3. The portrait on each denomination shows the same person as the old
bills did _____*so that*_____ the new money is familiar.

4. _____*Although*_____ the person in the portrait is the same, the portraits
themselves are different.

5. _____*While*_____ discussing the security measures, Treasury Department officials considered changing the color of the bills.

6. The bills are printed on the same paper as they were before
_____*because*_____ people can tell by the feel if the bills are real.

7. _____*When*_____ you look closely at one of the new bills, you can see
security fibers printed with the bill's amount.

8. The paper also has a watermark that is invisible _____*unless*_____ you
hold the bill up to the light.

9. The new bills do have simpler graphics _____*because*_____ the new security measures take up more space than the original design did.

10. _____*After*_____ so many years of the old design, the new bills seem
strange to many people.

- -

PRACTICE 2   Combining Sentences through Subordination

Combine each pair of sentences into a single sentence by using an appropriate
subordinating conjunction either at the beginning of or between the two sentences. Use a conjunction that makes sense with the two sentences, and add
commas where necessary. *Answers may vary. Possible edits are shown.*

TEACHING TIP This is a good
practice to do orally.

because composing

EXAMPLE: Most business executives now type their own letters. ~~Com-
posing~~ on a computer is faster than writing by hand.

1. Almost all college students used typewriters until the 1980s. *, when computers* ~~Computers~~ became more affordable.

2. Typewriters were used less often. *after computers* ~~Computers~~ became more widespread.

3. Computers offer many advantages. *, although there* ~~There~~ are also some drawbacks.

4. *If you* ~~You~~ have not saved what you have written. *, a* ~~A~~ power outage could cause you to lose your work.

5. *When computers* ~~Computers~~ became widely used in the 1980s. *, professors* ~~Professors~~ were surprised to hear students say, "The computer ate my paper."

6. *When you* ~~You~~ have written a rough draft of a paper. *, you* ~~You~~ should print it out.

7. Some people like to print out a document to proofread it. *because they* ~~They~~ fail to catch all their mistakes on the screen.

8. *While the* ~~The~~ quality of computer screens is getting better. *, people* ~~People~~ still complain about eyestrain.

9. *Even though spell-checking* ~~Spell-checking~~ programs prevent many errors. *, only* ~~Only~~ a person is able to recognize errors with soundalikes such as *their* and *there*.

10. Using a grammar-check program can also cause problems. *if writers* ~~Writers~~ assume that the computer understands grammar rules and do not check their work themselves.

• •

PRACTICE 3   Using Subordination

Complete each of the following sentences. *Answers may vary. Possible answers are shown.*

> **EXAMPLE:** Although most people may live to one hundred in the future, *those days are a long way off* .

1. *We have all heard stories of people who lived long lives* even though they smoked, ate meat every day, and drank alcohol regularly.

2. When someone lives to one hundred or older, *the story usually makes it into the news* .

3. Because very elderly people are unusual, *scientists are studying them to learn their secrets* .

4. *We will not understand why certain people live so long* until researchers learn more about the genetics of these individuals.

5. While some say it may be possible to develop drugs that greatly extend our lives, *many others are skeptical* .

6. *For now, most people will not live past one hundred* _____ unless they are very lucky.

7. *You will hear a lot of different stories* _____ if you ask very old people what they do every day to stay happy and healthy.

8. After my ninety-nine-year-old great-aunt wakes up every morning, *she reads the paper and takes a walk* _____.

9. Before she goes to bed, *she watches her favorite TV shows and has a beer* _____.

10. *I plan to do exactly what she does* _____ so that I can live to at least one hundred.

. . . .

Edit for Subordination

. . . .

PRACTICE 4   Editing Paragraphs for Subordination

In the following paragraphs, join the six pairs of underlined sentences using sub-ordinating conjunctions. Do not forget to punctuate correctly. There may be more than one correct answer. *Answers may vary. Possible edits are shown.*

(1) Washington, D.C., was the first city in the United States to im-plement a public bike-sharing program. *, although the* (2) ~~The~~ idea has been popular in Europe for years. (3) In fact, Paris has more than twenty thousand bikes available for people to rent and ride around the city. (4) Called SmartBike D.C., the Washington program costs citizens only $40 a year to join. (5) For that fee, they have access to any of the 120 bright-red three-speed bikes located in ten bike racks throughout the city. *since other* (6) After using the bikes for up to three hours, people must return them. (7) ~~Other~~ riders might be waiting.

(8) When cyclists are done with a bike, they return it to the nearest rack. *, and the* (9) The bikes have electronic locks. (10) ~~The~~ locks emit a signal if the bike is not returned.
since gasoline (11) Cycling has become much more popular in recent years. (12) ~~Gasoline~~ prices have increased. (13) A number of other cities are now considering bike-sharing programs. *because studies* (14) ~~Studies~~ show that these programs can reduce city traffic by 4 to 5 percent. (15) Some companies

are already creating similar programs to encourage their employees to exercise more and drive less. (16) Company leaders are aware that fit employees and a healthier environment are important goals. (17) ~~It~~ *even if it* means the company spends a little extra time, money, and effort to start and run a bike-sharing program.

· ·

PRACTICE 5   Editing Your Own Writing for Subordination

Edit a piece of your own writing for subordination. It can be a paper you are working on for this course, a paper you have already finished, a paper for another course, or a recent piece of writing from your work or everyday life. You may want to use the chart on page 467.

· ·

Chapter Review

LEARNING JOURNAL Did you find errors in your writing? What is the main thing you have learned about subordination that will help you? How would you explain subordination to someone else? What is unclear to you?

TEACHING TIP You can collect students' learning journals to find out what the class or individual students need more work on.

1. With subordination, you put a __*dependent word*__ in front of one of two related sentences.

2. List five common subordinating conjunctions. *Possible answers:* _____ *although, because, since, if, unless* _____

3. Write two sentences using subordination.

    _____

    _____

Chapter Test

TIP For advice on taking tests, see Appendix A.

Circle the correct choice to fill in each blank.

RESOURCES The *Testing Tool Kit* CD-ROM available with this book has even more tests.

1. _____ the candidate stepped up to the podium, a group of protesters began to shout criticisms of her.
    a. So that   **b.** As if   **c.** As

2. There were now neat rows of suburban homes _____ there had once been orange groves.
    a. where   **b.** as if   **c.** before

3. _____ you are sure that the lightning has stopped, don't let the kids get back into the pool.
    a. Until   **b.** Before   **c.** As if

4. Matt speaks out against glorifying college sports _____
he himself is the star of our football team.

    a. until   **(b.)** even though   **c.** unless

5. _____ we bought a snowblower, my son has not complained about having to shovel after storms.

    (a.) Since   **b.** Where   **c.** Unless

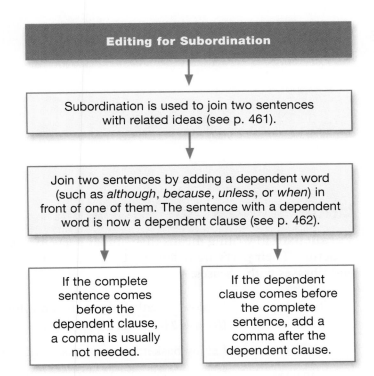

Parallelism

Balancing Ideas

THIS CHAPTER

- explains what parallelism is
- explains how to use parallelism when writing lists and comparisons
- explains how to write parallel sentences with paired words
- gives you practice writing parallel sentences

Understand What Parallelism Is

TIP To understand this chapter, you need to be familiar with basic sentence elements, such as nouns and verbs. For a review, see Chapter 21.

Parallelism in writing means that similar parts in a sentence have the same structure: Their parts are balanced. Use nouns with nouns, verbs with verbs, and phrases with phrases.

NOT PARALLEL	I enjoy basketball more than playing video games.
	[*Basketball* is a noun, but *playing video games* is a phrase.]
PARALLEL	I enjoy basketball more than video games.
PARALLEL	I enjoy playing basketball more than playing video games.
NOT PARALLEL	Last night, I worked, studied, and was watching television.
	[Verbs must be in the same tense to be parallel. *Was watching* has a different structure from *worked* and *studied*.]
PARALLEL	Last night, I worked, studied, and watched television.
PARALLEL	Last night, I was working, studying, and watching television.
NOT PARALLEL	This weekend, we can go to the beach or walking in the mountains.
	[*To the beach* should be paired with another prepositional phrase: *to the mountains*.]
PARALLEL	This weekend, we can go to the beach or to the mountains.

Practice Writing Parallel Sentences

Parallelism in Pairs and Lists

When two or more items in a series are joined by the word *and* or *or*, use a similar form for each item.

NOT PARALLEL   The professor assigned a chapter to read, practices to do, and writing a paper.

PARALLEL   The professor assigned a chapter to read, practices to do, and a paper to write.

NOT PARALLEL   The story was in the newspaper, on the radio, and the television.
[*In the newspaper* and *on the radio* are prepositional phrases. *The television* is not.]

PARALLEL   The story was in the newspaper, on the radio, and on the television.

. . . .

PRACTICE 1   Using Parallelism in Pairs and Lists

In each sentence, underline the parts of the sentence that should be parallel. Then, edit the sentence to make it parallel. *Answers may vary. Possible edits are shown.*

EXAMPLE: Coyotes roam the western mountains, the central plains,
                                                                        suburbs.
                and ~~they are in the suburbs of~~ the East Coast ~~of the United~~
                ~~States.~~

1. Wild predators, such as wolves, are vanishing because people hunt them
   take
   and ~~are taking~~ over their land.

2. Coyotes are surviving and ~~they do~~ well in the modern United States.
                              doing

3. The success of the coyote is due to its varied diet and ~~adapting easily~~.
                                                           adaptability

4. Coyotes are sometimes vegetarians, sometimes scavengers, and some-
   hunters
   times ~~they hunt~~.

5. Today, they are spreading and ~~populate~~ the East Coast for the first time.
                                 populating

6. The coyotes' appearance surprises and ~~is worrying~~ many people.
                                          worries

7. The animals have chosen an area ~~that is more populated and it's not as~~
                                    more populated and less wild than
   ~~wild as~~ their traditional home.

8. Coyotes can adapt to rural, suburban, or ~~even living in a city~~.
                                            urban life.

9. One coyote was identified, tracked, and ~~they~~ captured ~~him~~ in Central
   Park in New York City.

10. Suburbanites are getting used to the sight of coyotes ~~and hearing them~~.
                                                          and sound

. . . .

TIP For more practice with making sentences parallel, visit Exercise Central at **bedfordstmartins.com/ realwriting.**

RESOURCES *Additional Resources* contains tests and supplemental practice exercises for this chapter as well as a transparency master for the chart at the end.

TEACHING TIP Doing this practice orally allows students to hear problems with parallelism. The same is true of Practices 2, 3, and 5.

Parallelism in Comparisons

In comparisons, the items being compared should have parallel structures. Comparisons often use the word *than* or *as*. When you edit for parallelism, make sure that the items on either side of those words are parallel.

NOT PARALLEL	Driving downtown is as fast as the bus.
PARALLEL	Driving downtown is as fast as taking the bus.
NOT PARALLEL	To admit a mistake is better than denying it.
PARALLEL	To admit a mistake is better than to deny it. Admitting a mistake is better than denying it.

Sometimes you need to add or delete a word or two to make the parts of a sentence parallel.

NOT PARALLEL	A tour package is less expensive than arranging every travel detail yourself.
PARALLEL, WORD ADDED	*Buying* a tour package is less expensive than arranging every travel detail yourself.
NOT PARALLEL	The sale price of the shoes is as low as paying the regular price for two pairs.
PARALLEL, WORDS DROPPED	The sale price of the shoes is as low as the regular price for two pairs.

• •

PRACTICE 2   Using Parallelism in Comparisons

In each sentence, underline the parts of the sentence that should be parallel. Then, edit the sentence to make it parallel. *Answers may vary. Possible edits are shown.*

EXAMPLE: Leasing a new car may be less expensive than ~~to buy~~ *buying* one.

1. Car dealers often require less money down for leasing a car than for ~~the purchase of~~ *purchasing* one.

2. The monthly payments for a leased car may be as low as ~~paying for a loan~~ *loan payments*.

3. You should check the terms of leasing to make sure they are as favorable as ~~to buy~~ *the terms of buying*.

4. You may find that ~~to lease~~ *leasing* is a safer bet than buying.

5. You will be making less of a financial commitment by leasing a car than ~~to own~~ *by owning* it.

RESOURCES To gauge students' skills with parallelism, use the *Testing Tool Kit* CD-ROM available with this book.

6. Buying a car may be better than ~~a lease on~~ *leasing* one if you plan to keep it for several years.

7. A used car can be more economical than ~~getting~~ a new one.

8. However, ~~maintenance of~~ *maintaining* a new car may be easier than taking care of a used car.

9. A used car may not be as impressive as ~~buying~~ a brand-new vehicle.

10. To get a used car from a reputable source can be a better decision than ~~to buy~~ *to buy* a new vehicle that loses value the moment you drive it home.

Parallelism with Certain Paired Words

When a sentence uses certain paired words, called **correlative conjunctions**, the items joined by them must be parallel. These words link two equal elements and show the relationship between them. Here are the paired words:

both . . . and   neither . . . nor   rather . . . than

either . . . or   not only . . . but also

When you use the first part of a pair, be sure you always use the second part, too.

COMPUTER Students can use the find or search function to locate the first word in correlative conjunctions. They should read the sentences with those constructions carefully to make sure that the second word is present and that parallel structure is used.

NOT PARALLEL	Bruce wants *both* freedom *and* to be wealthy. [*Both* is used with *and*, but the items joined by them are not parallel.]
PARALLEL	Bruce wants *both* freedom *and* wealth.
PARALLEL	Bruce wants *both* to have freedom *and* to be wealthy.
NOT PARALLEL	He can *neither* fail the course and quitting his job is also impossible.
PARALLEL	He can *neither* fail the course *nor* quit his job.

PRACTICE 3   Using Parallelism with Certain Paired Words

In each sentence, circle the paired words and underline the parts of the sentence that should be parallel. Then, edit the sentence to make it parallel. You may need to change one of the paired elements to make the sentence parallel. *Answers may vary. Possible edits are shown.*

EXAMPLE: A cell phone can be (either) a lifesaver (or) ~~it can be annoying~~ *an annoyance*.

1. Fifteen years ago, most people (neither) had cell phones (nor) ~~did they want~~ *wanted* them.

2. Today, cell phones are (not only) used by people of all ages (but also) ~~are~~ carried everywhere.

3. Cell phones are not universally popular: Some commuters would (rather) ban cell phones on buses and trains (than) ~~being~~^be^ forced to listen to other people's conversations.

4. No one denies that a cell phone can be (both) useful (and) ~~convenience is a factor~~^convenient^.

5. A motorist stranded on a deserted road would (rather) have a cell phone (than)^be forced^ to walk to the nearest gas station.

6. When cell phones were first introduced, some people feared that they (either) caused brain tumors (or) ~~they~~ were a dangerous source of radiation.

7. Most Americans today (neither) worry about radiation from cell phones (nor)^fear^ other injuries.

8. The biggest risk of cell phones is (either) that drivers are distracted by them (or) ~~people getting~~^that people get^ angry at someone talking too loudly in public on a cell phone.

9. Cell phones probably do not cause brain tumors, but some experiments on human cells have shown that energy from the phones may (both) affect people's reflexes (and) ~~it might~~ alter the brain's blood vessels.

10. Some scientists think that these experiments show that cell phone use might have (not only) physical effects on human beings (but) ~~it also could influence mental processes~~^also mental ones^.

• •

PRACTICE 4   Completing Sentences with Paired Words

For each sentence, complete the correlative conjunction and add more information. Make sure that the structures on both sides of the correlative conjunction are parallel. *Answers may vary. Possible answers are shown.*

> **EXAMPLE:** I am both impressed by your company _and enthusiastic to work for you_.

1. I could bring to this job not only youthful enthusiasm _but also relevant experience_.

2. I am willing to work either in your main office _or in your San Francisco office_.

3. My current job neither encourages initiative _nor allows flexibility_.

4. I would rather work in a challenging job _than work in a boring one_.

5.   In college, I learned a lot both from my classes *and from other students*

_____ .

· ·

Edit for Parallelism

· ·

PRACTICE 5   Editing Paragraphs for Parallelism

Find and correct five parallelism errors in the following paragraphs.

(1) On a mountainous island between Norway and the North Pole is a special underground vault. (2) It contains neither gold *nor* ~~and~~ other currency. (3) Instead, it is full of a different kind of treasure: seeds. (4) They are being saved for the future in case something happens to the plants that people need to grow for food.

(5) More than 4.5 million types of seeds occupy this enormous vault. (6) Each sample has between one hundred and five hundred seeds, which means that the vault contains approximately 2.25 billion seeds. (7) *Storing* ~~To store~~ them is better than planting them. (8) Stored, they are preserved for future generations to plant. (9) On the first day that the vault's storage program began, 268,000 different seeds were deposited, put into sealed packages, and *collected* ~~collecting~~ into sealed boxes. (10) Some of the seeds were for maize (corn), while others were for rice, wheat, and barley.

(11) Although some people call it the "Doomsday Vault," many others see it as a type of insurance policy against starvation, in the case of a terrible natural disaster. (12) The vault's location keeps it safe from floods, earthquakes, and *storms* ~~storming~~. (13) Carefully storing these seeds not only will help ensure that people will have food to eat *but also will* ~~plus~~ make sure that important crops never go extinct.

TEAMWORK Have students form small groups. Then, have each group write five sentences that are not parallel. Each group should then exchange sentences with another group and correct the other group's sentences.

· ·

PRACTICE 6   Editing Your Own Writing for Parallelism

As a final practice, edit a piece of your own writing for parallelism. It can be a paper you are working on for this course, a paper you have already finished, a paper for another course, or a recent piece of writing from your work or everyday life. Record in your learning journal any problem sentences you find, along with their corrections. You may want to use the chart on page 475.

· ·

Chapter Review

1. Parallelism in writing means that *similar parts in a sentence have the same structure.*

2. In what three situations do problems with parallelism most often occur? *with pairs and lists, with comparisons, and with certain paired words*

3. What are two pairs of correlative conjunctions? *Possible answers: both/and, neither/nor*

4. Write two sentences using parallelism.

Chapter Test

Circle the correct choice for each of the following items.

1. If an underlined portion of this sentence is incorrect, select the revision that fixes it. If the sentence is correct as written, choose d.

   For our home renovation, we are planning to expand the kitchen,
                                                       A

   retile the bathroom, and we also want to add a bedroom.
           B   **C**

   a. add space to the kitchen   **c.** add a bedroom

   b. replace the tile in the bathroom   d. No change is necessary.

2. Choose the correct word(s) to fill in the blank.

   In my personal ad, I said that I like taking long walks on the beach, dining over candlelight, and _____ sculptures with a chainsaw.

   a. to carve   **b.** carving   c. carved

3. If an underlined portion of this sentence is incorrect, select the revision that fixes it. If the sentence is correct as written, choose d.

   To get her elbow back into shape, she wants exercising and not
      A   **B**

   to take pills.
     C

   a. To getting   c. taking pills

   b. to do exercises   d. No change is necessary.

4.   Choose the correct word(s) to fill in the blank.

The first-time homebuyer course teaches that _____ a home is often less expensive than renting one over the long term.

a. owning   **b.** have owned   **c.** to own

5.   Choose the correct words to fill in the blank.

You can travel by car, by plane, or _____.

a. boating is fine   **b.** by boat   **c.** on boat

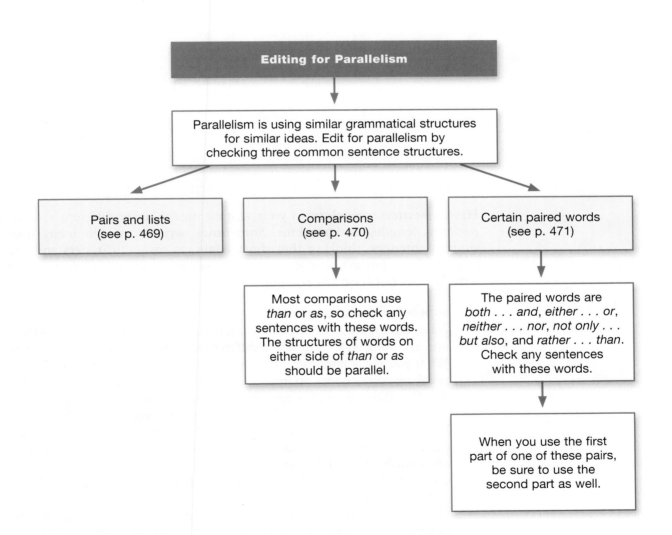

Editing for Parallelism

Parallelism is using similar grammatical structures for similar ideas. Edit for parallelism by checking three common sentence structures.

Pairs and lists
(see p. 469)

Comparisons
(see p. 470)

Certain paired words
(see p. 471)

Most comparisons use *than* or *as*, so check any sentences with these words. The structures of words on either side of *than* or *as* should be parallel.

The paired words are *both . . . and, either . . . or, neither . . . nor, not only . . . but also,* and *rather . . . than.* Check any sentences with these words.

When you use the first part of one of these pairs, be sure to use the second part as well.

32

Sentence Variety

Putting Rhythm in Your Writing

THIS CHAPTER
- gives you five ways to vary your sentences as you write
- gives you practice using those ways to achieve variety

Understand What Sentence Variety Is

Having **sentence variety** in your writing means using different sentence patterns, lengths, and rhythms. Sometimes, writers use too many short, simple sentences, thinking that short is always easier to understand than long. In fact, that is not true, as you can see in these examples, where the writing does not have any rhythm.

WITH SHORT, SIMPLE SENTENCES

Many people do not realize how important their speaking voice and style are. Speaking style can make a difference, particularly in a job interview. What you say is important. How you say it is nearly as important. Your speaking voice creates an impression. Mumbling is a bad way of speaking. It makes the speaker appear sloppy and lacking in confidence. Mumbling also makes it difficult for the interviewer to hear what is being said. Talking too fast is another bad speech behavior. The speaker runs his or her ideas together. The interviewer cannot follow them or distinguish what is important. A third common bad speech behavior concerns verbal "tics." Verbal tics are empty filler phrases like "um," "like," and "you know." Practice for an interview. Sit up straight. Look the person to whom you are speaking directly in the eye. Speak up. Slow down. One good way to find out how you sound is to leave yourself a voice-mail message. If you sound bad to yourself, you need practice speaking aloud. Do not let poor speech behavior interfere with creating a good impression.

TIP For more practice with sentence variety, visit Exercise Central at **bedfordstmartins.com/realwriting**.

PRACTICE 1   Starting Sentences with an Adverb

Edit each sentence so that it begins with an adverb. *Answers may vary. Possible answers are shown.*

Unfortunately, rabies
EXAMPLE: ~~Rabies unfortunately~~ remains a problem in the United States.

Once, rabies
1. ~~Rabies once~~ was a major threat to domestic pets in this country.

Now, the
2. ~~The~~ disease is ~~now~~ most deadly to wildlife such as raccoons, skunks, and bats.

Frequently, people
3. ~~People frequently~~ fail to have their pets vaccinated against rabies.

Mistakenly, they believe
4. ~~They believe mistakenly~~ that their dogs and cats are no longer in danger.

Worriedly, veterinarians note
5. ~~Veterinarians note worriedly~~ that wildlife with rabies can infect pets and people.

TIP Answers to odd-numbered practice items are on pages AK-1–10 at the back of the book.

PRACTICE 2   Starting Sentences with an Adverb

In each sentence, fill in the blank with an adverb that makes sense. Add a comma when necessary. There may be several good choices for each item. *Answers may vary. Possible answers are shown.*

EXAMPLE: _____*Luckily,*_____ a new method of vaccination may help reduce the amount of rabies in some wild animals.

1. _____*Recently,*_____ an oral vaccine that prevents rabies in raccoons and skunks has been developed.

2. _____*Often,*_____ the vaccine can be placed in bait that the animals like to eat.

3. _____*Thankfully,*_____ this method of vaccination has stopped the spread of rabies in coyotes in southern Texas.

4. _____*Additionally,*_____ it has saved humans' and pets' lives, public health officials agree.

5. _____*Unfortunately,*_____ the problem of rabies in bats has not yet been solved.

PRACTICE 3   Writing Sentences That Start with an Adverb

Write three sentences that start with an adverb. Use commas as necessary. Choose among the following adverbs: *often, sadly, amazingly, luckily, lovingly, aggressively, gently, frequently, stupidly.*

1. <u>*Answers will vary.*</u>

2. _____

3. _____

· ·

Join Ideas Using an *-ing* Verb

One way to combine sentences is to use a verb that ends in *-ing* to make one of the sentences into a phrase.

The *-ing* verb form indicates that the two parts of the sentence are happening at the same time. Add an *-ing* verb to the less important of the two sentences.

TEACHING TIP Explain to students that in their own writing they will need to consider the context when deciding which sentence contains the more important idea.

TWO SENTENCES	A pecan roll from our bakery is not dietetic. It contains eight hundred calories.
JOINED WITH -*ING* VERB FORM	*Containing* eight hundred calories, a pecan roll from our bakery is not dietetic.

To combine sentences this way, add *-ing* to the verb in one of the sentences and delete the subject. You now have a phrase that can be added to the beginning or the end of the other sentence, depending on what makes the most sense.

The fat content is also high, ~~It equals~~ *, equaling* the fat in a huge country breakfast.

If you add a phrase starting with an *-ing* verb to the beginning of a sentence, put a comma after it. If you add the phrase to the end of a sentence, you will usually need to put a comma before it, unless the phrase is essential to the meaning of the sentence.

If you put a phrase starting with an *-ing* verb at the beginning of a sentence, be sure the word that the phrase modifies follows immediately. Otherwise, you will create a dangling modifier.

TIP For more on finding and correcting dangling modifiers, see Chapter 28, and for more on joining ideas, see Chapters 29 and 30.

TWO SENTENCES	I ran through the rain. My raincoat got all wet.
DANGLING MODIFIER	Running through the rain, my raincoat got all wet.
EDITED	Running through the rain, I got my raincoat all wet.

· ·

PRACTICE 4   Joining Ideas Using an *-ing* Verb

Combine each pair of sentences into a single sentence by using an *-ing* verb. Add or delete words as necessary. *Answers may vary. Possible edits are shown.*

EXAMPLE: Some people read faces amazingly well, ~~They interpret~~ *, interpreting* nonverbal cues that other people miss.

TEACHING TIP Doing this practice orally will help students hear the correct formation. The same is true of Practices 6, 7, 9, 11, and 13.

1. A recent study ~~tested~~ *testing* children's abilities to interpret facial expressions. ~~The study~~ made headlines.

2. *Participating in the study, physically* ~~Physically~~ abused children ~~participated in the study.~~ They saw photographs of faces changing from one expression to another.

3. The children told researchers what emotion was most obvious in each face. *, choosing* ~~The children chose~~ among fear, anger, sadness, happiness, and other emotions.

4. The study also included nonabused children. *, serving* ~~They served~~ as a control group for comparison with the other children.

5. All of the children in the study were equally good at identifying most emotions. *, responding* ~~They all responded~~ similarly to happiness or fear.

6. Battered children were especially sensitive to one emotion on the faces. *, identifying* ~~These children identified~~ anger much more quickly than the other children could.

7. *Having* ~~The abused children have~~ learned to look for anger. *, the abused children* ~~They~~ protect themselves with this early-warning system.

8. Their sensitivity to anger may not help the abused children later in life. *, perhaps hurting* ~~It perhaps hurts~~ them socially.

9. *Tending* ~~The abused children tend~~ to run from anger they observe. *, abused children* ~~They~~ have difficulty connecting with people who exhibit anger.

10. The human brain works hard to acquire useful information. *, often hanging* ~~It often hangs~~ on to the information after its usefulness has passed.

• •

PRACTICE 5 Joining Ideas Using an *-ing* Verb

Write two sets of sentences, and join them using an *-ing* verb form.

EXAMPLE: a. <u>*Carol looked up.*</u>

b. <u>*She saw three falling stars in the sky.*</u>

Combined: <u>*Looking up, Carol saw three falling stars in the* </u>

<u>*sky.* </u>

1. a. <u>*Answers will vary.*</u>

b. _____

Combined: _____

2. a. _____

   b. _____

   Combined: _____

. . . .

Join Ideas Using a Past Participle

Another way to combine sentences is to use a past participle (often, a verb ending in -*ed*) to make one of the sentences into a phrase.

TIP For more on helping verbs, see Chapters 21 and 25. Chapter 25 also covers past participles.

TWO SENTENCES	Henry VIII was a powerful English king. He is *remembered* for his many wives.
JOINED WITH A PAST PARTICIPLE	*Remembered* for his many wives, Henry VIII was a powerful English king.

Past participles of irregular verbs do not end in -*ed*; they take different forms.

TWO SENTENCES	Tim Treadwell was *eaten* by a grizzly bear. He showed that wild animals are unpredictable.
JOINED WITH A PAST PARTICIPLE	*Eaten* by a grizzly bear, Tim Treadwell showed that wild animals are unpredictable.

Note that sentences can be joined this way when one of them has a form of *be* along with a past participle (*is remembered* in the first Henry VIII example and *was eaten* in the first Tim Treadwell example).

To combine sentences this way, delete the subject and the *be* form from the sentence that has the *be* form and the past participle. You now have a phrase that can be added to the beginning or the end of the other sentence, depending on what makes the most sense.

Subject   *be* form   Past participle

~~Henry VIII was~~ _Ddetermined to divorce one of his wives. ~~He~~ created the ``, Henry VIII``
Church of England because Catholicism does not allow divorce.

If you add a phrase that begins with a past participle to the beginning of a sentence, put a comma after it. If you add the phrase to the end of the sentence, put a comma before it.

If you put a phrase starting with a past participle at the beginning of a sentence, be sure the word that the phrase modifies follows immediately. Otherwise, you will create a dangling modifier. Sometimes, as in the example, you will need to change the word that the phrase modifies from a pronoun to a noun.

• •

PRACTICE 6   Joining Ideas Using a Past Participle

Combine each pair of sentences into a single sentence by using a past participle. *Answers may vary. Possible edits are shown.*

EXAMPLE: The oil company was forced to take the local women's
objections seriously. The oil company had to close for ten days
during their protest.

[handwritten: forced] *[handwritten: , the oil]*

1. *Angered by British colonial rule in 1929, the*
   The women of southern Nigeria were angered by British colonial rule in
   1929. They organized a protest.

2. *Covered with pipelines and oil wells,*
   Nigeria is now one of the top ten oil-producing countries. The nation is
   covered with pipelines and oil wells.

3. *Pumped* *, the*
   The oil is pumped by American and other foreign oil companies. The oil
   often ends up in wealthy Western economies.

4. *Stolen by corrupt rulers in many cases, the*
   The money from the oil seldom reaches Nigeria's local people. The cash
   is stolen by corrupt rulers in many cases.

5. *Polluted* *, the Nigerian countryside*
   The Nigerian countryside is polluted by the oil industry. The land then
   becomes a wasteland.

6. *Insulted* *, many Nigerians*
   Many Nigerians are insulted by the way the oil industry treats them.
   They want the oil companies to pay attention to their problems.

7. *Inspired* *, local Nigerian women*
   Local Nigerian women were inspired by the 1929 women's protests.
   They launched a series of protests against the oil industry in the summer
   of 2002.

8. The women prevented workers from entering or leaving two oil company
   offices. The offices were located in the port of Warri.

9. *Concerned* *, many workers at the oil company*
   Workers at the oil company were concerned about the women's threat
   to take their clothes off. Many workers told company officials that such
   a protest would bring a curse on the company and shame to its
   employees.

10. The company eventually agreed to hire more local people and to invest
    in local projects. The projects are intended to supply electricity and
    provide the villagers with a market for fish and poultry.

PRACTICE 7   Joining Ideas Using a Past Participle

Fill in the blank in each sentence with an appropriate past participle. *Answers will vary. Possible answers are shown.*

EXAMPLE: _____*Trusted*_____ by people around the world for centuries, herbs can be powerful medical tools.

1. Common American plants are made into medicine, such as Saint-John's-wort, _____*taken*_____ as an antidepressant.

2. _____*Made*_____ in laboratories, popular herbs are widely available in capsule form.

3. _____*Regarded*_____ as "natural" medicines, herbs are often believed to be harmless.

4. _____*Uninformed*_____ about the effects of herbal medicines, some people take them without understanding possible consequences.

5. Some herbs may interact badly with other drugs _____*prescribed*_____ by a doctor.

PRACTICE 8   Joining Ideas Using a Past Participle

Write two sets of sentences, and join them with a past participle.

EXAMPLE: a. *Chris is taking intermediate accounting.*

b. *It is believed to be the most difficult course in the major.*

Combined: *Chris is taking intermediate accounting, believed to be the most difficult course in the major.*

1. a. *Answers will vary.* _____

b. _____

Combined: _____

_____

2. a. _____

b. _____

Combined: _____

_____

Join Ideas Using an Appositive

An **appositive** is a noun or noun phrase that renames a noun. Appositives can be used to combine two sentences into one.

TWO SENTENCES	Fen-Phen was found to be toxic. It was a popular diet drug.
JOINED WITH AN APPOSITIVE	Fen-Phen, a popular diet drug, was found to be toxic.
	[The phrase *a popular diet drug* renames the noun *Fen-Phen*.]

To combine two sentences this way, turn the sentence that renames the noun into a noun phrase by dropping the subject and verb. The appositive phrase can appear anywhere in the sentence, but it should be placed before or after the noun it renames. Use a comma or commas to set off the appositive.

, a dangerous compound,
The drug caused a few deaths. ~~It was a dangerous compound.~~

• •

PRACTICE 9   Joining Ideas Using an Appositive

Combine each pair of sentences into a single sentence by using an appositive. Be sure to use a comma or commas to set off the appositive. *Answers may vary. Possible edits are shown.* *, perhaps the most famous work clothes in the world,*

EXAMPLE: Levi's jeans have looked the same for well over a century. ~~They are perhaps the most famous work clothes in the world.~~

1. Jacob Davis ~~was~~ a Russian immigrant working in Reno, Nevada, ~~He was~~ the inventor of Levi's jeans.

2. Davis came up with an invention *, the riveted seam,* that made work clothes last longer. ~~The invention was the riveted seam.~~

3. Davis bought denim from a wholesaler, ~~The wholesaler was~~ Levi Strauss.

4. In 1870, he offered to sell the rights to his invention to Levi Strauss for the price of the patent, ~~Patents then cost~~ about $70.

5. Davis joined the firm in 1873 and supervised the final development of its product, ~~The product was~~ the famous Levi's jeans.

6. Davis oversaw a crucial design element, ~~The jeans all had~~ orange stitching.

   Another
7. ~~The curved stitching on the back pockets was another~~ choice Davis made, *, the curved stitching on the back pockets,* ~~It~~ also survives in today's Levi's.

   A   *, the stitching on the pockets*
8. ~~The stitching on the pockets has been a~~ trademark since 1942, ~~It~~ is very recognizable.

9. During World War II, Levi Strauss temporarily stopped adding the pocket stitches because they wasted thread,. ~~It was~~ a valuable resource.

10. Until the war ended, the pocket design was added with a less valuable material,. ~~The company used~~ paint.

• •

PRACTICE 10 **Joining Ideas Using an Appositive**

Fill in the blank in each sentence with an appropriate appositive. *Answers will vary. Possible answers are shown.*

   EXAMPLE: The off-campus housing office, *a small room crowded with* *desperate students* , offered little help.

1. My sister, *a college freshman* , needed to find an apartment before she started school.

2. As she looked for a place to live, she faced a serious problem, *sky-high rents* .

3. Searching for apartments in the area near the campus, *a quiet, tree-lined neighborhood* , she found nothing suitable.

4. She applied for housing in a dormitory, *a high-rise on the campus* , but the waiting list already contained sixty-two names.

5. She finally found a place she could afford, *a dark, cramped apartment* , in a neighborhood with a high crime rate.

• •

Join Ideas Using an Adjective Clause

An **adjective clause** is a group of words with a subject and a verb that describes a noun. An adjective clause often begins with the word *who*, *which*, or *that*, and it can be used to combine two sentences into one.

TIP For more about adjectives, see Chapter 27.

TWO SENTENCES	Lauren has won many basketball awards. She is captain of her college team.
JOINED WITH AN ADJECTIVE CLAUSE	Lauren, *who is captain of her college team*, has won many basketball awards.

To join sentences this way, use *who*, *which*, or *that* to replace the subject in a sentence that describes a noun in the other sentence. You now have an adjective clause that you can move so that it follows the noun it describes. The sentence with the more important idea (the one you want to emphasize) should become the main clause. The less important idea should be in the adjective clause.

TEACHING TIP Explain to students that in their own writing they will need to consider the context when deciding which sentence contains the more important idea.

TIP Use *who* to refer to a person, *which* to refer to places or things (but not to people), and *that* for places or things.

Main clause   Adjective clause

, *which*

Rocío attributes her success to the Puente Project. ~~It~~ helped her meet the challenges of college.

[The more important idea here is that Rocío gives the Puente Project credit for her success. The less important idea is that the Puente Project helped her cope with college.]

NOTE: If an adjective clause can be taken out of a sentence without completely changing the meaning of the sentence, put commas around it.

Lauren, *who is captain of her college team,* has won many basketball awards.

[The phrase *who is captain of her college team* adds information about Lauren, but it is not essential; the sentence *Lauren has won many basketball awards* means almost the same thing as the sentence in the example.]

If an adjective clause is an essential part of a sentence, do not put commas around it.

Lauren is an award-winning basketball player who overcame childhood cancer.

[*Who overcame childhood cancer* is an essential part of this sentence. The sentence *Lauren is an award-winning basketball player* is different in meaning from the whole sentence in the example.]

· ·

PRACTICE 11   Joining Ideas Using an Adjective Clause

Combine each pair of sentences into a single sentence by using an adjective clause beginning with *who*, *which*, or *that*. *Answers will vary. Possible edits are shown.*

, who has been going to college for the past three years,

EXAMPLE: My friend Erin had her first child last June. ~~She has been going to college for the past three years.~~

1. While Erin goes to classes, her baby boy stays at a day-care center. , *which* ~~The day-care center~~ costs Erin about $100 a week.

2. Twice when her son was ill, Erin had to miss her geology lab. , *which* ~~The lab~~ is an important part of her grade for that course.

3. Occasionally, Erin's parents , who live about seventy miles away, come up and watch the baby while Erin is studying. ~~They live about seventy miles away.~~

4. Sometimes Erin feels discouraged by the extra costs. that ~~The costs~~ have come from having a child.

5. She feels that some of her professors who have never been parents themselves are not very sympathetic. ~~These are the ones who have never been parents themselves.~~

, who wants to be a good mother and a good student,
6. Erin understands that she must take responsibility for both her child and
her education. ~~She wants to be a good mother and a good student.~~

, which were once straight A's,
7. Her grades have suffered somewhat since she had her son. ~~They were
once straight A's.~~

, who hopes to go to graduate school someday,
8. Erin wants to graduate with honors. ~~She hopes to go to graduate school
someday.~~

, who is the most important thing to her,
9. Her son is more important than an A in geology. ~~He is the most important thing to her.~~

, who
10. Erin still expects to have a high grade point average, She has simply
given up expecting to be perfect.

- -

PRACTICE 12 Joining Ideas Using an Adjective Clause

Fill in the blank in each of the following sentences with an appropriate adjective
clause. Add commas, if necessary. *Answers will vary. Possible edits are shown.*

> **EXAMPLE:** The firefighters __who responded to the alarm__ entered
> the burning building.

1. A fire __that was probably caused by faulty wiring__ began in our house in
the middle of the night.

2. The members of my family __who were home at the time of the fire__
were all asleep.

3. My father __, who has always been a light sleeper,__ was the first to
smell smoke.

4. He ran to our bedrooms __, which were on the second floor,__
and woke us up with his shouting.

5. The house __, which was the only home I had ever lived in,__ was damaged,
but everyone in my family reached safety.

- -

Edit for Sentence Variety

- -

PRACTICE 13 Editing Paragraphs for Sentence Variety

Create sentence variety in the following paragraphs by joining at least two sentences in each of the paragraphs. Use several of the techniques covered in this
chapter. More than one right answer is possible. *Answers may vary. Possible
edits are shown.*

(1) When people go to football games, they frequently wear coats and hats. (2) If you are a Barrow Whalers' fan, you wear more than that. (3) ~~You put~~ *putting* on a parka, scarf, gloves, hat, and long underwear—in August! (4) The Whalers are the high school football team in Barrow, Alaska. (5) Barrow, ~~is~~ the northernmost city in the country, (6) ~~It~~ is also the coldest.

(7) Barrow, ~~is~~ a small city, (8) ~~It~~ has only about 4,500 residents. (9) Until 2006, the high school did not have a football team. (10) Then the superintendent, Trent Blankenship, and a computer teacher and former football coach, Mark Voss, had an idea. (11) ~~They suspected~~ *Suspecting* that a team might give some students a positive focus and decrease the school's dropout rate, (12) ~~They~~ *they* started a football program.

With wind chill temperatures dropping as low as 80 degrees below zero, being
(13) ~~Being~~ part of the team is not easy. (14) ~~Wind chill temperatures can drop as low as 80 degrees below zero.~~ (15) Bus drivers often park the school buses around the field, (16) ~~This arrangement provides~~ *providing* a wind barrier for players and the crowd.

• •

PRACTICE 14   Editing Your Own Writing for Sentence Variety

As a final practice, edit a piece of your own writing for sentence variety. It can be a paper you are working on for this course, a paper you have already finished, a paper for another course, or a recent piece of writing from your work or everyday life. Record in your learning journal any examples of short, choppy sentences you find, along with the edited versions of these sentences. You may want to use the chart on page 490.

• •

Chapter Review

LEARNING JOURNAL Did you find errors in your writing? What is the main thing you have learned about sentence variety that will help you? How would you explain how to vary sentences to someone else? What is unclear to you?

1. Having sentence variety means <u>*using different sentence patterns, lengths, and rhythms.*</u>

2. If you tend to write short, similar-sounding sentences, what five techniques should you try? <u>*starting some sentences with adverbs, combining sentences using an "-ing" verb, combining sentences using a past participle, combining sentences using an appositive, and combining sentences using an adjective clause*</u>

3. An <u>*appositive*</u> is a noun or noun phrase that renames a noun.

4. An ____*adjective*____ clause often starts with *who*, ____*which*____,

or ____*that*____. It describes a noun or pronoun.

5. Use commas around an adjective clause when the information in it is
(essential / (not essential)) to the meaning of the sentence.

TEACHING TIP You can collect students' learning journals to find out what the class or individual students need more work on.

Chapter Test

For each of the following sentence pairs, choose the answer that joins the sentences logically using one of the strategies in this chapter.

TIP For advice on taking tests, see Appendix A.

1. Luis straightened his tie. He waited to be called in for his job interview.
 a. Straightened his tie, Luis waited to be called in for his job interview.
 (b.) Straightening his tie, Luis waited to be called in for his job interview.

RESOURCES The *Testing Tool Kit* CD-ROM available with this book has even more tests.

2. The auditorium was noisy and chaotic. It was filled with people in Superman outfits.
 (a.) Filled with people in Superman outfits, the auditorium was noisy and chaotic.
 b. Filled with people in Superman outfits; the auditorium was noisy and chaotic.

3. My niece is a star softball player. She loves to watch baseball on TV.
 (a.) My niece, a star softball player, loves to watch baseball on TV.
 b. Starring as a softball player, my niece loves to watch baseball on TV.

4. Chocolate is a favorite sweet worldwide. It has compounds that might lower the risk of certain diseases.
 a. Chocolate is a favorite sweet worldwide, for it has compounds that might lower the risk of certain diseases.
 (b.) Chocolate, a favorite sweet worldwide, has compounds that might lower the risk of certain diseases.

5. The lawyer believed passionately in his client's innocence. He convinced the jury to come to a verdict of not guilty.
 (a.) The lawyer, who believed passionately in his client's innocence, convinced the jury to come to a verdict of not guilty.
 b. The lawyer believed passionately in his client's innocence, yet he convinced the jury to come to a verdict of not guilty.

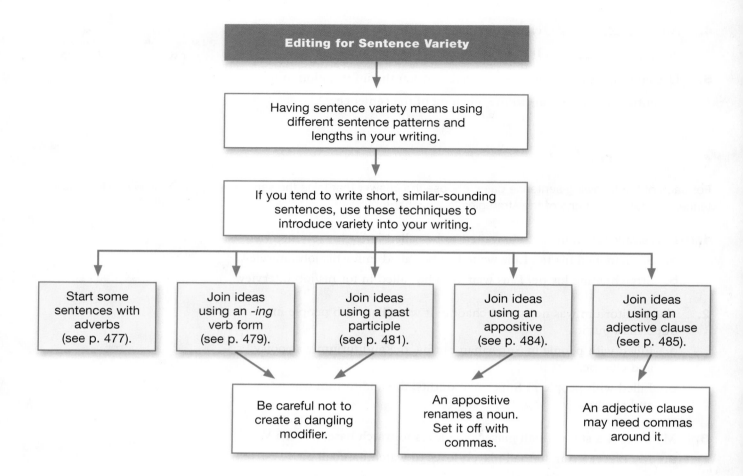

THIS CHAPTER

- explains four basic sentence patterns
- shows how to form negatives and questions
- explains the different kinds of pronouns and how to use them
- shows some verb tenses that can be tricky and gives you summary charts to refer to
- explains how to use articles and prepositions correctly

Formal English and ESL Concerns

Grammar Trouble Spots for Multilingual Students

Academic, or formal, English is the English you will be expected to use in college and in most work situations, especially in writing. If you are not used to using formal English, or if English is not your native language, this chapter will help you avoid the most common problems with key sentence parts.

NOTE: In this chapter, we use the word *English* to refer to formal English.

TIP For more on using formal English, see Chapter 3. In this chapter, subjects are underlined, and verbs are double-underlined.

Basic Sentence Patterns

Statements

Every sentence in English must have at least one subject and one verb **(S-V)** that together express a complete idea. (Some languages, such as Spanish and Italian, do not always use a subject because the subject is implied by the verb. In English, always include a subject.) The subject performs the action, and the verb names the action, as in the sentence that follows.

S V

The pitcher throws.

Other English sentence patterns build on that structure. One of the most common patterns is subject-verb-object **(S-V-O)**.

S V O

The pitcher throws the ball.

RESOURCES For additional support and exercises for ESL students, see *The Bedford/St. Martin's ESL Workbook*, Second Edition, available with this text. For tests on particular ESL trouble spots, see the *Testing Tool Kit* CD-ROM.

TEACHING TIP You may wish to assign this chapter to your class as a whole, especially if you have native students who speak nonstandard English. Even if they know the parts of speech, many students need extra practice with how those parts function in writing.

There are two kinds of objects.

DIRECT OBJECTS receive the action of the verb.

```
       S      V        DO
       |      |        |
The pitcher throws the ball.
```

[The ball directly receives the action of the verb *throws*.]

INDIRECT OBJECTS do not receive the action of the verb. Instead, the action is performed *for* or *to* the person.

```
       S      V    IO    DO
       |      |    |     |
The pitcher throws me the ball.
```

••

PRACTICE 1   Sentence Patterns

Label the subject (S), verb (V), direct object (DO), and indirect object (IO) in the following two sentences.

```
       S    V      DO
       |    |      |
```
1. John sent the letter.

```
       S    V    IO    DO
       |    |    |     |
```
2. John sent Beth the letter.

••

Note that the **S-V-O** pattern differs from the sentence patterns in some other languages. For example, in some languages (like Arabic) the pattern may be **S-O-V**; other languages do not have as strictly defined a word order (Spanish, Italian, and Russian, for example).

Another common sentence pattern is subject-verb-prepositional phrase. In standard English, the prepositional phrase typically follows the subject and verb.

TIP For more on prepositions, see pages 314–15. For more on the parts of sentences, see Chapter 21.

```
       S     V   Prepositional phrase
       |     |   |_____|
Lilah went to the movies.
```

••

PRACTICE 2   Using Correct Word Order

Read each of the sentences that follow. If the sentence is correct, write "C" in the blank to the left of it. If it is incorrect, write "I" and rewrite the sentence using correct word order.

TIP Answers to odd-numbered practice items are on pages AK-1–10 at the back of the book.

EXAMPLE: __*I*__ My friend to me gave a present.

Revision: *My friend gave me a present.*

<u> I </u> **1.** Presents I like very much.

     Revision: *I like presents very much.*

<u> I </u> **2.** To parties I go often.

     Revision: *I go to parties often.*

<u> I </u> **3.** To parties, I always bring a present.

     Revision: *I always bring a present to parties.*

<u> C </u> **4.** At my parties, people bring me presents, too.

     Revision: _____

<u> I </u> **5.** Always write to them a thank-you note.

     Revision: *I always write them a thank-you note.*

. . . .

Negatives

To form a negative statement, use one of these words, often with a helping verb such as *can/could, does/did, has/have,* or *should/will/would.*

never	nobody	no one	nowhere
no	none	not	

Notice in the example sentences that the word *not* comes *after* the helping verb.

SENTENCE	Dina can sing.
NEGATIVE	Dina ~~no can~~ sing. (cannot)

SENTENCE	The store sells cigarettes.
NEGATIVE	The store ~~no~~ sells cigarettes. (does not)

SENTENCE	Jonah talks too much.
NEGATIVE	Jonah not talks too much. (does)

SENTENCE	The teacher assigns homework.
NEGATIVE	The teacher ~~no~~ assigns homework. (does not)

SENTENCE	Bruce will call.
NEGATIVE	Bruce ~~no~~ will call. (not)

SENTENCE	Caroline walked.
NEGATIVE	Caroline ~~no~~ did walk. (not)

Common Helping Verbs

FORMS OF *BE*	FORMS OF *HAVE*	FORMS OF *DO*	OTHER VERBS
am	have	do	can
are	has	does	could
is	had	did	may
been			might
being			must
was			should
were			will
			would

TIP For more on helping verbs and their forms, see Chapter 25.

The helping verb cannot be omitted in expressions using *not*.

INCORRECT	The store *not sell* cigarettes.
CORRECT	The store *does not sell* cigarettes.
	[*Does*, a form of the helping verb *do*, must come before *not*.]
CORRECT	The store *is not selling* cigarettes.
	[*Is*, a form of *be*, must come before *not*.]

Double negatives are not standard in English.

INCORRECT	Bruce *will not call no one*.
CORRECT	Bruce *will not call anyone*.
CORRECT	Bruce *will call no one*.
INCORRECT	Shane *does not have no* ride.
CORRECT	Shane *does not have a* ride.
CORRECT	Shane *has no* ride.

When forming a negative in the simple past tense, use the past tense of the helping verb *do*.

did + *not* + Base verb without an *-ed* = Negative past tense

SENTENCE	I *talked* to Jairo last night.
	[*Talked* is the past tense.]
NEGATIVE	I *did not* talk to Jairo last night.
	[Note that *talk* in this sentence does not have an *-ed* ending because the helping verb *did* conveys that past.]

SENTENCE	Kerry *passed* the test.
NEGATIVE	Kerry *did not* pass the test.

. . . .

PRACTICE 3 Forming Negatives

Rewrite the sentences to make them negative.

EXAMPLE: Hassan's son is *not* talking now.

1. He *cannot* can say several words.
2. Hassan *does not* remembers when his daughter started talking.
3. He *does not* thinks it was at the same age.
4. His daughter was *not* an early speaker.
5. Hassan *does not* expects his son to be a genius.

. . . .

Questions

To turn a statement into a question, move the helping verb so that it comes before the subject. Add a question mark (**?**) to the end of the question.

STATEMENT	Johan *can go* tonight.
QUESTION	*Can* Johan *go* tonight?

If the only verb in the statement is a form of *be*, it should be moved before the subject.

STATEMENT	Jamie *is* at work.
QUESTION	*Is* Jamie at work?

If the statement does not contain a helping verb or a form of *be*, add a form of *do* and put it before the subject. Be sure to end the question with a question mark (**?**).

STATEMENT	Norah sings in the choir.	Tyrone goes to college.
QUESTION	*Does* Norah sing in the choir?	*Does* Tyrone go to college?

STATEMENT	The building burned.	The plate broke.
QUESTION	*Did* the building burn?	*Did* the plate break?

Notice that the verb changed once the helping verb *did* was added.

LANGUAGE NOTE: *Do* is used with *I, you, we,* and *they. Does* is used with *he, she,* and *it.*

EXAMPLES   *Do* [I/you/we/they] practice every day?

Does [he/she/it] sound terrible?

• •

PRACTICE 4   Forming Questions

Rewrite the sentences to make them into questions.

                        Does   ?
EXAMPLE: Brad knows how to cook.

Does he   ?
1. He makes dinner every night for his family.

Does he go   ?
2. He goes to the grocery store once a week.

Does he   ?
3. He uses coupons to save money.

Are there   ?
4. There are lots of coupons available online.

Does   ?
5. Brad saves a lot of money using coupons.

• •

There Is and *There Are*

English sentences often include *there is* or *there are* to indicate the existence of something.

There is a man at the door.   [You could also say, *A man is at the door.*]

There are many men in the class.   [You could also say, *Many men are in the class.*]

When a sentence includes the words *there is* or *there are*, the verb (*is, are*) comes before the noun it goes with (which is actually the subject of the sentence). The verb must agree with the noun in number. For example, the first sentence above uses the singular verb *is* to agree with the singular noun *man*, and the second sentence uses the plural verb *are* to agree with the plural noun *men*.

LANGUAGE NOTE: The *there is/there are* structure does not exist in some other languages, so speakers of those languages sometimes leave out these words when writing in English.

INCORRECT   My mother said much work to do.

Much work to do.

CORRECT   My mother said *there is* much work to do.

There is much work to do.

In questions, the word order in *there is* and *there are* is inverted.

STATEMENTS	*There is* plenty to eat.
	There are some things to do.
QUESTIONS	*Is there* plenty to eat?
	Are there some things to do?

. . . .

PRACTICE 5   Using *There Is* and *There Are*

In each of the following sentences, fill in the blank with *there is* or *there are*. Remember that these words are inverted in questions.

EXAMPLE: Although my parents are busy constantly, they say

_____*there is*_____ always more that can be done.

1. Every morning, _____*there are*_____ flowers to water and weeds to pull.

2. Later in the day, _____*there are*_____ more chores, like mowing the lawn or cleaning out the garage.

3. I always ask, "_____*Is there*_____ anything I can do?"

4. They are too polite to say that _____*there is*_____ work that they need help with.

5. If _____*there are*_____ more productive parents in the world, I would be surprised.

. . . .

Pronouns

Pronouns replace nouns or other pronouns in a sentence so that you do not have to repeat them. There are three types of pronouns:

TIP For more on pronouns, see Chapter 26.

    SUBJECT PRONOUNS serve as the subject of the verb (and remember, every English sentence *must* have a subject).

                            He
Rob is my cousin. ~~Rob~~ lives next to me.

    OBJECT PRONOUNS receive the action of the verb or are part of a prepositional phrase.

    Rob asked *me* for a favor.
    [The object pronoun *me* receives the action of the verb *asked*.]

    Rob lives next door *to me*.
    [*To me* is the prepositional phrase; *me* is the object pronoun.]

POSSESSIVE PRONOUNS show ownership.

<u>Rob</u> <u>is</u> *my* cousin.

Use the following chart to check which type of pronoun to use.

Pronoun Types

SUBJECT		OBJECT		POSSESSIVE	
SINGULAR	**PLURAL**	**SINGULAR**	**PLURAL**	**SINGULAR**	**PLURAL**
I	we	me	us	my/mine	our/ours
you	you	you	you	your/yours	your/yours
he/she/it	they	him/her/it	them	his/her/hers/its	theirs

| **RELATIVE PRONOUNS** |
| who, which, that |

The singular pronouns *he/she, him/her,* and *his/hers* show gender. *He, him,* and *his* are masculine pronouns; *she, her,* and *hers* are feminine.

Here are some examples of common pronoun errors, with corrections.

Confusing Subject and Object Pronouns

Use a subject pronoun for the word that *performs* the action of the verb, and use an object pronoun for the word that *receives* the action.

<u>Tashia</u> <u>is</u> a good student. ~~Her~~ *She* gets all A's.

[The pronoun performs the action *gets*, so it should be the subject pronoun, *she*.]

<u>Tomas</u> <u>gave</u> the keys to ~~she~~ *her*. <u>Banh</u> <u>gave</u> the coat to ~~he~~ *him*.

[The pronoun receives the action of *gave*, so it should be the object pronoun, *her* or *him*.]

Confusing Gender

Use masculine pronouns to replace masculine nouns and feminine pronouns to replace feminine nouns.

<u>Nick</u> <u>is</u> sick. ~~She~~ *He* has the flu.

[*Nick* <u>is</u> a masculine noun, so the pronoun must be masculine.]

The <u>jacket</u> <u>belongs</u> to Jane. <u>Give</u> it to ~~him~~ *her*.

[*Jane* is feminine, so the pronoun must be feminine.]

Leaving Out a Pronoun

Some sentences use the pronoun *it* as the subject or object. Do not leave *it* out of the sentence.

> *It is*
> ~~Is~~ a holiday today.
> ^

> *It will*
> Maria will bring the food. ~~Will~~ be delicious.
> ^

> *it*
> I tried calamari last night and liked ^ very much.

Using a Pronoun to Repeat a Subject

Pronouns *replace* a noun, so do not use both a subject noun and a pronoun.

> My father ~~he~~ is very strict.
> [*Father* is the subject noun, so the sentence should not also have the subject pronoun *he*.]

> The bus ~~it~~ was late.
> [*Bus* is the subject noun, so the sentence should not also have the subject pronoun *it*.]

Using Relative Pronouns

The words *who, which,* and *that* are **relative pronouns**. Use relative pronouns in a clause that gives more information about the subject.

- Use *who* to refer to a person or people.

  The man *who* lives next door plays piano.

- Use *which* to refer to nonliving things.

  The plant, *which* was a gift, died.

- Use *that* to refer to either people or nonliving things. (Note that *who* is the preferred pronoun to refer to a person or people.)

  The phone *that* I bought last week is broken.

  The job *that* I want pays well.

• •

PRACTICE 6 Using Correct Pronouns

Using the chart of pronouns on page 498, fill in the blanks with the correct pronoun. *Answers may vary. Possible answers are shown.*

> **EXAMPLE:** Tennis is popular, for _____*it*_____ is an exciting sport.

1. Since the first time I played tennis, I liked _____*it*_____ very much.

2. _____*My*_____ favorite player is John McEnroe.

3. _____*He*_____ is famous for his bad temper.

4. Even though he is now middle-aged, _____*his*_____ serve is perfect.

5. No matter how much I practice, _____*my*_____ serve will never be as good.

6. McEnroe got a lot of publicity when _____*he*_____ challenged Venus and Serena Williams to a match.

7. _____*They*_____ declined.

8. Venus said she didn't know if she could fit him into _____*her*_____ schedule.

9. Both of the sisters were busy with _____*their*_____ tournament matches.

10. Who is _____*your*_____ favorite tennis player?

• •

Verbs

Verbs have different tenses to show when something happened: in the past, present, or future.

    This section covers some common errors in verb usage and also has full coverage of the progressive tenses. In addition, this section contains timelines, examples, and common errors for the simple and perfect tenses. See Chapter 25 for full coverage of the simple tenses and the perfect tenses, as well as reference charts and practice exercises.

The Simple Tenses

Simple Present

Use the simple present to describe situations that exist now.

I like pizza.

I/You/We/They like pizza.

She/He likes pizza.

The third-person singular (*she/he*) of regular verbs ends in *-s* or *-es*. For irregular verb endings, see pages 385–88.

Simple Past

Use the simple past to describe situations that began and ended in the past.

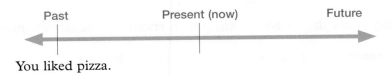

You liked pizza.

I/You/She/He/We/They like**d** pizza.

For regular verbs, the simple past is formed by adding either *-d* or *-ed* to the verb. For the past forms of irregular verbs, see the chart on pages 385–88.

Simple Future

Use the simple future to describe situations that will happen in the future. It is easier to form than the past tense. Use this formula for forming the future tense.

TIP For charts, explanations, and practices on the simple tense, including how to use it to form negatives and questions, see Chapter 25.

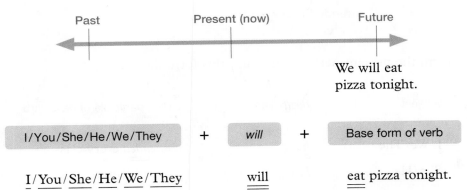

I/You/She/He/We/They   will   eat pizza tonight.

Common Errors in Using Simple Tenses

Following are some common errors in using simple tenses.

Simple Present.   Forgetting to add *-s* or *-es* to verbs that go with third-person singular subjects (*she/he/it*)

TIP The subject and the verb must agree in number. For more on subject-verb agreement, see Chapter 24.

INCORRECT   She know the manager.

CORRECT   She knows the manager.

Simple Past. Forgetting to add *-d* or *-ed* to regular verbs

INCORRECT	Gina work late last night.
CORRECT	Gina work**ed** late last night.

Forgetting to use the correct past form of irregular verbs (see the chart of irregular verb forms on pages 385–88).

INCORRECT	Gerard speaked to her about the problem.
CORRECT	Gerard **spoke** to her about the problem.

Forgetting to use the base verb without an ending for negative sentences

INCORRECT	She does not wants money for helping.
CORRECT	She does not **want** money for helping.

TIP Double negatives (*Johnetta will **not** call **no one***) are not standard in English. One negative is enough (*Johnetta will **not** call **anybody***).

The Perfect Tenses

Present Perfect

TIP For charts, explanations, and practices on the perfect tense, including how to use it to form negatives and questions, see Chapter 25.

Use the present perfect to describe situations that started in the past and are still happening.

To form the present perfect tense, use this formula:

Subject	+	has/have	+	Past participle of base verb
I/We/They		*have*		*attended* every class.
She/He		*has*		*attended* every class.

Note that *I/We/They* use *have*, and *she/he* use *has*.

Past Perfect

Use the past perfect to describe situations that began and ended before some other situation happened.

To form the past perfect tense, use this formula:

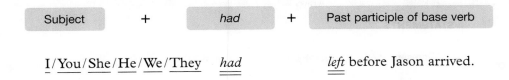

I/You/She/He/We/They *had* *left* before Jason arrived.

Future Perfect

Use the future perfect to describe situations that begin and end before another situation begins.

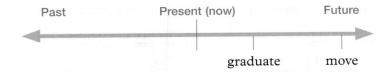

Use this formula to form the future perfect tense:

I/You/She/He/We/They *will have* *graduated* before moving.

Common Errors in Forming the Perfect Tense

Using *had* instead of *has* or *have* for the present perfect

INCORRECT	We **had** lived here since 2003.
CORRECT	We **have** lived here since 2003.

Forgetting to use past participles (with *-d* or *-ed* endings for regular verbs)

INCORRECT	She has attend every class.
CORRECT	She has attend**ed** every class.

Using *been* between *have* or *has* and the past participle of a base verb

INCORRECT	I have **been** attended every class.
CORRECT	I have attended every class.
INCORRECT	I will have **been** graduated before I move.
CORRECT	I will have graduated before I move.

TIP For more on the perfect tense, see Chapter 25. For a list of irregular verbs and their forms, see pages 385–88.

THE PROGRESSIVE TENSES

TENSE

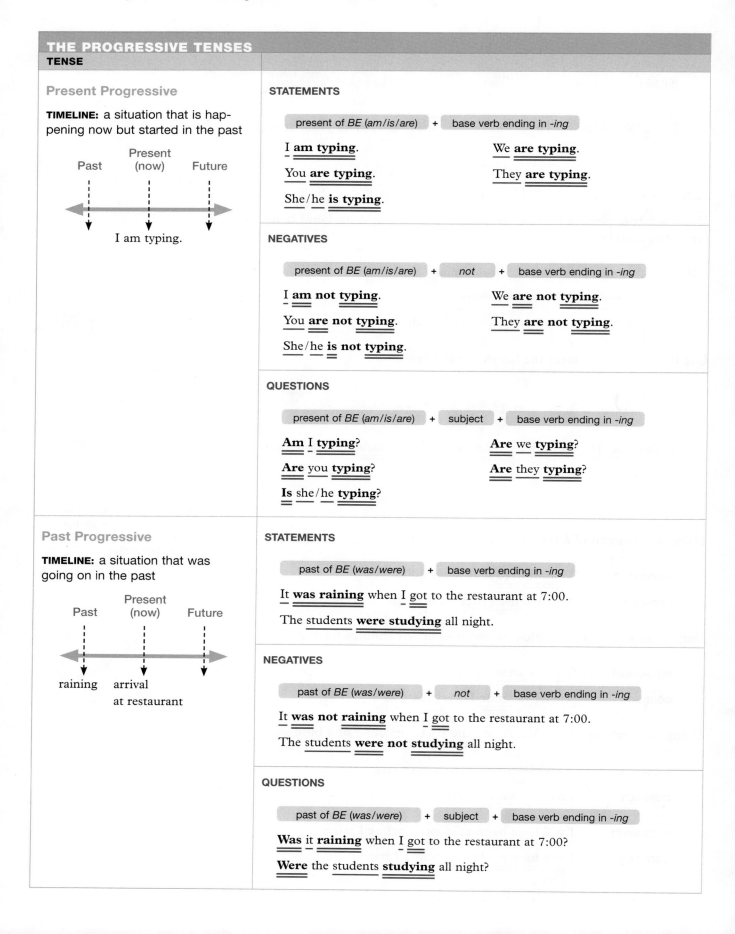

Present Progressive

TIMELINE: a situation that is happening now but started in the past

Past   Present   Future
         (now)

I am typing.

STATEMENTS

present of *BE* (*am/is/are*) + base verb ending in -*ing*

I **am typing**.   We **are typing**.

You **are typing**.   They **are typing**.

She/he **is typing**.

NEGATIVES

present of *BE* (*am/is/are*) + *not* + base verb ending in -*ing*

I **am not typing**.   We **are not typing**.

You **are not typing**.   They **are not typing**.

She/he **is not typing**.

QUESTIONS

present of *BE* (*am/is/are*) + subject + base verb ending in -*ing*

Am I **typing**?   **Are** we **typing**?

Are you **typing**?   **Are** they **typing**?

Is she/he **typing**?

Past Progressive

TIMELINE: a situation that was going on in the past

Past   Present   Future
         (now)

raining   arrival
          at restaurant

STATEMENTS

past of *BE* (*was/were*) + base verb ending in -*ing*

It **was raining** when I got to the restaurant at 7:00.

The students **were studying** all night.

NEGATIVES

past of *BE* (*was/were*) + *not* + base verb ending in -*ing*

It **was not raining** when I got to the restaurant at 7:00.

The students **were not studying** all night.

QUESTIONS

past of *BE* (*was/were*) + subject + base verb ending in -*ing*

Was it **raining** when I got to the restaurant at 7:00?

Were the students **studying** all night?

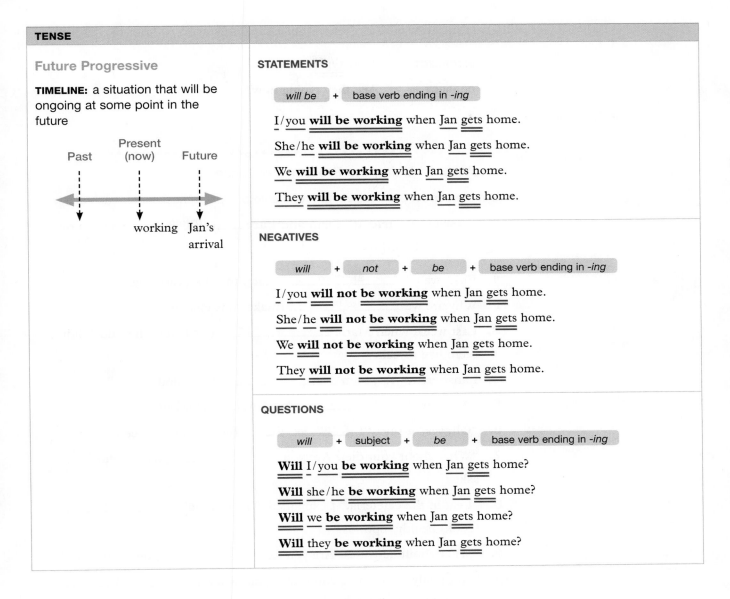

TENSE	
Future Progressive	**STATEMENTS**

Future Progressive

TIMELINE: a situation that will be ongoing at some point in the future

Past — Present (now) — Future

working — Jan's arrival

STATEMENTS

will be + base verb ending in *-ing*

I/you **will be working** when Jan gets home.

She/he **will be working** when Jan gets home.

We **will be working** when Jan gets home.

They **will be working** when Jan gets home.

NEGATIVES

will + *not* + *be* + base verb ending in *-ing*

I/you **will not be working** when Jan gets home.

She/he **will not be working** when Jan gets home.

We **will not be working** when Jan gets home.

They **will not be working** when Jan gets home.

QUESTIONS

will + subject + *be* + base verb ending in *-ing*

Will I/you **be working** when Jan gets home?

Will she/he **be working** when Jan gets home?

Will we **be working** when Jan gets home?

Will they **be working** when Jan gets home?

Common Errors in Forming the Present Progressive Tense

Forgetting to add *-ing* to the verb:

INCORRECT	I am type now.
	She/he is not type now.
CORRECT	I am typ**ing** now.
	She/he is not typ**ing** now.

Forgetting to include a form of *be* (*am/is/are*):

INCORRECT	He typing now.
	They typing now.
CORRECT	He **is** typing now.
	They **are** typing now.

Forgetting to use a form of *be* (*am/is/are*) to start questions:

INCORRECT	They <u>typing</u> now?
CORRECT	**<u>Are</u>** they <u>typing</u> now?

- -

PRACTICE 7   Using the Progressive Tense

Fill in the correct progressive form of the verb in parentheses after each blank.

> **EXAMPLE:** My friend Maria and I are _____*trying*_____ (try) to be healthier.

1. First, we are _____*starting*_____ (start) to walk every day.

2. Why are we _____*making*_____ (make) this change?

3. Last week, when Maria _____*was visiting*_____ (visit) me, she said I didn't seem like myself.

4. I answered, "Yes, I am _____*feeling*_____ (feel) kind of sad."

5. "Are you _____*sleeping*_____ (sleep) well?" she asked.

6. "Oh, yes," I said. "I _____*am getting*_____ (get) plenty of sleep."

7. "What about your diet? Are you _____*eating*_____ (eat) right?" she asked.

8. "I eat in the cafeteria," I explained. "They are always _____*cooking*_____ (cook) healthy options."

9. "What about activities? Are you _____*exercising*_____ (exercise) at all?"

10. "Not really, unless you count my brain while I am _____*studying*_____ (study)!" I admitted.

- -

PRACTICE 8   Forming Negative Statements and Questions

Rewrite the following sentences as indicated.

1. Betsy is golfing today. *Make the sentence a question:* Is Betsy golfing today?

2. It was snowing when we got up. *Make the sentence a negative statement:* It was not snowing when we got up.

3. You are going to the mall. *Make the sentence a question:* Are you going to the mall?

4. They are losing the game. *Make the sentence a negative statement:*

They are not losing the game.

5. Meriam was eating when you arrived. *Make the sentence into a question:*

Was Meriam eating when you arrived?

· ·

Modal (Helping) Verbs

Modal verbs are helping verbs that express the writer's attitude about an action. You do not have to learn too many modal verbs—just the eight in the chart that follows.

TIP For more on helping verbs, see Chapter 21.

MODAL (HELPING) VERBS		
GENERAL FORMULAS For all modal verbs. (More modal verbs shown below.)	**STATEMENTS** **Present:** subject + modal verb + base verb Dumbo can fly. **Past:** Forms vary—see below.	
	NEGATIVES **Present:** subject + modal verb + *not* + base verb Dumbo cannot fly. **Past:** Forms vary—see below.	
	QUESTIONS **Present:** modal verb + subject + base verb Can Dumbo fly? **Past:** Forms vary—see below.	
CAN Means *ability*	**STATEMENTS** **Present:** Beth **can** work fast. **Past:** Beth **could** work fast.	
	NEGATIVES **Present:** Beth **can**not work fast. **Past:** Beth **could** not work fast.	
	QUESTIONS **Present: Can** Beth work fast? **Past: Could** Beth work fast?	

(continued)

MODAL (HELPING) VERBS

COULD

Means *possibility*. It can also be the past tense of *can*.

STATEMENTS

Present: Beth **could** work fast if she had more time.

Past: Beth **could** have worked fast if she had had more time.

NEGATIVES

Can is used for present negatives. (See above.)

Past: Beth **could** not have worked fast.

QUESTIONS

Present: Could Beth work fast?

Past: Could Beth have worked fast?

MAY

Means *permission*

For past-tense forms, see *might*.

STATEMENTS

Present: You **may** borrow my car.

NEGATIVES

Present: You **may** not borrow my car.

QUESTIONS

Present: May I borrow your car?

MIGHT

Means *possibility*. It can also be the past tense of *may*.

STATEMENTS

Present (with *be*): Lou **might** be asleep.

Past (with *have* + past participle of *be*): Lou **might** have been asleep.

Future: Lou **might** sleep.

NEGATIVES

Present (with *be*): Lou **might** not be asleep.

Past (with *have* + past participle of *be*): Lou **might** not have been asleep.

Future: Lou **might** not sleep.

QUESTIONS

Might in questions is very formal and not often used.

MODAL (HELPING) VERBS

MUST Means *necessary*	**STATEMENTS** **Present:** We **must** try. **Past** (with *have* + past participle of base verb): We **must** have tried. **Past** (with *had* + *to* + base verb): We **had to** try.
	NEGATIVES **Present:** We **must** not try. **Past** (with *have* + past participle of base verb): We **must** not have tried.
	QUESTIONS **Present:** **Must** we try? Past-tense questions with *must* are unusual.
SHOULD Means *duty* or *expectation*	**STATEMENTS** **Present:** They **should** call. **Past** (with *have* + past participle of base verb): They **should** have called.
	NEGATIVES **Present:** They **should** not call. **Past** (with *have* + past participle of base verb): They **should** not have called.
	QUESTIONS **Present:** **Should** they call? **Past** (with *have* + past participle of base verb): **Should** they have called?
WILL Means *intend to* (future) For past-tense forms, see *might*.	**STATEMENTS** **Future:** I **will** succeed.
	NEGATIVES **Future:** I **will** not succeed.
	QUESTIONS **Future:** **Will** I succeed?

(continued)

MODAL (HELPING) VERBS

WOULD	
Means *prefer* or used to start a future request. It can also be the past tense of *will*.	**STATEMENTS** **Present:** I **would** like to travel. **Past** (with *have* + past participle of base verb): I **would** have traveled if I had had the money.
	NEGATIVES **Present:** I **would** not like to travel. **Past** (with *have* + past participle of base verb): I **would** not have traveled if it had not been for you.
	QUESTIONS **Present:** **Would** you like to travel? *Or* to start a request: **Would** you help me? **Past** (with *have* + past participle of base verb): **Would** you have traveled with me if I had asked you?

Common Errors with Modal Verbs

Following are some common errors in using modal verbs.

Using more than one helping verb:

INCORRECT	They **will can** help.
CORRECT	They **will** help. (future intention)
	They **can** help. (are able to)

Using *to* between the modal verb and the main (base) verb:

INCORRECT	Emilio **might to** come with us.
CORRECT	Emilio **might** come with us.

Using *must* instead of *had to* in the past:

INCORRECT	She **must** work yesterday.
CORRECT	She **had to** work yesterday.

Forgetting to change *can* to *could* in the past negative:

INCORRECT	Last night, I **can**not sleep.
CORRECT	Last night, I **could** not sleep.

Forgetting to use *have* with *could/should/would* in the past tense:

> **INCORRECT** Tara **should** <u>called</u> last night.
>
> **CORRECT** Tara **should have** <u>called</u> last night.

Using *will* instead of *would* to express a preference in the present tense:

> **INCORRECT** <u>I</u> **will** like to travel.
>
> **CORRECT** <u>I</u> **would** like to travel.

PRACTICE 9 Using Modal Verbs

Fill in the appropriate modal verbs in the sentences below. *Answers may vary. Possible answers are shown.*

> **EXAMPLE:** Lilly _____*would*_____ like to help the homeless.

1. What _____*should*_____ she do?

2. First, she _____*can*_____ find out what programs exist in her community.

3. For example, there _____*might*_____ be a chapter of Habitat for Humanity.

4. Religious organizations _____*might*_____ have started soup kitchens.

5. If she _____*cannot*_____ find anything in her community, she should contact a national organization, such as the National Coalition for the Homeless.

6. The organization _____*could*_____ definitely give her some ideas.

7. Also, she _____*should not*_____ feel as though she must do this alone.

8. Surely, there are other people who _____*will*_____ want to help.

9. How _____*can*_____ she get them involved?

10. She _____*must*_____ spread the word, perhaps through e-mail.

PRACTICE 10 Forming Negative Statements and Questions

Rewrite the following sentences as indicated.

1. You can help me. *Make the sentence a question:* <u>Can you help me?</u>

2. We might take the train to New York. *Make the sentence a negative statement:* <u>We might not take the train to New York.</u>

3. They should learn how to cook. *Make the sentence a question:* <u>Should they learn how to cook?</u>

4. They could take care of the dog. *Make the sentence a negative statement:*
   They could not take care of the dog.

5. Terrell would like to join us. *Make the sentence a question:* Would Terrell
   like to join us?

• •

PRACTICE 11 Using the Correct Tense

Fill in the blanks with the correct form of the verbs in parentheses, adding helping
verbs as needed. Refer to the verb charts if you need help. *Answers may vary.*
Possible answers are shown.

   EXAMPLE: Many critics __have argued__ **(argue) that** *Citizen Kane,*
   directed by Orson Welles, is the greatest movie ever made.

1. __Have__ you __seen__ (see) it?

2. If not, you __should rent__ (rent) it right away!

3. You might not want to watch a movie from 1941, but *Citizen Kane*
   __will convince__ (convince) you to give older films a chance.

4. The story __begins__ (begin) with the death of Charles Foster
   Kane, who was once a powerful man.

5. By the time of his death, Kane __had lost__ (lose) much of his
   power.

6. When he __died__ (die), he was alone in his mansion.

7. Charles's parents were poor, but he __inherited__ (inherit) a lot of
   money as a child.

8. His mother __sent__ (send) him east to live with a guardian,
   who was put in charge of the boy's fortune.

9. Kane __would__ not __have__ (have) access to the
   money until his twenty-fifth birthday.

10. Kane's fortune __did__ (do) not __consist__ (consist)
   only of money.

11. He also inherited a failing newspaper, *The Inquirer*, and __turned__
   (turn) it into a success.

12. In the beginning, his marriage was also a success, but his wife divorced
   him when she discovered he __was having__ (have) an affair.

13. At the time of the discovery, Kane __was running__ (run) for governor.

14. Because of the scandal, he __lost__ (lose) the election.

15. Kane married his mistress, but he __was__ (be) overly controlling with her.

16. She was so unhappy, she _____*tried*_____ (try) to commit suicide.

17. Her suicide attempt showed that he _*should have been*_ (be) kinder to her.

18. Eventually, his second wife _____*left*_____ (leave) him, too.

19. Kane's last word was "Rosebud." What _____*could*_____ (can) he ____*have meant*____ (mean) by that?

20. You ____*must watch*____ (watch) the movie to find out.

• •

PRACTICE 12   Using the Correct Tense

Fill in the blanks with the correct form of the verbs in parentheses, adding helping verbs as needed. Refer to the verb charts if you need help.

> EXAMPLE: _____*Have*_____ you _____*heard*_____ (hear) of snowboarding?

(1) Snowboarding is like skiing, except snowboarders _____*strap*_____ (strap) a single fiberglass board, instead of skis, onto their feet. (2) It is a winter sport because snowboarders, like skiers, ____*must wait*____ (wait) for snow. (3) In a November 5, 2002, article in *National Geographic Today*, Zoltan Istvan _____*reported*_____ (report) on a new sport: volcano boarding. (4) Volcano boarders _____*do*_____ not _____*need*_____ (need) to wait for snow. (5) If you ____*are looking*____ (look) for adventure, an active volcano will never disappoint you.

(6) Istvan first _____*got*_____ (get) the idea in 1995, when he ____*was sailing*____ (sail) past Mt. Yasur, an active volcano on an island off the coast of Australia. (7) For centuries, Mt. Yasur _____*has had*_____ (have) the reputation of being a dangerous volcano. (8) For example, it regularly _____*spits*_____ (spit) out lava bombs. (9) These large molten rocks _____*have*_____ often _____*struck*_____ (strike) visitors on the head. (10) _____*Can*_____ you _____*imagine*_____ (imagine) how much that ____*would hurt*____ (hurt)?

(11) There is a village at the base of Mt. Yasur. (12) When Istvan arrived with his snowboard, the villagers _____*did*_____ not _____*know*_____ (know) what to think. (13) He _____*made*_____ (make) his way to the volcano, _____*hiked*_____ (hike) up the highest peak, and rode his board all the way down. (14) After he _____*reached*_____ (reach) the bottom, Istvan admitted that volcano boarding is more difficult than snowboarding. (15) Luckily, no lava

bombs _____*fell*_____ (fall) from the sky, though the volcano
___*had erupted*___ (erupt) seconds before his descent. (16) Istvan hopes
this new sport ___*will become*___ (become) popular with snowboarders
around the world.

· ·

Gerunds and Infinitives

A **gerund** is a verb form that ends in *-ing* and acts as a noun. An **infinitive**
is a verb form that is preceded by the word *to*. Gerunds and infinitives cannot be the main verbs in sentences; each sentence must have another word
that is the main verb.

GERUND	<u>Mike</u> <u>loves</u> **swimming**.
	[*Loves* is the main verb, and *swimming* is a gerund.]
INFINITIVE	<u>Mike</u> <u>loves</u> **to run**.
	[*Loves* is the main verb, and *to run* is an infinitive.]

How do you decide whether to use a gerund or an infinitive? The decision often depends on the main verb in a sentence. Some verbs can be followed by either a gerund or an infinitive.

Verbs That Can Be Followed by Either a Gerund or an Infinitive

begin	hate	remember	try
continue	like	start	
forget	love	stop	

TIP To improve your ability to
write and speak standard
English, read magazines and
your local newspaper, and listen
to television and radio news
programs. Also, read magazines
and newspaper articles aloud;
this will help your pronunciation.

Sometimes, using a gerund or an infinitive after one of these verbs results in the same meaning.

GERUND	<u>Joan</u> <u>likes</u> **playing** the piano.
INFINITIVE	<u>Joan</u> <u>likes</u> **to play** the piano.

Other times, however, the meaning changes depending on whether you
use a gerund or an infinitive.

INFINITIVE	<u>Carla</u> <u>stopped</u> **helping** me.
	[This means that Carla no longer helps me.]

TIP For other problems with
verbs, see Chapter 25.

GERUND	<u>Carla</u> <u>stopped</u> **to help** me.
	[This means that Carla stopped what she was doing and helped me.]

Verbs That Are Followed by a Gerund

admit	discuss	keep	risk
avoid	enjoy	miss	suggest
consider	finish	practice	
deny	imagine	quit	

The politician risked **losing** her supporters.
Sophia considered **quitting** her job.

Verbs That Are Followed by an Infinitive

agree	decide	need	refuse
ask	expect	offer	want
beg	fail	plan	
choose	hope	pretend	
claim	manage	promise	

Aunt Sally wants **to help**.
Cal hopes **to become** a millionaire.

Do not use the base form of the verb when you need a gerund or an infinitive.

INCORRECT, BASE VERB	*Swim* is my favorite activity.
	[*Swim* is the base form of the verb, not a noun; it cannot be the subject of the sentence.]
CORRECT, GERUND	*Swimming* is my favorite activity.
	[*Swimming* is a gerund that can be the subject of the sentence.]
INCORRECT, BASE VERB	*Play* soccer is fun.
CORRECT, GERUND	*Playing* soccer is fun.
INCORRECT, BASE VERB	My goal is *graduate* from college.
CORRECT, GERUND	My goal is *graduating* from college.
CORRECT, INFINITIVE	My goal is *to graduate* from college.
INCORRECT, BASE VERB	I need *stop* at the store.
	[*Need* is the verb, so there cannot be another verb that shows the action of the subject, *I*.]
CORRECT, INFINITIVE	I need *to stop* at the store.

· ·

PRACTICE 13   Using Gerunds and Infinitives

Read the paragraphs, and fill in the blanks with either a gerund or an infinitive as appropriate. *Answers may vary. Possible answers are shown.*

EXAMPLE: If you want _____*to be*_____ (be) an actor, be aware that the profession is not all fun and glamour.

(1) When you were a child, did you pretend _____*to be*_____ (be) famous people? (2) Did you imagine _____*playing*_____ (play) roles in movies or on television? (3) Do you like _____*to take*_____ (take) part in plays? (4) If so, you might want _____*to make*_____ (make) a career out of acting.

(5) Be aware of some drawbacks, however. (6) If you hate _____*working*_____ (work) with others, acting may not be the career for you. (7) Also, if you do not enjoy _____*repeating*_____ (repeat) the same lines over and over, you will find acting dull. (8) You must practice _____*speaking*_____ (speak) lines to memorize them. (9) Despite these drawbacks, you will gain nothing if you refuse _____*to try*_____ (try). (10) Anyone who hopes _____*to become*_____ (become) an actor has a chance at succeeding through hard work and determination.

· ·

Articles

Articles announce a noun. English uses only three articles—*a, an,* and *the*—and the same articles are used for both masculine and feminine nouns.

> **LANGUAGE NOTE:** Articles (*a, an, the*) are not used in Russian or in many Asian languages. If you are not sure when to use an article or which one to use, pay close attention to this section.

Definite and Indefinite Articles

The is a **definite article** and is used before a specific person, place, or thing. *A* and *an* are **indefinite articles** and are used with a person, place, or thing whose specific identity is not known.

DEFINITE ARTICLE	*The* car crashed into the building. [A specific car crashed into the building.]
INDEFINITE ARTICLE	*A* car crashed into the building. [Some car, we don't know which one exactly, crashed into the building.]

DEFINITE ARTICLE	*The* band was loud.
	[A specific band was loud.]
INDEFINITE ARTICLE	*A* band was loud.
	[Some band was loud.]

When the word following the article begins with a vowel (*a, e, i, o, u*), use *an* instead of *a*.

An **o**ld car crashed into the building.

To use the correct article, you need to know what count and noncount nouns are.

Count and Noncount Nouns

Count nouns name things that can be counted, and they can be made plural, usually by adding *-s* or *-es*. **Noncount nouns** name things that cannot be counted, and they are usually singular. They cannot be made plural.

COUNT NOUN/SINGLE	I got a **ticket** for the concert.
COUNT NOUN/PLURAL	I got two **tickets** for the concert.
NONCOUNT NOUN	The Internet has all kinds of **information**.
	[You would not say, *The Internet has all kinds of information**s**.*]

Here is a brief list of several count and noncount nouns. In English, all nouns are either count or noncount.

COUNT	NONCOUNT	
apple/apples	beauty	money
chair/chairs	flour	postage
dollar/dollars	furniture	poverty
letter/letters	grass	rain
smile/smiles	grief	rice
tree/trees	happiness	salt
	health	sand
	homework	spaghetti
	honey	sunlight
	information	thunder
	jewelry	wealth
	mail	
	milk	

Use the chart that follows to determine when to use *a, **an**, **the***, or no article.

Articles with Count and Noncount Nouns

COUNT NOUNS		ARTICLE USED
SINGULAR		
Specific	→	*the*
		I want to read **the book** on taxes that you recommended.
		[The sentence refers to one particular book: the one that was recommended.]
		I cannot stay in **the sun** very long.
		[There is only one sun.]
Not specific	→	*a* or *an*
		I want to read **a** book on taxes.
		[It could be any book on taxes.]
PLURAL		
Specific	→	*the*
		I enjoyed **the books** we read.
		[The sentence refers to a particular group of books: the ones we read.]
Not specific	→	**no article or** *some*
		I usually enjoy **books**.
		[The sentence refers to books in general.]
		She found **some books**.
		[I do not know which books she found.]

NONCOUNT NOUNS		ARTICLE USED
SINGULAR		
Specific	→	*the*
		I put away **the food** we bought.
		[The sentence refers to particular food: the food we bought.]
Not specific	→	**no article or** *some*
		There is **food** all over the kitchen.
		[The reader does not know what food the sentence refers to.]
		Give **some food** to the neighbors.
		[The sentence refers to an indefinite quantity of food.]

• •

PRACTICE 14   **Using Articles Correctly**

Fill in the correct article (*a*, *an*, or *the*) in each of the following sentences. If no
article is needed, write "no article."

> **EXAMPLE:** I cannot go out tonight because I have _____*a*_____
>
> ton of homework.

1. _____*The*_____ school I attend is the best in the region.

2. The professors expect you to do a lot of _____*no article*_____ homework
   every night.

3. I do not mind because I have always enjoyed reading _____*no article*_____
   books.

4. The school also has _____*an*_____ excellent reputation for sports.

5. For example, our football team has ranked in _____*the*_____ top ten
   of our conference for forty years straight.

6. Three years ago, we won _____*the*_____ conference championship,
   but we have not been able to win it again.

7. It is exciting to go to _____*a*_____ football game during a winning
   season.

8. _____*The*_____ view from the stadium is nice, too. You can see all the
   way to the mountains.

9. When I first arrived, I made _____*no article*_____ friends quickly.

10. I will always remember _____*the*_____ good times I had here.

TEACHING TIP Have students,
in small groups, create two separate lists: one of count nouns
and the other of noncount
nouns. Then, ask students to
write two brief stories, each
using all the words from one
of the lists.

• •

PRACTICE 15   **Using Articles Correctly**

Edit the following paragraphs, adding, revising, or deleting articles as necessary.

>   *a*
> **EXAMPLE:** Jhumpa Lahiri is ~~the~~ fine writer.

                                  the
    (1) Have you ever heard of ~~an~~ author Jhumpa Lahiri? (2) Before
    the
she won ^ 2000 Pulitzer Prize for her short story collection, *Interpreter of
Maladies*, she was unknown. (3) However, *Interpreter of Maladies* has
                                                             a
been translated into twenty-nine different languages and became ~~the~~
bestseller around the world.

    (4) Lahiri was born in ~~the~~ England and raised in ~~the~~ Rhode Island,
but her parents were from ~~the~~ Calcutta, India, and held onto many traditions from the old country. (5) Although Lahiri visited India many times,

she felt removed from ^*the* country's culture as a child. (6) On the other hand, Lahiri admitted that while growing up in America, she felt that ~~an~~ ^*the* "Indian part" of her was "unacknowledged." (7) She identified neither as ~~the~~ ^*an* American nor as ~~the~~ ^*an* Indian. (8) She had to create ^*a* cultural identity for herself.

. . . .

Prepositions

A **preposition** is a word (such as *of, above, between, about*) that connects a noun, pronoun, or verb with other information about it. The correct preposition to use is often determined by idiom or common practice rather than by the preposition's actual meaning.

An **idiom** is any combination of words that is always used the same way, even though there is no logical or grammatical explanation for it. The best way to learn English idioms is to listen and read as much as possible and then to practice writing and speaking the correct forms.

Prepositions after Adjectives

TIP For more on prepositions, see Chapter 21.

Adjectives are often followed by prepositions. Here are some common examples.

afraid of	full of	scared of
ashamed of	happy about	sorry about/sorry for
aware of	interested in	tired of
confused by	proud of	
excited about	responsible for	

Peri is afraid ~~to~~ ^*of* walking alone.

We are happy ~~of~~ ^*about* Dino's promotion.

Prepositions after Verbs

Many verbs consist of a verb plus a preposition (or adverb). The meaning of these combinations is not usually the meaning the verb and the preposition would each have on its own. Often, the meaning of the verb changes completely depending on which preposition is used with it.

You must **take out** the trash. [*take out* = bring to a different location]

You must **take in** the exciting sights of New York City. [*take in* = observe]

Here are a few common examples.

call in (telephone)	You can *call in* your order.
call off (cancel)	They *called off* the party.
call on (ask for a response)	The teacher always *calls on* me.
drop in (visit)	*Drop in* the next time you are around.
drop off (leave behind)	Juan will *drop off* the car for service.
drop out (quit)	Many students *drop out* of school.
fight against (combat)	He tried to *fight against* the proposal.
fight for (defend)	We will *fight for* our rights.
fill out (complete)	Please *fill out* the form.
fill up (make full)	Do not *fill up* with junk food.
find out (discover)	Did you *find out* the answer?
give up (forfeit)	Do not *give up* your chance to succeed.
go by (visit, pass by)	I may *go by* the store on my way home.
go over (review)	Please *go over* your notes before the test.
grow up (mature)	All children *grow up*.
hand in (submit)	Please *hand in* your homework.
lock up (secure)	*Lock up* the apartment before leaving.
look up (check)	*Look up* the meaning in the dictionary.
pick out (choose)	*Pick out* a good apple.
pick up (take or collect)	Please *pick up* some drinks.
put off (postpone)	Do not *put off* starting your paper.
sign in (register)	*Sign in* when you arrive.
sign out (borrow)	You can *sign out* a book from the library.
sign up (register for)	I want to *sign up* for the contest.
think about (consider)	Simon *thinks about* moving.
turn in (submit)	Please *turn in* your homework.

• •

PRACTICE 16   Editing Prepositions

Edit the following sentences to make sure that the correct prepositions are used. Some sentences are correct; put "C" next to them.

   EXAMPLE: My instructor, Mr. Johnson, always calls ~~out~~ me.
                                                              on

1. Of course, my classmates are aware ~~at~~ this trend.
                                         of

2. I am so tired ~~with~~ them teasing me.
                    of

3. I wish they would grow up, and I have told them that. *C*

4. One day, I dropped ~~over~~ *in* at Mr. Johnson's office when he was about to leave.

5. "Hello, Seth!" he said. "Did you forget to hand ~~up~~ *in* your research paper in class?"

6. "No," I said, "I just want to say that your calling on me so much makes me a bit uncomfortable." *C*

7. "Oh," said Mr. Johnson thoughtfully. "I'm sorry ~~of~~ *about* that."

8. "Maybe you could start asking more of the other students to participate," I suggested. "I would certainly be happy ~~of~~ *about* that."

9. "Sure," said Mr. Johnson. "It will make them more responsible ~~on~~ *for* their homework, anyway."

10. "Thanks for your time," I said. "I'll go and let you lock ~~out~~ *up* now."

· ·

PRACTICE 17 **Editing Prepositions**

Edit the following paragraphs to make sure that the correct prepositions are used.

> **EXAMPLE:** Lucy is excited ~~for~~ *about* the coming weekend.

(1) She is almost finished with her English paper and will hand it ~~to~~ *in* on Friday. (2) She has been working hard on the paper and has begun to grow tired ~~with~~ *of* it. (3) At one point last week, she was so frustrated that she almost gave up. (4) Now, however, she is glad she fought ~~through~~ *against* that urge. (5) She forced herself to go ~~at~~ *over* the paper, and it is much better.

(6) As for this weekend, Lucy has a million things she wants to do. (7) Her friend Sylvie asked her to drop ~~over~~ *in* Friday night for a visit. (8) Saturday morning, she plans to sign ~~on~~ *up* for a gym membership. (9) Also, she might go ~~in~~ to the theater to see a movie. (10) Lucy was going to attend an event in the park on Sunday, but it has been called ~~out~~ *off*.

(11) Lucy is proud ~~with~~ *of* herself for finishing her paper. (12) She deserves a little rest and relaxation.

· ·

Chapter Review

1. What is a pronoun? *a word that replaces a noun or another pronoun*

What are the three types of English pronouns? *subject, object, possessive*

Use each of the types in a sentence. *Answers will vary.*

_____

_____

_____

What are five common pronouns? *Answers will vary.*

LEARNING JOURNAL Did you find errors in your writing? Record the type of errors in your learning journal, and review them before you edit your own writing.

2. Rewrite this sentence in the simple past and the simple future.

Melinda picks flowers every morning.

Past: *Melinda picked flowers yesterday. (or another past time)*

Future: *Melinda will pick flowers tomorrow. (or another future time)*

3. Rewrite this sentence so that it uses the perfect tense correctly.

They have call an ambulance. *They have called an ambulance.*

4. Using the progressive tenses, first rewrite this sentence as a question. Then rewrite the question in the past tense and in the future tense.

Chris is learning Spanish.

Question: *Is Chris learning Spanish?*

Past: *Was Chris learning Spanish?*

Future: *Will Chris be learning Spanish?*

5. Rewrite these sentences so that they use the modal verb correctly.

Jennifer should to help her mother. *Jennifer should help her mother.*

Yesterday, I cannot work. *Yesterday, I could not work.*

6. What is a gerund? *a verb form that ends in "-ing" and acts as a noun*

Write a sentence with a gerund in it. *Answers will vary.*

_____

7. What is an infinitive? *a verb form that is preceded by the word "to"*

Write a sentence with an infinitive in it. *Answers will vary.*

_____

8. Give an example of a count noun. _Answers will vary._ Give an example of a noncount noun. _Answers will vary._ Use each of the nouns in a sentence, using the correct article. _____

_____

_____

9. What is a preposition? _a word that connects a noun, pronoun, or verb with other information about it_

Write a sentence using a preposition. _Answers will vary._

_____

Chapter Test

TIP For advice on taking tests, see Appendix A.

RESOURCES The *Testing Tool Kit* CD-ROM available with this book has even more tests.

Circle the correct choice for each of the following items.

1. Choose the correct word(s) to fill in the blank.

You need _____ me if you have a problem.

   a. telling   **(b.)** to tell   **c.** told

2. Choose the sentence that has no errors.
   a. I have been written to my congressman three times, but I have never heard back from him.
   b. I have been writing to my congressman three times, but I have never heard back from him.
   (c.) I have written to my congressman three times, but I have never heard back from him.

3. Choose the sentence that has no errors.
   (a.) I walked five miles yesterday.
   b. I walk five miles yesterday.
   c. I walking five miles yesterday.

4. Choose the correct word to fill in the blank.

In January, they _____ to vacation in Florida.

   a. going   **b.** is going   **(c.)** are going

5. If an underlined portion of this sentence is incorrect, select the revision that fixes it. If the sentence is correct as written, choose d.

Pasquale <u>might to</u> get a job <u>at</u> his father's <u>construction</u> business.
                   A   B   C

a. might   **c.** constructing

b. on   **d.** No change is necessary.

6. Choose the correct word to fill in the blank.

Elena tells the funniest jokes. _____ always makes me laugh.

a. Her   **b.** Him   **c.** She

7. Choose the sentence that is in the correct order.

a. One pound of chocolate I ate last week.

b. I ate one pound of chocolate last week.

c. Chocolate one pound I ate last week.

8. If an underlined portion of this sentence is incorrect, select the revision that fixes it. If the sentence is correct as written, choose d.

<u>The</u> <u>healths</u> of our employees <u>is</u> very important.
 A   B   C

a. A   **c.** were

b. health   **d.** No change is necessary.

9. Choose the sentence that has no errors.

a. Was it snowing when you got to the mountain?

b. Snowing it was when you got to the mountain?

c. When you got to the mountain, snowing it was?

10. Choose the correct word to fill in the blank.

Because it rained, we called _____ the picnic.

a. on   **b.** in   **c.** off

EDITING

Part 6

Word Use

THIS CHAPTER

- explains two resources for finding words and their meanings
- explains and gives you practice avoiding four kinds of common word-choice problems

34

Word Choice

Using the Right Words

Understand the Importance of Choosing Words Carefully

In conversation, you show much of your meaning through facial expression, tone of voice, and gestures. In writing, you have only the words on the page to make your point, so you must choose them carefully. If you use vague or inappropriate words, your readers may not understand you. Carefully chosen words tell your readers exactly what you mean.

Two resources will help you find the best words for your meaning: a dictionary and a thesaurus.

TIP For fun podcasts with tips on grammar and usage, check out Grammar Girl's Quick and Dirty Tips for Better Writing on **bedfordstmartins.com/ realwriting.**

RESOURCES *Additional Resources* contains tests and supplemental practice exercises for this chapter.

Dictionary

You need a dictionary. A good paperback dictionary does not cost much, and a number of good dictionaries are now available free online. Dictionaries give you all kinds of useful information about words: spelling, division of words into syllables, pronunciation, parts of speech, other forms of words, definitions, and examples of use. Following is a sample dictionary entry.

Spelling and end-of-line division   Pronunciation   Parts of speech   Other forms

con • crete (kon´krēt, kong´-, kon-krēt´), *adj.*, *n.*, *v.* **-cret • ed,** —— Definition
-cret • ing, *adj.* **1.** constituting an actual thing or instance; real; per- —— Example
ceptible; substantial: *concrete proof.* **2.** pertaining to or concerned with

ESL ESL students may want to use a dictionary written especially for nonnative speakers (such as the *Longman Dictionary of American English*) in addition to a standard English dictionary.

realities or actual instances rather than abstractions; particular as opposed to general: *concrete proposals.* **3.** referring to an actual substance or thing, as opposed to an abstract quality: The words *cat*, *water*, and *teacher* are concrete, whereas the words *truth*, *excellence*, and *adulthood* are abstract. . . .

—*Random House Webster's College Dictionary*

Thesaurus

TIP To look up words online in both a dictionary and a thesaurus, go to **www.merriam-webster.com.**

A thesaurus gives **synonyms** (words that have the same meaning) for the word you look up. It comes in inexpensive and even electronic editions. Use a thesaurus when you cannot find the right word for what you mean. Be careful, however, to choose a word that has the precise meaning you intend. If you are not sure how a word should be used, look it up in the dictionary.

TIP For tools to build your vocabulary, visit the *Real Writing Student Center* at **bedfordstmartins.com/ realwriting.**

Concrete, *adj.* 1. Particular, specific, single, certain, special, unique, sole, peculiar, individual, separate, isolated, distinct, exact, precise, direct, strict, minute; definite, plain, evident, obvious; pointed, emphasized; restrictive, limiting, limited, well-defined, clear-cut, fixed, finite; determining, conclusive, decided.

—J. I. Rodale, *The Synonym Finder*

LANGUAGE NOTE: Make sure to use the right kinds of words in sentences: nouns when a person, place, or thing is meant, and adjectives when a description is meant.

INCORRECT	Everyone in the world wants happy.
	[*Happy* is an adjective, but a noun is needed in this case.]
	Smoking is not health.
	[*Health* is a noun, but an adjective is needed in this case.]
CORRECT	Everyone in the world wants **happiness**.
	Smoking is not **healthy**.

Practice Avoiding Four Common Word-Choice Problems

Four common problems with word choice may make it hard for readers to understand your point.

Vague and Abstract Words

Your words need to create a clear picture for your readers. Vague and abstract words are too general. They do not give your readers a clear idea of what you mean. Here are some common vague and abstract words.

Vague and Abstract Words

a lot	cute	nice	sweet
amazing	dumb	OK (okay)	terrible
awesome	good	old	thing
bad	great	pretty	very
beautiful	happy	sad	whatever
big	huge	small	young

COMPUTER Tell students they can use a computer's search or find function to locate these words in their own writing.

When you see one of these words or another general word in your writing, replace it with a concrete or more specific word. A **concrete** word names something that can be seen, heard, felt, tasted, or smelled. A **specific** word names a particular person or quality. Compare these two sentences:

VAGUE AND ABSTRACT	An old man crossed the street.
CONCRETE AND SPECIFIC	An eighty-seven-year-old priest stumbled along Main Street.

TEACHING TIP Take students to a spot on campus, and have them write descriptions of the same scene. Then, have them compare what they wrote, noting the use of concrete and specific language as well as of vague and abstract words.

The first version is too general to be interesting. The second version creates a clear, strong image. Some words are so vague that it is best to avoid them altogether.

VAGUE AND ABSTRACT	It is awesome.
	[This sentence is neither concrete nor specific.]

PRACTICE 1 Avoiding Vague and Abstract Words

In the following sentences, underline any words that are vague or abstract. Then, edit each sentence by replacing the vague or abstract words with concrete, specific ones. You may invent any details you like. *Answers may vary. Possible edits are shown.*

TIP For more practice on choosing words effectively, visit Exercise Central at **bedfordstmartins.com/ realwriting.**

EXAMPLE: I think it would be neat to be a farmer. *I think it would be fascinating to be a farmer.*

1. It would be hard to grow some kinds of crops. *It would be challenging to grow some kinds of crops.*

2. Taking care of cows would take a lot of work. *Taking care of cows would mean long hours of feeding and milking them.*

3. You would have to do bunches of things for them. *You would have to clean their stalls, feed them, milk them, etc.*

RESOURCES To gauge students' word-choice skills, use the *Testing Tool Kit* CD-ROM available with this book.

4. Not using chemicals to grow things is <u>cool</u>. <u>*Not using chemicals to grow things is better for people and for the environment.*</u>

5. Planting seeds would take <u>tons of time</u>. <u>*Planting seeds is time-consuming.*</u>

6. I <u>bet</u> the fields look <u>really pretty</u> early in the morning. <u>*I imagine that the fields look beautiful early in the morning.*</u>

7. The food that you grew would probably taste <u>great</u>. <u>*The food that you grew would probably taste fresh.*</u>

8. Living out in the country sounds <u>awesome</u>, <u>for sure</u>. <u>*Living out in the country sounds fun.*</u>

9. I would do a <u>decent</u> job of taking care of <u>stuff</u>. <u>*I would do an excellent job taking care of the farm, the animals, and the crops.*</u>

10. Being a farmer would be <u>amazing</u>. <u>*Being a farmer would be rewarding.*</u>

· ·

Slang

TEAMWORK Students can collaborate to list slang words and then translate them into formal English.

Slang, informal and casual language, should be used only in informal situations. Avoid it when you write, especially for college classes or at work. Use language that is appropriate for your audience and purpose.

SLANG	EDITED
S'all good.	Everything is going well.
Dawg, I don't deserve this grade.	Professor, I don't deserve this grade.

· ·

PRACTICE 2   Avoiding Slang

In the following sentences, underline any slang words. Then, edit the sentences by replacing the slang with language appropriate for a formal audience and purpose. Imagine that you are writing to a boss where you work. *Answers may vary. Possible edits are shown.*

       Hello,   *to*
EXAMPLE: ~~Yo~~, Randy, I need to talk ~~at~~ you for a minute.

1. That reference letter you wrote for me was ~~really awesome sweet.~~ *helpful and much appreciated.*

2. I am grateful because the one my English instructor did for me ~~sucked.~~ *was not helpful.*

3. She said I thought I was ~~all that~~, but that is not true. *conceited*

4. I would be ~~down with doing~~ a favor for you in return if you need it. *happy to do*

5. Maybe you and I could ~~hang sometime~~ one of these weekends? *spend time together*

6. I know we cannot be best ~~buds~~, but we could ~~shoot some hoops or something.~~ *friends* *play basketball.*

7. You could let me know ~~whazzup~~ when I see you at work next week. *what you have planned*

8. If you are too stressed, do not ~~go all emo on me.~~
   get upset.
   relax

9. Just ~~chill out~~ and forget about it.

10. ~~Text~~ me when you get ~~a mo.~~
    Contact   *a chance*

. . . .

Wordy Language

People sometimes use too many words to express their ideas. They may think that using more words will make them sound smart, but too many words can weaken a writer's point.

WORDY	I am not interested *at this point in time*.
EDITED	I am not interested now.
	[The phrase *at this point in time* uses five words to express what could be said in one word: *now*.]
WORDY	*In the opinion of this writer*, I think the directions are clear.
	[The phrase *in the opinion of this writer* is not necessary and weakens the statement.]
WORDY	The suspect was evasive and *avoided answering the questions*.
EDITED	The suspect was evasive.
	[The words *evasive* and *avoided answering the questions* repeat the same idea without adding anything new.]

Common Wordy Expressions

WORDY	EDITED
As a result of	Because
Due to the fact that	Because
In spite of the fact that	Although
It is my opinion that	I think (*or just make the point*)
In the event that	If
The fact of the matter is that	(*Just state the point.*)
A great number of	Many
At that time	Then
In this day and age	Now
At this point in time	Now
In this paper I will show that . . .	(*Just make the point; do not announce it.*)
Utilize	Use

COMPUTER Students can use a computer's search or find function to locate these phrases (or others like them) in their writing.

PRACTICE 3 Avoiding Wordy Language

In the following sentences, underline the wordy or repetitive language. Then, edit each sentence to make it more concise. Some sentences may contain more than one wordy phrase. *Answers may vary. Possible edits are shown.*

EXAMPLE: Sugar substitutes are a popular diet choice for people ~~of all ages~~ when they are searching for ways to ~~cut down on all of~~ [reduce] the calories they ingest ~~on a daily basis.~~ [each day.]

1. ~~It is a well-known fact that~~ [Dieting] dieting is difficult for most people.

2. ~~Due to the fact that~~ [Because] people are trying to cut calories, sugar substitutes are used in sodas, snacks, and other products.

3. ~~The fact of the matter is that these~~ [These] substitutes provide a sweet taste, but without the calories of sugar or honey.

4. ~~A great number of~~ [Many] researchers have stated ~~at this time~~ that such substitutes are not ~~necessarily~~ safe or healthy to use in large quantities.

5. ~~Some of the current~~ [Current] experts ~~on the matter are of the opinion~~ [believe] that sugar substitutes can cause cancer, allergies, and other serious health problems.

6. ~~At this point in time, other~~ [Other] experts ~~on the same subject~~ believe that using these substitutes maintains a person's addiction to sugar and leads people to eat more junk food.

7. Despite these warnings, ~~negative evaluations, and critical opinions~~ from the experts, nearly 200 million people consume sugar-free or low-calorie products each year.

8. ~~In this day and age, people~~ [People] are consuming an average of four of these items each day.

9. ~~In spite of the fact that~~ [Although] people know sugar is bad for them, their tastes will probably not change ~~anytime in the near future.~~ [soon.]

10. ~~It is my opinion that it~~ [It] would be better if people just learned to consume foods that do not contain sweeteners of any kind.

Clichés

Clichés are phrases used so often that people no longer pay attention to them. To get your point across and to get your readers' attention, replace clichés with fresh language.

CLICHÉS	EDITED
I cannot *make ends meet*.	I do not have enough money to live on.
My uncle *worked his way up the corporate ladder*.	My uncle started as a shipping clerk but ended up as a regional vice president.
This roll is *as hard as a rock*.	This roll is so hard I could bounce it.

Common Clichés

as big as a house	few and far between	spoiled brat
as light as a feather	hell on earth	starting from scratch
better late than never	last but not least	sweating blood/bullets
break the ice	no way on earth	too little, too late
crystal clear	110 percent	24/7
a drop in the bucket	playing with fire	work like a dog
easier said than done		

COMPUTER Students can use a computer's search or find function to locate these phrases (or others like them) in their writing.

- -

PRACTICE 4   Avoiding Clichés

In the following sentences, underline the clichés. Then, edit each sentence by re-placing the clichés with fresh language. *Answers will vary. Possible edits are shown.*

> > > > excruciating
EXAMPLE: Riding a bicycle one hundred miles a day can be ~~hell on~~
> work extremely hard. ^
~~earth~~ unless you are willing to ~~give 110 percent~~.

TIP Hundreds of clichés exist. To check if you have used one, go to **www.clichesite.com**.

 devote every bit of your strength to the challenge
1. You have to persuade yourself to ~~sweat blood and work like a dog~~ for up
  ^
to ten hours.

 It is impossible to
2. ~~There's no way on earth you can~~ do it without extensive training.
  ^

 the very last mile,   an enormously difficult task.
3. Staying on your bike until ~~the bitter end,~~ of course, is ~~easier said than~~
  ^   ^
~~done.~~

 maintain your determination
4. It is important to ~~keep the fire in your belly~~ and keep your goal of finish-
 always present
ing the race ~~crystal clear~~ in your mind.
  ^

5. No matter how long it takes you to cross the finish line, remind yourself
 finishing at all is a tremendous achievement.
that it's ~~better late than never.~~
  ^

6. Even if you are not a champion racer, training for a bike race will keep
 in top physical condition.
you ~~fit as a fiddle.~~
  ^

continue to

7. It may take discipline to make yourself train, but you should ~~keep your~~
  work hard.
     ^
  ~~nose to the grindstone.~~

protect themselves

8. Bike racers should always ~~play it safe~~ by wearing helmets.
             ^
       watch carefully

9. When you train for road racing, ~~keep an eye peeled~~ for cars.
                    ^
       injured   *killed!*

10. You do not want to end up ~~flat on your back~~ in the hospital or ~~six feet~~
                    ^   ^

   ~~under!~~

TIP See Chapter 26 for more
advice on using pronouns.

A FINAL NOTE: Language that favors one gender over another or that assumes that only one gender performs a certain role is called *sexist*. Such language should be avoided.

SEXIST	A doctor should politely answer *his* patients' questions.
	[Not all doctors are male, as suggested by the pronoun *his*.]
REVISED	A doctor should politely answer *his or her* patients' questions.
	Doctors should politely answer *their* patients' questions.
	[The first revision changes *his* to *his or her* to avoid sexism. The second revision changes the subject to a plural noun (*Doctors*) so that a genderless pronoun (*their*) can be used. Usually, it is preferable to avoid *his or her*.]

Edit for Word Choice

PRACTICE 5   Editing for Word Choice

Find and edit six examples of vague or abstract language, slang, wordy language, or clichés in the following paragraphs.   *Answers may vary. Possible edits are shown.*

most unusual

(1) Imagine spending almost two weeks living in the ~~coolest~~ home in
                             ^
the world. (2) That is what scientist Lloyd Godson did when he lived at
the bottom of a lake in Australia for thirteen days. (3) While ~~there is no~~
  not
~~way on earth~~ I would want to do that, it ~~sure~~ sounds fascinating.
           ^

(4) Godson's home was an eight-by-eleven-foot-long yellow steel box
that he dubbed the BioSUB. (5) His air supply came from the algae
plants growing inside the BioSUB. (6) Divers brought him food, water,
  supplies
and other ~~junk~~ through a manhole built in the bottom of his underwater
       ^
home. (7) To keep busy, he rode on an exercise bicycle, which created
electricity for him to recharge his laptop and run the lights for his plants.
(8) He used his computer to talk to students all over the world and to
watch movies.

(9) Godson paid for this experiment with money he had won in the "Live Your Dream" contest. (10) ~~At this point in time, I have to say that~~
For
~~for~~ most people, the BioSUB home would be less appealing than a regular, aboveground room, apartment, or house. (11) Indeed, by the time
and
his two weeks were over, Godson was ready to come up, feel the sunshine and wind on his face again, ~~and "smell the roses."~~

- -

PRACTICE 6   Editing Your Own Writing for Word Choice

As a final practice, edit a piece of your own writing for word choice. It can be a paper you are working on for this course, a paper you have already finished, a paper for another course, or a recent piece of writing from your work or everyday life. Record in your learning journal any problem sentences you find, along with their corrections. You may want to use the chart on page 538.

- -

Chapter Review

1. What two resources will help you choose the best words for your meaning? *a dictionary and a thesaurus*

2. What are four common word-choice problems? *vague and abstract words, slang, wordy language, and clichés*

3. Replace vague and abstract words with _____*concrete*_____ and _____*specific*_____ words.

4. When is it appropriate to use slang in college writing or in writing at work? _____*never*_____

5. Give two examples of wordy expressions. *Answers will vary.*

LEARNING JOURNAL Did you find problems with word choice in your writing? What is the main thing you have learned about word choice that will help you? What is unclear to you?

TEACHING TIP You can collect students' learning journals to find out what the class or individual students need more work on.

Chapter Test

For each of the following items, choose words or sentences that are specific and appropriate for a formal (academic or work) audience.

1. Choose the item that uses words most effectively.
   a. My dorm is just an OK place to study.
   (b.) My dorm is so noisy and full of activity that it is difficult to study there.
   c. My dorm is not where I go when I want to study.

TIP For advice on taking tests, see Appendix A.

RESOURCES The *Testing Tool Kit* CD-ROM available with this book has even more tests.

2. Choose the best words to fill in the blank.

I am afraid all of your hard work did not _____.

(a.) solve our problem   **b.** do the trick   **c.** do it for us

3. Choose the best word(s) to fill in the blank.

Kevin was extremely _____ about his new job.

a. juiced   **b.** turned on   **(c.)** enthusiastic

4. Choose the item that uses words most effectively.
  a. I like that thing Nikki does whenever she scores a goal.
  b. I like the way Nikki goes nuts whenever she scores a goal.
  (c.) I like the way Nikki does a backflip whenever she scores a goal.

5. Choose the item that uses words most effectively.
  a. In the event that you are ever in River City, stop by to see me.
  (b.) If you are ever in River City, stop by to see me.
  c. If by chance you are ever in River City, stop by to see me.

Editing for Word Choice

In writing, you have only your words to help you get your point across, so choose them carefully.

Two resources are invaluable for finding the best word.

A dictionary helps with spelling and gives definitions and examples.

A thesaurus gives synonyms for the word you look up.

Avoid these four word-choice problems:

Vague and abstract words (see p. 530)

Slang (see p. 532)

Wordy language (see p. 533)

Clichés (see p. 534)

Commonly Confused Words

Avoiding Mistakes with Soundalike Words

Understand Why Certain Words Are Commonly Confused

People often confuse certain words in English because they sound alike and may have similar meanings. In speech, words that sound alike are not a problem. In writing, however, words that sound alike may be spelled differently, and readers rely on the spelling to understand what you mean. Edit your writing carefully to make sure that you have used the correct words.

- **Proofread carefully**, using the techniques discussed on page 551.
- **Use a dictionary** to look up any words you are unsure about.
- **Focus on finding and correcting mistakes** you make with the twenty-seven sets of commonly confused words covered in this chapter.
- **Develop a personal list of soundalike words** you confuse often. In your learning journal, record words that you confuse in your writing and their meanings. Before you turn in any piece of writing, consult your personal word list to make sure you have used words correctly.

RESOURCES *Additional Resources* contains tests and supplemental exercises for this chapter.

Practice Using Commonly Confused Words Correctly

Study the different meanings and spellings of these twenty-seven sets of commonly confused words. Complete the sentence after each set of words, filling in each blank with the correct word.

TIP Some commonly confused words sound similar but not exactly alike, such as *conscience* and *conscious*, *loose* and *lose*, and *of* and *have*. To avoid confusing these words, practice pronouncing them correctly.

539

TIP For tools to build your vocabulary, visit the *Real Writing Student Center* at **bedfordstmartins.com/ realwriting**.

A/An/And

a: used before a word that begins with a consonant sound

A friend of mine just won the lottery.

an: used before a word that begins with a vowel sound

An old friend of mine just won the lottery.

and: used to join two words

My friend *and* I went out to celebrate.

A friend *and* I ate at *an* Italian restaurant.

Other lottery winners were _____*an*_____ algebra teacher _____*and a*_____ bowling team.

Accept/Except

accept: to agree to receive or admit (verb)

I will *accept* the job offer.

except: but, other than

All the stores are closed *except* the Quik-Stop.

I *accept* all the job conditions *except* the low pay.

Do not _____*accept*_____ gifts from clients _____*except*_____ those who are also personal friends.

TIP For more practice using commonly confused words correctly, visit Exercise Central at **bedfordstmartins.com/ realwriting**.

Advice/Advise

advice: opinion (noun)

I would like your *advice* before I make a decision.

advise: to give an opinion (verb)

Please *advise* me what to do.

Please *advise* me what to do; you always give me good *advice*.

If you do not like my _____*advice*_____, please _____*advise*_____ me how to proceed.

Affect/Effect

affect: to make an impact on, to change something (verb)

The whole city was *affected* by the hurricane.

effect: a result (noun)

What *effect* will the hurricane have on the local economy?

TIP Thinking "*the effect*" will help you remember that *effect* is a noun.

Although the storm will have many negative *effects*, it will not *affect* the price of food.

The _____*effect*_____ of the disaster will _____*affect*_____ many people.

Are/Our

are: a form of the verb *be*

The workers *are* about to go on strike.

our: a pronoun showing ownership

The children played on *our* porch.

My relatives *are* staying at *our* house.

_____Our_____ new neighbors _____are_____ moving in today.

TEACHING TIP It is helpful to complete these sentences as a class or to assign them as homework and then go over them in class. Have students read the sentences aloud so that they can focus on differences in pronunciation.

By/Buy

by: next to or before

Meet me *by* the entrance.

Make sure the bill is paid *by* the fifteenth of the month.

buy: to purchase (verb)

I would like to *buy* a new CD player.

When I walk *by* the cottage, I know I would like to *buy* it.

_____By_____ next year, I will be able to _____buy_____ a washing machine.

Conscience/Conscious

conscience: a personal sense of right and wrong (noun)

Jake's *conscience* would not allow him to cheat.

conscious: awake, aware (adjective)

The coma patient is now *conscious*.

I am *conscious* that it is getting late.

The judge was *conscious* that the accused had acted according to his *conscience* even though he had broken the law.

The man said he was not _____conscious_____ that what he had done was illegal, or his _____conscience_____ would not have let him do it.

TIP Remember that one of the words is *con-science*; the other is not.

Fine/Find

fine: of high quality (adjective); feeling well (adjective); a penalty for breaking a law (noun)

This jacket is made of *fine* leather.

After a day in bed, Jacob felt *fine*.

The *fine* for exceeding the speed limit is fifty dollars.

find: to locate, to discover (verb)

Did Clara *find* her glasses?

I *find* gardening to be a *fine* pastime.

Were you able to _____find_____ a place to store your _____fine_____ jewelry?

Its/It's

its: a pronoun showing ownership

The dog chased *its* tail.

it's: a contraction of the words *it is*

It's about time you got here.

It's very hard for a dog to keep *its* teeth clean.

_____ It's _____ no surprise that the college raised _____ its _____ tuition.

Knew/New/Know/No

knew: understood; recognized (past tense of the verb *know*)

I *knew* the answer, but I could not think of it.

new: unused, recent, or just introduced (adjective)

The building has a *new* security code.

know: to understand; to have knowledge of (verb)

I *know* how to bake bread.

no: used to form a negative

I have *no* idea what the answer is.

I never *knew* how much a *new* car costs.

The _____ new _____ teacher _____ knew _____ many of her students already.

There is _____ no _____ way Tom could _____ know _____ where Celia is hiding.

I _____ know _____ that there is _____ no _____ cake left.

Loose/Lose

loose: baggy; relaxed; not fixed in place (adjective)

In hot weather, people tend to wear *loose* clothing.

lose: to misplace; to forfeit possession of (verb)

Every summer, I *lose* about three pairs of sunglasses.

If the ring is too *loose* on your finger, you might *lose* it.

I _____ lose _____ my patience with _____ loose _____ rules in schools.

Mind/Mine

mind: to object to (verb); the thinking or feeling part of one's brain (noun)

Toby does not *mind* if I borrow his CDs.

Estela has a good *mind*, but often she does not use it.

mine: belonging to me (pronoun); a source of ore and minerals (noun)

>   That coat is *mine*.

>   My uncle worked in a coal *mine* in West Virginia.

That writing problem of *mine* was on my *mind*.

If you do not _____*mind*_____, the gloves you just took are _____*mine*_____.

Of/Have

of: coming from; caused by; part of a group; made from (preposition)

>   The leader *of* the band played bass guitar.

have: to possess (verb; also used as a helping verb)

>   I *have* one more course to take before I graduate.

>   I should *have* started studying earlier.

The president *of* the company should *have* resigned.

Sidney could _____*have*_____ been one _____*of*_____ the winners.

NOTE: Do not use *of* after *would, should, could,* and *might.* Use *have* after those words (*would have, should have*).

Passed/Past

passed: went by or went ahead (past tense of the verb *pass*)

>   We *passed* the hospital on the way to the airport.

past: time that has gone by (noun); gone by, over, just beyond (preposition)

>   In the *past*, I was able to stay up all night and not be tired.

>   The snow fell *past* my window.

This *past* school year, I *passed* all of my exams.

Trish _____*passed*_____ me as we ran _____*past*_____ the one-mile marker.

Peace/Piece

peace: no disagreement; calm

>   Could you quiet down and give me a little *peace*?

piece: a part of something larger

>   May I have a *piece* of that pie?

The feuding families found *peace* after they sold the *piece* of land.

To keep the _____*peace*_____, give your sister a _____*piece*_____ of candy.

Principal/Principle

principal: main (adjective); head of a school or leader of an organization (noun)

Brush fires are the *principal* risk in the hills of California.

Ms. Edwards is the *principal* of Memorial Elementary School.

Corinne is a *principal* in the management consulting firm.

principle: a standard of beliefs or behaviors (noun)

Although tempted, she held on to her moral *principles*.

The *principal* questioned the delinquent student's *principles*.

The _____*principal*_____ problem is that you want me to act against my _____*principles*_____.

Quiet/Quite/Quit

quiet: soft in sound; not noisy (adjective)

The library was *quiet*.

quite: completely; very (adverb)

After cleaning all the windows, Alex was *quite* tired.

quit: to stop (verb)

She *quit* her job.

COMPUTER Tell students that although a spell checker won't help them with the spelling of most of these words, they can use the search or find function to find every instance of the words they have trouble with.

After the band *quit* playing, the hall was *quite quiet*.

If you would _____*quit*_____ shouting and be _____*quiet*_____, you would find that the scenery is _____*quite*_____ pleasant.

Right/Write

right: correct; in a direction opposite from left (adjective)

You definitely made the *right* choice.

When you get to the stoplight, make a *right* turn.

write: to put words on paper (verb)

Will you *write* your phone number for me?

Please *write* the *right* answer in the space provided.

You were _____*right*_____ to _____*write*_____ to the senator.

Set/Sit

set: a collection of something (noun); to place an object somewhere (verb)

Paul has a complete *set* of Johnny Cash records.

Please *set* the package on the table.

sit: to rest in a chair or other seatlike surface; to be located in a particular place

> I need to *sit* on the sofa for a few minutes.

> The shed *sits* between the house and the garden.

If I *sit* down now, I will not have time to *set* the plants outside.

Before you _____ *sit* _____ on that chair, _____ *set* _____ the magazines on the floor.

Suppose/Supposed

suppose: to imagine or assume to be true

> I *suppose* you would like something to eat.

> *Suppose* you won a million dollars.

supposed: past tense of *suppose*; intended

> Karen *supposed* Thomas was late because of traffic.

I *suppose* you know that Rita was *supposed* to be home by 6:30.

I _____ *suppose* _____ you want to leave soon because we are _____ *supposed* _____ to arrive before the guests.

Than/Then

than: a word used to compare two or more things or persons

> It is colder inside *than* outside.

then: at a certain time; next in time

> I got out of the car and *then* realized the keys were still in it.

Clara ran more miles *than* she ever had before, and *then* she collapsed.

Back _____ *then* _____, I smoked more _____ *than* _____ three packs a day.

Their/There/They're

their: a pronoun showing ownership

> I borrowed *their* clippers to trim the hedges.

there: a word indicating location or existence

> Just put the keys *there* on the desk.

> *There* are too many lawyers.

they're: a contraction of the words *they are*

> *They're* about to leave.

There is a car in *their* driveway, which indicates that *they're* home.

_____ *Their* _____ beach house is empty except for the one week that _____ *they're* _____ vacationing _____ *there* _____.

TIP If you are not sure whether to use *their* or *they're*, substitute *they are*. If the sentence does not make sense, use *their*.

Though/Through/Threw

though: however; nevertheless; in spite of (conjunction)

Though he is short, he plays great basketball.

through: finished with (adjective); from one side to the other (preposition)

I am *through* arguing with you.

The baseball went right *through* the window.

threw: hurled; tossed (past tense of the verb *throw*)

She *threw* the basketball.

Even *though* it was illegal, she *threw* the empty cup *through* the window onto the road.

_____*Though*_____ she did not really believe it would bring good luck, Jan _____*threw*_____ a penny _____*through*_____ the air into the fountain.

To/Too/Two

to: a word indicating a direction or movement (preposition); part of the infinitive form of a verb

Please give the message *to* Sharon.

It is easier *to* ask for forgiveness than *to* get permission.

too: also; more than enough; very (adverb)

I am tired *too*.

Dan ate *too* much and felt sick.

That dream was *too* real.

two: the number between one and three (noun)

The lab had only *two* computers.

They went *to* a restaurant and ordered *too* much food for *two* people.

When Marty went _____*to*_____ pay for his meal, the cashier charged him _____*two*_____ dollars _____*too*_____ much.

Use/Used

use: to employ or put into service (verb)

How do you plan to *use* that blueprint?

TIP Writing *use to* instead of *used to* is a common error. Train yourself not to make it.

used: past tense of the verb *use*. *Used to* can indicate a past fact or state, or it can mean "familiar with."

He *used* his lunch hour to do errands.

He *used* to go for a walk during his lunch hour.

She *used* to be a chef, so she knows how to *use* all kinds of kitchen gadgets.

She is also *used* to improvising in the kitchen.

Tom _____*used*_____ the prize money to buy a boat; his family

hoped he would _____*use*_____ it for his education, but Tom was

_____*used*_____ to getting his way.

Who's/Whose

who's: a contraction of the words *who is*

    Who's at the door?

whose: a pronoun showing ownership

    Whose shoes are these?

Who's the person *whose* car sank in the river?

The student _____*whose*_____ name is first on the list is the one

_____*who's*_____ in charge.

TIP If you are not sure whether to use *whose* or *who's*, substitute *who is*. If the sentence does not make sense, use *whose*.

Your/You're

your: a pronoun showing ownership

    Did you bring *your* wallet?

you're: a contraction of the words *you are*

    You're not telling me the whole story.

You're going to have *your* third exam tomorrow.

_____*Your*_____ teacher says _____*you're*_____ good with numbers.

TIP If you are not sure whether to use *your* or *you're*, substitute *you are*. If the sentence does not make sense, use *your*.

· ·

PRACTICE 1   Using the Right Word

In each of the following items, circle the correct word in parentheses.

1. I just cannot (accept / except) your decision.

2. She (use / used) to live next door.

3. (Their / There / They're) on (their / there / they're) way to the mountains.

4. The baby has more toys (than / then) he knows what to do with.

5. You should always act in accordance with your (principals / principles).

6. After cheating on the test, she had a guilty (conscience / conscious).

7. His enthusiasm (knows / nos) (know / no) bounds.

8. Are you going to (your / you're) class today?

9. I should (of / have) left (are / our) car at the garage.

10. I need to (buy / by) some food for dinner.

· ·

Edit for Commonly Confused Words

PRACTICE 2   Editing for Commonly Confused Words

Edit the following paragraphs to correct eighteen errors in word use.

(1) More and more women are purchasing handguns, against the ~~advise~~ *advice* of law enforcement officers. (2) Few of these women are criminals or plan to commit crimes. (3) They ~~no~~ *know* the risks of guns, and they ~~except~~ *accept* those risks. (4) They buy weapons primarily because ~~their~~ *they're* tired of feeling like victims. (5) They do not want to contribute ~~too~~ *to* the violence in ~~are~~ *our* society, but they also realize that women are the victims of violent attacks far ~~to~~ *too* often. (6) Many women ~~loose~~ *lose* ~~they're~~ *their* lives because they cannot fight off ~~there~~ *their* attackers. (7) Some women have made a ~~conscience~~ *conscious* decision to arm themselves for protection.

(8) But does buying a gun make things worse rather ~~then~~ *than* better? (9) Having a gun in ~~you're~~ *your* house makes it three times more likely that someone will be killed there—and that someone is just as likely to be you or one of your children as a criminal. (10) Most young children cannot tell the difference between a real gun and a toy gun when they ~~fine~~ *find* one. (11) Every year, ~~their~~ *there* are tragic examples of children who accidentally shoot and even kill other youngsters while they are playing with guns. (12) A mother ~~who's~~ *whose* children are injured while playing with her gun will never again think that a gun provides ~~piece~~ *peace* of mind. (13) Reducing the violence in ~~are~~ *our* society may be a better solution.

PRACTICE 3   Editing Your Own Writing for Commonly Confused Words

As a final practice, edit a piece of your own writing for commonly confused words. It can be a paper you are working on for this course, a paper you have already finished, a paper for another course, or a recent piece of writing from your work or everyday life. Add any misused words you find to your personal list of the soundalike words you confuse most often.

TEACHING TIP Ask students for a few more commonly confused words. Start them off by putting one set on the board, and then list others that they suggest.

Chapter Review

1. What are four strategies you can use to avoid confusing words that sound alike or have similar meanings? _Proofread carefully, use a dictionary to look up any words you are unsure about, find and correct mistakes you make with the twenty-seven sets of commonly confused words, and develop a personal list of soundalike words you confuse often._

LEARNING JOURNAL Record your personal list of commonly confused words, and look at it when you edit your own writing.

2. What are the top five commonly confused words on your personal list? _Answers will vary._

Chapter Test

Use the words in parentheses to correctly fill in the blanks in each of the following sentences.

TIP For advice on taking tests, see Appendix A.

1. The coin machine will _____accept_____ any coins _____except_____ foreign ones. (*accept, except*)

2. _____They're_____ going to arrive _____there_____ late, but they will be sure to bring all of _____their_____ tools. (*their, there, they're*)

RESOURCES The *Testing Tool Kit* CD-ROM available with this book has even more tests.

3. There is _____too_____ much confusion in our department now that _____two_____ supervisors have been asked _____to_____ perform the same job. (*to, too, two*)

4. Everyone thinks _____you're_____ going to get a perfect score on _____your_____ exam. (*your, you're*)

5. The veterinarian told me _____it's_____ not necessary to wash a cat because a cat keeps _____its_____ own fur clean. (*its, it's*)

36

Spelling

Using the Right Letters

THIS CHAPTER
- gives you strategies for finding and correcting spelling errors
- gives you methods to become a better speller
- gives you memory aids for mastering spelling rules
- gives you a list of one hundred commonly misspelled words to use as a reference

Finding and Correcting Spelling Mistakes

Some extremely smart people are poor spellers. Unfortunately, spelling errors are easy for readers to spot, and they make a bad impression. You can improve your spelling in several ways. First, learn to find and correct spelling mistakes in your writing by using the following strategies.

Use a Dictionary

When proofreading your papers, consult a dictionary whenever you are unsure about the spelling of a word. *Checking a dictionary is the single most important thing you can do to improve your spelling.*

Use a Spell Checker—with Caution

All word-processing programs have spell checkers. A spell checker finds and highlights a word that may be misspelled, suggests other spellings, and gives you the opportunity to change the spelling of the word. (Most word-processing programs automatically highlight potentially misspelled words.) Use a spell checker after you have completed a piece of writing but before you print it out.

Never rely on a spell checker to do your editing for you. A spell checker ignores anything it recognizes as a word, so it will not help you find words that are misused or misspellings that are also words. For example, a spell checker would not highlight any of the problems in these phrases:

Just *to* it.	(Correct: Just *do* it.)
pain in the *nick*	(Correct: pain in the *neck*)
my writing *coarse*	(Correct: my writing *course*)

Use Proofreading Techniques

Use some of the following proofreading techniques to focus on the spelling of one word at a time. Different techniques work for different people, so try them all and then decide which ones work best for you.

TIP For more spelling practice, visit Exercise Central at **bedfordstmartins.com/ realwriting**.

- Print out your paper before proofreading. (Many writers find it easier to detect errors on paper than on a computer screen.)

- Put a piece of paper under the line that you are reading.

- Cut a "window" in an index card that is about the size of a long word (such as *misunderstanding*), and place it over your writing to focus on one word at a time.

- Proofread your paper backward, one word at a time.

- Print out a version of your paper that looks noticeably different: Make the words larger, make the margins larger, triple-space the lines, or do all of these.

- Read your paper aloud. This strategy will help you if you tend to leave words out.

- Exchange papers with a partner and proofread each other's papers, identifying only possible misspellings. The writer of the paper should be responsible for checking the spelling and correcting any errors.

Make a Personal Spelling List

Set aside a section of your course notebook or learning journal for your spelling list. Every time you edit a paper, write down the words that you misspelled. Every couple of weeks, go back to your spelling list to see if your problem words have changed. Are you misspelling fewer words in each paper?

For each word on your list, create a memory aid or silly phrase to help you remember the correct spelling. For example, if you often misspell *a lot*, you could think, "*a lot* is a lot of words."

TEACHING TIP Telling students they will have to turn in their spelling lists reinforces the importance of their making them. If you have time, you can make up individualized spelling quizzes. Premade quizzes are included in the *Testing Tool Kit* CD-ROM available with this book.

Three Strategies for Becoming a Better Speller

Learning to find and correct your spelling mistakes is only half the battle. You also need to become a better speller so that you do not make so many mistakes in the first place. Here are several good strategies.

Master Commonly Confused Words

Chapter 35 covers twenty-seven sets of words that are commonly confused because they sound similar, such as *write* and *right* or *its* and *it's*. If you can master these commonly confused words, you will avoid many spelling mistakes.

Learn Six Spelling Rules

This section covers spelling situations in which people often think, *What do I do here?* If you can remember the rules, you can correct many of the spelling errors in your writing.

Before the six rules, here is a quick review of vowels and consonants.

VOWELS: *a, e, i, o,* and *u*

CONSONANTS: *b, c, d, f, g, h, j, k, l, m, n, p, q, r, s, t, v, w, x,* and *z*

The letter *y* can be either a vowel or a consonant. It is a vowel when it sounds like the *y* in *fly* or *hungry*. It is a consonant when it sounds like the *y* in *yellow*.

Rule 1.   "*I* before *e*, except after *c*. Or when sounded like *a*, as in *neighbor* or *weigh*."

Many people repeat this rhyme to themselves as they decide whether a word is spelled with an *ie* or an *ei*.

> **pie**ce (*i* before *e*)
>
> rec**ei**ve (except after *c*)
>
> **ei**ght (sounds like *a*)

TEAMWORK For each rule, have students give three additional examples of words that follow the rule. This exercise can be done in small groups or pairs.

EXCEPTIONS: *either, neither, foreign, height, seize, society, their, weird*

Rule 2.   Drop the final *e* when adding an ending that begins with a vowel.

> hop**e** + ing = hoping
>
> imagin**e** + ation = imagination

Keep the final *e* when adding an ending that begins with a consonant.

> achiev**e** + ment = achievement
>
> definit**e** + ly = definitely

EXCEPTIONS: *argument, awful, simply, truly,* and others

Rule 3.   When adding an ending to a word that ends in *y*, **change the *y* to *i*** when a consonant comes before the *y*.

lonely + est = loneliest

happy + er = happier

apology + ize = apologize

likely + hood = likelihood

Do not change the *y* when a vowel comes before the *y*.

boy + ish = boyish

pay + ment = payment

survey + or = surveyor

buy + er = buyer

EXCEPTIONS:

1. When adding *-ing* to a word ending in *y*, always keep the *y*, even if a consonant comes before it: stu**dy** + ing = stud**y**ing.

2. Other exceptions include *daily, dryer, said,* and *paid.*

Rule 4.   When adding an ending that starts with a vowel to a one-syllable word, follow these rules.
   Double the final consonant only if the word ends with a consonant-vowel-consonant.

trap + ed = trap**p**ed

d**rip** + ed = drip**p**ed

knit + ed = knit**t**ed

fat + er = fat**t**er

   Do not double the final consonant if the word ends with some other combination.

VOWEL-VOWEL-CONSONANT	VOWEL-CONSONANT-CONSONANT
cl**ean** + est = cleanest	sl**ick** + er = slicker
p**oor** + er = poorer	te**ach** + er = teacher
cl**ear** + ed = cleared	l**ast** + ed = lasted

Rule 5.   When adding an ending that starts with a vowel to a word with two or more syllables, follow these rules.
   Double the final consonant only if the word ends with a consonant-vowel-consonant and the stress is on the last syllable.

sub**mit** + ing = submi**t**ting

oc**cur** + ence = occur**r**ence

pre**fer** + ed = prefer**r**ed

Do not double the final consonant in other cases.

prob**lem** + atic = prob**lem**atic

unders**tand** + ing = unders**tand**ing

of**fer** + ed = of**fer**ed

Rule 6. **Add -*s*** to most words, including words that end in *o* preceded by a vowel.

MOST WORDS	WORDS THAT END IN VOWEL PLUS *O*
book + **s** = book**s**	vid**eo** + **s** = vid**eo**s
college + **s** = college**s**	ster**eo** + **s** = ster**eo**s
jump + **s** = jump**s**	ra**dio** + **s** = ra**dio**s

Add -*es* to words that end in *o* preceded by a consonant and words that end in *s*, *sh*, *ch*, or *x*.

WORDS THAT END IN CONSONANT PLUS *O*	WORDS THAT END IN *S*, *SH*, *CH*, OR *X*
pota**to** + **es** = pota**to**es	clas**s** + **es** = clas**s**es
he**ro** + **es** = he**ro**es	pu**sh** + **es** = pu**sh**es
go + **es** = go**es**	ben**ch** + **es** = ben**ch**es
	fa**x** + **es** = fa**x**es

EXCEPTIONS: *pianos*, *solos*, and others

Consult a List of Commonly Misspelled Words

Use a list like the one below as an easy reference to check your spelling.

One Hundred Commonly Misspelled Words

absence	appetite	business	conscious
achieve	argument	calendar	convenient
across	athlete	career	cruelty
aisle	awful	category	daughter
a lot	basically	chief	definite
already	beautiful	column	describe
analyze	beginning	coming	develop
answer	believe	commitment	dictionary

different	guidance	necessary	secretary
disappoint	harass	ninety	separate
dollar	height	noticeable	sincerely
eighth	humorous	occasion	sophomore
embarrass	illegal	perform	succeed
environment	immediately	physically	successful
especially	independent	prejudice	surprise
exaggerate	interest	probably	truly
excellent	jewelry	psychology	until
exercise	judgment	receive	usually
fascinate	knowledge	recognize	vacuum
February	license	recommend	valuable
finally	lightning	restaurant	vegetable
foreign	loneliness	rhythm	weight
friend	marriage	roommate	weird
government	meant	schedule	writing
grief	muscle	scissors	written

Chapter Review

1. What are two important tools for good spelling? _a dictionary and a_
spelling list

2. What three strategies can you use to find and correct spelling mistakes?
Use a spell checker, use proofreading techniques, and check your
personal spelling list.

3. What three strategies can you use to become a better speller?
Master commonly confused words, learn the six spelling rules, and
consult a list of commonly misspelled words.

LEARNING JOURNAL What are your spelling demons? How will you remember to spell them correctly?

Chapter Test

In each sentence, fill in the blank with the correctly spelled word.

TIP For advice on taking tests, see Appendix A.

1. Your joining us for dinner is a pleasant _____ .

   a. suprise   **b.** surprize   **c.** surprise

RESOURCES The *Testing Tool Kit* CD-ROM available with this book has even more tests.

2. When can I expect to _____ the package?

    a. recieve   **b.** receive   **c.** reeceive

3. Is the fax _____ right now?

    a. transmiting   **b.** transmitting   **c.** transsmiting

4. Colin's roommate is _____ weird.

    a. definately   **b.** definitely   **c.** definitly

5. After my doctor diagnosed my injury, she _____ me to a physical therapist.

    a. refered   **b.** reffered   **c.** referred

6. We will have to go in _____ cars.

    a. separate   **b.** seperate   **c.** sepurate

7. I have not seen her since _____ grade.

    a. eith   **b.** eigth   **c.** eighth

8. The date is circled on the _____.

    a. callender   **b.** calendar   **c.** calander

9. Dana got her _____ last week.

    a. lisense   **b.** liscence   **c.** license

10. That ring is _____.

    a. valuble   **b.** valuable   **c.** valueble

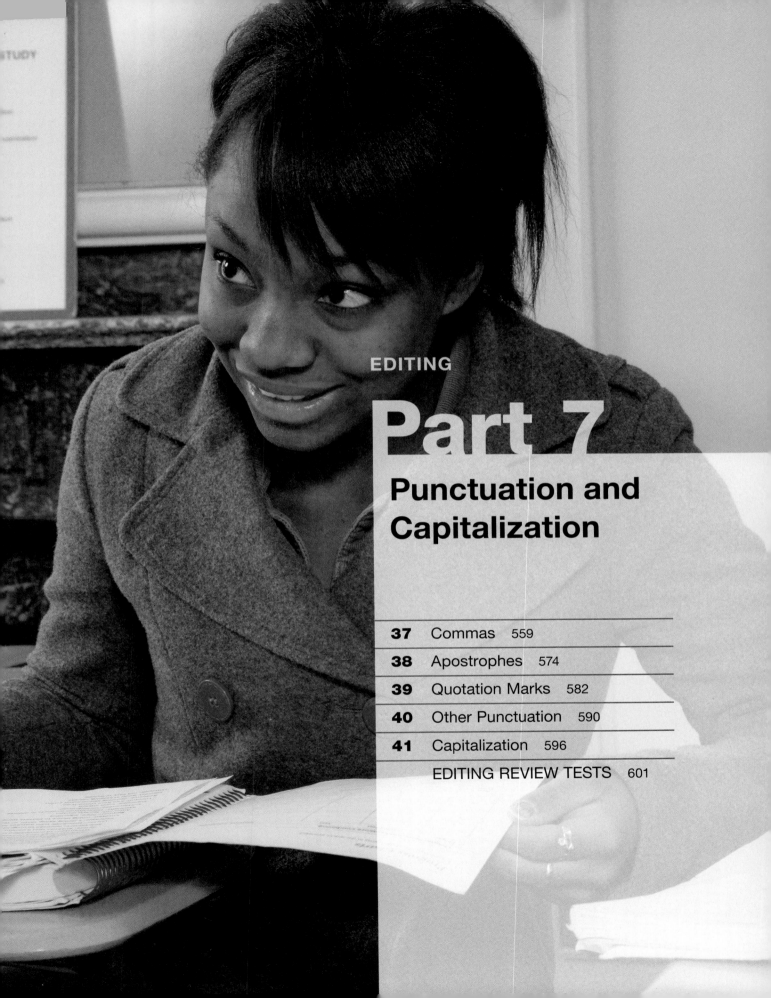

EDITING

Part 7

Punctuation and Capitalization

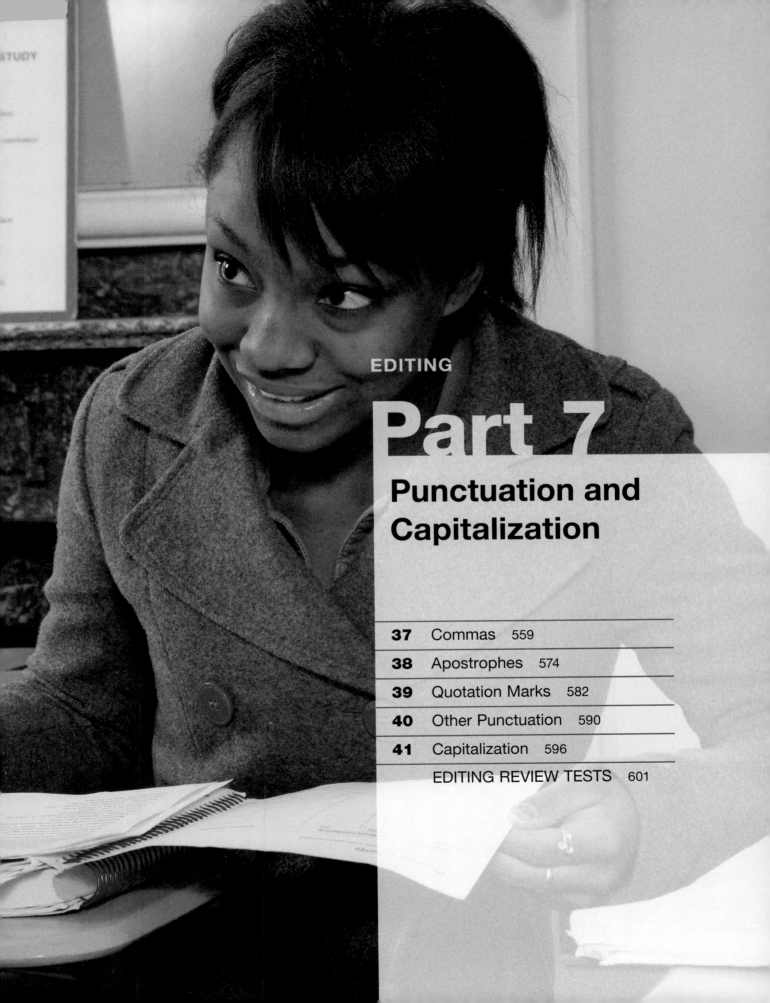

EDITING

Part 7

Punctuation and Capitalization

THIS CHAPTER

- shows you how and where to use commas (and tells you where *not* to use them)
- gives you practice using commas correctly

37

Commas (,)

Understand What Commas Do

Commas (,) are punctuation marks that help readers understand a sentence. Read aloud the following three sentences. How does the use of commas change the meaning?

NO COMMA	When you call Sarah I will start cooking.
ONE COMMA	When you call Sarah, I will start cooking.
TWO COMMAS	When you call, Sarah, I will start cooking.

Commas signal particular meanings to your readers, so it is important that you understand when and how to use them.

TIP For fun podcasts with tips on grammar and usage, check out Grammar Girl's Quick and Dirty Tips for Better Writing on **bedfordstmartins .com/realwriting**.

RESOURCES For instructor resources, go to **bedfordstmartins .com/rewritingbasics**.

Practice Using Commas Correctly

Commas between Items in a Series

Use commas to separate the items in a series (three or more items). This includes the last item in the series, which usually has *and* before it.

TIP How does a comma change the way you read a sentence aloud? Many readers pause when they come to a comma.

| Item | , | Item | , | Item | , | and | Item |

To get from South Dakota to Texas, we will drive through *Nebraska*, *Kansas*, and *Oklahoma*.

We can *sleep in the car, stay in a motel,* or *camp outside.*

As I drive, I see many beautiful sights, such as *mountains, plains,* and *prairies.*

NOTE: Writers do not always use a comma before the final item in a series. In college writing, however, it is best to include it.

Commas between Coordinate Adjectives

Coordinate adjectives are two or more adjectives that independently modify the same noun and are separated by commas.

Conor ordered a big, fat, greasy burger.

The diner food was cheap, unhealthy, and delicious.

Do *not* use a comma between the final adjective and the noun it describes.

INCORRECT	Joelle wore a long, clingy, red, dress.
CORRECT	Joelle wore a long, clingy, red dress.

Cumulative adjectives describe the same noun but are not separated by commas because they form a unit that describes the noun. You can identify cumulative adjectives because separating them by *and* does not make any sense.

The store is having its *last storewide clearance* sale.
[Putting *and* between *last* and *storewide* and *storewide* and *clearance* would make an odd sentence: The store is having its *last* and *storewide* and *clearance* sale. The adjectives in the sentence are cumulative adjectives and should not be separated by commas.]

In summary:

- **Do** use commas to separate two or more **coordinate adjectives.**
- **Do not** use commas to separate **cumulative adjectives.**

TEACHING TIP Write this incorrectly punctuated sentence on the board: *My daughter is a fast aggressive, and competitive soccer player.* Read it aloud (as if it were correctly punctuated), and ask students if they can hear where the missing comma should go.

TIP For more practice using commas correctly, visit Exercise Central at **bedfordstmartins** **.com/realwriting.**

. . . .

PRACTICE 1 Using Commas in Series and with Adjectives

Edit the following sentences by underlining the items in the series and adding commas where they are needed. If a sentence is already correct, put a "C" next to it.

EXAMPLE: Sales of our fruit juices have expanded in the Northeast, the South, and the Midwest.

1. Continued expansion depends on our ability to promote novelty beverages such as papaya, mango, and boysenberry juices in grocery stores and restaurants.

2. The juices are good alternatives to soda because they are <u>natural</u>,<u>nutri-tious</u>, and <u>healthy</u>.

3. In California, we are doing well because many Californians are open to <u>new</u>,<u>healthful</u> products.

4. In these areas, our increase in market share over the past three years has been <u>7 percent</u>,<u>10 percent</u>,and <u>7 percent</u>.

5. As we enter new markets, we expect <u>similar</u>,<u>steady</u>,<u>increasing</u> growth.

6. In each section of the country, <u>the regional sales director will develop a plan</u>,<u>his or her assistant will communicate the plan</u>,and <u>local salespeople will implement the plan</u> for that area.

7. We want to target New England states such as <u>Connecticut</u>,<u>Massachu-setts</u>,and <u>Maine</u>, where attitudes about fruit juice are similar to those in <u>Seattle</u>,<u>Portland</u>,and <u>other Northwest cities</u>.

8. Our advertising should emphasize <u>our small-scale production methods</u>, <u>our commitment to quality</u>, and <u>our juices' delicious flavor</u>. *C*

9. We should <u>set up displays</u>,<u>provide free samples of our juices</u>,and <u>sponsor contests</u>.

10. <u>Careful planning</u>, <u>hard work</u>, and <u>individual initiative</u> will ensure the growth of our company. *C*

RESOURCES To gauge students' punctuation skills, use the *Testing Tool Kit* CD-ROM available with this book.

Commas in Compound Sentences

A **compound sentence** contains two complete sentences joined by a coordinating conjunction: *and, but, for, nor, or, so, yet.* Use a comma before the joining word to separate the two complete sentences.

TIP Remember the coordinating conjunctions with *FANBOYS: for, and, nor, but, or, yet,* and *so.* For more information, see Chapter 29.

Sentence	**,**	*and, but, for, nor, or, so, yet*	Sentence.

I called my best friend, and she agreed to drive me to work.

I asked my best friend to drive me to work, but she was busy.

I can take the bus to work, or I can call another friend.

LANGUAGE NOTE: A comma alone cannot separate two sentences in English. Doing so creates a run-on (see Ch. 23).

> ### Editing for Correct Comma Usage: Using Commas in Compound Sentences
>
> ---
>
> **Find**
>
> Many college <u>students</u> <u>are</u> the first in their families to go to college (and) their <u>relatives</u> <u>are</u> proud of them.
>
> 1. To determine if the sentence is compound, **underline** subjects, and **double-underline** the verbs.
> 2. **Ask:** Is the sentence compound? Yes.
> 3. **Circle** the word that joins them.
>
> ---
>
> **Edit**
>
> Many college students are the first in their families to go to college, and their relatives are proud of them.
>
> 4. **Put a comma** before the word that joins the two sentences.

PRACTICE 2   Using Commas in Compound Sentences

Edit the following compound sentences by adding commas where they are needed. If a sentence is already correct, put a "C" next to it.

> **EXAMPLE:** Marika wanted to get a college education, but her husband did not like the idea.

TIP Answers to odd-numbered practice items in this chapter begin on page AK-8 at the back of the book.

1. Marika's hospital volunteer work had convinced her to become a physical therapist, but she needed a college degree to qualify. C

2. Deciding to apply to college was difficult for her, so she was excited when she was admitted.

3. She had chosen the college carefully, for it had an excellent program in physical therapy.

4. Marika knew the courses would be difficult, but she had not expected her husband to oppose her plan.

ESL Because different languages have different intonation patterns, students should not rely on intonation alone to decide where to put commas.

5. They had been married for twelve years, and he was surprised that she wanted a career. C

6. She tried to tell him about the exciting things she was learning, but he did not seem interested.

7. It was hard for her to manage the house and keep up with her classes, but he would not help. *C*

8. Maybe he was upset that she wanted more education than he had,or perhaps he was afraid they would grow apart.

9. She did not want to have to choose between her husband and an education,and she did not have to.

10. They talked about their problems,and now he thinks her career might even help their marriage.

· ·

Commas after Introductory Word Groups

Use a comma after an introductory word or word group. An introductory word group can be a word, a phrase, or a clause. The comma lets your readers know when the main part of the sentence is starting.

Introductory word or word group	,	Main part of sentence.

INTRODUCTORY WORD: *Yesterday,* I went to the game.

INTRODUCTORY PHRASE: *By the way,* I do not have a babysitter for tomorrow.

INTRODUCTORY CLAUSE: *While I waited outside,* Susan went backstage.

· ·

PRACTICE 3   Using Commas after Introductory Word Groups

In each item, underline introductory words or word groups. Then, add commas after introductory word groups where they are needed. If a sentence is already correct, put a "C" next to it.

> **EXAMPLE:** According to most medical researchers, the chance of the AIDS virus being spread through athletic contact is low.

1. As we all know,AIDS is spread mainly through sexual contact and through drug use that involves the sharing of needles.

2. Nonetheless,some people feel that all college athletes should be tested for HIV.

3. Since basketball star Magic Johnson revealed in 1991 that he is HIV-positive,an NBA player must be removed from a game if he is bleeding.

4. Once the wound is properly bandaged,the player is allowed to return to the game.

5. Not surprisingly, many college sports follow similar rules.

6. However, requiring athletes to leave a contest when they are bleeding is quite different from forcing them to be tested for HIV. *C*

7. According to some student athletes, mandatory HIV testing would violate their civil liberties.

8. Using the same argument, many student athletes object to being tested for the use of drugs. *C*

9. In their view, student athletes should be treated no differently than other students. *C*

10. In this case, some would say that public health is more important than civil liberties.

Commas around Appositives and Interrupters

An **appositive** comes directly before or after a noun or pronoun and re-names it.

TIP For more on appositives, see Chapter 32.

Lily, *a senior*, will take her nursing exam this summer.

The prices are outrageous at Beans, *the local coffee shop*.

An **interrupter** is an aside or transition that interrupts the flow of a sentence and does not affect its meaning.

My sister, *incidentally*, has good reasons for being late.

Her child had a fever, *for example*.

Putting commas around appositives and interrupters tells readers that these elements give extra information but are not essential to the meaning of a sentence. If an appositive or interrupter is in the middle of a sentence, set it off with a pair of commas, one before and one after. If an appositive or interrupter comes at the beginning or end of a sentence, separate it from the rest of the sentence with one comma.

By the way, your proposal has been accepted.

Your proposal, *by the way*, has been accepted.

Your proposal has been accepted, *by the way*.

NOTE: Sometimes an appositive is essential to the meaning of a sentence. When a sentence would not have the same meaning without the appositive, the appositive should not be set off with commas.

The actor *John Travolta* has never won an Academy Award.

[The sentence *The actor has never won an Academy Award* does not have the same meaning.]

Editing for Correct Comma Usage:
Using Commas to Set Off Appositives and Interrupters

Find

Tamara my sister-in-law moved in with us last week.

1. **Underline** the subject.
2. **Underline** any appositive (which renames the subject) or interrupter (which interrupts the flow of the sentence).
3. **Ask:** Is the appositive or interrupter essential to the meaning of the sentence? *No.*

Edit

Tamara, my sister-in-law, moved in with us last week.

4. If it is not essential, **set it off with commas**.

- -

PRACTICE 4 Using Commas to Set Off Appositives and Interrupters

Underline all the appositives and interrupters in the following sentences. Then, use commas to set them off.

> **EXAMPLE:** Harry, an attentive student, could not hear his teacher because the radiator in class made a constant rattling.

1. Some rooms, in fact, are full of echoes, dead zones, and mechanical noises that make it hard for students to hear.

2. The American Speech-Language-Hearing Association, experts on how noise levels affect learning abilities, have set guidelines for how much noise in a classroom is too much.

3. The association recommends that background noise, the constant whir-ring or whining sounds made by radiators, lights, and other machines, be no more than 35 decibels.

4. That level, 35 decibels, is about as loud as a whispering voice fifteen feet away.

5. One study found a level of 65 decibels, the volume of a vacuum cleaner, in a number of classrooms around the country.

6. Other classroom noises came, for example, from ancient heating systems, whirring air-conditioning units, rattling windows, humming classroom computers, buzzing clocks, and the honking of traffic on nearby streets.

7. An increasing number of school districts are beginning to pay more attention to acoustics, the study of sound, when they plan new schools.

8. Some changes, such as putting felt pads on the bottoms of chair and desk legs to keep them from scraping against the floor, are simple and inexpensive.

9. Other changes, however, can be costly and controversial, such as buying thicker drapes, building thicker walls, or installing specially designed acoustic ceiling tiles.

10. School administrators, often parents themselves, hope that these improvements will result in a better learning environment for students.

Commas around Adjective Clauses

An **adjective clause** is a group of words that begins with *who, which,* or *that*; has a subject and a verb; and describes a noun right before it in a sentence. Whether or not an adjective clause should be set off from the rest of the sentence by commas depends on its meaning in the sentence.

If an adjective clause can be taken out of a sentence without completely changing the meaning of the sentence, put commas around the clause.

> Lily, *who is my cousin,* will take her nursing exam this summer.
>
> Beans, *which is the local coffee shop,* charges outrageous prices.
>
> I complained to Mr. Kranz, *who is the shop's manager.*

TEACHING TIP Ask students to explain what is meant by "essential" in this context. Help them see that essential (restrictive) phrases and clauses generally answer the question "Which one?" If they are taken out, the meaning of the sentence can change completely.

If an adjective clause is essential to the meaning of a sentence, do not put commas around it. You can tell whether a clause is essential by taking it out and seeing if the meaning of the sentence changes significantly, as it would if you took the clauses out of the following examples.

> The only grocery store *that sold good bread* went out of business.
>
> Students *who do internships* often improve their hiring potential.
>
> Salesclerks *who sell liquor to minors* are breaking the law.

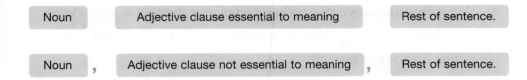

| Noun | Adjective clause essential to meaning | Rest of sentence. |

| Noun | , | Adjective clause not essential to meaning | , | Rest of sentence. |

**Editing for Correct Comma Usage:
Using Commas to Set Off Adjective Clauses**

Find

The woman <u>who had octuplets</u> received much publicity.

1. **Underline** any adjective clause (a word group that begins with *who*, *which*, or *that*).
2. **Read** the sentence without this clause.
3. **Ask:** Does the meaning change significantly without the clause? Yes.

Edit

The woman who had octuplets received much publicity.

4. If the meaning *does* change, as in this case, **do not put in commas**. (Add commas only if the meaning *does not* change.)

PRACTICE 5   Using Commas to Set Off Adjective Clauses

Edit the following sentences by putting commas around adjective clauses where they are needed. Remember that if an adjective clause is essential to the meaning of a sentence, do not use commas. If a sentence is already correct, put a "C" next to it.

> **EXAMPLE:** Maintaining a healthy weight, which is a wise decision, is
>
> becoming more important to teens.

1. Unfortunately, many young people turn to fad diets that involve drastic
   decreases in food intake. C

2. Teens who cut down too much on nutrients can eventually do damage to
   their bodies. C

3. Diet drinks, which often have fewer calories, deprive people of essential
   vitamins and minerals.

4. Nutritional studies, which were conducted over the course of two years, have shown that young women tend to be much more involved with dieting than young men are.

5. Young people, who tend to make snap decisions, can learn to make healthier food choices.

6. Examples of snacks that are high in nutrition include dried fruit and nuts, fruit smoothies, and fresh vegetables. *C*

7. Parents, who are often frustrated at their children's diets, can also help their kids make healthier choices.

8. Of course, exercise, which burns calories and works muscles, is also an important element of maintaining a healthy weight.

9. Experts from different organizations, who all seem to agree on the issue, recommend that young people exercise three times a week.

10. Parents who provide a good role model for their children can play one of the most helpful parts of all. *C*

Other Uses for Commas

Commas with Quotation Marks

TIP For more on quotation marks, see Chapter 39.

Quotation marks are used to show that you are repeating exactly what someone said. Use commas to set off the words inside quotation marks from the rest of the sentence.

> "Let me see your license," demanded the police officer.
>
> "Did you realize," she asked, "that you were going eighty miles per hour?"
>
> I exclaimed, "No!"

Notice that a comma never comes directly after a quotation mark.

When quotations are not attributed to a particular person, commas may not be necessary.

> "Pretty is as pretty does" never made sense to me.

Commas in Addresses

Use commas to separate the elements of an address included in a sentence. However, do not use a comma before a zip code.

> My address is 2512 Windermere Street, Jackson, Mississippi 40720.

If a sentence continues after the address, put a comma after the address.

> I moved here from Detroit, Michigan, when I was eighteen.

Commas in Dates

Separate the day from the year with a comma. If you give just the month and year, do not separate them with a comma.

> My daughter was born on November 8, 2004.
>
> The next conference is in August 2011.

If a sentence continues after the date, put a comma after the date.

> On April 21, 2012, the contract will expire.

Commas with Names

Put commas around the name of someone you are addressing by name.

> Don, I want you to come look at this.
>
> Unfortunately, Marie, you need to finish the report by next week.

Commas with Yes or No

Put commas around the word *yes* or *no* in response to a question.

> Yes, I believe you are right.

• •

PRACTICE 6 Using Commas in Other Ways

Edit the following sentences by adding commas where they are needed. If a sentence is already correct, put a "C" next to it.

> **EXAMPLE:** On August 12, 2006, beachfront property was badly damaged by a fast-moving storm.

1. Some homeowners were still waiting to settle their claims with their insurance companies in January 2007. *C*

2. Rob McGregor of 31 Hudson Street, Wesleyville, is one of those homeowners.

3. Asked if he was losing patience, McGregor replied, "Yes, I sure am."

4. "I've really had it up to here," McGregor said. *C*

5. His wife said, "Rob, don't go mouthing off to any reporters."

6. "Betty,˄I'll say what I want to say,˄" Rob replied.

7. An official of Value-Safe Insurance of Wrightsville,˄Ohio,˄said the company will process claims within the next few months.

8. "No,˄there is no way we can do it any sooner,˄" the official said.

9. Customers unhappy with their service may write to Value-Safe Insurance, P.O. Box 225, Wrightsville, Ohio 62812. *C*

10. The company's home office in Rye,˄New York,˄can be reached by a toll-free number.

Edit for Commas

PRACTICE 7   Editing for Commas

Edit the following paragraphs by adding commas where they are needed.

(1) One of the nation's grocery store chains,˄Whole Foods Market,˄ recently made an important business decision. (2) As of April 22,˄2008,˄ they stopped asking customers if they wanted paper or plastic bags. (3) The store,˄which cares about environmental issues,˄now offers only paper bags made from recycled paper.

(4) The president of Whole Foods stated,˄"We estimate we will keep 100 million new plastic grocery bags out of our environment between Earth Day and the end of this year." (5) The company also sells cloth bags, hoping to encourage shoppers to bring their own reusable bags with them when they go shopping.

(6) Experts believe that plastic bags do a great deal of damage to the environment. (7) They clog drains,˄harm wildlife,˄and take up an enormous amount of space in the nation's landfills. (8) It takes more than a thousand years for a plastic bag to break down, and Americans use 100 billion of them every single year. (9) According to the experts,˄ that works out to more than 330 bags for every single person in the United States.

PRACTICE 8   Editing Your Own Writing for Commas

As a final practice, edit a piece of your own writing for comma usage. It can be a paper you are working on for this course, a paper you have already finished, a paper for another course, or a recent piece of writing from your work or everyday life. In your learning journal, record any examples of sentences with comma problems that you find, along with edited versions of those sentences.

. . . .

Chapter Review

1. A comma (,) is a _punctuation mark_ that helps readers understand a sentence.

2. How do you use commas in these three situations?

   In a series of items, _use commas to separate three or more items._

   In a compound sentence, _use a coordinating conjunction and a comma_
   to make two sentences into one.

   With an introductory word or word group, _use a comma after the word,_
   clause, or phrase.

3. An appositive comes before or after a noun or pronoun and _renames the_
   noun or pronoun.

4. An interrupter is an _aside or transition_ that interrupts the flow of a sentence.

5. Put commas around an adjective clause when it is ___not essential___ to the meaning of a sentence.

6. How are commas used with quotation marks? _Use commas to set off_
   the words inside quotation marks from the rest of the sentence.

7. In a date with the month, the day, and the year, a comma goes _between_
   the day and the year.

LEARNING JOURNAL Did you find comma errors in your writing? What is the main thing you have learned about using commas that will help you? What is unclear to you?

TEACHING TIP Collect students' learning journals to find out what the class or individual students need more work on.

Chapter Test

Circle the correct choice for each of the following items.

1. If an underlined portion of this sentence is incorrect, select the revision that fixes it. If the sentence is correct as written, choose d.

   The company <u>owners, for</u> your <u>information are</u> planning to inspect
                    A   B

   our <u>department this</u> afternoon.
             C

   a. owners for   **c.** department, this
   b. information, are   **d.** No change is necessary.

TIP For advice on taking tests, see Appendix A.

RESOURCES The *Testing Tool Kit* CD-ROM available with this book has even more tests. For Editing Review Tests, see pages 601–10.

2. Choose the item that has no errors.

  a. Digital cameras are easy, to use but they do not necessarily improve people's pictures.

  (b.) Digital cameras are easy to use, but they do not necessarily improve people's pictures.

  c. Digital cameras are easy to use, but, they do not necessarily improve people's pictures.

3. Choose the item that has no errors.

  a. If you do not file your income tax forms by April 15, 2010 you could face penalties.

  (b.) If you do not file your income tax forms by April 15, 2010, you could face penalties.

  c. If you do not file your income tax forms by April 15 2010 you could face penalties.

4. If an underlined portion of this sentence is incorrect, select the revision that fixes it. If the sentence is correct as written, choose d.

Henry's <u>favorite hobbies</u> <u>are watching birds,</u> collecting <u>stamps, and</u>
        A   B   C
fixing up old cars.

  a. favorite, hobbies   **c.** stamps and

  b. are watching, birds   **(d.)** No change is necessary.

5. Choose the item that has no errors.

  (a.) Roger, who teaches dance at a local studio, will be my partner for the ballroom competition.

  b. Roger who teaches dance at a local studio will be my partner for the ballroom competition.

  c. Roger who teaches dance at a local studio, will be my partner for the ballroom competition.

6. If an underlined portion of this sentence is incorrect, select the revision that fixes it. If the sentence is correct as written, choose d.

Feeling <u>adventurous, Alexia</u> <u>tasted the</u> guava, <u>mango and</u> passion
         A   B   C
fruit.

  a. adventurous Alexia   **(c.)** mango, and

  b. tasted, the   **d.** No change is necessary.

7. Choose the item that has no errors.

    a. I discovered that Lansing, Michigan was the hometown of four people at the party.

    b. I discovered that Lansing Michigan, was the hometown of four people at the party.

    (c.) I discovered that Lansing, Michigan, was the hometown of four people at the party.

8. If an underlined portion of this sentence is incorrect, select the revision that fixes it. If the sentence is correct as written, choose d.

Just to be <u>different I</u> <u>decided to</u> wear a top <u>hat to</u> all of my classes
             A   B   C

today.

    (a.) different, I   **c.** hat, to

    b. decided, to   **d.** No change is necessary.

9. Choose the item that has no errors.

    a. "If you follow my instructions precisely" said the manager, "I will consider you for a promotion."

    b. "If you follow my instructions precisely," said the manager "I will consider you for a promotion."

    (c.) "If you follow my instructions precisely," said the manager, "I will consider you for a promotion."

10. If an underlined portion of this sentence is incorrect, select the revision that fixes it. If the sentence is correct as written, choose d.

No Bob, I cannot <u>swim, paddle</u> a <u>kayak, or</u> steer a sailboat.
  A   B   C

    (a.) No, Bob,   **c.** kayak or

    b. swim paddle   **d.** No change is necessary.

38

Apostrophes (')

THIS CHAPTER
- explains how to use apostrophes
- gives you practice using apostrophes correctly

Understand What Apostrophes Do

TIP For fun podcasts with tips on grammar and usage, check out Grammar Girl's Quick and Dirty Tips for Better Writing on **bedfordstmartins .com/realwriting.**

An **apostrophe (')** is a punctuation mark that either shows ownership (*Susan's*) or indicates that a letter has been intentionally left out to form a contraction (*I'm, that's, they're*). Although an apostrophe looks like a comma (,), it is not used for the same purpose, and it is written higher on the line than commas are.

apostrophe'   comma,

Practice Using Apostrophes Correctly

Apostrophes to Show Ownership

TIP *Singular* means one; *plural* means more than one.

Add -'s to a singular noun to show ownership even if the noun already ends in -s.

Karen's apartment is on the South Side.

They all followed the *college's* rules.

James's roommate is looking for him.

If a noun is plural and ends in -s, just add an apostrophe. If it is plural but does not end in -s, add -'s.

My *books'* covers are falling off.

[more than one book]

RESOURCES *Additional Resources* contains tests and supplemental exercises for this chapter. For additional instructor resources, go to **bedfordstmartins.com/ rewritingbasics.**

The *twins'* father was building them a playhouse.
[more than one twin]

The *children's* toys were broken.

The *men's* locker room is being painted.

The placement of an apostrophe makes a difference in meaning.

My *sister's* six children are at my house for the weekend.
[one sister who has six children]

My *sisters'* six children are at my house for the weekend.
[two or more sisters who together have six children]

Do not use an apostrophe to form the plural of a noun.

Gina went camping with her *sister's* and their children.

All of the *highway's* to the airport are under construction.

Do not use an apostrophe with a possessive pronoun. These pronouns already show ownership (possession).

Is that bag *your's*?   No, it is *our's*.

Possessive Pronouns

my	his	its	their
mine	her	our	theirs
your	hers	ours	whose
yours			

The single most common error with apostrophes and pronouns is confusing *its* (a possessive pronoun) with *it's* (a contraction meaning "it is"). Whenever you write *it's*, test correctness by replacing it with *it is* and reading the sentence aloud to hear if it makes sense.

• •

PRACTICE 1   Using Apostrophes to Show Ownership

Edit the following sentences by adding -'s or an apostrophe alone to show ownership and by crossing out any incorrect use of an apostrophe or -'s.

> **EXAMPLE:** People must respect other people's need's for personal
>
> space.

TIP For more practice using apostrophes correctly, visit Exercise Central at **bedfordstmartins.com/ realwriting.**

TIP Answers to odd-numbered practice items for this chapter appear on page AK-9 at the back of the book.

1. A person's feelings about personal space depend on his or her's culture.

2. Personal space is especially important in cultures' that are formal and reserved.

3. Putting your face too close to another's is considered rude.

4. Fistfights often are preceded by someone's aggressive violation of some- one else's space.

5. The expression "Get out of my face!" is a warning meant to prevent the confrontation's violent conclusion.

6. A dog's interaction with a member of it's own species can follow a similar pattern; dogs are determined to defend what is their's.

7. The hair on dogs' neck's may stand on end.

8. A researcher's recent work examines various species' personal space.

9. For example, seagulls' positions on a log follow a pattern similar to that of people lined up waiting for a bus.

10. Studies show that an animal's overcrowded environment can lead to violent behavior.

· ·

Apostrophes in Contractions

TIP Ask your instructor if contractions are acceptable in papers.

A **contraction** is formed by joining two words and leaving out one or more of the letters. When writing a contraction, put an apostrophe where the letter or letters have been left out, not between the two words.

> *She's* on her way. = *She is* on her way.

> *I'll* see you there. = *I will* see you there.

Be sure to put the apostrophe in the right place.

> It *doesn't* really matter.

LANGUAGE NOTE: Contractions that include a *be* verb cannot be followed by the base verb or the helping verbs *can, does,* or *has.*

INCORRECT	She's *work* late. He's *has* sick.
CORRECT	She's *working* late. He's sick.

Common Contractions

aren't = are not	she'll = she will
can't = cannot	she's = she is, she has
couldn't = could not	there's = there is
didn't = did not	they'd = they would, they had
don't = do not	they'll = they will
he'd = he would, he had	they're = they are
he'll = he will	they've = they have
he's = he is, he has	who'd = who would, who had
I'd = I would, I had	who'll = who will
I'll = I will	who's = who is, who has
I'm = I am	won't = will not
I've = I have	wouldn't = would not
isn't = is not	you'd = you would, you had
it's = it is, it has	you'll = you will
let's = let us	you're = you are
she'd = she would, she had	you've = you have

ESL Because contractions are often new to ESL students, you may want to advise them to avoid all contractions in college work that they are submitting for a grade. They should use apostrophes only to show ownership.

. . . .

PRACTICE 2 **Using Apostrophes in Contractions**

Read each sentence carefully, looking for any words that have missing letters. Edit these words by adding apostrophes where needed and crossing out incorrectly used apostrophes.

> **EXAMPLE:** Although we observe personal space boundaries in our daily lives, they're not something we spend much time thinking about.

1. You'll notice right away if a stranger leans over and talks to you so that his face is practically touching yours.

2. Perhaps you'd accept this kind of behavior from a family member.

3. There isn't one single acceptable boundary we'd use in all situations.

4. An elevator has its own rules: Don't stand right next to a person if there is open space.

5. With coworkers, we're likely to keep a personal space of four to twelve feet.

RESOURCES To gauge students' punctuation skills, use the *Testing Tool Kit* CD-ROM available with this book.

6. We'll accept a personal space of four feet down to eighteen inches with friends.

7. The last sixteen inches are reserved for people we're most intimate with.

8. When people hug or kiss, they're willing to surrender their personal space to each other.

9. A supervisor who's not aware of the personal space boundaries of his or her employees might make workers uncomfortable.

10. Even if the supervisor doesn't intend anything by the gestures, it's his or her responsibility to act appropriately.

Apostrophes with Letters, Numbers, and Time

Use -'s to make letters and numbers plural. The apostrophe prevents confusion or misreading.

> In Scrabble games, there are more *e*'s than any other letter.

> In women's shoes, size *8*'s are more common than size *10*'s.

Use an apostrophe or -'s in certain expressions in which time nouns are treated as if they possess something.

> She took four *weeks*' maternity leave after the baby was born.

> This *year*'s graduating class is huge.

PRACTICE 3 Using Apostrophes with Letters, Numbers, and Time

Edit the following sentences by adding apostrophes where needed and crossing out incorrectly used apostrophes.

> **EXAMPLE:** When I returned to work after two weeks' vacation, I had what looked like a decade's worth of work in my box.

1. I sorted letters alphabetically, starting with *A*'s.

2. There were more letters by names starting with *M*'s than any other.

3. When I checked my e-mail, the screen flashed 48's to show that I had forty-eight messages.

4. My voice mail wasn't much better, telling me that in two weeks' time I had received twenty-five messages.

5. I needed another week's time just to return all the phone calls.

Edit for Apostrophes

∙ ∙

PRACTICE 4   Editing for Apostrophes

Edit the following paragraphs by adding two apostrophes where needed and crossing out four incorrectly used apostrophes.

(1) Have you noticed many honeybee's when you go outside? (2) If not, it is'nt surprising. (3) For reasons that scientists still don't quite understand, these bees have been disappearing all across the country. (4) This mass disappearance is a problem because bees are an important part of growing a wide variety of flowers, fruits, vegetables, and nuts as they spread pollen from one place to another.

(5) In the last year, more than one-third, or billions, of the honeybees in the United States' have disappeared. (6) As a consequence, farmers have been forced either to buy or to rent beehives for their crops. (7) Typically, people who are in the bee business ship hives to farmers' fields by truck. (8) The hives often have to travel hundreds of miles.

(9) Scientist's have been trying to find out what happened to the once-thriving bee population. (10) They suspect that either a disease or chemicals harmed the honeybees. (11) As part of their research, scientists are taking samples from different hives to study. (12) They are eager to find out what caused bee's to disappear so that they can help reverse the trend, if possible.

∙ ∙

PRACTICE 5   Editing Your Own Writing for Apostrophes

As a final practice, edit a piece of your own writing for apostrophes. It can be a paper you are working on for this course, a paper you have already finished, a paper for another course, or a recent piece of writing from your work or everyday life. In your learning journal, record any examples of sentences with apostrophe problems that you find, along with edited versions of these sentences.

∙ ∙

Chapter Review

1. An apostrophe (') is a punctuation mark that either shows
_____ownership_____ or indicates that a letter or letters have been intentionally left out to form a _____contraction_____ .

2. To show ownership, add _____'s_____ to a singular noun, even if the noun already ends in -*s*. For a plural noun, add an ___apostrophe___ alone if the noun ends in -*s*; add _____'s_____ if the noun does not end in -*s*.

3. Do not use an apostrophe with a ___possessive___ pronoun.

4. Do not confuse *its* and *it's*. *Its* shows ___ownership___; *it's* is a ___contraction___ meaning "it is."

5. A ___contraction___ is formed by joining two words and leaving out one or more of the letters.

6. Use -'s to make letters and numbers ___plural___.

7. Use an apostrophe or -'s in certain expressions in which ___time nouns___ are treated as if they possess something.

LEARNING JOURNAL Did you find errors in your writing? What is the main thing you have learned about apostrophes that will help you? How would you explain the *it's/its* rule to someone? What is unclear to you?

TEACHING TIP Collect students' learning journals to find out what the class or individual students need more work on.

TIP For advice on taking tests, see Appendix A.

RESOURCES The *Testing Tool Kit* CD-ROM available with this book has even more tests. Also, for cumulative Editing Review Tests, see pages 601–10.

Chapter Test

Circle the correct choice for each of the following items.

1. If an underlined portion of this sentence is incorrect, select the revision that fixes it. If the sentence is correct as written, choose d.

   I've always believed that <u>its</u> a crime to use software that you <u>haven't</u>
   <u>A</u>   B   C
   paid for.

   a. Ive   **c.** havent
   (b.) it's   **d.** No change is necessary.

2. Choose the item that has no errors.
   a. The thieves boldness made them a lot of money, but it eventually landed them in jail.
   b. The thieves's boldness made them a lot of money, but it eventually landed them in jail.
   (c.) The thieves' boldness made them a lot of money, but it eventually landed them in jail.

3. Choose the item that has no errors.
   a. By playing that slot machine, your throwing away money.
   (b.) By playing that slot machine, you're throwing away money.
   c. By playing that slot machine, youre' throwing away money.

4.   If an underlined portion of this sentence is incorrect, select the revision
that fixes it. If the sentence is correct as written, choose d.

The house is now <u>Renee's</u>, but <u>she'll</u> regret having an address with
          A   B

five <u>3s</u> in it.
     C

   a. Renees   **(c.)** 3's

   b. sh'ell   **d.** No change is necessary.

5.   Choose the item that has no errors.

   (a.) Her eighteen months' service overseas has somehow made her seem
older.

   b. Her eighteen month's service overseas has somehow made her seem
older.

   c. Her eighteen months service overseas has somehow made her seem
older.

39

Quotation Marks (" ")

THIS CHAPTER
- explains how quotation marks are used
- gives you practice using quotation marks correctly

Understand What Quotation Marks Do

TIP For fun podcasts with tips on grammar and usage, check out Grammar Girl's Quick and Dirty Tips for Better Writing on **bedfordstmartins .com/realwriting.**

Quotation marks (" ") always appear in pairs. Quotation marks have two common uses in college writing: They are used with direct quotations, and they are used to set off titles.

Direct quotations exactly repeat, word for word, what someone said or wrote, and **indirect quotations** restate what someone said or wrote, but not word for word. Quotation marks are used only for direct quotations.

> **DIRECT QUOTATION**   He said, "You should get the downtown bus."
>
> **INDIRECT QUOTATION**   He said that I should get the downtown bus.

Practice Using Quotation Marks Correctly

Quotation Marks for Direct Quotations

RESOURCES *Additional Resources* contains tests and supplemental exercises for this chapter.

When you write a direct quotation, use quotation marks around the quoted words. These tell readers that the words used are exactly what was said or written.

1. "I do not know what she means," I said to my friend Lina.

2. Lina asked, "Do you think we should ask a question?"

3. "Excuse me, Professor Soames," I called out, "but could you explain that again?"

4. "Yes," said Professor Soames. "Let me make sure you all understand."

5. After further explanation, Professor Soames asked, "Are there any other questions?"

When you are writing a paper that uses outside sources, use quotation marks to indicate where you quote the exact words of a source.

TIP For more on incorporating outside source material through quoting and other methods, see Chapter 20.

> We all need to become more conscientious recyclers. A recent editorial in the *Bolton Common* reported, "When recycling volunteers spot-checked bags that were supposed to contain only newspaper, they found a collection of nonrecyclable items such as plastic candy wrappers, aluminum foil, and birthday cards."

When quoting, writers usually use words that identify who is speaking, such as *I said to my friend Lina* in the first example on the previous page. The identifying words can come after the quoted words (example 1), before them (example 2), or in the middle of them (example 3). Here are some guidelines for capitalization and punctuation.

GUIDELINES FOR CAPITALIZATION AND PUNCTUATION

- Capitalize the first letter in a complete sentence that is being quoted, even if it comes after some identifying words (example 2 on the previous page).

TEACHING TIP As you go over the first two rules on capitalization, put a sentence on the board without any quotation marks. Ask students where the quotation marks should go and which letters should be capitalized.

- Do not capitalize the first letter in a quotation if it is not the first word in a complete sentence (*but* in example 3).

- If it is a complete sentence, and it is clear who the speaker is, a quotation can stand on its own (second sentence in example 4).

- Identifying words must be attached to a quotation; they cannot be a sentence on their own.

- Use commas to separate any identifying words from quoted words in the same sentence.

- Always put quotation marks after commas and periods. Put quotation marks after question marks and exclamation points if they are part of the quoted sentence.

TIP For more on commas with quotation marks, see Chapter 37.

- If a question mark or exclamation point is part of your own sentence, put it after the quotation mark.

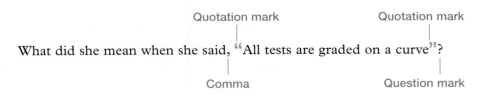

Setting Off a Quotation within Another Quotation

Sometimes, when you directly quote someone, part of what that person said quotes words that someone else said or wrote. Put single quotation marks (' ') around the quotation within a quotation so that readers understand who said what.

> The student handbook says, "Students must be given the opportunity to make up work missed for legitimate reasons."

> Terry told his instructor, "I am sorry I missed the exam, but that is not a reason to fail me for the term. Our student handbook says, 'Students must be given the opportunity to make up work missed for legitimate reasons,' and I have a good reason."

● ●

PRACTICE 1   Punctuating Direct Quotations

Edit the following sentences by adding quotation marks and commas where needed.

TIP For more practice using quotation marks correctly, visit Exercise Central at **bedford stmartins.com/realwriting**.

EXAMPLE: A radio journalist asked a nurse at a critical-care facility, "Do you feel that the medical community needlessly prolongs the life of the terminally ill?"

1. "If I could quickly answer that question," the nurse replied, "I would deserve an honorary degree in ethics."

RESOURCES To gauge students' punctuation skills, use the *Testing Tool Kit* CD-ROM available with this book.

2. She added, "But I see it as the greatest dilemma we face today."

3. "How would you describe that dilemma?" the reporter asked the nurse.

4. The nurse said, "It is a choice of when to use our amazing medical technology and when not to."

5. The reporter asked, "So there are times when you would favor letting patients die on their own?"

6. "Yes," the nurse replied, "I would."

7. The reporter asked, "Under what circumstances should a patient be allowed to die?"

8. "I cannot really answer that question because so many variables are involved," the nurse replied.

9. "Is this a matter of deciding how to allocate scarce resources?" the reporter asked.

TIP Answers to odd-numbered practice items in this chapter appear on page AK-9 at the back of the book.

10. "In a sense, it is," the nurse replied. "As a colleague of mine says, 'We should not try to keep everyone alive for as long as possible just because we can.'"

● ●

No Quotation Marks for Indirect Quotations

When you report what someone said or wrote but do not use the person's exact words, you are writing an indirect quotation. Do not use quotation marks for indirect quotations. Indirect quotations often begin with the word *that*.

TEAMWORK Have students interview one another on a controversial issue that you have chosen. The interviewer should write up the interview using direct and indirect quotations.

INDIRECT QUOTATION	DIRECT QUOTATION
Sam said that there was a fire downtown.	Sam said, "There was a fire downtown."
The police told us to move along.	"Move along," directed the police.
Tara told me that she is graduating.	Tara said, "I am graduating."

PRACTICE 2 Punctuating Direct and Indirect Quotations

Edit the following sentences by adding quotation marks where needed and crossing out quotation marks that are incorrectly used. If a sentence is already correct, put a "C" next to it.

> **EXAMPLE:** Three days before her apartment was robbed, Jocelyn told a friend, "I worry about the safety of this building."

1. "Have you complained to the landlord yet?" her friend asked.

2. "Not yet," Jocelyn replied, "although I know I should."

3. Jocelyn phoned the landlord and asked him to install a more secure lock on the front door. C

4. The landlord said that "he felt the lock was fine the way it was."

5. When Jocelyn phoned the landlord after the burglary, she said, "I know this would not have happened if that lock had been installed."

6. "I am sorry," the landlord replied, "but there is nothing I can do about it now."

7. Jocelyn asked a tenants' rights group whether she had grounds for a lawsuit. C

8. The person she spoke to said that "she probably did."

9. "If I were you," the person said, "I would let your landlord know about your plans."

10. When Jocelyn told her landlord of the possible lawsuit, he said that he would reimburse her for the lost items. C

Quotation Marks for Certain Titles

When you refer to a short work such as a magazine or newspaper article, a chapter in a book, a short story, an essay, a song, or a poem, put quotation marks around the title of the work.

NEWSPAPER ARTICLE	"College Tuition to Rise 25 Percent"
SHORT STORY	"The Awakening"
ESSAY	"Why Are We So Angry?"

Usually titles of longer works, such as novels, books, magazines, newspapers, movies, television programs, and CDs, are italicized. The titles of sacred books such as the Bible or the Koran are neither underlined nor surrounded by quotation marks.

BOOK	*The Good Earth*
NEWSPAPER	*Washington Post*

[Do not italicize or capitalize the word *the* before the name of a newspaper or magazine, even if it is part of the title: I saw that in the *New York Times*. But do capitalize *The* when it is the first word in titles of books, movies, and other sources.]

TIP For more information on citing sources, see Chapter 20.

If you are writing a paper with many outside sources, your instructor will probably refer you to a particular system of citing sources. Follow that system's guidelines when you use titles in your paper.

NOTE: Do not enclose the title of a paragraph or an essay that you have written in quotation marks when it appears at the beginning of your paper. Do not italicize it either.

· ·

PRACTICE 3   Using Quotation Marks for Titles

Edit the following sentences by adding quotation marks around titles as needed. Underline any book, magazine, or newspaper titles.

EXAMPLE: After the terrorist attacks of September 11, 2001, the 1,200 radio stations belonging to Clear Channel Communications were asked not to play songs with a political message, such as "Imagine" by John Lennon.

1. In 2002, Bruce Springsteen released his first new album in years, containing songs like "Worlds Apart" that dealt with the terrorist attacks on the United States.

2. "The Missing," a review of the Springsteen album in the New Yorker magazine, found Springsteen's new songs unusual because they did not include many specific details about people, as older Springsteen songs like "Born in the U.S.A." had done.

3. No one made that complaint about "John Walker's Blues," a song by Steve Earle based on the story of the young American captured while fighting for the Taliban in Afghanistan.

4. Earle was condemned by some for writing from Walker's point of view; a New York Post headline claimed, "Twisted Ballad Honors Tali-Rat."

5. As a Time magazine article, "Don't Even Tell These Guys about Eminem," pointed out, the controversy was peculiar because it occurred before Earle's song had even been released, and those objecting had apparently neither heard the song nor read its lyrics.

Edit for Quotation Marks

PRACTICE 4 Editing for Quotation Marks

Edit the following paragraphs by adding twelve sets of quotation marks where needed and crossing out the two sets of incorrectly used quotation marks. Correct any errors in punctuation.

(1) When Ruiz first came into my office, he told me that he was a poor student. (2) I asked, "What makes you think that?"

(3) Ruiz answered, "I have always gotten bad grades, and I do not know how to get any better." (4) He shook his head. (5) "I have just about given up."

(6) I told him that "there were some resources on campus he could use and that we could work together to help him."

(7) "What kind of things are you talking about?" asked Ruiz. (8) "What exactly will I learn?"

(9) I said, "There are plenty of programs to help you. (10) You really have no excuse to fail."

(11) "Can you be a little more specific?" he asked.

(12) "Certainly," I said. (13) I told him about the survival skills program. (14) I also pulled out folders on study skills, such as managing time, improving memory, taking notes, and having a positive attitude. (15) "Take a look at these," I said.

(16) Ruiz said, "No, I am not interested in that. (17) And I do not have time."

(18) I replied, "That is your decision, Ruiz, but remember that education is one of the few things that people are willing to pay for and not get." (19) I paused and then added, "It sounds to me like you are wasting the money you spent on tuition. (20) Why not try to get what you paid for?"

(21) Ruiz thought for a moment, while he looked out the window, and finally told me that "he would try."

(22) "Good," I said. (23) "I am glad to hear it."

. . . .

PRACTICE 5   Editing Your Own Writing for Quotation Marks

As a final practice, edit a piece of your own writing for quotation marks. It can be a paper you are working on for this course, a paper you have already finished, a paper for another course, or a recent piece of writing from your work or everyday life. In your learning journal, record any examples you find of mistakes in the use of quotation marks. Also, write down the edited versions of these sentences.

. . . .

Chapter Review

LEARNING JOURNAL Did you find quotation mark errors in your writing? How would you explain the use of quotation marks in direct and indirect quotes? What is unclear to you?

TEACHING TIP Collect students' learning journals to find out what the class or individual students need more work on.

1.   Quotation marks look like this: _____ " " _____ . They always appear in (pairs)/ threes).

2.   A direct quotation exactly _____ repeats _____ what someone (or some outside source) said or wrote. (Use)/ Do not use) quotation marks around direct quotations.

3.   An indirect quotation restates what someone said or wrote, but not word for word _____.

(Use /(Do not use) quotation marks with indirect quotations.

4.   To set off a quotation within a quotation, use single quotation marks _____.

5.   Put quotation marks around the titles of short works such as (give four examples) Answers will vary. Possible answers: short stories, poems, songs, articles _____.

6.   For longer works such as magazines, novels, books, newspapers, and so on, _____ italicize _____ the titles.

Chapter Test

Circle the correct choice for each of the following items.

TIP For advice on taking tests, see Appendix A.

1. If an underlined portion of this sentence is incorrect, select the revision that fixes it. If the sentence is correct as written, choose d.

    Do you think <u>she</u> was serious when she <u>said, "Leave</u> the building
          A   B

    <u>immediately?"</u>
      C

RESOURCES The *Testing Tool Kit* CD-ROM available with this book has even more tests. Also, for cumulative Editing Review Tests, see pages 601–10.

    a. "she"
    b. said "Leave
    c. immediately"?
    d. No change is necessary.

2. Choose the item that has no errors.
    a. "You need to strengthen that knee," Dr. Wheeler warned, "so be sure to do all of your exercises".
    b. "You need to strengthen that knee," Dr. Wheeler warned, so be sure to do all of your exercises.
    c. "You need to strengthen that knee," Dr. Wheeler warned, "so be sure to do all of your exercises."

3. Choose the item that has no errors.
    a. Eric pointed at an article titled 'New Alternative Fuel in Your Backyard.'
    b. Eric pointed at an article titled New Alternative Fuel in Your Backyard.
    c. Eric pointed at an article titled "New Alternative Fuel in Your Backyard."

4. If an underlined portion of this sentence is incorrect, select the revision that fixes it. If the sentence is correct as written, choose d.

    The man said, "I'm sorry, <u>officer, but</u> did I hear you correctly when
                                A

    you <u>said, "Drive</u> into that <u>ditch'?"</u>
        B   C

    a. officer, "but
    b. said, 'Drive
    c. ditch?'"
    d. No change is necessary.

5. Choose the item that has no errors.
    a. Rachel told the security guard that she needed to enter the building for official business.
    b. Rachel told the security guard that "she needed to enter the building for official business."
    c. Rachel told the security guard that she "needed to enter the building for official business."

40

Other Punctuation
(; : () -- -)

THIS CHAPTER
- explains what five other punctuation marks are and how they are used
- gives you practice using punctuation correctly

Understand What Punctuation Does

TIP For fun podcasts with tips on grammar and usage, check out Grammar Girl's Quick and Dirty Tips for Better Writing on **bedfordstmartins .com/realwriting**.

Punctuation helps readers understand your writing. If you use punctuation incorrectly, you send readers a confusing—or, even worse, a wrong—message. This chapter covers five punctuation marks that people sometimes use incorrectly because they are not quite sure what these are supposed to do.

Practice Using Punctuation Correctly

Semicolon ;

Semicolons to Join Closely Related Sentences

RESOURCES *Additional Resources* contains tests and supplemental exercises for this chapter.

Use a semicolon to join two closely related sentences and make one sentence.

> In an interview, hold your head up and do not slouch; it is important to look alert.

> Make good eye contact; looking down is not appropriate in an interview.

> **LANGUAGE NOTE:** Using a comma instead of a semicolon to join two sentences would create a run-on (see Ch. 23).

Semicolons When Items in a List Contain Commas

Use semicolons to separate items in a list that itself contains commas. Otherwise, it is difficult for readers to tell where one item ends and another begins.

> For dinner, Bob ate an order of onion rings; a sixteen-ounce steak; a baked potato with sour cream, bacon bits, and cheese; a green salad; and a huge bowl of ice cream with fudge sauce.

> Because one item, *a baked potato with sour cream, bacon bits, and cheese*, contains its own commas, all items need to be separated by semicolons.

TEACHING TIP Caution students not to use semicolons unless they feel certain about how they are used. Since many students use semicolons as a default solution when trying to increase sentence complexity, they end up overusing or misusing them.

Colon :

Colons before Lists

Use a colon after an independent clause to introduce a list. An independent clause contains a subject, a verb, and a complete thought. It can stand on its own as a sentence.

> Many companies had booths at the computer fair: Apple, Microsoft, IBM, and Dell, to name just a few.

> The fair featured a vast array of software: financial-management applications, games, educational CDs, college-application programs, and so on.

Colons before Explanations or Examples

Use a colon after an independent clause to let readers know that you are about to provide an explanation or example of what you just wrote.

> The fair was overwhelming: too much hype about too many things.

> I picked up something I have been looking for: a new game.

A colon follows an independent clause. One of the most common misuses of colons is to use them after a phrase instead of an independent clause. Watch out especially for colons following the phrases *such as* or *for example*.

INCORRECT	Tonya enjoys sports that are sometimes dangerous. For example: white-water rafting, wilderness skiing, rock climbing, and motorcycle racing.
CORRECT	Tonya enjoys sports that are sometimes dangerous: white-water rafting, wilderness skiing, rock climbing, and motorcycle racing.
INCORRECT	Jeff has many interests. They are: bicycle racing, sculpting, and building musical instruments.

TIP See Chapter 37 (Commas), Chapter 38 (Apostrophes), and Chapter 39 (Quotation Marks) for coverage of these punctuation marks. For more information on using semicolons to join sentences, see Chapter 29.

CORRECT   Jeff has many interests: bicycle racing, sculpting, and building musical instruments.

Colons in Business Correspondence and before Subtitles

Use a colon after a greeting (called a *salutation*) in a business letter and after the standard heading lines at the beginning of a memorandum.

Dear Mr. Hernandez:

To: Pat Toney
From: Susan Anker

Colons should also be used before subtitles—for example, "Running a Marathon: The Five Most Important Tips."

Parentheses ( )

TEACHING TIP Advise students that although an occasional set of parentheses is fine, too many are distracting.

Use parentheses to set off information that is not essential to the meaning of a sentence. Parentheses are always used in pairs and should be used sparingly.

My grandfather's most successful invention (and also his first) was the electric blanket.

When he died (at the age of ninety-six), he had more than 150 patents registered.

Dash --

Dashes can be used like parentheses to set off additional information, particularly information that you want to emphasize. Make a dash by writing or typing two hyphens together. Do not put extra spaces around a dash.

The final exam--worth 25 percent of your total grade--will be next Thursday.

A lively review session--come one, come all--will begin in an hour.

A dash can also indicate a pause, much like a comma does.

My uncle went on long fishing trips--without my aunt and cousins.

Hyphen -

Hyphens to Join Words That Form a Single Description

Writers often join two or more words that together form a single description of a person, place, or thing. To join the words, use a hyphen.

Being a stockbroker is a high-risk career.

Michelle is the ultimate decision-maker in our department.

Jill is a lovely three-year-old girl.

When writing out two-word numbers from twenty-one to ninety-nine, put a hyphen between the two words.

Seventy-five people participated in the demonstration.

Hyphens to Divide a Word at the End of a Line

Use a hyphen to divide a word when part of the word must continue on the next line.

Critics accused the tobacco industry of increasing the amounts of nico-tine in cigarettes to encourage addiction and boost sales.

If you are not sure where to break a word, look it up in a dictionary. The word's main entry will show you where you can break the word: *dic • tio • nary*. If you still are not confident that you are putting the hyphen in the right place, do not break the word; write it all on the next line.

TIP Most word processing programs automatically put a whole word on the next line rather than hyphenating it. When you write by hand, however, you need to hyphenate correctly.

Edit for Punctuation

· ·

PRACTICE 1   Editing for Other Punctuation Marks

Edit the following paragraphs by adding semicolons, colons, parentheses, dashes, and hyphens when needed. Circle the punctuation marks that you add. In some places, more than one type of punctuation may be acceptable. *Answers may vary. Possible edits are shown.*

TIP For more practice using the types of punctuation covered in this chapter, visit Exercise Central at **bedfordstmartins.com/ realwriting**.

(1) When John Wood was on a backpacking trip to Nepal in 1998, he discovered something he had not expected: only a few books in the nation's schools. (2) He knew that if the students did not have the materials they needed, it would be much harder for them to learn. (3) They did not need high-tech ~~high tech~~ supplies as much as they needed old-fashioned ~~old fashioned~~ books. (4) Wood decided that he would find a way to get those books.

(5) Two years later, Wood founded Room to Read, an organization dedicated to shipping books to students who needed them. (6) Since then, the group has donated more than 3 million books. (7) One of Wood's first shipments was carried to students on the back of a yak. (8) Many others arrived in a Cathay Pacific Airlines plane.

(9) Along with the books, Room to Read has also built almost three hundred schools and has opened five thousand libraries. (10) Different companies donate books to the organization; Scholastic, Inc., recently sent 400,000 books to Wood's group. (11) Money to fund all of these efforts comes through various fund-raisers: read-a-thons, auctions, and coin drives.

· ·

PRACTICE 2   Editing Your Own Writing for Punctuation

As a final practice, edit a piece of your own writing for semicolons, colons, parentheses, dashes, and hyphens. It can be a paper you are working on for this course, a paper you have already finished, a paper for another course, or a piece of writing from your work or everyday life. You may want to try more than one way to use these punctuation marks in your writing. In your learning journal, record any examples of sentences you edited, showing the sentences both before and after you edited them.

· ·

Chapter Review

1.   Semicolons (;) can be used to _join closely related sentences into one sentence_ and to _separate items in a list that itself contains commas_.

2.   Colons (:) can be used in what three ways? _after an independent clause to introduce a list, after an independent clause to provide an explanation or example of what you just wrote, and after a greeting in a business letter or memo heading and before subtitles_

3.   A colon in a sentence must always be used after an _independent clause_.

4.   Parentheses ( ) set off information that is _not essential_ to a sentence.

5.   _Dashes (--)_ also set off information in a sentence, usually information that you want to emphasize.

6.   Hyphens (-) can be used to join two or more words that together _form a single description_ and to _break_ a word at the end of a line.

Chapter Test

Circle the correct choice for each of the following items.

TIP For advice on taking tests, see Appendix A.

RESOURCES The *Testing Tool Kit* CD-ROM available with this book has even more tests.

1. Choose the item that has no errors.
   a. Our car trip took us through Pittsburgh, Pennsylvania, Wheeling, West Virginia, and Bristol, Tennessee.
   (b.) Our car trip took us through Pittsburgh, Pennsylvania; Wheeling, West Virginia; and Bristol, Tennessee.
   c. Our car trip took us through Pittsburgh; Pennsylvania, Wheeling; West Virginia, and Bristol; Tennessee.

2. If an underlined portion of this sentence is incorrect, select the revision that fixes it. If the sentence is correct as written, choose d.

   Gary's dog (a seventeen-year-old easily won first prize in the Elderly
   　　　　　　　　　　　A

   Dog Show; she had the shiniest coat and the most youthful step.
   　　　B　　　　　　　　　　　C

   (a.) (a seventeen-year-old)   c. coat: and
   b. Show-she   d. No change is necessary.

3. Choose the item that has no errors.
   (a.) As our computer specialist, you have three tasks: fixing malfunctioning computers, teaching people to use their computers, and not making any problem worse.
   b. As our computer specialist: you have three tasks, fixing malfunctioning computers, teaching people to use their computers, and not making any problem worse.
   c. As our computer specialist, you have three tasks: fixing malfunctioning computers, teaching people to use their computers (and not making any problem worse).

4. Choose the item that has no errors.
   a. Is there such a thing as a low-stress-job?
   (b.) Is there such a thing as a low-stress job?
   c. Is there such a thing as a low stress-job?

5. If an underlined portion of this sentence is incorrect, select the revision that fixes it. If the sentence is correct as written, choose d.

   You will have five and only five minutes to leave the office before the
   　　　　　　　A　　　　　　　　　　　B　　　　　　C

   alarm sounds.

   (a.) five—and only five—   c. before; the
   b. to: leave   d. No change is necessary.

Capitalization

Using Capital Letters

THIS CHAPTER
- explains three important rules of capitalization
- gives you practice capitalizing correctly

Understand Three Rules of Capitalization

TIP For fun podcasts with tips on grammar and usage, check out Grammar Girl's Quick and Dirty Tips for Better Writing on **bedfordstmartins.com/realwriting**.

RESOURCES *Additional Resources* contains tests and supplemental exercises for this chapter.

If you can remember the following rules, you will avoid the most common errors of capitalization.

THE THREE RULES OF CAPITALIZATION

Capitalize the first letter

- Of every new sentence
- In names of specific people, places, dates, and things
- Of important words in titles

Practice Capitalization

Capitalization of Sentences

TEACHING TIP Remind students that they should not write or type in all capital letters because it will be more difficult for them to recognize and edit their capitalization errors.

Capitalize the first letter of each new sentence, including the first word of a direct quotation.

The superintendent was surprised.

He asked, "What is going on here?"

Capitalization of Names of Specific People, Places, Dates, and Things

The general rule is to capitalize the first letter in names of specific people, places, dates, and things. Do not capitalize a generic name such as *college* as opposed to the specific name: *Carroll State College*. Look at the examples for each group.

People

Capitalize the first letter in names of specific people and in titles used with names of specific people.

SPECIFIC	NOT SPECIFIC
Jean Heaton	my neighbor
Professor Fitzgerald	your math professor

SPECIFIC	NOT SPECIFIC
Dr. Cornog	the doctor
Aunt Pat, Mother	my aunt, your mother

The name of a family member is capitalized when the family member is being addressed directly: Happy Birthday, *Mother*. In other instances, do not capitalize: It is my *mother's* birthday.

The word *president* is not capitalized unless it comes directly before a name as part of that person's title: *President* Barack Obama.

Places

Capitalize the first letter in names of specific buildings, streets, cities, states, regions, and countries.

SPECIFIC	NOT SPECIFIC
Bolton Town Hall	the town hall
Arlington Street	our street
Dearborn Heights	my hometown
Arizona	this state
the South	the southern region
Spain	that country

Do not capitalize directions in a sentence.

Drive *south* for five blocks.

Dates

Capitalize the first letter in the names of days, months, and holidays. Do not capitalize the names of the seasons (winter, spring, summer, fall).

SPECIFIC	NOT SPECIFIC
Wednesday	tomorrow
June 25	summer
Thanksgiving	my birthday

ESL Ask ESL students to identify any English capitalization rules that differ from the rules in their first language.

LANGUAGE NOTE: Some languages, such as Spanish, French, and Italian, do not capitalize days, months, and languages. In English, such words must be capitalized.

INCORRECT	I study russian every monday, wednesday, and friday from january through may.
CORRECT	I study **Russian** every **Monday**, **Wednesday**, and **Friday** from **January** through **May**.

Organizations, Companies, and Groups

SPECIFIC	NOT SPECIFIC
Taft Community College	my college
Microsoft	that software company
Alcoholics Anonymous	the self-help group

Languages, Nationalities, and Religions

SPECIFIC	NOT SPECIFIC
English, Greek, Spanish	my first language
Christianity, Buddhism	your religion

The names of languages should be capitalized even if you aren't referring to a specific course.

I am taking psychology and *Spanish*.

Courses

SPECIFIC	NOT SPECIFIC
Composition 101	a writing course
Introduction to Psychology	my psychology course

Commercial Products

RESOURCES To gauge students' capitalization skills, use the *Testing Tool Kit* CD-ROM available with this book.

SPECIFIC	NOT SPECIFIC
Diet Pepsi	a diet cola
Skippy peanut butter	peanut butter

Capitalization of Titles

When you write the title of a book, movie, television program, magazine, newspaper, article, story, song, paper, poem, and so on, capitalize the first word and all important words. The only words that do not need to be capitalized (unless they are the first word) are *the*, *a*, *an*, coordinating conjunctions (*and*, *but*, *for*, *nor*, *or*, *so*, *yet*), and prepositions.

TIP For more on punctuating titles, see Chapter 39. For a list of common prepositions, see page 315.

> *I Love Lucy* was a long-running television program.

> Both *USA Today* and the *New York Times* are popular newspapers.

> "Once More to the Lake" is one of Chuck's favorite essays.

Chapter Review

1. Capitalize the ____first letter____ of every new sentence.

2. Capitalize the first letter in names of specific ____people____, ____places____, ____dates____, and ____things____.

3. Capitalize the first letter of ____important words____ in titles.

LEARNING JOURNAL Did you find capitalization errors in your writing? What is the main thing you have learned about capitalization that will help you? What is unclear to you?

TEACHING TIP Collect students' learning journals to find out what the class or individual students need more work on.

Chapter Test

Circle the correct choice for each of the following items.

TIP For advice on taking tests, see Appendix A.

1. Choose the item that has no errors.
  a. My daughter's school, Spitzer High School, no longer sells pepsi and other sodas in its vending machines.
  b. My daughter's school, Spitzer high school, no longer sells pepsi and other sodas in its vending machines.
  c. My daughter's school, Spitzer High School, no longer sells Pepsi and other sodas in its vending machines.

RESOURCES The *Testing Tool Kit* CD-ROM available with this book has even more tests. Also, for cumulative Editing Review Tests, see pages 601–10.

2. If an underlined portion of this sentence is incorrect, select the revision that fixes it. If the sentence is correct as written, choose d.

Will our company <u>President</u> speak at the <u>annual meeting</u>, or will
　　　　　　　　　　　A　　　　　　　　　　　　　B

<u>Dr. Anders?</u>
　C

a. president   **c.** doctor Anders
b. Annual Meeting   **d.** No change is necessary.

3. Choose the item that has no errors.
   a. Which Library do you go to, Hill Library or Barry Township Library?
   b. Which library do you go to, Hill Library or Barry Township Library?
   c. Which library do you go to, Hill library or Barry Township library?

4. If an underlined portion of this sentence is incorrect, select the revision that fixes it. If the sentence is correct as written, choose d.

In my <u>english 99</u> class <u>last summer</u>, we read some interesting essays
　　　　A　　　　　　　　　　B

by <u>famous authors.</u>
　　C

a. English 99   **c.** Famous Authors
b. last Summer   **d.** No change is necessary.

5. If an underlined portion of this sentence is incorrect, select the revision that fixes it. If the sentence is correct as written, choose d.

Of the states in the <u>East</u>, one can travel the farthest <u>North</u> in <u>Maine.</u>
　　　　　　　　　　　A　　　　　　　　　　　　　　　　B　　　C

a. east   **c.** maine
b. north   **d.** No change is necessary.

Editing Review Test 1

The Four Most Serious Errors (Chapters 21–25)

DIRECTIONS: Each of the underlined word groups contains one or more errors. As you locate and identify each error, write its item number on the appropriate line below. Then, edit the underlined word groups to correct the errors. If you need help, turn back to the chapters indicated.

Answers may vary. Possible edits are shown.

Two fragments _____2, 9_____   Two verb problems _____10, 16_____

Two run-ons _____8, 15_____   Four subject-verb
                                      agreement errors _____4, 6, 11, 14_____

    1 Every time you step outside, you are under attack. **2** ~~Which~~ *You* ~~you~~ may not know what is hitting you, but the attack is truly happening. **3** Invisible storms of sky dust rain down on you all the time. **4** It does not matter if the sun is shining, and the sky *is* ~~are~~ bright blue. **5** The dust is still there.

    6 Sky dust *consists* ~~consist~~ of bug parts, specks of hair, pollen, and even tiny chunks of comets. **7** According to experts, 6 million pounds of space dust settle on the earth's surface every year. **8** You will never notice it; scientists, however, are collecting it in order to learn more about weather patterns and pollution. **9** *Scientists use* ~~Using~~ sophisticated equipment like high-tech planes and sterile filters to collect dust samples.

    10 Dan Murray, a geologist at the University of Rhode Island, has *begun* ~~began~~ a new project that invites students and teachers to help collect samples of cosmic dust. **11** Murray says that collecting the dust particles *is* ~~are~~ quite simple. **12** It starts with a researcher setting up a small, inflatable swimming pool. **13** Next, this investigator leaves the pool out in the open for forty-eight hours. **14** Finally, the researcher uses a special type of tape to pick up whatever *has* ~~have~~ settled over time. **15** The tape is put into a beaker of water to dissolve. *A* microscope is used to analyze what comes off the tape. **16** The information *found* ~~finded~~ there will help scientists predict insect seasons, measure meteor showers, or even catch signs of global warming.

Editing Review Test 2

The Four Most Serious Errors (Chapters 21–25)

DIRECTIONS: Each of the underlined word groups contains one or more errors. As you locate and identify each error, write its item number on the appropriate line below. Then, edit the underlined word groups to correct the errors. If you need help, turn back to the chapters indicated.

Answers may vary. Possible edits are shown.

Two fragments _____5, 12_____   Two verb problems _____4, 16_____

Three run-ons _____6, 9, 14_____   Three subject-verb
agreement errors _____1, 8, 17_____

     1 Most people spend many hours a day indoors, so windows and natural light <u>is</u> *are* important to their health. **2** Light helps people feel connected to the world around them. **3** However, traditional windows allow the loss of heat in winter and of cool air in summer; the result is high energy costs to maintain office buildings and homes at comfortable temperatures. **4** Architects and designers <u>knowed</u> *know* this fact, so they have developed energy-efficient "smart windows." **5** <u>Shifting from clear to dark and back again.</u> *Smart windows shift* **6** Some smart windows change from clear to dark <u>with a touch of a button others change automatically in response to the intensity of the outside light.</u>

     7 Their design and engineering make smart windows *chromogenic*, or able to change colors. **8** <u>Smart windows shifts to darker colors</u> *shift* when they are given a small electrical charge. **9** <u>The darker the room, the more it remains cool the sun does not warm it.</u> *The* **10** Smart windows take only a minute or so to darken.

     11 Although these smart windows save energy, they may not be ready for the market **12** <u>For a few more years.</u> *for* **13** At present, designers face some resistance from potential customers who distrust the technology. **14** <u>Another obstacle is the price tag, this new technology remains expensive.</u> *. This* **15** To deal with both of these issues, developers are starting small. **16** <u>They were creating motorcycle and ski helmets with face masks that switch between dark and clear.</u> *are* **17** <u>They hopes that handy products like these will help the new technology gain wide acceptance.</u> *hope*

Editing Review Test 3

The Four Most Serious Errors (Chapters 21–25)
Other Grammar Concerns (Chapters 26–33)

3

DIRECTIONS: Each of the underlined word groups contains one or more errors. As you locate and identify each error, write its item number on the appropriate line below. Then, edit the underlined word groups to correct the errors. If you need help, turn back to the chapters indicated.

Answers may vary. Possible edits are shown.

Two fragments	3, 6	Two verb problems	1, 5
One run-on	10	Two pronoun errors	2, 8
One adjective error	11	One parallelism error	13
Two subject-verb agreement errors	16, 17		

1 Flying an airplane across the Atlantic Ocean may have been a miracle almost a century
                                                                        is
ago, but today it ~~be~~ quite commonplace. **2** When a man named Maynard Hill decided to do it,
                                        it   *He gave*
however, most people told him ~~he~~ simply could not be done. **3** ~~Giving~~ it a try despite everyone's

doubts. **4** His persistence was rewarded when TAM-5, his eleven-pound model airplane, flew
                                                                    set
from Canada to Ireland in approximately thirty-nine hours. **5** TAM-5's flight ~~sat~~ world records

not only for the longest distance but also for the longest time ever flown by this type of airplane.
It followed
6 ~~Following~~ the same path as the first nonstop flight across the ocean in 1919.

        7 This successful trip was not Hill's first attempt, by any means. **8** He started *his* ~~its~~ project a

decade ago, and he lost several planes trying to complete the journey. **9** Finally, in August
                                                                    ;
2003, he made a fifth attempt. **10** He tossed the TAM-5 into the air once airborne, it was
                                                            best
guided by remote control on the ground. **11** It was the ~~most best~~ version he had made. **12** It

soared to a cruising altitude of almost a thousand feet, and at that point a computerized

autopilot took over.
                                                                                hoped
        13 For days, the flight crew watched the clock, followed the TAM-5's progress, and ~~hopes~~

for the best. **14** A crowd of fifty people waited on the shore in Ireland to watch the TAM-5's

landing. **15** When it appeared on the horizon, a cheer went up. **16** Today, model plane
                remember   *was*
enthusiasts ~~remembers~~ his feat. **17** Even though the plane ~~were~~ made out of nothing more than

balsa wood, fiberglass, and plastic film, it flew right into history that August afternoon.

Editing Review Test 4

The Four Most Serious Errors (Chapters 21–25)
Other Grammar Concerns (Chapters 26–33)

DIRECTIONS: Each of the underlined word groups contains one or more errors. As you locate and identify each error, write its item number on the appropriate line below. Then, edit the underlined word groups to correct the errors. If you need help, turn back to the chapters indicated.

Answers may vary. Possible edits are shown.

Two fragments _____2, 7_____   One run-on _____6_____

One subject-verb agreement error ___4___   One pronoun error _____3_____

One misplaced/dangling modifier ___8___   Two coordination/
                                                  subordination errors _____5, 9_____

One use of inappropriately
informal or casual language _____11_____

    1 Almost half a century after U.S. astronauts last walked on the moon, the National Aeronautics and Space Administration (NASA) has built another manned spacecraft to land in the same place. **2** ~~Taking~~ *The spacecraft took* years to build and cost $104 billion. **3** ~~They~~ *It* will carry four astronauts and a large amount of supplies. **4** Called a CEV, its initials *are* is an abbreviation for "crew exploration vehicle."

    5 The CEV was built for moon trips, ~~because~~ *although* it is also designed to travel to Mars and the International Space Station. **6** It is three times larger than the old Apollo spaceships*;* it is more rugged, too. **7** ~~Powered~~ *It is powered* through a series of solar panels, along with liquid methane fuel.

    8 During this mission, *set to launch in 2018,* astronauts will be able to stay on the moon's surface for four to seven days*,* ~~set to launch in 2018.~~ **9** The CEV will operate without a crew when in orbit, ~~but~~ *so* no one has to stay behind while the others go out to explore. **10** In the future, NASA hopes to build a permanent space base on the moon. **11** Establishing outposts would one day enable astronauts to take ~~cool~~ *important* journeys to other planets and beyond.

Editing Review Test 5

The Four Most Serious Errors (Chapters 21–25)
Other Grammar Concerns (Chapters 26–33)
Word Use (Chapters 34–36)

5

DIRECTIONS: Each of the underlined word groups contains one or more errors. As you locate and identify each error, write its item number on the appropriate line below. Then, edit the underlined word groups to correct the errors. If you need help, turn back to the chapters indicated.

Answers may vary. Possible edits are shown.

One run-on _____13_____   One verb problem _____5_____

One word-choice error _____11_____   Two pronoun errors _____2, 8_____

One adjective error _____9_____   One spelling error _____16_____

One subject-verb agreement error ___4___   One misplaced/dangling modifier ___15___

Two commonly
confused word errors _____13, 18_____

    1 How do you celebrate the New Year? **2** Some people watch television on New Year's
Eve so that <u>he can see the glittering ball drop in New York's Time Square.</u> *(they)* **3** Others invite
friends and family over to celebrate with special foods or fireworks.

    4 The New Year <u>are</u> *(is)* celebrated all over the world in a variety of ways. **5** For example, in
Australia, people <u>spended</u> *(spend)* the day in fun, outdoor activities such as picnics, trips to the beach,
and rodeos. **6** After all, it is summertime there in January. **7** In Spain, people eat a dozen
grapes at midnight. **8** They eat one each time the clock chimes because <u>she believe it will bring</u> *(they)*
good luck for the New Year. **9** The people of Denmark have <u>the unusualest</u> tradition. *(an unusual)* **10** On
New Year's Eve, they throw old dishes at the doors of their friends' homes. **11** <u>If you find a lot</u>
<u>of broken junk</u> *(dishes)* in front of your house in the morning, you are well-liked. **12** Wearing all new
clothes is the way many Koreans celebrate the start of the New Year. **13** In Germany, people
leave food on <u>there plates, this practice is meant to ensure that their kitchens will be full of food</u> *(their ;)*
for the coming New Year.

    14 Not all countries celebrate the New Year on January 1. **15** <u>~~Setting off firecrackers, the~~</u> *(The)*
holiday is celebrated later by the Chinese people, *(, by setting off firecrackers.)* **16** <u>The date of the New Year depends on the</u>
<u>lunar calander</u> *(calendar)* and usually falls somewhere between January 21 and February 20. **17** The
Chinese often have a big parade with colorful floats of dancing dragons. **18** <u>The mythical</u>
<u>creatures are supposed to be cymbals</u> *(symbols)* of wealth and long life.

Editing Review Test 6

6

The Four Most Serious Errors (Chapters 21–25)
Other Grammar Concerns (Chapters 26–33)
Word Use (Chapters 34–36)

DIRECTIONS: Each of the underlined word groups contains one or more errors. As you locate and identify each error, write its item number on the appropriate line below. Then, edit the underlined word groups to correct the errors. If you need help, turn back to the chapters indicated.
Answers may vary. Possible edits are shown.

One run-on _____4_____

One subject-verb agreement error ___8___

One parallelism error _____1_____

Two commonly confused word errors ____3, 13____

One use of inappropriately informal or casual language ____6____

One verb problem _____2_____

One pronoun error _____9_____

Two spelling errors _____7, 14_____

    1 The idea of being able to unlock your car, turn on a light, or ~~starting~~ *start* your computer just by waving your hand sounds like something out of a science fiction novel. **2** Thanks to advancements in technology, the futuristic idea has ~~became~~ *become* a reality. **3** Some people are *already* ~~all ready~~ able to accomplish routine actions in this unusual way. **4** They do not have special powers*;* they have special computer chips embedded inside their bodies. **5** These high-tech chips help people do daily tasks with little or no effort.

    6 Known as RFIDs, which stands for "radio frequency identification devices," the chips are *extremely* ~~way~~ small. **7** They are as tiny as a *piece* ~~peice~~ of rice, have small antennas that send signals, and can be painlessly implanted and worn under the skin. **8** Health care workers ~~uses~~ *use* the chips in a variety of life-saving ways. **9** For example, emergency medical workers can scan the chips in accident victims to determine *their* ~~his~~ blood type or allergies.

    10 For security reasons, some parents have their children wear RFIDs on backpacks, bracelets, or ID tags. **11** Through a cell phone signal, the chips automatically let the parents know when their children have reached and left school or other destinations. **12** Even some pets are now equipped with these computer chips. **13** If the pet runs away or gets lost, *then* ~~than~~ its owners can track down their pet more easily by using the chip. **14** Although many people think these chips have great *potential,* ~~potental,~~ others worry that the government will eventually use them to spy on people.

Editing Review Test 7

The Four Most Serious Errors (Chapters 21–25)
Other Grammar Concerns (Chapters 26–33)
Word Use (Chapters 34–36)
Punctuation and Capitalization (Chapters 37–41)

7

DIRECTIONS: Each of the underlined word groups contains one or more errors. As you locate and identify each error, write its item number on the appropriate line below. Then, edit the underlined word groups to correct the errors. If you need help, turn back to the chapters indicated.
Answers may vary. Possible edits are shown.

One run-on ____3____   One verb problem ____8____

One apostrophe error ____7____   One pronoun error ____2____

One adverb error ____9____   One quotation mark error ____10____

One subject-verb agreement error ____13____ One capitalization error ____6____

One comma error ____11____   One semicolon error ____4____

    1 People in the United States drink a great deal of soda every single day. **2** In fact, the
average American drinks 557 cans of ~~them~~ *it* a year. **3** The problem with regular soda is that it is
full of sugar and caffeine *. It* it can add many empty calories to a person's diet. **4** Under pressure
from parents, many school administrators have banned soda*;* eliminating it from cafeterias and
vending machines.

    5 In response, companies such as Coca-Cola and PepsiCo are making some changes to
their products. **6** For instance, they are creating sodas that have added ~~Vitamins~~ *vitamins*, such as B3,
B6, and B12. **7** The ~~company's~~ *companies* are also planning to include magnesium, zinc, and other
minerals to improve the nutritional value of their beverages.

    8 Consumers have ~~buyed~~ *bought* less soda in recent years and have been drinking more water
and juices instead. **9** In an effort to lure people back to soda, companies are ~~quick~~ *quickly* attempting
to make their drinks healthier. **10** "We want to reinvent carbonated soft drinks*,"* says John
Compton, president of PepsiCo. **11** However*,* nutrition experts are doubtful. **12** Adding a few
trace ingredients to a sugary, caffeinated soft drink does not make this beverage a healthy
choice. **13** People's diets should ~~includes~~ *include* more fruit and vegetables, rather than just a different
type of soda.

Editing Review Test 8

The Four Most Serious Errors (Chapters 21–25)
Other Grammar Concerns (Chapters 26–33)
Word Use (Chapters 34–36)
Punctuation and Capitalization (Chapters 37–41)

DIRECTIONS: Each of the underlined word groups contains one or more errors. As you locate and identify each error, write its item number on the appropriate line below. Then, edit the underlined word groups to correct the errors. If you need help, turn back to the chapters indicated.

Answers may vary. Possible edits are shown.

One run-on _____5_____	One semicolon error _____1_____
One pronoun error _____13_____	One verb problem _____4_____
One comma error _____14_____	One adverb error _____10_____
One apostrophe error _____9_____	One spelling error _____11_____
One use of inappropriately informal or casual language _____11_____	One parallelism error _____12_____
One capitalization error _____6_____	One hyphen error _____7_____

1 If it seems as though places in the United States are more crowded lately, it might be because the country's population recently hit 300 million. **2** The nation has the third-largest population in the world. **3** Only China and India have more people. **4** Experts *believe* ~~belief~~ that by 2043 there will be 400 million people in the United States.

5 The country is growing rapidly because people are having more babies *and* more people are moving to the United States. **6** The *Northeast* ~~northeast~~ is the most populated area within the country. **7** It took *fifty-two* ~~fifty two~~ years for the country's population to go from 100 million to 200 million. **8** It took only thirty-nine years to rise from 200 million to its current 300 million. **9** If *experts'* ~~experts~~ statistics are correct, it will take even less time for the population of the United States to reach 400 million.

10 Some people worry that the United States is growing too ~~quick.~~ *quickly.* **11** Researchers predict some ~~super scary possibilitys.~~ *frightening possibilities.* **12** They state that if the population grows too large, it will stress available land, deplete water resources, and ~~it can~~ increase air pollution. **13** ~~Its~~ *Their* concerns are valid ones; in the meantime, the population just keeps growing. **14** Although this country is large, future generations may be squeezed in more tightly than the present generation can imagine.

Editing Review Test 9

The Four Most Serious Errors (Chapters 21–25)
Other Grammar Concerns (Chapters 26–33)
Word Use (Chapters 34–36)
Punctuation and Capitalization (Chapters 37–41)

9

DIRECTIONS: Each of the underlined word groups contains one or more errors. As you locate and identify each error, write its item number on the appropriate line below. Then, edit the underlined word groups to correct the errors. If you need help, turn back to the chapters indicated.
Answers may vary. Possible edits are shown.

One fragment _____7_____	One spelling error _____9_____
One run-on _____10_____	One hyphen error _____4_____
One pronoun error _____13_____	One semicolon error _____8_____
One parallelism error _____14_____	One parenthesis error _____12_____
One commonly confused word error ___3___	One word-choice error _____2_____

1 Whenever you have to write a paper, a letter, or any other document for work or school, you probably head toward the computer. **2** ~~In this day and age,~~ ^*Today,*^ most people reach for keyboards faster than they pick up pens. **3** At one elementary school in Scotland, however, the ~~principle,~~ ^*principal,*^ Bryan Lewis, is taking a different approach. **4** He feels that neat handwriting is still an important skill, so he has his students write not only by hand but also with ~~old fashioned~~ ^*old-fashioned*^ fountain pens.

5 Fountain pens were used in schools long ago and lately have been regaining popularity because they are refillable. **6** A writer using a fountain pen dips the point into a little ink bottle, **7** ^*, drawing*^ ~~Drawing~~ ink up into the barrel of the pen, as needed. **8** Today, a writer simply throws an empty pen away, and gets a new one.

9 So far, Principal Lewis is pleased with the results of his ~~experimint.~~ ^*experiment.*^ **10** He reports that students are taking more care with their work; their self-esteem has improved as well. **11** He stresses to teachers all over the world that the ability to produce legible handwriting remains a necessary skill. **12** Lewis is happy with the improvement he sees in his students' writing (and in his own writing, too. **13** He knows that computers are here to stay and that ~~it~~ ^*they*^ will not disappear. **14** However, he believes the practice with fountain pens helps students to focus, to write faster, and ~~they can~~ ^*to*^ feel proud of themselves.

Editing Review Test 10

The Four Most Serious Errors (Chapters 21–25)
Other Grammar Concerns (Chapters 26–33)
Word Use (Chapters 34–36)
Punctuation and Capitalization (Chapters 37–41)

DIRECTIONS: Each of the underlined word groups contains one or more errors. As you locate and identify each error, write its item number on the appropriate line below. Then, edit the underlined word groups to correct the errors. If you need help, turn back to the chapters indicated.

Answers may vary. Possible edits are shown.

One subject-verb agreement error ____11____   One spelling error ____7____

One pronoun error ____4____   One comma error ____14____

One coordination/subordination error ____2____   One semicolon error ____13____

One colon error ____9____   One apostrophe error ____12____

One commonly confused word error ____15____

1 When Shaun Ellis decided that he wanted to learn more about wolves, he made a radical life change. **2** He decided to live with the wolves ~~yet~~ *and* imitate their wild lifestyle as closely as he possibly could. **3** For eighteen months, he lived with three wolf pups that had been abandoned. **4** He pretended to be ~~its~~ *their* mother in many ways. **5** He worked to teach them the skills they would need to survive in the wild. **6** It certainly was not an easy way to live. **7** Ellis shared an outdoor pen with the pups, and it had no heat or ~~beding.~~ *bedding.* **8** To keep warm on the cold nights, he had to snuggle with the young wolves.

9 In order to communicate with them, Ellis learned how to/ growl, snarl, and howl. **10** He also learned how to use body positions and facial expressions in order to get a message across to the animals. **11** While living with the wolves, he also ~~try~~ *tried* to eliminate any emotion because animals do not feel things as human beings do. **12** This ~~mans~~ *man's* transition back to regular life was quite difficult for him.

13 Ellis's unorthodox methods have earned him criticism from his colleagues; but he firmly believes that his techniques led to valuable knowledge about wolves. **14** He has founded, the Wolf Pack Management organization in England. **15** Its goal is to get captive wolves released back into the wild and ~~than~~ *then* use what was learned to help the animals avoid future conflicts with humans.

READINGS

Part 8

Readings for Writers

42

Narration

In this part of the book (this chapter through Chapter 50), you will find twenty-seven essays that demonstrate the types of writing you studied in Part 2 of this book. The first essay in each chapter is written by a student; the next two are by professional writers.

These readings are more than just good models of writing. They tell great stories, argue passionately about controversial issues, and present a wide range of perspectives and information. These essays can also provide you with ideas for your own writing, both in and out of school. Most important, they offer you a chance to become a better reader and writer by seeing how others write.

Each essay in this chapter uses narration to get its main point across to the reader. As you read these essays, consider how they achieve the four basics of good narration that are listed below and discussed in Chapter 10.

■■ Four Basics of Good Narration
■■

1 It reveals something of importance to the writer (the main point).

2 It includes all of the major events of the story (primary support).

3 It brings the story to life with details about the major events (secondary support).

4 It presents the events in a clear order, usually according to when they happened.

Monique Rizer
When Students Are Parents

PREDICT: What do you think Rizer will write about?

_____

_____

Monique Rizer graduated from Gonzaga University with a journalism degree in 2001 and received an M.S. in information management from Syracuse University. As the mother of a young son while in college, Rizer was presented with an unusual challenge, one that she says inspired her to "share a unique experience about college life and offer suggestions on how to support other non-traditional students." She also kept an anonymous blog while her husband was deployed to Iraq, sharing her stories and experiences with other military spouses. She offers this encouragement for other student writers: "Read. Read. Read. Along with just writing frequently to build that muscle, reading is probably just as important."

GUIDING QUESTION
Do you know about resources that could help you on your campus?

VOCABULARY DEVELOPMENT
The words in **boldface** are defined at the bottom of the page. Underline the words as you read them.

IDEA JOURNAL Write about your first day in a college class.

Crammed behind my desk, I **fidgeted**[1] and shifted my eyes to observe the other students in the room. I tried not to look the way I felt—like I didn't belong there with them. I couldn't help noticing that all the other women were wearing shorts, sandals, flirty summer dresses: appropriate clothes for a warm September day. I tugged at the baggy clothes hiding my **postpartum**[2] weight. I thought of my six-week-old son and hoped I would make it home to nurse him at the scheduled time.

It was the summer of 1998. I was a twenty-year-old new mother and wife, and it was my first day of class, though not my first day of college. I had begun my long journey through higher education three years before, but my plans to attend full time after high-school graduation were put on hold when financial difficulties forced my family of eight to move. I then found a local community college and felt prepared to start again, but instead, the registration papers sat abandoned in my car, where I practically lived since home was a thirty-two-foot trailer filled with seven other people. In the summer of 1996, I packed my bags and left to live on my own; I enrolled again the next spring and had my son in July 1998. I knew I had to stay in school and go full time. I wanted more for my son and myself, even though I wasn't exactly sure what "more" was at the time.

That commitment to finish college has paid off. Today I have a bachelor's degree in journalism from Gonzaga University and a master's degree in information management from Syracuse University. During my years in school, my son kept me focused and ignited my ambition to be a better student. In my experience, there is no better motivation to finish college and to appreciate the **marrow**[3] of the experience than a child whose future depends on your decisions. I had to continue to use my education to give him a better life and to set an example for him to follow. I also had to finish what

1

2

3

---

1. fidget: to move nervously, fuss   **2. postpartum:** referring to the time shortly after childbirth   **3. marrow:** the tissue that fills the cavities of bones; the innermost, essential part my mother didn't: She had me at nineteen and gave in to pressure to quit college and go to work.

Inspired to earn better grades and get involved on the campus, I sacrificed the necessary free time to stay ahead with my studies. I wasn't the only one taking on that challenge: One day, I saw a fellow parent in the parking lot, struggling to get her baby out of her car. She was rushing to a group project, and having been a parent in college for nearly a year by that time, I knew she could do without the distraction of toting and keeping an eye on her new son. I had met her only once, through a classmate, but in a moment of bonding, I offered to babysit for her. She hesitantly, but gratefully, accepted. At first, I was surprised that she allowed me to watch her new baby—after all, we didn't really know each other. But we were both moms and students who could not turn down a helping hand.

Nearly two years later, after transferring schools when my husband was accepted into law school, I met another student when my son and her two daughters were **wreaking**[4] playful **havoc**[5] in the college bookstore. Lugging my books and chasing three pairs of little feet, I found her hunched over, looking for her own textbooks. I asked her, "Are you a student here?"—and within minutes our kids had a play date. Soon we met many families like ours, and I finally felt as though we had a community. We held organized playgroups, and several of us joined the same YMCA to work out together and swim with the kids. It was a perfect blend of college and family life.

The years I worked toward my graduate degree while my husband worked through law school were the hardest but the best. All of the student families latched onto one another for support and friendship because we understood what it was like to need financial aid to cover the cost of diapers. We could **commiserate**[6] about coordinating schedules to accommodate both swimming lessons for the kids and study sessions for ourselves. We gave one another scholarship information and scoops on the most family-friendly professors. We offered each other a place to laugh or cry about our hectic lives.

Still, I often felt like an outsider on the campus. Instead of a dorm, I needed my own apartment. Grocery shopping and cooking took the place of eating and socializing at the cafeteria. I pared down my extracurricular involvement to the basics, doing enough to stay plugged into the student body and to give me things to put on my résumé—like writing articles for the campus newspaper, participating in writing competitions, and attending conferences—but not so much that it interfered with my home life.

I never found sufficient guidance among administrators in the financial-aid and other offices. It wasn't until my senior year, for instance, that I learned I could include day care as a living expense in my aid budget—and it wasn't anyone at the university who told me, but the information was part of a scholarship program. I was thrilled but wondered why no one had told me that before. Fortunately, I had been able to rotate family members to babysit up until that point; had I needed to rely on three years of day care,

4

5

6   **SUMMARIZE:** How did the student parents help each other?

_____

_____

7

8   **REFLECT:** Have you learned what resources are available to you on campus?

_____

_____

---

4. wreak: to bring about   **5. havoc:** chaos, disorder   **6. commiserate:** to express sympathy with or understand the feelings of others the cost would have exceeded $13,000. The administration didn't seem to understand that anyone capable of handling parenthood and college is a student well worth that investment of time and energy.

Information for student parents on available resources, such as nearby 9 day-care centers or housing, is a great help. A designated **liaison**[7] in student affairs can also be very useful. And, of course, financial aid is always welcome. Gonzaga University, where I completed my undergraduate work, gave a small discount on tuition if both parents attended. We took advantage of a range of offerings, including discounts at the local Y and reduced-price health benefits for our sons, to make life a little easier.

The personal support I received from other students and professors, 10 too, made finishing my degree not only possible but all the sweeter. A friend offered to help one day when my son and I both came down with stomach flu. While we were **quarantined**[8] in the one bedroom in our apartment, she cleaned up and cooked us dinner. I was shocked that a single girl would give up her evening to help me out on a school night when I knew she had other things to do. Needless to say, she became a close friend and a constant source of support.

While a good friend can get you over the bumps, a great scholarship 11 can let you soar. I was part of the first class of Gates Millennium Scholars, an honor that inspired me to earn a graduate degree and relieved me of most of my financial burdens. I know this type of outside assistance is rare, but I hope to see more institutions support student parents. It takes more than motivation to complete a degree with a family in tow.

I feel a tremendous sense of accomplishment, and I have learned so 12 many lessons about myself. I want to help other young parents achieve their educational goals, and I see a bright future for my boys (I have two now). And I keep telling my mom that she doesn't have to live vicariously through me—she can return to college anytime she wants.

IDENTIFY: What is Rizer's purpose in writing this essay?

_____

_____

• •

SUMMARIZE AND RESPOND

In your reading journal or elsewhere, summarize the main point of "When Students Are Parents." Then, go back and check off the support for this idea. Next, write a brief summary of the essay. Finally, write a brief response to the reading. What do you think was the most significant resource or factor in Rizer's success as a parent-student?

• •

CHECK YOUR COMPREHENSION

1. An alternate title for this essay could be

   a. "Students Who Are Parents Just Don't Fit In."

   b. "Professors Appreciate Students Who Are Parents."

7. liaison: a person who serves as a link or connection between two or more parties
8. quarantine: to isolate in order to prevent the spread of disease

    c. "Parents Can Earn College Degrees, Too."

    d. "Student and Mother Feels like 'Special Exhibit.'"

2. The main point of this essay is that

    a. with the right resources and attitude, parents can pursue higher education.

    b. parents make better students than those who do not have children.

    c. distance learning programs are a great help to parents who are students.

    d. students who are also parents cannot really become part of a college's community.

3. What is Rizer's point in mentioning her mother, as well as her child?

    a. Rizer wants readers to contrast her own ambition, intelligence, and level of education with her mother's.

    b. Rizer wants to show how she succeeded, despite her mother's disapproval toward parents who seek higher education.

    c. Rizer sees herself as having completed the educational journey her mother began but never finished.

    d. Rizer wants to show how much easier it is for a parent to get a degree now than it was in her mother's time.

4. Does this essay include the Four Basics of Good Narration? Why or why not?

5. Look back at the **boldface** vocabulary you underlined, and write sentences using these words: *fidget* (para. 1); *wreak* (5); *commiserate* (6); *liaison* (9).

TIP For tools to build your vocabulary, visit the *Real Writing Student Center* at **bedfordstmartins.com/realwriting**.

READ CRITICALLY

1. In the opening paragraph, Rizer emphasizes how she did not belong in a college program or fit in with other students: She hid her postpartum weight and worried about her baby's nursing schedule. How does her attitude toward her child and toward her status as a student-parent change during the essay?

2. Why is it important that Rizer met other students who are also parents?

3. How do the choices that Rizer's mother made differ from Rizer's own path? How do her mother's choices motivate her?

4. Rizer contrasts the support of other student-parents with what she found in university financial-aid offices. Why do you think she does this—and how is it connected with her career ambitions stated at the end of the essay?

5. In the final paragraph, Rizer writes that she has learned lessons about herself. Based on the progress and details of her narrative, what do you think those lessons are?

· ·

WRITE

WRITE A PARAGRAPH: Write a paragraph that recounts a time when you felt like an outsider, as Rizer did when she attended class as a new parent. Like Rizer, include details about what made you feel so different from others and how you responded to the situation.

WRITE AN ESSAY: In an essay, narrate an account of a challenging experience you have had that provided you with lessons, as Rizer's time as a parent and a student did. What was the experience? What did you learn?

· ·

Walter Scanlon
It's Time I Shed My Ex-Convict Status

Walter F. Scanlon (b. 1937) began working with alcohol and drug abusers after he had himself sought out and entered a twelve-step program upon his release from prison. Scanlon had dropped out of high school and then spent more than a decade in hospitals, in jail, and on the streets. Today, he holds a bachelor's degree from Pace University, an M.B.A. from the New York Institute of Technology, and a Ph.D. in psychology from Columbus University. In addition to being a specialist in workplace and family interventions for people with drug, alcohol, and other problems, he lectures widely. With Nick Lessa, he coauthored *Wiley Concise Guides to Mental Health: Substance Use Disorders* (2005).

Scanlon observes that "there were long periods in my life when most decisions were made for me, not by me. Writing gave me a way to circumvent all that was happening around me and better understand what was happening within me." In the following essay, Scanlon tells the story of the changes in his life over the past thirty years. (For more on Walter Scanlon and an example of his writing at work, see pp. 210–11.)

VOCABULARY DEVELOPMENT
The words in **boldface** are defined at the bottom of the page. Underline them as you read.

IDEA JOURNAL Tell about a time when you overcame a difficulty in your life.

REFLECT: What is the purpose of the background information in paragraphs 1 and 2? Is it effective?

GUIDING QUESTION
Why does Scanlon feel that he should be able to shed his ex-convict status? Is his personal story convincing?

Thirty years ago I decided to drastically turn my life around. With a   1
state-issued olive suit on my back, a high-school equivalency diploma, and $40 travel money in my pocket, I became an ex-convict. I had done my time—almost five years in all—and now had the opportunity to **redeem**[1] myself. I felt almost optimistic. As the huge outer gate of New York state's Clinton Prison slammed behind me, the discharge officer bid me farewell: "Get your act together," he bellowed with a mix of sincerity and humor. "I don't want to see you back here any time soon." A Department of Corrections van sat rumbling at the prison's checkpoint—my ride to the Greyhound bus depot.

1. **redeem:** to save, make up for

As we pulled away, the towering walls, razor wire, and iron gates of the prison grew even more awesome, and the looming gun towers more **ominous**.[2] It was a bright early autumn morning, my thirty-second birthday was days away, and the last ten years of my life had been spent in and out of men's shelters, hospitals, and prisons. I wanted to make it this time.

Alcohol and other drugs had been my failing. Realizing I would need help, I sought an organization of other recovering addicts. Within a few days I landed a job in a metal-plating factory and rented a tiny furnished room. On the urging of a new friend who had a similar past, I soon took my first college course. My first grade was a disappointing C, but before long I was scoring A's and B's. I also got better jobs, eventually landing a counseling job in a substance-abuse treatment program. On job applications, I left questions about past arrests and convictions blank. I had read that this would probably go unnoticed, and if it didn't, it would be better to discuss such matters in person. Time passed, and in a few short years, I completed college. I went on to get my master's degree, and using my graduate thesis as its foundation, I wrote a book on drugs in the workplace.

Today I live a full life, enjoying what most people enjoy: movies, books, theater, good food, and good friends. My significant other is a South Asian woman, and her diverse circle of friends has enriched my life. My annual income as a substance-abuse specialist is **adequate**,[3] my standing in the community is solid, and my commitment to continued recovery is permanent.

All of these qualities notwithstanding, I remain, **irrevocably**,[4] an ex-convict. Although the years have removed all but hazy memories of addiction, hospitalizations, street living, and prison, I secretly carry the baggage of a former offender. As my qualifications for higher-level positions grew, so, too, did the potential for a more detailed **scrutiny**[5] of my past. Opportunities for better jobs that colleagues took for granted were not so available to me. On virtually every job application, the question continued to haunt me: "Have you ever been convicted of a felony or misdemeanor or denied bond in any state?" Staring blankly at the application, I would often wonder, will this nightmare ever end? For minorities, who have a higher rate of incarceration, the nightmare is even more likely to occur.

To the average person, the ex-convict is an individual of questionable character. And without the experience of meeting a rehabilitated offender, there is little chance that this image will change. It is reinforced by the fact that the only thing usually newsworthy about an ex-convict is bad news — another arrest.

Yet the real news is that many former offenders are, like me, rehabilitated members of society. No one would guess at our pasts. We don't deserve **kudos**[6] for not committing crimes, but our failings should not **supersede**[7] decades of personal growth and responsible citizenship. Unfortunately, that's often what happens.

Under employment discrimination laws, hiring decisions cannot be made on the basis of age, sex, or the color of a person's skin. A job applicant does not have to reveal a disability or medical condition, including former

2

3

IDENTIFY: Put an X by Scanlon's educational and job accomplishments in this paragraph.

4

REFLECT: Why does Scanlon give the reader these details?

_____

_____

5

IDENTIFY: Underline the sentence that explains why Scanlon was not eligible for higher-level positions.

6

TEACHING TIP Point out to students how Scanlon gives plenty of examples in the course of telling his story — for instance, examples of how he turned his life around after prison and of the challenges he faced while doing so.

7

8

---

2. ominous: threatening   **3. adequate:** sufficient, enough   **4. irrevocably:** permanently   **5. scrutiny:** inspection   **6. kudos:** credit, praise   **7. supersede:** replace drug dependence. Employability is based on the ability to perform the essential function of the job. Yet the former offender, whose past may be directly related to substance abuse, is expected to reveal his **transgression**.[8]

No one is born an ex-convict; the title is earned, and the individual 9 must accept responsibility. Yet wouldn't it be nice if there were an ex-ex-con status? It would feel good not to panic at the sight of a job application and that dreaded question: "Have you ever been convicted of a felony or misdemeanor or denied bond in any state?" This question, without exclusionary criteria ([for example,] within the last ten years), serves no one's interest. To those of us who have paid our debt to society, it's a form of discrimination that undermines our efforts to continue to rebuild our lives.

REFLECT: How might discrimination against ex-convicts hurt their efforts "to continue to rebuild" their lives?

_____

_____

- -

SUMMARIZE AND RESPOND

In your reading journal or elsewhere, summarize the main point of "It's Time I Shed My Ex-Convict Status." Then, go back and check off the support for this idea. Next, write a brief summary of the essay. Finally, write a brief response to the reading. Should ex-convicts, like Scanlon, be able to shed their status?

- -

CHECK YOUR COMPREHENSION

1. An alternate title for this essay could be
   a. "Once an Ex-Convict, Always an Ex-Convict."
   b. "Paying a Debt to Society."
   c. "Rehabilitation Rights."
   d. "Employment Discrimination against Ex-Convicts." *(circled)*

2. The main idea of this essay is that
   a. alcohol and drug use can lead to crime and time in prison.
   b. ex-convicts should not have to reveal their status on job applications. *(circled)*
   c. ex-convicts can be rehabilitated.
   d. ex-convicts make good employees.

3. What does Scanlon mean when he writes that "our failings should not supersede decades of personal growth and responsible citizenship"?
   a. Ex-convicts who have worked hard to enter society should not be held back by their past mistakes. *(circled)*
   b. Ex-convicts need to grow more and prove that they are responsible citizens before they are forgiven for their mistakes.
   c. Mistakes of ex-convicts should always be remembered.
   d. Ex-convicts need to learn from their mistakes.

4. Look back at the **boldface** vocabulary you underlined, and write sentences using the following words: *redeem* (para. 1); *ominous* (2); *adequate* (4); *scrutiny* (5); *supersede* (7).

8. **transgression:** violation of the law

· ·

READ CRITICALLY

1. What is Scanlon's tone in this essay?

2. In paragraph 6, according to Scanlon what could be done to begin to change the image of ex-convicts? What reinforces the image most people have of ex-convicts?

3. In paragraph 8, what does Scanlon feel should be the basis of employment? Do you agree with him?

4. In paragraph 9, Scanlon writes that asking a question about conviction "without exclusionary criteria . . . serves no one's interest." Why do you think he added the term "exclusionary criteria" to his statement?

5. What are some of Scanlon's accomplishments after he served his time? Do these help to support his main point? Why or why not?

· ·

WRITE

WRITE A PARAGRAPH: Write a paragraph that tells about a time when you did something wrong and tried to make up for it, but still had it held against you.

TIP For a sample narration paragraph, see page 121.

WRITE AN ESSAY: Scanlon uses personal experience in this essay to make a point about discrimination against ex-convicts. To support his thesis, he uses many specific details. In your essay, write about a time when you felt discriminated against in some way. Like Scanlon, share your personal experience, and include details and examples that allow the reader to understand your point of view.

· ·

Pat Conroy
Chili Cheese Dogs, My Father, and Me

The writing of Pat Conroy (b. 1945) draws heavily on his life experiences. *The Water Is Wide* (1972) recounts his days teaching at a one-room school in South Carolina. *The Great Santini* (1976) describes the difficulty of growing up with a strict military father. Several of Conroy's books have been made into movies. The most famous of these films is *The Prince of Tides* (1991), which was based on Conroy's 1986 novel of the same name. His most recent books are *My Losing Season* (2002), about the basketball team at the Citadel; *The Pat Conroy Cookbook: Recipes of My Life* (2005), a mix of food writing and memoir; and the novel *South of Broad* (2009).

In the following essay, Conroy uses narration to tell a story about two important relationships—with food and with his father—and how they came together.

TEACHING TIP Students should see that this essay has three parts: (1) the story of the author's sixth birthday, (2) the story of his first visit to Chicago, and (3) the story of his final days with his father.

IDEA JOURNAL Describe a relationship of yours that has changed over time.

GUIDING QUESTION
What is the significance of chili cheese dogs in the narrator's relationship with his father?

VOCABULARY DEVELOPMENT
The words in **boldface** are defined at the bottom of the page. Underline them as you read.

When I was growing up and lived at my grandmother's house in Atlanta, my mother would take us after church to The Varsity, an institution with more religious significance to me than any cathedral in the city. Its food was celebratory, fresh, and cleansing to the soul. It still remains one of my favorite restaurants in the world. 1

I had then what I order now—a habit that has not **deviated**[1] since my sixth birthday in 1951, when my grandmother, Stanny, ordered for me what she considered the picture-perfect Varsity meal: a chili cheese hot dog, onion rings, and a soft drink called "The Big Orange." 2

On that occasion, when my family had finished the meal, my mother lit six candles on a cupcake she had made, and Stanny, Papa Jack, my mother, and my sister Carol sang "Happy Birthday" as I blushed with pleasure and surprise. I put together for the first time that the **consumption**[2] of food and celebration was a natural and fitting combination. It was also the first time I realized that no one in my family could carry a tune. 3

REFLECT: Based on paragraph 4, how would you describe the father's personality?

_____

_____

When my father returned home from the Korean War, he refused to believe that The Varsity—or the American South, for that matter—could produce a hot dog worthy of consumption. My Chicago-born father was a fierce **partisan**[3] of his hometown, and he promised me that he would take me to eat a real "red hot" after we attended my first White Sox game. 4

That summer, we stayed with my dad's parents on the South Side of Chicago. There, I met the South Side Irish for the first time on their own turf. My uncles spent the summer teasing me about being a southern hick as they played endless games of **pinochle**[4] with my father. Then, my father took me for the **sacramental**[5] rite of passage: my first major league baseball game. We watched the White Sox beat the despised Yankees. 5

After the game, my father drove my Uncle Willie and me to a place called Superdawg to get a red hot. He insisted that the Superdawg sold the best red hots in the city. When my father handed me the first red hot I had ever eaten, he said, "This will make you forget The Varsity for all time." That summer, I learned that geography itself was one of the great **formative**[6] shapers of identity. The red hot was delicious, but in my lifetime I will never **forsake**[7] the pleasure of The Varsity chili cheese dog. 6

When my father was dying of colon cancer in 1998, he would spend his days with me at home on Fripp Island, South Carolina, then go back to Beaufort at night to stay with my sister Kathy, who is a nurse and was in charge of his medications. Since I was responsible for his daily lunch, I told him I would cook him anything he wanted as long as I could find it in a South Carolina supermarket. 7

"Anything, pal?" my father asked. 8

"Anything," I said. 9

PREDICT: What do you think will happen next?

_____

_____

Thus, the last days between a hard-core Marine and his edgy son, who had spent his career writing about horrific father-son relationships, 10

---

1. **deviated:** changed   2. **consumption:** using; eating (in the case of food)
3. **partisan:** one who takes sides   4. **pinochle:** a card game popular in the mid-1900s
5. **sacramental:** sacred   6. **formative:** giving form to   7. **forsake:** to give up

became our best days as we found ourselves united by the glorious subject of food.

My father was a simple man with simple tastes, but he was well-traveled, and he began telling me his life story as we spent our long hours together. The first meal he ordered was an egg sandwich, a meal I had never heard of but one that kept him alive during the **Depression**.[8] He told me, "You put a fried egg on two slices of white bread which has been spread with ketchup."

"It sounds **repulsive**,"[9] I said.

"It's delicious," he replied.

When Dad spoke of his service in Korea, I fixed him kimchi (spicy pickled vegetables), and when he talked about his yearlong duty on an aircraft carrier on the Mediterranean, I made **spaghetti carbonara**[10] or **gazpacho**.[11] But most of the time, I made him elaborate sandwiches: salami or baloney tiered high with lettuce, tomatoes, and red onions. The more elaborate I made them, the more my father loved them.

He surprised me one day by asking me to make him some red hots, done "the Chicago way, pal." That day, I called Superdawg and was surprised that it was still in business. A very pleasant woman told me to dress the red hots with relish, mustard, onion, and hot peppers with a pickle on the side. "If you put ketchup on it, just throw it in the trash," she added.

The following week, he surprised me again by ordering up some chili cheese dogs, "just like they make at The Varsity in Atlanta." So I called The Varsity and learned step by step how to make one of their scrumptious chili cheese dogs.

When my father began his quick, slippery **descent**[12] into death, my brothers and sisters drove from all directions to sit six-hour shifts at his bedside. We learned that watching a fighter pilot die is not an easy thing. One morning, I arrived for my shift and heard screaming coming from the house. I raced inside and found Carol yelling at Dad: "Dad, you've got to tell me you're proud of me. You've got to do it before you die."

I walked Carol out of the bedroom and sat her down on the sofa. "That's Don Conroy in there, Carol—not **Bill Cosby**,"[13] I said. "You've got to learn how to translate Dad. He says it, but in his own way."

Two weeks before my father died, he presented me with a gift of infinite price. I made him the last chili cheese dog from The Varsity's recipe that he would ever eat. When he finished, I took the plate back to the kitchen and was shocked to hear him say, "I think the chili cheese dog is the best red hot I've ever eaten."

There is a translation to all of this, and here is how it reads: In the last days of his life, my father was telling me how much he loved me, his oldest son, and he was doing it with food.

11

12

13

14

15

16

17 **REFLECT:** Why does Carol act as she does here?

_____

_____

18

19

20 **SUMMARIZE:** How do the father's words show that he loves his son?

_____

_____

---

8. Depression: a serious economic downturn lasting from 1929 until the late 1930s
9. repulsive: disgusting   **10. spaghetti carbonara:** pasta with a sauce of cream, eggs, and bacon   **11. gazpacho:** a cold vegetable soup from Spain   **12. descent:** a way down; a passage down to   **13. Bill Cosby:** the actor who played a wise, kind father in a 1980s TV comedy

• •

SUMMARIZE AND RESPOND

In your reading journal or elsewhere, summarize the main point of "Chili Cheese Dogs, My Father, and Me." Then, go back and check off the support for this idea. Next, write a brief summary of the essay. Finally, write a brief response to the reading. What impression does Conroy create of his changing relationship with his father?

• •

CHECK YOUR COMPREHENSION

1. An alternate title for this essay could be
    a. "My Father, the Fighter Pilot."
    (b.) "How My Father Told Me He Loved Me."
    c. "How I Learned to Love Chili Cheese Dogs."
    d. "The Varsity vs. Superdawg."

2. The main point of this essay is that
    a. chili cheese dogs are better tasting than red hots.
    b. men can learn to be excellent and creative cooks.
    (c.) people can communicate their affection for others in indirect ways.
    d. only when a parent is dying does a child learn what that parent is really like.

3. What is Conroy's point in telling the story of his sister Carol's angry outburst toward their father (para. 17)?
    a. He wants readers to understand that he comes from a family in which yelling is common.
    b. He wants to show the kind of relationship he has with his sister.
    c. He wants readers to see that anger is not useful in dealing with parents.
    (d.) He wants to show how difficult it is for his father to express feelings for his children.

4. Look back at the **boldface** vocabulary you underlined, and write sentences using the following words: *deviated* (para. 2); *consumption* (3); *formative* (6); *repulsive* (12); *descent* (17).

• •

READ CRITICALLY

1. What details show the change in Conroy's father's attitude toward The Varsity's chili cheese dogs? What is the significance of this change?

2. What three stories does Conroy narrate in this essay? When does he shift to telling about his father's last days? How do you know?

3. Based on details from the essay, describe the ways in which father and son are "united by the glorious subject of food"?

4.   Beginning in paragraph 8, Conroy includes a number of direct quotations from himself and his father. What is the effect of Conroy's presenting this dialogue?

5.   Though this essay tells a sad story overall, it has some humorous moments. What are they, and how did they affect you?

• •

WRITE

WRITE A PARAGRAPH: Write a paragraph that tells about a time when a particular food played a special role during a family celebration, such as a birthday or a holiday. Like Conroy, include details about family members and your own response to the occasion.

WRITE AN ESSAY: In an essay, trace the history of your relationship with an older family member or someone else who has played a significant role in your life. As Conroy does in writing about his relationship with his father, tell specific stories about your times with this person, and suggest ways in which your relationship changed over time.

• •

43

Illustration

Each essay in this chapter uses illustration to get its main point across to the reader. As you read these essays, consider how they achieve the four basics of good illustration that are listed below and discussed in Chapter 11 of this book.

▪▪ Four Basics of Good Illustration

1 It has a point.
2 It gives specific examples that show, explain, or prove the point.
3 It gives details to support the examples.
4 It uses enough examples to get the point across to the reader.

Rose Martinez
Reality TV

Rose Martinez wrote the following piece for an assignment in a college writing class at Passaic County Community College, where she is pursuing a degree. She is working for a large regional bank, which is community-service oriented, a focus that Martinez likes. The bank has remained in good financial shape because it has concentrated on lending to people in the community rather than getting into riskier mortgages and loans. At home, Martinez has two children, both of whom are scoring in the upper 90th percentile of state tests in reading, language arts, and math. She applies what she has learned in college about the importance of reading to raising her children and believes that is what has helped them perform so well. She helps her children with their reading, reads herself, and reads along with them. After they have finished a reading assignment, she asks them questions to make sure they understand. They enjoy reading together.

GUIDING QUESTION
What examples does Martinez give of how reality television can be good?

Reality TV is fun to watch, but it can also be helpful. For example, *The Super Nanny* helps parents change their children's bad behaviors. Another program, *Trading Spaces*, helps people organize themselves. Reality TV is fun, but it is also **productive**[1] because it educates people and gives them real-world skills.

Many reality TV programs offer sound advice for viewers. For example, *Trading Spaces* gives expert advice about how to design and organize houses or apartments. Viewers learn to use their money wisely by reusing old furniture and other items. In one episode, people sanded down a dresser to uncover a beautiful oak wood that needed just a polished finish. Another program, *The Super Nanny*, provides **strategies**[2] to help parents discipline their children. The expert walks into a household where the children have no self-control. One program showed children who hit and screamed at their elders. By the end of the show, the children had learned to communicate with others about what they felt and what they needed. Watching reality TV helps viewers in several ways with parenting and with their homes.

Additionally, reality TV educates people about how to get ideas and how to deal with real-life situations. For instance, *Trading Spaces* shows people how to store their necessary possessions so that they are easily used. It also shows people that some of their stuff should be **discarded**.[3] The contestants are able to make better use of their possessions, be more organized, and reduce **clutter**.[4] With more **efficient**[5] organization, people have more time: They can clean up faster, start new projects, and have more time for themselves and their families. Reality TV gave them techniques for improving their everyday lives.

Also, reality TV promotes good teamwork, such as in *The Super Nanny*. For example, one episode showed how parents can work together to control **time-outs**[6] for their children. If one parent placed the child in a time-out, he or she would be in charge of making sure the child sat through the time-out session but could use the other parent for **reinforcement**.[7] By the end of the show, both the parents and the children behaved better and had a more **harmonious**[8] family. Thus, reality TV shows that if you work as a team, you can accomplish your goals.

1

VOCABULARY DEVELOPMENT The words in **boldface** are defined at the bottom of the page. Underline the words as you read them.

2

IDEA JOURNAL Write about a television show you like, and give examples of why it is good.

3

4

IDENTIFY: What are three examples that Martinez gives of how reality TV can be good?

_____

_____

---

1. productive: helpful; getting positive results   **2. strategies:** plans or methods for obtaining a specific goal   **3. discarded:** thrown away or rejected   **4. clutter:** disorder; jumble of stuff   **5. efficient:** performing or functioning with the least waste of time, energy, and effort   **6. time-outs:** short breaks for children from the action, often for bad behavior   **7. reinforcement:** support   **8. harmonious:** showing agreement in feeling, attitude, or action; forming a pleasingly consistent whole

REFLECT: What real-world skills have you learned from reality TV?

_____

_____

Some reality TV programs are very useful and can be used in everyday 5 life. I learned to use an organizing system to work as a team with my family to complete household chores. Working together has built a better relationship in my family. As a result, we can compare ourselves to the ending of _The Super Nanny_, where the family looks happier with their progress of working together. We also have more time for ourselves because we are more efficient. For example, our children work as a team to clean up their rooms, and my husband and I divide the rest of the chores. Reality TV programs are both fun and productive to watch because they teach people important strategies for improving their real-life situations.

. . . .

SUMMARIZE AND RESPOND

In your reading journal or elsewhere, summarize the main point of "Reality TV." Then, go back and check off the support for this idea. Next, write a brief summary of the essay. Finally, write a brief response to the reading. Do you think "reality television" truly represents reality?

. . . .

CHECK YOUR COMPREHENSION

1. An alternate title for this essay could be
    a. "Why Reality TV Is So Entertaining."
    b. "Reality TV and Everyday Life."
    c. "Reality TV: Entertaining _and_ Informative."
    d. "Reality TV Promotes Good Families."

2. The main point of this essay is that
    a. people need to watch television to become educated.
    b. people's lives are too cluttered and inefficient.
    c. television viewing promotes harmonious families.
    d. reality television can be educational and useful.

3. Why does Martinez discuss using an organizing system with her family?
    a. She wants to emphasize how disorganized her family is.
    b. She wants to show the kind of relationship she has with her family.
    c. She wants to give an example of reality television helping her and her family.
    d. She wants to show how her whole family enjoys watching reality television shows.

4. Does this essay include the Four Basics of Good Illustration? Why or why not.

5. Look back at the **boldface** vocabulary you underlined, and write sentences using these words: _productive_ (para. 1); _strategies_ (2); _efficient_ (3); _reinforcement, harmonious_ (4).

TIP For tools to build your vocabulary, visit the _Real Writing Student Center_ at **bedfordstmartins.com/ realwriting**.

• •

READ CRITICALLY

1. Martinez focuses on "reality TV." What is "reality television," and how is it different from—or similar to—other kinds of television programming?

2. According to Martinez, these shows are not only fun to watch but also instructive. Do you think that television programs have an obligation to be educational or useful for viewers? Why or why not?

3. What transitional words and phrases does Martinez use to shift from one example to the next? How do they help her focus her paragraphs and structure her essay, as a whole?

4. In paragraph 5, Martinez claims that she has learned a specific organizing system that helps her work as a team with her family. Where else might she have learned such skills or strategies, other than from television?

5. Do you agree with the thesis of this essay? What possible problems might arise from the idea that "reality TV educates people about how to get ideas and how to deal with real-life situations" (para. 3)?

• •

WRITE

WRITE A PARAGRAPH: Write a paragraph that illustrates a lesson, skill, or strategy you learned from a source that is not usually seen as educational. Like Martinez's example at the end of her essay, your own example should be specific and concrete.

WRITE AN ESSAY: Write an essay examining what values, attitudes, or skills people generally learn from watching television—or a specific kind of TV programming. What attitude do you think viewers should take toward television's educational value?

• •

Dianne Hales
Why Are We So Angry?

PREDICT: After reading the title, what do you expect this essay to do?

_____

_____

Dianne Hales specializes in writing about mental health, fitness, and other issues related to the body and mind. She contributes regularly to *Parade* magazine and *Ladies Home Journal*, and she has written several college-level health textbooks. In her critically acclaimed book *Just like a Woman* (2000), she examined assumptions about the biological differences between women and men. Most recently, she authored *La Bella Lingua: My Love Affair with Italian, the World's Most Enchanting Language* (2009). Both the American Psychiatric Association and the American Psychological Association have presented Hales with awards for excellence in writing. In addition, she has earned an

Exceptional Media Merit Award (EMMA) from the National Women's Political Caucus for health reporting. She lives in Marin County, California.

In the following article, Hales uses vivid examples to illustrate the "rage" phenomenon. She reports on the causes and results of the apparent increase in out-of-control anger—and explains what can be done to relieve the problem.

GUIDING QUESTION

Does the author present specific and plentiful examples to answer the question that she poses in her title?

Something snapped inside Jerry Sola during his evening commute 1 through the Chicago suburbs two years ago. When the driver in front of the fifty-one-year-old salesman suddenly slammed on his brakes, Sola got so **incensed**[1] that he gunned his engine to cut in front of the man. Still steaming when both cars stopped at a red light, Sola grabbed a golf club from the backseat and got out.

"I was just about to smash his windshield or do him some damage," 2 the brawny, 6-foot-1 former police officer recalls. "Then it hit me: 'What in God's name am I doing? I'm really a nice, helpful guy. What if I killed a man, went to jail, and destroyed two families over a crazy, trivial thing?' I got back into my car and drove away."

Like Sola, more and more Americans are feeling pushed to the break- 3 ing point. The American Automobile Association's Foundation for Traffic Safety says incidents of violently aggressive driving—which some **dub**[2] "mad driver disease"—rose 7 percent a year in the 1990s. Airlines are reporting more outbursts of sky rage. And sideline rage has become widespread: A Pennsylvania kids' football game ended in a brawl involving more than one hundred coaches, players, parents, and fans. In a particularly tragic incident that captured national attention, a Massachusetts father—angered over rough play during his son's hockey practice—beat another father to death as their children watched.

No one seems **immune**[3] to the anger epidemic. Women fly off the 4 handle just as often as men, though they're less likely to get physical. The young and the infamous, such as musicians Sean "Puffy" Combs and Courtney Love—both sentenced to anger-management classes for violent outbursts—may seem more **volatile**,[4] but even senior citizens have erupted into "line rage" and pushed ahead of others simply because they felt they had "waited long enough" in their lives.

"People no longer hold themselves **accountable**[5] for their bad behav- 5 ior," says Doris Wilde Helmering, a therapist and author of _Sense Ability_. "They blame anyone and everything for their anger."

It's a mad, mad world. Violent outbursts are just as likely to occur 6 in leafy suburbs as in crowded cities, and even **idyllic**[6] vacation spots are not immune. "Everyone everywhere seems to be hotter under the collar these days," observes Sybil Evans, a conflict-resolution expert in New York

---

1. incensed: angered   **2. dub:** to call   **3. immune:** protected against
4. volatile: explosive   **5. accountable:** responsible   **6. idyllic:** peaceful

City, who singles out three primary **culprits**[7]: time, technology, and tension. "Americans are working longer hours than anyone else in the world. The cell phones and pagers that were supposed to make our lives easier have put us on call 24/7/365. Since we're always running, we're tense and low on patience. And the less patience we have, the less we monitor what we say to people and how we treat them."

Ironically,[8] the recent boom times may have brought out the worst in some people. "Never have so many with so much been so unhappy," observes Leslie Charles, author of *Why Is Everyone So Cranky?* "There are more of us than ever, all wanting the same space, goods, services, or attention. Everyone thinks, 'Me first. I don't have time to be polite.' We've lost not only our civility but our tolerance for inconvenience."

The sheer complexity of our lives also has shortened our collective fuse. We rely on computers that crash, drive on roads that gridlock, place calls to machines that put us on endless hold. "It's not any one thing but lots of little things that make people feel like they don't have control of their lives," says Jane Middleton-Moz, a therapist and author. "A sense of helplessness is what triggers rage. It's why people end up kicking ATM machines."

Getting a grip. When his lawn mower wouldn't start, a St. Louis man got so angry that he picked it up by the handle, smashed it against the patio, and tore off each of its wheels. Playing golf, he sometimes became so enraged that he threw his clubs 50 feet up the fairway and into the trees and had to get someone to retrieve them. In anger-therapy sessions with Doris Wilde Helmering, he learned that such outbursts accomplish nothing. "Venting" may make you feel better—but only for a moment.

"**Catharsis**[9] is worse than useless," says Brad Bushman, a psychology professor at Iowa State University whose research has shown that letting anger out makes people more aggressive, not less. "Many people think of anger as the psychological equivalent of the steam in a pressure cooker: It has to be released, or it will explode. That's not true. The people who react by hitting, kicking, screaming, and swearing just feel more angry."

Over time, temper tantrums sabotage physical health as well as psychological **equanimity**.[10] By churning out stress hormones like adrenaline, **chronic**[11] anger revs the body into a state of combat readiness, multiplying the risk for stroke and heart attack—even in healthy individuals. In one study by Duke University researchers, young women with "*Jerry Springer Show*–type anger," who tended to slam doors, curse, and throw things in a fury, had higher cholesterol levels than those who reacted more calmly.

How do you tame a toxic temper? The first step is to figure out what's really making you angry. Usually the rude sales clerk is the final straw that unleashes bottled-up fury over a more difficult issue, such as a divorce or a domineering boss. Next, monitor yourself for early signs of exhaustion

---

7. **culprits:** guilty ones   8. **ironically:** opposite to what is or might be expected
9. **catharsis:** release of emotional tension   10. **equanimity:** balance
11. **chronic:** habitual

Marginal notes (right column):

PREDICT: Pick one of the culprits; how do you think Hales in subsequent paragraphs will show it to be a cause of anger?

_____

_____

7

IDENTIFY: According to this paragraph, what triggers rage?   8

_____

_____

9

10

SUMMARIZE: In your own words, summarize how letting anger out creates problems.   11

_____

_____

12

IDENTIFY: Underline the sentence that presents a solution to releasing anger.

TEACHING TIP In addition to providing vivid examples, this article traces the causes and effects of what appears to be an increase in angry outbursts. If you are also teaching the cause-and-effect chapters (17 and 50), you might want to point to this essay as an example of how these (and other) writing strategies can be mixed.

or overload. While stress alone doesn't cause a blow-up, it makes you more **vulnerable**[12] to overreacting.

When you feel yourself getting angry, control your tongue and your 13 brain. "Like any feeling, anger lasts only about three seconds," says Doris Wilde Helmering. "What keeps it going is your negative thinking." As long as you focus on who or what irritated you—like the oaf who rammed that grocery cart into your heels—you'll stay angry. "Once you come to understand that you're driving your own anger with your thoughts," adds Helmering, "you can stop it."

Since his roadside **epiphany**,[13] Jerry Sola has conscientiously worked 14 to rein in his rage. "I am a changed person," he says, "especially behind the wheel. I don't listen to the news on the car radio. Instead, I put on nice, soothing music. I force myself to smile at rude drivers. And if I feel myself getting angry, I ask a simple question: 'Why should I let a person I'm never going to see again control my mood and ruin my whole day?'"

· ·

SUMMARIZE AND RESPOND

In your reading journal or elsewhere, summarize the main point of "Why Are We So Angry?" Then, go back and check off the support for this idea. Next, write a brief summary of the essay. Finally, write a brief response to the reading. Can you identify with the angry people Hales writes about in this essay? Have you ever been one of them?

· ·

CHECK YOUR COMPREHENSION

1. An alternate title for this essay could be
    a. "Anger Management."
    b. "Road Rage."
    c. "Investigating the Anger Epidemic."
    d. "The Breaking Point."

2. The main point of this essay is that
    a. anger is a widespread occurrence in today's society.
    b. anger is most common in sports.
    c. people should enroll in anger-management courses.
    d. road rage must stop.

3. What do experts say about releasing anger?
    a. Releasing anger reduces frustration.
    b. Hitting a pillow is a simple way to release anger.
    c. Releasing anger is not productive.
    d. People in the suburbs are most likely to release anger.

12. vulnerable: open to damage or attack   **13. ephiphany:** a sudden understanding of something

4. Look back at the **boldface** vocabulary you underlined, and write sentences using the following words: *immune* (para. 4); *accountable* (5); *chronic* (11); *vulnerable* (12).

. . . .

READ CRITICALLY

1. Based on your personal experience and observations, do the examples presented in this essay seem realistic?

2. Throughout the essay, Hales presents information gained from therapists and experts. Does this information strengthen Hales's main point? Would the essay be just as effective without it?

3. What role does technology play in creating anger?

4. Do the steps presented under "How do you tame a toxic temper?" (paras. 12 and 13) seem like a workable solution? Why or why not?

5. Hales begins her essay with the example of Jerry Sola and ends with it. Why do you suppose she uses this technique?

. . . .

WRITE

WRITE A PARAGRAPH: Write a paragraph about a location where you have seen people exhibit their anger. Identify the location, and provide concrete examples of the way people show their anger.

WRITE AN ESSAY: Write an essay about a time when either you or someone you knew lost control. What happened? Give concrete examples of the loss of control. What were the consequences? Did you learn anything from the experience about expressing anger? Feel free to include the ideas you wrote about in your reading journal for Summarize and Respond.

TIP For a sample illustration paragraph, see page 139.

. . . .

James Verini

Supersize It

James Verini writes for the *Los Angeles Times*, the *New York Observer*, and other publications. He lives in New York.

In this essay, originally published in the online magazine *Slate*, Verini gives examples of how spaces, clothing, and even caskets are being "supersized" to accommodate ever-larger Americans.

GUIDING QUESTION
How would you describe the examples the author presents to illustrate the trend he describes? Do you think he intends any of them to be funny?

IDEA JOURNAL What do you think are some of the causes of increasing obesity in the United States?

PREDICT: At this point, what kinds of examples do you think the author will provide?

_____

_____

VOCABULARY DEVELOPMENT
The words in **boldface** are defined at the bottom of the page. Underline these words as you read them.

IDENTIFY: List one example of how manufacturers are making seating bigger.

_____

_____

George Farquhar[1] once said that necessity was the mother of invention, but we know that to be nonsense, really: Who needs an iPod that holds 10,000 songs? There is, however, one area of life in which technology keeps step with nature—the size of things. As we Americans are getting bigger (the Centers for Disease Control and Prevention in Atlanta estimates that roughly a third of Americans are overweight, with 20 percent of us qualifying as obese), so, too, is our stuff. 1

Take our seats, for instance. Irwin Seating, a Michigan company that supplies the AMC and Regal cinema chains, has found that the movie theater industry now demands increasingly wide seats: The standard width used to be 19 inches, but now, according to Irwin, the **benchmark**[2] is 23 inches. A popular Irwin model, "the Ambassador," is 23 inches wide, includes flip-up arms for easy access, and a drink holder wide enough to hold a 44-ounce soda. 2

The trend continues into every corner of our sitting lives. Cars are getting larger, of course—the 2004 Ford Excursion fits eight average-size passengers (or roughly six obese ones). And apparently so are the people driving them—the Excursion's driver's seat is 40 inches wide. The same goes for our places of worship. Thomas McElheny, the CEO of Church Plaza, a manufacturer of "worship furniture" based in Florida, says that whereas 18 inches per worshipper used to be the **allotment**[3] when fitting for pews, most churches now require 21 inches. Church Plaza's pews have been made to support an almost miraculous 1,700 pounds per seat. "The last thing you want is the tragedy of a chair collapsing in church," McElheny says. 3

But it's not only more sitting space we require. We also need more room to get into and out of the places where we're sitting, or working, or shopping, as the case may be. Revolving doors are thus getting wider. The average width for revolving doors used to be about 6 feet, or 3 feet per compartment. But these days, says Tim Mohl, of Horton Automatics, a revolving-door maker in Corpus Christi, Texas, he rarely installs anything narrower than 8 feet. "We're just figuring that people are a little larger now." Horton has models that stretch up to 18 feet, particularly popular with Las Vegas casinos. 4

Horton also makes those extra-large automatic sliding doors you find in the new breed of superbig supermarkets—where, not surprisingly, the aisles have also widened. Supermarket aisles used to be about 5 feet wide; they are now 7 to 7½ feet. This trend is not meant to **accommodate**[4] larger shoppers, according to industry insiders, but rather to allow for larger carts, which range in size from pretty big (over 3 feet in width) to, in stores such as Costco, platform-on-wheels big (designed to carry several hundred pounds of food). The larger carts allow for larger products—the 4-gallon drum of mayonnaise, the jumbo pack of pork chops—which are made for bargain shoppers with larger appetites. 5

So are the huge stores making us huge? Or are they huge because we are? Is it even possible to say? Trying to determine cause and effect, one 6

---

1. George Farquhar: Irish playwright (1678–1707)   **2. benchmark:** a standard
3. allotment: an assigned share   **4. accommodate:** to hold comfortably

inevitably[5] finds oneself in a kind of What Came First **conundrum,**[6] the Fried Chicken or the Extra-Large Egg?

Unfortunately, none of the designers or executives I spoke to was able to answer these questions. Nor did the federal government have much to offer. While it's true that certain things in America (elevators, wheelchair ramps) are more plentiful and bigger these days thanks to the Americans with Disabilities Act, when it comes to larger people, the ADA is not very helpful. The only place where obesity seems to be addressed on the ADA Web site is in the "Myths and Facts" section—"MYTH: The ADA protects people who are overweight. FACT: Just being overweight is not enough. . . . The Department has received only a handful of complaints about obesity."

But let's get to the important question: What to wear while you're shopping in the 7½-foot-wide supermarket aisle or watching a movie in the 23-inch Irwin Ambassador?

For football enthusiasts, Russell Athletic now makes an XXXXXL (that's five X's) team jersey. This fits a 62-inch-wide chest and an even larger belly, if the jersey's mesh-blend stretchiness is put to full use. But high-end **clothiers**[7] have also come to recognize the value of getting into plus sizes, which now account for about 5 percent to 10 percent of the male clothing market and, by some estimates, as much as 20 percent of the female market. At Rochester Big & Tall, the country's largest clothing store chain for the plus-size male, you can now purchase clothing made by Ralph Lauren, Burberry, and even suits by Ermenegildo Zegna (whose advertisements feature the wafer-thin actor Adrien Brody).

There's no question the market for products custom-made for the heavy set is **burgeoning.**[8] If Tiffany can't supply you with a suitable plus-size band, you can find one at Winged Elephant, a Kent, Washington, jewelry designer that offers rings, necklaces, bracelets, and "hair-sticks" for the "style-conscious BBW"—that's Big, Beautiful Woman. A Bearville, New York, company called Amplestuff offers XL umbrellas, XL bicycle helmets, seat-belt extenders for car and airplane seats, leg lifters (for those who can't lift their own), and the Ample-Sponge, a brick-sized sponge attached to a bendable plastic handle specially designed for reaching between folds of flesh. Amplestuff's motto: "Make your world fit you!"

Finally, in the event that you should **succumb to**[9] the heart disease, diabetes, or risk of stroke that the CDC warns are several times more likely to occur with obesity, you can take **solace**[10] that even death can be made to fit. At Goliath Casket Inc., in Indiana, orders for specially made double-wide caskets have skyrocketed, says a spokesperson for the company. Goliath introduced a 52-inch model in July (a standard casket is 24 inches wide), and it is already on back order, despite the casket's own weight—200 pounds— the $1,000-plus cost of shipping it out of state, and the fact that it can only be towed on the back of a flatbed truck. (Goliath admits that, as yet, no known hearses can carry its double-wide model.)

7   **SUMMARIZE:** In your own words, what is the author saying in this paragraph?

_____

_____

8   **DISCUSSION** You might ask students about Verini's purpose and intended audience. Also, how does he use humor to make his point?

9

10   **REFLECT:** Which example in paragraphs 10 and 11 do you find most surprising?

_____

_____

11

---

5. inevitably: eventually; unavoidably   **6. conundrum:** a difficult problem
7. clothiers: clothing sellers   **8. burgeoning:** growing steadily   **9. succumb to:** to die from   **10. solace:** comfort

If we reduced the size of our stuff, would we shrink **accordingly**[11]?   12
Maybe, maybe not. But in the meantime, there's one thing we can be sure
of: We're more comfortable. Who wants to return to the days when you had
to squeeze by other patrons in the supermarket? **Commodiousness**[12]
means comfort. Roominess is happiness. Bigger is better.

• •

SUMMARIZE AND RESPOND

In your reading journal or elsewhere, summarize the main point of "Supersize It."
Then, go back and check off the support for this idea. Next, write a brief summary of the essay. Finally, write a brief response to the reading. Do you think that
the number of overweight Americans should be a matter of concern? Are manufacturers right to make bigger products to suit the obese?

• •

CHECK YOUR COMPREHENSION

1. An alternate title for this essay could be
    a. "Bigger People, Bigger Products." *(circled)*
    b. "The Many Inconveniences Faced by a Heavier Population."
    c. "The Risks of Obesity."
    d. "How Marketers Respond to Consumer Demand."

2. The main point of this essay is that
    a. manufacturers must always meet the needs of consumers, no matter
       what the consequences are.
    b. Americans today are able to be more comfortable than they were in
       years past.
    c. Americans' increasing obesity is reflected in the size of the goods
       that are being manufactured. *(circled)*
    d. the increasing size of stores is one clear cause of many Americans'
       gaining weight.

3. Which of the following points does Verini *not* make in the essay?
    a. Some businesses market their products exclusively to larger-sized
       Americans.
    b. In general, it is increasingly difficult for overweight people to find
       fashionable clothing. *(circled)*
    c. It is estimated that 20 percent of Americans weigh more than is good
       for their health.
    d. Many movie theaters and churches are providing attendees with
       more ample seat room.

4. Look back at the **boldface** vocabulary you underlined, and write sen-
    tences using the following words: *accommodate* (para. 5); *inevitably* (6);
    succumb, solace (11); *accordingly* (12).

11. accordingly: in the same way   **12. commodiousness:** spaciousness

READ CRITICALLY

1. How would you describe Verini's tone here? What is his attitude toward the trend he describes?

2. What transitional words and phrases does Verini use to signal shifts from one example to another? How do these transitions help him to focus his paragraphs?

3. In paragraphs 6 and 12, Verini poses several questions. What is the purpose of these questions? What do they suggest about the author's larger purpose in writing the essay?

4. In paragraphs 2, 3, and 10, Verini puts phrases in quotation marks and offers direct quotations from one manufacturer and from two other manufacturers' Web sites. What is the effect of these uses of quotation?

5. Does Verini provide an effective introduction for his essay? Does his closing provide a satisfying conclusion? Why or why not?

WRITE

WRITE A PARAGRAPH: Write a paragraph about a trend you've observed among people in your peer group. The trend might involve something physical—such as clothing or a type of hairstyle—or it might involve an attitude, a belief, or a common problem. In developing your paragraph, be sure to provide specific examples from your experience and observations.

WRITE AN ESSAY: Write an essay about a national trend in sports, in television programming, or in human behavior, such as the way people relate to one another in public. Like Verini, give specific examples of this trend, and provide clear transitions from one example to the next.

44

Description

Each essay in this chapter uses description to get its main point across to the reader. As you read these essays, consider how they achieve the four basics of good description that are listed below and discussed in Chapter 12 of this book.

■■ Four Basics of Good Description

1 It creates a main impression—an overall effect, feeling, or image—about the topic.

2 It uses specific details to support the main impression.

3 It supports those examples with details that appeal to the five senses: sight, hearing, smell, taste, and touch.

4 It brings a person, place, or physical object to life for the reader.

Brian Healy
First Day in Fallujah

Brian Healy is currently pursuing a degree in business management from Florida Community College. Although a typical writing process includes submitting a piece to several rounds of revision, Healy decided to "revise this essay as little as possible." He says, "I felt that given the topic, I should go with what I first wrote so that it would show more dirty truth than be polished to perfection." He values the role of emotion in writing and exhorts others not to "write for the sake of writing, [but to] write because you are passionate about it."

GUIDING QUESTION
What events affected Healy?

The year was 2004, and I was a young, 21-year-old Marine Corporal on my second tour of Iraq. I had been in the country for five months and was not enjoying it any more than the first time. From the first time I had set foot in Iraq, I perceived it as a foul-smelling **wasteland**[1] where my youth and, as I would soon find out, my innocence were being **squandered**.[2] I had been in a number of firefights, roadside bomb attacks, and mortar and rocket attacks; therefore, I had thought I had seen it all. So when the word came down that my **battalion**[3] was going to Fallujah to drive through the center of the city, I was as **naïve**[4] as a child on the first day of school. The lesson of that first day would be taught with blood, sweat, and tears, learned through pain and suffering, and never forgotten.

At 2:00 in the morning on November 10, the voice of my commander pierced the night: "Mount up!" Upon hearing these words, I boarded the Amtrak transport. I heard a loud "clank, clank," the sound of metal hitting metal as the ramp closed and sealed us in. Sitting shoulder to shoulder, we had no more room to move than sardines in a very dark can. The diesel fumes choked our lungs and burned our throats. There was a sudden jolt as the metal beast began to move, and with each bump and each turn, I was thrown from side to side inside the beast's belly with only the invisible bodies of my comrades to steady myself. I thought back to my childhood, to a time of carefree youth. I thought how my father would tell me how I was the cleanest of his sons. I chuckled as I thought, "If only he could see me now, covered in sweat and dirt and five days away from my last shower."

I was violently jerked back into the present with three thunderous explosions on the right side of the Amtrak vehicle. We continued to move faster and faster with more intensity and urgency than before. My heart was racing, pounding as if it were trying to escape from my chest when we came to a screeching halt.

With the same clank that sealed us in, the ramp dropped and released us from our can. I ran out of the Amtrak nearly tripping on the ramp. There was no moon, no street light, nothing to pierce the blanket of night. Therefore, seeing was almost completely out of the question. However, what was visible was a scene that I will never forget. The massive **craters**[5] from our bombs made it seem as if we were running on the surface of the moon. More disturbing were the dead bodies of those enemies hit with the bombs. Their bodies were strewn about in a frenzied manner: a leg or arm here, **torso**[6] there, a head **severed**[7] from its body. Trying to avoid stepping on them was impossible. Amidst all this and the natural "**fog of war**,[8]" we managed to get our bearings and move toward our **objective**.[9] We were able to take the

1

VOCABULARY DEVELOPMENT
The words in **boldface** are defined at the bottom of the page. Underline the words as you read them.

IDEA JOURNAL Write about a time you were very frightened.

PREDICT: What do you think the next paragraph will be about?

2 _____
_____

3

4 **IDENTIFY:** Underline some of the vivid images.

---

1. wasteland: an area that is uncultivated and barren, or devastated by natural disasters or war   **2. squandered:** wasted; not used to good advantage   **3. battalion:** an army unit   **4. naïve:** unsophisticated; lacking experience, judgment, or information
5. craters: shallow, bowl-shaped depressions on a surface, caused by an impact or explosion   **6. torso:** the trunk of a human body   **7. severed:** cut or divided from
8. fog of war: a term describing the general uncertainty that soldiers experience during military operations   **9. objective:** a goal or target

entrance to a government complex located at the center of the city, and we did so in fine style. "Not so tough," we all thought. We would not have to wait long until we would find out how insanely foolish we were.

As the sun began to rise, there were no morning prayers, no loudspeakers, and no noise at all. This, of course, was odd since we had become accustomed to the sounds of Iraq in the morning. However, this silence did not last long and was shattered as the enemy released hell's **wrath**[10] upon us. The enemy was **relentless**[11] in its initial assault but was unable to gain the advantage and was slowly pushed back.

As the day dragged on, the enemy fought us in an endless cycle of attack and retreat. There was no time to relax as rocket-propelled **grenades**[12] whistled by our heads time and time again. Snipers' bullets skipped off the surface of the roof we were on. While some bullets tore through packs, radios, and boots and clothing, a lucky few found their mark and ripped through flesh like a hot knife through butter.

Suddenly, there was a deafening crack as three 82-millimeter mortars rained upon us, throwing me to the ground. The dust blacked out the sun and choked my lungs. I began to rise only to be thrown back down by a rocket-propelled grenade whizzing just overhead, narrowly missing my face. At this point, it seemed clear to me that there was no end to this enemy. In the windows, out the doorways, through alleyways, and down streets, they would run. We would kill one, and another would pop up in his stead, as if some factory just out of sight was producing more and more men to fight us.

As the sun fell behind the horizon, the battle, which had so suddenly started, ended just as swiftly. The enemy, like moths to light, were nowhere to be seen. The rifles of the Marines, which were so active that day, were silent now. We were puzzled as to why it was so quiet. My ears were still ringing from that day's events when the order came down to hole up for the night. There was no sleep for me that night; the events of the day made sure of that. I sat there that cold November night not really thinking of anything. I just sat in a **trance**,[13] listening to small firefights of the battle that were still raging: a blast of machine gun fire, **tracer rounds**,[14] and air strikes. **Artillery**[15] flying through the air gave the appearance of a laser light show. Explosions rattling the earth lit my comrades' faces. As I looked over at them, I did not see my friends from earlier in the day; instead, I was looking at old men who were wondering what the next day would bring. I wondered if I would survive the next day.

The battle for Fallujah would rage on for another three weeks. The Marines of the First Battalion Eighth Marine Regiment would continue to fight with courage and honor. As each day of the battle passed, I witnessed new horrors and acts of bravery, of which normal men are not capable.

5

6

7

8

9

IDENTIFY: What senses has Healy used in his description?

_____

_____

---

10. **wrath:** strong, fierce anger; angry vengeance   11. **relentless:** steady; persistent; unyielding   12. **grenades:** handheld explosives   13. **trance:** a dazed or bewildered condition; a state seemingly between sleeping and waking   14. **tracer rounds:** ammunition containing a substance that causes bullets or rounds to trail smoke or fire so as to make their path visible and show a target for other shooters   15. **artillery:** large, crew-operated weapons

However, none of those days would have the **impact**[16] on me that that first day did.

The battle is over, but for the men who were there, it will never end. It is fought every day in their heads and in voices of friends long gone, all the while listening to the screams and **taunts**[17] of people who know nothing of war but would call these men terrorists.

10 **REFLECT:** What effect does this essay have on you?

_____

_____

· ·

SUMMARIZE AND RESPOND

In your reading journal or elsewhere, summarize the main point of "First Day in Fallujah." Then, go back and check off the support for this idea. Next, write a brief summary of the essay. Finally, write a brief response to the reading. Although Healy writes about the chaotic and violent aspects of war, does he also make his battle experience meaningful?

· ·

CHECK YOUR COMPREHENSION

1. An alternate title for this essay could be
    a. "The United States at War in the Middle East."
    b. "Changed Forever in the Fog of War."
    c. "Liberating Fallujah and Iraq."
    d. "A News Update from Iraq."

2. The main point of this essay is that
    a. the United States should make military service a requirement for all citizens.
    b. the writer has maintained his innocence, despite having experienced combat.
    c. combat is intense, frightening, and confusing, and its effects change soldiers.
    d. the war in Iraq is unwinnable because the number of enemies there is infinite.

3. Why does Healy recall his father's remark that Healy was "the cleanest of his sons"?
    a. Healy wants the reader to know how infrequently soldiers bathe.
    b. This memory shows Healy's change from the child he once was.
    c. Healy wants to show how well he adapted to conditions in Iraq.
    d. Healy thinks his father would be disappointed at how dirty he has become.

4. Does this essay include the Four Basics of Good Description? Why or why not?

16. **impact:** influence; an effect; a collision   17. **taunts:** scornful insults, jeering, or ridicule

TIP For tools to build your vocabulary, visit the *Real Writing Student Center* at **bedfordstmartins.com/ realwriting**.

5.   Look back at the **boldface** vocabulary you underlined, and write sentences using these words: *squander*, *naïve* (para. 1); *severed* (4); *relentless* (5); *impact* (9).

READ CRITICALLY

1.   In giving his description of combat, how does Healy appeal to his readers' different senses? Provide specific examples.

2.   How would you characterize the tone of "First Day in Fallujah," and why?

3.   Healy opens his essay by describing himself as "a young, 21-year-old Marine Corporal." How does he change during the course of his account? What is the difference between "lost" innocence and "squandered" innocence?

4.   In paragraph 9, Healy says that his battalion fought with "courage and honor" and that he witnessed "new horrors and acts of bravery, of which normal men are not capable." What does he mean by "normal"?

5.   In the conclusion of his essay, Healy writes that the battle is still fought every day in the heads of these soldiers and "in voices of friends long gone." What experience is he writing about here?

WRITE

WRITE A PARAGRAPH: Write a descriptive paragraph that recounts a personal experience that transformed you and made you less innocent or naïve.

WRITE AN ESSAY: At the very end of his narrative, Healy refers to people who "know nothing of war but would call these men terrorists." Write an essay that considers the value of reading accounts such as Healy's: Do they help us "know" war? Did his essay change the way you understand soldiers, combat, and war, generally?

David M. Dosa
A Day in the Life of Oscar the Cat

David Dosa, M.D., M.P.H., is an assistant professor of medicine at the Warren Alpert Medical School of Brown University. He attended medical school at the George Washington University and completed his residency at University Hospitals at the University of Pittsburgh. As a doctor, his specialties include geriatrics, dementia care, and nursing home medicine, areas that relate to his essay "A Day in the Life of Oscar the Cat." The story, which first appeared in the *New England Journal of Medicine* in July 2007, tells the story of a hospice cat with the "uncanny knack for predicting when nursing home patients are going to die." *Making the Rounds with Oscar*, a book based on his experiences with Oscar, will be published in 2010 by Hyperion.

GUIDING QUESTION
At what point do you begin to realize that Oscar's walk around the nursing home has a purpose?

Oscar the Cat wakens from his nap, opening a single eye to survey his kingdom. From atop the desk in the doctor's charting area, the cat peers down the two wings of the nursing home's advanced **dementia**[1] unit. **All quiet on the western and eastern fronts**.[2] Slowly, he rises and **extravagantly**[3] stretches his two-year-old frame, first backward and then forward. He sits up and considers his next move.

In the distance, a resident approaches. It is Mrs. P., who has been living on the dementia unit's third floor for three years now. She has long forgotten her family, even though they visit her almost daily. Moderately **disheveled**[4] after eating her lunch, half of which she now wears on her shirt, Mrs. P. is taking one of her many aimless strolls to nowhere. She glides toward Oscar, pushing her walker and **muttering**[5] to herself with complete **disregard**[6] for her surroundings. **Perturbed**,[7] Oscar watches her carefully and, as she walks by, lets out a gentle hiss, a rattlesnake-like warning that says, "leave me alone." She passes him without a glance and continues down the hallway. Oscar is relieved. It is not yet Mrs. P.'s time, and he wants nothing to do with her.

Oscar jumps down off the desk, relieved to be once more alone and in control of his **domain**.[8] He takes a few moments to drink from his water bowl and grab a quick bite. Satisfied, he enjoys another stretch and sets out on his rounds. Oscar decides to head down the west wing first, along the way sidestepping Mr. S., who is slumped over on a couch in the hallway. With his lips slightly **pursed**,[9] he snores peacefully—perhaps **blissfully**[10] unaware of where he is now living. Oscar continues down the hallway until he reaches its end and Room 310. The door is closed, so Oscar sits and waits. He has important business.

Twenty-five minutes later, the door finally opens, and out walks a nurse's aide carrying dirty linens. "Hello, Oscar," she says. "Are you going inside?" Oscar lets her pass, then makes his way into the room, where there are two people. Lying in a corner bed and facing the wall, Mrs. T. is asleep in a **fetal position**.[11] Her body is thin and wasted from the breast cancer that has been eating away at her organs. She is mildly **jaundiced**[12] and has

---

IDEA JOURNAL Describe how you felt when you were very sick.

VOCABULARY DEVELOPMENT
The words in **boldface** are defined at the bottom of the page. Underline the words as you read them.

---

1. dementia: loss of memory, concentration, judgment, and other mental abilities caused by head injuries, tumors, or illnesses such as Alzheimer's disease   **2. *All Quiet on the Western Front*:** a famous book and movie about a veteran of World War I
3. extravagantly: in a rich or luxurious way   **4. disheveled:** untidy or disorderly
5. muttering: talking softly to oneself   **6. disregard:** not paying attention to or noticing   **7. perturbed:** annoyed or puzzled   **8. domain:** a territory that one controls or rules   **9. pursed:** wrinkled or puckered   **10. blissfully:** with extreme happiness
11. fetal position: a position in which the body is curled up like an unborn fetus
12. jaundiced: colored yellow because of illness

REFLECT: What do you think Oscar is doing by observing the patients?

_____

_____

not spoken in several days. Sitting next to her is her daughter, who glances up from her novel to warmly greet her visitor. "Hello, Oscar. How are you today?"

Oscar takes no notice of the woman and leaps up onto the bed. He   5
surveys Mrs. T. She is clearly in the terminal phase of illness, and her breathing is labored. Oscar's examination is interrupted by a nurse, who walks in to ask the daughter whether Mrs. T. is uncomfortable and needs more morphine. The daughter shakes her head, and the nurse retreats. Oscar returns to his work. He sniffs the air, gives Mrs. T. one final look, then jumps off the bed and quickly leaves the room. Not today.

Making his way back up the hallway, Oscar arrives at Room 313. The   6
door is open, and he proceeds inside. Mrs. K. is resting peacefully in her bed, her breathing steady but shallow. She is surrounded by photographs of her grandchildren and one from her wedding day. Despite these **keepsakes**,[13] she is alone. Oscar jumps onto her bed and again sniffs the air. He pauses to consider the situation, and then turns around twice before curling up beside Mrs. K.

PREDICT: Why do you think the nurse leaves the room quickly?

_____

_____

One hour passes. Oscar waits. A nurse walks into the room to check on   7
her patient. She pauses to note Oscar's presence. Concerned, she hurriedly leaves the room and returns to her desk. She grabs Mrs. K.'s chart off the medical-records rack and begins to make phone calls.

Within a half hour, the family starts to arrive. Chairs are brought into   8
the room, where the relatives begin their **vigil**.[14] The priest is called to deliver **last rites**.[15] And still, Oscar has not budged, instead purring and gently **nuzzling**[16] Mrs. K. A young grandson asks his mother, "What is the cat doing?" The mother, fighting back tears, tells him, "He is here to help Grandma get to heaven." Thirty minutes later, Mrs. K. takes her last earthly breath. With this, Oscar sits up, looks around, then departs the room so quietly that the grieving family barely notices.

On his way back to the charting area, Oscar passes a plaque mounted   9
on the wall. On it is engraved a **commendation**[17] from a local hospice agency: "For his compassionate **hospice**[18] care, this plaque is awarded to Oscar the Cat." Oscar takes a quick drink of water and returns to his desk to curl up for a long rest. His day's work is done. There will be no more deaths today, not in Room 310 or in any other room for that matter. After all, no one dies on the third floor unless Oscar pays a visit and stays awhile.

NOTE: *Since he was adopted by staff members as a kitten, Oscar the Cat has had an unexplainable ability to predict when residents are about to die. He has presided over the deaths of more than 25 residents on the third floor of Steere House Nursing and Rehabilitation Center in Providence, Rhode Island. His presence at the bedside is viewed by physicians and nursing home staff as a reliable indicator of impending death, allowing staff members to adequately notify families. Oscar has also provided companionship to those who would otherwise have died alone.*

13. **keepsake:** an item that reminds a person of someone or something   14. **vigil:** a wait or watch   15. **last rites:** a religious ritual performed before a person dies
16. **nuzzling:** snuggling up to   17. **commendation:** an award or a compliment for service   18. **hospice:** a health-care place or program for the terminally ill that focuses on pain control and emotional support for patients and their families

• •

SUMMARIZE AND RESPOND

In your reading journal or elsewhere, summarize the main point of "A Day in the Life of Oscar the Cat." Then, go back and check off the support for this idea. Next, write a brief summary of the essay. Finally, write a brief response to the reading. What seems to be the attitude of doctors, nurses, patients, and their families toward Oscar the cat?

• •

CHECK YOUR COMPREHENSION

1. An alternate title of this essay could be
    a. "The Cat Who Hissed at Doctors, Nurses, and Patients."
    b. "Oscar: The Cat Who Gives Hospice Care."
    c. "Cats Are People, Too."
    d. "Oscar the Cat: Helping to Cure Terminal Illnesses."

2. The main point of this essay is
    a. to show that cats are like human beings in almost every way.
    b. that Oscar is a remarkable cat with a vital role at this hospice.
    c. that dogs may be loyal and friendly, but cats are more intelligent.
    d. that doctors are sometimes so overwhelmed that they need help from pets.

3. Why does the writer show Oscar hissing at one patient and ignoring the family member of another patient?
    a. Dosa wants to show how unfriendly cats are, in general.
    b. Dosa wants to show that stray cats never adjust to new surroundings.
    c. Dosa wants to show that Oscar is focused and serious when working.
    d. Dosa wants to show that patients are often uncomfortable around Oscar.

4. Look back at the **boldface** vocabulary you underlined, and write sentences using these words: *extravagantly* (para. 1); *disregard, perturbed* (2); *vigil* (8); *commendation* (9).

• •

READ CRITICALLY

1. Does "A Day in the Life of Oscar the Cat" have a thesis? Can you state it in your own words?

2. Dosa primarily provides a description of Oscar and an account of his typical workday. How would you summarize the larger point or purpose of this essay, in your own words?

3. How would you describe the attitude of the hospice staff, the patients, and the patients' families toward Oscar? What specific details give you this impression?

4. Oscar works in a human environment and appears to have some human qualities, but he is not actually a human being. In his description, how does Dosa convey both these aspects of the cat?

5. In paragraph 8, Dosa includes part of a conversation between the relatives of a patient who is dying as Oscar nuzzles and purrs beside her. Why does the author include these remarks? How do they add to our impression of Oscar?

WRITE

WRITE A PARAGRAPH: Write a paragraph that describes a pet, or any other animal you have ever seen. In the description, include your response to the animal (affectionate, fearful, humorous). Use physical details that appeal to at least three of the five senses: sight, hearing, smell, taste, and touch.

WRITE AN ESSAY: In an essay, recount an experience you have had in any health-care facility such as the doctor's office or a hospital. Try to recall what you saw, tasted, touched, smelled, and heard there in order to describe the environment and the experience as vividly as possible. If the experience was emotional in any way (frightening, comforting, humorous), include those responses, as well.

Eric Liu
Po-Po in Chinatown

Eric Liu is a graduate of Yale University and Harvard Law School and currently teaches at the University of Washington's Evans School of Public Affairs. He is a former speechwriter for President Bill Clinton and also served as the president's Deputy Domestic Policy Advisor. Liu has written several books on a range of subjects and edited the Norton anthology *Next: Young American Writers on the New Generation* (1994). His book *The Accidental Asian: Notes of a Native Speaker* (1999) was selected as a *New York Times* Notable Book and was also featured in the PBS documentary *Matters of Race*. His most recent book is *Imagination First: Unlocking the Power of Possibility*, which he coauthored with Scott Noppe-Brandon.

GUIDING QUESTION
What picture do you form of Po-Po and the author's attitude toward her?

For more than two decades, my mother's mother, Po-Po, lived in   1
a **cinder-block**[1] one-bedroom apartment on the edge of New York's

1. cinder-block: a concrete block

Chinatown.[2] She was twenty floors up, so if you looked straight out of the main room, which faced north, one block appeared to melt into the next, all the way to the spire of the **Empire State Building**[3] off in the distance. This was a saving grace, the view, since her own block down below was not much to look at. Her building, one of those interchangeable towers of 1970s public housing, was on the lower east side of the **Lower East Side**,[4] at the corner of South and Clinton Streets. It was, as the Realtors say, only minutes from the Brooklyn Bridge and the South Street Seaport, although those **landmarks**,[5] for all she cared, might as well have been in Nebraska. They weren't part of the world Po-Po inhabited, which was the world that I visited every few months during the last years of her life.

My visits followed a certain pattern. I'd get to her apartment around noon, and when I knocked on the door, I could hear her **scurrying**[6] with excitement. When she opened the door, I'd be struck always as if for the first time, by how tiny she was: four feet nine and shrinking. She wore loose, baggy clothes, nylon, and ill-fitting old glasses that covered her soft, wrinkled face. It was a face I recognized from my own second-grade class photo. *Eh, Po-Po, ni hao maaa?* She offered a giggle as I bent to embrace her. With an impish smile, she proclaimed my American name in her **Yoda**-like[7] voice: *Areek.* She got a kick out of that. As she shuffled to the kitchen where Li Tai Tai, her caregiver, was preparing lunch, I would head to the bathroom, trained to wash my hands upon entering Po-Po's home.

In the small bath were the accessories of her everyday life: a **frayed**[8] toothbrush in a plastic Star Trek mug I'd given her in 1979, stiff washrags and aged pantyhose hanging from a clothesline, medicine bottles and hair dye cluttered on the sinktop. I often paused for a moment there, looking for my reflection in the filmy, clouded mirror, taking a deep breath or two. Then I would walk back into the main room. The place was neat but basically grimy. Some of the furniture—the lumpy couch, the coffee table with old magazines and **congealed**[9] candies, the lawn chair where she read her Chinese newspaper through a magnifying glass—had been there as long as I could remember. The windowsill was crammed with plants and flowers. The only thing on the thickly painted white wall was a calendar. *Your house looks so nice*, I'd say in a tender tone of **Mandarin**[10] that I used only with her. On a tray beside me, also surveying the scene, was a faded black-and-white portrait of Po-Po as a beautiful young woman, dressed in Chinese costume. *Lai chi ba*, Po-Po would say, inviting me to eat.

Invariably,[11] there was a banquet's worth of food awaiting me on the small kitchen table: *hongshao* stewed beef, a broiled fish with scallions and ginger, a leafy green called *jielan*, a soup with chicken and winter melon and radishes, tofu with ground pork, stir-fried shrimp still in their salty shells.

2

3

4

VOCABULARY DEVELOPMENT
The words in **boldface** are defined at the bottom of the page. Underline the words as you read them.

IDEA JOURNAL Describe an older relative's apartment or house.

IDENTIFY: What senses has the author used so far in his description?

_____

_____

---

2. Chinatown: a section of New York City with a large population of Chinese immigrants
3. Empire State Building: a famous skyscraper in New York City   **4. Lower East Side:** a neighborhood in New York City traditionally known for its immigrant population
5. landmarks: buildings with historical importance   **6. scurrying:** moving quickly
7. Yoda: a small, elderly creature from the *Star Wars* movies   **8. frayed:** worn out, with threads raveling   **9. congealed:** jelled or hardened   **10. Mandarin:** the official language of China   **11. invariably:** always; without exception

Po-Po ate sparingly, and Li Tai Tai, in her mannerly Chinese way, **adamantly**[12] refused to dine with us, so it was up to me to attack this meal. I **gorged**[13] myself, loosening my belt within the half hour and sitting back dazed and short of breath by the end. No matter how much I put down, Po-Po would express disappointment at my **meager**[14] appetite.

As I ate, she chattered excitedly, pouring forth a **torrent**[15] of opinions   5 about politics in China, Hong Kong pop singers, the latest developments in Taiwan. After a while, she'd move into stories about people I'd never met, distant relations, half-brothers killed by the Communists, my grandfather, who had died when I was a toddler. Then she'd talk about her friends who lived down the "F" train in **Flushing**[16] or on the other side of Chinatown and who were dying one by one, and she'd tell me about seeing Jesus after she'd had a cancer operation in 1988, and how this blond Jesus had materialized and said to her in Chinese, *You are a good person, too good to die now. Nobody knows how good you are. Nobody appreciates you as much as I do.* I would sit quietly then, not sure whether to smile. But just as she approached the **brink**,[17] she would take a sip of 7-Up and swerve back to something in the news, perhaps something about her heroine, the Burmese **dissident**[18] aunt **Aung San Kyi**.[19] She was an incredible talker, Po-Po, using her hands and her eyes like a performer. She built up a tidal momentum, relentless, imaginative, **spiteful**[20] like a child.

I generally didn't have much to say in response to Po-Po's commen-   6 tary, save the occasional Chinese-**inflected**[21] *Oh?* and *Wah!* I took in the **lilt**[22] of her **Sichuan**[23] accent and relied on context to figure out what she was saying. In fact, it wasn't until I brought my girlfriend to meet Po-Po that I realized just how vague my comprehension was. *What did she say?* Carroll would ask. *Um, something about, something, I think, about the president of Taiwan.* Of course, I'm not sure Po-Po even cared whether I understood. If I interrupted, she'd cut me off with a hasty *bushide—no, it's not that*—a habit I found endearing in small doses but that my mother, over a lifetime, had found maddening.

If there was a lull, I might ask Po-Po about her health, which would   7 prompt her to spring up from her chair and, bracing herself on the counter, kick her leg up in the air: *I do this ten times every morning at five*, she would proudly say in Chinese. *Then this*, she'd add, and she would stretch her arms out like little wings, making circles with her fingertips. *And last week, I had a headache, so I rubbed each eye like this thirty-six times.* Pretty soon, I was out of my chair, too, laughing, rubbing, kicking, as Po-Po schooled me in her system of exercises and home remedies. We did this every visit, like a ritual.

REFLECT: Why do you think the author finds Po-Po endearing while his mother found her maddening?

_____

_____

12. **adamantly:** in a stubborn or unyielding manner   13. **gorge:** to eat a huge amount
14. **meager:** deficient; of a very small amount   15. **torrent:** a violently flowing stream, river, or downpour of rain   16. **Flushing:** a neighborhood in New York City
17. **brink:** the edge, as of a cliff   18. **dissident:** a protester; one who disagrees with a political establishment   19. **Aung San Suu Kyi:** a Nobel Peace Prize–winning human rights activist from Burma   20. **spiteful:** mean-spirited   21. **inflected:** accented in a certain way   22. **lilt:** a pleasant varation in the pitch of one's speech
23. **Sichuan:** a province of south-central China

Time moved so slowly when I was at Po-Po's. After lunch, we might sit   8
on the couch next to each other or go to her room so she could tell me
things that she didn't want Li Tai Tai to hear. We would rest there, digesting,
our conversation turning more mellow. I might pull out of my bag a small
keepsake[24] for her, a picture of Carroll and me, or a souvenir from a recent
vacation. She would show me a bundle of poems she had written in classical
Chinese, scribbled on the backs of small cardboard rectangles that come
with travel packs of Kleenex. She would recount how she'd been inspired to
write this poem or that one. Then she would open a spiral notebook that she
kept, stuffed with news clippings and filled with **idioms**[25] and sentences she
had copied out of the Chinese newspaper's daily English lesson: *Let's get a
move on. I don't like the looks of this.* At my urging, she'd read the sentences
aloud, **tentatively**.[26] I would praise her warmly, she would chuckle, and
then she might show me something else, a photo album, a book about
qigong.[27]

One day, she revealed to me her own way of prayer, demonstrating how   9
she sat on the side of her bed at night, and clasped her hands, bowing as if
before Buddha, repeating in fragile English, *God bless me? God bless me? God
bless me?* Another time, she urgently recited to me a short story that had
moved her to tears, but I understood hardly a word of it. On another visit,
she fell asleep beside me, her glasses still on, her chin tucked into itself. And
so the hours would pass, until it was time for me to go—until, that is, I decided it was time to go, for she would have wanted me to stay forever—and
I would hold her close and stroke her knotted back and tell her that I loved
her and that I would miss her, and Po-Po, too modest to declare her heart
so openly, would nod and press a little red envelope of money into my hand
and say to me quietly in Chinese, *How I wish I had wings so I could come to
see you where you live.*

. . . .

SUMMARIZE AND RESPOND

In your reading journal or elsewhere, summarize the main point of "Po-Po in Chinatown." Then, go back and check off the support for the idea. Next, write a brief
summary of the essay. Finally, write a brief response to the reading. Do you think
Liu enjoyed these visits with his grandmother? Why or why not?

. . . .

CHECK YOUR COMPREHENSION

1.   An alternate title for this essay could be
      a. "Memories of My Chinese Grandmother."
      b. "My Grandmother's Dirty Apartment."

---

24. **keepsake:** a reminder of something past   25. **idioms:** words or sayings specific to
a region   26. **tentatively:** uncertainly; hesitantly   27. **qigong:** a traditional Chinese
practice of meditation and self-healing

    c. "Confessions of a Chinese American Grandmother."

    d. "An Immigrant Story."

2. The main point of this essay is that

    a. the language barrier between Liu and his Chinese grandmother made their relationship nearly impossible.

    b. New York is a city full of immigrant neighborhoods, such as Chinatown.

    c. Liu's grandmother liked to talk, but her anger and inability to learn English made it impossible for her to feel at home in America.

    (d.) Liu's grandmother was a complex, funny, and opinionated woman, and his memories of visiting her remain with him.

3. Why does Liu mention the 1979 plastic Star Trek mug in his grandmother's bathroom?

    a. It shows how his grandmother had abandoned her Chinese heritage.

    b. His grandmother loved watching American television.

    (c.) It shows how time stood still in her apartment.

    d. It shows that his grandmother had good health habits.

4. Look back at the **boldface** vocabulary you underlined, and write sentences using these words: *adamantly, meager* (para. 4); *torrent, spiteful* (5); *tentatively* (8).

· ·

READ CRITICALLY

1. In paragraph 3, Liu writes that his grandmother's apartment was "neat but basically grimy." What do you think that distinction means? How do the details in the essay support this claim?

2. Liu appeals to his reader's senses throughout the essay. Find specific examples in the text where he appeals to at least three of the five senses (sound, sight, taste, touch, and smell). How do they contribute to the overall impression of "Po-Po in Chinatown"?

3. Liu writes in paragraph 5 that his grandmother "built up a tidal momentum" when she talked. In what specific ways does Liu's writing evoke her excited chatter for the reader?

4. In paragraph 6, Liu writes that he's not sure if his grandmother even cared if he understood what she said to him. What does this say about their relationship, and how is it related to the larger point of the essay?

5. At the conclusion of the essay, Liu writes that he would tell his grandmother he loved her but that she was "too modest to declare her heart so openly." How does he give an impression of his grandmother's love, even though she never tells him explicitly?

WRITE

WRITE A PARAGRAPH: Write a paragraph that vividly describes the home, apartment, or living space of a close friend or relative. Like Liu, include details that show how the person's home reflects his or her personality, life, and relationships.

WRITE AN ESSAY: Liu writes that his visits to his grandmother "followed a certain pattern," which he then recounts in the essay. Write an essay in which you describe the pattern of your own regular visits or meetings with a friend, relative, or group of people. Try to show how this order of events reveals important aspects of your relationship with the person or people you visit.

45

Process Analysis

Each essay in this chapter uses process analysis to get its main point across to the reader. As you read these essays, consider how they achieve the four basics of good process analysis that are listed below and discussed in Chapter 13 of this book.

■■ Four Basics of Good Process Analysis

1. It tells readers what process the writer wants them to know about and makes a point about it.
2. It presents the essential steps in the process.
3. It explains the steps in detail.
4. It presents the steps in a logical order (usually time order).

Jasen Beverly
My Pilgrimage

Jasen Beverly is the author of the essay "My Pilgrimage," a piece he began for an introductory college English class. While publication was not an original goal of his, he was later encouraged to seek a larger audience beyond his class. Before submitting the essay, Beverly spent two weeks editing his work, working through several drafts and aiming each time "to make it better with every draft." In addition to a series of revisions, he also looks to his friends for editorial support with his writing and "to make sure it is never too wordy or sugar-coated."

GUIDING QUESTION
Why does Beverly title his essay "My Pilgrimage"?

I'm tired and scared as hell. I've been running from this thing for who knows how long, but now I'm trapped. I crouch into a fetal position as the monster approaches me. With a closer look, I realize it's my best friend trying to kill me. He lifts his arm and cocks the gun back. Without words, he pulls the trigger.

The sound of a newly received instant message wakes me up. It's only 6:30 in the morning, so I'm hesitant to check the instant message. Minutes later, I roll over and reach for my phone. I slowly wipe the crust from my eyes and begin to read, "Wakey, wakey, eggs and bakey . . . skoo time!" reads the IM from my Mexican friend. I slide my phone open and reply with a quick "aiight," before I proceed to pass out again. Just as I begin to reconnect with my dream, at about 6:45, I'm interrupted once more. This time, it is a loud repeated banging at my bedroom door.

Without thoughts or words, I roll out of bed, grab my cloth and towel, and head for the bathroom. Upon reaching the bathroom, I hop into the shower. When my shower ends, I am forced to rush through both the grooming and dressing processes because there is a massive cold front sweeping through my apartment. This cold front is caused by a lack of heat in the apartment. This, in turn, is caused by what I like to call "hard times."

By 7:20, all is well, and I am ready to begin my **pilgrimage**[1] to Bunker Hill Community College for my first day of college. I leave my apartment with my hoodie unzipped, backpack half on, while trying fast to detangle my headphones for use. As I walk down the street, the frigid air begins to take its toll. My whole face is stinging as if it was being poked, the air circulating inside my shirt. I immediately slip my headphones into my pocket and zip my hoodie. I tie my hood tightly around my eyes. My hood cuts off my **peripheral**[2] vision but keeps all unwanted air off my face. Now I finish untangling my headphones and plug them into my phone. I quickly browse my list of albums before choosing one to listen to. This morning, I choose John Legend's *Once Again*. The music is soothing; it puts me in the zone as I continue the short trek to the bus stop.

While waiting patiently at the bus stop, I begin to **ponder**.[3] My first thought is, "How much longer will I be here waiting for the bus?" Next, I ask myself, "Am I even going to be able to sit when I get on the bus?" As this thought leaves my head, I see a bus coming down Columbia Road.

I enter the bus, tap my **Charlie Card**[4] on the target area, and begin to walk away. Shortly after, a stranger taps me on my leg as I walk by. When I look back, he is pointing to the fare box. I walk back and notice the driver

1 VOCABULARY DEVELOPMENT The words in **boldface** are defined at the bottom of the page. Underline the words as you read them.

2 IDEA JOURNAL Write about a trip you make so often that you do not usually think about the many steps involved.

IDENTIFY: What kind of introductory technique does Beverly use?

_____

_____

3 TEACHING TIP If you have covered narration, point out to students that this essay is also a narration.

4 IDENTIFY: What detail gives you information about Beverly's financial situation?

_____

_____

---

1. **pilgrimage:** a long journey, often made to some sacred place as an act of religious devotion   2. **peripheral:** to the sides of a person's main line of sight   3. **ponder:** to think about   4. **Charlie Card:** a plastic pass card used to pay fares on Boston's public transportation

saying something. I'm not able to make out what he is saying because I have my headphones on. My card must not have been processed correctly. I re-tap my card on the target area. This time, I wait for it to register before walking away. I spot a seat in the back of the bus, so I fill it. Once I sit, I look around at the other people on the bus. I feel as if everyone is looking at me, so I close my eyes and let the music soothe my mind. When the bus pulls into Andrews Station, I stand and exit the bus. I walk down the stairs and wait for the train to arrive.

REFLECT: Why does Beverly think about the business-people?

_____

_____

When it arrives, it is packed with an uncountable number of business-   7
people taking a trip to the Financial District. In fact, it is so packed that I prefer to wait for the next train. While waiting, I begin to think about all of the businesspeople. I ask myself, "How long did they have to attend college to put themselves into the position they're in now?" As the next train pulls into the station, I notice it is much like the last, but this time I squeeze myself into the middle of the car. Luckily for me, Downtown Crossing, my stop, is only three stops away.

Upon reaching Downtown Crossing at 7:45, I exit the train and begin   8
to watch as people dart down the long corridor in hopes of catching the train. This becomes the highlight of the morning as I watch the doors slam in people's faces. There's no explaining the humor of watching people who have tried so hard, panting angrily as the train leaves without them. After this joyous moment, I proceed to transfer from the Red Line to the Orange Line.

SUMMARIZE: What kind of student was Beverly in high school?

_____

_____

Standing on the Orange Line platform, I recognize a few familiar faces.   9
They belong to students of Charlestown High School. I laugh, knowing that school for them began at 7:20. Then I begin to **reminisce**[5] about my own CHS experiences. I think about all my suspension hearings, the work I refused to do, and how easy it was to get by doing the bare minimum. Only the cold draft of the approaching train brings me back to reality.

I step on the train and position myself against the door. I could sit, but   10
I figure it is too short a ride to get comfortable. One by one, the stops come and go: State, Haymarket, and then North Station. The train seems to be on an effortless glide as it starts to move toward Community College.

My stomach begins to **churn**[6] as I start the last phase of my pilgrim-   11
age. The last phase consists of walking out of the train station, down the walkway, and into Bunker Hill Community College. I compare this walk to the walk death row inmates take before they are executed. As I take this walk, I begin to ask myself, "What the ---- are you doing here?" Within seconds, my sensible half answers, "You're here so that you don't have to live like the rest of your family. The rest of your friends are in school, and Lord knows half of them aren't half as smart as you. Lastly, we already paid for this, so get it done." With BHCC right in front of me, I take a deep breath and end this pilgrimage by entering the **mecca**[7] that will start me on the path of reaching my **pinnacle**.[8]

---

5. reminisce: to think back or recollect   **6. churn:** to stir powerfully   **7. mecca:** a place that many people want to visit; a center of activity (Mecca is an Islamic holy city in Saudi Arabia)   **8. pinnacle:** the highest point or achievement snapped apart, first at its weakest point and then **disintegrating**[4] rapidly from there as the tidal force became stronger than the chemical bonds holding your body together. You would be reduced to a bunch of disconnected atoms. Those atoms would be stretched into a line and continue in a processional march. As Tyson described it, you would be "**extruded**[5] through space like toothpaste being squeezed through a tube." No one knows for certain what happens to those atoms once they reach the center, or "singularity," of a black hole.

In a small black hole—like the one predicted by the LHC **doomsayers**[6]—this **dissolution**[7] would occur almost immediately. In fact, for all but the largest black holes, dissolution would happen before a person even crossed the event horizon, and it would take place in a matter of billionths of a second.   5

The more matter—and people—a black hole gobbled up, the bigger it would get. That could have the effect of making it less spectacularly deadly. As a black hole increases in size, the differences in gravitational force inside become less dramatic. If you fell into a truly gigantic black hole, the rate of change—and resulting tidal force—might not be enough to rip your body apart until after you had crossed the event horizon.   6

If you fell into a large enough black hole, your last moments would be a little bit like being on the inside of a **distorted**,[8] one-way mirror. No one outside would be able to see you, but you would have a view of them. Meanwhile, the gravitational pull would bend the light weirdly and distort your last moments of vision.   7

• •

SUMMARIZE AND RESPOND

In your reading journal or elsewhere, summarize the main point of "What Happens If You Fall into a Black Hole?" Then, go back and check off the support for this idea. Next, write a brief summary of the essay. Finally, write a brief response to the reading. Although it's extremely unlikely that anyone would ever die in this way, do you think it's fascinating or worthwhile to consider the process? Why or why not?

• •

CHECK YOUR COMPREHENSION

1. An alternate title for this essay could be

   a. "The Many Dangers of Black Holes."

   b. "The Most Spectacular Way to Die in Space."

   c. "Collider in Switzerland May Cause Black Hole."

   d. "New Scientific Experiments May Explain Black Holes."

---

4. disintegrate: to break up into tiny parts because of impact or decay   **5. extruded:** forced out or pressed out   **6. doomsayer:** a person who predicts a disaster in the near future   **7. dissolution:** separation into smaller parts   **8. distorted:** pulled or twisted out of shape

2. The main point of this essay is to
   - **a.** show what would happen to a person in a black hole.
   - **b.** calm fears that the new Swiss collider will destroy the world.
   - **c.** prove that it is impossible to go faster than the speed of light.
   - **d.** give advice on how to survive if you fall into a black hole.

3. Why is it impossible for anyone to escape from a black hole?
   - **a.** Black holes are all over the universe.
   - **b.** Black holes get larger as they swallow more matter and people.
   - **c.** Escape would require a person to exceed the speed of light.
   - **d.** Doomsayers warn that escaping would destroy Earth.

4. Look back at the **boldface** vocabulary you underlined, and write sentences using these words: *phenomenon* (para. 3); *disintegrate* (4); *dissolution* (5); *distorted* (7).

READ CRITICALLY

1. The article refers to people who are worried that the LHC will create a black hole and destroy the world. Do you think the author agrees with their concerns? Why or why not?

2. In paragraph 4, Malone describes in detail how death would occur if a person were sucked into a black hole. What emotional effect does this have? Does the explanation seem serious, sad, detached, or humorous?

3. Malone is writing about the complex subjects of astronomy and physics. How do her style, tone, and word choice make the material relatively easy to understand?

4. What, if anything, seems hard to understand or confusing in "What Happens If You Fall into a Black Hole?" and why?

5. What overall effect do you think Malone wants this essay to have on her readers?

WRITE

WRITE A PARAGRAPH: It is highly improbable that anyone will ever die through the process that Malone describes. Write a paragraph about an unlikely or even impossible event that interests or frightens you, regardless of whether your fear is reasonable or not. It may even be your recollection of a childhood fear. You may title it "What Happens If _____ ?"

WRITE AN ESSAY: Write a process analysis essay about something scientific or technical that you know about but that others may not. The essay could describe a process you have read about or one that you have learned and use in your everyday life. For example, you might explain how to create a blog or a MySpace page to an older person you know. Make sure to explain the steps in detail and to present them in a logical order.

46

Classification

Each essay in this chapter uses classification to get its main point across to the reader. As you read these essays, consider how they achieve the four basics of good classification that are listed below and discussed in Chapter 14 of this book.

Four Basics of Good Classification

1 It makes sense of a group of people or items by organizing them into categories.

2 It has a purpose for sorting the people or items.

3 It categorizes using a single organizing principle.

4 It gives detailed examples or explanations of what fits into each category.

Vanessa Radzimski

Vanessa the Vegetarian

Vanessa Radzimski wrote the following essay as an assignment for a writing class at Florida Community College, Jacksonville, from which she graduated in 2009. As a meteorology major at Florida State University, Radzimski is interested in the technical side of writing, as she writes that "lab reports and scientific findings are an important component" of her future profession. Of her own writing, Radzimski says that she always aims "to have clear and clean language" in her essays. Throughout the process of revision, she seeks the advice of her professors and encourages other student writers to "be patient, challenge yourself, and always know that your professor is there for a reason!"

GUIDING QUESTION
What are the different types of vegetarians, and what does each type eat?

VOCABULARY DEVELOPMENT
The words in **boldface** are defined at the bottom of the page. Underline the words as you read them.

IDEA JOURNAL How would you title an essay about yourself ("[your name] the _____")?

PREDICT: What do you think the essay will discuss?

_____

_____

There are many different types of vegetarians. Some vegetarians eat dairy, egg, and fish products, while others do not. Some vegetarians will not buy any animal products. There is no specific **regimen**[1] that you have to follow when you are a vegetarian. It is a personal choice that many people make, be it for health or for **humanitarian**[2] purposes.

When I was twelve, I decided I wanted to stop eating red meat. I remember that day very clearly. My parents were watching the news, and a story about **mad cow disease**[3] in Canada was aired. Being the **paranoid**[4] pre-teen that I was, I decided that I was going to get mad cow disease if I kept eating red meat. My parents were telling me how the disease was found in Canada and how I wouldn't get it, but I didn't believe them. After I cut out red meat, I ate poultry products for a couple of years. I never thought I would cut out meat completely, but when I was fourteen, I woke up one morning and decided I would stop eating all types of meat. The decision was not popular in my family. My father, especially, was against the idea. Despite his arguments, I kept to my decision. The day after my Thanksgiving dinner in 2003, I officially became a vegetarian. Since then, I have learned a lot about my new lifestyle. There are specific definitions for different types of vegetarians.

IDENTIFY: Underline the definition of *ovovegetarian*.

Ovovegetarians consume egg products but no dairy products. Some people choose an ovovegetarian diet because they are **lactose**[5]-intolerant. Basically, their bodies are allergic to lactose, the key ingredient in dairy products. Ovovegetarians do not eat cheese, milk, butter, yogurt, or any food made with milk or cream. The humanitarian reason for being an ovovegetarian is that many cows are kept pregnant all the time so that they produce milk. Also, many cows are separated from their calves, which denies calves their mothers' milk.

IDENTIFY: Underline the definition of *lactovegetarian*.

Lactovegetarians consume dairy products but not egg products, the opposite of ovovegetarians. Lactovegetarians eat cheeses, yogurt, milk, and milk products. A health reason for choosing a lactovegetarian diet is to lower cholesterol. There are also spiritual and humanitarian reasons for avoiding eggs, including the mistreatment of hens. Many Eastern religions, such as Hinduism and Buddhism, practice lactovegetarianism.

IDENTIFY: Underline the definition of *vegan*.

The most extreme vegetarians are vegans, who do not eat meat, dairy, eggs, or any sort of animal by-product. Many won't consume even honey

---

1. regimen: a program of diet, exercise, or treatment that tries to preserve or restore good health **2. humanitarian:** helping to improve the welfare or happiness of people or animals **3. mad cow disease:** a brain disorder affecting cows **4. paranoid:** having extreme, irrational fear or distrust **5. lactose:** a sugar found in milk because the bees that produce honey are kept in captivity. Vegans do not wear fur coats or leather jackets, nor do they carry leather purses or wallets. Many vegans will not wear leather shoes. Nutritionally, being a vegan is a challenge because it is difficult to get all the vitamins and minerals a body needs. Vegans must carefully plan in order to get balanced daily nutrition.

I am an ovolactovegetarian, so I eat basically anything except meat. I do not eat beef, poultry, fish, or shellfish. Still, I have to be conscious of getting necessary vitamins and minerals in my diet, especially protein, iron, Vitamin B, and zinc. My favorite way to get the nutrients I need is through soy products. Many soy products taste like food I used to eat before I became a vegetarian. Morningstar Farms makes a wide variety of delicious vegetarian foods such as hot dogs, corn dogs, chicken and soy burgers, buffalo wings, and breakfast sausages. They provide lots of protein and have fewer calories and fat than the non-vegetarian versions.   6

People become vegetarians for many different reasons such as **ethical**[6] and health. I did it for both these reasons. I do feel that harming animals is cruel and that it should not be done just so that we humans can eat. There are so many other ways to eat and stay healthy other than eating a steak dinner. I also became a vegetarian so that I could keep my weight down. I am a ballerina and must stay thin. By being a vegetarian, I am able to control my weight and still enjoy delicious foods without worrying so much about the high calorie content in non-vegetarian diets.   7

    REFLECT: Do you know any vegetarians? What type are they, and why did they make the choice?

For me, being a vegetarian is not at all stressful. I cannot imagine eating meat again. I have avoided it for so many years now that it seems alien. I do not try to convince others to become vegetarians because it is a personal choice. I wake up every morning knowing that I am living a healthy lifestyle while also living with a good decision I made years ago.   8

SUMMARIZE AND RESPOND

In your reading journal or elsewhere, summarize the main point of "Vanessa the Vegetarian." Then, go back and check off the support for this idea. Next, write a brief summary of the essay. Finally, write a brief response to the reading. Did Radzimski's essay change your view of vegetarians or vegetarianism in any way?

CHECK YOUR COMPREHENSION

1. An alternate title for this essay could be
    a. "Eating Meat: Unethical, Unhealthy, and Disgusting."
    b. "Why I Am a Vegetarian."
    c. "When Parents Disapprove of Our Choices."
    d. "Mad Cow Disease Must Be Stopped."

6. ethical: dealing with morals, or questions of right and wrong in behavior

2. The main point of the essay is that
   a. eating meat is cruel to helpless animals.
   b. humanitarians should not eat meat.
   c. vegetarians often stop eating meat because of allergies.
   (d.) people become vegetarians for various reasons.

3. Why did the writer first decide to stop eating meat?
   a. She wanted to lose weight for her dance classes.
   b. She wanted to please her family and friends.
   (c.) She was afraid of getting mad cow disease.
   d. She developed an allergy to beef and poultry.

4. Does this essay include the Four Basics of Good Classification? Why or why not?

5. Look back at the **boldface** vocabulary you underlined, and write sentences using these words: *regimen*, *humanitarian* (para. 1); *paranoid* (2); *ethical* (7).

READ CRITICALLY

1. How does the writer organize her essay? How does she classify the varieties of vegetarianism?

2. In paragraph 2, Radzimski refers to herself as a "paranoid pre-teen." How have her reasons for her choice changed since then?

3. What is Radzimski's attitude toward people who eat meat? What is her attitude toward other kinds of vegetarians?

4. Being a vegetarian can cause some difficulties, according to the writer. What are they?

5. In paragraph 7, Radzimski writes that some people become vegetarians for "ethical" reasons. How are our personal eating habits related to moral questions of right and wrong?

WRITE

WRITE A PARAGRAPH: Write a paragraph that describes a category of food that you do not like to eat. Be specific about the foods in this category, as well as your reasons for not eating them.

WRITE AN ESSAY: Radzimski writes that she likes being a vegetarian because the diet leads to a "healthy lifestyle." Write an essay that categorizes the various strategies that people in general (or you, specifically) use to lead healthier lives. You may include more obvious classifications like exercise, but try to think of three or four other "regimens" as well.

Stephanie Ericsson

The Ways We Lie

Stephanie Ericsson was born in 1953 and raised in San Francisco. She has lived in a variety of places, including New York, Los Angeles, London, Mexico, the Spanish island of Ibiza, and Minnesota, where she currently resides. Ericsson's life took a major turn when her husband died suddenly, leaving her two months pregnant. She began a journal to help her cope with the grief and loss and later used her writing to help others with similar struggles. An excerpt from her journal appeared in the *Utne Reader*, and her writings were later published in a book entitled *Companion through the Darkness: Inner Dialogues on Grief* (1993). About her book, Ericsson writes, "It belongs to those who have had the blinders ripped from their eyes, who suddenly see the lies of our lives and the truths of existence for what they are."

In "The Ways We Lie," which also appeared in the *Utne Reader* and is taken from her follow-up work, *Companion into the Dawn: Inner Dialogues on Loving* (1994), Ericsson continues her search for truth by examining and classifying our daily lies.

GUIDING QUESTION
As you read this essay, pay attention to the examples Ericsson provides. What examples of lying can you think of from your own experience?

The bank called today, and I told them my deposit was in the mail, X1 even though I hadn't written a check yet. It'd been a rough day. The baby I'm pregnant with decided to do aerobics on my lungs for two hours, our three-year-old daughter painted the living-room couch with lipstick, the IRS put me on hold for an hour, and I was late to a business meeting because I was tired.

I told my client that the traffic had been bad. When my partner came X2 home, his **haggard**[1] face told me his day hadn't gone any better than mine, so when he asked, "How was your day?" I said, "Oh, fine," knowing that one X more straw might break his back. A friend called and wanted to take me to lunch. I said I was busy. Four lies in the course of a day, none of which I felt X the least bit guilty about.

We lie. We all do. We exaggerate, we **minimize,**[2] we avoid **confrontation,**[3] we spare people's feelings, we conveniently forget, we keep secrets, we justify lying to the big-guy institutions. Like most people, I **indulge**[4] in small falsehoods and still think of myself as an honest person. Sure I lie, but it doesn't hurt anything. Or does it?

I once tried going a whole week without telling a lie, and it was paralyzing. I discovered that telling the truth all the time is nearly impossible. It means living with some serious consequences: The bank charges me $60 in overdraft fees, my partner **keels**[5] over when I tell him about my **travails,**[6] my client fires me for telling her I didn't feel like being on time, and my

VOCABULARY DEVELOPMENT
The words in **boldface** are defined at the bottom of the page. Underline the words as you read them.

IDEA JOURNAL Think of another common human behavior. Break it into categories, and give examples for each category.

IDENTIFY: In the first two paragraphs, the author provides four examples of lies she has told. Put an X by these examples.

REFLECT: Do you agree that there "must be some merit to lying"? Why or why not?

_____

_____

---

1. haggard: drawn, worn out   **2. minimize:** to reduce   **3. confrontation:** an argumentative meeting   **4. indulge:** to become involved in   **5. keel:** to fall over
6. travails: painful efforts; tribulations

friend takes it personally when I say I'm not hungry. There must be some merit to lying.

But if I justify lying, what makes me any different from slick politicians or the corporate robbers who raided the S&L industry? Saying it's OK to lie one way and not another is **hedging**.[7] I cannot seem to escape the voice deep inside me that tells me: When someone lies, someone loses.   5

What far-reaching consequences will I, or others, pay as a result of my lie? Will someone's trust be destroyed? Will someone else pay *my* **penance**[8] because I ducked out? We must consider the *meaning of our actions*. Deception, lies, capital crimes, and **misdemeanors**[9] all carry meanings. *Webster's* definition of *lie* is specific: 6

1.   a false statement or action especially made with the intent to deceive;

2.   anything that gives or is meant to give a false impression.

A definition like this implies that there are many, many ways to tell a lie. Here are just a few.   7

The White Lie

The white lie assumes that the truth will cause more damage than a simple, harmless untruth. Telling a friend he looks great when he looks like hell can be based on a decision that the friend needs a compliment more than a **frank**[10] opinion. But, in effect, it is the liar deciding what is best for the lied to. Ultimately, it is a vote of no confidence. It is an act of subtle **arrogance**[11] for anyone to decide what is best for someone else.   8

Yet not all circumstances are quite so cut and dried. Take, for instance, the sergeant in Vietnam who knew one of his men was killed in action but listed him as missing so that the man's family would receive indefinite compensation instead of the lump-sum **pittance**[12] the military gives widows and children. His intent was honorable. Yet for twenty years this family kept their hopes alive, unable to move on to a new life.   9

Facades

We all put up **facades**[13] to one degree or another. When I put on a suit to go to see a client, I feel as though I am putting on another face, obeying the expectation that serious businesspeople wear suits rather than sweatpants. But I'm a writer. Normally, I get up, get the kid off to school, and sit at my computer in my pajamas until four in the afternoon. When I answer the phone, the caller thinks I'm wearing a suit (although the UPS man knows better).   10

But facades can be destructive because they are used to seduce others into an illusion. For instance, I recently realized that a former friend was a liar. He presented himself with all the right looks and the right words and offered lots of new consciousness theories, fabulous books to read, and fascinating insights. Then I did some business with him, and the time came   11

TEACHING TIP Have small groups diagram the essay. Discuss whether all the categories in the essay are really lies (for example, is stereotyping really a lie?). What other categories should the author have included? Have students record the ways they lie and share their responses at the next class meeting (anonymously, if necessary). Classify the responses according to category.

IDENTIFY: Underline the main point of this paragraph. What example does Ericsson use to support it?

_____

_____

---

7. hedging: avoiding the question   **8. penance:** a penalty to make up for an action
9. misdemeanors: minor violations of rules   **10. frank:** honest; direct   **11. arrogance:** belief in one's superiority   **12. pittance:** a small amount   **13. facades:** masks

for him to pay me. He turned out to be all talk and no walk. I heard a **plethora**[14] of reasonable excuses, including in-depth descriptions of the big break around the corner. In six months of work, I saw less than a hundred bucks. When I confronted him, he raised both eyebrows and tried to convince me that I'd heard him wrong, that he'd made no commitment to me. A simple investigation into his past revealed a crowded graveyard of disenchanted former friends.

Ignoring the Plain Facts

In the sixties, the Catholic Church in Massachusetts began hearing complaints that Father James Porter was sexually molesting children. Rather than relieving him of his duties, the **ecclesiastical**[15] authorities simply moved him from one parish to another between 1960 and 1967, actually providing him with a fresh supply of unsuspecting families and innocent children to abuse. After treatment in 1967 for **pedophilia**,[16] he went back to work, this time in Minnesota. The new **diocese**[17] was aware of Father Porter's obsession with children, but they needed priests and recklessly believed treatment had cured him. More children were abused until he was relieved of his duties a year later. By his own admission, Porter may have abused as many as a hundred children.

12 **SUMMARIZE:** In your own words, summarize the example in this paragraph in one or two sentences.

_____

_____

Ignoring the facts may not in and of itself be a form of lying, but consider the **context**[18] of this situation. If a lie is *a false action done with the intent to deceive*, then the Catholic Church's conscious covering for Porter created irreparable consequences. The church became a **coperpetrator**[19] with Porter.

13

Stereotypes and Clichés

Stereotype and cliché serve a purpose as a form of shorthand. Our need for vast amounts of information in **nanoseconds**[20] has made the stereotype vital to modern communication. Unfortunately, it often shuts down original thinking, giving those hungry for truth a candy bar of misinformation instead of a balanced meal. The stereotype explains a situation with just enough truth to seem unquestionable.

14

All the *isms* — racism, sexism, ageism, et al. — are founded on and fueled by the stereotype and the cliché, which are lies of exaggeration, omission, and ignorance. They are always dangerous. They take a single tree and make it a landscape. They destroy curiosity. They close minds and separate people. The single mother on welfare is assumed to be cheating. Any black male could tell you how much of his identity is **obliterated**[21] daily by stereotypes. Fat people, ugly people, beautiful people, old people, large-breasted women, short men, the mentally ill, and the homeless all could tell you how much more they are like us than we want to think. I once admitted to a group of people that I had a mouth like a truck driver. Much to my surprise, a man stood up and said, "I'm a truck driver, and I never cuss." Needless to say, I was humbled.

15

14. **plethora:** excess   15. **ecclesiastical:** relating to a church   16. **pedophilia:** sexual abuse of children   17. **diocese:** a district or churches under the guidance of a bishop   18. **context:** a surrounding situation   19. **coperpetrator:** the helper of a person who commits an action   20. **nanoseconds:** billionths of a second
21. **obliterated:** wiped out

PREDICT: Pause just as you start the "Out-and-Out Lies" section. How do you think Ericsson might define such lies?

_____

_____

REFLECT: Think back on your answer to the question on page 667 about whether lying ever has any merit. Have your views on this issue changed? Why or why not?

_____

_____

Out-and-Out Lies

Of all the ways to lie, I like this one the best, probably because I get tired of 16 trying to figure out the real meanings behind things. At least I can trust the bald-faced lie. I once asked my five-year-old nephew, "Who broke the fence?" (I had seen him do it.) He answered, "The murderers." Who could argue?

At least when this sort of lie is told it can be easily confronted. As the 17 person who is lied to, I know where I stand. The bald-faced lie doesn't toy with my perceptions—it argues with them. It doesn't try to refashion reality; it tries to **refute**[22] it. *Read my lips* . . . No **sleight**[23] of hand. No guessing. If this were the only form of lying, there would be no such thing as floating anxiety or the adult-children of alcoholics movement.

These are only a few of the ways we lie. Or are lied to. As I said earlier, 18 it's not easy to entirely eliminate lies from our lives. No matter how **pious**[24] we may try to be, we will still **embellish**,[25] hedge, and omit to lubricate the daily machinery of living. But there is a world of difference between telling functional lies and living a lie. Martin Buber once said, "The lie is the spirit committing treason against itself." Our acceptance of lies becomes a cultural cancer that eventually **shrouds**[26] and reorders reality until moral garbage becomes as invisible to us as water is to a fish.

How much do we tolerate before we become sick and tired of being 19 sick and tired? When will we stand up and declare our *right* to trust? When do we stop accepting that the real truth is in the fine print? Whose lips do we read this year when we vote for president? When will we stop being so **reticent**[27] about making judgments? When do we stop turning over our personal power and responsibility to liars?

Maybe if I don't tell the bank the check's in the mail I'll be less tolerant 20 of the lies told to me every day. A country song I once heard said it all for me: "You've got to stand for something or you'll fall for anything."

• •

SUMMARIZE AND RESPOND

In your reading journal or elsewhere, summarize the main point of "The Ways We Lie." Then, go back and check off the support for this idea. Next, write a brief summary of the essay. Finally, write a brief response to the reading. What did it make you think about or feel? Do you agree with Ericsson's claim that we all tell lies every day? Provide examples from your own experience that support this idea.

• •

CHECK YOUR COMPREHENSION

1.   An alternate title for this essay could be

    a.   "Lying Never Hurt Anyone."

    b.   "The Check's in the Mail: The Greatest Lie of All."

---

22. refute: to deny   **23. sleight:** a skillful trick   **24. pious:** religious
25. embellish: to decorate   **26. shroud:** to cover, conceal   **27. reticent:** reserved; silent; reluctant

    c. "Justification for Lying."

    d. "Lies in Our Lives."

2. The main point of this essay is that

    a. small lies are OK because everyone lies.

    b. we should reevaluate the role that lies play in our lives.

    c. lies told by someone you trust are the worst.

    d. to trust and be trusted, we must refuse to lie.

3. What distinction does Ericsson make between telling a functional lie and living a lie?

    a. Telling a functional lie makes someone feel bad, and living a lie cheats big institutions.

    b. Telling a functional lie is relatively harmless, but living a lie can have serious consequences.

    c. Telling a functional lie has no merit, and living a lie is a good idea.

    d. Telling a functional lie is honest, and living a lie is dishonest.

4. Look back at the **boldface** vocabulary you underlined, and write sentences using these words: *confrontation* (para. 3); *penance* (6); *obliterate* (15); *embellish* (18); *reticent* (19).

· ·

READ CRITICALLY

1. Describe Ericsson's tone in this essay. For example, what is her tone in paragraph 1 when she tells us that "the baby I'm pregnant with decided to do aerobics on my lungs for two hours"?

2. How does Ericsson organize her essay? How does she classify the ways we tell lies?

3. What images does Ericsson associate with telling lies? Select one that you like, and explain why.

4. What is Ericsson's attitude toward lying? What examples in the essay support your answer?

5. In paragraph 16, Ericsson writes, "At least I can trust the bald-faced lie." What do you think she means by trusting a lie?

· ·

WRITE

WRITE A PARAGRAPH: Write a paragraph that describes another category of lies. Be sure to provide examples for your readers.

WRITE AN ESSAY: Write an essay that continues Ericsson's classification of the ways we lie. Provide detailed examples from your experiences—or the experiences of people you know—for at least two of the categories she provides.

Develop two new categories of your own. Feel free to include the ideas you wrote about in your reading journal for Summarize and Respond.

• •

Carolyn Foster Segal

The Dog Ate My Disk, and Other Tales of Woe

Carolyn Foster Segal (b. 1950) is an associate professor of English at Cedar Crest College in Pennsylvania, where she teaches creative writing, American literature, and film; she also serves as an adviser for the writing minor. In addition to teaching, Segal has published fiction, poetry, and popular and critical essays. She has recently written a series of eleven essays on academic life for the *Chronicle of Higher Education*.

The following essay classifies students' excuses for late course work. Segal notes, "I am not talking about all students or all excuses here. There are certainly legitimate—and sometimes devastating—reasons for missing a deadline; on the other hand, it's quite possible that a few readers might feel guilty." Her essay clearly touched a nerve with other instructors, hundreds of whom sent their own stories of student excuses to Segal after the piece appeared.

GUIDING QUESTION
What creative categories of student excuses does Segal present? Are the examples within each category concrete and specific?

IDEA JOURNAL Can you recall a common excuse that you may have used in school or college in the past or have heard others use?

VOCABULARY DEVELOPMENT The words in **boldface** are defined at the bottom of the page. Underline the words as you read them.

PREDICT: Predict the type of family excuses Segal will give in this paragraph.

——————————————

——————————————

Taped to the door of my office is a cartoon that features a cat explaining to his **feline**[1] teacher, "The dog ate my homework." It is intended as a gently humorous reminder to my students that I will not accept excuses for late work, and it, like the lengthy warning on my syllabus, has had absolutely no effect. With a show of energy and creativity that would be admirable if applied to the (missing) assignments in question, my students persist, week after week, semester after semester, year after year, in offering excuses about why their work is not ready. Those reasons fall into several broad categories: the family, the best friend, the evils of dorm life, the evils of technology, and the totally bizarre.

The Family. The death of the grandfather/grandmother is, of course, the grandmother of all excuses. What heartless teacher would dare to question a student's grief or **veracity**[2]? What heartless student would lie, wishing death on a revered family member, just to avoid a deadline? Creative students may win extra extensions (and days off) with a little careful planning and fuller plot development, as in the sequence of "My grandfather/grandmother is sick"; "Now my grandfather/grandmother is in the hospital"; and finally, "We could all see it coming—my grandfather/grandmother is dead."

1

2

1. feline: catlike   **2. veracity:** truthfulness

Another favorite excuse is the "family emergency," which (always) goes like this: "There was an emergency at home, and I had to help my family." It's a lovely **sentiment**,[3] one that **conjures**[4] up images of **Louisa May Alcott's**[5] little women rushing off with baskets of food and copies of *Pilgrim's Progress*, but I do not understand why anyone would turn to my most irresponsible students in times of trouble.

The Best Friend. This heartwarming concern for others extends beyond the family to friends, as in, "My best friend was up all night and I had to (a) stay up with her in the dorm, (b) drive her to the hospital, or (c) drive to her college because (1) her boyfriend broke up with her, (2) she was throwing up blood [no one catches a cold anymore; everyone throws up blood], or (3) her grandfather/grandmother died."

At one private university where I worked as an **adjunct**,[6] I heard an interesting spin that incorporated the **motifs**[7] of both best friend and dead relative: "My best friend's mother killed herself." One has to admire the cleverness here. A mysterious woman in the prime of her life has allegedly committed suicide, and no professor can prove otherwise! And I admit I was moved, until finally I had to point out to my students that it was amazing how the simple act of my assigning a topic for a paper seemed to drive large numbers of otherwise happy and healthy middle-aged women to their deaths. I was careful to make that point during an off week, during which no deaths were reported.

The Evils of Dorm Life. These stories are usually fairly predictable; almost always feature the evil roommate or hallmate, with my student in the role of the innocent victim; and can be summed up as follows: <u>My roommate, who is a horrible person, likes to party, and I, who am a good person, cannot concentrate on my work when he or she is partying.</u> Variations include stories about the two people next door who were running around and crying loudly last night because (a) one of them had boyfriend/girlfriend problems; (b) one of them was throwing up blood; or (c) someone, somewhere, died. A friend of mine in graduate school had a student who claimed that his roommate attacked him with a hammer. That, in fact, was a true story: it came out in court when the bad roommate was tried for killing his grandfather.

The Evils of Technology. The computer age has revolutionized the student story, inspiring almost as many excuses as it has Internet businesses. Here are just a few electronically enhanced explanations:

- The computer wouldn't let me save my work.
- The printer wouldn't print.
- The printer wouldn't print this disk.
- The printer wouldn't give me time to proofread.
- The printer made a black line run through all my words, and I know you can't read this, but do you still want it, or wait, here take my disk. File name? I don't know what you mean.

3. sentiment: expression of feeling   **4. conjure:** to summon, create   **5. Louisa May Alcott:** a nineteenth-century American author best known for the novel *Little Women*   **6. adjunct:** part-time instructor   **7. motifs:** patterns

IDENTIFY: Underline the sentence in which Segal summarizes stories about "the evils of dorm life."

TEACHING TIP In a class discussion, ask students to list other excuses offered for missing or delayed classwork. Students may not feel comfortable discussing excuses they themselves have used, so ask them to list ones they have heard of. Then discuss how these various excuses might be classified.

- I swear I attached it.

- It's my roommate's computer, and she usually helps me, but she had to go to the hospital because she was throwing up blood.

- I did write to the newsgroup, but all my messages came back to me.

- I just found out that all my other newsgroup messages came up under a diferent name. I just want you to know that its really me who wrote all those messages, you can tel which ones our mine because I didn't use the spelcheck! But it was yours truley :) Anyway, just in case you missed those messages or dont belief its my writing, I'll re-peat what I sad: I thought the last movie we watched in clas was borring.

REFLECT: How "bizarre" is the excuse presented in this paragraph? Is it too bizarre to be believable?

The Totally Bizarre. I call the first story "The Pennsylvania Chain 8 Saw Episode." A commuter student called to explain why she had missed my morning class. She had gotten up early so that she would be wide awake for class. Having a bit of extra time, she walked outside to see her neighbor, who was cutting some wood. She called out to him, and he waved back to her with the saw. Wouldn't you know it, the safety catch wasn't on or was broken, and the blade flew right out of the saw and across his lawn and over her fence and across her yard and severed a tendon in her right hand. So she was calling me from the hospital, where she was waiting for surgery. Luckily, she reassured me, she had remembered to bring her paper and a stamped envelope (in a plastic bag, to avoid bloodstains) along with her in the ambu-lance, and a nurse was mailing everything to me even as we spoke.

That wasn't her first absence. In fact, this student had missed most of 9 the class meetings, and I had already recommended that she withdraw from the course. Now I suggested again that it might be best if she dropped the class. I didn't harp on the absences (what if even some of the story were true?). I did mention that she would need time to recuperate and that mak-ing up so much missed work might be difficult. "Oh, no," she said, "I can't drop this course. I had been planning to go on to medical school and be-come a surgeon, but since I won't be able to operate because of my accident, I'll have to major in English, and this course is more important than ever to me." She did come to the next class, wearing—as evidence of her recent trauma—a **bedraggled**[8] Ace bandage on her left hand.

REFLECT: How do you imag-ine Segal reacted when she read this final excuse?

You may be thinking that nothing could top that excuse, but in fact I 10 have one more story, provided by the same student, who sent me a letter to explain why her final assignment would be late. While recuperating from her surgery, she had begun corresponding on the Internet with a man who lived in Germany. After a one-week, whirlwind Web romance, they had agreed to meet in Rome, to **rendezvous**[9] (her phrase) at the **papal**[10] Easter Mass. Regrettably, the time of her flight made it impossible for her to attend class, but she trusted that I—just this once—would accept late work if the pope wrote a note.

8. bedraggled: messy, untidy   **9. rendezvous:** to meet   **10. papal:** relating to the pope of the Roman Catholic Church

SUMMARIZE AND RESPOND

In your reading journal or elsewhere, summarize the main point of "The Dog Ate My Disk, and Other Tales of Woe." Then, go back and check off the support for this idea. Next, write a brief summary of the essay. Finally, write a brief response to the reading. What did it make you think about or feel? Do you agree with Segal's sense that students make up stories about why they do not have their homework? Provide examples from your own experience to support your position.

CHECK YOUR COMPREHENSION

1. An alternate title for this essay could be
    a. "Computer Cop-Outs."
    b. "Homework Hassles."
    c. "How to Lie Effectively."
    (d.) "Excuses: The Old, the New, and the Creative."

2. The main point of this essay is that
    (a.) students have never-ending and often bizarre excuses for not submitting required work.
    b. teachers often downgrade late assignments.
    c. the more bizarre excuse a student gives, the less likely that the teacher can prove the student is lying.
    d. teachers should issue strong warnings and penalties to prevent students from handing in assignments late.

3. Which excuse can students expand upon to get further deadline extensions?
    a. Best friend
    b. Technology
    c. Dorm life
    (d.) Family

4. Look back at the **boldface** vocabulary you underlined, and write sentences using these words: *veracity* (para. 2); *sentiment* (3); *motif* (5); *bedraggled* (9); *rendezvous* (10).

TIP For tools to build your vocabulary, visit the *Real Writing Student Center* at **bedfordstmartins.com/ realwriting.**

READ CRITICALLY

1. How would you describe the tone of this essay?

2. Do Segal's categories seem logical and appropriate for the examples she provides?

3. Which category seems the most developed? The least developed?

4. What gives Segal authority to write about this subject?

5. What do you suppose Segal means by the phrase "the grandmother of all excuses" in paragraph 2?

. . . .

WRITE

TIP For a sample classification paragraph, see page 188.

WRITE A PARAGRAPH: Think of another category that Segal could have included in this essay. Using that category, create a topic sentence, and write a paragraph that provides concrete examples of student excuses.

WRITE AN ESSAY: Consider one of your roles in life—as an employee, a child, a parent, a boyfriend, a girlfriend, and so on. Then, brainstorm and categorize excuses for not doing something that you are supposed to do as part of that role—such as coming to work or doing assigned chores. Next, as Segal does, write an essay in which you present and develop each category with examples.

. . . .

47

Definition

Each essay in this chapter uses definition to get its main point across to the reader. As you read these essays, consider how they achieve the four basics of good definition that are listed below and discussed in Chapter 15 of this book.

TIP For tools to build your vocabulary, visit the *Real Writing Student Center* at **bedfordstmartins.com/ realwriting**.

■■
■■ Four Basics of Good Definition

1 It tells readers what is being defined.

2 It presents a clear basic definition.

3 It uses examples to show what the writer means.

4 It gives details about the examples that readers will understand.

John Around Him

Free Money

John Around Him grew up on a reservation in South Dakota. He wrote the following essay for a writing class he took when he was a student at Bunker Hill Community College in Boston. Before enrolling at BHCC, John had served as a Marine in Iraq, so he qualified for financial aid. In 2008, he transferred from BHCC to Dartmouth College, from which he expects to graduate in 2012. As a writer, Around Him is interested in education and Native American issues, and he plans to pursue a career in education, which he knows will require a lot of writing. Before beginning an essay, he says that he often looks to his friends as a sounding board for his ideas and potential topics be-cause "they give a different window in which to see my ideas." When offering advice to fellow student writers, Around Him writes, "Through writing you may discover who you are, so have fun while doing it."

GUIDING QUESTION
How does a student get financial aid for college?

Free money: The words almost take your breath away. For the average 1 college student, the idea is especially appealing. The weight of college tuition, in combination with the cost of food, rent, and other living expenses, makes the climb toward educational success appear almost impossible. However, assistance in the form of financial aid is available to help lighten the load.

Financial aid is money to help pay for college tuition or other expenses 2 while going to college. Financial aid comes in an **array**[1] of programs, from federal and state funding to scholarships. Federal financial aid is the source most students use. It is available in the form of grants, student loans, and the Federal Work-Study Program. A grant really is free money, while a student loan has to be repaid when a student either completes college or stops going. The Federal Work-Study Program allows students to earn money while attending college. In 2008, the budget for Federal Pell Grants was about $15 billion. In that same year, the student loan budget was $72.8 billion, and the work-study program's budget was $980 million.

To apply for federal financial aid, students must fill out the Free Ap- 3 plication for Federal Student Aid (FAFSA), available at your college's finan-cial aid office or online (Google FAFSA). In order to receive aid, a student must meet the following **criteria**:[2] be a U.S. citizen or eligible non-citizen of the United States with a valid social security number; have a high school diploma or have passed the General Education Development (GED) test; and be enrolled in a degree program, taking a minimum of six credits. Men between the ages of eighteen and twenty-six must have registered in the **selective service**.[3]

Using the information provided in the FAFSA, the federal government 4 calculates each applicant's Expected Family Contribution (EFC). The EFC is calculated with a formula based on the student's income or, if the student is a **dependent**,[4] the family's income and **assets**.[5] For students who are de-pendents but do not receive financial support from their parents, the EFC can be a problem because counting family income might make the student ineligible. However, that is the formula. Other **factors**[6] include the number of family members in the household and number of family members in college. Last year, I applied for financial aid but did not qualify because, ac-cording to the financial aid office at my college, I made too much money. Nevertheless, I will continue to apply for financial aid.

1. array: a large range of a particular kind of thing   **2. criteria:** standards by which something is judged or decided   **3. selective service:** a system that requires all men between the ages of eighteen and twenty-six to register so that the federal government has information available about potential soldiers in case of war   **4. dependent:** a person who relies on someone for money or other support   **5. assets:** total financial resources, such as cash and property   **6. factors:** elements that contribute to a process, a result, or an accomplishment

Students should always apply for financial aid, but many do not. Much of the money available is not used because students do not know about it or fill out the proper forms. Looking around and going to your college's financial aid office is worth the time required because there really is free money. For example, there are scholarships for health-care programs, for business programs, for graduate programs, to name just a few. My goal is to finish my two-year degree and transfer to a four-year college. In order to do this, I need to have a plan and prepare myself by researching schools to find out which ones are suitable for me. Then, I can find out what courses I need to take to graduate and to transfer with as many credits as possible. I won't do this alone: I will take advantage of the various services available at my college, including meeting with my adviser. I will apply to many sources of financial aid, because getting my degree will be very expensive.

Clearly, the price tag for higher education is very high, and most students cannot afford it without assistance. I know that the money is available, and some of it is free. However, as the saying goes, "Nothing in life is free," and that means that getting what I need requires effort. It is my responsibility to work hard to find that money, along with working hard to get good grades.

5 **REFLECT:** Have you visited your college's financial aid office?

6 **REFLECT:** What services does your college offer?

SUMMARIZE AND RESPOND

In your reading journal or elsewhere, summarize the main point of "Free Money." Then, go back and check off the support for this idea. Next, write a brief summary of the essay. Finally, write a brief response to the reading. Do you think federal and state governments do enough to help college students financially?

CHECK YOUR COMPREHENSION

1. An alternate title for this essay could be
  a. "Nothing in Life Is Free."
  b. "Wealthy Students Should Not Receive Financial Aid."
  c. "Students Need to Learn to Save Money."
  d. "Students Should Take Advantage of Financial Aid."

2. The main point of this essay is that
  a. many financial resources are available to students.
  b. the federal government should increase aid to college students.
  c. the selective service is a requirement for financial aid.
  d. students should be less financially dependent on their families.

3. In the past, the writer was denied financial aid for college because
  a. he had not registered for selective service.
  b. he was not a U.S. citizen.
  c. he made too much money.
  d. he missed the deadline for applying.

4. Does this essay include the Four Basics of Good Definition? Why or why not?

5. Look back at the **boldface** vocabulary you underlined, and write sentences using these words: *array* (para. 2); *criteria* (3); *dependent, assets, factors* (4).

READ CRITICALLY

1. What do you think Around Him wants his readers to do with the information in this essay?

2. In paragraph 1, the writer says that college tuition and expenses can make getting an education "appear almost impossible." Do you agree, and do you think higher education is too expensive?

3. Around Him lists and explains the requirements students must meet in order to receive federal or state financial aid. Do these requirements seem reasonable? Why or why not?

4. Do you think it is fair that some students are ineligible for financial aid because their parents have too much money?

5. Although this essay encourages students to seek financial support, how does it also suggest that they take responsibility for their education?

WRITE

WRITE A PARAGRAPH: Around Him refers to the saying "Nothing in life is free." Write a paragraph that either supports this saying or argues against it. You may draw on a personal experience to make your point.

WRITE AN ESSAY: Around Him argues that students "should always apply for financial aid." Who do you think should receive "free money" to go to college? In an essay, define the kinds of students who should receive the most financial assistance for college expenses.

Michael Thompson
Passage into Manhood

Michael Thompson is a consultant, child psychologist, and author. His 1999 book *Raising Cain: Protecting the Emotional Life of Boys* (1999), cowritten with Dan Kindlon, was the inspiration for a PBS documentary of the same name. Both the book and the documentary, which was hosted by Thompson, explore boys' emotional development and the negative consequences of common misunderstandings about them. Thompson's other books include *Speaking of Boys: Answers to the Most-Asked Questions about*

Raising Sons (2000), *Mom, They're Teasing Me: Helping Your Child Solve Social Problems* (2002), *The Pressured Child: Helping Your Child Achieve Success in School and in Life* (with Teresa Barker, 2004), and *It's a Boy! Your Son's Development from Birth to Age 18* (2008).

In "Passage into Manhood," which appeared in the *Boston Globe* in 2005, Thompson gets one young man's definition of manhood, raising questions about what our society does—and, more important, does not do—to prepare boys to become men.

GUIDING QUESTION

What is necessary for the passage into manhood, according to the author?

1   The boy sitting next to me on the plane from Toronto to North Bay was seventeen years old, a rising high school senior with a slight beard. He had the **misfortune**[1] to sit next to a child psychologist, a so-called expert on boys, who would pester him with questions for the entire trip about how he was spending his summer, and why. "This is kind of like a final exam," he observed, trying to get me to **relent**,[2] but I wouldn't let go.

2   After he had **gamely**[3] answered a number of my questions about the summer camp to which he was headed, I sprang the big one on him, the question I have asked many boys his age. "Do you consider yourself to be a man?"

3   "Yes," he replied immediately. Then he caught himself, hesitating momentarily before declaring with **conviction**:[4] "Well, no. But I will be in August!"

4   What could a seventeen-year-old boy do between the last week of June and August that he could **anticipate**[5] would make him a man? American culture doesn't have any universal **ritual**[6] that sees a boy through that psychologically difficult passage from boyhood to manhood. Many boys, actually, almost every boy, struggles with what it means to become a man. Boys (or young men, if you prefer) of seventeen, nineteen, and into their early twenties wrestle with the riddle: What test do I have to pass to become a man, and who will be able to recognize that I have reached that point? My young companion thought he had found an answer.

5   It turned out that he was going to **embark**[7] the next morning on a fifty-day canoeing trip that would take him and nine companions through lakes, rivers, rapids, mud, and **ferocious**[8] mosquitoes, all the way up to Hudson's Bay, a distance of six hundred miles. He and his friends had been preparing for this by developing wilderness skills for the last four years at their camp. They would carry all of their own food, they would take risks, and they would suffer. Toward the end of their journey they would see the **Northern lights**[9] and would visit an **Inuit**[10] settlement. They might see moose and wolves, but, he told me, they were not going to be tourists. "This isn't about seeing wild animals," he asserted.

6   What was his definition of manhood? "It's taking responsibility," he said. "At the end of the day, it's taking responsibility and taking things you've learned from others and creating your own self."

VOCABULARY DEVELOPMENT The words in **boldface** are defined at the bottom of the page. Underline the words as you read them.

IDEA JOURNAL Write about a personal experience that you felt marked a passage from youth to adulthood. What happened, and how did the experience change you?

REFLECT: In paragraph 3, why do you suppose the boy answered "yes" and then changed his mind?

_____

_____

IDENTIFY: Paragraph 5 provides several examples. Check off the experiences that the boy expects to have.

IDENTIFY: In paragraphs 6 and 7, underline the boy's definitions of manhood.

1. **misfortune:** bad luck   2. **relent:** to give up; to stop   3. **gamely:** enthusiastically
4. **conviction:** a strong belief or feeling   5. **anticipate:** to expect   6. **ritual:** a ceremony or rite of passage   7. **embark:** to go on board; to make a start   8. **ferocious:** fierce; menacing   9. **Northern lights:** a colorful display of lights in the sky, caused by solar winds   10. **Inuit:** native people of North America

"It's about finishing a **grueling portage**,"[11] he said. "It's about doing   7
work and getting a result."

Didn't he get that from school and varsity athletics? No. Though he did   8
well in school and had bright college prospects, school didn't address his
hunger to be a man, not even playing sports. "After sports you go home,
take a shower, and watch TV." When he was canoe tripping, he felt as if he
made a **sustained**[12] effort that connected him to all the men who had ca-
noed before him at that camp for more than one hundred years.

Could he find the experience he sought among his friends back home?   9
What were they doing this summer? "Hanging out. They're playing video
games," he said. They didn't get it. "It's frustrating. You try to explain to
them how great it is. You tell them about paddling all day, and cooking your
own food, about the mosquitoes, and carrying a wood canoe, and they say,
'What, are you crazy?'"

This young about-to-be man described his father as a "good guy," his   10
mother as a hardworking professional, and his step-father as financially successful, but none of them seemed to hold the key to helping him become a
man. American culture has no universal ritual for helping boys move from
boyhood to manhood. Jewish boys have their **bar mitzvahs**,[13] Mormon
boys have their year of missionary service, other boys sign up for the military. Yet every boy **yearns**[14] to be a man, and traditional societies always
took boys away from their parents to pass an initiation rite. We no longer
have such rituals, but boys still wonder: What is the test, where do I find it,
how do I pass it, and who will recognize that moment when I pass from
boyhood to manhood? We fail to provide a meaningful, challenging path that
speaks to the souls of a majority of boys.

The key to his manhood lay with the counselors who accompany him   11
on the journey and with his companions whose lives he would protect and
who would, in turn, look out for him. Past the rain, the bugs, the smelling
bad, he would discover his manhood in community and in the kind of challenge that only nature offers up.

Our plane journey over, I wished him luck. And then I couldn't get our   12
conversation out of my mind. While a demanding canoe trip is not for every
boy, I'm certain that every boy is searching for a test. You can find the test
by taking on anything that requires commitment and courage. However,
there is something that happens out-of-doors that strips you down to the
essentials: safety, companionship, a shared sense of mission. You set aside
the busyness and crap of daily life, and then you can think about what it actually means to be a man.

• •

SUMMARIZE AND RESPOND

In your reading journal or elsewhere, summarize the main point of "Passage into
Manhood." Then, go back and check off support for this idea. Next, write a brief

SUMMARIZE: In a sentence or
two (in your own words), sum
up the point that the author
makes in paragraph 10.

TEACHING TIP Write "man" on
one side of the board and
"woman" on the other. Then,
ask students to call out the
names of people (famous or
otherwise) that they consider to
be ideal men and women, and
write the names down. Students
should give at least one reason
for their choices; write the reasons down as well. Next,
discuss the similarities and differences among the people and
reasons listed. Did students
give different reasons for the
different genders? If so, what
do the differences suggest
about what society values in
men versus women?

11. **grueling portage:** a difficult journey that requires the carrying of supplies
12. **sustained:** continuous; ongoing   13. **bar mitzvahs:** ceremonies marking Jewish
boys' thirteenth birthdays and the beginning of their religious responsibilities
14. **yearn:** to want, desire

summary of the essay. Finally, write a brief response to the reading. Do you agree with the author about what is needed for boys to make the passage into manhood?

● ●

CHECK YOUR COMPREHENSION

1. An alternate title for this essay could be
   a. "American Boys Overwhelmed by Adult Responsibilities."
   b. "One Teen's Story of His Passage into Manhood."
   c. "The Path to Manhood: A Difficult Journey for Most Boys."
   d. "American Boys Need a Meaningful Path to Manhood."

2. The main point of this essay is that
   a. undergoing a wilderness challenge is the only real way to become a man.
   b. young men should be able to define for themselves what it means to be a man, even if most people would disagree.
   c. going through a significant ritual or test makes boys feel like men, but American culture fails to provide such paths.
   d. American boys should be given a bar mitzvah or be required to perform missionary service.

3. What challenge was the boy Thompson spoke with about to take on?
   a. A boating competition
   b. A fifty-day canoeing trip
   c. A hiking and biking tour
   d. A Canadian triathalon

4. Look back at the **boldface** vocabulary you underlined, and write sentences using the following words: *relent* (para. 1); *conviction* (3); *anticipate* (4); *sustained* (8); *yearn* (10).

● ●

READ CRITICALLY

1. In paragraph 2, the author asks the boy what he considers to be a "big" question: Does the boy consider himself to be a man? Why does the author consider this to be a big question, and do you agree? Why or why not?

2. How do you define manhood or womanhood? How is your definition similar to or different from that provided by the boy Thompson speaks to?

3. In paragraph 10, Thompson argues, "We fail to provide a meaningful, challenging path [to adulthood] that speaks to the souls of a majority of boys." Do you agree? Why or why not? What other possible paths to manhood are not mentioned by Thompson?

4. Why, according to Thompson, are outdoor challenges especially useful for boys making the passage toward manhood? Do you share his view?

5.   Why do you suppose Thompson is interested in the opinions of one young person he meets on a plane? How do the quotations from the boy contribute to the point of Thompson's essay?

· ·

WRITE

TIP For a sample definition paragraph, see page 205.

WRITE A PARAGRAPH: Write a paragraph that gives at least two pieces of advice to a boy who is about to become a man or to a girl who is about to become a woman. The person could be a brother or sister, a son or daughter, or a friend. Or you could imagine a boy or girl to address the advice to. Be sure to explain why each piece of advice is important, and give examples to show what you mean.

WRITE AN ESSAY: Write an essay that defines what it is to be a man or a woman. Use examples from your personal experience to help define the concept. If you answered question 2 under Read Critically, you might want to use some of the insights from that question to develop your essay. Explain why you think Thompson, or the boy he interviewed, might agree or disagree with your definition.

· ·

Janice E. Castro with Dan Cook and Cristina Garcia
Spanglish

Janice E. Castro is an assistant professor in the Medill New Media Program at Northwestern University. She worked as a reporter for *Time* for more than twenty years and started the magazine's health policy beat. After the publication of her book *The American Way of Health: How Medicine Is Changing, and What It Means to You* (1994), she became the managing editor of *Time*'s online division.
        Castro wrote "Spanglish" while at *Time* with the help of Dan Cook and Cristina Garcia. In the essay, she defines the language created when Spanish and English speakers come together in our blended culture.

GUIDING QUESTION
What are some of the reasons the authors provide for the rise of the use of Spanglish?

VOCABULARY DEVELOPMENT
The words in **boldface** are defined at the bottom of the page. Underline the words as you read them.

REFLECT: The authors include several Spanish terms in the first paragraph. What do you think they mean?

In Manhattan a first-grader greets her visiting grandparents, happily   1
exclaiming, "Come here, *siéntate*!" Her **bemused**[1] grandfather, who does not speak Spanish, nevertheless knows she is asking him to sit down. A Miami personnel officer understands what a job applicant means when he says, "*Quiero un* part time." Nor do drivers miss a beat reading a billboard alongside a Los Angeles street advertising CERVEZA—SIX-PACK!

This free-form blend of Spanish and English, known as Spanglish, is   2
common **linguistic currency**[2] wherever concentrations of Hispanic Amer-

1. **bemused:** surprised and a bit confused   2. **linguistic currency:** typical speech

icans are found in the U.S. In Los Angeles, where 55 percent of the city's 3 million inhabitants speak Spanish, Spanglish is as much a part of daily life as sunglasses. Unlike the broken-English efforts of earlier immigrants from Europe, Asia, and other regions, Spanglish has become a widely accepted conversational mode used casually—even playfully—by Spanish-speaking immigrants and native-born Americans alike.

Consisting of one part Hispanicized English, one part Americanized Spanish, and more than a little **fractured syntax**,[3] Spanglish is a bit like a Robin Williams comedy routine: a crackling line of cross-cultural **patter**[4] straight from the **melting pot**.[5] Often it enters **Anglo**[6] homes and families through the children, who pick it up at school or at play with their young Hispanic **contemporaries**.[7] In other cases, it comes from watching TV; many an Anglo child watching *Sesame Street* has learned *uno dos tres* almost as quickly as one two three.

Spanglish takes a variety of forms, from the Southern California Anglos who bid farewell with the utterly silly "*hasta la* bye-bye" to the Cuban American drivers in Miami who *parquean* their *carros*. Some Spanglish sentences are mostly Spanish, with a quick detour for an English word or two. A Latino friend may cut short a conversation by glancing at his watch and excusing himself with the explanation that he must "*ir al* supermarket."

Many of the English words transplanted in this way are simply hardier than their Spanish counterparts. No matter how distasteful the subject, for example, it is still easier to say "income tax" than *impuesto sobre la renta*. At the same time, many Spanish-speaking immigrants have adopted such terms as *VCR*, *microwave*, and *dishwasher* for what they view as largely American **phenomena**.[8] Still other English words convey a cultural context that is not **implicit**[9] in the Spanish. A friend who invites you to *lonche* most likely has in mind the brisk American custom of "doing lunch" rather than the **languorous**[10] afternoon break traditionally implied by *almuerzo*.

Mainstream Americans exposed to similar hybrids of German, Chinese, or Hindi might be mystified. But even Anglos who speak little or no Spanish are somewhat familiar with Spanglish. Living among them, for one thing, are 19 million Hispanics. In addition, more American high school and university students sign up for Spanish than for any other foreign language.

Only in the past ten years, though, has Spanglish begun to turn into a national slang. Its popularity has grown with the explosive increases in U.S. immigration from Latin American countries. English has increasingly collided with Spanish in retail stores, offices and classrooms, in pop music, and on street corners. Anglos whose ancestors picked up such Spanish words as *rancho*, *bronco*, *tornado*, and *incommunicado*, for instance, now freely use such Spanish words as *gracias*, *bueno*, *amigo*, and *por favor*.

Among Latinos, Spanglish conversations often flow easily from Spanish into several sentences of English and back.

Spanglish is a sort of code for Latinos: the speakers know Spanish, but their **hybrid**[11] language reflects the American culture in which they live.

---

3. **fractured syntax:** language that breaks grammatical rules   4. **patter:** quick speech
5. **melting pot:** a blending of people from different cultures   6. **Anglo:** a white, English-speaking person   7. **contemporaries:** peers   8. **phenomena:** strange experiences or things   9. **implicit:** understood but not expressed directly
10. **languorous:** long and relaxing   11. **hybrid:** a combination of two things

IDEA JOURNAL How important do you think it is for non-Hispanics in the United States to understand at least some Spanish?

SUMMARIZE: In your own words, describe how Spanglish differs from the broken English of earlier immigrants to the United States.

PREDICT: Based on the first part of the first sentence of paragraph 4, how do you suppose the authors will go on to develop this paragraph?

Many lean to shorter, clipped phrases in place of the longer, more graceful expressions their parents used. Says Leonel de la Cuesta, an assistant professor of modern languages at Florida International University in Miami: "In the U.S., time is money, and that is showing up in Spanglish as an economy of language." Conversational examples: *taipiar* (type) and *winshi-wiper* (windshield wiper) replace *escribir a màquina* and *limpiaparabrisas*.

Major advertisers, eager to tap the estimated $134 billion in spending 10 power **wielded**[12] by Spanish-speaking Americans, have ventured into Spanglish to promote their products. In some cases, attempts to sprinkle Spanish through commercials have produced embarrassing **gaffes**.[13] A Braniff Airlines ad that **sought**[14] to tell Spanish-speaking audiences they could settle back *en* (in) luxuriant *cuero* (leather) seats, for example, **inadvertently**[15] said they could fly without clothes (*encuero*). A fractured translation of the Miller Lite slogan told readers the beer was "Filling, and less delicious." Similar **blunders**[16] are often made by Anglos trying to impress Spanish-speaking pals. But if Latinos are amused by mangled Spanglish, they also recognize these goofs as a sort of friendly acceptance. As they might put it, *no problema*.

· ·

SUMMARIZE AND RESPOND

In your reading journal or elsewhere, summarize the main point of "Spanglish." Then, go back and check off the support for this idea. Next, write a brief summary of the essay. Finally, write a brief response to the reading. Was the term *Spanglish* new to you, or were you already familiar with it? What did you find most interesting about the essay? Did you find any of it amusing?

· ·

CHECK YOUR COMPREHENSION

1. An alternate title for this essay could be

    a. "The Influence of Hispanic Americans on U.S. Culture."

    b. "The Economic Power of Hispanic Americans."

    c. "How Language Changes over the Course of Time."

    (d.) "A New Cross-Cultural 'Language.'"

2. The main point of this essay is that

    a. most Hispanic American children find it easy to learn English.

    (b.) Spanglish is becoming common wherever speakers of Spanish and English come together.

    c. many Hispanic Americans prefer to speak to one another in Spanish than in English.

    d. Spanglish is a kind of code for Hispanic Americans that distinguishes them from other English speakers.

12. wielded: held   **13. gaffes:** mistakes   **14. sought:** wanted to; looked for
15. inadvertently: by mistake; not intentionally   **16. blunders:** mistakes

3. Which of the following is *not* a reason cited in the essay for the rise of Spanglish?

    a. Some English terms refer to things that Hispanic Americans regard as essentially American.

    b. In many cases, an English term is shorter than its Spanish counterpart.

    c. The mixture of English and Spanish reflects the hybrid culture in which Hispanic Americans live.

    (d.) People who speak both English and Spanish are naturally going to switch back and forth.

4. Look back at the **boldface** vocabulary you underlined, and write sentences using the following words: *implicit* (para. 5); *hybrid* (9); *wield, inadvertently, blunder* (10).

- -

READ CRITICALLY

1. Do the authors give enough examples of what they mean by *Spanglish*? Do they provide enough details about the examples to help readers understand their definition? Why or why not?

2. Whom would you say the authors see as the primary audience for this essay? What makes you think so?

3. The authors suggest that many Anglos can understand Spanglish and even speak it themselves. To what extent do you believe that this is the case?

4. How would you evaluate the authors' final paragraph? Why do you suppose they chose to conclude as they do?

5. This essay was first published in 1988. Since then, the Hispanic population of the United States has grown even larger. What would you point to as some further ways that Hispanic culture has influenced mainstream American culture?

- -

WRITE

WRITE A PARAGRAPH: Write a paragraph that defines an expression common to your group of friends, your workplace, your region, or some other group to which you belong. As you draft, assume that your readers are not familiar with the expression or its special use within your group. In developing your paragraph, consider using contrast, as the authors of "Spanglish" do in paragraph 2, and choose clear examples to communicate your meaning.

WRITE AN ESSAY: In an essay, define a concept that is important to a culture to which you belong. You might, for example, choose to define *success*, *diversity*, or some other concept in terms of U.S. culture. Or you might choose to define a concept that has a special significance at your job, in a hobby you have, or in your ethnic culture. Before you begin to draft, be sure to define your audience. If your readers will already be somewhat familiar with the concept, you will need to bring your own particular slant to the definition to maintain their interest. If readers will be unfamiliar with the concept, you will need to give enough background for your definition.

• •

48

Comparison and Contrast

Each essay in this chapter uses comparison and contrast to get its main point across to the reader. As you read these essays, consider how they achieve the Four Basics of Good Comparison and Contrast that are listed below and discussed in Chapter 16 of this book.

■■
■■ **Four Basics of Good Comparison and Contrast**

1 It uses subjects that have enough in common to be compared or contrasted in a useful way.

2 It serves a purpose—either to help readers make a decision or to understand the subjects.

3 It presents several important, parallel points of comparison or contrast.

4 It arranges points in a logical order.

Jackie Davison
Happy Birthday, Sis!

Jackie Davison Linstead, a student when she wrote this essay, graduated from California State University, Fullerton, with a degree in English and is currently a high school English teacher. She says her ideas for her writing often "stem from real life," and she looks to include "slices of life" in her writing, creating an emotional connection with her reader. When giving advice to other student writers, Davison writes: "Writing is a labor of love. It is irritating, all-consuming, and enjoyable all at the same time. . . . There is no greater feeling than to read over your work and think, 'That's it! That's what I meant to say!'"

GUIDING QUESTION
What are some differences between Jackie and her sister?

VOCABULARY DEVELOPMENT
The words in **boldface** are defined at the bottom of the page. Underline the words as you read them.

IDEA JOURNAL Compare yourself with a brother or sister.

My sister and I share the same last name—Davison—a name that will 1 forever be confused with Davidson, prompting video store clerks and Department of Motor Vehicle employees to make cracks about how we must be related to **Harley-Davidson**.[1] We roll our identical brown eyes and flash each other a smile, and there our similarities end. Always growing up in the same small room, my sister **camouflages**[2] into her surroundings like a ladybug perched on a red rose, while I'm more like a hyena screaming in a library.

With her nose in a book, my sister radiates a Zen-like stillness, a peace- 2 ful silence that would shame even Buddha. Classical music whispers through the invisible room divider, lingering and lulling the otherwise **static**[3] air. **Monet**'s[4] **pastel**[5] posters accent the **sparsely**[6] decorated white walls, working like around-the-clock tranquility pills. However, a visitor need make only a 180-degree turn to see a completely different territory: my side of the room.

My side is anything but calm. Screaming to be noticed, the art almost 3 comes out from the walls, with posters of far-off places on my travel list. Van Morrison rocks through the air, as I try to shake my sister into anger, or at least action. She, forever outsmarting me, however, gracefully dons her headphones and continues with the peaceful, predictable musical patterns of **Chopin**[7] and **Mozart**.[8] Under her breath, she mutters, "Thanks be to God," that our days of sharing a room will soon be over.

IDENTIFY: Does the essay use part-to-part or whole-to-whole organization?

_____

_____

I call my sister The Thinker, like **Auguste Rodin**'s[9] famous statue, 4 because he must have had someone like her in mind as he worked. Her thoughts are carefully **doled out**[10] like food during the Great Depression, offering only what is needed to **sustain**[11] another. With focused, undivided attention, she refuses to cook breakfast while discussing politics or catch up on the cell phone while driving to work. She chooses each word carefully.

In contrast, I could break priceless statues as I forget that my huge 5 backpack, loaded with heavy books, is an agent of destruction. Without a thought, I spin around to say something, while my backpack destroys everything in its path. I hurl it into the middle of a room, paying no attention to what it may shatter on its airborne path. My actions are anything but focused: They're more like lyrics to Beatles songs written under the influence of drugs.

The Thinker is rarely distracted from her very organized plans. She has 6 a plain leather binder that holds her schedule, planned to the minute. Even researching a world event, complete with journal searches and radio reports,

---

1. **Harley-Davidson:** a type of motorcycle   2. **camouflage:** to hide by changing her appearance to fit her surroundings   3. **static:** not in motion   4. **Monet:** a French Impressionist painter   5. **pastel:** delicate, soft, and pale in color   6. **sparsely:** thinly 7. **Chopin:** a Polish-born French composer and pianist   8. **Mozart:** an Austrian composer   9. **Auguste Rodin:** a French sculptor whose most famous work was *The Thinker* 10. **doled out:** distributed, as charity   11. **sustain:** to support or keep up

is scheduled into its **allotted**[12] twenty-two minutes. Her binder is her life, neatly divided into days and minutes. She moves through life with great **precision**.[13]

I have a planner, too. It is three years old, and the dates are all off, leaving me days late for appointments and confused about what day my birthday is this year. I have never sent a birthday card on time and am always scribbling little apologies for being late, once again. I once joked that there should be whole boxes of **belated**[14] event cards for people like me. My sister saw no humor in this, seeing my belatedness as a lack of respect for family and friends. However, we have recently bridged our differences.

I was both shocked and delighted when my sister, with a girlish grin, handed over my birthday present, three days late! Biting my tongue to keep from asking her to clock in at the door and deduct points for lack of punctuality, I tore into the perfectly color-coordinated, neatly wrapped package, decorated with **elaborate**,[15] curlicued ribbon. Not surprisingly, my ribbons are always limp and frazzled, like a perm gone wrong.

As I saw my first black leather day planner, identical to hers, The Thinker said, "I have taken the liberty of adding all of your important dates, just to get you started. I'm sorry it's late."

My sister's birthday is in four days. I have already bought the card, a hilarious one, and wrapped her present. Though my sister and I, with our identical brown eyes, see the glass differently, half empty and half full, we can finally drink from the same glass. Happy Birthday, Sis.

REFLECT: Are you more like the author or her sister? How?

_____

_____

7

8

9

10

. . . .

SUMMARIZE AND RESPOND

In your reading journal or elsewhere, summarize the main point of "Happy Birthday, Sis!" Then, go back and check off the support for this idea. Next, write a brief summary of the essay. Finally, write a brief response to the reading. Whom do you have more in common with, Jackie Davison or her sister?

. . . .

CHECK YOUR COMPREHENSION

1. An alternate title for this essay could be
    a. "The Ladybug and the Hyena."
    b. "The Bull in the China Shop."
    c. "My Perfect Sister."
    d. "Rock Music vs. Classical Music."

2. The main point of this essay is that
    a. the author and her sister seem like opposites, but they are not so different after all.

12. **allotted:** assigned or set aside for a specific use   13. **precision:** exactness; strictness   14. **belated:** coming after the expected time   15. **elaborate:** having carefully arranged parts or details

    b. the author does not understand her sister's orderly life or her love of peace and quiet.

    c. both the author and her sister are happy that their days of sharing a room are over.

    d. the author is an optimist, but her sister is a pessimist.

3. The author calls her sister "The Thinker" because

    a. her sister is a straight-A student but does not seem to have any emotions.

    b. her sister loves Auguste Rodin and music by classical composers.

    (c.) she thinks Rodin had someone like her sister in mind when he made the sculpture.

    d. her sister plans her life to the minute, using a plain leather binder for her schedule.

4. Does this essay include the Four Basics of Good Comparison and Contrast? Why or why not?

5. Look back at the **boldface** vocabulary you underlined, and write sentences using these words: *static, sparsely* (para. 2); *sustain* (4); *allotted* (6); *belated* (7).

TIP For tools to build your vocabulary, visit the *Real Writing Student Center* at **bedfordstmartins.com/ realwriting.**

- -

READ CRITICALLY

1. What specific details does the author provide to give a clear sense of her sister?

2. What do the author and her sister have in common?

3. According to the author, her sister thinks that being late with birthday or holiday cards and presents shows "a lack of respect for family and friends" (para. 7). Do you agree?

4. What gift does the author's sister give her, and why is it meaningful? Why is it significant that her sister gives her a birthday gift three days late?

5. Which of these sisters do you have more in common with?

- -

WRITE

WRITE A PARAGRAPH: In showing her sister's personality and her own, the author points to specific objects (such as a leather binder) and preferences (such as their musical choices) that reveal their differences. Write a paragraph comparing two objects or preferences in your life and how they explain your personality.

WRITE AN ESSAY: The author has written a comparison/contrast essay about her sister and their relationship. Choose a person in your life—a family member or a friend, for example—and write your own comparison/contrast essay, exploring your differences. As the author does, try to include how you bridge these differences.

- -

Judith Ortiz Cofer

Don't Misread My Signals

Judith Ortiz Cofer is a Puerto Rican author and the Regents' and Franklin Professor of English and Creative Writing at the University of Georgia, where she has taught since 1984. She earned a B.A. in English from Augusta College and an M.A. in English from Florida Atlantic University. In 2007, she was awarded an honorary doctorate in human letters from Lehman University in New York City. Cofer's works span across literary genres, including books of poetry, novels, autobiographical writing, and collections of short stories and essays. Her work has appeared in numerous literary journals and is often anthologized and included in textbooks.

GUIDING QUESTION
How do people's assumptions about Cofer, based on her appearance, differ from who she is?

1   On a bus to London from Oxford University, where I was earning some graduate credits one summer, a young man, obviously fresh from a pub, approached my seat. With both hands over his heart, he went down on his knees in the aisle and broke into an Irish **tenor**'s[1] **rendition**[2] of "**Maria**"[3] from *West Side Story*.[4] I was not amused. "Maria" had followed me to London, reminding me of a prime fact of my life: You can leave the island of Puerto Rico, master the English language, and travel as far as you can, but if you're a **Latina**,[5] especially one who so clearly belongs to **Rita Moreno**'s[6] gene pool, the island travels with you.

2   Growing up in New Jersey and wanting most of all to belong, I lived in two completely different worlds. My parents designed our life as a **microcosm**[7] of their **casas**[8] on the island—we spoke Spanish, ate Puerto Rican food bought at the **bodega**,[9] and practiced strict Catholicism complete with Sunday mass in Spanish.

3   I was kept under tight **surveillance**[10] by my parents, since my virtue and modesty were, by their cultural equation, the same as their honor. As teenagers, my friends and I were lectured constantly on how to behave as proper senoritas. But it was a conflicting message we received, since our Puerto Rican mothers also encouraged us to look and act like women by dressing us in clothes our Anglo schoolmates and their mothers found too "mature" and **flashy**.[11] I often felt humiliated when I appeared at an American friend's birthday party wearing a dress more suitable for a semiformal. At Puerto Rican festivities, neither the music nor the colors we wore could be too loud.

---

1. tenor: the highest range of the adult male voice   **2. rendition:** a performance
3. "Maria": a song from *West Side Story* about one of the main Puerto Rican characters
4. *West Side Story*: a 1957 Broadway musical, made into a film in 1961   **5. Latina:** a female Latin American living in the United States   **6. Rita Moreno:** a Puerto Rican actress who played in *West Side Story*   **7. microcosm:** a world in miniature   **8. casa:** Spanish for "house"   **9. bodega:** Spanish for "small grocery store"   **10. surveillance:** a watch kept over a person or group of people   **11. flashy:** showy

VOCABULARY DEVELOPMENT
The words in **boldface** are defined at the bottom of the page. Underline the words as you read them.

IDEA JOURNAL Compare the way you dress now with how you dressed ten years ago and what each kind of style says about you.

IDENTIFY: As you read, check off customs and details that made the author different.

_____

_____

I remember Career Day in high school, when our teachers told us to 4 come dressed as if for a job interview. That morning, I **agonized**[12] in front of my closet, trying to figure out what a "career girl" would wear, because the only model I had was **Marlo Thomas**[13] on TV. To me and my Puerto Rican girlfriends, dressing up meant wearing our mothers' **ornate**[14] jewelry and clothing.

At school that day, the teachers **assailed**[15] us for wearing "everything 5 at once"—meaning too much jewelry and too many accessories. And it was painfully obvious that the other students in their tailored skirts and silk blouses thought we were hopeless and **vulgar**.[16] The way they looked at us was a taste of the cultural clash that awaited us in the real world, where **prospective**[17] employers and men on the street would often misinterpret our tight skirts and bright colors as a **come-on**.[18]

REFLECT: What are some customs your family has that others may find odd?

It is custom, not **chromosomes**,[19] that leads us to choose scarlet over 6 pale pink. Our mothers had grown up on a tropical island where the natural environment was a riot of primary colors, where showing your skin was one way to keep cool as well as to look sexy. On the island, women felt free to dress and move **provocatively**[20] since they were protected by the traditions and laws of a Spanish Catholic system of morality and **machismo**,[21] the main rule of which was, "You may look at my sister, but if you touch her, I will kill you." The extended family and church structure provided them with a circle of safety on the island; if a man "wronged" a girl, everyone would close in to save her family honor.

Off-island, signals often get mixed. When a Puerto Rican girl who is 7 dressed in her idea of what is attractive meets a man from **mainstream**[22] culture who has been trained to react to certain types of clothing as a sexual signal, a clash is likely to take place. She is seen as a Hot Tamale, a sexual **firebrand**.[23] I learned this lesson at my first formal dance when my date leaned over and painfully planted a sloppy, overeager kiss on my mouth. When I didn't respond with sufficient passion, he said in a resentful tone, "I thought you Latin girls were supposed to mature early." It was the first time I would feel like a fruit or vegetable—I was supposed to ripen, not just grow into womanhood like other girls.

These **stereotypes**,[24] though rarer, still surface in my life. I recently 8 stayed at a classy metropolitan hotel. After having dinner with a friend, I was returning to my room when a middle-aged man in a tuxedo stepped directly into my path. With his champagne glass extended toward me, he exclaimed, "*Evita!*"[25]

---

12. agonize: to worry about   **13. Marlo Thomas:** an American actress who played a modern single woman on the television show *That Girl*, which ran from 1966 to 1971
14. ornate: decorated with complex patterns   **15. assail:** to attack   **16. vulgar:** common; crude; lacking in good taste   **17. prospective:** likely to become; expected
18. come-on: flirting   **19. chromosomes:** material that carries genes or biological traits from parent to child   **20. provocatively:** in a way that causes a response or calls forth feelings, thoughts, or actions   **21. machismo:** a strong or exaggerated sense of manliness or power   **22. mainstream:** ideas and behaviors considered to be normal
23. firebrand: a person who is passionate about a particular cause   **24. stereotypes:** conventional and oversimplified ideas, opinions, or images   **25. Evita:** a musical and film about Eva Perón, Argentina's first lady from 1946 to 1952

Blocking my way, he bellowed the song "Don't Cry for Me, Argentina." 9
Playing to the gathering crowd, he began to sing loudly, a **ditty**[26] to the tune
of "La Bamba"—except the lyrics were about a girl named Maria whose
exploits[27] all rhymed with her name and **gonorrhea**.[28]

REFLECT: Have you ever
been stereotyped? How?
_____
_____

I knew that this same man—probably a corporate executive, even 10
worldly by most standards—would never have **regaled**[29] a white woman
with a dirty song in public. But to him, I was just a character in his universe
of "others," all cartoons.

Still, I am one of the lucky ones. There are thousands of Latinas with- 11
out the privilege of the education that my parents gave me. For them, every
day is a struggle against the **misconceptions**[30] **perpetuated**[31] by the myth
of the Latina as a whore, domestic worker, or criminal.

Rather than fight these **pervasive**[32] stereotypes, I try to replace them 12
with a more interesting set of realities. I travel around the United States
reading from my books of poetry and my novel. With the stories I tell, the
dreams and fears I examine in my work, I try to get my audience past the
particulars of my skin color, my accent, or my clothes.

I once wrote a poem in which I called Latinas "God's brown daugh- 13
ters." It is really a prayer of sorts, for communication and respect. In it,
Latin women pray "in Spanish to an Anglo God with a Jewish heritage," and
they are "**fervently**[33] hoping that if not **omnipotent**,[34] at least He be
bilingual."

* * *

SUMMARIZE AND RESPOND

In your reading journal or elsewhere, summarize the main point of "Don't Misread
My Signals." Then, go back and check off the support for this idea. Next, write a
brief summary of the essay. Finally, write a brief response to the reading. Have
you ever misread signals, stereotyped someone, or gotten the wrong impression
of someone? How did it occur?

* * *

CHECK YOUR COMPREHENSION

1. An alternate title for this essay could be
   a. "My Name Is Not 'Maria.'"
   b. "Learning to Embrace Stereotypes."
   c. "The Struggles of Immigrant Life."
   d. "The Benefits of a Good Education."

---

26. **ditty:** a short, simple song   27. **exploits:** bold and daring actions   28. **gonorrhea:** a sexually transmitted disease   29. **regale:** to entertain   30. **misconceptions:**
false opinions based on lack of understanding   31. **perpetuate:** to keep, preserve
32. **pervasive:** widespread   33. **fervently:** passionately   34. **omnipotent:** all-
powerful

2. The main point of this essay is that
   a. young Puerto Rican women often dress in a flashy, provocative way.
   b. Cofer dislikes musicals like *West Side Story* and *Evita*.
   (c.) Cofer has faced common misunderstandings about Latinas.
   d. Cofer's parents kept a strict watch over their daughters.

3. Cofer includes accounts of strangers singing to her because
   a. she likes getting attention from men.
   (b.) the stories are good examples of stereotyping.
   c. these men show a strict morality and machismo.
   d. in Puerto Rico, it is common for men to sing in public.

4. Look back at the **boldface** vocabulary you underlined, and write sentences using these words: *prospective* (para. 5); *misconception, perpetuate* (11); *pervasive* (12); *fervently* (13).

. . . .

READ CRITICALLY

1. Who do you suppose is Cofer's intended audience for this essay? Why?

2. The title of the essay is "Don't Misread My Signals." What specific examples does she provide of people misreading her?

3. In paragraph 3, Cofer refers to receiving "conflicting messages." What are they, and how do they cause difficulties?

4. Cofer is writing about stereotypes of Latinas. Where do these images and ideas seem to come from? How do they distort reality?

5. According to Cofer, she has a "privilege" that many other Latinas do not have. What is her privilege, and what does this advantage allow her to do?

. . . .

WRITE

WRITE A PARAGRAPH: Cofer is writing, in part, about being misunderstood. Write a paragraph in which you recall a time when people have misunderstood you or have gotten the wrong idea about your behavior, background, appearance, or words. Contrast the misunderstanding with the reality of the situation, and try to understand the source of the mistake.

WRITE AN ESSAY: Cofer focuses primarily on misunderstandings or myths about Latinas. But there are many other stereotypes in our culture as well. Choose and describe a common stereotype that you think is mistaken; then, compare and contrast those stereotypical images or ideas with a more accurate portrait of reality. For example, you might write about the way women are portrayed in some rap songs versus how they really are.

. . . .

Deborah Tannen

Gender Patterns Begin at the Beginning

 Deborah Tannen (b. 1945) earned a doctorate in linguistics from the University of California, Berkeley, in 1979, and she now teaches linguistics at Georgetown University. She has written on communication in doctor-patient relationships and across cultures, but her most popular books have focused on communication and gender. *You Just Don't Understand: Men and Women in Conversation* (1990) was number one on the *New York Times* bestseller list for eight months. She has also published, among many other books, *Talking from 9 to 5* (1994), in which she discusses how different communication styles affect men and women in the workplace. Her most recent book is *You Were Always Mom's Favorite! Sisters in Conversation throughout Their Lives* (2009).

Following is an excerpt from Tannen's book *I Only Say This Because I Love You* (2001). Comparing the communication styles of men and women, she shows how patterns learned at an early age can affect not only how adults interact but also how parents relate to their opposite-sex children.

GUIDING QUESTION

What does Tannen see here as the main difference between the way women and girls communicate with one another and the way men and boys do?

1   **Genderspeak**[1] creates confusion between parents and children of the opposite sex just as surely as it does between parents themselves. For mothers, having sons can be a mystery, just as having daughters can be a mystery for fathers. The seeds of these confusions are planted in the different ways boys and girls relate to their friends while growing up. So adults who were girls and adults who were boys often have greater automatic understanding of the children who were the same kind of children they were.

2   Some years ago, I conducted a research project in which I asked pairs of best friends, boys and girls, to take chairs into a room and talk. When I show clips from these tapes to audiences, they always laugh at the contrast. In the first clip, two five-year-old girls sit directly facing each other. They lean in toward each other; one reaches out to adjust the other's headband; and both talk **intently**[2] while keeping their gazes fixed steadily on each other's faces.

3   Then come the five-year-old boys, who look lost and **antsy**[3] in their little chairs. Sitting side by side, they never look directly at each other—never turn toward each other at all. They bounce in their seats as they talk about what they'd rather be doing—activities like blowing up the house (but only the upstairs, where I have forced them to sit and talk, not the downstairs, where the Nintendo is). A few moments after this sequence, the boys were up out of their chairs, running around the room. I quickly called

VOCABULARY DEVELOPMENT The words in **boldface** are defined at the bottom of the page. Underline the words as you read them.

IDEA JOURNAL What differences have you observed between women and men in terms of how they communicate?

PREDICT: Based on the first two sentences of this paragraph, what do you think Tannen will do in the paragraphs that follow?

_____

_____

IDENTIFY: What pattern of comparison and contrast does Tannen use to organize paragraphs 2 and 3?

_____

_____

1. **genderspeak:** Tannen's word for the differing communication styles of women and men
2. **intently:** with great interest or attention   3. **antsy:** restless

a halt to the taping when I saw, from my seat beside the camera operator outside the room, that one of the boys had lifted his small plastic chair above his head and was running with it straight toward the camera.

Then come the ten-year-olds. The girls sit and face each other, talking intently; they never take their eyes off each other's faces. The boys sit side by side, awkwardly shifting and squirming, and their eyes never meet: When one turns his head slightly toward the other, the other is always looking away.

The fifteen-year-olds always spark laughter. The girls sit directly facing each other, their gazes fixed **unswervingly**[4] on each other's faces as one describes to the other a gift she bought for a friend. Then come the boys, sitting side by side, leaning forward. One boy rests his elbows on his knees and looks at the floor; the other rests his right foot on his left knee as he plays with his shoelace, keeping his eyes firmly fixed on his foot rather than on his friend.

You can observe similar patterns on a sunny day when pairs of women and men are sitting outside having lunch, or just about anywhere friends are lounging in a casual setting: The women sit face-to-face and keep their eyes focused on each other's faces as they talk **incessantly**;[5] the men sit at angles or side by side and look around them while talking **intermittently**.[6]

These different patterns often lead to confusion and frustration between women and men: The woman complains, "You're not listening to me," to a man who is not looking at her, and the man feels wrongly accused. He would be uncomfortable if the person he was talking to looked too intently at him. If it's a man, the direct gaze feels like a challenge; if it's a woman, it feels like flirting. But many women perceive the lack of direct gaze as a failure of listening—which to them is the most important gift a person can give. A letter published by *Newsweek* following an article regarding women's sexuality reflected this value: "Now, if only the pharmaceutical companies could develop a drug to increase blood flow to men's ears," wrote Julie Wash, "*that* would be the women's Viagra."

Imagine a scene in a kitchen when the kids come home from school. Mother and daughter sit at the kitchen table facing each other. The mother asks what happened at school, and the daughter tells her. She talks about the teacher, her friends, and the conversations they had. In another kitchen a mother asks the same question of her little boy and gets in reply the equivalent of the 1950s popular book title: "*Where did you go?*" "*Out.*" "*What did you do?*" "*Nothing.*" But there is hope: Instead of expecting their sons to sit opposite them and talk, many mothers find they are more likely to hear information they are interested in while doing something with their sons, like driving in the car or weeding the garden. One mother on hearing me say this exclaimed, "That's true! And my son is only four!"

Many fathers understand this automatically. David Reimer, a man who was raised as a girl following a surgical accident that destroyed his genital organ, tells of the moment when he was nearly fifteen and his parents revealed to him the truth of his birth. The teenager, who up until then knew

REFLECT: What do you think of Tannen's characterization of the behavior of men and women? How accurate do you think it is?

_____

_____

IDENTIFY: Underline the main point of paragraph 7.

SUMMARIZE: What, according to Tannen, should mothers do to get their sons to communicate with them?

_____

_____

4. **unswervingly:** without moving   5. **incessantly:** without stopping   6. **intermittently:** not continuously; occasionally

herself as a girl named Brenda, suspected something was up when her father picked her up and suggested they get some ice cream instead of going straight home. Looking back, David recalls that his first thought was that something dreadful had happened to his parents or his brother: "Usually when there was some kind of disaster in the family, good old dad takes you out in the family car for a cone or something. So I was thinking, 'Is Mother dying? Are you guys getting a divorce? Is everything OK with Brian?'" In other words, the teenager immediately sensed that the father was setting the stage for a **momentous**[7] **revelation**[8]—probably involving a family member—by arranging for them to sit side by side, with eyes fixed straight ahead.

SUMMARIZE AND RESPOND

In your reading journal or elsewhere, summarize the main point of Tannen's essay. Then, go back and check off the support for this idea. Next, write a brief summary of the essay. Finally, write a brief response to the reading. To what extent does your own experience match with Tannen's observations? In your opinion, how significant are the differences she describes?

CHECK YOUR COMPREHENSION

1. An alternate title for this essay could be
   a. "As Boys and Girls Communicate, So Do Men and Women."
   b. "Gender as a Force in the Development of One's Personality."
   c. "Why Mothers and Daughters Communicate Better than Fathers and Sons."
   d. "The Hardest Thing about Communicating with Adolescents."

2. The main point of this essay is that
   a. little boys have short attention spans, while little girls generally have better concentration.
   b. differences in communication styles between men and women can be traced back to childhood.
   c. a woman may think a man is not listening to her because the man is not looking at her directly.
   d. as people get older, they learn to communicate more effectively with the opposite sex.

3. Tannen describes the tapes of the five-year-old, ten-year-old, and fifteen-year-old boys and girls to show
   a. why her audiences always laugh at the contrast between the boys and the girls.
   b. how the communication styles of boys and girls change over time.

---

7. momentous: of great importance   **8. revelation:** something revealed or disclosed

      c. the consistency of differences in communication styles between boys and girls.

      d. how she uses videotape in her research about communication differences.

4. Look back at the **boldface** vocabulary you underlined, and write sentences using these words: *intently* (para. 2); *incessantly, intermittently* (6); *momentous* (9).

· ·

READ CRITICALLY

1. Who do you suppose is Tannen's intended audience for this essay? Why?

2. How effective do you find Tannen's descriptions of the children she videotaped (paras. 2–5)? Pick out some passages that you think work well, and explain why you think they do.

3. Tannen writes that their different communication patterns "often lead to confusion and frustration between women and men" (para. 7). How accurate do you find this observation? Think, perhaps, about how men and women communicate when they are not with one another physically— when using the telephone or e-mail, for example. How similarly or differently do they communicate then?

4. In paragraph 8, Tannen contrasts the way a daughter communicates with a mother with the way a son does. Do you agree that the contrast in communication styles is as sharp as she describes?

5. Evaluate Tannen's final paragraph. How effective is it as a conclusion to the essay? What purpose is served by the extended example she offers here?

· ·

WRITE

WRITE A PARAGRAPH: Write a paragraph describing some other difference in behavior between boys and girls of the same age. Be sure to describe this differing behavior clearly and in detail.

WRITE AN ESSAY: Tannen focuses exclusively on differences between girls and boys, and women and men. Write an essay on the behavior of males and females in a particular situation (or in various situations), but try not to limit yourself to contrasts; consider similarities as well. Be sure to develop a clear thesis that makes a general point about the behavior of women and men, and support this point using specific examples from your own observations and experiences.

· ·

49

Cause and Effect

Each essay in this chapter uses cause and effect to get its main point across to the reader. As you read these essays, consider how they achieve the four basics of good cause and effect that are listed below and discussed in Chapter 17 of this book.

■■
■■■ **Four Basics of Good Cause and Effect**

1 The main point reflects the writer's purpose: to explain causes, effects, or both.

2 If the purpose is to explain causes, the writing presents real causes.

3 If the purpose is to explain effects, it presents real effects.

4 It gives readers detailed examples or explanations of the causes or effects.

Ruth Russell

The Wounds That Can't Be Stitched Up

Ruth Russell graduated from the University of Massachusetts at Amherst in 2005, after majoring in media art and English. "The Wounds That Can't Be Stitched Up" is a true story that Russell first wrote about in a community college writing class. She later sent the essay to *Newsweek*, which published it in the "My Turn" column. Of the response it received, Russell notes, "It was gratifying to have young students recognize me and stop to say a few words about how the essay made them think differently about drinking and driving." She advises other student writers to "take a chance and speak out" and notes that "English professors can be a writer's best friend."

GUIDING QUESTION
How does what happened affect the author?

VOCABULARY DEVELOPMENT
The words in **boldface** are defined at the bottom of the page. Underline the words as you read them.

IDEA JOURNAL Write about an event or a situation that strongly affected you.

IDENTIFY: How do the first two paragraphs work together to create an effect?

_____

_____

PREDICT: What do you think the next paragraphs will be about?

_____

_____

IDENTIFY: Check the effects on the author's family members.

1   It was a mild December night. Christmas was only two weeks away. The evening sky was overcast, but the roads were dry. All was quiet in our small town as I drove to my grandmother's house.

2   I heard the sirens first. Red lights and blue lights **strobed**[1] **in tandem.**[2] Ambulances with their interiors lit like television screens in a dark room flew by, escorted by police cruisers on the way to the hospital.

3   When I arrived at my gram's, she was on the porch steps struggling to put on her coat. "Come on," she said breathlessly. "Your mother has been in an accident." I was seventeen then, and it would take a long time before sirens lost their power to reduce me to tears. Twenty-three years have passed, but only recently have I realized how deeply affected I was by events caused by a drunk driver so long ago.

4   When the accident occurred, my youngest brother was eight. He was sitting in the back seat of our family's large, sturdy sedan. The force of the crash sent him flying headlong into the back of the front seat, leaving him with a grossly swollen black eye. He was admitted to the hospital for observation. He didn't talk much when I visited him that night. He just sat in the bed, a lonely little figure in a darkened hospital room.

5   My sister, who was twelve, was sitting in the front seat. She confided to me later how much she missed the beautiful blue coat she'd been wearing at the time. It was an early Christmas present, and it was destroyed beyond repair by the medical personnel who cut if off her body as they worked to save her life. She had a severely **fractured**[3] skull that required immediate surgery. The resulting facial scar became for our family a permanent reminder of how close she came to dying that night.

6   My mother was admitted to the intensive-care unit to be stabilized before her multiple facial cuts could be stitched up. Dad tried to prepare me before we went in to see her by telling me that she looked and sounded worse than she was. One eye was temporarily held in place by a bandage wrapped around her head. Her lower lip hideously **gaped,**[4] exposing a mouthful of broken teeth. **Delirious,**[5] she cried out for her children and apologized for an accident she neither caused nor could have avoided, an accident that happened when her car was hit head-on by a drunk driver speeding down the wrong side of the road in a half-ton truck with no headlights.

7   My dad, my brothers, my sister, and I spent Christmas at the hospital visiting my mother. Sometimes, she was so out of it from medication that

---

1. strobed: pulsed or flashed on and off with intense bursts of light   **2. in tandem:** together   **3. fractured:** broken or split   **4. gaped:** was opened widely
5. delirious: in a disturbed state of mind caused by illness or intoxication

she barely recognized us. We celebrated two of my brothers' birthdays—one only days after Christmas and the other in early January—there, too.

I remember watching the police escort the drunk driver out of the hospital the night of the accident. He looked about 35 years old, but his face was so **distorted**[6] by rage and alcohol that I could only guess. A bandaged wrist was his only visible injury. He kept repeating that he'd done nothing wrong as several officers tried to get him into the cruiser waiting outside the emergency room exit.   8

The man was jailed over the weekend and lost his license for 30 days for driving under the influence. I don't know if that was his first alcohol-related traffic violation, but I know it wasn't the last. Now and then, I'd see his name in the court log of our local paper for another DUI and wonder how he could still be behind the wheel.   9

Sometimes when I tell this story, I'd be asked in an **accusatory**[7] tone if my mom and siblings were wearing seat belts. I think that's a lot like asking a rape victim how she was dressed. The answer is no. This all happened before seat-belt awareness campaigns began. In fact, if they had been in a smaller car, seat belts or not, I believe my mother and sister would have died.   10

Many local people who know the driver are surprised when they hear about the accident, and they are quick to defend him. They tell me he was a war hero. His parents aren't well. He's an alcoholic. Or my favorite: "He's a good boy when he doesn't drink."   11

Two years ago, I discovered this man had moved into my apartment building. I felt vaguely **apprehensive**,[8] but I believed the accident was ancient history. Nothing could have prepared me for what happened next.   12

It was a mild afternoon, just a few days before Christmas. I had just started down the back staircase of the building, on my way to visit my son, when I recognized my neighbor's new pickup truck as it roared down the street. The driver missed the entrance to our shared parking lot. He reversed crookedly in the road, slammed the transmission into forward, then quickly pulled into his parking space. Gravel and sand flew as he stomped on the brakes to halt his truck just inches from where I stood frozen on the staircase. As he staggered from his vehicle, he looked at me and asked drunkenly, "Did I scare you?"   13

REFLECT: What is the long-term effect of the accident on the author?

_____

_____

• •

SUMMARIZE AND RESPOND

In your reading journal or elsewhere, summarize the main point of "The Wounds That Can't Be Stitched Up." Then, go back and check off the support for this idea. Next, write a brief summary of the essay. Finally, write a brief response to the reading. What did this essay make you think or feel? How did the details that Russell included contribute to this overall impression?

---

6. distorted: twisted and misshapen   **7. accusatory:** said in a way that assigns blame or fault   **8. apprehensive:** uneasy or fearful that something bad might happen

• •

CHECK YOUR COMPREHENSION

1. An alternate title for this essay could be
    a. "The Lasting Damage Done by Drunk Drivers."
    b. "Alcohol, Driving, and Holidays Don't Mix."
    c. "Drinking and Driving: A Deadly Cocktail."
    d. "A Most Memorable Christmas Holiday."

2. The main point of this essay is that
    a. Russell's family suffered severe consequences, but the person responsible for the accident did not.
    b. people with drug and alcohol addictions should not be held accountable for their actions, no matter how damaging.
    c. when families experience catastrophes, they must stick together for support.
    d. even if you are careful behind the wheel, driving a car is still very dangerous.

3. Why does Russell mention the weather and the dry roads in her introductory paragraph?
    a. She wants to give a realistic impression of small-town life in America.
    b. These details show that road conditions were not a factor in the accident.
    c. In good weather, accidents should never happen.
    d. The conditions allowed rescue personnel to save her mother and siblings.

4. Does this essay include the Four Basics of Good Cause and Effect? Why or why not?

5. Look back at the **boldface** vocabulary you underlined, and write sentences using these words: *in tandem* (para. 2); *delirious* (6); *distorted* (8); *accusatory* (10); *apprehensive* (12).

TIP For tools to build your vocabulary, visit the *Real Writing Student Center* at **bedfordstmartins.com/ realwriting**.

• •

READ CRITICALLY

1. According to the essay, what are both the short-term and long-term effects of drunk driving?

2. What is Russell's attitude toward the man who caused the accident? How can you tell?

3. In paragraph 10, the writer makes a comparison between her mother and siblings and rape victims. Does this analogy seem convincing and accurate? Why or why not?

4. Russell writes that local people are sometimes "quick to defend" the drunk driver. Why do you think that is the case? What effect does this attitude have on Russell?

5. The essay ends with a question. What do you think the answer is? What effect does this conclusion have?

· ·

WRITE

WRITE A PARAGRAPH: Sometimes, our intentions lead to unintended consequences. Write a paragraph in which you describe an experience where your choices, behavior, or words had a different effect than you planned or desired.

WRITE AN ESSAY: Russell writes that she realized "only recently" how "deeply affected" she was by the drunk-driving accident years before. Write an essay about an incident in your own life that still affects you now, or had consequences only after some time had passed.

· ·

Pat Wingert
Uniforms Rule

 Pat Wingert earned a B.S. in journalism from the University of Illinois, Champaign–Urbana, and learned her craft working for the Pulitzer Prize–winning columnist Mike Royko at the *Sun-Times*. She became a reporter at the paper herself and later worked for the *Chicago Tribune*. After nine years at the two Chicago newspapers, she left her native city for the Washington bureau of *Newsweek* in 1986 and has worked there ever since. Wingert has cowritten many cover stories over the years on issues related to children, families, and education. In "Uniforms Rule," originally from *Newsweek* (October 1999), Wingert examines how and why uniforms and other dress codes affect public-school safety and student behavior.

IDEA JOURNAL What do you think about schools that require students to wear uniforms?

GUIDING QUESTION
Why would wearing a uniform influence students' behavior?

Kiara Newsome's spotless navy jumper and **demure**[1] white blouse won't win raves on the runways. But to school reformers, the six-year-old is a real trendsetter. This fall, Kiara and her classmates at P.S. 15 on Manhattan's Lower East Side joined hundreds of thousands of students in the nation's largest school system and **donned**[2] uniforms for the first time.

Kiara likes her new duds "'cause they're pretty." Her mother, Alelia, is happy because "it's much easier to find the clothes in the morning." Educa-

1

2

VOCABULARY DEVELOPMENT
The words in **boldface** are defined at the bottom of the page. Underline the words as you read them.

---

1. demure: proper; prim   **2. don:** to put on

SUMMARIZE: Summarize the reasons in paragraphs 2 and 3 in favor of school uniforms.

_____

_____

TEACHING TIP Have students circle the effects of the trend toward requiring schoolchildren to wear uniforms. Then ask them to double-underline the causes of the trend. Have them list at least two additional causes or effects that Wingert has not mentioned and then prepare a response to Wingert's essay in which they either support the trend or oppose it.

tors in New York and around the country believe uniforms could also solve some of the toughest problems facing schools today. In the aftermath of the Littleton, Colorado, shootings, many see dress codes as a cheap and simple way to make schools safer. This fall, Los Angeles, Chicago, Miami, Boston, Houston, Cleveland, and Washington, D.C., all have a majority of their students in uniforms. "It's spreading to the suburbs now," says Vince Ferrandino, president of the National Association of Elementary School Principals. "It's become a national **phenomenon**."[3]

Proponents[4] say clothing rules eliminate the baggy gang-inspired look 3 that makes it easy for students to smuggle in weapons, drugs, and other banned items. Dress codes also make it easier to spot intruders. "Last week this boy walked into our cafeteria in jeans, and we knew right away he wasn't one of ours," says Ramond Rivera, an elementary-school principal in El Paso, Texas, whose students wear uniforms. "We immediately escorted him out."

Researchers say there's very little hard evidence that uniforms improve 4 students' behavior or academic success. They do, however, affect student attitudes. One of the best studies compared two middle schools in Charleston County, South Carolina, one with a uniform policy, the other without. A survey of more than 300 sixth to eighth graders revealed that uniformed students gave their schools higher scores. "Although school uniforms do not represent a **panacea**[5] for all society's problems," says the lead researcher, Richard K. Murray, a principal in Dorchester, South Carolina, "research now shows that school uniforms do significantly affect student perceptions of school climate."

Keith King of the University of Cincinnati recently published a review 5 of research on the effectiveness of dress codes. He says that overall, students in uniforms "felt more like a team." That's important, King says, because "the No. 1 protective factor against school violence is having a student feel connected to his school and that he fits in."

IDENTIFY: Underline the sentences that identify a positive effect of uniforms in middle schools and high schools.

Uniforms are getting the most attention at middle and high schools, 6 where security and school unity are big issues, along with the extremes of current teen fashion: spaghetti-strap tanks, face painting, body piercing. "You'd be amazed at the amount of time administrators have been spending on what kids are wearing to school," says Susan Galletti, a middle-school specialist at the National Association of Secondary School Principals [NASSP]. "With uniforms, all that is eliminated, and they can spend more time on teaching and learning."

IDENTIFY: Underline the sentence that presents the courts' decision about uniforms in schools.

While some schools stick to traditional plaids and navy blue, others 7 allow polo shirts, chinos, and even capri pants. Still, teens in the **throes**[6] of adolescent rebellion often object and in a few cases, they've even sued for the freedom to choose their own clothes. "The older kids get, the more aware they are of their rights," says Stephen Yurek, general counsel of the NASSP. "If you try to restrict what they can say or wear, you'll start hearing that their rights are being violated." Yurek says the courts have made it clear

---

3. **phenomenon:** an occurrence or a circumstance   4. **proponents:** those in favor of something   5. **panacea:** a remedy for all problems or diseases; a cure-all
6. **throes:** a painful struggle

that students don't have the same rights inside school as they do outside; clothing requirements are not considered a violation of their freedom of expression if there's a **valid**[7] educational reason for imposing them. To avoid legal hassles, though, most schools will provide uniforms to poor students who can't afford to buy them, and many allow parents to opt out if they have religious objections.

Educators say the best way to get kids to accept uniforms is to start in the early grades. Noelle Ebright, sixteen, a student at Wilson High School in Long Beach, California, has been wearing a uniform for eight years. "I've slowly adapted to it," she says. This year, she says, "all I have to do is grab some khaki bottoms and a white shirt with a collar and I'm out of the house." Still, she admits, "if I had my personal preference, of course I would prefer not to wear one. Any kid would." **8**

Some adults sympathize. Norman Isaacs, principal of Millikan Middle School in Sherman Oaks, California, has resisted uniforms. He believes clothing gives teachers insights into what's happening with individual students. "Our counselors and teachers monitor the way kids are dressed," he says. "If we see a big change in the way a student dresses, that sends up a signal and tells us we need to address that person." **9**

Other critics say they fear the spread of uniforms will smother student creativity. But experienced educators have learned that kids often dream up truly inspired **loopholes**.[8] El Paso's Rivera remembers the girl who came to school wearing contact lenses that gave her the appearance of having yellow cat eyes. It wasn't a strict violation; no one had thought to include contacts in the dress code. Still, he says, "We had to put a stop to that. . . . It was a distraction to every kid in her class." And a real eye-opener for the principal. **10**

REFLECT: Wingert offers an example of a creative loophole. Based on your experience, what other loopholes might students create?

_____

_____

• •

SUMMARIZE AND RESPOND

In your reading journal or elsewhere, summarize the main point of "Uniforms Rule." Then, go back and check off the support for this idea. Next, write a brief summary of the essay. Finally, write a brief response to the reading. What did it make you think or feel? Do you have an opinion on the subject? Do you think wearing uniforms could result in better student behavior?

• •

CHECK YOUR COMPREHENSION

1. An alternate title for this essay could be

   a. "School Uniforms Kill Student Creativity."

   b. "Dress Codes and Public Schools."

   c. "School Uniforms and Student Behavior."

   d. "School Uniforms and Freedom of Expression."

---

7. valid: correct; supported by fact   **8. loopholes:** ways to get around a rule

2. The main point of this essay is that
   a. teenagers do not care what they wear to school.
   b. school uniforms have a positive effect on student attitudes.
   c. schools that require uniforms are stricter than schools that do not.
   d. wearing a school uniform cuts down on the time required to get ready for school in the morning.

3. According to research, what is one effect of wearing school uniforms?
   a. Uniforms make students feel as if they are part of a team and fit in.
   b. Uniforms make students feel as though they are in grade school.
   c. Students will always find loopholes in the dress code.
   d. Uniforms will cause an increase in body piercing.

4. Look back at the **boldface** vocabulary you underlined, and write sentences using the following words: *demure* (para. 1); *proponent* (3); *throes, valid* (7); *loophole* (10).

READ CRITICALLY

1. According to Wingert, what are the effects of wearing school uniforms? What has caused schools to adopt school uniform policies?

2. Why don't the courts consider requiring school uniforms a violation of students' freedom of expression? Do you agree or disagree with this view?

3. How can wearing school uniforms improve school safety?

4. Can you tell from the essay what Wingert's attitude toward school uniforms is? How would you describe the tone of the essay?

5. As a parent, how would you react if your child were required to wear a uniform to school? How would you react if you were required to wear a uniform to class? Is your response different, and if so, why?

WRITE

TIP For a sample cause/effect paragraph, see page 239.

WRITE A PARAGRAPH: Write a paragraph about what causes students at a particular grade level to feel alienated from their schools or classmates.

WRITE AN ESSAY: Write an essay that explores the possible effects of a high school dropping its uniform policy and allowing students to wear whatever they choose. If you addressed this issue in Summarize and Respond, feel free to use those ideas.

John Tierney

Yes, Money Can Buy Happiness

A well-known columnist for the *New York Times* since 1990, John Tierney has an extensive background in news writing. After graduating with a degree in American studies from Yale University, Tierney reported for a series of publications, including the *Bergen Record*, the *Washington Star*, and *Science* magazine. He then worked for several years as a freelance writer, reporting on six continents and publishing articles in more than fifteen national newspapers and magazines. As a columnist for the Science Times section of the *New York Times*, Tierney says he uses his blog "to check out new research and rethink conventional wisdom about science and society."

GUIDING QUESTION

In the essay, how does money buy happiness?

1   Yes, money can buy happiness, but probably not in the way you imagined. Spending it on yourself may not do much for your spirits, but spending it on others will make you happier, according to a report from a team of social psychologists in the new issue of *Science*.

2   The researchers **confirmed**[1] the joys of giving in three separate ways. First, by surveying a national sample of more than 600 Americans, they found that spending more on gifts and charity **correlated**[2] with greater happiness, whereas spending more money on oneself did not. Second, by tracking sixteen workers before and after they received profit-sharing bonuses, the researchers found that the workers who gave more of the money to others ended up happier than the ones who spent more of it on themselves. In fact, how the bonus was spent was a better predictor of happiness than the size of the bonus.

3   The final bit of evidence came from an experiment in which 46 students were given either $5 or $20 to spend by the end of the day. The ones who were instructed to spend the money on others—they bought toys for siblings, treated friends to meals, and made donations to the homeless—were happier at the end of the day than the ones who were instructed to spend the money on themselves.

4   "These experimental results," the researchers conclude, "provide direct support for our causal argument that spending money on others promotes happiness more than spending money on oneself." The social psychologists—Elizabeth Dunn and Lara Aknin of the University of British Columbia, Vancouver, and Michael Norton of Harvard Business School—also conclude that "how people choose to spend their money is at least as important as how much money they make."

5   I asked Dr. Dunn if she had any advice for readers on how much to spend on others. Her reply was, "I think even minor changes in spending

VOCABULARY DEVELOPMENT The words in **boldface** are defined at the bottom of the page. Underline the words as you read them.

IDEA JOURNAL Write about a time when you did something good for someone and how you felt afterward.

TEACHING TIP If you have discussed illustration, point out that paragraphs 2 and 3 use illustration.

SUMMARIZE: Summarize the three causes of positive feelings.

_____

_____

---

1. confirm: to prove the truth   **2. correlate:** to be related to or have a connection with habits can make a difference. In our experiment with college students, we found that spending just $5 **prosocially**[3] had a **substantial**[4] effect on happiness at the end of the day. But I wouldn't say that there's some fixed amount that everyone should spend on others. Rather, the best bet might be for people to think about whether they can push themselves to devote just a little more of their money to helping others."

But why wouldn't people be doing that already? Because most people   6
don't realize the personal benefits of charity, according to Dr. Dunn and her colleagues. When the researchers surveyed another group of students, they found that most of the respondents predicted that personal spending would make them happier than spending the money on other people.

REFLECT: Do you agree that charity always makes people feel better?

_____

_____

Perhaps that will change as word of these experiments circulates—   7
although that prospect raises another question, which I put to Dr. Dunn: If people started giving away money chiefly in the hope of making themselves happier, as opposed to wanting to help others, would they still **derive**[5] the same happiness from it?

"This is a fascinating question," she replied. "I certainly hope that tell-   8
ing people about the emotional benefits of prosocial spending doesn't completely erase these benefits; I would hate to be responsible for the **downfall**[6] of joyful prosocial behavior."

REFLECT: Answer the questions in paragraph 9.

_____

_____

Do you have any theories on the joys of giving? Any reports of your   9
own experiments? Or any questions you'd like to ask the researchers? Dr. Dunn, in keeping with the results of her experiments, has generously offered to provide some answers free of charge.

• •

SUMMARIZE AND RESPOND

In your reading journal or elsewhere, summarize the main point of "Yes, Money Can Buy Happiness." Then, go back and check off the support for this idea. Next, write a brief summary of the essay. Finally, write a brief response to the reading. How do you see the relationship between money and happiness in your own life, both now and as you look toward the future?

• •

CHECK YOUR COMPREHENSION

1.   An alternate title for this essay could be

  a. "Profit-Sharing Proves Profitable for Employees and Employers."

  b. "Spending Money on Others Can Increase Your Happiness."

  c. "Charity Should Begin and End at Home."

  d. "Study Finds That Money Is the Key to Happiness."

---

3. prosocially: in a manner that is intended to benefit another person, as in cases of helping or sharing   **4. substantial:** significant   **5. derive:** to get something from
6. downfall: a loss of power or status

2. The main point of this essay is that

  (**a.**) people are often happier when they spend money on others, rather than on themselves.

  b. people are beginning to give more money to charity because they realize that such generosity is a source of happiness.

  c. scientists are fascinated by the spending habits of the American people.

  d. even in a bad economy, people should continue their charitable giving.

3. According to the article, why don't people spend more money on others than they already do?

  a. Human beings are selfish and therefore do not like giving.

  b. People mostly like to be charitable during the holiday season.

  c. College students do not make a good sample for a scientific study.

  (**d.**) Most people do not realize the personal benefits of charity.

4. Look back at the **boldface** vocabulary you underlined, and write sentences using these words: *confirm* (para. 2); *substantial* (5); *derive* (7); *downfall* (8).

· ·

READ CRITICALLY

1. Tierney suggests in his opening paragraph that money can buy happiness, "but probably not in the way you imagined." Do you find the results of these studies surprising? Why or why not?

2. Tierney writes that spending money "on yourself may not do much for your spirits." How do people generally spend money to change their mood or lift their "spirits"?

3. Social psychologists in the article conclude that "how people spend their money is at least as important as how much money they make" (para. 4). Does this seem true to you? What other factors might social psychologists take into account, as far as discovering the relationship between money and happiness?

4. How does Tierney structure this essay, in terms of explaining the experiments, the conclusions, and their implications?

5. What apparently common human flaw or flaws does this article highlight in paragraph 8?

· ·

WRITE

WRITE A PARAGRAPH: The scientist in the article says she hopes people will "think about whether they can push themselves to devote just a little more of their money to helping others." Will this article change your attitude about charity or cause you to alter your behavior in any way? Write a paragraph explaining your answer.

WRITE AN ESSAY: Tierney's article explores "the emotional benefits of prosocial spending." Have you ever experienced these "benefits"? Write an essay in which you examine an experience where you spent money on or helped others. Did the action cause the effects that scientists found in their studies?

50

Argument

The essays in this chapter use argument to make clear their positions on the subject of snitching. There are three essays, one written by a student and two written by professional writers. Each of the three writers offers a different viewpoint on the subject of snitching, and as you read, pay close attention to how each writer interprets what snitching is. Consider how the writer achieves the four basics of good argument that are listed below and discussed in Chapter 18 of this book.

Four Basics of Good Argument

1   It takes a strong and definite position.
2   It gives good reasons and supporting evidence to defend the position.
3   It considers opposing views.
4   It has enthusiasm and energy from start to finish.

Your instructor may assign one, two, or all three of the essays, and each is followed by a series of questions and writing assignments based on the individual essay. However many of the essays your instructor assigns, ask yourself the following questions as you read each one:

1.   How does the author define snitching?

2.   What effect does the author think snitching has on the community?

3.   Is the author in favor of snitching or against it?

4.   What is the basic support for each author's opinion?

Answering all four questions for each of the readings will allow you to build your own understanding of the issue and have a body of information to work with if your instructor assigns the writing assignment on page 725 that draw on all three of the essays. You can compare the authors' arguments to form your own position and write your own argument. Pay particular attention to the way that Alexandra Natapoff, the author of the third essay, talks about snitching: Her interpretation of it differs from Robert Phansalkar's and Bill Maxwell's interpretations.

Whatever position you take on the subject, you will have learned to look beyond the surface to more fully understand how to examine an issue before making a well-formed argument that puts forth your own stand on the issue.

Robert Phansalkar
Stop Snitchin' Won't Stop Crime

 Robert Phansalkar graduated from the University of Wisconsin in 2007 with degrees in languages and cultures of Asia and political science and is currently pursuing a J.D. from Fordham Law School. He wrote the essay "Stop Snitchin' Won't Stop Crime" when he was a student at UW, and it first appeared in the UW student newspaper, the *Badger Herald Weekly*. Of the piece, he says he explores "issues facing minorities in law enforcement," a topic that connects to his overall concerns as a writer: "Law and social justice issues interest me the most because these play off of fundamental issues of fairness. It is rare to find someone who does not have an opinion, developed or not, on these issues."

GUIDING QUESTION
How would Phansalkar define snitching, and what is his position on the Stop Snitchin' movement?

VOCABULARY DEVELOPMENT
The words in **boldface** are defined at the bottom of the page. Underline the words as you read them.

IDEA JOURNAL Write about a time you "snitched" on someone.

The "Stop Snitchin'" movement is a reaction to racial profiling and   1 racism in police actions. Now widespread and promoted by many, it began with a homemade DVD called *Stop Snitching*, hosted by a rapper known as Skinny Suge. It featured a number of rappers and others who threatened violence against people who gave the police any information about crimes. Among the people in the DVD was Carmelo Anthony, an NBA star, whose participation helped the DVD gain media attention. Now there are Web sites, T-shirts, and lots of other items that promote the Stop Snitchin' campaign. The movement **maintains**[1] that until the system reflects real justice, minorities should willfully avoid helping police with ongoing investigations, regardless of circumstance or crime. While many support the movement, maintaining that silence in the face of injustice is more honorable than co-

---

1. maintain: to believe; to state

operation, the cities suffer as witnesses fail to give any information they have about crimes. Stop Snitchin' does not stop crime.

While the movement has developed into rappers' sales and perceived "**street cred**,"[2] it has also blossomed into an unfortunate force that **hinders**[3] crime prevention. For example, Cameron Giles, known as Cam'ron or Killa Cam, was shot multiple times during an attempted carjacking, but he refused to give police information about the suspects. Avoiding the police encourages the very kind of lawlessness that is all too common in cities **riddled**[4] with gang violence. At the movement's Web site, stopsnitchin.com, rappers and others complain about their experiences in rough, violent neighborhoods, but they promote it with Stop Snitchin'.

2

It is difficult to connect how refusing to contribute to investigations helps the problem. Even if the Stop Snitchin' movement isn't aiming to lower crime rates, not cooperating with police certainly does not help the neighborhoods that these rappers grew up in, which makes their support of the movement all the more confusing. If people actually want to reduce gang violence in the neighborhoods and have a shot at breaking boundaries and moving beyond poverty and violence, why allow criminals to run wild? Why not work to promote successful and peaceful neighborhoods? Most of the rappers and other supporters of Stop Snitchin' believe that the justice system is based on racism and that cooperating with the police actually threatens innocent people because snitchers lie to save themselves.

3

IDENTIFY: Where does the author acknowledge the opposing view?

_____

_____

Certainly, racism in law enforcement practices is a **legitimate**[5] issue that needs to be addressed, but simply not cooperating with the institutions that exist to protect people is a **ludicrous**[6] solution. Turning your back on the system ensures one thing: The system will continue to not work for you. Expecting change to happen when you look away is precisely the kind of **mentality**[7] that rarely accomplishes anything and draws more heat than if you were working positively to effect change in your community.

4

Instead of rapping about not snitching on real criminals, why not rap about not committing crimes? Why not rap about improving the systems of inequality and injustice through positive action? Stop Snitchin' doesn't answer any of these questions, and even though the movement **defies**[8] the logic of self-preservation, it continues because nobody has the courage to stand up and say what really happened.

5

SUMMARIZE: What is the author's basic argument? Do his reasons support his position?

_____

_____

• •

SUMMARIZE AND RESPOND

In your writing journal or elsewhere, summarize the main point of "Stop Snitchin' Won't Stop Crime." Then, go back and check off the support for this idea. Next, write a brief summary of the essay. Finally, write a brief response to the reading. Why would a campaign like "Stop Snitchin'" be popular or persuasive?

2. street cred: trustworthiness and value as seen by young, urban people, especially in hip-hop culture   **3. hinder:** to cause difficulties or delays   **4. riddled:** spread throughout   **5. legitimate:** real; valid   **6. ludicrous:** laughable   **7. mentality:** a way of thinking   **8. defy:** to go against; to disagree with

● ●

CHECK YOUR COMPREHENSION

1. An alternate title for this essay could be

   a. "Turning Your Back on the System Ensures More Crime and Injustice."

   b. "High-Crime Communities Need Jobs and Schools, Not Snitches."

   c. "Hip-Hop Stars and Athletes Must Strive to Be Better Role Models."

   d. "Silence in the Face of Injustice Is More Honorable Than Cooperation."

2. The main point of this essay is that

   a. too many people are using the Internet to promote illegal behavior.

   b. racism is not a problem in the United States, although many people claim it still exists.

   c. refusing to cooperate with the police will not change the legal system or prevent crime.

   d. snitches threaten innocent people because they often lie to save themselves.

3. According to the writer, rappers might have a more positive effect if they would

   a. rap about fixing inequalities and work to create peaceful neighborhoods.

   b. discourage people from snitching, even though this will make cities less safe.

   c. join with professional athletes to speak out against carjacking.

   d. stop complaining about racism.

4. Does this essay include the Four Basics of Good Argument? Why or why not?

5. Look back at the **boldface** vocabulary you underlined, and write sentences using these words: *maintain* (para. 1); *hinder* (2); *legitimate, mentality* (4); *defy* (5).

TIP For tools to build your vocabulary, visit the *Real Writing Student Center* at **bedfordstmartins.com/ realwriting**.

● ●

READ CRITICALLY

1. How would you state the thesis of Phansalkar's essay in your own words?

2. Does the writer acknowledge and address views other than his own? Where and how does he do this?

3. Who is the audience for this essay? What readers does the writer want to persuade? How do you know?

4. Why does Phansalkar include the example of rapper Cameron Giles (para. 2), who was shot during a carjacking? What point does it make?

5. Phansalkar ends his essay by questioning the "courage" of those who participate in or support the "Stop Snitchin'" campaign. Why does he do this? What effect does it have?

. . . .

WRITE

As Phansalkar writes, NBA player Carmelo Anthony participated in the "Stop Snitchin'" campaign. Do you think star athletes and other celebrities have an obligation to be law-abiding role models? Should society hold them to a higher standard than private citizens? Write a paragraph or an essay that takes a position on this issue.

. . . .

Bill Maxwell
Start Snitching

Bill Maxwell is an internationally syndicated columnist and editorial writer for the *St. Petersburg Times* in St. Petersburg, Florida. After receiving a B.A. from Bethune-Cookman College, he went on to earn a master's and a doctoral degree from the University of Chicago before he began teaching in 1973. His diverse background as an educator and a writer is evident in the many publications for which he has written, including the *Fort Pierce Tribune*, the *Gainesville Sun*, and the *St. Petersburg Times*. He wrote the essay "Start Snitching" in September 2007 for the *St. Petersburg Times* in response to the deaths of several black men from the community.

GUIDING QUESTION
What does Maxwell's Wall of Black Death represent to him? How does it relate to snitching?

1 Cedric "C. J." Mills. Isaiah Brooks. Tedric Maynor. Felicia Hines. Vinson Phillips. Kurt Anthony Bryant. Amuel Murph. Alfonso Williams. These names are forever **inscribed**[1] on my private "Wall of Black Death." My wall contains the names of black people killed by other black people, along with those believed to have been killed by fellow blacks, in the Tampa Bay area since May. I will update the **roster**[2] as soon as new deaths are reported. More are sure to follow. I do not have answers as to how to stop blacks from killing their **brethren**.[3] But I do have an answer for catching some, if not all, of these murderers. Snitch.

VOCABULARY DEVELOPMENT
The words in **boldface** are defined at the bottom of the page. Underline the words as you read them.

IDEA JOURNAL Are you surprised when you read about gang murders? Why or why not?

REFLECT: What effect does the list of names have?

_____

_____

1. inscribed: listed; written   **2. roster:** a list of people   **3. brethren:** brothers; men within the same race, nationality, or group

Nationwide, too many blacks refuse to help the police identify, find, 2
and arrest killers in their communities. To enjoy a decent quality of life in
their communities, blacks must begin to help the police. Studies show that
homicides,[4] especially unsolved homicides, **destabilize**[5] low-income communities. Needless to say, many of the nation's black communities have individuals and families with low incomes. Businesses that can provide jobs
for unemployed residents and provide the **amenities**[6] that other areas take
for granted are **wary**[7] of locating in black communities where homicide
rates are high.

IDENTIFY: What kinds of evidence does the author use?

_____

_____

A recent *St. Petersburg Times* article reported that a group of Tampa 3
black residents have organized an effort to stop the "don't snitch" culture
that permits killers to remain free. Many of the organizers are related in some
way to a youngster killed by a fellow black. Consider this sobering portrait of
blacks and homicide and other serious crimes from a recent U.S. Bureau of
Justice Statistics report: Although blacks comprised only 13 percent of the
population in 2005, they were victims of about 49 percent of all homicides.
The bureau estimated that 16,400 murders occurred in the United States in
2005. Of that number, 8,000 victims were black, 93 percent of those victims
were killed by other blacks, and 77 percent of those murders involved firearms. Most black victims were between ages 17 and 29.

Many people, including police officials I have spoken with, say that fear 4
prevents most blacks from snitching. I agree that some residents remain silent out of fear, but I suspect that the fear factor receives too much weight.
I have come to believe that an untold number of blacks have grown as insensitive to black-on-black murders as they have to other black-on-black
crimes. For one thing, the high number of homicides in their communities
have made many blacks **inured**[8] to all but the most sensational killings that
receive a lot of press.

REFLECT: Does the information in paragraphs 4 and 5
surprise you?

_____

_____

"I expect somebody to shoot somebody every week around here," a St. 5
Petersburg woman who lives in a **predominantly**[9] black neighborhood said
a few weeks ago when I asked if she had known a man who had been killed
recently. "I don't go near my windows at night. They shoot guns around
here all the time. I don't pay attention when they say somebody got shot. I
just try to make sure it won't be me one of these days."

I am not a **sociologist**,[10] but I suspect that many blacks in high-crime 6
communities have all the symptoms of the abused person **syndrome**:[11] We
have been cruel toward one another for so long we have **internalized**[12] the
belief that such cruelty is normal. Those of us who have internalized the
cruelty think nothing of treating other blacks likewise, thus **perpetuating**[13]
the cycle without **apparent**[14] end. Each day I open the newspaper and
switch on TV news, I **brace**[15] myself for yet another murder. With each killing, I feel sadness, regret, helplessness, anger, and shame—shame of being
associated with such people in any way.

4. homicides: murders   **5. destabilize:** to make unsteady or cause something to fail
6. amenities: comforts, conveniences, or pleasures   **7. wary:** cautious   **8. inured:**
accustomed to or used to   **9. predominantly:** mainly   **10. sociologist:** a person
who studies the origin, development, and other aspects of human society   **11. syndrome:** a disorder or an illness   **12. internalize:** to make something part of your core
beliefs or attitudes   **13. perpetuate:** to continue   **14. apparent:** obvious
15. brace: to prepare for

Because I regularly write about this issue, I receive a lot of hate mail   7
from both whites and blacks. White letter-writers remind me that blacks are
"animals" and "cause all of America's social problems." Black letter-writers
see me as the "enemy of the people" and a "sell-out" because I condemn
blacks for killing one another without taking into account the nation's history of racism. To whites, I have nothing to say. To blacks, I have one message: We need to start snitching. Only we can stop black-on-black murders.
Until then, I will be adding names to the Wall of Black Death.

REFLECT: Does the race of
the author have an effect on
the way you read this essay?
Why or why not?

_____

_____

SUMMARIE AND RESPOND

In your reading journal or elsewhere, summarize the main point of "Start Snitching." Then, go back and check off the support for this idea. Next, write a brief
summary of the essay. Finally, write a brief response to the reading. Maxwell
speculates that "an untold number of blacks" have become "insensitive to black-
on-black murders." As a result, they refuse to snitch. What other reasons would
you suggest account for this reluctance to work with the police?

CHECK YOUR COMPREHENSION

1. An alternate title for this essay could be

   a. "Snitching and the 'Wall of Black Death.'"

   b. "Black Communities Must Provide More Jobs and Amenities."

   c. "Stop Racist Hate Mail."

   d. "Most Black Murder Victims Are between 17 and 29."

2. The main point of this essay is that

   a. only the most sensational killings now capture the attention of African Americans.

   b. Maxwell lives in fear of speaking out about snitching because he gets
   so much angry mail.

   c. white people have become indifferent to the crime and violence in
   America's black communities.

   d. African Americans must cooperate with police to help reduce black-
   on-black violence.

3. According to Maxwell, what is one of the reasons African Americans do
not snitch?

   a. They have been persuaded by calls from black celebrities and athletes to avoid speaking to the police about black-on-black crime.

   b. The police do not listen to the concerns of people living in predominantly black neighborhoods.

   c. People in black communities prefer to enforce their own justice when
   they catch suspected criminals and do not wish to bother the police.

   d. Many blacks are insensitive to black-on-black murders, having internalized the belief that such behavior is "normal."

4. Look back at the **boldface** vocabulary you underlined, and write sentences using these words: *wary* (para. 2); *predominantly* (5); *syndrome, perpetuate, apparent* (6).

. . . .

READ CRITICALLY

1. Why does Maxwell open his essay with this list of names? Do you find the introduction effective? Why or why not?

2. What effects does black-on-black violence have on communities, according to Maxwell?

3. How does the quotation in paragraph 5 help Maxwell's argument? Which of his claims does it support?

4. Does the writer acknowledge or address competing points of view in his essay?

5. In the concluding paragraph, Maxwell refers to his hate mail and claims that he has "nothing to say" to the whites who write him hate mail. Why do you think he refuses to address these letter writers?

. . . .

WRITE

In the conclusion of his essay, Maxwell refers to the "hate mail" he receives from two general categories of letter writers. Write a paragraph or essay that addresses and responds to the claims of either one of these groups. How would you engage them in a civil and meaningful discussion?

. . . .

Alexandra Natapoff

Bait and Snitch: The High Cost of Snitching for Law Enforcement

Alexandra Natapoff is a law professor at Loyola Law School in Los Angeles, California, where she teaches criminal law and criminal procedure. She graduated cum laude with a B.A. from Yale University and earned her J.D. with distinction at Stanford Law School. Before becoming a professor, Natapoff worked as an assistant federal public defender in Baltimore, Maryland; while there, she founded the Urban Law & Advocacy Project. As a scholar and writer, Natapoff is interested in the criminal justice system, as well as race and the law and administrative law. She is considered "a nationally recognized expert on snitching in the criminal justice system."

GUIDING QUESTION
How does Natapoff define snitching?

From Baltimore to Boston to New York; in Pittsburgh, Denver, and Milwaukee, kids are sporting the **ominous**[1] fashion statement, "Stop Snitchin'," prompting local fear, outrage, and fierce arguments over crime. Several trials have been disrupted by the T-shirts; some witnesses refuse to testify. With cameo appearances in the growing **controversy**[2] by NBA star Carmelo Anthony of the Denver Nuggets and the rapper Lil Kim, snitching is making urban culture headlines.

The "Stop Snitchin'" T-shirt drama looks, at first, like a **dust-up**[3] over a simple **counterculture**[4] message launched by some urban criminal **entrepreneurs**;[5] that friends don't snitch on friends. But it is, in fact, a symptom of a more **insidious**[6] reality that has largely escaped public notice.

For the last 20 years, state and federal governments have been creating criminal snitches and setting them loose in poor, high-crime communities. The **backlash**[7] against snitches reflects a growing national recognition that snitching is dangerous public policy—producing bad information, endangering innocent people, letting dangerous criminals off the hook, compromising the **integrity**[8] of police work, and **inciting**[9] violence and distrust in socially **vulnerable**[10] neighborhoods.

The heart of the snitching problem lies in the secret deals that police and prosecutors make with criminals. In investigating drug offenses, police and prosecutors rely heavily—and sometimes exclusively—on criminals willing to trade information about other criminals in exchange for **leniency**.[11] Many snitches avoid arrest altogether, thus continuing to use and deal drugs and commit other crimes in their neighborhoods, while providing information to the police. As drug **dockets**[12] swell and police and prosecutors become increasingly dependent on snitches, high-crime communities are filling up with these active criminals who will turn in friends, family, and neighbors in order to "work off" their own crimes.

Critics of the T-shirts tend to dismiss the "stop snitching" sentiment as pro-criminal and antisocial, a subcultural expression of misplaced loyalty. But the T-shirts should be **heeded**[13] as evidence of a failed public policy. Snitching is an **entrenched**[14] law-enforcement practice that has become **pervasive**[15] due to its crucial role in the war on drugs. This practice is favored not only by police and prosecutors, but by legislatures: **Mandatory**[16] minimum sentences and restrictions on judges make snitching one of the only means for defendants to negotiate in the face of rigid and **drastic**[17]

---

1 **VOCABULARY DEVELOPMENT** The words in **boldface** are defined at the bottom of the page. Underline the words as you read them.

IDEA JOURNAL Write about a law or practice that you think is unfair.

2

3 **IDENTIFY:** How does the author define snitching?

_____

_____

4 **IDENTIFY:** Check the reasons the author gives to show that snitching is a bad practice.

5

---

1. **ominous:** threatening   2. **controversy:** an argument; a conflict of opinion
3. **dust-up:** a fight   4. **counterculture:** opposed to established culture   5. **entrepreneur:** a person who starts or manages a business   6. **insidious:** dangerous while appearing harmless   7. **backlash:** a strong or sudden violent reaction toward something
8. **integrity:** morality, honesty, and legality   9. **inciting:** urging on; encouraging
10. **vulnerable:** easily harmed   11. **leniency:** mildness; softness; tolerance
12. **docket:** a list of legal cases to be tried   13. **heed:** to pay attention to   14. **entrenched:** deeply dug in; secure   15. **pervasive:** widespread   16. **mandatory:** required   17. **drastic:** extreme

sentences. But the policy has turned out to be a **double-edged sword**.[18] Nearly every drug offense involves a snitch, and snitching is increasingly displacing more traditional police work, such as undercover operations and independent investigation.

According to some agents and prosecutors, snitching is also slowly crippling law enforcement: "Informers are running today's drug investigations, not the agents," says veteran DEA [Drug Enforcement Administration] agent Celerino Castillo. "Agents have become so dependent on informers that the agents are at their mercy." 6

The government's traditional justification for creating criminal snitches— "we-need-to-flip-little-fishes-to-get-to-the-Big-Fish"—is at best an ideal and mostly the **remnant**[19] of one. Today, the government lets all sorts of criminals, both big and little, trade information to escape punishment for nearly every kind of crime, and often the snitches are more dangerous than the targets. 7

Snitching thus puts us right **through the looking glass**:[20] Criminals direct police investigations while avoiding arrest and punishment. Nevertheless, snitching is ever more popular with law enforcement: It is easier to "flip" defendants and turn them into snitches than it is to fight over their cases. For a criminal system that has more cases than it can prosecute, and more defendants than it can **incarcerate**,[21] snitching has become a convenient case-management tool for an institution that has bitten off more than it can chew. 8

And while the government's snitching policy has gone mostly unchallenged, it is both damaging to the justice system and socially expensive. Snitches are famously unreliable: A 2004 study by the Northwestern University Law School's Center on Wrongful Convictions reveals that 46 percent of wrongful death penalty convictions are due to snitch misinformation— making snitches the leading cause of wrongful conviction in capital cases. Jailhouse snitches routinely **concoct**[22] information; the system gives them every **incentive**[23] to do so. Los Angeles snitch Leslie White infamously avoided punishment for his crimes for years by **fabricating**[24] confessions and **attributing**[25] them to his cellmates. 9

REFLECT: Why is this paragraph's evidence persuasive?

_____

_____

Snitches also undermine law-enforcement legitimacy—police who rely on and protect their informants are often perceived as favoring criminals. In a growing number of public **fiascos**,[26] snitches actually invent crimes and criminals in order to provide the government with the information it demands. In Dallas, for example, in the so-called "fake drug scandal," paid informants set up innocent Mexican immigrants with fake drugs (gypsum) while police falsified drug field tests in order to inflate their drug-bust statistics. 10

Finally, as the T-shirt controversy illustrates, snitching worsens crime, violence, and distrust in some of the nation's most socially vulnerable com- 11

---

18. double-edged sword: something that can have both good and bad consequences **19. remnant:** a piece or part of   **20. through the looking glass:** a place or situation where things happen in a way that is the opposite of expectations   **21. incarcerate:** to put in jail   **22. concoct:** to make up or invent something   **23. incentive:** a reason to do **24. fabricate:** to make up or invent someone   **26. fiasco:** a complete failure   **25. attribute:** to give credit to munities. In the poorest neighborhoods, vast numbers of young people are in contact with the criminal justice system. Nearly every family contains someone who is in prison, under supervision, or has a criminal record. In these communities, the law-enforcement policy of pressuring everyone to snitch can have the **devastating**[27] effect of tearing families and social networks apart. **Ironically,**[28] these are the communities most in need of positive role models, strong social institutions, and good police-community relations. Snitching undermines these important goals by setting criminals loose, creating distrust, and compromising police integrity.

The "Stop Snitchin'" T-shirts have drawn local fire for their perceived threat to law-abiding citizens who call the police. But in the outrage over that perceived threat, the larger message of the shirts has been missed: Government policies that favor criminal snitching harm the communities most in need of law-enforcement protection.

12 **ANALYZE:** How are the author's opinions different from Phansalkar's (pp. 714–15)?

_____

_____

While snitching will never be **abolished,**[29] the practice could be substantially improved, mostly by lifting the veil of secrecy that shields law-enforcement practices from public scrutiny. As things stand, police and prosecutors can cut a deal with a criminal; turn him into a snitch or cut him loose; forgive his crimes or resurrect them later; release him into the community; or decide to pick him up. They do all this at their discretion, without legal rules, in complete secrecy, with no judicial or public accountability. As a result, we have no idea whether snitching even reduces crime or actually increases it, and we can only guess at the collateral harms it imposes on high-crime communities.

13

The government should reveal snitching's real costs, including data on how many snitches are released into high-crime neighborhoods and what sorts of snitch crimes are forgiven. The government should also be required to establish the concrete benefit of a policy that releases some criminals to catch others, by accounting for how much crime actually gets stopped or solved by snitch information. Only then can we rationally evaluate how much government-sponsored snitching makes sense. Until we can know the real value of snitching, the T-shirts remain an important reminder that this particular cure for crime may be as bad as the disease.

14 **REFLECT:** Does the author present a good argument? Has she changed your mind?

_____

_____

• •

SUMMARIZE AND RESPOND

In your reading journal or elsewhere, summarize the main point of "Bait and Snitch: The High Cost of Snitching for Law Enforcement." Then, go back and check off the support for this idea. Next, write a brief summary of the essay. Finally, write a brief response to the reading. The writer discusses the popularity of "Stop Snitchin'" T-shirts, which some say are pro-criminal and antisocial. Why do you think that crime and criminals—whether organized crime, "urban criminal entrepreneurs," or even western outlaws—have had such a lasting appeal in American popular culture?

27. devastating: overwhelming; destructive   **28. ironically:** in a way that goes against expectations or a desired outcome   **29. abolish:** to end

. . . .

CHECK YOUR COMPREHENSION

1. An alternate title for this essay could be
    a. "The United States Needs to Build More Prisons."
    b. "Snitching Undermines Law Enforcement and Harms Communities."
    c. "Law Enforcement Authorities Must Take Steps to Ban 'Stop Snitchin'' T-Shirts."
    d. "Too Many Snitches Cut Deals with the Police and Escape Justice."

2. The main point of this essay is that
    a. the U.S. justice system is weak, which means that too many criminals go unpunished.
    b. the police and other legal authorities are overwhelmed by the number of drug offenders.
    c. policies that favor criminal snitching harm the legal system and do damage to many communities.
    d. snitching is an unfortunate but necessary part of our justice system.

3. According to Natapoff, the heart of the snitching problem lies in
    a. the communities that choose to protect criminals rather than bring them to justice.
    b. American prisons, which are overcrowded.
    c. police officers, judges, and politicians who incarcerate too many innocent people.
    d. the secret deals that police and prosecutors make with criminals.

4. Look back at the **boldface** vocabulary you underlined, and write sentences using these words: *controversy* (para. 1); *integrity* (3); *mandatory* (5); *concoct* (9); *abolish* (13).

. . . .

READ CRITICALLY

1. Natapoff argues that critics of the "Stop Snitchin'" T-shirts misunderstand their meaning. What is the misunderstanding? What do the T-shirts actually represent, according to Natapoff?

2. In paragraph 3, the writer claims that the practice of using "criminal snitches" hurts the "integrity of police work." What do you think that means?

3. The writer argues that the reliance on snitches has led to "public fiascos" (para. 10). How does she support this claim?

4. How does Natapoff use statistics in this essay, and how do they support her argument?

5. What practical steps does Natapoff propose at the conclusion of this essay? Does the essay convince you that they are necessary? Why or why not?

WRITE

The immediate focus of this essay is the role of snitching in the police and criminal justice system. But the figure of the "snitch," "rat," informant, or even "tattletale" has almost always been one that many people dislike. Why do you think that is the case, even if such informants and "snitches" can help bring criminals to justice or, more generally, stop bad things from happening? Write a paragraph or essay that addresses these issues.

WRITE USING READINGS

Write an essay either in favor of or against snitching, drawing upon the opinions and evidence given in the essays by Phansalkar, Maxwell, and Natapoff. You may want to quote directly from any of the three essays or paraphrase their arguments. Whichever position you take, you should take the opposing position into consideration by referring to one of the authors who disagrees with your opinion. In your concluding paragraph, review the reasons you have given to support your position.

TIP For more on quoting and paraphrasing, see Chapter 20.

Appendix A: Succeeding on Tests

Adam Moss
DeVry, South Florida

This appendix will help you prepare for any testing situation, increasing your confidence and your chances of success.

Understand Testing Myths and Facts

Test makers do not set out to create test questions that will trip you up or confuse you. That is one of many common myths about tests. Here are some others.

MYTH: Test makers pick obscure topics for reading passages to confuse you.

FACT: Test makers often avoid very common topics because they do not want students who are familiar with those topics to have an unfair advantage.

MYTH: Tests often have hidden patterns, and if you can just figure out these patterns, you will get a good score.

FACT: Tests answers rarely follow a pattern, and if they do, the pattern is often hard to figure out, and you will waste time trying. The best strategy is good preparation.

MYTH: Some people are just good at taking tests, but I am not one of them.

FACT: Students who are good at tests are usually those who have learned to manage their anxiety and to be "test wise": They know what to find out about the test, they know how to study, and they know how to read and answer test questions. In other words, they are informed about and prepared for tests. You, too, can be a good test taker if you learn the strategies that are discussed in the pages that follow.

Understand What to Do Before and During Tests

Before the Test

To do well on a test, take the time to gather information that will help you study effectively.

Ask Questions

Although your instructors will not give you the test questions in advance, most will give you general information that will help you prepare. Ask a few key questions, and write down the answers.

- What subjects are on the test or what chapters are covered? If the test has more than one part, do you have to take all the parts or just some?

- What kinds of questions appear on the test? Question types include multiple choice, true/false, matching, short answer, and essay. Many tests combine several types of questions.

- How much time do you have for the entire test? How much time do you have for each section? Are there breaks between sections?

- What should you review? The text? Handouts? Lecture notes? Something else?

- Is the test paper-and-pencil or computerized? If it will be paper-and-pencil, practice that format. If it will be computerized, practice that. In some cases, your teacher may be able to provide or refer you to sample tests on paper or on a computer. See also the suggestions in the next section.

- What materials are you required or allowed to bring? Do you need pens, pencils, or both? Can you use notes or the textbook? Are you allowed to use a calculator? Do you need to bring an ID? Are you required to provide your own scratch paper?

- What score do you need to achieve to pass, and are you allowed to retake the test?

- For objective tests, will you be penalized for guessing answers?

Study Effectively

Once you have collected information about the test you are about to take, write out a plan of what you need to study and follow it. The following tips will also help you study effectively.

- Choose a good place to study. Find a straight-backed chair and table in the dining room or kitchen and study there, or study in the library or another quiet place with similar conditions. Be careful about studying in bed or on the sofa; you may fall asleep or lose concentration.

- Use test-specific study materials like "prep" books and software, if they are available. These materials often include old, real test questions and usually have full practice tests. Be sure to get an up-to-date book to ensure that any recent changes to the test are covered. Also, your instructor may have practice tests. Note that this textbook has sample tests at the end of each grammar chapter, as well as cumulative Editing Review tests on pages 601–10. Additionally, grammar practices are available at **bedfordstmartins.com/realwriting** and on a CD-ROM available with this book, *Exercise Central to Go.*

- Visit Web sites with practice tests. Following are some sites that have samples of tests required in certain states: the CUNY/ACT Basic Skills Test, **www.lehman.edu/provost/enrollmentmgmt/testing/act.html**; the Florida College Basic Skills Exit Test, **net3.valenciacc.edu/pss/Grammar/FCBSET/fcbset_wr_01.htm**; Florida's College Level Academic Skills Test (CLAST), **www.dianahacker.com/bedhandbook6e/subpages/add_clast.html**; the Georgia Regents' Test, **www2.gsu.edu/~wwwrtp/index94.htm**; and the Texas Higher Education Assessment (THEA), **www.thea.nesinc.com**.

- Make up and answer your own test questions. Try to think like your instructor or the test writer.

- Take a test-preparation class if one is available. Many schools offer free or reduced-cost classes to students preparing for entrance or exit tests.

- If your test is going to be timed, try to do a sample test within a time limit. Grab an egg timer from the kitchen and set it for a time similar to that of the test.

- Use all the study aids available to you: chapter reviews, summaries, or highlighted terms in your textbook; handouts from your instructor; study guides; and so on. Also, many schools have writing centers that offer tutoring or study-skills worksheets. Check out your school's resources. Your tuition pays for these services, so you should take advantage of them.

- Learn what study strategies work best for you. Some students find that copying over their notes is effective because they are doing something active (writing) as they review the material. Other students find that reading their notes aloud helps them to remember the ideas. Still others find that drawing a concept helps them remember it.

- Study with other students in your class. By forming a study group, you can share each other's notes and ideas.

- Don't give up! The key to studying well is often to study until you are "sick" of the material. Whatever pain you feel in studying hard will be offset by the happiness of doing well on the test.

Reduce Test Anxiety

Everyone gets test anxiety. The trick is to manage your nerves instead of letting them control you. Turn your nervousness into positive energy, which can sharpen your concentration. Also, the following tips can help.

- Study! Study! Study! No test-taking strategies or anxiety-reducing techniques can help if you do not know the material. Think about a job you do well. Why don't you get nervous when you do it, even under pressure? The answer is that you know how to do it. Similarly, if you have studied well, you will be more relaxed as you approach a test.

- Eat a light meal before the test; overeating can make you uncomfortable or sleepy. Consider including protein, which can help your brain work better. Do not consume too much caffeine or sugar, however. Be especially wary of soft drinks, because they contain both. Take a bottle of water with you if you are allowed to. Sipping water as you work will help you stay hydrated, especially during long testing periods.

- Take the test at a time that is good for you, if possible. For example, if you are a "morning person," take the test early in the day. With computerized testing, more and more schools offer flexible test schedules or individual appointments. If you can choose your testing time, do not take the test after a long day of work or if you are very tired.

- Get to the test early. Nothing is more stress-inducing than arriving late, and you might miss the valuable pretest instructions. Also, you may not be allowed to take the test at all if you arrive too late.

- Resist the urge to discuss the test with others before you begin. Anxiety can be contagious, and others who are less prepared can make you needlessly nervous.

- Be sure to breathe deeply, in through your nose and out through your mouth. When you get nervous, your breathing becomes rapid and shallow. By controlling your breathing, you can reduce your nervousness.

- Think positive thoughts. Do not think about how terrible it will be if poor test scores keep you from getting accepted into school, advancing to the next class, or getting a new job. Instead, remind yourself of how much you know and how well prepared you are. Harness your energy and believe in yourself.

During the Test

TIP For more tips on understanding test directions, see Chapter 1.

As the test begins, it is important to listen to any directions your instructor or test monitor gives. Resist the temptation to start flipping through the test as soon as you get it; if you are not paying attention, you might miss important instructions that are not included in the written directions.

Also, it is important to monitor your time. Many test takers lose track of time and then complain, "I didn't have time to finish." Do not let that happen to you. After you have listened to the directions, survey the whole test, unless you are told not to do so. This way, you will know how many parts the test has, what kinds of questions are asked, and, in some cases, how many points each part or question is worth. Then, make a time budget.

Look at one student's time budget.

	MINUTES (55 TOTAL)
Part 1: 10 multiple-choice questions (2 point each)	5
Part 2: 10 fill-ins (3 points each)	10
Part 3: 2 paragraphs to edit (10 points each)	15
Part 4: 1 paragraph to write (30 points)	20
Final check of work	5

Here is a good strategy for taking this test:

1. Do items in Parts 1 and 2 that you know the answers to; do not spend time on items for which you do not know the answer immediately. (However, if you are not penalized for guessing, you may want to fill in answers; you can always change them later.)

2. Move on to Part 3, making all the edits you can and leaving at least twenty minutes for Part 4.

3. Write the paragraph for Part 4. Reread it to fix any problems you see.

4. Go back and try to answer questions from Parts 1 and 2 that you were unsure of.

5. If you have time, do a final check of your work.

Do not work too slowly or too quickly. Spending too much time on questions can lead to "overthinking" and a loss of attention. You have only so much energy, so use it wisely. However, rushing is as big a problem as overthinking. Test designers sometimes make the first choice in a multiple-choice question appear correct, while the truly correct answer is presented later. This approach trips up students who do not take the time to read each question and answer carefully.

Understand How to Answer Different Types of Test Questions

The general strategies just described will help you on any test. However, it is equally important to develop strategies to attack specific types of questions. Following are some ways to approach typical kinds of questions.

Multiple Choice

-   Read the directions carefully. Most tests allow only one answer choice per question, but some tests allow multiple responses.

-   For each question, see if you can come up with an answer before looking at the answer choices.

- Be sure to read all answer choices. Answer A may seem correct, but B, C, or D may be a better answer.

- Use the process of elimination, ruling out those answers that you know are incorrect first. Your odds of guessing correctly will increase with every answer eliminated.

- Stick with your first choice unless you are sure it is wrong. Your initial thinking will often be correct.

- If there is no penalty for guessing, try to answer even those questions for which you are unsure of the answer. If there is a penalty, make an educated guess, a guess based on having narrowed the choices to one or two.

- Many students fear "all of the above" and "none of the above" questions, but you can actually use them to your advantage. If you know that any single answer is correct, you can eliminate "none of the above"; likewise, if you know that any single answer is incorrect, you can eliminate "all of the above." If you know that more than one answer is correct, you can safely choose "all of the above."

- Be sure to interpret questions correctly. A question that asks "Which of the following is not true?" is actually asking "Which of the following is false?" Consider the following example.

    Which of the following instruments does not belong in an orchestra?
    a. tympani drum
    b. cello
    c. electric guitar
    d. oboe

    The question is asking which instrument is *not* in an orchestra, but students who do not read carefully may miss the word *not* and choose incorrectly. The correct answer is C.

- Pay attention when there are two similar but opposite answers. The following example question is based on a reading passage not shown here.

    Which of the following is true based on the passage you have read?
    a. Drug abusers who enter treatment under legal pressure are as likely to benefit from it as those who enter treatment voluntarily.
    b. Drug abusers who enter treatment under legal pressure are less likely to benefit from it than are those who enter treatment voluntarily.
    c. Drug abusers who have committed crimes should be treated only in high-security facilities.
    d. Drug abusers can overcome their addictions more easily if they get treatment in isolated facilities.

Answer options A and B say the opposite things, so one of them must be eliminated as incorrect. In this case, A happens to be the correct answer.

■ Usually, you can eliminate two answers that say the same thing in different words. If one is true, the other must be too. You cannot choose both of them, unless the test allows you to select more than one answer.

> Upton Sinclair's novel *The Jungle* was famous for its stark view of what?
>
> a.   unsafe and filthy working conditions in the American meat-packing industry
> b.   the situation of poor and jobless Americans during the Great Depression
> c.   the events of the last days of the Vietnam War
> d.   working-class Americans and their plight during the Depression era

Answers B and D can clearly be eliminated because they contain the same idea. If one were to be correct, the other would automatically be correct as well. Eliminate these two choices. The correct answer is A.

■ Keep in mind that longer and more detailed answers are often the correct ones. Test makers may put less time and effort into creating the wrong answer choices. See the example below.

> One role of hemoglobin in the bloodstream is to
>
> a.   fight disease.
> b.   bind to oxygen molecules and carry them to cells.
> c.   help form blood clots.
> d.   carry proteins to cells.

Answer choice B is the longest and most detailed answer, and it is the correct choice. Always be sure, however, to read every answer option, for it is not always the case that the longest one is correct.

■ Be aware of absolute statements that include words like *all*, *always*, *every*, *everyone*, *never*, *none*, and *only*. They are rarely the correct answer. The following example question is based on a reading passage not shown here.

> Which of the following statements is true based on the reading passage?
>
> a.   Catheter-based infections are less treatable than other hospital infections.
> b.   Methicillin-resistant *Staphylococcus aureus* is always more serious than regular *Staphylococcus aureus*.

c. Methicillin-resistant *Staphylococcus aureus* is treatable, but fewer antibiotics work against it than against other staph infections.

d. Hand-washing plays a small role in preventing the spread of staph infections.

B contains the word "always," suggesting that there are no exceptions. This is not true; therefore, B can be eliminated. C happens to be the correct answer.

True-False

- You have a 50 percent chance of guessing correctly, so it is usually wise to guess on true-false questions.

- There are usually more true answers than false answers on a test. Start with the presumption that an item is true, and then look for information that may make it false.

- If any part of a question is false, the whole question is false. Students tend to focus on just the true section. Even though most of the statement below is correct, the mistake in the third name, which should read "*Santa Maria*," is enough to make the whole statement false.

    True or false? In 1492, Christopher Columbus reached the New World with three ships: the *Niña*, the *Pinta*, and the *Santa Dominga*.

- Be aware that statements with absolute words like *all*, *always*, *never*, and *none* are usually false (see p. A-7).

- However, "possibility" words like *most*, *often*, *probably*, *some*, *sometimes*, and *usually* often indicate true answers. Since penguins do not always live in cold climates, and the word *usually* allows for these exceptions, the following statement is true.

    True or false? Penguins usually live in cold climates.

- Beware of cause-and-effect statements that may seem true at first but that show a false cause. In the following example, it is true that a koala is both a marsupial and eats eucalyptus leaves, but it not a marsupial *because* it eats eucalyptus leaves.

    True or false? A koala bear is a marsupial because it eats eucalyptus leaves.

Reading Comprehension Questions

These questions are usually based on a paragraph (or paragraphs) that you have to read. Follow these tips for success:

- Read all the questions before reading the passage. This will help you pay attention to important points as you read.

- Understand that you must "read for speed." Reading passages are the number one time killer on tests. If you take too long to read, you will use up much of your time.

- On a related point, try to absorb whatever you can, and do not stop on any one word or idea. Chances are that the questions will not require a perfect understanding of the word(s) you are finding difficult.

- Take a "leap of faith" when answering reading comprehension questions. Sometimes, students will agonize over a question even if they are fairly sure they know the right answer. In this case, take an educated guess and move on.

Essay Questions and Timed Writing Assignments

Many students think essay questions are harder than other types of questions, but they actually offer a little more flexibility because there is not just one limited answer. There are, however, certain standards you need to follow. These are described in the following sections.

Understand the Essay Rubric

Most standardized or departmental essay tests have their own scales, called *rubrics*. Rubrics show what elements graders look for and rate in an essay answer or timed writing, and they often present the number of possible points for each element. Rubrics are often available from a college's testing center, writing center, or learning lab. Also, instructors often include scoring rubrics as part of the course syllabus.

Regardless of the particular rubric used, every essay test is graded based on similar fundamentals.

> **TIP** When considering the length of your answer, be especially careful with paragraphs. Some test graders penalize short paragraphs, even if they are well written.

Understand the Question

Every writing test comes with a topic or set of topics from which you must choose one. Read the topic(s) and directions and make sure you understand whether a single paragraph or a whole essay is required. Is there a minimum or maximum length for the paragraph or essay? How many words should it be? How much time do you have, and does that include "prewriting" time?

Then, read the question/topic carefully, looking for **key words** that tell you

- what subject to write on
- how to write about it
- how many parts your answer should have

Follow Key Writing Steps Using Standard Essay Structure

Once you understand the question or topic, plan your answer, using prewriting to get ideas and at least three major support points. (See Chapter 6.)

Introduction
Include a thesis sentence stating your main point.

Supporting paragraph 1
with topic sentence

Supporting paragraph 2
with topic sentence

Supporting paragraph 3
with topic sentence

Conclusion

As you begin to write, bear in mind that your test essay, just like other essays you write, should have the parts shown in the chart at the left. Follow this process to complete the essay:

1.   Try to write a scratch outline based on your prewriting. This should include your thesis statement and at least three support points. The outline doesn't have to be in complete sentences.

2.   Write an introduction, concluding with your thesis statement.

3.   Write your body paragraphs. Each paragraph should begin with a topic sentence based on the support points you wrote for step 1. You should include at least three minor supporting details in each body paragraph.

4.   Finish with a short concluding paragraph. It should refer back to your main point and make an observation.

5.   If you have time, revise and proofread your essay, looking for any grammar errors and other issues. Usually, it is acceptable to make corrections by crossing out words and neatly writing the correction above.

Use *Real Writing* to Succeed on Standardized Tests

Many standardized, departmental, and state exams (like those listed on p. A-3) test for the same basic skills, whether through multiple-choice questions, essay questions, or other items. Following is a list of typical skills tested and where you can get help in *Real Writing*.

SKILL	CHAPTER IN *REAL WRITING*
Writing/Essay Questions	
Using thesis statements and topic sentences (main ideas)	5
Using adequate and relevant support	6
Arranging ideas in a logical order	7
Writing unified sentences/paragraphs	9
Using effective transitions	9
Choosing appropriate words	34
Avoiding confused or misused words	35
Taking a position on an issue (typical in essay exams)	18
Reading	
Understanding readings	2 (and the "Readings for Writers" section of *Real Writing with Readings*)

Appendix B:
Solving Problems

Writing in the Real World/Solving a Problem (Writing Assignment 3 in Chapters 10–18) offers you the opportunity to solve real-world problems by working alone or as a part of a team. Your instructor will probably decide whether you will do these assignments independently or in groups.

Problem solving and teamwork are important in today's workplace as well as in your college courses and in everyday life, so this is great real-world practice.

This section will explain both what these skills are and how to use them effectively.

Problem Solving

Problem solving is the process of identifying a problem and figuring out a reasonable solution.

Problems range from minor inconveniences like finding a rip in the last clean shirt you have when you are running late to more serious problems such as being laid off from your job. While such problems disrupt our lives, they also give us opportunities to tackle difficult situations with confidence.

Too often people are paralyzed by problems because they do not have strategies for attacking them. However, backing away from a problem rarely helps solve it. When you know how to approach a challenging situation, you are better able to take charge of your life.

Problem solving consists of five basic steps, which can be used effectively by both individuals and groups of people.

The Problem-Solving Process

Understand the problem.

You should be able to say or write it in a brief statement or question.

EXAMPLE:

Your ten-year-old car needs a new transmission, which will cost at least $750. Do you keep the car or buy a new one?

Identify people or information that can help you solve the problem (resources).

EXAMPLES:

- Your mechanic
- Friends who have had similar car problems
- Car advice from print or Web sources

↓

List the possible solutions.

EXAMPLES:

- Pay for the transmission repair.
- Buy a new car.

↓

Evaluate the possible solutions.

1. Identify the steps each solution would require.
2. List possible obstacles for each solution (like money or time constraints).
3. List the advantages and disadvantages of the solutions.

EXAMPLES (considering only advantages and disadvantages):

- Pay for the transmission repair.

    Advantage: This option would be cheaper than buying a new car.

    Disadvantage: The car may not last much longer, even with the new transmission.

- Buy a new car.

    Advantage: You will have a reliable car.

    Disadvantage: This option is much more expensive.

↓

Choose the most reasonable solution, one that is realistic — the simpler the better. Be able to give reasons for your choice.

SOLUTION: Pay for the transmission repair.

REASONS: You do not have money for a new car, and you do not want to assume more debt. Opinions from two mechanics indicate that your car should run for three to five more years with the new transmission. At that point, you will be in a better position to buy a new car.

Teamwork

Teamwork is working with others to achieve a common goal. Working with others to solve a problem has many benefits: more possible solutions, more people to share the work, more ideas and perspectives. But effective teamwork involves more than simply meeting with people: You need to understand and apply good teamwork skills. For example, sports teams don't win merely because the individual players are talented; they win because the individual players pool their individual talents into a coordinated whole. Each player on the team works hard, but each player also supports and cooperates with other players. Players may also discuss strategies together to help ensure the team's success. The same is true of teamwork in other arenas as well.

Following are some basics to keep in mind when you are part of a team.

BASICS OF EFFECTIVE TEAMWORK

- The team establishes ground rules that ensure each person on the team can contribute.
- Members listen to each other and respect different points of view.
- Although one person may function as team leader, all individuals play an equal role and are equally appreciated.
- Members recognize that they must depend on one another.
- All members contribute and feel responsible for their own work because it affects the outcomes of the team's efforts.

Answers to Odd-Numbered Editing Exercises

Chapter 21

Practice 21-1, page 313

Possible answers: (1) rare, nest, of (3) complained, but, across, them (5) of, return, nest

Practice 21-2, page 315

Answers: **1.** Subject: company; prepositional phrase: without a chief executive officer **3.** Subject: people; prepositional phrase: on the short list of candidates **5.** Subject: man; prepositional phrase: from a bankrupt firm **7.** Subject: appearance; prepositional phrase: before the members of the board **9.** Subject: workforce; prepositional phrase: within the company

Practice 21-3, page 318

Answers: **1.** Subject: Egyptians; verb: invented (action verb) **3.** Subject: they; verb: bowled (action verb) **5.** Subject: alley; verb: opened (action verb) **7.** Subject: alley; verb: offers (action verb) **9.** Subject: people; verb: would think (helping verb + main verb)

Practice 21-4, page 320

Answers and possible edits: **1.** Complete. **3.** Incomplete; Because mother had taught me to cook spaghetti, I felt I could do this. **5.** Incomplete; I chose a luscious cherry pie from the bakery. **7.** Incomplete; Landing face down in the cherry pie was messy. **9.** Incomplete; And then she started to laugh at the ridiculous sight.

Practice 21-6, page 321

Answers and possible edits: (1) Subject: travel; verb: fascinates (3) Subject: he; verb: thought (5) Subject: he; verb: is (7) Subject: He; verb: has. He has the company of millions of other people and me, too. (9) Subject: names; verb: travel (11/12) Subject: Planetary Society; verb: flew. In 1996, the Planetary Society flew the names of members into space using the Mars *Pathfinder*. (13) Subject: individuals; verb: signed (15) Subject: people; verb: submit. Now people submit names on the Internet by filling out a form. (17) Subject: names; verb: go (19) Subject: people; verb: have placed (20/21) Their names are on a CD which could survive for billions of years. (23) Subject: we; verb: will travel (24/25) After signing up, we received colorful certificates to print out to tell about our mission. (27) Subject: grandpa and I; verb: travel

Practice 21-7, page 322

Answers and possible edits: (1) pen (3) walked, tossed, on (5) class, new (7) quickly, groceries (9) but (11) hopefully (13) in

Chapter 22

Practice 22-2, page 329

Answers and possible edits: **1. Because** I have gathered these stones from different places, they each have a special meaning for me. **3.** I was taking a long walk with my grandfather **in** the neighborhood park near his house. **5. When** he showed me the rock, we both smiled because it had marks that made it look like a smiley face. **7. Although** the rock is brown and gray on one side, the other side is made up of beautiful purple amethyst crystals. **9.** It is a flat tan rock **with** a picture of a horse sketched on it with a Magic Marker.

Practice 22-3, page 330

Answers and possible edits: **For many hundreds of years**, people have used natural remedies to heal an illness. They eat chicken soup **because it is healthy and helps the immune system**. People are not the only ones **who like chicken soup**. Two pandas are fed chicken soup to help maintain their health **in the Wuhan Zoo in central China**. The animals had been moved in June **because their habitat had been damaged by an earthquake**. They faced a challenge adjusting to their new home. Then, during a national holiday, many visitors came **to the zoo to see the pandas**. The animals got tired and stressed **when so many people crowded around their area**. Zookeepers cooked up chicken soup **because colder weather was on the way**. They boiled the chicken for twelve hours, **which seems like a long time but helped increase the flavor**. The keepers were not sure the pandas would enjoy the soup. Each panda ate over two pounds of soup **in giant dishes along with their regular diet**.

Practice 22-4, page 332

Answers and possible edits: (1) Correct (3/4) In 1931, Plennie Wingo set out on an ambitious journey **walking** backward around the world. (5) Correct; **wearing** (6/7) After eight thousand miles, Wingo's journey was interrupted by a war in Pakistan, **ending** his ambitious journey. (8/9) Hans Mullikan spent more than two years in the late 1970s traveling to the White House by crawling from Texas to Washington, D.C., **taking** time out to earn money as a logger and a Baptist minister. (10/11) Alvin Straight, suffering from poor eyesight, traveled across the Midwest on a lawnmower, **looking** for his long-lost brother.

Practice 22-5, page 334

Answers and possible edits: (1) Correct (3/4) Many Web sites show you how **to make** personalized stamps. (5) **To be**; correct (6/7) Many parents use the sites after their children are born to make stamps to put on birth announcements. (8/9) Photo stamps of grandchildren are great gifts **to give** to grandparents. (11) Correct (13/14) It costs more than twice as much as regular stamps **to order** stamps with personal photos.

Practice 22-6, page 336

Answers and possible edits: (1/2) Being a smart consumer can be difficult, **especially when making a major purchase.** (3/4) **At car dealerships, for example, important information is often in small type, like finance charges or preparation charges.** (5/6) Advertisements also put negative information in small type, **such as a drug's side effects.** (7/8) Credit card offers often use tiny, hard-to-read print for the terms of the card, **like interest charges and late fees, which can really add up.** (9/10) Phone service charges can also be hidden in small print, **like limits on text messaging and other functions.** (11) Correct as is; sentence is an explanation.

Practice 22-7, page 336

Answers and possible edits: **1.** Fragment: To add to their income. To add to their income, publishers are placing advertisements in their games. **3.** Fragment: Across the finish line. One character, a race-car driver, drove his ad-covered car across the finish line. **5.** Fragment: Worrying that ads are distracting. Worrying that ads are distracting, some publishers are trying to limit the number of ads per game. **7.** Fragment: Like grocery carts and restroom walls. These players are used to seeing ads in all kinds of places, like grocery carts and restroom walls. **9.** Fragment: To strike a balance between profitable advertising and high game quality. To strike a balance between profitable advertising and high game quality is what publishers want.

Practice 22-8, page 337

Answers and possible edits: **1.** Although he was in failing **health, in** 1853, he was appointed lighthouse keeper at Lime Rock in Newport. Many lighthouse keepers were forced to leave family behind when they assumed their **duties because** the lighthouses were in remote locations and the living situations were poor. At first, Lime Rock had only a **shed for** the keeper and a temporary lantern for light. **3.** Some called her "The Bravest Woman in **America," for** saving eighteen lives during her time of service. She became famous, and many important people came to see **her, for** example, President Ulysses S. Grant. All the ships anchored in the harbor tolled their **bells to** honor her after her death.

Practice 22-9, page 338

Possible edits: (1/2) Thank you so much for taking the time to meet with me this past Wednesday. (3) I am more excited than ever about the administrative assistant position at Fields Corporation. (5) Correct (6/7) With my strong organizational skills, professional experience, and friendly personality, I'm sure that I would be an asset to the company. (8/9) Because of my strong interest in the position, I hope you will keep me in mind. (10/11) Please let me know if you need any other information, like references or a writing sample.

Chapter 23

Practice 23-2, page 347

Answers and possible edits: **1.** CS (comma splice); Farmers have been trying to keep hungry birds out of their crops for centuries; the first scarecrow was invented for this reason. **3.** FS (fused sentence); Recently, a group of berry farmers tried something new. They brought in bigger birds called falcons. **5.** FS (fused sen-

tence); Because these starlings are frightened of falcons, they fly away when they see these birds of prey in the fields. They need to get where they feel safe. **7.** FS (fused sentence); A falconer, or a person who raises and trains falcons, keeps an eye on the birds during the day. He makes sure they only chase away the starlings instead of killing them. **9.** FS (fused sentence); In recent years, the falcons have also been used in landfills to scatter birds and other wildlife. Some have even been used at large airports to keep flocks of birds away from landing airplanes.

Practice 23-3, page 349

Possible edits: **1.** In most cultures, popular <u>foods</u> <u>depend</u> greatly on availability and tradition, so <u>people</u> <u>tend</u> to eat old familiar favorites. **3.** In many societies, certain <u>foods</u> <u>are allowed</u> to age, for this <u>process</u> <u>adds</u> flavor. **5.** As an American, <u>you</u> <u>might</u> not like such eggs, or the <u>thought</u> of eating them <u>might</u> even <u>revolt</u> you. **7.** Many <u>Koreans</u> <u>love</u> to eat kimchee, a spicy aged cabbage, but <u>Americans</u> often <u>find</u> the taste odd and the smell overpowering. **9.** <u>Americans</u> on a visit to Kyrgyzstan <u>consider</u> themselves brave for tasting kumiss, but local <u>children</u> <u>drink</u> it regularly.

Practice 23-4, page 352

Answers and possible edits: **1.** The <u>National Basketball Association</u> (NBA) has used basketballs made out of leather for decades, although <u>it</u> recently <u>decided</u> to use ones made out of a synthetic material instead. **3.** While this was a reasonable idea, <u>it</u> <u>did</u> not <u>work</u> as planned. **5.** To find out what was not working with the basketballs, the <u>NBA</u> <u>talked</u> to several scientists since <u>they</u> <u>know</u> a great deal about how everyday items work. **7.** Though the plastic <u>ball</u> <u>was</u> easier to grip when it was dry, <u>it</u> <u>lost</u> friction and <u>was</u> harder to hold once it got wet. **9.** Until the <u>researchers</u> <u>analyzed</u> the differences between the leather and synthetic basketballs, <u>they</u> <u>did</u> not <u>realize</u> that the logo printed on the plastic ones also made them bounce improperly.

Practice 23-5, page 354

Possible edits: **1.** Even though jumbo-sized airplanes can hold up to 500 people, they are now being designed with only 300 seats. **3.** Another way to add room is to eliminate the phones on the seatbacks since hardly anyone uses those phones anyway. **5.** New design features will also make passengers feel more comfortable. These include softer lighting and larger overhead luggage bins. **7.** The most noticeable difference in the new planes will be the large windows. They will be 19 inches high and 11 inches wide. **9.** Something about being able to see more of our surroundings puts us at ease; at least that is what the airlines hope.

Practice 23-6, page 355

Answers and possible edits: (1) Correct (3) A team of Japanese scientists followed a group of sperm whales to locate the rare squids. The whales like to eat the eight-legged creatures. (5) From aboard their research ship, the team located the squids thousands of feet under the water. The scientists lowered bait over the side to attract them. (7) Correct (9) Correct (11) Correct (13) Correct

Practice 23-7, page 355

Possible edits: (1) I'm writing to you because I was seriously overcharged for the Star 3 MP3 player I ordered from your Web site last week. (3) If you check out any competitors' sites, you will see that

no one expects people to pay that much money for the Star model. The prices are never higher than $165.
(5) Sincerely,
Chris Langley

Chapter 24

Practice 24-2, page 364

Answers: **1.** Subject: sleep; verb: is **3.** Subject: lights; verb: were **5.** Subject: home; verb: has **7.** Subject: student; verb: does **9.** Subject: you; verb: are

Practice 24-3, page 364

Answers: **1.** Subject: stars; verb: are **3.** Subject: I; verb: do **5.** Subject: you; verb: have **7.** Subject: one; verb: is **9.** Subject: Orion; verb: is

Practice 24-4, page 366

Answers: **1.** Prepositional phrase: from a job or family commitments; verb: makes **3.** Prepositional phrase: with cable television; verb: want **5.** Prepositional phrase: from all parts of our society; verb: are **7.** Prepositional phrase: across America; verb: sleep **9.** Prepositional phrase: of us; verb: need

Practice 24-5, page 367

Answers: **1.** Dependent clause: that hired my cousins. The restaurant that hired my cousins is not treating them fairly. **3.** Dependent clause: who supervises the morning shift. Correct **5.** Dependent clause: whose hand was injured slicing potatoes. Ramón, whose hand was injured slicing potatoes, needs to have physical therapy. **7.** Dependent clause: who cleaned his wound and put in his stitches at the hospital. The doctors who cleaned his wound and put in his stitches at the hospital expect him to pay for the medical treatment. **9.** Dependent clause: whose English is not yet perfect. My cousins, whose English is not yet perfect, feel unable to leave their jobs.

Practice 24-6, page 369

Answers: **1.** Subject joined by: and; verb: share **3.** Subject joined by: and; verb: are **5.** Subject joined by: or; verb: provides **7.** Subject joined by: or; verb: finds **9.** Subject joined by: or; verb: costs

Practice 24-7, page 371

Answers: **1.** Subject: everyone; verb: remembers; prepositional phrase: none **3.** Subject: one; verb: realizes; prepositional phrase: of you **5.** Subject: someone; verb: knows; prepositional phrase: in your family **7.** Subject: one; verb: plans; prepositional phrase: of your relatives **9.** Subject: someone; verb: connects; prepositional phrase: in this class

Practice 24-8, page 374

Edits: **1.** What is the best reason to study music? **3.** Correct **5.** Here are a guitar, a saxophone, and a piano. **7.** What time of day do you usually practice? **9.** What musician do you admire most?

Practice 24-9, page 374

Answers: **1.** The shoppers who take on this work earn money for checking on a store's quality of service. **3.** Chain stores across the nation hire mystery shoppers. **5.** What reasons motivate a person to become a mystery shopper? **7.** Others say they have only one reason: the money they are paid. **9.** One does not have to pay a fee to become a mystery shopper.

Practice 24-10, page 375

Answers: (1) You probably do not have a mirror at your computer desk, but if you did, you might notice something about yourself you had not been aware of before. (3) Correct (5) Correct (7) Everyone who studies these trends is concerned. (9) Correct (11) Everyone, according to experts, needs to sit up straight while at the computer, take frequent breaks to get up and walk around, and carry less in his or her backpack.

Practice 24-11, page 376

Possible edits: (1) Dear Professor Connors, (3) In my humble opinion, it is one of the best classes this college offers. (5) I plan to graduate with a degree in business and economics, so your class is important to me. (7) I would sure appreciate it. (9) If I cannot get into your class this semester, I will have to rearrange my schedule so that I can take it next semester instead. (11) You are great, professor.

Chapter 25

Practice 25-2, page 382

Answers: **1.** Subject: classes; verb: require **3.** Subject: employees; verb: agree **5.** Subject: job; verb: pays **7.** Subject: he; verb: wonders **9.** Subject: bicycle; verb: allows

Practice 25-3, page 383

Answers: **1.** displayed **3.** annoyed, seemed **5.** assumed **7.** learned, remained **9.** disappeared, passed

Practice 25-4, page 384

Answers: **1.** have; received **3.** have; climbed **5.** had; handed **7.** have; purchased **9.** has; saved

Practice 25-5, page 388

Answers: **1.** have **3.** is **5.** are **7.** has **9.** have

Practice 25-6, page 390

Answers: **1.** was **3.** was **5.** was **7.** were

Practice 25-7, page 390

Answers: **1.** began **3.** gave **5.** knew **7.** left **9.** shut

Practice 25-8, page 391

Edits: **1.** In 1900, my great-grandfather grew wheat and raised a few cattle on his farm in Wyoming. **3.** The family did not have much money, and they hoped for good weather every year. **5.** One year, high winds blew down the barn, and hailstones broke their windows. **7.** Somehow, they kept going in spite of their difficulties.

Practice 25-9, page 391

Answers: **1.** had become **3.** had begun **5.** had grown **7.** have put **9.** has run

Practice 25-10, page 393

Answers: **1.** have begun **3.** needed **5.** have spent **7.** have expressed **9.** have kept

Practice 25-11, page 394

Answers: **1.** had been **3.** had become **5.** encouraged **7.** spent **9.** had refined

Practice 25-12, page 397

Possible edits: **1.** The owners were going to close some shelters. **3.** Animal lovers started a campaign. **5.** News teams filmed the animals. **7.** Animal lovers across the state staged a protest. **9.** The legislature restored some funds.

Practice 25-13, page 398

Answers: **1.** Verbs: take, wanted; correct verb: wants **3.** Verbs: feel, were blinking, making; correct verb: felt **5.** Verbs: included, offers; correct verb: offered **7.** Verbs: provide, advised; correct verb: advise **9.** Verbs: use, liked, get; correct verb: like

Practice 25-14, page 399

Edits: **1.** Many of Sheena's friends were getting tattoos ten years ago. **3.** Sheena was twenty-two when she went to the tattoo parlor. **5.** Her sister liked the tattoo, but her mother fainted. **7.** Dermatologists have seen the development of a new trend toward tattoo removal. **9.** That technique left scars. **11.** Six months ago, Sheena started to have treatments to remove her tattoo.

Practice 25-15, page 399

Edits: (1) When you think about a farm, you probably imagine acres of cornfields and stalls full of noisy animals. (3) Some experts believe that farms of the future will be found inside the top floors of a city's tallest skyscrapers. (5) Indoor city gardening not only would help make places become more self-sufficient but also could provide new uses for the variety of abandoned buildings that are found scattered throughout large cities. (7) Correct (9) Although this technology is not currently available, architects have been toying with possible designs. (11) It will be about five to ten years before all of these ideas will be commonplace.

Practice 25-16, page 400

Possible edits: **1.** Dear Dr. Kerrigan, (3) I became sick about a day ago. (5) Also, I have a high fever, and I am very tired. (7) I look forward to seeing you during my appointment.

Chapter 26

Practice 26-1, page 412

Answers: **1.** Pronoun: they; noun: stars **3.** Pronoun: it; noun: sky; pronoun: they; noun: stars **5.** Pronoun: its; noun: International Dark Sky Association **7.** Pronoun: they; noun: cities and towns **9.** Pronoun: they; noun: birds

Practice 26-2, page 414

Answers: **1.** his or her **3.** its **5.** he or she no longer works **7.** himself or herself **9.** he or she

Practice 26-3, page 416

Answers: **1.** their **3.** its **5.** its **7.** their **9.** its

Practice 26-4, page 418

Possible edits: **1.** My doctor referred me to a physical therapist, who said I needed to exercise more. **3.** I tried a lower fat diet along with the exercising, but this combination did not really work either. **5.** Therefore, I started eating fats again and stopped consuming carbs, but these methods were not a permanent solution. **7.** Last week, I overheard my Uncle Kevin talking to my brother, and my uncle explained how he stayed slender even while traveling a lot. **9.** He says it is not hard to pack carrots or apples for a trip, so anyone can plan in advance.

Practice 26-5, page 420

Edits: **1.** Young people sometimes take advertisements too literally. **3.** People who see or hear an advertisement have to think about the message. **5.** A recent study said that parents can help kids overcome the influence of advertising.

Practice 26-6, page 423

Edits: **1.** In 1974, George Foreman was the heavyweight boxing champion, and he and Muhammad Ali agreed to a fight for the title. **3.** Because American officials considered Mobutu a strong anticommunist, they and he were allies, but Mobutu was a dictator who stole money intended for his impoverished country. **5.** Foreman angered the people of Zaire immediately when he and his German shepherd dog were seen getting off the airplane. **7.** The people loved Muhammad Ali, and pictures of him and his group in Zaire showed adoring crowds everywhere. **9.** Ali may have feared losing the fight, but when he and Foreman finally got in the ring, Ali took punch after punch.

Practice 26-7, page 425

Edits: **1.** In addition, I was nowhere near as well equipped for camping as she. **3.** Correct **5.** He seemed to believe that we were more experienced than they. **7.** They all hurried past us, but Hannah kept hiking just as slowly as I. **9.** When Hannah and I saw the group running back toward us, I was more alarmed than she.

Practice 26-8, page 426

Answers: **1.** whom **3.** who **5.** who

Practice 26-9, page 428

Possible edits: **1.** A writing tutor must know his or her way around college writing assignments. **3.** Students signing up for tutoring at the writing center may not be in their first semester of college. **5.** The writing-center tutor is careful not to correct his or her students' papers. **7.** Every student has to learn to catch his or her own mistakes. **9.** No student gets his or her grade on a paper from a writing tutor.

Practice 26-10, page 428

Possible edits: **1.** My class received their term paper grades yesterday. **3.** I usually get better grades than he, but he does not usually fail. **5.** When Gene went to the department office, the office assistant told him where to find Mr. Padilla. **7.** The paper contained language that was unusual for Gene. **9.** Mr. Padilla, who typed some passages from Gene's paper into a search engine, found two online papers containing sentences that were also in Gene's paper. **11.** Gene told my girlfriend and me later that he did not realize that borrowing sentences from online sources was plagiarism. **13.** Anyone doing Internet research must be especially careful to document his or her sources, as Gene now knows. **15.** Mr. Padilla will let Gene take the class again and will help him avoid accidental plagiarism, and Gene said that no one had ever been more relieved than he to hear that news.

Practice 26-11, page 429

Edits: (1) Correct (3) Correct (5) Correct (7) Correct (9) Correct (11) Correct

Chapter 27

Practice 27-1, page 436

Answers: **1.** *Stubborn* modifies *smokers*. **3.** *Typical* modifies *smoker*. **5.** *Terrible* modifies *effect*. **7.** *Strongly* modifies *smell*. **9.** *Large* modifies *dose*.

Practice 27-2, page 438

Answers: **1.** more relaxed   **3.** easiest   **5.** harder   **7.** closer   **9.** Calmer

Practice 27-3, page 439

Answers: **1.** *Well* modifies *communicate.*   **3.** *Well* modifies *feel.*   **5.** *Well* modifies *see.*   **7.** *Well* modifies *hear.*   **9.** *Good* modifies *solution.*

Practice 27-4, page 440

Answers: **1.** worst   **3.** better   **5.** better   **7.** worse   **9.** worse

Practice 27-5, page 441

Possible edits: (1) Every day, many people log on to play one of the most popular computer games of all time, *World of Warcraft.* (3) More than 11 million players participate in the game every month, according to the most recent figures. (5) Correct (7) Correct (9) Each side tends to think it is better than the other one. (11) Correct (13) Players must proceed carefully to stay in the game and increase their overall power and abilities.

Chapter 28

Practice 28-1, page 445

Edits: **1.** I still write in a diary about all kinds of personal things and private observations.   **3.** Any story that is entertaining might show up in my blog.   **5.** Wanting the video to be funny, I had invited to the birthday party my loudest, wildest friends.   **7.** Unfortunately, the battery in the video recorder that Tim loaned me died.   **9.** I explained how I would include in the blog the funny story about the failed videotaping.

Practice 28-2, page 446

Possible edits: **1.** While I was preparing a big family dinner, the oven suddenly stopped working.   **3.** With everyone trying to help, the kitchen was crowded.   **5.** Discouraged, we almost canceled dinner.   **7.** Correct   **9.** When I returned to the crowd in the kitchen, family members still surrounded the oven.

Practice 28-3, page 447

Possible edits: (1) Correct (3) Because students have to plan ahead for the whole day and often need books, extra clothes, and on-the-go meals, their backpacks get heavier and heavier. (5) Researchers from the University of Pennsylvania and the Marine Biological Laboratory have recently invented a new type of backpack. (7) Correct (9) Correct (11) Correct (13) Correct

Chapter 29

Practice 29-1, page 452

Possible answers: **1.** or   **3.** so   **5.** and   **7.** but   **9.** so

Practice 29-2, page 453

Possible edits: **1.** Many professionals use e-mail to keep in touch with clients and contacts, so they must be especially careful not to offend anyone with their e-mail messages.   **3.** Employees may have time to send personal messages from work, but they should remember that employers often have the ability to read their workers' messages.   **5.** No message should be forwarded to everyone in a sender's address book, and senders should ask permission before adding someone to a mass-mailing list.   **7.** Typographical errors and misspellings in e-mail make the message appear less profes-sional, yet using all capital letters—a practice known as *shouting*—is usually considered even worse.

Practice 29-3, page 455

Answers: **1.** Too much exposure to the sun can cause skin cancer; using tanning booths has similar risks.   **3.** It is easy to ignore long-term health dangers; the desire to look good is tempting.   **5.** Ultraviolet light can injure the eyes; tanning-salon patrons should always wear protective goggles.

Practice 29-4, page 455

Possible edits: **1.** One such group is the sea gypsies, who spend a lot of time swimming and diving; therefore, their eyes have adapted to seeing underwater.   **3.** Objects often look vague under the surface; also, people are hard to recognize.   **5.** Parents in this culture teach their children to dive deep into the ocean; in fact, from an early age, the children collect clams, sea cucumbers, and pearls from the ocean floor.   **7.** Scientists believe that the sea gypsies' eyes have adapted to an underwater environment; in addition, their excellent vision may also have a genetic component.   **9.** Sea gypsies can also make their pupils constrict; as a result, they can see objects measuring less than a quarter of an inch.

Practice 29-5, page 457

Possible answers: **1.** , and   **3.** ; however,   **5.** , nor   **7.** ; then,   **9.** , so

Practice 29-6, page 458

Possible edits: (1/2) Identity theft is becoming an increasingly serious problem, and teenagers are frequent victims of this crime. (3) Correct (4/5) Young people are common targets because they are relatively inexperienced, trusting, and disorganized; in addition, they usually have clean credit records. (7/8) Experts recommend that teens always leave their Social Security cards at home at all times; in fact, credit cards and checkbooks should never be taken to parties or other social gatherings. (9) Correct (10/11) Teenagers make many purchases online and use peer-to-peer file-sharing programs such as LimeWire to download music and movies, so they become especially easy prey for identity thieves who steal bank account numbers and loan information. (13) Correct (15/16) It can take years to get everything straightened out, and the process can cost more than $1,000. (17) Correct (19/20) Thieves got away with nearly $100 million last year; therefore, people, especially teenagers, must protect themselves before they become part of future statistics about this crime.

Chapter 30

Practice 30-1, page 463

Possible answers: **1.** because   **3.** so that   **5.** While   **7.** When   **9.** because

Practice 30-2, page 463

Possible edits: **1.** Almost all college students used typewriters until the 1980s, when computers became more affordable.   **3.** Computers offer many advantages, although there are also some drawbacks.   **5.** When computers became widely used in the 1980s, professors were surprised to hear students say, "The computer ate my paper."   **7.** Some people like to print out a document to proofread it because they fail to catch all their mistakes on the screen.   **9.** Even though spell-checking programs prevent many errors, only a person is able to recognize errors with soundalikes such as *their* and *there.*

Practice 30-3, page 464

Completed sentences might read as follows: **1.** We have all heard stories of people who lived long lives even though they smoked, ate meat every day, and drank alcohol regularly.   **3.** Because very elderly people are unusual, scientists are studying them to learn their secrets.   **5.** While some say it may be possible to develop drugs that greatly extend our lives, many others are skeptical.   **7.** You will hear a lot of different stories if you ask very old people what they do every day to stay happy and healthy.   **9.** Before she goes to bed, she watches her favorite TV shows and has a beer.

Practice 30-4, page 465

Possible edits: (1/2) Washington, D.C., was the first city in the United States to implement a public bike-sharing program, although the idea has been popular in Europe for years. (3) Correct (5) Correct (6/7) After using the bikes for up to three hours, people must return them since other riders might be waiting. (9/10) The bikes have electronic locks, and the locks emit a signal if the bike is not returned. (11/12) Cycling has become much more popular in recent years since gasoline prices have increased. (13/14) A number of other cities are now considering bike-sharing programs, because studies show that these programs can reduce city traffic by 4 or 5 percent. (15) Correct (16/17) Company leaders are aware that fit employees and a healthier environment are important goals even if it means the company spends a little extra time, money, and effort to start and run a bike-sharing program.

Chapter 31

Practice 31-1, page 469

Answers and possible edits: **1.** Parts that should be parallel: hunt/are taking over. Wild predators, such as wolves, are vanishing because people hunt them and take over their land.   **3.** Parts that should be parallel: varied diet/adapting easily. The success of the coyote is due to its varied diet and adaptability.   **5.** Parts that should be parallel: spreading/populate. Today, they are spreading and populating the East Coast for the first time.   **7.** Parts that should be parallel: more populated/it's not as wild as. The animals have chosen an area more populated and less wild than their traditional home.   **9.** Parts that should be parallel: identified/tracked/they captured him. One coyote was identified, tracked, and captured in Central Park in New York City.

Practice 31-2, page 470

Answers and possible edits: **1.** Parts that should be parallel: for leasing/for the purchase of one. Car dealers often require less money down for leasing a car than for purchasing one.   **3.** Parts that should be parallel: the terms of leasing/to buy. You should check the terms of leasing to make sure they are as favorable as the terms of buying.   **5.** Parts that should be parallel: by leasing/to own. You will be making less of a financial commitment by leasing a car than by owning it.   **7.** Parts that should be parallel: used car/getting a new one. A used car can be more economical than a new one. **9.** Parts that should be parallel: a used car/buying a brand-new vehicle. A used car may not be as impressive as a brand-new vehicle.

Practice 31-3, page 471

Answers and possible edits: **1.** Paired words: neither/nor. Parts that should be parallel: had cell phones/did they want them. Fifteen years ago, most people neither had cell phones nor wanted them.   **3.** Paired words: rather/than. Parts that should be parallel: ban cell phones on buses and trains/being forced to listen to other people's conversations. Cell phones are not universally popular: Some commuters would rather ban cell phones on buses and trains than be forced to listen to other people's conversations.   **5.** Paired words: rather/than. Parts that should be parallel: have a cell phone/to walk to the nearest gas station. A motorist stranded on a deserted road would rather have a cell phone than be forced to walk to the nearest gas station.   **7.** Paired words: neither/nor. Parts that should be parallel: worry about radiation from cell phones/other injuries. Most Americans today neither worry about radiation from cell phones nor fear other injuries.   **9.** Paired words: both/and. Parts that should be parallel: affect people's reflexes/it might alter the brain's blood vessels. Cell phones probably do not cause brain tumors, but some experiments on human cells have shown that energy from the phones may both affect people's reflexes and alter the brain's blood vessels.

Practice 31-4, page 472

Possible edits: **1.** I could bring to this job not only youthful enthusiasm but also relevant experience.   **3.** My current job neither encourages initiative nor allows flexibility.   **5.** In college, I learned a lot both from my classes and from other students.

Practice 31-5, page 473

Possible edits: (1) Correct (3) Correct (5) Correct (7) Storing them is better than planting them. (9) On the first day that the vault's storage program began, 268,000 different seeds were deposited, put into sealed packages, and collected into sealed boxes. (11) Correct (13) Carefully storing these seeds not only will help ensure that people will have food to eat but also will make sure that important crops never go extinct.

Chapter 32

Practice 32-1, page 478

Edits: **1.** Once, rabies was a major threat to domestic pets in this country.   **3.** Frequently, people fail to have their pets vaccinated against rabies.   **5.** Worriedly, veterinarians note that wildlife with rabies can infect pets and people.

Practice 32-2, page 478

Possible answers: **1.** Recently   **3.** Thankfully   **5.** Unfortunately

Practice 32-4, page 479

Possible edits: **1.** A recent study testing children's abilities to interpret facial expressions made headlines.   **3.** The children told researchers what emotion was most obvious in each face, choosing among fear, anger, sadness, happiness, and other emotions.   **5.** All of the children in the study were equally good at identifying most emotions, responding similarly to happiness or fear.   **7.** Having learned to look for anger, the abused children protect themselves with this early-warning system.   **9.** Tending to run from anger they observe, abused children have difficulty connecting with people who exhibit anger.

Practice 32-6, page 482

Possible edits: **1.** Angered by British colonial rule in 1929, the women of southern Nigeria organized a protest.   **3.** Pumped by American and other foreign oil companies, the oil often ends up in wealthy Western economies.   **5.** Polluted by the oil industry, the Nigerian countryside becomes a wasteland.   **7.** Inspired by the 1929 women's protests, local Nigerian women launched a series of protests against the oil industry in the summer of 2002.   **9.** Concerned about the women's threat to take their clothes off, many workers at the oil company told company officials that such a protest would bring a curse on the company and shame to its employees.

Practice 32-7, page 483

Possible answers: **1.** taken **3.** Regarded **5.** prescribed

Practice 32-9, page 484

Possible edits: **1.** Jacob Davis, a Russian immigrant working in Reno, Nevada, was the inventor of Levi's jeans. **3.** Davis bought denim from a wholesaler, Levi Strauss. **5.** Davis joined the firm in 1873 and supervised the final development of its product, the famous Levi's jeans. **7.** Another choice Davis made, the curved stitching on the back pockets, also survives in today's Levi's. **9.** During World War II, Levi Strauss temporarily stopped adding the pocket stitches because they wasted thread, a valuable resource.

Practice 32-10, page 485

Possible answers: **1.** a college freshman **3.** a quiet, tree-lined neighborhood **5.** a dark, cramped apartment

Practice 32-11, page 486

Possible edits: **1.** While Erin goes to classes, her baby boy stays at a day-care center, which costs Erin about $100 a week. **3.** Occasionally, Erin's parents, who live about seventy miles away, come up and watch the baby while Erin is studying. **5.** She feels that some of her professors who have never been parents themselves are not very sympathetic. **7.** Her grades, which were once straight A's, have suffered somewhat since she had her son. **9.** Her son, who is the most important thing to her, is more important than an A in geology.

Practice 32-12, page 487

Possible answers: **1.** that was probably caused by faulty wiring **3.** , who has always been a light sleeper, **5.** , which was the only home I had ever lived in,

Practice 32-13, page 487

Possible edits: (1) Correct (2/3) If you are a Barrow Whaler's fan, you wear more than that, putting on a parka, scarf, gloves, hat, and long underwear—in August! (5/6) Barrow, the northernmost city in the country, is also the coldest. (7/8) Barrow, a small city, has only about 4,500 residents. (9) Correct (11/12) Suspecting that a team might give some students a positive focus and decrease the school's dropout rate, they started a football program. (13/14) With wind chill temperatures dropping as low as 80 degrees below zero, being part of the team is not easy. (15/16) Bus drivers often park the school buses around the field, providing a wind barrier for players and the crowd.

Chapter 33

Practice 33-1, page 492

Answers: **1.** Subject: John; verb: sent; direct object: letter

Practice 33-2, page 492

Answers and edits: **1.** Incorrect; I like presents very much. **3.** Incorrect; I always bring a present to parties. **5.** Incorrect; I always write them a thank-you note.

Practice 33-3, page 495

Possible edits: **1.** He cannot say several words. **3.** He does not think it was at the same age. **5.** Hassan does not expect his son to be a genius.

Practice 33-4, page 496

Possible edits: **1.** Does he make dinner every night for his family? **3.** Does he use coupons to save money? **5.** Does Brad save a lot of money using coupons?

Practice 33-5, page 497

Answers: **1.** there are **3.** Is there **5.** there are

Practice 33-6, page 499

Possible answers: **1.** it **3.** He **5.** my **7.** They **9.** their

Practice 33-7, page 506

Answers: **1.** starting **3.** was visiting **5.** sleeping **7.** eating **9.** exercising

Practice 33-8, page 506

Answers: **1.** Is Betsy golfing today? **3.** Are you going to the mall? **5.** Was Meriam eating when you arrived?

Practice 33-9, page 511

Possible answers: **1.** should **3.** might **5.** cannot **7.** should not **9.** can

Practice 33-10, page 511

Answers: **1.** Can you help me? **3.** Should they learn how to cook? **5.** Would Terrell like to join us?

Practice 33-11, page 512

Possible answers: **1.** Have [you] seen **3.** will convince **5.** had lost **7.** inherited **9.** would [not] have **11.** turned **13.** was running **15.** was **17.** should have been **19.** could [he] have meant

Practice 33-12, page 513

Possible answers: **1.** strap **3.** reported **5.** are looking **7.** has had **9.** have [often] struck **11.** Correct **13.** made, hiked **15.** fell, had erupted

Practice 33-13, page 516

Possible answers: **1.** to be **3.** to take **5.** Correct **7.** repeating **9.** to try

Practice 33-14, page 519

Answers: **1.** The **3.** no article **5.** the **7.** a **9.** no article

Practice 33-15, page 519

Edits: **1.** Have you ever heard of the author Jhumpa Lahiri? **3.** However, *Interpreter of Maladies* has been translated into twenty-nine different languages and became a bestseller around the world. **5.** Although Lahiri visited India many times, she felt removed from the country's culture as a child. **7.** She identified neither as an American nor as an Indian.

Practice 33-16, page 521

Edits: **1.** Of course, my classmates are aware of this trend. **3.** Correct **5.** "Hello, Seth!" he said. "Did you forget to hand in your research paper in class?" **7.** "Oh," said Mr. Johnson thoughtfully. "I'm sorry about that." **9.** "Sure," said Mr. Johnson. "It will make them more responsible for their homework, anyway."

Practice 33-17, page 522

Edits: **1.** She is almost finished with her English paper and will hand it in on Friday. **3.** Correct **5.** She forced herself to go over the paper, and it is much better.   **7.** Her friend Sylvie asked her to drop in Friday night for a visit.   **9.** Also, she might go to the theater to see a movie.   **11.** Lucy is proud of herself for finishing her paper.

Chapter 34

Practice 34-1, page 531

Answers and possible edits: **1.** hard; It would be challenging to grow some kinds of crops.   **3.** do bunches of things for them; You would have to clean their stalls, feed them, milk them, etc. a few responsibilities.   **5.** tons of time; Planting seeds is time-consuming.   **7.** great; The food that you grew would probably taste fresh.   **9.** decent, stuff; I would do an excellent job taking care of the farm, the animals, and the crops.

Practice 34-2, page 532

Answers and possible edits: **1.** really awesome sweet; That reference letter you wrote for me was helpful and much appreciated.   **3.** all that; She said I thought I was conceited but that is not true.   **5.** hang sometime; Maybe you and I could spend time together one of these weekends?   **7.** whazzup; You could let me know what you have planned when I see you at work next week.   **9.** chill out; Just relax and forget about it.

Practice 34-3, page 534

Answers and possible edits: **1.** Wordy language: It is a well-known fact that; Dieting is difficult for most people.   **3.** Wordy language: The fact of the matter is that; These substitutes provide a sweet taste, but without the calories of sugar or honey.   **5.** Wordy language: Some of the current, on the matter are of the opinion; Current experts believe that sugar substitutes can cause cancer, allergies, and other serious health problems.   **7.** Wordy language: negative evaluations, and critical opinions; Despite these warnings from the experts, nearly 200 million people consume sugar-free or low-calorie products each year.   **9.** Wordy language: In spite of the fact that, anytime in the near future; Although people know sugar is bad for them, their tastes will probably not change soon.

Practice 34-4, page 535

Answers and possible edits: **1.** Clichés: sweat blood; work like a dog. You have to persuade yourself to devote every bit of your strength to the challenge for up to ten hours.   **3.** Clichés: the bitter end; easier said than done. Staying on your bike until the very last mile, of course, is an enormously difficult task.   **5.** Cliché: better late than never. No matter how long it takes you to cross the finish line, remind yourself that finishing at all is a tremendous achievement.   **7.** Cliché: keep your nose to the grindstone. It may take discipline to make yourself train, but you should continue to work hard.   **9.** Cliché: keep an eye peeled. When you train for road racing, watch carefully for cars.

Practice 34-5, page 536

Answers and possible edits: (1) Imagine spending almost two weeks living in the most unusual home in the world. (3) While I would not want to do that, it sounds fascinating. (5) Correct (7) Correct (9) Correct (11) Indeed, by the time his two weeks were over, Godson was ready to come up and feel the sunshine and wind on his face again.

Chapter 35

Practice 35-1, page 547

Answers: **1.** accept   **3.** They're; their   **5.** principles   **7.** knows; no   **9.** have; our

Practice 35-2, page 548

Possible edits: **1.** (1) More and more women are purchasing handguns, against the advice of law enforcement officers. (3) They know the risks of guns, and they accept those risks. (5) They do not want to contribute to the violence in our society, but they also realize that women are the victims of violent attacks far too often. (7) Some women have made a conscious decision to arm themselves for protection. (9) Having a gun in your house makes it three times more likely that someone will be killed there—and that someone is just as likely to be you or one of your children as a criminal. (11) Every year, there are tragic examples of children who accidentally shoot and even kill other youngsters while they are playing with guns. (13) Reducing the violence in our society may be a better solution.

Chapter 37

Practice 37-1, page 560

Answers: **1.** Continued expansion depends on our ability to promote novelty beverages such as papaya, mango, and boysenberry juices in grocery stores and restaurants.   **3.** In California, we are doing well because many Californians are open to new, healthful products.   **5.** As we enter new markets, we expect similar, steady, increasing growth.   **7.** We want to target New England states such as Connecticut, Massachusetts, and Maine, where attitudes about fruit juice are similar to those in Seattle, Portland, and other Northwest cities.   **9.** We should set up displays, provide free samples of our juices, and sponsor contests.

Practice 37-2, page 562

Answers: **1.** Correct   **3.** She had chosen the college carefully, for it had an excellent program in physical therapy.   **5.** Correct   **7.** Correct   **9.** She did not want to have to choose between her husband and an education, and she did not have to.

Practice 37-3, page 563

Answers: **1.** As we all know, AIDS is spread mainly through sexual contact and through drug use that involves the sharing of needles.   **3.** Since basketball star Magic Johnson revealed in 1991 that he is HIV-positive, an NBA player must be removed from a game if he is bleeding.   **5.** Not surprisingly, many college sports follow similar rules.   **7.** According to some student athletes, mandatory HIV testing would violate their civil liberties.   **9.** Correct

Practice 37-4, page 565

Answers: **1.** Some rooms, in fact, are full of echoes, dead zones, and mechanical noises that make it hard for students to hear.   **3.** The association recommends that background noise, the constant whirring or whining sounds made by radiators, lights, and other machines, be no more than 35 decibels.   **5.** One study found a level of 65 decibels, the volume of a vacuum cleaner, in a number of classrooms around the country.   **7.** An increasing number of school districts are beginning to pay more attention to acoustics, the study of sound, when they plan new schools.   **9.** Other changes, however, can be costly and controversial, such as buying thicker drapes, building thicker walls, or installing specially designed acoustic ceiling tiles.

Practice 37-5, page 568

Edits: **1.** Correct   **3.** Diet drinks, which often have fewer calories, deprive people of essential vitamins and minerals.   **5.** Young people, who tend to make snap decisions, can learn to make healthier food choices.   **7.** Parents, who are often frustrated at their children's diets, can also help their kids make healthier choices.   **9.** Experts from different organizations, who all seem to agree on the issue, recommend that young people exercise three times a week.

Practice 37-6, page 569

Answers: **1.** Correct **3.** Asked if he was losing patience, McGregor replied, "Yes, I sure am." **5.** His wife said, "Rob, don't go mouthing off to any reporters." **7.** An official of Value-Safe Insurance of Wrightsville, Ohio, said the company will process claims within the next few months. **9.** Correct

Practice 37-7, page 570

Edits: (1) One of the nation's grocery store chains, Whole Foods Market, recently made an important business decision. (3) The store, which cares about environmental issues, now offers only paper bags made from recycled paper. (5) Correct (7) They clog drains, harm wildlife, and take up an enormous amount of space in the nation's landfills. (9) According to the experts, that works out to more than 330 bags for every single person in the United States.

Chapter 38

Practice 38-1, page 575

Answers: **1.** A person's feelings about personal space depend on his or her culture. **3.** Putting your face too close to another's is considered rude. **5.** The expression "Get out of my face!" is a warning meant to prevent the confrontation's violent conclusion. **7.** The hair on dogs' necks may stand on end. **9.** For example, seagulls' positions on a log follow a pattern similar to that of people lined up waiting for a bus.

Practice 38-2, page 577

Answers: **1.** You'll notice right away if a stranger leans over and talks to you so that his face is practically touching yours. **3.** There isn't one single acceptable boundary we'd use in all situations. **5.** With coworkers, we're likely to keep a personal space of four to twelve feet. **7.** The last sixteen inches are reserved for people we're most intimate with. **9.** A supervisor who's not aware of the personal space boundaries of his or her employees might make workers uncomfortable.

Practice 38-3, page 578

Answers: **1.** I sorted letters alphabetically, starting with A's. **3.** When I checked my e-mail, the screen flashed 48's to show that I had forty-eight messages. **5.** I needed another week's time just to return all the phone calls.

Practice 38-4, page 579

Edits: (1) Have you noticed many honeybees when you go outside? (3) Correct (5) In the last year, more than one-third, or billions, of the honeybees in the United States have disappeared. (7) Typically, people who are in the bee business ship hives to farmers' fields by truck. (9) Scientists have been trying to find out what happened to the once-thriving bee population. (11) Correct

Chapter 39

Practice 39-1, page 584

Answers: **1.** "If I could quickly answer that question," the nurse replied, "I would deserve an honorary degree in ethics." **3.** "How would you describe that dilemma?" the reporter asked the nurse. **5.** The reporter asked, "So there are times when you would favor letting patients die on their own?" **7.** The reporter asked, "Under what circumstances should a patient be allowed to die?" **9.** "Is this a matter of deciding how to allocate scarce resources?" the reporter asked.

Practice 39-2, page 585

Answers: **1.** "Have you complained to the landlord yet?" her friend asked. **3.** Correct **5.** When Jocelyn phoned the landlord after the burglary, she said, "I know this would not have happened if that lock had been installed." **7.** Correct **9.** "If I were you," the person said, "I would let your landlord know about your plans."

Practice 39-3, page 586

Edits: **1.** In 2002, Bruce Springsteen released his first new album in years, containing songs like "Worlds Apart" that dealt with the terrorist attacks on the United States. **3.** No one made that complaint about "John Walker's Blues," a song by Steve Earle based on the story of the young American captured while fighting for the Taliban in Afghanistan. **5.** As a *Time* magazine article, "Don't Even Tell These Guys about Eminem," pointed out, the controversy was peculiar because it occurred before Earle's song had even been released, and those objecting had apparently neither heard the song nor read its lyrics.

Practice 39-4, page 587

Answers: (1) Correct (3) Ruiz answered, "I have always gotten bad grades, and I do not know how to get any better." (5) "I have just about given up." (7) Correct (9) I said, "There are plenty of programs to help you. (11) "Can you be a little more specific?" he asked. (13) Correct (15) "Take a look at these," I said. (17) And I do not have time." (19) I paused and then added, "It sounds to me like you are wasting the money you spent on tuition. (21) Ruiz thought for a moment, while he looked out the window, and finally told me that he would try. (23) "I am glad to hear it."

Chapter 40

Practice 40-1, page 593

Edits: (1) When John Wood was on a backpacking trip to Nepal in 1998, he discovered something he had not expected: only a few books in the nation's schools. (3) They did not need high-tech supplies as much as they needed old-fashioned books. (5) Correct (7) Correct (9) Correct (11) Money to fund all of these efforts comes through various fund-raisers: read-a-thons, auctions, and coin drives.

Acknowledgments, continued

Bill Maxwell. "Start Snitching." From the *St. Petersburg Times*, September 30, 2007. © 2007 St. Petersburg Times. All Rights Reserved.

Alexandra Natapoff. "Bait and Snitch: The High Cost of Snitching, for Law Enforcement." From *Slate .com* December 12, 2005. www.slate.com/id/2132103. Reprinted by permission of the author.

Tara Parker-Pope. "How to Boost Your Willpower." From *The New York Times*, December 10, 2007. © 2007 The New York Times. All rights reserved. Used by permission and protected by the Copyright Laws of the United States. The printing, copying and redistribution, or transmission of the Material without express permission is prohibited. www.nytimes.com.

Robert Phansalkar. "Stop Snitchin' Won't Stop Crime." From *The Badger Herald*, May 1, 2007. Copyright © 2007 The Badger Herald, Inc. Reprinted by permission of the publisher.

Monique Rizer. "When Students Are Parents." Originally published in *The Chronicle of Higher Education*, December 16, 2005. Reprinted by permission of the author.

Ruth Russell. "The Wounds That Can't Be Stitched Up." Originally published in *Newsweek*, December 20, 1999. Copyright © 1999 by Ruth Russell. Reprinted by permission of the author.

Walter Scanlon. "It's Time I Shed My Ex-Convict Status." Originally published in *Newsweek*, February 21, 2000 issue. © 2000 Newsweek, Inc. All rights reserved. Used by permission and protected by the Copyright Laws of the United States. The printing, copying and redistribution, or transmission of the Material without express permission is prohibited. www.newsweek.com.

Carolyn Foster Segal. "The Dog Ate My Disk, and Other Tales of Woe." Originally published in *The Chronicle of Higher Education*, August 11, 2000. Reprinted by permission of the author.

Deborah Tannen. "Gender Patterns Begin at the Beginning." From *I Only Say This Because I Love You: How the Way We Talk Can Make or Break Family Relationships Throughout Our Lives*. Copyright © 2001 by Deborah Tannen. Used by permission of Random House, Inc. All rights reserved.

Michael Thompson. "Passage into Manhood." Originally published in the *Boston Globe*, July 26, 2005. Used by permission of Michael Thompson.

John Tierney. "Yes, Money Can Buy Happiness." Originally published in *The New York Times*, March 20, 2008 issue. Copyright © 2008 The New York Times. All rights reserved. Used by permission and protected by the Copyright Laws of the United States. The printing, copying, redistribution or retransmission of the Material without permission is prohibited. www.nytimes.com.

James Verini. "Supersize It." Originally published in *Slate* magazine, March 3, 2004. Used by permission of the author.

Pat Wingert. "Uniform Rule." Originally published in *Newsweek*, October 4, 1999 issue. © 1999 Newsweek, Inc. All rights reserved. Used by permission and protected by the Copyright Laws of the United States. The printing, copying, redistribution, or retransmission of the Material without express written permission is prohibited. www.newsweek.com.

Photo/Art Credits

Title page and part photos: Jonathan Stark.

Pages 8–9: Courtesy Montgomery County Community College.

Page 10: nurse: © John Nordell / The Image Works: lab technician: © AGStockUSA, Inc. / Alamy: physical therapist: © Mira / Alamy.

Page 22: © Somos/Veer/Getty Images.

Page 23: © Alex Segre / Alamy.

Page 31: *Left;* © David Young-Wolff/PhotoEdit. *Right;* © Robert Brenner/PhotoEdit. Chapters 4–9 Chelsea Wilson/Nick Brown photographs: Pelle Cass.

Page 140: © The Daily Texan/Caleb Miller.

Page 151: Courtesy Urban College of Boston.

Page 156: © The Daily Texan.

Page 189: © Jenn Ackerman.

Page 207: © David Jennings/The Image Works.

Page 223: © Harrison Diamond/Florida Alligator.

Page 237: Copyright © 2009 by Consumers Union of U.S., Inc. Yonkers, NY 10703-1057, a nonprofit organization. Reprinted with permission from the January 2009 issue of CONSUMER REPORTS® for educational purposes only. No commercial use or reproduction permitted. www.ConsumerReports.com.

Page 242: © Daily Tarheel/Kate Napier.

Page 256: Photo by Ryan Garza Journal Staff Photographer © 2008 The Flint Journal. All Rights Reserved. Reprinted with permission.

Page 261: © Josh Ferrin/joshferrin.com.

Page 300: Courtesy Hoodia Maxx.

Page 301: © 2010 Mayo Foundation for Medical Education and Research (MFMER). All rights reserved.

Page 621: © AP Photo/Lou Krasky.
Page 629: Courtesy Dianne Hales.
Page 642: Courtesy Dr. David Dosa.
Page 646: © Barbara Kinney.
Page 656: © Evan Leslie /The New York Times.
Page 660: Courtesy Noreen Malone.
Page 667: Copyright © 2009 Stephanie Ericsson. Reprinted by the permission of Dunham Literary as
   agents of the author.
Page 680: © Ming/Courtesy Michael Thompson.
Page 684: Courtesy Northwestern University.
Page 693: Courtesy University of Georgia/Peter Frey.
Page 697: © Stephen Voss.
Page 705: Courtesy Workman Publishing Company.
Page 709: Courtesy of The New York Times.
Page 717: © Michelle Gray—stpetephotos.com.
Page 720: Courtesy Alexandra Natapoff.

Index

Useful Editing and Proofreading Marks

This chart lists typical marks and abbreviations that instructors use to correct and comment on your papers. You can also use these marks to edit and review your own work or in peer review. If your instructor uses different symbols for some errors, write them in the left-hand column for future reference.

YOUR INSTRUCTOR'S SYMBOL	STANDARD SYMBOL	HOW TO REVISE OR EDIT (numbers in boldface are chapters where you can find help)
	adj	Use correct adjective form **Ch. 27**
	adv	Use correct adverb form **Ch. 27**
	agr	Correct subject-verb agreement or pronoun agreement **Chs. 24 and 26**
	awk	Awkward expression: edit for clarity **Ch. 9**
	cap or triple underline [example]	Use capital letter correctly **Ch. 41**
	case	Use correct pronoun case **Ch. 26**
	cliché	Replace overused phrase with fresh words **Ch. 34**
	coh	Revise paragraph or essay for coherence **Ch. 9**
	coord	Use coordination correctly **Ch. 29**
	cs	Comma splice: join the sentences correctly **Ch. 23**
	dev	Develop you paragraph or essay more completely **Chs. 4 and 6**
	dm	Revise to avoid a dangling modifier **Ch. 28**
	frag	Attach the fragment to a sentence or make it a sentence **Ch. 22**
	fs	Fused sentence: join the two sentences correctly **Ch. 23**
	ital	Use italics **Ch. 39**
	lc or diagonal slash [Example]	Use lowercase **Ch. 41**
	mm	Revise to avoid a misplaced modifier **Ch. 28**
	pl	Use the correct plural form of the verb **Ch. 25**
	ref	Make pronoun reference clear **Ch. 26**
	ro	Run-on sentence; join the two sentences correctly **Ch. 23**
	sp	Correct the spelling error **Ch. 36**
	sub	Use subordination correctly **Ch. 30**
	sup	Support your point with details, examples, or facts **Ch. 6**
	tense	Correct the problem with verb tense **Ch. 25**
	trans	Add a transition **Ch. 9**
	w	Delete unnecessary words **Ch. 34**
	wc	Reconsider your word choice **Ch. 34**
	?	Make your meaning clearer **Ch. 9**
	^ ,	Use comma correctly **Ch. 37**
	; : ( ) - —	Use semicolon/colon/parentheses/hyphen/dash correctly **Ch. 40**
	" "	Use quotation marks correctly **Ch. 39**
	^	Insert something
	[exaample]	Delete something
	⌒ [words example]	Change the order of letters or words
	¶	Start a new paragraph
	# [example words]	Add a space
	⌒ [ex ample]	Close up a space

Useful Lists, Checklists, and Charts